In Our Image and Likeness

Volume 2

IDEAS OF HUMAN NATURE SERIES

Charles Trinkaus: In Our Image and Likeness (2 volumes)

Other titles in preparation

Erratum

The frontispiece, illustrating the façade of San Petronio at Bologna, represents *La Condanna al Lavoro*, by Iacopo della Quercia, not *La Creazione dell 'Uomo*.

Detail from Iacopo della Quercia's *La Creazione dell' Uomo* from the façade of San Petronio at Bologna, executed between 1425 and 1438.

In Our Image and Likeness

Humanity and Divinity in
Italian Humanist Thought

by Charles Trinkaus

IN 2 VOLUMES

Volume 2

Et Deus dixit: 'Faciamus Hominem
ad imaginem et similitudinem
nostram.' Genesis i, 26

The University of Chicago Press

Standard Book Number: 226-81245-6
Library of Congress Catalog Card Number: 77-76532
The University of Chicago Press, Chicago 60637
Constable & Co Ltd, London WC2

Published 1970
Printed in Great Britain

Contents

VOLUME I

VOLUME II

Part III.
Four Philosophers on the Condition of Man: The Impact of the Humanist Tradition

IX. Humanist Themes in Marsilio Ficino's Philosophy of Human Immortality

The Florentine, Marsilio Ficino, 1433–99, made one of the most important humanist contributions to the history of human thought with his complete translation of Plato and his subsequent translations of the ancient Neoplatonists. In this task he was completely a humanist in method and aspiration. Ficino, however, had also received an early training in scholastic philosophy, although from a teacher whose ideas were indeed somewhat influenced by humanism. He was none the less thoroughly conversant with scholastic Aristotelianism through his early education. Ficino, however, became possibly the leading philosopher of the Renaissance primarily on the basis of his own study of Plato and the Neoplatonists for which his serious effort to make a philosophically adequate translation of Plato was a superlative preparation.[1]

In elaborating his Christian-Platonic philosophical ideas Ficino necessarily had to enter into and develop many of the questions that had been central to scholastic philosophy and which had to some extent been avoided or even ridiculed by the humanists of the fourteenth and fifteenth centuries. There were to be sure some notable exceptions, and Salutati and Valla must of course be counted among these exceptions, although whether this entitles them to be called 'philosophers' does not seem a question in which we need to become involved.

Our interest in the thought of the humanists, in particular their religious and anthropological thought, has been centrally to discover some of the ways in which a new and more positive evaluation of human experience and human capacity, that was part and parcel of late medieval and Renaissance life, was assimilated into the religious preconceptions and practices of the age. Our quest has been a theoretical and not a practical one, for, of course, the same process of adjustment was taking place on the level of action, both individual and collective. The consequences were apparent both in the spread of new popular attitudes and behaviour-patterns and in the most crucial events of civil and ecclesiastical history. We, however, have been looking for new or altered theoretical postures within the context of religious thought and current ideas of human nature – postures, moreover, that could enjoy a certain freedom in their elaboration since they were undertaken by 'humanists', mostly men without obligations or commitments to traditional scholastic intellectual categories or to the compulsions of ecclesiastical discipline.

One must not minimise the crucial importance of these two kinds of freedom which the humanist movement enjoyed on a *de facto* basis, although it was true, of course, both that the traditional philosophical categories exercised an influence on the humanists and that certain of them were members of religious orders or ordained as clergy. On the other hand, the romantic and revolutionary conceptions of the humanists' role in European thought has long been proven untenable. In utilising the particular methodologies of their profession, in turning perhaps more freely but certainly not newly to classical literary and philosophical sources, in praising their own approaches and castigating those of the older learned professions, they were simultaneously enjoying the comparatively unformed and uninstitutionalised character of the practice of humanism and engaging in an obvious kind of self-reassurance and self-justification. They could not alter the historical and biographical facts of their existence within a particular cultural environment with its established and fervently entertained religious notions and modes of social, economic and political life. They were men of their time. It speaks for their importance, however, that they increasingly gave their own colouration to their time, led it toward their own particular resolution or lack of resolution of its crucial problems and questions. The point is that in fact the questions that interested them as men of their time and to which they could apply their special talents and humanistic faculties were those that were central not just to the humanists but to the general experience of their time.

It has been our thesis that the traditional way in which human life was conceived and the way in which it was integrated into the Christian religious outlook was inherently unsatisfactory to many men of learning of the later Middle Ages; that, furthermore, the Italian humanists from Petrarch on were involved in the effort to restructure this conception and this mode of integration. It was not simply that the norms of modern life ran against both the teachings of the Church and the consciences of individuals as sinful, but even more that what from one perspective was admirable and desirable, from another was despicable and evil. Consequently an undesirable pyschological condition emerged. Men, on the one hand, might be denounced as wicked and sinful, and on the other hand, their denouncers might be charged with hypocrisy, as may be seen in the humanist treatises on this theme.[2] Worst of all was the state of distrust and despair which we have seen so vividly deplored by Petrarch.

Another consequence of the attrition of earlier medieval modes of integrating secular and religious life was the absence of adequate moral and political means for ordering a human existence now oriented towards expansion and achievement in this world. To develop such secular moralities and political legalities something other than total condemnation of the secular activities of men was necessary. In the absence of new restraints and regulatory norms, or in the presence of heavily challenged secular ones, it was easier to have recourse to violence, exploitation, oppression and conquest than to develop new and more adequate perspectives. The disorders, wars, violence and political disasters of the closing Middle Ages and the Renaissance without any doubt made for an increase of pessimism and distrust of man, rendered it more difficult to evolve the necessary new syntheses of human action and religious conception, and at the same time did not make the simpler, older medieval formulas any more convincing. We have seen evidence of this state of mind, also, in such humanists as Petrarch, Facio, Poggio and Garzoni.[3]

But the major need was for an outlook which would discriminate between the actions of men that deserved religious sanction and those which should be subject to condemnation. There was not and could not be either a blanket endorsement of human behaviour of any sort or a blanket condemnation of life in this world such as emanated from the pen of Innocent III. To the minds of many thinkers of the Renaissance, a new Christian reconciliation which extended the range of admirable human activity was essential, one even that extended the range of such activity to its utmost, one, moreover, that no longer would make a sharp and fatal distinction between clergy and laity. The effect of such new integrations would be not only to render licit and Christianly admirable a whole series of activities and achievements of which the men of those times were justly proud anyhow, but to provide a new inducement to faith and religious fervour within a point of view which made the Christian religion compatible with the more human values history had imposed on the men of those times and rooted in them. It was a two-fold need both for the sanctioning of human capacity and achievement and for a renewed faith now seen to be supportive rather than condemnatory of the dreams and actions of men.

We have examined such solutions in a number of humanists and have had the temerity to characterise them, as our title suggests, as a vision of man in the image of God. But we have not done so without much justification in the reversion to the exegesis of the *Genesis* story of man's creation and the stress on human divinization through the Incarnation. It is our claim, here, in connection with Marsilio Ficino, that he too made the construction of such a synthesis his central task. What we aim to do is to show from certain limited aspects of his writings how his philosophy fits into this particular context. It is not at all our thought to reconstruct his philosophy as a whole, which has been so cogently done by Kristeller and discussed by so many others.[4]

In his preface to his *Theologia platonica*[5] addressed to Lorenzo de' Medici, Ficino makes clear that his double purpose is to reinforce the worship of God and to bring about a new understanding of the nature of man. Both the new moral pursuits of the humanists and the older naturalistic investigations should lead to the first goal. And to follow the insights of Plato was to be consistent with the same purpose, 'since he never dealt with any subject whether ethics or dialectics or mathematics or physics which he did not soon lead back towards the contemplation and worship of God with fullest piety'. But where was God chiefly to be discovered within the range of man's ordinary, not divinely inspired, experience except in the human soul?

> But since he considers the soul to be like a mirror in which the image of the divine countenance is readily reflected, for that reason [Plato], while he

> diligently sought God himself through His separate vestiges, continually turned towards the mirror of the soul knowing that that oracular saying 'know thyself' most potently urges that whoever wished to know God should first know himself. As a consequence anyone who seriously studies the Platonic writings, which I have now translated entirely into Latin, will, of course, discover all things, but especially these two things out of all the rest, the pious worship of the known God and the divinity of souls. . . .[6]

Thus for Ficino Platonism seems to mean the discovery of the divinity of man as an image of God, and of God Himself through this human image.

But this, of course, was also the theme of many humanist treatises on man and God written without the aid of Plato. Rather, as we have seen, the humanists tended to find their inspiration in (among others) St. Augustine. Ficino adds that in these discoveries to be gained from the study of Plato there

> consists a universal understanding of things and the basis of all life and complete happiness, especially since Plato spoke about these things in such a way that Aurelius Augustinus chose him, since he was the nearest of all to Christian truth, as the one out of all the (number of) philosophers who might be imitated, and asserted that by changing a few things the Platonists would be Christians.[7]

Thus Ficino too, as is well known, was of an Augustinian persuasion which he found compatible with Platonism. Thus also it was his purpose to pursue the two subjects of the renewed worship of God and the discovery of His image in the human soul in this work which should therefore properly be called *Platonic Theology on the Immortality of Souls*. It was moreover his special hope

> that in the very divinity of the created mind, as a mirror in the middle of all things, we might on the one hand gaze upon the works of the Creator Himself, and also contemplate and worship the mind.

He also had a further purpose which is of historical significance; he wished to convince 'at least by the Platonic reasonings that support religion' those in his day 'who did not easily cede to the one authority of divine law', and he also wished to convince those 'who impiously separate the study of philosophy too much from holy religion' that they erred in this as much as if they separated the love of wisdom from respect for it, or true knowledge from a right will.[8] In other words he wished to combat secularism as such, and he also was opposed to the separation of the study of philosophy in the universities' arts faculties from the exposition of revelation based on faith.

Let us turn to this latter epistemological and methodological question first. In the passage just cited we can recognise the same objection to an objective and impersonal study of philosophy in separation from the goal of making the reader a better, more religious person that we first encountered in Petrarch's criticism of the cult of Aristotle in his own day. One can also agree that this argument was used by many humanists on behalf of the rhetorical ends of persuasion which were part of their arts. While it is apparently true that Ficino, like the humanists, continually insisted that the end of philosophy was a deepened faith, an ennobled life and truer happiness, and that, as Kristeller has shown, he attempted to put himself at the centre of a circle of lay piety,[9] there is also an essential difference between his attitude and Petrarch's, and this despite Petrarch's protestations of faith in the unknown philosophy of Plato which was indeed well known to Ficino. Many of the humanists, and, as I have sought to show, especially Petrarch, while criticising the naturalistic determinism of certain scholastic schools, and definitely the philosophy of Averroes, were in fact in agreement with certain aspects of fourteenth-century nominalism, whether they were aware of this or would admit to it, or not. They did not agree with nominalism insofar as it reached its conclusions by essentially dialectical means, but they did agree with the anti-realist conclusions of nominalism. The truths of the Christian religion could not be established by the faulty methods of secular logic but had to be accepted on the basis of revelation and held in faith. The humanist scepticism concerning philosophical demonstration of religious truth led them to the same position as the nominalists and bred an inclination to fideism in both of them.

Now Ficino in speaking of those who separated the study of philosophy from religion was doubtless also referring to the so-called Averroists and to the natural philosophers who did, indeed, make a separation between the truths of faith and the truths of philosophy, although this is not to say they believed in a so-called 'double-truth'. Ficino's antagonism to Averroes in Book XV of his *Theologia* is well known. But it is also true, although less attention has been paid to it, that his entire philosophy implies an opposition to nominalism. He could not possibly teach the doctrine of Platonic ideas, which was the historical original of philosophical realism, and have anything to do with that still dominant theological school of his own day, and this makes Heiko Oberman's attempt to find parallels between Ficino and such nominalists as Gabriel Biel and Ockham untenable.[10] Thus while he could agree with the humanists that faith and morals must be the end of thought, and that will must play at least an equal role to that of the intellect,[11] Ficino is compelled to disagree with those humanists such as Petrarch and Lorenzo Valla, and perhaps even Giannozzo Manetti, who resorted either to fideism or to Scriptural fundamentalism. And it is very possible that the antagonism between Ficino's philosophy and the nominalistic tendencies of Quattrocento theology is of far greater historical importance than his differences with the natural philosophers, of which much more has been made. For if the natural philosophers chose not to pronounce upon theological questions, and to accept them on faith, still they continued to uphold the role of rational thought in constructing tenable images of the universe, whereas the epistemological scepticism of nominalistic dialectic and theology delivered both the historical-moral and the spiritual realms to a fideistic or a positivistic acceptance of arbitrary power – the *potentia absoluta* of God and the absolute sovereignty of the prince or *lo stato*. Moreover, the anti-nominalistic implications of Ficino's philosophy did battle with the future of western philosophy as much as its past, whereas so-called 'Averroism', as both Randall and Vasoli have suggested, represented a vestigial survival in the Renaissance of a non-dynamic hieratic freezing of the cosmos and was essentially conservative with regard to the imperative intellectual problems of the Renaissance. Although attempts have been made to connect Ficino's Platonism with far too many developments of early modern culture, science and religion, those who claim that the significance of Renaissance Platonism lay in its effort to consider the spiritual world of God and the human soul as one with the natural universe [using 'natural' in a sense other than Ficino's application of it to the corporeal], and in its attempted conjoining of the subjective and the objective realms, do not seem to have been wrong. I have especially in mind Cassirer and Kristeller.

Ficino's philosophy then in its scope and intent is monumental, and it is also to a very great extent a seamless garment which makes it extremely difficult to deal with any single aspect of it without consideration of the whole. As indicated above, I will, nevertheless, temeritously pluck out certain sections that have special relevance in showing his relationship to the Renaissance humanist conceptions of man and God, although his philosophy as a whole has equally specific relevance to the general problem of man and God. Passing over his first five books of the *Theologia*, where the rational soul is established as a third essence lying between the corporeal and the divine, as the linkage between the lower and the upper realms, as by general and compelling abstract considerations immortal, as life itself, as the mistress and psychic dominator of the corporeal and the physiological, let us look at Ficino's more concrete consideration of the relationship of the soul and the body. Specifically, in books six, seven and eight, respectively, he seeks to establish the three-fold functioning of the human soul *in* the body, *through* the body and *independently* of the body *through itself.* The first concerns the so-called vegetative functions of human (and any other animate) existence: generation, nutrition and metabolic growth; the second human action utilising the five external senses and the internal images derived from these senses; the third human action by the pure force of the soul without sense impressions or internal images utilising only incorporeal things as objects of investigation. 'Thus you have natural action, sensibility and intelligence' as the three functions of the human soul in the body.[12]

Although book six is concerned with 'natural action', formally, he first engages in a general refutation of psychic materialism, or, perhaps more appropriately, 'corporealism'. And this is important to notice because it brings out the extent to which his central effort to prove psychic dominance in man (and other creatures) is also bound up with the effort to disprove a physiological or corporeal autonomy by means of basically epistemological arguments. He has, of course, learned this from Plato whose discussions of ontology rarely are detached from the attempt to prove that the alternative viewpoint is untenable because of an epistemological or gnoseological flaw in its argument. Ficino first of all lists four types of materialistic psychology: that the soul is made up of corpuscles of one or another of the elements or some combination of them – the atomist theory; or that it is not a body but a physical quality such as heat, as certain Stoics and others think; or a more intense point of quality lodged in some part of the body as other Stoics and certain others think; or as a point of quality diffused through the body as a kind of corporeal predisposition as another Hellenic school would have it.[13]

Last of all, however, are those who did not assign the soul to the first two levels of being, which constitute Ficino's ontology, namely matter and [physical] quality, but regard it as non-material and non-physicalistic, as something indivisible, that is an integral whole which we properly call 'individual' [although his Latin word *individuum* is more literal], but present in every part of the body, produced by an incorporeal author, and dependent only on the power of the agent and not on any quality of matter. Non-materiality, integrity and agency thus are attributed to the soul by the ancients which Ficino follows – the so-called *prisci theologi*, which we discuss elsewhere in this book – Zoroaster, Mercury, Orpheus, Aglaophemus, Pythagoras, and then Plato, 'in whose traces the natural philosopher Aristotle followed to a large extent'.[14]

It will be recalled that Manetti, who certainly admired Aristotle, also felt called upon to refute the materialist conceptions of the soul, but he followed Aristotle and Cicero as guides in doing this.[15] Ficino is not breaking new ground in seeking to demonstrate the spirituality and the immortality of the soul, and, in the quality of agency, its subjectivity or selfhood, although he is, perhaps, repeating on a more rigorous philosophical level what Cicero did more rhetorically rather than literally imitating him. Where Ficino does, indeed, represent something new and different from the preceding humanist tradition of discussions of man, from Salutati to Manetti (and also including most definitely Valla who insisted on the non-materiality and subjectivity of the soul), was in the independence of his scholarship [still relative, of course] and most of all in his confronting of the problem on the basis of Platonic epistemology. It is not his categories that are Platonic, for these are borrowed from Plotinus and from Aristotle, the vegetative, sensitive, and intellective souls, and from St. Augustine, and curiously pass over Plato's trilogy of appetite, passion and intellect which do not at all exactly correspond to Aristotelian categories; it is rather that his insight, nurtured by his study of Plato, of the way in which human experience leads to certain philosophical conclusions, and the ways in which experience itself has to be modified and corrected in order to pass from false, relativistic and merely subjective opinion, to philosophically validated truth, is newly Platonic.

In this way Ficino is able to show how the nature of the mind-body problem itself shapes the answers at which men arrive concerning the mind. Natural action sets in from the moment of conception through foetal life; sensibility only begins at birth; intelligence rarely begins even at the age of thirty when many men still remain boys. But if one inquires what the soul is from the context of natural action, or physiological functioning, the natural answer based on experience would be that it was physiological since psychic force only touched the body. Moreover, if the nature of the soul is sought by regarding its functioning in relation to the external senses, a similar answer would be forthcoming because it is natural enough to conceive of the soul visually through the eyes, aurally through the ears, and so on. But even if the internal sense with the images of the phantasy is considered, it has nothing but material images to go on. So long as human consciousness does not pass beyond physiological, sensual and imaginative experience it will only come to materialistic conclusions. Even if the mind itself is asked, after dismissing 'these three preceptors as though they were sophists' it too would give a corporeal answer because it is so involved in corporeal experience.[16]

But if the mind is consulted with regard to the soul in a pure state, unchained to the body and unsoiled by vices,

> the mind will immediately reply that the soul is not only incorporeal but divine. O soul, you are something grand if you are not filled with petty things, you are the finest if evil displeases you, the most beautiful if ugly things horrify you, eternal if you disdain the temporal. Since you are of such qualities, if you wish to discover yourself, look for yourself there where those qualities exist. Great things are only there where no spatial limits are imposed; excellence where nothing adverse happens; the most beautiful where there is nothing dissonant; eternal where there is no defect. Therefore seek yourself outside of the material world. But in order to seek and find yourself beyond the world, fly beyond, indeed look beyond; for you are outside the world when you regard the entire world.[17]

This passage with its epistemological meaning is the original of Pico della Mirandola's much better known encomium of the multi-potentiality of man in his famous *Oration on the Dignity of Man.* But Ficino's further explanation makes it clear that man's potentiality depends on his insights. When his experience leads him to limited insights, he becomes a being in accord with those materialistic notions; when his intellect lifts him through philosophical knowledge to the larger and universal insights, man finds his being in them. He immediately alludes to Plato's metaphor of the cave where men see only the shadows of realities and the sunlight where the philosopher sees things as they are. And he also alludes, or so it seems to me, to another Platonic passage where the saying is attributed to Protagoras that 'Man is the measure of all things.' For, as we shall see, Ficino is trying, like Plato, to show how man is the measure according to how he experiences, and how he permits himself to experience, so that he has the possibilities of transcending the limits of his own experience in the mental act of recognising this [rather than remaining limited to them as Plato accused Protagoras of thinking]. These are, indeed, Platonic dialectics which Ficino is following, but their relevance and the strength of their appeal in the discussions of his day should not be underestimated.

> But you think that you are in the lowest place of the world because, indeed, you do not see yourself flying beyond the ether, but you see your shadow, the body, here below, like when a boy looking into the depth of a well thinks he sees himself down there because he does not look at himself but at his reflection; or as if a bird flying in the air thinks it is flying along the ground when it sees its shadow on the ground. Therefore leave the insubstantiality of this shadow and turn towards yourself. For thus you will turn to fullness. You should know that there is enormous amplitude in spirit but infinite thinness in body, as I would put it. From this it may be seen that numbers which approach the spiritual nature, since they also are non-spatial, measure and number according to form both corporeal and incorporeal things and are nothing else but images of unity itself, but that unity is incorporeal since everything corporeal is multiple. Numbers, I say, are spiritual, and increase without end although they do not decrease without end. Magnitude on the contrary has a limit in increasing but none in decreasing.[18]

In other words, by an act of thought such as is involved in mathematics man can transcend the limits by which he is enclosed by sense judgements. Thus by sight alone men think the sun is two cubits wide, that the sky is immobile though it runs most rapidly, that the shore rather than the ship moves. And the other senses make equally gross errors. 'Who will correct the errors of the senses? Reason. But what emends and perfects is more noble than what is emended.' By reason the existence of the incorporeal can be judged, but sense judgement can only come to materialistic conclusions. And judging by one sense alone, such as sight, we deny the existence of sounds. And all the senses conspiring together will deny that anything exists in nature which is not corporeal.

> Nevertheless, reason, refuting all of these illusory conclusions, shows that something incorporeal also exists and truly so, and this conclusion is much truer than that of the senses which naturally condemn each other and are refuted by it. For what is more stupid than to claim that we excel the animals in reason and then to admit that the things exist which we perceive through the sense and which some animals perceive much more acutely than we do, and at the same time to contend that what we learn by the eye of reason is nothing?

Whoever uses reason so that he is more deceived by it than by sense must not be considered the king of other creatures. So he rejects the conclusions of the petty philosophers who, limited by the judgement of sense, cannot think the soul is incorporeal and divine.[19]

These philosophers

> should at last be made aware that it is their long experience with the body that made them so corporeal that they understandably know nothing except the body or things derived from the body. Let them be purified and they will perceive pure things. May they some day experience within themselves, for they can if they only wish to, what they have long sought in the world. They certainly perceive things that are of a composite nature and many forms within the composite. They further seek some separated forms outside the composite. They themselves are composites of soul and body. They possess life passed from the soul of the body; they also possess a life of the soul itself thriving within itself. They should despise the one but prize the other. They should lead an intellectual life separate from the body, and once separate they will attain immediately to the separate forms, and they will soon prove by fact that Socratic opinion that there are forms in themselves perfect beyond the imperfect forms which adhere to subjects, and these form unformed subjects. And they will learn that the unique way not only of attaining but of possessing the incorporeal is to render themselves incorporeal, that is to withdraw the mind from movement, sense, affect,

> and corporeal imagination as far as they are able. For thus experience itself will establish first how it is to be pure soul, that is reason living with itself and turning itself avidly about the light itself of truth. Secondly how it is to be an angel, that is pure intellect now enjoying the infused light of truth. Third, [how it is] when the soul itself as though it were an angel enjoys the full light of truth, perceives God at once as the truth lighting and enjoying itself by itself, then light itself enjoying its own truth, and at last joy itself lighting by its own truth.[20]

Thus Ficino proposes here again, what is, of course, central to his philosophy, the introspection of an interior experience which teaches the independent existence of the psychic functioning in abstraction or separation from the body.[21] It will be recalled, of course, that St. Augustine made this central to his own establishment of the dominance of spirit and subjectivity in the universe, and that the Augustinian, Gregory of Rimini, utilised the same thought to establish the existence of psychic realities which had been denied by some of the fourteenth-century nominalists by a similar kind of corporeal epistemology to that Ficino is criticising here.[22] Ficino leads this process of finding a new transcendent experience, that frees the mind from the body and gives it previously denied insights, on to his advocacy of meditation. All of this he regarded as a counter-education or counter-*paideia* to the experience limited to the corporeal. 'We begin to recognise that the error of the uneducated is for the most part born from the experience of the body when we conceive of a certain education contrary to it.'[23] This he seeks to establish through an example drawn from Avicenna who imagined a man educated without recourse to the senses, which he follows with a long citation of his own translation of the allegory of the cave from the seventh book of Plato's *Republic*.[24]

We have thus by too long an exposition, but far shorter than Ficino's and necessarily but unfortunately passing over much of interest, shown how he has resorted to a confrontation of those philosophies that deny mental and spiritual realities because they are able to reduce the thought-process to the sensual or the physiological. He has seen that this is an epistemological consequence of having too limited an experience and education, which he is seeking in his entire philosophy to overcome. The analogy to the less systematic humanist efforts to overcome nominalistic scepticism, as well as the more systematic Augustinianism of Gregory of Rimini, on the one hand, shows the context within which

Ficino must be considered. On the other hand, it was his merit to see how arguments drawn from the Platonists and the Neoplatonists could strengthen and systematise these positions, which, repudiating the metaphysical naturalism of natural philosophy, felt uncomfortable in the alternative nominalism, and sought by an affirmation and analysis of subjectivity to re-establish the possibility of knowing universals and knowing the truth. It should be clear that Ficino in repudiating so-called Averroism, in making use of Thomas Aquinas, does so in a decidedly Augustinian way, and that his repudiation of nominalism also began where nominalism began, with the experience of the individual. But in place of the limited and limiting epistemology of nominalist theology, he sought to develop a positive structure of spiritual reality discernible in the internal life of man.

It should not, however, be thought because he argued so effectively against corporeal thinking that he regarded the human body entirely with disdain. He thought of man, it is certainly true, predominantly as a spiritual being, a rational, immortal soul. But he also saw man as having a place in the chain of being characterised by a middle position between eternal spirits outside of the body, or angels, and mortal spirits in a body, or animals. Man, therefore, was a rational soul existing in a body but immortal. But, he asked, 'is the human body endowed with such dignity that it deserves to receive an immortal mind as its guest? Without any doubt'. He then proceeds to state most of the traditional arguments in praise of the human body that we have encountered in the treatises on the dignity of man. One should not be disturbed if animals are given special physical endowments for their protection and nourishment.

> For nature did not wish to deform the delicate harmony of our body, nor was she able to supply innumerable means of protection and other instruments for the infinite actions of men which follow from the infinity of man's thinking, but, as Aristotle says, when she gave mind and hand she gave all arts and all instruments,

whereas the more specialised actions of animals are directed to a single limited end. The body is a suitable hospice for the soul

> on account of its erect posture, not looking at the ground but upward and as though recognising heaven as properly its own country, on account of

> the marvellous beauty of all the various members, and because the finer elements of fire and air have a larger role in us; this is also indicated by the agility of the body, by the height of the figure and its erect look, and especially by the most harmonious complexion, or total composition which is shown by the delicate, soft, firm and brilliant suppleness of the flesh which could only exist with the most precise balance of the elements.[25]

Man is surpassed by animals in sight, hearing and smell, but not in taste and touch, which is shown by the extent of human indulgence in eating, drinking and sex, which men pursue more avidly than animals because they feel more sharply.[26] Man also has a larger brain and a warmer heart. All of these together with the specific balance of elements in man make possible his greater mental activity. Man's internal composition also is such as to relieve him of the necessity of horns, furs, feathers.

> Let us conclude therefore that man is born for contemplation, as Anaxagoras said, since his brain and the rest of his body is so constituted that it continually serves the office of contemplation which requires a supple brain and a harmonious complexion of the body. . . . But since the balance of our body is so great and so sublime that it seems to imitate the harmony of the heavens, it is no wonder that a celestial soul for a time inhabits this building so similar to heaven.

The soul descends by intermediate stages into the body, by means of eternal ethereal bodies and spirit.

> Thus it is well that the immortal soul is joined to mortal bodies through that immortal ethereal body. It dwells in it eternally but in this earthly one for a short time only, so that the soul deservedly ought to be called a god or a star surrounded with a cloud or a daemon, not an inhabitant of the earth but a guest.[27]

Ficino's central purpose as a philosopher was to demonstrate the immortality and divinity of the human soul. For a number of humanists the immortality of the soul, and for some even its divinity, was alleged as a major argument on behalf of the dignity and excellence of man. Ficino, turning the proposition around, argued in the thirteenth and fourteenth books of the *Theologia platonica* that the many signs of the dignity and excellence of man, or more specifically the human rational soul, were themselves evidence of the immortality and divinity of the soul. Although he would thus range himself with those humanists who followed the more traditional ecclesiastical arguments for man's dignity as resting in his heavenly destiny rather than with those who emphasised his earthly achievements, nonetheless, in these two books Ficino gives a remarkable picture of the greatness of human nature as manifested in its this-worldly capacities and achievements. Of course, in the earlier books, he brought forth many more strictly philosophical arguments for the immortality of souls, but in these two books he also resorted to the type of argument previously used by the humanists, namely, that the nature of human existence can be comprehended only on the assumption of a deep conviction of immortality within man. If this were to prove not to be true, all man's efforts would be ridiculous and in vain. It is the nature of man and of human existence that provides his most forceful argument for divinity. I think it is possible therefore to claim that Ficino's exposition of the dignity and excellence of man is genuinely the culmination of the previous humanists' efforts not only in the sense that many major arguments are recapitulated but also because it goes beyond them in the depth, extent and completeness of its vision of man. Man is conceived of not only as the *image* of God, but as a veritable divinity – a god on earth and a god in the world to come.

He begins book XIII with a consideration, again, of psychic dominance in man's life, in this case the dominance of the lowest elements of the soul, the affects of the 'phantasy', over the body itself.[28] We saw above how he borrowed the Aristotelian categories of vegetative, sensitive and intellective souls. Here he follows Neoplatonic divisions of the soul into three parts, which are, in fact, much more characteristic of his own thinking. One of his clearest expositions of the parts of the soul and of their relationship with the prevailing orders of the cosmos occurs in the middle of chapter 2 of this book, where he wishes to account for man's power of prophecy by stating the relationship of the parts of the human soul to the orders of causes in the universe. 'Three orders of things seem to pertain to the human soul: providence, fate and nature. Providence is the succession of minds [or intelligences], fate the succession of souls, nature the succession of bodies.'[29] The soul in turn consists of the *mens*, or intellect, which is linked with and participates in providence, the *rational soul,* which has a position of independence in the middle, and the *idolum* or phantasy or imagination which gathers and organizes the impressions of the five senses into images. Below this is the body. Man is linked to the order of fate through the phantasy, to the order of nature through the body.[30]

Thus Ficino is compelled by the nature of the problem to set forth the relationship of the freedom and dignity of man to the determining orders of causes in the universe, as we saw Salutati earlier doing. And, as the latter insisted, Ficino also affirms man's freedom in the midst of these orders.

> Therefore the soul is above fate through mind, and in the order of providence only, in such a way that it imitates its superiors and together with them governs inferior beings. For the soul, as though a participant in providence, according to the model of divine governance rules itself, and governs the home, the community, the arts and the animals. Through the *idolum* the soul is in the order of fate, similarly, but it is not under fate. . . . Thus the soul is placed in the laws of providence, fate, and nature not only passively but also as an actor. . . . Although in these three parts [of ourselves] we are partially bound to the order of things and partially not bound, in a fourth we are entirely free and our own. This is the reason which we locate in the middle between the mind, the head of the soul, and the idolum, the foot of the soul.[31]

The essence of man is, according to Ficino, embodied in the reason.

> For the *mind* is within the soul not in so far as it is soul in the proper sense but as something angelic and as though occupied by supernal minds. The *idolum* also of the soul, that is the guiding power over the body, is not the function of the pure soul but of the soul verging towards the body. But *reason* is interposed, a certain proper force of true souls through which they proceed from the principles of things in temporal succession to the conclusions in a universal concept, they resolve effects into their causes, and again deduce effects from their causes, and arrive also at a particular concept after the model of a universal consideration.

The Platonists say that the force of reason

> is related to intelligence in such a way as we see speech is related to the soul, and it is involved in perpetual and free movement. Finally that rational faculty, which is the proper nature of the true soul, is not determined for some one thing for it wanders up and down in free movement. . . . For although through the mind, the *idolum* and nature we are linked in some way to a common order of things, . . . still through the reason we are entirely our own law, and as though free we may follow whatever of these parts we wish. Sometimes reason adheres to the intellect and then it rises into providence, sometimes it follows the *idolum* and nature and there it submits to fate by a certain love while trusting the senses it is distracted

> hither and yon by the charm of sensible things, and sometimes excluding the others it retires within itself where it examines other things by argumentation or investigates itself. To so great an extent that middle and proper power of the soul is both free, and restless. And whenever something comes into the range of our extreme parts, as into the mind, the *idolum* or our nature, it is possible for the soul immediately to perceive it, but it is not aware of perceiving it before it passes into this middle power. For since it is through this intermediary power that we are men, indeed that we ourselves are, whatever pertains to it, most evidently pertains to men.[32]

This is how Ficino structured the soul and linked it to the cosmic orders, and how he also provided an autonomous centre of free action and choice in man in the rational soul, which, unlinked to the cosmos, was free to become whatever man wished, and in this sense was not a 'microcosm'. As we suggested above, Ficino, following Plotinus, anticipated Pico della Mirandola in this conception of man as free from cosmic bonds, though it has usually been claimed that Pico was original in this position.[33] However, let us return to his discussion of the capacity of the human soul to dominate the body, moving upward from the affects of the phantasy in his original order, through the other powers of the soul.

The affects of the phantasy are the four commonly so considered: desire, pleasure, fear and pain. Ficino's treatment of them shows a remarkable psychological sophistication. To demonstrate their powers over the body he presents for each a series of examples of what we would call psycho-somatic occurrences.

> These four emotions entirely dominate the body since they change it in all sorts of ways. Moreover these are motions of the soul itself, for as the soul judges something to be good or bad, so it desires, enjoys, fears or sorrows. Whence it follows that the nature of the body is entirely subject to the movements of the soul.

The body easily yields to the soul because it is less earthy in its complexion than the bodies of other animals, and having more of the sublimer elements, is a receptacle for the celestial soul. This is shown also by the fact that intellectuals such as Aristotle, Pyrrho, Speusippus, Carneades, Chrysippus and Plotinus were of a delicate constitution and often ill. Plato 'adds that the most powerful emotions of the soul even dissolve and disintegrate the body, which happens not only in the course of an affect but also during intense speculation'.[34]

Movements within the soul or the body can affect the other in different ways, some penetrating and others not. Heat or cold may affect the body but not the soul. But some things are so physically tense that the soul notices them. The soul may speculate tranquilly without influencing the body, but a violent movement of the intelligence or the phantasy toward something harmful or useful will make itself felt in the body.

> Certainly when through some affect of the soul movements occur in the body they seem to happen not through the force of the body but through the empire of the soul. For the body has no power of acting and receives movements transmitted by the soul without delay. . . . To become aware and to judge are acts of the soul. And so the soul is disturbed through its own actions and not through the violence of the body, and hence it moves itself and is not moved by the body. This may be plainly seen in that the body is always agitated by a more vigorous cogitation or affection of the soul, and it cannot resist it, whereas the soul is not necessarily changed in its condition by a passion or suffering of the body.[35]

Turning to the affects of the reason, he divides these into the examples of philosophers, poets, priests and prophets who were able by the intensity of their mental activity to transcend the body.[36] Epimenides slept fifty years – that is he lived detached from the senses; Pythagoras and Zoroaster for twenty. Socrates and Plato both could go into periods of abstraction. Archimedes was unaware of the battle around him because he was so intent on his study of geometry. Plotinus, Heraclitus and Democritus also retreated from the senses. Plato in the *Phaedrus* wrote that the intelligence of philosophers acquired wings which helped them fly toward God. Such men were usually of the melancholy temperament and, possessing a greater portion of earth in their makeup, could more easily withdraw their soul from other things

> to what was their own and fixing it in contemplation bring it to bear on penetrating to the centre of things. Nevertheless, neither the planets nor the humours of this sort do these things as though efficient causes but either offer the occasion or drive away the obstacles; rather it is the soul itself which unaided and freely accomplishes these actions. Certainly the empire of the mind is great which is freed from the fetters of the body by its own power. Great is the richness of the mind for as often as it desires precious treasures of God and nature, it draws them from its own breast and not from the bowels of the earth.[37]

The affection of the mind is also shown in the fury of poetic inspiration, as Plato has shown in the *Phaedrus* and in *Ion*. Whereas individual arts are acquired over a long period of time without the aid of God, poets such as Orpheus, Homer, Hesiod and Pindar insert signs of all the arts in their works. Many compose in madness and afterwards do not know what they have said, as if God had used them as musical instruments. The best poets were not erudite prudent men but those struck with divine madness. God picks inept men for this to show that poetry is a divine gift.[38]

Priests also manifested the power of the intellect to transcend the body. St. Paul was lifted to the third heaven in divine abstraction. The disciples in one day were transformed from fishermen into theologians. 'All antiquity witnesses that, before these times, many priests under the influence of demons were delivered into divine transports and made marvellous pronouncements.'[39] Moreover, there are many other kinds of holy men and prophets who are able to remove the mind from the body and be in many places at once, and in the three times of past, present and future simultaneously. Ficino brought his discussion of the three orders of succession in the cosmos – providence, fate and nature – into his discussion here, and showed, as we saw above, how intellect, phantasy and corporeal nature corresponded to each, with the reason freely autonomous. But it is through these connections of the intellect with providence that the power of prophecy, of poetry, of the priesthood and of the philosopher (corresponding to Plato's four kinds of madness in the *Phaedrus*) took place. He devotes the rest of this long chapter to discussing seven types of withdrawal from the body or *vacatio*.[40]

Ficino's theory of prophecy is interesting, as it shows that man by putting aside his concerns with his own course of life, which are in the control of the rational soul, by stepping out of his role of free active being in other words, can relate to the orders of causes in the universe of which, as we have seen above, he is a participant through his intelligence, his *idolum* or his nature.

> When that influx of minds finds our reason emptied or free for the intellect, it shows it something of those things which pertain to universal knowledge of eternal matters or to the government of the universe, so that it foresees either the law of God and the orders of angels or the return of the ages and

> the revolutions of kingdoms. When the impulse of the *idola* and of the natures comes upon an entirely emptied reason and phantasy, something is revealed to it concerning the vicissitudes of times and the disturbances of the elements so that it can foresee future rains, earthquakes and similar things.[41]

It is very difficult to exhaust the consciousness sufficiently to open the soul to these influences. And the dreams and sleep of many men engaged in active involvement in the affairs of this life and of the world prove to Ficino that the true philosophical 'shaman', or a true prophet and sage, is very rare indeed. For instance,

> There are also many men who despise the voluptuous life but who are nevertheless intent on civil affairs or avid for power and fame. In them while sleeping the phantasy is lulled for a time but the reason goes on dealing with both private and public affairs and is occupied greatly with them. There are some who are contemptuous of pleasure and of human glory as well, but given to the investigation of divine and natural questions. In their sleep not only the phantasy stops for a time but also the anxious consultation of the active reason. But that customary investigation of the speculative reason revives, so that we seem either to be measuring the heavens or dividing the elements or numbering the species of animals. To none of these whom we have listed is prophecy generally suitable, even though these last philosophers truly think while sleeping and sometimes make discoveries, which they have long sought while awake but have not found, because the reason is more tranquil.[42]

The true prophet must abandon even these highest human concerns.

> Nor are those entirely lacking, although very few such are found, who having tamed pleasure and neglecting civil affairs so order their life that they burn with a desire for acquiring the truth, yet despair of being able to find it through the human vestiges which the dubious mind of the natural philosophers commonly is accustomed to trust. Hence they dedicate themselves to God in such a way that they do nothing. With eyes opened and purified they wait especially for what divinely may be shown them, and this Socrates is said to have advised and practiced. These are called pious men and religious. Their soul is more withdrawn while awake than that of any others, in sleep it is entirely withdrawn. Therefore the supernal impulse is easily observed by them.[43]

Having shown in the first two chapters of this book how man can rise above and control his animal nature through his phantasy, and how he can extract himself from his rational soul in order to be in touch with providence, fate and nature, in the third chapter (in a passage reminiscent of Manetti's eulogy of the works of man) he returns to man as the expression of the rational soul, actively changing and re-creating the world of nature about him by means of art and industry.

> The other animals either live without art, or have each one single art to the use of which they do not turn by their own power but are dragged by a law of fate. The sign of this is that they gain nothing from time for the work of making things. On the contrary men are the inventors of innumerable arts which they practise according to their own decision. This is shown by the fact that individuals practise many arts, change, and become more expert by extensive exercise, and what is marvellous, human arts make by themselves whatever nature itself makes, so that we seem not to be servants of nature but competitors.

Zeuxis painted grapes so that birds flew to them. Apelles painted a horse and a dog so that passing horses neighed and dogs barked. Praxiteles made a marble Venus in a temple of the Indies so beautiful that it could hardly be preserved from the lusty glances of passers-by. Archytas of Tarentum, following the rules of mathematics, made a wooden dove, inflated it with air and it flew. The Egyptians made statues of gods which according to Hermes Trismegistus walked and spoke. Archimedes of Syracuse made a brass celestial sphere in which the seven planets moved as they do in the heavens, and it revolved as the heavens do. The pyramids of the Egyptians, the buildings of the Greeks and Romans, the workshops in metal and glass may also be mentioned. 'Man at last imitates all the works of divine nature and perfects, corrects and modifies the works of lower nature.'[44]

There is in Ficino an irrepressible admiration for the works of human industry with which he was surrounded in Renaissance Florence. And much as he encouraged and advocated a life of contemplation transcending the earthly concerns of man, he cannot help seeing in man's mastery of the world, so apparent to the eye of a man of the Renaissance, further evidence of man's similarity to God if not of his divinity itself. Ficino's praise of *homo faber* is fulsome, and in the light of the more frequent emphasis on his inwardness we shall report it fully.

> The force of man is almost similar to the divine nature since man by himself, that is through his intelligence and skill, governs himself without being in the least limited by his physical nature and imitates the individual works of

the higher nature. And he has so much less need than the beasts for the aid of inferior nature as he is endowed by nature with fewer natural aids to bodily protection than the animals, but he himself provides his own supply of food, clothing, bedding, housing, furnishings and arms. Hence he supports himself by his own capacity more richly than nature preserves the beasts. In connection with this an indescribable variety of pleasures are developed for delighting the five senses of the body which we invent for ourselves by our own talents. The animals are enclosed in the narrowest limits of nature. Our soul is concerned not only with the necessities of the body like beasts subjected to the rule of nature, but with various delights of the senses as though a kind of food for the phantasy. And the soul not only flatters its phantasy with these various pleasures while daily seducing it with various games as if for jest, but meanwhile also the cogitative reason acts seriously, and it comes out eager to propagate its own progeny, and to show how strong its own inventive genius is through various silk and woollen textiles, paintings, sculptures and buildings. In composing these works it often respects no bodily comforts, no pleasing of the senses, since it sometimes willingly undergoes hardship and trouble, but it also expands and proves its productive power.

In these industrial arts it may be observed how man everywhere utilises all the materials of the universe as though all were subject to man. He makes use, I say, of the elements, the stones, metals, plants and animals, and he transforms them into many shapes and figures, which animals never do. Nor is he content with one element or a few, as animals, but he uses all as though he was master of all. He tramps the earth, he sails the water, he ascends in the air by the highest towers, as I pass over the feathers of Daedalus or Icarus. He alone lights fire and uses his familial hearth, especially appreciating it. Correctly only a celestial animal is delighted by a celestial element. With celestial virtue he ascends the heavens and measures them. With supercelestial intelligence he transcends the heaven. But man not only uses the elements, he adorns them, which no brute does. How marvellous the cultivation of the earth through all the world. How stupendous the structures of buildings and cities. How ingenious his works of irrigation. He acts as the vicar of God, since he inhabits all the elements and cultivates all, and present on earth, he is not absent from the ether. Indeed he employs not only the elements but all the animals of the elements, terrestrial, aquatic, and flying, for food, comfort and pleasure, and the supernal and celestial ones for learning and the miracles of magic. He not only uses the animals but he rules them. It is possible that some animals by means of the weapons received from nature may sometimes either attack men or escape the attacks of men; man however gets his weapons from himself and avoids the attacks of wild beasts and defeats and tames them. Who ever saw any men kept under the rule of animals such as everywhere we see herds both of the most savage as well as the milder animals obeying men their entire life. He does not only rule the animals cruelly, but he also governs, fosters and teaches them. Universal providence is proper to God who is the universal cause. Therefore man who universally provides for all things living and not living is a certain god. He is the god without doubt of the animals since he uses all of them, rules them, and teaches some of them. He is established also as god of the elements since he inhabits and cultivates them all. He is, finally, the god of all materials since he handles all, and turns and changes them. Anyone who dominates the body in so many and such great things and acts as the vicar of immortal God is without doubt immortal.[45]

The wonder is that with such a paean of praise to the status of civilised man, Ficino was not satisfied with his earthly condition. For this passage, a development out of the one we first quoted from Petrarch, resembling in many ways the superlatives of Manetti, is a culmination, as it were, of Renaissance encomiums of man as the builder and ruler of the earthly realm. It is, moreover, a literal application of the vision of man as the image of God! He adds, however, another important side of man's earthly role, which to be sure was not neglected by Manetti, nor by the Florentine civic humanists, and which is a quality that Ficino considers far superior to those of industrial man – *homo faber*.

But the arts of this type, although they mould the matter of the universe and command the animals, and thus imitate God, the creator of nature, are nevertheless inferior to those arts which imitating the heavenly kingdom undertake the responsibility of human government. Single animals scarcely suffice for the care of themselves or briefly of their offspring. But man alone so abounds in perfection that he rules himself first, which no beasts do, then governs his family, administers the state, rules peoples and commands the entire world. And as though born for ruling he is entirely impatient of servitude. Add that he will submit to death for the sake of the public good, which animals do not do, since trusting in the strength of common and eternal good he despises these single mortal goods.[46]

But man in his ascent upwards transcends both the mechanical and civil arts by developing the liberal intellectual ones.

But the arts of this sort may seem to someone to pertain to this present life, although such great care is not necessary for this present life but rather regards the imitation of divine providence. Let us consider therefore those arts which not only are not necessary for bodily nourishment but are very offensive to it, such as all the liberal sciences whose study enervates the body and restricts the comforts of life. The subtle computation of numbers, the meticulous description of figures, the most obscure movement of lines, the mysterious consonance of music, long observation of the stars, the study of natural causes, the investigation of enduring things, the eloquence of orators, the madness of poets – in all of these the soul of man despises the ministry of the body as though he one day would be able and now already begins to live without the aid of the body.[47]

In this movement away from his earth-bound condition, however, Ficino still perceives great glory in man's constructive capacity. Not anyone can understand the principles and methods underlying a work constructed by a skilled artisan but only someone who is endowed with talent in that art. Thus only a man of similar genius is able to understand how Archimedes constructed his spheres.

Since therefore man sees the order of the heavens, whence and where they move and by what measures and what they bring about, who will deny that he is endowed with a genius, as I would put it, that is almost the same as that of the Author of the heavens, and that man would be able to make the heavens in some way if he only possessed the instruments and the celestial material, since he does make them now, although out of other material, yet very similar in structure?[48]

Certainly Ficino is in this aspiration and confidence historically prophetic of modern man's efforts to understand and restructure physical reality itself.

The human soul was endowed with four great gifts that made these achievements in the arts possible: speed of perception, the widest and almost indelible memory, the cleverest prediction of future things, the use of innumerable words. Here that admired talent of the age of humanism, the use of words, came in for special praise by Ficino, also.

Finally the use of speech and writing especially proper to man indicates a certain divinity of mind present in us which animals lack. Thus without speech we would live like beasts and mute men. Hence speech is granted to us for a certain more excellent task, namely as the interpreter of the mind, and herald and infinite messenger of infinite discoveries.[49]

Valla, as we saw above, wished to identify himself with the Epicurean tradition by claiming that animals also share man's mental and psychic powers. Ficino attempts to answer Epicurus, that if animals had speech and hands we would see their intelligence, by claiming that while animals do have a limited intelligence which enables them to search for nourishment and a rudimentary set of sounds sufficient to express their confused concepts,

> the mind of man, however, the inventress of innumerable and different things, is supported by the use of innumerable words, as though by a certain worthy interpreter of itself, and it is furnished with hands as well which are most apt instruments for making the innumerable inventions of the mind; indeed the same nature would have given these instruments to animals also if there were in them an interior craftsman who would use such instruments. Therefore the mind in comprehending conceives of as many things in itself as God in knowing makes in the world. By speaking it expresses as many into the air; with a reed it writes as many on paper. By making it constructs as many in the material of the world. Therefore he would be proven mad who would deny that the soul, which in the arts and in governing competes with God, is divine.[50]

Whereas Lorenzo Valla, the most influential philologist of the Renaissance, claimed that man was distinguished from the animals by the gift of immortality, Ficino, the foremost advocate of immortality in the Renaissance, at this point gave ironically greater emphasis to the gift of language than Valla had done. Ficino's statement also echoes Cicero's argument in the second book of *On the Nature of the Gods*, though he makes no allusion to this as a source.

We shall not enter into his discussion of the fourth sign of man's immortality and divinity, his working of miracles, except to indicate that Ficino also considered this in the context of human mastery over all parts of the earthly and the cosmic environment.

> The human mind vindicates to itself a right to divinity not only in forming and shaping matter through the methods of arts, as we have said, but also in transmuting the species of things by command, which work is indeed called a miracle, not because it is beyond the nature of our soul, when it is made an instrument of God, but because, since it is something great and rarely done, it generates admiration. Here we marvel that the souls of men dedicated to God rule the elements, call upon the winds, force the clouds to rain, chase away fogs, cure the diseases of human bodies and the rest. These plainly were done in certain ages among various peoples, as poets sing, historians narrate, and those who are the most excellent of philosophers, especially the Platonists, do not deny, the ancient theologians testify, above all Hermes and Orpheus, and the later theologians also prove by word and deed.[51]

Although the specific influence of the Hermetic tradition in the formation of Ficino's notions of natural magic was no doubt central, as Frances Yates, D. P. Walker and others claim,[52] it is important to note that here in the *Theologia platonica* Ficino leads up to magic through man's rational, artistic, productive and scientific capacities. Here it is regarded essentially as a divinely aided extension of the rational and psychic, even proto-divine, powers with which man is endowed. In the later *Libri de vita,* which these scholars utilise, the context is medical and more purely magical. Besides, as we have seen, through the linkage of man to providence through the intellect, to fate through the phantasy, and to nature through the body, man is in possession of certain miraculous forces without resort to theurgy or talismans.

Having demonstrated by his four signs that souls dominate bodies, Ficino moved towards an even more strenuous demonstration of the soul's immortality – that it strives to become God in twelve different ways corresponding to twelve 'gifts', or characteristics, of God. Here the conception of man as living in the image of God is made completely explicit through the notion that the characteristic directions of human *conatus* are all towards deification. God is, and man strives to be: [1] one, true and good; [2] everything; [3] the creator of the universe; [4] above all; [5] in all; [6] always. God does, and man strives to: [7] provide for all; [8] administer justly; [9] persevere with fortitude in his state of being; [10] deal temperately and smoothly; [11] live richly and joyously; [12] see, admire and worship himself.[53] Moreover this effort is a natural appetite of the human species:

> The entire striving of our soul is that it become God. Such striving is no less natural to men than the effort to flight is to birds. For it is always in men everywhere. Likewise it is not a contingent quality of some men but follows the nature itself of the species. ... Therefore the human effort to become God can some day be fulfilled. For who but God, Himself, whom we seek, would have inserted this into our souls? who, since He alone is the author of the species, inserts a proper appetite into the species.[54]

Ficino alludes to the Biblical tradition in asserting finally that man in becoming eternal does in truth become God.

> For if the mind lifts itself as much higher for the sake of contemplating spiritual things as it removes itself farther from corporeal things, if the supreme end which the intelligence can attain is the very substance of God, it follows

that then at length the mind is able to draw near the divine substance, when it will be totally alienated from mortal senses. Therefore the soul, freed from the chains of this body, and departing in purity, does in a certain mode become God. God, however, and the eternity of God are the same. Therefore by a similar method it becomes eternity and even more it becomes eternal. This is that state which John, the theologian, called to become similar to God, and Paul to be transformed into the image of God.[55]

In man's natural striving towards divinity, Ficino argues, there is first manifested a natural desire to know the truth and to possess the good. But in knowing and possessing any truth or good, we are not satisfied with less than the first of these categories, so mankind restlessly seeks one after the other until it can come to rest in the first truth and first good which is God. 'Therefore we desire God Himself. But what do we most strongly desire in God? That we may become similar to Him.' All things, in accordance with their level of being, strive to become like God. Man, therefore, strives to become like God through his intellect and his will. In knowing something the intellect transforms itself into the image of the thing known. Thus in truly comprehending God, the intellect becomes the image of God. 'Therefore our end is to see God through the intellect, having seen God to enjoy Him through the will, since our *summum bonum* is the highest object of our highest power or the most perfect action concerning it.'[56] This is his essential argument concerning man's striving to become God in relation to the first and chief quality of God. He supports it with arguments from Aristotle, St. Thomas, Plato and Cicero. But his own main concern is to show that this striving towards the first truth and first good is a 'natural appetite'. This he does by comparing it to the natural appetite of all the different levels of existence, but chiefly the bodily, whose natural appetite is for food and sexual union.

But indeed the body demands food at rare intervals, sexual union even more rarely. But we desire the true and the good at every moment. For we are always desirous of new things, imaginations and reasons. We always open our eyes to whatever is occurring, and we are excessively delighted with distant and wide vistas, indeed we are only happy with what is immense. Always we bend our ears to whatever is to be heard, which infants do and adults, educated and uneducated, and artisans in any industry, guided by nature. Moreover the lust for sexuality can be moderated, the greed for eating diminished, but the desire for truth and goodness never. Indeed those decrease with age but these increase. Consider further that those corporeal objects are desired on account of something else, these, however, for their own sake. Therefore as much more natural as the desire for the true and the good is than the desire for food and sex, that much more is it provided by nature that it will entirely achieve its end.[57]

It is important to Ficino to assert that the end of this natural desire will be achieved by individuals, although they will restlessly seek it without fulfilment in this life. He cannot agree here with Averroes who denies that the intellect can attain its end in individuals but asserts that it only can attain it collectively in all men. But there is no single intellect in all men who are continually quarrelling with each other, nor does a desired condition of the soul come simultaneously to all men. And when individuals are blind to the divine, the collectivity is also blind. We cannot imagine the divine forms out of natural substances at our wish. For natural substances decline toward matter but the divine ones do not. Thus Averroes is wrong on two counts: one that there is a collective mind that can perceive what individuals cannot, and two that divine things can be understood through natural things. The mind itself must be lifted and informed with divinity, but this must happen in individuals. This, of course, was a very important issue to Ficino and to his times. As we shall see, Pomponazzi attempted to solve the same problem by preserving the individuality of the human intellect but denying its natural potentiality for immortality. Ficino wants both, as did St. Thomas, with whom Pomponazzi argued, also. But there is an important difference in Ficino's insistence that our striving towards goodness and truth was a natural appetite which informed all of our actions and eventually led upwards towards immortality.[58]

The next sign of man's attempt to achieve divinity could be more concretely demonstrated. It is man's multipotentiality in his effort to become everything. Again Ficino has stated in advance of Pico's more succinct expression the underlying thought of this idea.

Man leads the life of a plant in so far as in eating he indulges the body, the life of an animal when he flatters his senses, the life of a man in so far as he consults reason in human affairs, the life of heroes as he investigates natural phenomena, the life of demons when he engages in mathematical speculation, the life of angels according as he inquires into divine mysteries, the life of God as far as he does all for the sake of God. The soul of every man experiences all these things in a certain way in himself, although each in his own way, and so mankind strives to become all beings since it leads the lives of all beings.

And he quotes the same passage from the *Asclepius* with which Pico begins his oration, significantly linking the same idea of multipotentiality to the Asclepian passage as Pico was to do.

Hermes Trismegistus marvelled at this so much that he said 'A great miracle is man, an animal to be venerated and adored who knows the race of demons as if he was related by nature, and who changes into God as if he himself were a god.'

In this striving for totality of being man seeks to know all and to enjoy all through intellect and will. The mind in knowing something becomes the thing it knows;

when the intellect seeks to know all things and in knowing them dresses itself entirely in their form, the consequence is that it seeks to become all things, hence it attempts to become God, in whom are all things, when it attempts to become all.[59]

The will in seeking to enjoy all things strives to unite with them. But unlike the intellect, the will seeks all things in their concrete particularity whereas the intellect knows them in their abstract universality. 'For both become all things, the intellect all true things, the will all good things. But the intellect is united to things by transferring the things into itself, the will on the contrary by transferring itself into the things.' This is a dialectically different statement from those of Duns Scotus, Salutati, and Valla discussed above, where it is argued that man is shaped by things through the intellect but shapes things through the will. The preoccupation with the dynamics of the movements of the human soul in relation to the world is patent, however, in all of them.[60]

Man also attempts to emulate God in making all things, as he said above in connection with the arts, and to conquer all things. As he also said above, man is impatient of servitude.

Even if he is forced to serve, he hates his lord, since to serve is contrary to his nature. Moreover, he strives with all his might to conquer in any thing, and is ashamed to be bested in the least thing or the most trivial games, as though it was contrary to the natural dignity of man; and the affect of shame and respect peculiar to mankind shows that there is hidden in us something of I do not know what grandeur which it would be wicked to violate and which is most worthy of respect.

This emphasis on man's desire to win, on his competitiveness, we have encountered in other humanists. Valla especially stressed it, and enjoyed striving for *victory* as a kind of ultimate goal of human fruition. Manetti however made this same desire to excel and fear of being bested by others the source of man's troubles and sin. Ficino also speaks of 'victory' in relation to Alexander seeking other worlds to conquer:

> But in what pertains to the desire for victory, the immense magnificence of our soul may manifestly be seen from this, that he will not be satisfied with the empire of this world, if, having conquered this one, he learns that there remains another world which he has not yet subjugated. . . . Thus man wishes no superior and no equal and will not permit anything to be left out and excluded from his rule. This status belongs to God alone. Therefore he seeks a divine condition.[61]

In an age where conquest and the struggle for personal political power was forcibly impressed on everyone's consciousness Ficino was able to single out and admire an instinct for victory in man as one of the marks of attempted self-deification. Moreover there is nothing servile about his stress on freedom. Equally topical were the two following signs treated in his next chapter, man's desire to be everywhere and his desire always to be – ubiquity and duration. The first, which selects the Renaissance zeal for discovery and exploration and travel as a sign of immortality is quickly dealt with.

> God is everywhere . . . and always. Man desires to be everywhere. For he uses the four elements, as we have said. He measures the earth and the heavens, and he sounds the hidden depths of Tartarus. The heavens do not seem too high to him, as I borrow the words of Hermes, nor the centre of the earth deep. No intervals of time or place prevent him from running through all things whatever they are in whatever times and places. No wall dulls or weakens his glance. He is content with no frontier. He yearns to command everywhere and to be praised everywhere. And so he strives to be, as God, everywhere.

The vividness of Ficino's description is the mark of the relevance of his attempt to incorporate this most contemporary sense of human experience into a new theological and anthropological vision. As Burckhardt, Gentile and Cassirer so well saw, this is truly the Renaissance's image of man.[62]

And so also is Ficino's vision of fame. For him the desire for fame is the desire to perdure. Man seeks to be always, as God is, in two ways.

First he attempts to remain through all future time in the speech of men, and mourns that he is not able to have been celebrated also in past ages and that he cannot be honoured in the future by all the nations of men and by all kinds of animals. Everyone, youths as well as adults, the ignorant and the educated, seek this with all their force and zeal, and they seek it the more ardently the more excellent their genius. What all men desire, and especially the superior ones, is desired by them as a good by a natural law. . . . Now there is no profit in praise which is not heard. That is why the human species predicts that it will not be deprived of sense in a future age, since it often even despises the present life so that it might be praised by posterity.[63]

To this kind of immortality through celebrity and fame during all the centuries, which humanist rhetoric claimed it especially conferred, he added his second type, which is a natural instinct both to be and to survive. All being and life shares in this in accord with its particular nature.

The Creator of nature, moreover, balanced knowledge with essence, appetite with knowledge, and the attainment of the end with appetite. Therefore just as the animal knows only temporal existence in accord with the capacity of his nature, and according to his nature desires temporal existence, so our soul in the magnificence of its own nature knows eternal existence and naturally desires it.[64]

God also manifested his being through his prudence, justice, fortitude and temperance. These four cardinal virtues were considered, therefore, also as signs of man's divinity by Ficino. Men seek to acquire them universally, but different men seek them by different ways. Ficino seems to adopt a Stoic position here, regarding the striving for virtue as something natural to man through seeds sown in him by God.

God, who is Himself the exemplary virtue, affects the human soul from the beginning with certain seeds and incitements of the virtues, by which we are conveniently prepared through the human virtues, that is the civil, the purgatorial and the virtues of the already purified soul, for the exemplary and divine virtues.[65]

The virtues, however, receive comparatively small emphasis in Ficino whose vision of the ambience of man was more cosmic and metaphysical than ethical and social. But his next divine endowment is one to which he devotes a lengthy and very revealing discussion.

We may add, as we posited, that the life of God is the most opulent and the most joyous. For He alone is the sum of wealth and the height of pleasure who is the source of all goods, lacking nothing. Therefore if all men seek after the sum of riches and the highest pleasure, they are striving to become gods.[66]

To Ficino it is a special characteristic of the human species, of human nature, not to be satisfied with sufficient goods and pleasures to maintain the body and spirit at a suitable level of existence, but unlike the other living creatures man 'thinks he has acquired but little of them while even the least remains to be acquired.' Prudent men think that the riches and pleasures of God consist in the treasures of intelligence and virtue and seek only these, but also in the extreme. Imprudent men, like Midas and Xerxes, seek to enjoy material goods, but extremely, and offer prizes to those who can invent new pleasures. They are envious of the life they imagine the gods possess, and in this sense seek to be gods. 'They do not serve the body but damage it, and unaware of bodily troubles, they do not obey the body, but envious of divine happiness, they strive to take over for themselves this immense supply of goods and pleasures.' And meanwhile they lose their bodies, afflict their souls and disturb their lives. And none, neither the prudent nor the imprudent, are able to find the treasures they seek in this life. Unlike all the other forms of life, and that of our body also which relaxes and rests when its physical and sensual needs are satisfied, the human soul never rests and is always restless.

> But meanwhile the intellectual reason eagerly seeks the causes of things and anxiously consults on the execution of actions, or the imaginative reason invents and demands new pleasures. It is spurred on by repentance, troubled by suspicion.

Then comes his declaration that this is characteristic of man.

> Anxiety of this sort is peculiar to man, himself, since it arises from the characteristic powers of the human soul, not from the corporeal elements, nor the animal powers which have been satisfied in us, as we said. That is why man alone in this present condition of life never relaxes, he alone in this place is not content. Therefore man alone is a wanderer in these regions, and in the journey itself he can find no rest, while he seeks the heavenly fatherland, which all of us seek, although because of the variety of opinions and choices we seek it by many roads.

Here is the Faustian image of man, with its endless lust and *Wanderlust*, driven on by an insatiability of soul, not body.[67]

For Ficino this restless seeking carries with it a metaphysical imperative that the human soul should find its goal of immortality and divinity. Not in this present life, of course, for we seek as our natural habitat and end a good which is pure, whole and stable. And here the soul is distracted toward the bodily and cannot be pure. It cannot be whole here, because the soul cannot know and possess all goods. It cannot be stable, because man faces innumerable obstacles to his actions and seeks all his life for a happiness which eludes him. And, on the other hand, whenever a man attains a moment of joy, 'as if we were exiles, we fall into sadness, although we do not know the cause of our sadness or think of it.' It is surprising how romantic this outlook is, and how profoundly Ficino has penetrated the true psychology of his contemporaries who, with all their zest for accomplishment, had concealed in themselves a worm of discontent. Even human society seems to Ficino to have been provoked into existence by this incapacity of man to face his own loneliness.

> It follows from this that man is unable to live alone, for in the society of other men and the multiple variety of diversions we think we are able to expel the hidden and perpetual sadness. But alas, too frequently we are deceived. Certainly in the middle of our pleasant games we sometimes sigh, and having played the games we depart all the sadder.

The pleasures are sought not for their own sake but as anodynes and compensations.

> We also offer to the mind thirsty for nectar, that is the joy of the fatherly vision, the lethal waters of the river Lethe, while we engage in the shadowy games of the corporeal pleasures, which are false pleasures not only because they are most brief and full of worries but because they are mixed with suffering, since an ungratified appetite is a certain kind of pain. . . . Therefore it is understandable that earthly pleasures do not bring fulfilment to the soul, but only titillate it.

To Ficino this world and this life with its shadowy, tantalizing not-quite satisfactions seemed literally to be Plato's cave of shades and shadows. 'Euripides rightly called this life "the dream of a shade".'[68]

Ficino's sensitivity to the psychological and spiritual qualities of humanity comes forth in his discussion of the last divine endowment in men – that they aspire toward divinity and imitate God in loving and worshipping themselves, 'for all men not only do what all other creatures do, they love and protect themselves, but they also worship themselves with great intensity as though they were worshipping certain divine spirits'. Ficino's conception of human self-esteem goes far beyond simple hedonistic and utilitarian notions, because he sees the complex and awesome image that men create of themselves in their inner consciousness. Wise men worship their own mind as though it was a dependency of God and refuse to soil it with external and bodily concerns.

> They think it a sacrilege to pollute the august majesty of their own mind, as though it was a divine statue, with vile thoughts and earthly filth. Indeed this natural notion generates the sense of shame and modesty in human kind, so that we not only revere the presence of other men as though of gods, but the conscience of our own mind, as Pythagoras teaches, as though the face of God.

Conscience drives us to repentance even when we do not fear punishment, and the memory of our good deeds causes us to rejoice as if the celestial soul was horrified by the stains of earthly vices. Even unwise men do this, though less intensely, and the very mad persist in their own opinions as though they were divine decrees.

> Finally, all men honour the most excellent souls and those deserving the best from mankind as though they were divine while in this life, and when they are freed from the body they adore them as certain gods most dear to the supreme God. The ancients called them heroes.[69]

To this apotheosis and worship of man's higher nature is linked, as a second mode of imitating God's own self-love, the worship of God Himself by men, in sentiment, deed, word, sanctuaries and sacrifices.

> Plato in the *Protagoras* considered it a special indication of our divinity that we alone as participants in divine destiny on account of a certain kinship know and desire God as our Creator, invoke and love Him as a father, revere Him as a king, fear Him as a master.

If God did not respond to all the ways men express their wish to worship Him, it would be strange and contrary to divine nature, indeed. For who would dare say God despises human affairs as unimportant?[70]

Ficino embarks here on a complex argument to show that the purposive quality of human life, which is manifested in the providential works of man, must correspond to the real existence of the underlying purpose which prompts mankind so to act. As in the case of the workman it is the comfortable dwelling that leads him to build the house, to conceive its form and shape its materials. This purposive, teleological force is also present in plants and animals. Ficino puts forth a pre-Lamarckian notion that all parts of nature must have a pre-existing function. Thus it is the divine mind which provides the goal of all purposes of the will, and as the end of all is the cause of all. God, 'this divine farmer', supplies the underlying impulses of nature which determine natural forms and processes.

> Why should He then despise men who alone on earth do not despise divine majesty? Far be it. If God does not neglect even the least part of the world, certainly he does not despise mankind which is so precious a part of the world that it is the intermediary of temporal and eternal things according as it understands the eternal and organises the temporal; it is so close to God that insinuating itself into the secrets of the divine mind it knows this work of God, namely the order of the universe. Comprehension of the world order is more excellent than that order itself, since this kind of order is made and directed by intelligence. If our soul is more excellent than the world because of knowledge, it will also be more excellent through life. By the power of life that is separable from the body, it can also be separated from the body by its operation and transcend the world by what I would call the force of super-mundane life.[71]

All of this is to prove from man's great god-like powers of understanding and directing the universe, which are a kind of divinity and immortality, that it is unthinkable that man will not be immortal and divine. 'If the soul feels God, why does not God also feel the soul, especially since God gave this very force and action of feeling to the soul and preserves and leads it?' 'Besides if the soul ascends to God, why shouldn't God somehow descend to the soul?'

> Hence many men give up all, all men certainly many, of the comforts of temporal life for love or suspicion or fear of God. God therefore ought to recompense these temporal goods with eternal. None of the other animals, indeed, abstains from present goods on account of an avidity for future things. Thus it would be brought about that man would be the most stupid of all animals as well as the most miserable, if he enjoyed neither the present life nor the future.

All of this is unthinkable to Ficino, overwhelmed as he is by what he feels is man's own sense of his divinity. The argument, however, is reminiscent of Valla's celestial 'Epicureanism'.[72]

But he expands in still another way on the evidence of man's religiosity as an argument for his immortality. He even goes so far as to take over the same argument Lorenzo Valla used concerning the intelligence of man and animals. Earlier we have seen that Ficino argued that animal intelligence was extremely rudimentary and limited and that he thought man's power of speech and his hands differentiated him from animals.[73] Now he wishes to assert, as did Valla, that the only characteristic of man different in kind (not degree) from the animals is man's religiosity, which necessarily must correspond to his immortality. The comparison with Valla may be carried even further, at least in this particular context of Ficino's writings. Both men were convinced of immortality and heavenly fruition of man's life because of the strength of their sentiments of human immortality. Of course it must be added that Ficino sought to supply many of the metaphysical arguments and proofs elsewhere in his writings which Valla professed to think baseless. But perhaps, in the final analysis, it was the depth of their conviction arising from their feeling that man had to be immortal, or all the drives of his nature would be in vain, that explains their respective outlooks.

> As Aristotle shows in the twelfth book of his *De animalibus* [i.e. *De partibus animalium*, II, x, 4.], his works are the most evident testimony that man is superior to the animals. Let us inquire therefore in what particular endowment he is most outstanding. He certainly seems to excel in talent for the arts and government, especially since, as we have declared before, men vary their works since they themselves are the creators and not the instruments of another workman. Animals, however, do not make variations in what they do because they are instruments of a productive nature rather than possessing an art themselves. But although we excel other animals in the capacity for art and government, nevertheless this activity is common to us and to the animals. But it is necessary, when the human species is distinguished from the animals, for it to have some distinctive perfection of its own in which animals do not in any sense participate. Will this be speech? But animals imitate speech with gestures, cries and songs. Will it be reason? Reason, certainly, but not every operation of reason, for practical reason has certain traces in the animals, through signs of art and government. Speculative reason concerning natural things seems also to have some vestiges in animals. For they also cure themselves by the choice of certain foods and remedies, and as foreseeing future seasons they show signs of the future and change places in order to avoid the dangers of future times, although they are rather led to this by nature than lead. What therefore remains that is entirely man's

alone? The contemplation of divine things. For no animal shows any sign of having a religion, so that the lifting of the mind towards God, the king of heaven, is proper to us, just as the erectness of the body towards heaven is confined to us. And divine worship is nearly as natural to men as neighing to horses or barking to dogs.[74]

It should not lessen our estimation of Ficino's tremendous admiration for man that in embracing the myriad manifestations of human potency and aspiration in his day he conceived of man as fundamentally religious by nature, yearning for immortality, striving to be a god in all of his thoughts and actions, and necessarily realising his dreams. Certainly this is one of the most far-reaching visions of man to be produced in the Renaissance, in a sense an epitome and summary and a culmination of them all. But it was one that was not satisfied with either the limitations placed by the external conditions of life on man's aspirations or the limited results the human mind and will could attain in this life. Ficino necessarily had to aspire higher. Nor was he satisfied merely to put forth this exalted vision of man in the image of God. He was compelled to construct a philosophy which he considered adequate to support it. He found it necessary to go beyond dream, poetry and rhetoric. But in so doing he sustained the dreams, poetry and rhetoric of many artists, writers and thinkers of an entire ensuing age who found in his philosophy the rational shape and the justification for pursuing their aspiration towards human grandeur in a world that seemed naturally divine. He assimilated these trends of fourteenth- and fifteenth-century humanist speculation about man and God and transformed them into a shape that the less political, more religious and more systematic sixteenth century could use.

It has been the contention of a number of recent scholars that Ficino's influence on the ensuing age was due more to his elaboration of a new kind of 'spiritual' magic than to his philosophy of human immortality. While the chief proponents of this view have been the English scholars, D. P. Walker and Frances Yates, of the Warburg Institute, the interest of a number of continental scholars such as Eugenio Garin, Cesare Vasoli, and François Secret have over the past twenty years been directed towards the exploration of the relationship of humanism and Renaissance philosophy to the quasi-magical traditions of Hermetism and the Cabala.[75] The position of Marsilio Ficino and of Giovanni Pico della Mirandola have been central to all of these discussions, especially Ficino's *De vita*, a modern edition of which has been announced by Garin and is eagerly awaited.

These are all important studies. However, they raise certain crucial questions of interpretation of Renaissance thought. Although not all of the scholars engaged in these researches might agree with her, a statement by Frances Yates in her book on *Giordano Bruno and the Hermetic Tradition* does raise the relevant question in a challenging form. She says that she 'has only hinted in a partial and fragmentary way . . . at a theme which I believe may be of absolutely basic importance for the history of thought – namely, Renaissance magic as a factor in bringing about fundamental changes in the human outlook'.[76] By Renaissance magic Miss Yates means the modifications and transformations of traditional, medieval magical notions and practices by Ficino, chiefly under the influence of Hermetic texts such as *Asclepius*, the Hermetic magical tradition, and possibly even such a writing as the Arabic *Picatrix*. The nature of the transformation in this tradition was, according to her, and to Walker as well, a liberation of man from the deterministic Ptolemaic astrology through new forms of magic which sought to draw down counter-influences to the astrologically predetermined ones. Thus Ficino sought to combat his Saturnine nature and destiny by means of talismans attracting Jovial and Venereal spirits.

Miss Yates continues with her broad application of this development in a paragraph that asserts that the Greeks, despite their scientific aptitudes and discoveries, 'never took wholeheartedly, with all their powers, the momentous step which western man took at the beginning of the modern period of crossing the bridge between the theoretical and the practical, of going all out to apply knowledge to produce operations'. With this statement, in the very broad and general sense in which she intends it, I can certainly agree. I suspect also that she is right in suggesting that the reason the Greeks 'did not *want* to operate' was a matter of the will, since they did not wish to risk losing the higher status that 'pure rational and philosophical speculation' conferred on them as 'the only occupation worthy of the dignity of man'.[77] Although she does not say so, it is well known also that the Italian humanists perpetuated this attitude in their adoption of the word *humanitas* and its adjective *humanius* to designate the scholarly disciplines they themselves practised, which, following both Roman and Greek traditions, they regarded as that which rendered man peculiarly human. I am not sure that I can agree with her, however, when she says that 'The Middle Ages carried on this attitude in the form that theology is the crown of philosophy and the true end of man is contemplation; any wish to operate can only be inspired by the devil.'[78] This is true of only one of the medieval traditions – the high scholastic Thomist; and it is not even entirely true about it. Moreover, as we have seen, the humanists also had a high regard for operation, or better, action, in the spheres of politics and morals, and, as this book has been emphatically arguing, the humanists in their views of man, despite the theoretical role implied by their taking over the classical term of *humanitas*, predominantly laid stress on the human will and operation. It is enough to recall our major figures, Petrarch, Salutati, Valla, Manetti and Morandi. Moreover such emphases on a 'civic' humanism as Hans Baron's and Garin's, although they are too exclusively political and republican, justly affirm the role of the *vita activa* and the will.

Miss Yates proceeds to give central emphasis in her interpretation to the role of will in the Renaissance, but she attributes this role to the 'magic' stemming from Hermetism and the Cabala.

> Quite apart from the question of whether Renaissance magic could, or could not, lead on to genuine scientific procedures, the real function of the Renaissance Magus in relation to the modern period (or so I see it) is that he changed the will. It was now dignified and important for man to operate; it was also religious and not contrary to the will of God that man, the great miracle, should exert his powers. It was this basic psychological reorientation towards a direction of the will which was neither Greek nor medieval in spirit, which made all the difference.

The emotional sources of this new attitude she suggests lay in 'the religious excitement caused by the re-discovery of the *Hermetica*, and their attendant *Magia*', as well as that associated with the Cabala. 'It is magic as an aid to gnosis which begins to turn the will in the new direction.' Even Copernicus may have been inspired by the 'Hermetic impulse'. 'Thus "Hermes Trismegistus" and the Neoplatonism and Cabalism associated with him, may have played during his period of glorious ascendance over the mind of western man a strangely important role in the shaping of human destiny.'[79]

Fundamentally this point of view seems to me an exaggerated one. Yet it is difficult to deny or disagree with many items and aspects of it, particularly since Miss Yates is a very careful scholar in this field, as is her colleague D. P. Walker. She also offers the most comprehensive study of Renaissance Hermetism to date in her book, although medieval and Renaissance references prior to Ficino are neglected. Moreover both scholars point out how closely magic comes in this form to religion, and this point of view explicitly argues that fundamental new conceptions of man and his role in the world could not, in this period, be dissociated from religion. We have been endeavouring to prove exactly this.

Where I do disagree and am obliged to say so clearly is on the question of the exact nature and the sources of this new attitude, as well as of its dating.

I do not wish to minimise the importance of Marsilio Ficino or of Giovanni Pico della Mirandola in Renaissance thought, but I do wish to place their sometimes startlingly stated ideas in their proper historical context. Ficino, at least, with all of his metaphors and his mysteries, was a conscientious expounder of his philosophy, and he has the great merit of seeking a philosophical demonstration of his new vision of man as made in the image of God in man's origin as a species, in his potentiality and in his destiny. But the humanists, at least certain very influential ones, anticipated an extensive array of the arguments he used in demonstrating this, as I believe I have now shown. Moreover, the humanists were drawing on a medieval and a patristic tradition for this, just as the Renaissance Platonists also were.

What remains are the questions of magic and of the influence and impact of the *Hermetica.* While it is perfectly true that the humanists did not elaborate this new kind of magic that Ficino set forth in his *V.C.C.* [i.e. *De vita coelitus comparanda*] as Walker fondly abbreviates it, it seems to me wrong to suggest, as I believe Miss Yates does, that the humanists were immune, because of their scholarly proclivities and desire for historical and textual accuracy, to the charms of magic.[80] My mentor, Lynn Thorndike, has left me completely open to the notion or the discovery that practically any man of learning, scholar or scientist could manage to retain, and fit into what may seem to us otherwise incompatible attitudes, a trust in, an acceptance and belief, even a practice, of a wide range of magics. Moreover we do know that while many of the humanists sought to emphasize the role of divine providence and of human will over against astrological determinism, as for instance Salutati did in his *De fato*, they also freely and openly accepted the existence of natural magical linkages between the material world and the heavens, the presence and continual activities of animated spirits, both demonic and angelic, the existence and occurrence of miracles by both divine and demonic intervention. I do not say that the humanists advocated or practised magic on a wide scale at all, or that they came anywhere near Ficino's trust and confidence in what he believed were his new magical discoveries – spiritual and only very improbably demonic, as both Walker and Yates rather reluctantly admit.

What I question here is the need for the discovery of magic, or even this new kind of Hermetic and Cabalistic magic, as a basis for men asserting in the Renaissance a new confidence in human operative and theoretical powers and a new vision of an apotheosised mankind. The existence of the latter, of course, I accept, but I question this explanation of it. After all, as their treatises show, they did have *Genesis* and they did have the doctrine of the Incarnation available to interpret in this way. They did not need 'Hermes Trismegistus' to show them the way.

However, despite the importance of Ficino's translations of the previously untranslated parts of the *Hermetica* (and the importance of Lazzarelli's too), the text that Yates lays most stress on was well known throughout the Middle Ages and the Renaissance, namely the *Asclepius* in the Latin translation attributed to Apuleius. In a later chapter in Part IV of this book we deal with this question again in what seems to me is its proper historical context, and that is the continuity between the medieval and early humanist tradition of a *theologia poetica* and that of a *theologia platonica*, and the true origin of the legend of the *prisci theologi* in that of the *prisci poetae*.[81]

It must be granted that the distinctions between magic, the various types of magic, Gnosticism and Hermetism, various kinds of mysticism, divinely produced miracles, with or without human agency, faith in the preternatural, but particularly religious faith, can become very tenuous. It would be folly to argue that Ficino was a devotee of mysticism rather than magic, as some scholars have held, or of magic rather than mysticism. Despite the care with which the scholastic theologians sought to set up viable distinctions – and perhaps their firmness and clarity in doing so is a measure of their greatness – the Middle Ages and the Renaissance frequently blurred the differences. And especially was this the case where there was a great effort at synthesis, where the tendency which we have today called syncretism has taken place. Marsilio Ficino knew the scholastic distinctions, but he was also eager to find points in common between the various traditions. Miss Yates is quite right in stressing his excitement and in seeking to recapture his state of mind on encountering some of the ideas in the *Hermetica* that seemed to parallel those of the Scriptures and Christian theology. But to suggest that this made him a pagan, or that without knowing it he betrayed his own faith to pagan ideas seems to me a difficult position to uphold.

I do not believe that there has been a single phase in the history of Christianity, from the time of St. Paul, in which Christianity was not permeated with notions that could be found in other religions and traditions. Sometimes there was a direct influence, or an unconscious one; sometimes there was merely an independent elaboration of ideas that were similar because human experience itself was similar. Where there is a deliberate and self-conscious effort to discover the usable common elements in another tradition – as was the case with Scholastic Aristotelianism and with Renaissance Platonism – there are bound to be exaggerations and fears concerning the interpretation one's colleagues are making, and even actual overt departure from the Christian orthodoxies, patristic, Catholic, Protestant. It is important to be aware of the impact and the concatenation and the consequential controversies that occur when this happens. But it is also important, and perhaps today more important, to see what a particular movement of thought adds up to in its own terms, for such is the way its originators and practitioners were concerned with it. Archaism has never meant anything but a desire to transform the contemporary.

Let us then recognise that Marsilio Ficino was an extraordinarily potent thinker as a result of his capacity, desire and practice of drawing from all those intellectual and religious traditions that were available to him in the fifteenth century, and those as well that he, himself, made available through his translations from the Greek, namely Thomism, Augustinianism, Ockhamism, Epicureanism, Ciceronian humanism, the *Hermetica*, Plato, the Neoplatonists, the *Orphica*, the *Chaldean Oracles*, the Platonising Arabic and Jewish thinkers who had been translated in the Middle Ages, particularly Avicenna and Avicebron, but also including Averroes, and many others, and not to forget the Scriptures. Several of these strands he quotes with such frequency that given scholars have elected to identify his thought with one of these particular sects or thinkers.

While I do not think it is possible to avoid recognising the tremendous importance of Plato's writings as interpreted by Plotinus in this thinking, I do think that it is a mistake to hunt down the mysterious and all-explaining source. He should rather be seen for what he was, one of those seminal thinkers who for good or ill left their mark on an entire epoch, figures such as Plato and Aristotle, Epicurus, Panaetius, Posidonius, Cicero and Plotinus in antiquity; St. Augustine, St. Thomas, William of Ockham in the Middle Ages; Descartes, Kant and Hegel in modernity. He is more akin to Augustine and Hegel in the sense of attempting to create a new all-comprehensive mode of viewing man and God and the cosmos by combining the partial truths of the many preceding traditions into a new revelation or synthesis. At the same time, like all of these others, he seems in some sense to betray or not to understand fully the predecessors he utilises, or he transforms them into something that their devotees find objectionable. This does not lessen his importance as a figure who sought to give a new order to the manifold and conflicting trends of his time, an order, which to this historian, at least, seems to correspond to deep and persistent aspirations of that age.

I must, however, hasten to add that I do not wish to claim that Ficino's Platonism truly summarises the Renaissance, for no one can or has done that. I am merely saying that he was the one thinker who sought and achieved an amazingly comprehensive synthesis in that age. This synthesis did not leave him unopposed to many other currents nor unopposed by them in turn. Nor were these currents or individuals themselves unimportant. What I have already said and will say about some of them should suffice.

X. Giovanni Pico della Mirandola on the Place of Man in the Cosmos: Egidio da Viterbo on the Dignity of Men and Angels

There was one tradition to which Ficino was able to give lip service but could not make his own – the Hebraic.[1] As we know, and as we shall discuss in some detail in the next part of this book, Giannozzo Manetti was the first significant Hebraist among western thinkers of the Renaissance.[2] Manetti, although to some degree influenced by the philological cogency of certain Biblical interpretations based not only on the Hebraic original but on the Jewish exegetical works with which he was familiar, at the same time held himself aloof from the philosophical and theological doctrines of contemporary and medieval Judaism, which he continued to regard as a debased and inferior religious tradition in addition to its fundamental perfidy.[3] Pico della Mirandola was far superior to Manetti as a Hebraist, and certainly a far more imaginative and gifted thinker.[4] As a philosopher,[5] which Manetti was not, Pico sought like Ficino to produce a grand synthesis. Whether he was originally dependent on Ficino for this ambitious purpose, which I doubt, there can be no doubt that he took all that Ficino could give him, first from his writings and then from him personally, and then added to and broadened the scope of the Ficinian synthesis in at least two significant respects. One was his recognition of the underlying Neoplatonic and mystical nature of the so-called Averroist doctrine of the possible intellect as universal rather than individual. This doctrine he apparently learned from one of his teachers of Hebrew lore, Elia del Medigo, while he, Pico, was a student at Padua.[6] The other, and perhaps more significant, addition was the mystical and esoteric medieval Jewish tradition of the Cabala.

This chapter is concerned with Pico's vision of the dignity of man. For purpose of comparison with the preceding humanist tradition his famous and much cited, but wrongly called *Oration on the Dignity of Man* might be utilised, and it will be. It was an inaugural oration intended to precede his defence of the nine hundred theses he offered for debate in Rome, and the greatest part of its content deals with the question of the inter-relatedness and universality of the partial truths of the many traditions in the history of mankind, and with the universal truth that can be found hidden in them.[7]

The 'dignity of man', as is well known, was held by Pico to consist in the condition that man was not created as a fixed part of the structure of the universe, but was given a role by God, after the universe itself was completed, of viewing it and admiring its Maker. Man was to be in this view the earthly image of God, and the being that helped the deity maintain the subjectivity of His own being by sharing it to some degree with a creature whose nature was to rise above nature into subjectivity. This subjectivity comprised man's freedom to participate in the universe at whatever level and in whatever condition he chose. Man could debase himself to the pure materiality of the elements, vegetate with the flowers in the biological processes of life, nutrition and growth, indulge his senses with the animals on the psychically more complicated level of perception and imagination, rise with reason to the spheres of the heavens, ascend beyond them to the supercelestial realm of the intelligences or angels, by using his intellect. Here he would closely approach towards becoming akin to God Himself.[8]

One can see that these are ideas in which Marsilio Ficino, at least, preceded him, for, as we have shown in the preceding chapter,[9] Ficino also regarded man's possession of reason as a condition that freed man from and allowed him to transcend the three kinds of determinism built into the universe – providential, fatal and natural. They are also ideas which one can find adumbrated in Manetti's treatise and in Facio's, without, to be sure, the rhetorical sharpness of this non-rhetorician.[10] They are to be found in St. Augustine's *De quantitate animae*,[11] and also in one of two patristic treatises on the condition of man which were available in Latin translation in the Middle Ages and the Renaissance, but which I have not found directly cited by any of the humanists. The one which contains Pico's ideas of the multipotentiality and freedom of man is Gregory of Nyssa's extension of his brother St. Basil's treatise on the creation, the *Hexaemeron*. The other treatise, frequently confused with Gregory's, was written by Nemesius of Emesa. As we reported above, these existed and circulated in the Middle Ages, Gregory in a fifth-century, Nemesius in eleventh-and twelfth-century versions.[12] Pico's conception of man's role as to view the beauty of the creation was also to be found in Philo Judaeus.[13]

Pico seems to have written his *Oration* in 1486. In 1488–9 he wrote his commentary on the first chapter of *Genesis*, called, unlike so many before him, *Heptaplus* (rather than *Hexaemeron*, six days), as describing God's six days of labour and the *seventh* of rest.[14] This work is important and interesting in many different connections, but it is particularly of concern to us because it indicates once again that the Renaissance discussions of the dignity of man belong in the context of the exegesis of *Genesis* i:26. Pico's exposition also shows that his vision of the dignity of man, expressed in the oration, refers to man before the Fall and after the Incarnation, although part of man's freedom was his freedom to fall, and Pico's view of the sacred history of mankind is anything but successional and chronological.

In this work the influence of cabalistic notions of the universe are prominent, especially the division of the cosmos into the three parts of the elementary world of nature, the celestial world of the planets and the angelic world of the intelligences, within which existed the fourth world of man.[15] But, as Pico is concerned to prove, this does not really differ from the universe as Pseudo-Dionysius the Areopagite and the Platonic philosophers conceived it. And the fact that this is the cabalistic cosmos becomes for that reason of less significance, since also its conception was formed under the influence of the same late classical conceptions that entered into Neoplatonism and the Pseudo-Dionysius. Without reference to the Cabala, Ficino also divides his cosmos into the three deterministic systems of the divine intelligences characterised by providence, the fatal celestial spheres of the planets, the natural world of the elements governed by natural laws.[16] Pico adds to the first three the fourth world of man. But here again he seems to agree with Ficino, if he need not have specifically followed him. Moreover in the *Heptaplus* Pico stresses that man is a microcosm, whereas it is sometimes stressed that Pico abandoned the microcosm notion.[17]

> There is, moreover, besides the three which we have described, another fourth world in which all those things are to be found which are in the others. This is man himself, who for that reason is also called by the name of 'every creature' in the Gospel, as the catholic doctors say, for although the Gospel is to be preached to men, but not to animals and angels, yet it is commanded by Christ that it be preached to every creature. It is a trite saying in the schools that man is a lesser world in whom there is seen to be a body mixed from the elements and a celestial spirit and the vegetable soul of plants and the senses of brutes and reason and the angelic intelligence and the likeness of God.

It will therefore be in his fourth book that his principle discussion of man is to be found. But he conceives of the work as a whole as divided into seven books corresponding to the work of the six days and the rest on the seventh, and he also divides each book into seven chapters on the same principle, in as much as each major division of the cosmos and the work of the creation corresponds in its sub-divisions to all seven. The first four books deal with the three parts of the universe – elementary, celestial and angelic – and the fourth world of man. The fifth book deals with the sequence of these worlds and their concord of discords or discordant harmony. The sixth book deals with inter-relationships between the worlds and all things, the seventh with the ultimate felicity from which all creation descends and returns, God, beatitude, and the Incarnation which closes the circle between Creator and created. Within the books the sixth chapter of the sixth day is devoted also to man who was created on the sixth day, and the seventh deals with Christ as the exemplar of man. Therefore we must also turn to the sixth and seventh chapters of each book.

Christ as the Incarnate God has a special relationship to the discussion of man on the principle, which he borrows from Ficino, of the *primum in aliquo genere*, stressed by Kristeller in *The Philosophy o, Marsilio Ficino*. This application of Christ as the exemplar of man is set forth in the seventh chapter of book one, which is very brief and we quote it in its entirety.[18]

> Moreover, just as the absolute consummation of all inferior things is man, so the absolute consummation of all men is Christ. If, therefore, as the

philosophers say, from the one which is the most perfect in any kind all perfection for the others of the same order is derived as if from a spring, no one can doubt that from the Man, Christ, the perfection of all goodness in all men is derived; this is to say that the Spirit has been given to Him alone without measure, so that we all receive it from his plenitude. You may see beyond any doubt that this prerogative is owed to Him as to God and man, and this is also peculiar to Him as a man and is a fitting and legitimate privilege.

Man's dignity derives therefore both from his origin and from his restoration by the coming of the divine-human exemplar. It also derives in his more literal account of the creation of the elements in book one, from man's creation on the sixth day [the sixth chapter]. 'Supreme and prince of all is man in whom the nature of the corruptible world comes to the end of its development and signals its finish.'[19] And man's perfection is exemplified by Christ who is the 'first of man's kind'.

His second book delineates the spheres of the planets, the firmament, the crystalline and the empyrean, as well as the stars and signs of the zodiac. This celestial world of living beings culminates in a description of its soul, which in chapter six is modelled on the human soul.

Now prepared to declare that the [corporeal nature of the heavens] is endowed with a rational soul, he allegorically recalls man, not such a one as is weak and earthly and visible, but such as the one by whom, as Plotinus said, that visible man is ruled. . . . The Scriptures accord with our exposition for in them all angelic and rational nature is designated as man. . . . God therefore added to the celestial machine a live and rational substance, participating in intelligence, and, hence in His own image and likeness, he wished it to rule over these animated bodies of which we recently spoke, that is over all the stellar signs and planets which are so ruled by his nod and obey his command in such a way that there is no delay and no disobedience.[20]

The significance of this notion is that he conceives of the world anthropomorphically and as essentially subjective and animated from God, through the angels, the celestial bodies, down to man. The stars and planets do not in his view exercise a material influence over men's lives, but they can exercise a spiritual one. His chapter seven is a protest against a materialistic astrological determinism.

This noble creature ought to be exalted and celebrated by us; but if we are not forgetful of the Platonic doctrine, as I pass over the theologians in silence,

> our souls have been tempered by the Supreme Craftsman, God, in the same mixing bowl and from the same elements with the celestial souls; let us watch out then that we do not wish to be slaves of those whom nature wished to be our brothers. Nor should we measure our condition according to weak body, for this man is not that weak and earthly thing which we see, as is written in the *Alcibiades*, but he is soul, he is intellect, which exceeds every circuit of heaven, every course of time.

The stars cannot rule us by their material parts which are as vile as ours, so that we should beware of worshipping the work of the artificer as more perfect than its author.

> Therefore let us fear, love and venerate Him in whom, as Paul said, are all created things both visible and invisible, who is the beginning in whom God made heaven and earth, that is Christ.
>
> Therefore let us form not stellar images in metals but the image of the Word of God in our souls.[21]

Book three on the angelic world seeks to show the correspondence of cabalistic doctrine and that of the Pseudo-Dionysius on the celestial hierarchies and how they also conformed to the Hermetic and Platonic writings. The contemporary Jews he commands to stand on the traditions of their ancient fathers [meaning, of course, the quite recent doctrines of the medieval cabalistic mysticism].

> Finally whatever we find to be alien to evangelic truth we shall confute according to our ability, and whatever is holy and true we shall transfer from the synagogue as from an unjust possessor to ourselves, the legitimate Israelites.[22]

The theory of a cosmos populated and administered by angelic hierarchies was peculiarly compatible with Pico's vision of a subjectively shaped universe. And after he has explained how the creation and nature of the angels can be inferred from the words of *Genesis*, and after he has divided the angelic hierarchies into three groups of three according to the waters above the firmament [those functioning in the super-celestial world of intelligences] those of the firmament which guide and direct the heavens, and those of the waters beneath the firmament [cf. *Genesis* i:6–7],[23] he dwells on the functions of these three lower orders. Principalities watch over republics and monarchs, archangels care for the mysteries and the sacred ceremonies, angels are guardians to individual men. This, as in the case of Facio and Manetti, was a mark of human excellence.[24]

But Pico carries the doctrine further.

> We should not understand otherwise concerning these angels which look after sublunary affairs. For different ones care for different corporeal things and others preside over other human actions, since, just as the Platonists, so also our theologians believe that various spiritual substances have been placed in charge of the various affairs of this corruptible world by God. With regard to this Augustine also asserted that there is no visible thing among us over which an angelic power does not rule and all bodies are constantly ruled through a rational spirit of life.

Gregory the Great, Origen and Damascenus also are cited.

> But just as all these things below man refer to man, so also the care of the angels for these things is subordinated to man and powerfully serves him, zealously caring for human affairs and aiding our weakness as much, indeed, as we allow them, so that we may lead a pious and happy life.[25]

The angels of the lower waters thus wash and purify us; the middle hierarchy illuminate the celestial region for our benefit; the supercelestial angels by a vivifying fire perfect and fecundate us for such great happiness, 'that they generate not just health-bringing herbs, but the Saviour himself, and thus not one virtue, but Christ, the plenitude of all virtues is formed in us'.[26]

Finally, in his last chapter, he comes to the question debated in the medieval commentaries on the *Sentences*, whether man was ultimately higher than the angels. As we have seen, his entire treatment of the ministerial functioning of the angels is directed towards mankind. They are the agents of an ever-beneficent divine providence towards man. This would suggest that man, the object of their ministrations, must occupy a higher place. Moses in his narrative, interpreted so that it may yield its meaning concerning the angelic world,

> finally remembers man, not because man is an angel, but because he is the end and term of the angelic world just as in treating of the corruptible nature he also places man in it not as part of this nature but as its beginning and head. From this it derives that the treatment of man pertains to the three worlds, to that which is proper to him and to both extremes, namely the incorporeal and the elementary of which he is the mean in such a way that he is the end of the one and the beginning of the other. But I see a trap has been prepared for our exposition, since it is added that man should rule over

> the fishes of the sea, the birds and the animals. For if that signifies for us an angelic nature, in what way can it be true what is written, that man, who is diminished from the angels, excels these, as the philosophers know and the prophet testifies? Let Him assist us and break the trap Who also broke Satan beneath our feet. Jesus Christ the first-born of all creatures will certainly break this trap and loose and solve every knot. For human nature is not only so sublimated in Him in whom all divinity corporeally dwelt, so that the man, Christ, in accord with his humanity, if we believe Dionysius, taught, illuminated and perfected angels, rendering himself, as Paul said, as much better than the angels as the name which he inherited is higher than theirs, but also all of us to whom the power has been given to become sons of God through the grace whose giver is Christ are able to soar beyond the angelic dignity.[27]

The significance of this statement by Pico should not be missed. Similar ones had been made by humanists before him, some of which we have seen, and one, Valla's, we shall see in a later chapter. Ficino had also taken this position.[28] It will be recalled that the common, but not the universal position of the scholastics of the thirteenth century had been that by status and essence the angels possessed greater dignity than man, but that man in the qualified sense that he might obtain salvation might be said to be higher than the angels. However, man's ontological position kept him essentially lower in the hierarchy.[29] Renaissance ideas of freedom that have frequently been stressed with reference to Pico's declaration in his oration, rest ultimately on a change in this exegesis. If man does not occupy a fixed status, then his deification, or apotheosis, is metaphysically possible. This is the meaning which Ficino and Pico gave to man's status. Reason, according to Ficino, permitted man to be free from the three deterministic systems of providence, fate and nature, which controlled man's intellect, imagination and body. Pico rests his claim on apologetic and theological grounds more than on philosophical ones, since the Incarnation and the humanity of Christ does in fact contradict the metaphysics of the cosmos, and Christ came for the benefit of Man. Moreover, through his continuous subjectivisation, or personalisation, of the elements of his cosmos, Pico is essentially undermining the metaphysical order. Man has become the model for the rational beings that animate the celestial bodies, for the angels, and, shall we say it?, for divinity itself.

His fourth book deals with the fourth world of man. One must recognise a certain lack of clarity in his organisational schema. The fourth is the middle book of seven, and man is in his view, as in Ficino's, the node or centre of the cosmos. But man was created, according to *Genesis*, on the sixth day. Each book follows through the seven days of creation and rest in its seven chapters, so that the fourth chapter of the fourth book is the exact centre of the work, if it is conceived of like an acrostic, as Pico conceived of it. But he is unable to make his exegesis of *Genesis* come out thus neatly. The work of each day of creation has its allegorical correspondence to an aspect of man's nature.

> After we have shown sufficiently the treatment of every part of the world by the prophet and of every nature celestial, angelic and corruptible, it remains, if we recall our promises, to reinterpret the entire reading concerning man in order to prove by this act that there is no statement in this whole work which does not comprehend the hidden senses and deepest truths concerning the three worlds of which we have spoken and concerning the nature of man as well.

And this interpretation is no less meritorious since it enables man to know himself, as, passing over the Delphic saying, Plato proved in his *Alcibiades*. 'And certainly his study is false and arrogant, who, ignorant of himself and not knowing whether he can know anything, boldly affects the knowledge of things that are so far from himself.' It is only by self-knowledge that man can arrive at knowledge of the Father and the fatherland. So he would follow the traces left in the narrative of Moses rather than the traces of animal existence in man.[30]

Following the opening lines of *Genesis* declaring the creation of heaven and earth,

> Man is made from body and from rational soul. Rational soul is called heaven, for Aristotle calls heaven an animal moved by itself, and as the Platonists prove our soul is a self-moving substance. . . . The heaven is moved in an orbit; the rational soul transferring itself from causes to effects and again returning from effects to causes revolves in the orbit of reasoning. . . . The body is called earth because it is earthy and a heavy substance. Therefore, as Moses wrote, being made from *humus* gives the name 'human' to man. But between the earthly body and the heavenly substance of the soul a middle link was needed which should couple together such distant natures; for this function that thin and spiritual corpuscle which both physicians and philosophers call spirit was assigned; this, as Aristotle wrote, is both more divine in nature than the elements and corresponds to the proportions of heaven; this [Moses] called light, which designation could not agree more

with the position of the philosophers and physicians whose common opinion is that it is of an especially lucid substance and that in nothing more than light does it rejoice, be kindled and recreated. . . . Let us now return to the words of the Prophet according to whom we first see heaven and earth created, the extremes, that is, of our substance, the rational force and the earthly body, which finally, when light has been made, that is the lucid spirit is added, are so united that from the evening and the morning, that is from the nocturnal nature of the body and the matutinal nature of the soul, man becomes one. And since, as we have shown, through this light all vital and sensual virtue descends to our earth, rightly before the birth of light the earth was empty and void, and heaven could not grant to it the benefits of movement and life except through the mediation of light. Therefore he immediately adds the cause of the emptiness, since namely up to this point darkness lay over it, light not yet having been created.[31]

We have quoted at length from his first chapter in order to illustrate his method of exegesis and application of the words of *Genesis* to the explanation of the nature of man. He thus proceeds through the succeeding days. Particularly important to him was the work of the second day where God made the firmament and divided the waters below it from those above it, and called the firmament sky. He has mentioned so far three parts of the human substance – the rational, the corporeal and the 'spirit'. There are, says Pico, two more, the sensual through which we communicate with the animals below us, and the intellect through which we communicate with the angels above the heavens. Reason is called heaven, and thus the waters above the firmament correspond to the intellect and the waters below to the sense. The intellect is properly symbolised by the waters over the heavens, since it reveals a very great truth about the soul. 'For a higher and indeed divine intellect illumines the intellect which is in us, and it either is God, as some say, or else a mind closely related to man, as almost all Greeks, as the Arabs and many Hebrews wish.' Jewish philosophers and Alpharabi call it the Spirit of the Lord.

Neither was it without cause that before He established man from soul and body by the link of light [expounded as 'spirit'], he [Moses] recalled [the extension of the Spirit over the waters, but it was done for this purpose,] that we should not by some chance believe that the Spirit is not present in our intellect except when it is linked to the body.[32]

The third chapter discusses man's sensual nature symbolised as the waters that flow beneath the heavens, or reason.

For all sensitive virtues flow together into what we call common sense (which Aristotle locates in the heart) as rivers into the sea. Nor do we say absurdly that the five senses of the body which we see, hearing, sight, taste, touch and smell, are diffused as though five Mediterraneans, from that sea entering within the continent of the body.

This flow of the senses is what gives life and nourishment to the body.

Rightly, after that congregating of the waters he brings forth the land green and flourishing. For senses have been granted by nature to all mortals for the sake of procuring the life and safety of the body, so that they may know through them what things are harmful and what are health-bringing; then having learned this, through the appetite annexed to the senses they reject the former, desire the latter; finally, through the conjoined motor power they flee evil and pursue useful things. The eyes see food, the nostrils smell it, the feet approach, the hands grab, the palate tastes it. We say all this in order that we might know how aptly there is conjoined by the establishment of the waters, that is of the sensitive powers, to the earth, which has long meant the body to us, a fertile happiness.[33]

Pico therefore does not show a total rejection of the physiological level of human existence, although of course he regards it as the lowest and the most temporary. But he continues in its praise in the very next fourth chapter on the fourth day.

This according to his acrostical scheme is the very centre of the work, but not fitting the six labours, it also deals with man's physical beauties and faults symbolised by the fourth day's work of creating night and day, darkness and light, moon and sun. 'But since the rational nature is distinguished by many virtues and powers, what has been said will suffice for its bare substance. Now we must speak of its beauty and royal ornamentation, so to say.' These are symbolised by the text speaking of the moon, sun and stars placed in the firmament.

And indeed more recent philosophers would perhaps interpret the sun as the active intellect and the moon as that which is in potentiality, but since we disagree greatly with them, we shall meanwhile so expound the text that the soul, in that part which turns to the upper waters, to the Spirit of the Lord, especially because it lights up everything, may be called the sun; in that part which refers to the lower waters, that is the sensual powers whence it contracts some stain of infection, it may have the name of moon. . . . Moreover, because while we wander away from the fatherland and live in the night and darkness of this present life we make greatest use of that part which is turned towards the senses and thence have opinions more than knowledge, but when the day of future life shines, turned away from the senses towards the divine, we shall know by means of that other superior part, it is rightly said that our sun rules the day and our moon the night.

This is meant to correspond with the Platonic doctrine which makes the sun *dianoia*, and the moon *doxa*.[34]

The fifth day, on which God created the reptiles, fish of the sea and birds of the air, Pico utilises to discuss, not man's cognitive powers as heretofore, but his affective ones, the seats of concupiscence and anger. 'These he designated through the beasts and the irrational kinds of living creatures because they are common to us with the beasts and, what is more unhappy, often impel us to a brutish life.' It is not difficult to believe the paradox of the Pythagoreans that evil men change into brutes. But a reading of Moses shows that these beasts are to be subdivided and distinguished. Some are produced from the waters below the heavens and some from the land. The waters signify the sensual part which is under the heavens and subject to reason. The land is the fragile and earthly body surrounding us. Some senses apply more to the body and others to the interior sense which philosophers call the phantasy. Pico distinguishes thus between a purely physiological sensation and a psychological imaginary one. Those concerned with food and sex are the bodily senses which are given to men in order to preserve the body through nutrition and the species through reproduction. They may be used for necessity but not for pleasure, and therefore they are symbolised by cattle and wild animals.

> But we refer to the waters, that is the sense of imagination, those affections which can be called more spiritual and which are the progeny of our cognition rather than of our flesh; of this kind are those which call us to honours, anger, to revenge and other emotions related to these. These are necessary and useful to the moderate user, for one must become angry but within limits, and revenge often does the work of justice; and each one should guard his own dignity not refusing honours which are gathered by honourable means.

This statement of recognition of the partial value of the affects is important because it makes clear that Pico wishes to avoid the dualistic condemnation of the physiological and affective levels of life. In fact he warns against the danger of falling into Manichaeism.

> I say this because God created and having created blessed these animals which signify the sensual appetites, so that we do not consider them bad in their

own nature and believe with the Manicheans that they were created by an evil principle and not rather by the good God. All these therefore are good and necessary to man but we in exceeding their limits and transforming them into ambition, fury, passionateness and pride make into evil by our own guilt what He the Best established as best.[35]

What he has said thus far about man, he claims fits perfectly with what follows on the sixth day: that man was made by God in His own image in order that he might rule over the fishes, the birds and the beasts.

And indeed we have disputed about man already above, but now we first know in him that image of God through which the rule and command of the beasts is given to him. Man is thus established by nature so that reason might master the senses and arrest with its law all fury and appetite of both anger and lust. But having destroyed the image of God by the blemish of sin, miserable and unhappy, we begin to be slaves of our own beasts and with the Chaldean king to dwell with them, to crawl on the ground, desirous of earthly things, forgetful of the fatherland, forgetful of the Father, forgetful of the kingdom and of our pristine dignity given to us as a privilege. In other words man, when he was in honour, did not know it but now he has been reduced to the stupid cattle and made similar to them.[36]

Thus it is quite clear that to Pico the Fall of man removed his primeval dignity and honoured place in the universe.

But chapter seven, always devoted to the Incarnation as symbolised by God's rest, will restore man's dignity:

But just as all of us in the first Adam, who obeyed Satan more than God, and whose sons we are according to the flesh, deformed from men degenerated into brutes, so in the newest Adam Jesus Christ, who fulfilled the will of the Father and defeated the spiritual iniquities with his own blood, whose sons we are all according to the spirit, reformed by grace we are regenerated by man into adoption as sons of God, if only the prince of darkness and of this world, as in Him, so in us finds nothing.[37]

Clearly man's great dignity of having been made as Adam in the image of God exists for Pico only before the Fall and after the Resurrection. Yet it does now exist in man through Christ the new Adam.

In his fifth book he deals with the order of the creation, this time following *Genesis* more literally in the order of days. He comes to man properly in the sixth chapter, not in the fourth. And in fact he now says that man is not a fourth world but a completion and tieing together of the first three, which brings him back closer to Ficino's position.

> Hitherto we have spoken of the three supercelestial, celestial and sublunary worlds. Now we are concerned with man concerning whom it is written, 'Let us make man in our image', who is not so much a fourth world as if some new creation, but the completion and binding together of the three we have named.

In this consideration of man Pico magnifies him as essential not only to the binding together of the cosmos but as an earthly god who acts as a surrogate of the Creator. It is a custom, he says, for earthly kings when they have founded a magnificent and noble city to place their own image in the middle of it for all to see and admire. 'Hardly otherwise do we see that God the ruler of all has done, Who having constructed the whole machine of the world, established man last of all in its midst, formed in His image and likeness.' But, he adds, it is an arduous question why man has this privilege of being the image of God. God is invisible and incorporeal so that man is made in his image in that part of him where he is most similar to God, namely in his soul in which the image of the Trinity is represented.[38]

This exegesis is a very old one, going back to St. Augustine, *De Trinitate* and his *De Genesi ad litteram*. But the image of the Trinity is more powerfully placed in the angels as they have more of similarity and relationship to the divine nature.

> We moreover are seeking something peculiar to man from which the dignity proper to him and the image of the divine substance may be found to be common to him and no other creature. What else can this be except that the substance of man (as some Greek interpreters also hold) comprehends in himself the substances of all natures and the plenitude of the entire universe through his very existence? I say through his very existence, moreover, because both angels and any other intelligent creature contains in itself everything in a certain way, in as much as it knows everything being full of the forms and reasons of all things. But indeed just as God, not only because He knows all things but because He unites and collects in Himself the whole perfection of the true substance of things, so man also (although differently, as we shall show, otherwise he would be God not the image of God) brings together and co-unites all natures of the entire world to the integrity of his own substance. This we can say of no other creature, whether angelic, celestial, or sensible.[39]

Here then is an even fuller statement of man's dignity as lying, not now in his freedom, but in his total comprehension in his own substance of all the substances of the universe. This concept is similar to that of the microcosm but seems to be a vastly extended version of it, since, like Ficino's concept of man as the node of the universe, Pico seems to conceive of man as the cement which pulls it together – a spiritual and subjective and not a material one. It is a conception which is metaphysical in nature but also seems to transcend metaphysics and rest ultimately on a theological vision fed by his Christian faith and his exegesis of *Genesis*.

Man, however, is not God. He wants this to be clear.

> There is, moreover, this diversity between man and God, that God contains all things in Himself as the principle or beginning of all, man, however, contains all things in himself as the middle of all; from this it happens that in God everything is of a better kind than in themselves, in man inferior things are nobler in condition, but the superior degenerate. . . .

Man is, however, a microcosm in the sense that he enumerates all the parts of the universe as contained within him, but man also has them at his service, both the elements and the beasts beneath him, and the celestial souls and the angels, as we saw earlier, above him.

> It is a truly divine possession of all these natures at the same time flowing into one, so that it pleases us to exclaim with Hermes, 'A great miracle, O Asclepius, is man.' The human condition can especially be glorified for this reason, through which it happens that no created substance disdains to serve him. To him the earth and the elements, to him the animals are ready for service, for him the heavens fight, for him the angelic minds procure safety and goodness, if indeed it is true as Paul wrote that all ministering spirits are sent in ministry on account of those who are destined as heirs of salvation. No wonder that he is loved by all in whom all recognise something of their own, indeed their whole selves and all their possessions.[40]

This vision of man, fulsome as it is, should be noticed to be a metaphysical and a religious vision of man as demi-god, and not a vision of man as an active earthly creature making himself a ruler and knower of all. I do not think the appellation of *Magus*, which Miss Yates wishes to apply to this conception of man, is fitting, because it is surprisingly non-operative, extraordinarily passive, almost statuesque, with man almost literally seen as the emblem of God in the middle of the world with all its parts and creatures doing him service.[41] I have said it is metaphysical and religious, though I have argued above that it is more theological than ontological. Pico's theology is a Scriptural-Exegetical one which seeks to find correspondences between his religious vision of an animated cosmos, populated with angels and demons and stellar souls and animals, as well as with mankind, and a fairly undifferentiated and unelaborated synthesis of Platonic, Neoplatonic and Aristotelian metaphysical systems. But I find it difficult to regard this as genuinely philosophical; it is rather the utilisation of a rather wide-flung net-full of philosophical positions for his essentially religious vision. Similarly, and perhaps more easily, he is able to blend in the quasi-poetic, visionary systems of the so-called *prisca theologia* of Zoroaster, Hermes Trismegistus and Orpheus, regarded as non-Hebraic and non-Christian prophets, contemporary in age with Moses, who were divinely inspired by the same one Hebrew-Christian God, but whose visions were less than fully orthodox because they were obscured and polluted by vulgar paganism. All of this we discuss below in Part IV in our chapters on the *theologia poetica* and on the inter-relationship of Hebrew, Pagan and Christian traditions, but there is need to mention it here.[42]

Pico, in contrast to Ficino, stressed the importance of a distinction between theology and philosophy, whereas the latter, following the example of St. Augustine, felt that either one that fully carried through its task would necessarily reach conclusions identical with those of the other. Yet there is in Pico, as he actually presents his arguments, a far greater blurring of the differences than there is in fact in Ficino. Possibly this is because Pico's very theology is not really a theology resting on the logical analysis of the consequences of certain revealed aspects of divinity but is far more a brilliant application of the method of allegorical exegesis that was so popular in the Middle Ages – possibly more so in the eleventh and twelfth centuries than in the more scholastic thirteenth, and possibly because some of those very Neoplatonic sources that so delighted Pico were also utilised by men such as Bernard Sylvester and permeated the mentality of lesser figures. Pico's theology is, in fact, *theologia poetica*, as Wind has so happily stressed,[43] and, as we know, he promised but did not write a work by that name. His famous *Commento* on the *Canzone d'amore* of Girolamo Benivieni typifies his penchant for drawing out the abstract relationships symbolised by the concrete imagery and action of a myth. What we have seen above of his method in deriving a complete idea of human nature through an allegorical interpretation of the six days' work of creation in

Genesis i, is also illustrative of his method and his mentality. It should be said, however, that in this present instance of the practice of what E. R. Curtius called 'Biblical Poetics', he is not entirely arbitrary in finding applications of the language of *Genesis*, but is able to weave the image of the cosmos and of the cosmogony contained there more readily into his philosophy of man because he also believes in the correspondence and involvement of the parts of man with the parts of the universe, and he also believes that the universe, like man, is alive and quivering with soul.

We have been arguing in these last paragraphs that Pico's image of man is basically a religious image, and also a poetic one, and that it was not an operative image because it was not an experimental-magical one. Man was a miracle and performed his miracles by a kind of self-hypnotic visionary experience in which he lifted himself by the wings of his imagination to the divine world beyond even the angelic one, and he summoned to him the angelic powers, and the stellar souls, and charmed the passionate beasts like some modern Orpheus to do his bidding. Pico's vision of man has far more in common with the mythological-poetic tradition and with Hebrew, pagan and Christian mysticism than it does with the *vita activa et operosa* of the Renaissance whether manifested by the statesman, the businessman, the craftsman, the lawyer, the physician, the publicly-employed humanist secretary, the astrologer, or the Aristotelian natural-philosopher. In the previous chapter I suggested that Ficino's vision of man was Faustian. Pico does to be sure have some of the same elements in his dream of calling the angels to his service, as Frances Yates has properly suggested, but he lacks the earthliness, the practicality and the cunning of Faust in his dealings with Mephistopheles. The equally dreamy Ficino betrays more familiarity with them. Again I say Pico's is a poetic vision.

Let us look now at the seventh chapter of this fifth book, for it shows how this view of man with the universe loving and serving him is framed and limited by the religious doctrine from which it drew its chief support – the Incarnation. Man who is served by both terrestrial and celestial things 'because he is both the link and the node of the heavenly and the earthly' can have peace with both these parts of the universe only if he has peace within himself between his own corresponding parts. He should beware, therefore, of not knowing how great is his own dignity.

> We should hold it always before the eyes of our soul as a certain, demonstrated and indubitable truth; for just as all things favour us when we observe the law that has been given to us, so if by sin or transgression of the law we defect from our course, we will have all things adverse to us and hostile enemies. It is quite rational that, according as we do injury not only to ourselves but to the universe that we comprise in ourselves, and to God the omnipotent author of His world, we should experience everything that is in the world, also, and in the first place God, as the most potent avengers and terrible punishers for the injury received.[44]

Man does not only have the universe at his beck and call but must confront its savage justice if he sins. But his sin consists of a failure to know his own dignity.

There rests on man the awful responsibility of holding the universe together in harmonious peace.

> They are answerable for having violated the universe and having committed *lèse-majesté* towards God whose image they have soiled with the most fetid stain of iniquity. . . . It entirely exceeds every kind of madness that we should believe that it is permitted to anyone placed in some city, decorated with the highest honours, to sin against its prince, against the entire republic deserving so well of him, without punishments; should he not rather be immediately delivered to the lictors and executioners to be tortured or to the multitude of the people in order to be stoned.[45]

The lictors and executioners of this divine republic are the evil demons commanded by Satan.

Man therefore in his sinful humility and suffering needs divine mercy to counteract cosmic justice. And this is revealed in the verse, 'If a sinner repents all the angels exult in joy.'

> Here is the open explanation of this mystery which has been hidden for ages – that our nature corrupted in the first Adam and degraded from its condition will be restored by the cross of Christ. For it was also fitting that He who is the image of the invisible God, the first-born of all creatures, in whom the universe is founded, should be linked to him in an ineffable union who was made in the image of God, who is the linkage of every creature, in whom the universe is completed. If all nature was imperilled with man, his fall ought not to be ignored nor his reparation accomplished by any other than Him through whom all nature was established.[46]

The story of man's dignity is also the story of the creation and potential perfection of the cosmos, of its threatened disaster, and its redemption by the incarnate God-Man along with fallen man himself. Pico cannot separate his religious vision from his metaphysical cosmic vision, nor either of them from his vision of man.

Although we have basically completed our exposition, Pico has not completed his explanation of man and the cosmos, since he must add a sixth and seventh book to complete his seven days. The sixth book deals with the inter-relationship of the parts of the universe, and it is especially important for bringing out in a rhetorically sharper way his conception of man as the unifying linkage in the world, and of Christ as the divine saviour which makes it possible for man to resume this role after his fall. The doctrine of Christ as the Mediator is naturally of great importance in any Neoplatonic approach to Christianity, and perhaps Pico's language in his seventh chapter of this book can add to what we have already shown. He says that the lower waters divided from the upper by the firmament cannot enjoy the benefits of the upper without the intercession of the heavens or firmament between them. So there can be no coupling of the extremes of the universe, 'except through that nature which, a middle between the extremes, contains both within itself, that is, unites the extremes smoothly with themselves because it has united them before within himself through the property of his own nature'. This, of course, is done both by man and by Christ, Who is foolishness to the Gentiles and a scandal to the Jews.

> Man cannot be joined to God except through Him who, since he joined man to God in himself, was made the true mediator; so He can attach men to God in such a way that as in Him the Son of God took on human form, so through Him men may become sons of God.[47]

And again in the final chapter of all, the seventh of the seventh book, he stresses that through the sacrament of Baptism and Christ's sacrifice on the cross, men are once again, by the conversion of the Jews and Gentiles and their subsequent sacramental washings,

> reformed in the image of God. For if Baptism makes sons of God, and the Son moreover is the image of the Father, is not the virtue of the whole Trinity operating in Baptism that which said 'Let us make man in our image'? If therefore we are in the image of God, we are also Sons, if sons, we are also heirs of God, coheirs with Christ. . . .

Who are sons? Quoting Paul, he says,

> those who live in the Spirit, these are the sons of God, these the brothers of Christ, these destined to the eternal heritage which they shall possess as the reward both of faith and of a life well-done, happily, in the celestial Jerusalem.[48]

Of Pico's orthodoxy there could have been doubts, but of his Christianity, none.

Our treatment of Pico, here, has focused on his central writing within the tradition of Christian and Renaissance Platonist exegesis of *Genesis* i:26. The *Heptaplus*, by covering the entire six days of the creation and the seventh day of rest [*Genesis* i:–ii:3], allowed him to put together in a concentration of interpretative fervour what frequently fell into three works – a cosmology and natural history based on the first five days, a treatment of the dignity of man based on the sixth, and Pico's own addition of the seventh day as the occasion for dealing with the Fall of man and his far more significant restoration and potential divinisation through the Incarnation. We have sought to show how extraordinarily anthropocentric Pico reveals his vision of the universe and its three worlds, of God and man, Creator and created image, Redemptor and redeemed to have been. And to be sure a different picture might emerge from consideration of his *Conclusiones*, *Apologia*, *De ente et uno* or *Disputationes adversus astrologiam divinatricem*. Pico was a philosopher trained and a philosopher by intention. Nonetheless in the work studied here (which, as we claim, is cognate also to his *Oratio de dignitate hominis*), theological vision and exegetical enthusiasm are uppermost.

Moreover, we have not especially stressed the idea of multipotential freedom of metaphysical choice, which is so prominent in the *Oration*, because we have wished to emphasise, paradoxically perhaps, the extent of his inter-involvement of man's nature with the levels of being of his cosmos. Both in his attempt to project this view of man's vast freedom from metaphysical involvement and simultaneous elaboration of that involvement itself, it seems to us that he has not departed as far from the more scholarly and the more soberly and methodologically philosophical Ficino as contemporary scholarship insists.

Pico, by the far-flung circulation of his *Oration*, particularly in the nineteenth and twentieth centuries but also in the Renaissance, has come to symbolise a Renaissance liberation of the human spirit from an earth-born determinism. But this vision is only one side of his thought, and he had it in common with Ficino. Moreover, we have tried to show that while both Pico and Ficino were prone to utilise some of the more ecstatic passages from both the Hermetic and the Neoplatonic writings, that their ideas also derived from the Christian-Augustinian tradition which, in one aspect of it at least, provided the basic notions for the Renaissance conception of the dignity of man. Not only did the tradition of the Augustinian *Genesis* exegesis and the Trinitarian conception of the human soul as imaging the divine Trinity find full elaboration in Renaissance Platonism, but many of the supporting arguments and themes, philosophical or rhetorical, the label does not matter, had previously been asserted in the humanist discussions of the condition of man, his misery and his dignity, both in the Facian and the Manettian directions. And the emphasis on immortality and a heavenly destiny and fruition borne on the cathexis of the human will towards God was also prominent in Petrarch, Salutati and Valla. Possibly Ficino was able to draw into the context of his philosophy the stress on the worldly achievements of man such as Manetti had offered more effectively than Pico. Possibly Pico remained closer to the more literal exegetical and theological arguments we observed in Facio in his dependence on Antonio da Barga. Without wishing in the least to dim the glory of these two potent Renaissance philosophers who certainly exceeded their humanist predecessors by far in their mental energy, capacity for comprehensive synthesis of ideas and sustained philosophical argumentation, it seems to me important to reassert, concretely and specifically as I have sought to do, rather than just impressionistically and argumentatively, their contextual and thematic dependence on the humanists of the fourteenth and fifteenth centuries for their centrally important conceptions of man and his dynamic potentiality for transforming nature and his own nature in a universe where God is a Trinitarian Spirit and man possesses His image for his own spirit.

We should not in this overlook the importance of the effort made by the Platonists to draw on a far wider range of traditions and we have included some chapters on this phase of their thought in Part IV below.[49] Nor should we forget, as well, that the more specifically

Latin, western, Augustinian tradition had behind it the syncretistic tendencies of Greek patristic thought with its own high visions of the place of man in the universe – Origen, Nemesius of Emesa, Gregory of Nyssa, Johannes Damascenus, the Philonic exegesis in the background. The western tradition also had Lactantius and the Ciceronian-Stoic projection of human dignity in *The Nature of the Gods*.[50] Finally there was the Hermetic tradition, both the theological and the magical, which completely fascinated Ficino and Pico. We have stated our attitude towards the contemporary stress on this tradition above.[51] It was one of several conspiring influences (or they were made by Ficino and Pico to conspire). I am not willing to say that Hermetism was the one, or the chief, or the most potent and influential tradition that entered into the formation of Ficino's and Pico's thought. Possibly a hundred years later it was for Giordano Bruno and Tommaso Campanella. Of that I cannot judge.

Of more immediate interest and concern, as a kind of appendix to this chapter, and at the same time a rounding off of a theme with which we began our consideration of the Renaissance discussions of the dignity of man in Part II above,[52] is the treatment of the comparative dignity of man and angels by Egidio da Viterbo, 1469–1532. Egidio, who was made a Cardinal by Leo X and took a prominent part in the Lateran Council, was possibly a student of Ficino but very briefly.[53] Nevertheless, he absorbed a rather impressive knowledge of Plato and the Renaissance Platonist ideas and set himself up as an apostle of a Platonic and anti-Aristotelian approach to theology within the Church itself. Possibly it was his antagonism as a member of the Augustinian Hermits of which he was Prior General to the prominence of the Dominicans and their Thomistic Aristotelianism which motivated him. But the depth of his knowledge went far beyond mere controversialism.

Egidio's commentary on the *Sentences* 'according to the mind of Plato', published in part by Eugenio Massa, is a strangely interesting work, more for its style and the methodology of its thought than for its actual ideas. Egidio was one of the leading ecclesiastical orators of his day, famous for his polished, erudite, humanistic sermons. He represented a genuine penetration of the new humanist rhetoric and classicism into the centres of churchly power. Egidio had close relations with both Julius II and Leo X. His commentary is important also because of his constant reiteration of his theological arguments in terms of the classical myths of the gods and heroes, a sort of *theologia poetica* in reverse where he translates the meanings back into the myths. This, too, he took from humanist and Platonist circles. His treatment of the Lombard was fragmentary, arriving only at Book I, Distinction XVIII. And, at that, he does not follow the *Sentences* very systematically, instead, paralleling its arguments by his own.

Massa has published his selection twice: once under the title, 'The Soul and Man in Egidio da Viterbo and in the Classical and Medieval Sources', as part of the volume, *Unedited Humanistic Texts on the 'De Anima'*, edited by Garin (series ed. Castelli) in 1951. Massa's second publication, with only minor changes, was in 1954 under the title *The Metaphysical Foundations of the 'Dignity of Man'*.[54] Without very much discussion of either the *De anima* or *The Dignity of Man*, Massa's useful introduction on the texts stresses the dynamic rather than the hierarchic character of Egidio's views of man in the cosmos.

What, in fact, Egidio does do, is to revive the traditional discussions of the relative dignity of man and angel which was a standard part of earlier scholastic commentaries on the *Sentences*, as we reported above. The third section of Egidio's commentary,[55] to follow Massa's divisions, uses arguments drawn from Plato, but essentially recapitulating the traditional Augustinian position, to demonstrate that the image of God in man is in man's soul, since by man, one must mean man's soul. After citing Aristotle that the soul is the form of man, and human actions are to be attributed to man rather than to the soul only, he argues:

> Others, on the contrary, overturn all this: first of all they believe that man is not the whole but the soul only, and they make the body an organ of man, not a part. Plato, indeed, was the chief spokesman for this position. ... Those therefore who believe with Plato think that the whole man (for so they call the soul) was born according to the image of God, and they hold that the divine Word both rightly and properly said that man was made according to the image of God; others cannot defend this position unless they understand that it is said in the sense of form, so that when they say this it is necessary for them to say that Moses did not speak properly.[56]

Egidio's fifth section is entitled, 'The Image of Angels is More Excellent than the Image of Man'. Here he argues that although from the fact that it was conceded to man to become the Son of God 'the human condition would seem not only to equal but even to excel the nature of the gods [i.e. angels]', if we compare not those things which happen to man 'but human nature itself to the nature of the celestial gods, there is no one who would not see that the gods and the image of the gods must be placed far above men and the human image'. All immortals are superior to mortals, just as incorporeal things are superior to corporeal and the soul is more precious than the body. A more powerful operation argues a more powerful nature. Therefore then angels are far superior to men. They are also far more similar to God 'since they are pure and simple acts as is demonstrated in the *Metaphysics*, which indeed does not fit the nature of man'. Therefore angels are superior both in nature and image.

> Nor are those things relevant which were said above against this, for the argument is about nature, not about a unique accident of nature; for when things are compared, their natures are compared, or those affections of nature which arise from internal sources of nature. But the fact that man is made into God does not derive from the internal affection of nature but from the external mercy of God.[57]

Typically setting up the argument on Aristotelian grounds, he is eager to demolish it from Platonic [i.e. Augustinian] arguments. The next section is 'The Image is in a Certain Way Stronger in Man than in the Angel'.[58] Man restlessly wishes to prove that he can excel the angels. Because men are better than animals, it does not mean that animals are not stronger or more effective than men in certain powers and faculties. While angels may excel men by their natures it is in man's destiny and movement that he excels the angels.[59]

> But in those matters which make for divine friendship and the blessed life no one doubts that men are placed above the immortal gods. For the sins of men procure forgiveness, those of the gods falling from heaven never procure it.

Moreover these angels serve us as guardians.

> For Plato also teaches in the first book of the *Republic* that all shepherds should be concerned not with their own needs but those of their flock; but the tenth book of the *Laws* makes gods shepherds of men; by this fact they are necessarily inferior to us, for always the worse serve the better, as Plato argued in *Gorgias*.[60]

His ultimate argument is in terms of the superiority of the joys awaiting men in their triumphal fruition in heaven.

> Finally the gods in the blessed life which they perpetually enjoy have one force only, the bare mind alone by which they enjoy a bare blessedness; we, besides the gifts of the mind, also enjoy the divine and blessed delights of the body which are fitting for the citizens of the most sacred and blessed city. To this must be added the rewards for labours and merits; for all of these must be taken into account: nothing of these things can be hoped for by the gods who are not able either to labour or to risk their life for a republic or a prince, to seek death or oppose the body to dangers. Therefore since it is not given to these to engage in struggle, triumph and victory is also denied them. From such arguments it may be sufficiently established that while parts of nature are conceded to the gods, there are indeed many in which necessarily the gods cede to mortals and as much as they are higher than us by nature, by so much we are better than they are in many things.[61]

With these arguments of Egidio, which recapitulate many arguments of the humanists, as well as those of Augustine and of those scholastics who favoured the dignity of man over the angels, we are reminded of the long theological tradition of discussion of the dignity of man. In his efforts to support it from the works of Plato against the use of Aristotle on the contrary side, we may observe the influence of Renaissance Platonism back into the original scholastic context of the argument. We can also recognise the ultimate direction of the impact that this humanist assertion of the centrality of man in religious and moral thought had in late Renaissance ecclesiastical circles. As Wind has reminded us,[62] Martin Luther was a visitor in the house of the Augustinian order in Rome during the time when Egidio was its Prior General. This was also when he was engaged in writing this work. It may seem a far cry from the golden circles of Julius II and Leo X and such classicising rhetoricians and theologians as Egidio to Luther's repudiation of aught but the purest Biblical tradition. None the less it is possible to suggest that there may have been certain underlying features in common characterised, perhaps, by the wish to find a genuine reconciliation between the will, the feelings, the passions of men and their ultimate destiny of fruition divinely offered and graciously granted them. The influence of St. Augustine lay equally strong on Renaissance and Reformation.

XI. Pietro Pomponazzi on the Condition of Earthly Man

It is impossible to consider the emergence of new views of the nature of man in the Renaissance and of the efforts to relate them to the divine image of God and the Christian teachings on human destiny without considering, though perhaps not as fully as it deserves, the remarkable assertion of an autonomous, naturalistic vision of man by Pietro Pomponazzi of Mantua, 1462–1525.[1] Pomponazzi developed his views in the course of his career as a natural philosopher, lecturing at Padua, Ferrara and eventually at Bologna. Undoubtedly, from the point of view of the history of philosophy, his ideas must be regarded and treated as developing out of the contrasting interpretations of Aristotle that were current in his own time, but which had provided since the thirteenth century the major approaches to the nature of man and of the human soul in the arts faculties of the medieval and Renaissance universities. These interpretations were chiefly those influenced by the great Arabic scholar of Cordoba, Ibn Rush'd, or Averroes, and those which sought to uphold the Christianised interpretation of Aristotle that had been developed by Thomas Aquinas. There also existed a third position, which has not entered particularly into the discussions of Pomponazzi, perhaps, because it was by then so weakly represented in Italy, namely the nominalism and terminism developed by Ockham and his followers and rivals in the fourteenth century.

Undoubtedly from the genetic point of view of the evolution of philosophical ideas Pomponazzi's elaboration of an interpretation of Aristotle's *De anima* which denied that the highest part of the human soul, the possible intellect, was immortal either in the sense of being part of a universal separate substance, as Averroes held, or as part of an individual, immortal soul, as the Christian, Thomas, taught, was of prime importance and a signal achievement. It not only freed philosophy from theology, a freedom which natural philosophers and dialectians had strenuously but tenuously maintained since the thirteenth century, but it laid the basis for an immanent, empirical this-worldly treatment of the world of man in the philosophy of the enlightenment and of the nineteenth century.[2]

Pomponazzi's achievement, however, is also and often viewed within the cultural context of humanism and the Italian Renaissance, and it will be from this perspective that we shall attempt to discuss it, just as we tried to do in the case of Marsilio Ficino, also an outstanding Renaissance philosopher. No evidence has as yet come forth that Pomponazzi himself engaged in any kind of discussion with contemporary humanists, nor is there direct evidence that he knew or cited their works, although this latter would not be conclusive since he frequently referred to particular philosophical positions without identifying them or their author. I should like, however, to juxtapose his ideas with those of an Italian humanist who wrote on a similar theme nearly fifty years previous to the publication of Pomponazzi's *De immortalitate animae*, and interestingly enough a Bolognese humanist, Benedetto Morandi, who was discussed above.[3] I am not suggesting, and I would not want to suggest, that Morandi exercised any kind of influence on Pomponazzi, if indeed the latter had ever heard of him. What does seem to emerge, however, and seems to be of significance is that Morandi's ideas grew in the context of the discussions of Aristotelians in this university centre north of the Appennines, discussions directly involving the inter-relationship of religious doctrines and Aristotelian concepts which he alluded to in his second treatise against Garzoni.

It may be recalled that Morandi, although he affirmed and reaffirmed Christian teachings concerning the end of man as the fruition of beatitude, concerning man's creation in the divine image, his fall, and his reparation by the divine assumption of human nature, was at pains to make clear that he was arguing on behalf of a 'human happiness' of which man was capable in his natural condition of being human, rather than sub-human animal condition or super-human angelic state or even the fruition of the blest in paradise. Morandi was, perhaps, not sufficiently involved and engaged as an Aristotelian philosopher to be concerned to take a position on Averroes versus Thomas, but he freely cites Aristotle, Averroes, Avicenna and especially Albertus Magnus, rather than Thomas. His opponent Garzoni, on the other hand, was both a protégé of Lorenzo Valla and a great admirer of the *Doctor Angelicus*. Thus we do not have from Morandi the crucial argument produced by Pomponazzi on the mortality of the possible intellect as an inseparable material form of the sensitive soul and the body, for Morandi was dealing with the happiness, not the mortality, of man. Moreover, we also do not have any attempt to argue that the immortality of the soul can be demonstrated by natural reason, so that he was not concerned to uphold either the point of view of the Averroists or of the Thomists.

What Morandi does stress over and over again are two things: first that from a non-Christian, pagan perspective certain attitudes in conformance with the nature of man were perfectly natural, such as Cato's suicide, and second that an Aristotelian or even a Stoic conception of morality has much to justify it from a human, although perhaps not from a Christian, point of view.[4] He does not, in other words, follow the lines of the Thomistic effort to synthesise Christian and Aristotelian ethics, as did certain humanists as well, such as Leonardo Bruni, but he looks at these positions as subject to analysis and acceptance or rejection in terms of human reason and the principles of logic alone.

Secondly, Morandi stresses, as Pomponazzi also does, that the human condition is an autonomous condition that must be viewed in its own terms rather than by imposing on it the values appropriate to either animals or to angels, which he accuses Garzoni of doing. I believe that this position is a crucial one in Pomponazzi's own line of argumentation and reflects his underlying attitude toward life; it is also the fundamental basis of his argument concerning the mortality of the soul, for those who seek to establish its immortality, he feels, wish to transgress the bounds of the human and to make man into something non-human, either angelic or bestial. While Morandi recognised, as we have shown above, that the philosopher and intellectual approaches the angelic or divine conditions, and that the man who allows himself to develop into a habitual sinner becomes animal-like, he also wishes to make it clear that these are comparative terms. This he does in the following passage which we shall set alongside of a statement by Pomponazzi:

Indeed happiness is a comparative term and has degrees; nor does it consist in an indivisible whole but of a number of things [*connumerata*], as Aristotle said, that is if even the least good is added, it becomes greater. Only God has supreme, infinite, incomprehensible and ineffable beatitude. Nevertheless angelic happiness is not therefore nothing. But neither does the magnitude of angelic happiness destroy the human of which man is capable. The happiness of mortals approaches closer to that which is of the angels than the angelic to the divine, because there can be no proportion between the finite and the infinite, whereas the former have limits and are comparable. Thus numbers and magnitudes may be compared in such a way that they do not mutually cancel each other but [so that they] may be said to be either greater or lesser. . . . Mediate things compared to those which are higher lose the force of their character but if they are compared to inferior things, no one will deny that their kind exists. Hence angelic happiness will be nothing in respect to that which is God's, but compared with the happiness of man, it suppresses it. But if you compare man to the other living creatures, he will not lack his own, human happiness itself, on account of the dignity of the intellect and because all things of nature are subject to his use and command, and, as Aristotle says, man is the end of natural things for whose sake nature produces them.[5]

Pomponazzi also makes numerous comparisons of the status and condition of man showing that man may be given the qualifications of a higher or lower being but only relatively, not absolutely. Indeed, his entire argument about the mortality of the intellect is made by reiterating the distinction between man's relative immortality and absolute mortality in intellect.

But if man is at times called immortal, this is understood relatively, since it is said, in *De partibus* ii, chapter 10: 'Man alone among mortals partakes in the highest degree of divinity.' Compared to other mortals he can be called immortal, for, as has been said, man is halfway between the gods and the beasts. Whence just as grey compared to black is called white so man compared to the beasts can be called God and immortal, but not truly and unqualifiedly.[6]

Pomponazzi expresses himself differently on the subject of human happiness, however, than Morandi did, although there are certain very significant similarities as well. Pomponazzi's whole attitude towards human life needs to be explored. In the *De immortalitate animae* he attempts to meet those objections to his position which are not strictly speaking philosophical but are rather arguments pointing out the untenable consequences of holding that man is mortal. He presents these objections in Chapter XIII and answers them in Chapter XIV. If it is not too complicated to make a double comparison here, we should like to point out that the objections, or some of them, at least, seem to be drawn directly from Marsilio Ficino's arguments in *Theologia Platonica*, also called *De immortalitate animorum*, which Pomponazzi seems to have known. However, the arguments can also be found in many other places which he probably did not know, such as Facio's *De hominis excellentia* discussed above. We shall consider only the first objection, which is the most substantial, namely that if the soul is not immortal it will have no final end and hence will not become happy. This position is sustained by exactly the argument we saw Facio use,[7] namely that man, unlike the beasts, is unable to achieve any contentment in this life but is always restlessly striving for knowledge. Ficino, of course, adds the good to the true as the goals of man's striving, which can only be satisfied by the attainment of the absolute. But here is Pomponazzi's summary of the argument:

> Moreover, who will assert this knowledge to be happiness, since in happiness we are at peace, but in this we are tossed about and not at peace? . . . Moreover, in striving for this knowledge how many arts, how many sciences, how many labours, how many sleepless nights are needful? . . . Further, since the time needed for producing such happiness is very great, and the way of arriving at it most difficult, for a man ought to renounce the body almost completely while he is in the body; and he is doubtful of the outcome, and even after he has succeeded he may lose it in a moment, by dying or going mad or by some other chance; how then will that not be more truly called unhappiness than happiness? Wherefore many have not unreasonably said, if the human soul is mortal, the condition of man is far worse than that of any beast, considering the weakness of man in regard to his body, which is subject to so many infirmities, and the restlessness of his soul, which is ever turning this way and that.[8]

The last sentence will be recognised as an almost direct echo of the first sentence of Ficino's great work. But it was also a frequent argument of those humanists and ecclesiastics who asserted the 'misery of the human condition', as we saw above, and specifically Garzoni.

We have shown that the answer of the humanists to this position was to assert the dignity of man. But some stressed that man's dignity lay exclusively in his immortality towards which he strove, and which he attained in accord with the Christian revelation. Others emphasised that man's actions in this life were themselves demonstrations of his great excellence of which the next life was but an augmentation and a culmination.[9] Ficino, as a Platonic philosopher, as we have seen, placed his greatest stress on the ultimate achievement of immortality, but in arguing on behalf of the truth of immortality he produced a picture of human action and striving in this world which was exceptionally laudatory and admiring.[10] Morandi also was admiring of man but more modestly. Rather he saw in human progress and the works of civilisation the mark that man was fulfilling his needs in an autonomous way in this world in accord with his nature, and that despite his troubles he must be considered happy. Human civilisation, with its industry and progress, its works of the intellect, was also viewed as wholly admirable.[11]

Pomponazzi does not offer such a forthright picture of human achievements. He seems to be well aware of the troubles and pains that men experience. He is far more pessimistic about the condition of man than Morandi, or even Ficino, was, and has surprisingly little confidence in the powers of the intellect.

> But if it is said that we greatly vilify the human intellect, when we assert that it is hardly the shadow of intellect, to this it is replied, that truly in comparison with the Intelligences it is a shadow. . . . But if you compare the intellect with the other things that are generated and corrupted, it will obtain the first rank of nobility, although the body is very weak and subject to an almost infinite number of infirmities, and is of a worse condition than almost all beasts, as Pliny the Elder shows very ably in his *Natural History*. Add, besides, that man is either a subject or else rules others. If he is a subject let him consider his lot most miserable, since of a thousand thousand rulers hardly one is found of even moderate virtue; indeed, almost always those established in power are mad, ignorant and filled with every sort of vice. How hard indeed is this kind of fate is plain enough, since no race of animals is thus oppressed by one of its own species. But if he rules others, how unjust a tyranny is both Plato in the *Republic* and Aristotle in the *Politics* make clear at sufficient length. . . . Let him then who so greatly magnifies man not consider what he does not experience but those things which he knows and has before his eyes.[12]

Pomponazzi's pessimism, though, as we shall see, it was not absolute, is nonetheless striking. It was offered almost as an acceptance of the challenge of those he saw arguing that, without immortality, man would be the most miserable of creatures. Indeed man is, he seems to say. But he has a more specific answer to this specific objection, not in Chapter 12 from which the above passage was taken, but in Chapter 14. If the end of man is not immortality and its accompaniments, then what is it seen in sublunary, purely natural terms? Pomponazzi's answer, as always, is complex and highly qualified. First, in keeping with his previous statements,

> there must be assigned to each thing as its end not what is good to a greater degree, but only according to what suits its nature, and has a due proportion to it. For although it is better to sense than not to sense, it does not suit a stone; for then it would no longer be a stone. Whence also in assigning an end to man, if it were such as we should assign to God and the Intelligences, that would not be fitting, since he would thus not be man.

Man in other words must be considered strictly after his own nature and not after the image of God. Nor can Pomponazzi tolerate the notion of Ficino, Pico and others that man is a chameleon capable of taking on a multiplicity of natures.[13]

'Secondly, it must be accepted . . . that the whole human race can be compared to one single man.' Pomponazzi here shifts the argument in a startling way from the individual to the human collective. Although he objected to the Averroistic doctrine of a collective possible intellect shared in by each individual and vindicated the human intellect as individual though mortal, he here seems to feel, unlike Aristotle's insistence on the individuality of human ends in the *Ethics*, and more like Plato's collectivism in the *Republic*, that man collectively seeks a good of the species through differentiated individual contributions, functioning organically and harmoniously together like the parts of the human body.

> Just as Plato says in the *Timaeus* that God gave to each what is best for it and for the whole, in the same way we must think of the whole human race. For the whole human race is like a single body composed of different members, also with different functions, yet ordered to the common advantages of the human race. . . . Nor can all be of equal perfection, but to some are given functions more perfect, to some less perfect. And were this inequality destroyed, either the human race would perish, or it would persist with great difficulty.[14]

Thus in subordinating individual ends or functioning to that of the whole Pomponazzi also disagrees with Thomas Aquinas' statement in *Summa contra Gentiles* that, unlike other creatures, man is given his end as an individual rather than as species.[15]

But Pomponazzi proceeds to qualify this assertion of functional inequality by saying that at the same time all men have certain things in common. 'For otherwise they would not be parts of one genus and with a tendency towards a single common good . . .' But the individual functioning and ends must definitely be orchestrated into a harmonious whole so that the inequality of man does not produce discord. 'A commensurate diversity among men generates the perfect, the beautiful, the suitable, and the delightful; but an incommensurate diversity the contrary.'[16]

What then are these differentiated ends that must be harmonised for the good of the whole, and what do men have in common? All men share in the three intellects classified by Aristotle: the theoretical, the practical, and the productive, but there is great diversity not only in their endowments of the first and the last but in the ways in which these operate in a practical sense. There may be some theoretical knowledge in all men, but only a few are philosophers and intellectuals. Productive ability may be far more widespread throughout the working masses of mankind, but even the sage needs it even if to a slight extent. It is the middle or 'practical' intellect in which all seem to share equally in endowment. Thus, the men engaged in using the speculative intellect are like the heart of the human race, whereas the productive faculty is so common that even some beasts share in it. 'Yet the practical or operative intellect is truly fitting for men.'[17]

How do these intellects function as ends? 'We say that the end of the human race in general is to participate in these three intellects by which men communicate with each other and live together . . .' But the practical intellect is the most important, since, in his use of the Aristotelian term, this refers to human 'action' which consists primarily of the moral virtues. '[E]very man should possess it perfectly. For in order that the human race be rightly preserved, every man must be morally virtuous and as far as possible lack vice. . . .' As we can see emerging, Pomponazzi is moving towards making the moral life the life of man *per se*, but not in the context of a religious vision of salvation and damnation. Rather morality is essential for the maintenance of human civilisation, the collective whole of human life on a truly human, neither animal nor angelic, level. It is the moral life, rather than the life of the intellect or the life of the producer that is distinctively human.

> Wherefore the universal end of the human race is to participate relatively in the speculative and the productive intellects, but perfectly in the practical. For the whole would be most perfectly preserved if all men were righteous and good, but not if all were philosophers or smiths or builders.[18]

But on the other hand, the end of the human individual as well as that of the race also consists in virtue. For not everyone can serve the whole theoretically or productively, but

> if man is mortal, every man can have the end which suits man universally. . . . Happiness then does not consist in the theoretical power of demonstration, as suitable for the whole human race, but as suiting its principal part. And though the other parts cannot arrive at such happiness, they are still not wholly deprived of all happiness, since they can possess something of the theoretical and something of the productive, and the practical perfectly. For farmer or smith, destitute or rich, if his life be moral, can be called happy, and truly so called, and can depart contented with his lot. . . . Hence the human race is not frustrated in its end, unless it make itself so.[19]

Although Pomponazzi draws this argument for the universality of man's moral vocation seemingly from Aristotle's *Ethics* VI, 5, and Plato's *Republic* IV, 420b, although the argument for the inequality of the productive and speculative intellects similarly is drawn from *Politics* IV, 4, and the *Republic* IV, 442c, there seems to be another source involved. Pomponazzi does not cite Plato's *Protagoras* 320d and 323d where the myth of the gifts of Prometheus and of Hermes are set forth, though it seems unlikely that he did not know it. For here also the gifts of productivity and the intellect are unevenly distributed, but all men share the capacity for moral virtue sent to them by Zeus through Hermes. Thus, just as Pomponazzi was ready to modify his Aristotelianism in a Stoic direction, he may also have shaped his ideas of man's condition after the original humanist vision of Protagoras.[20]

As to the charge, which echoed Ficino's statement, 'that the condition of man would be far worse than that of any brute' if man did not attain immortality,

> surely in my opinion that is not said philosophically, since the work of beasts, though they bring content to their kind, are here preferred to the restless works of the intellect. Who would prefer to be a stone or a stag of long life, rather than a man of however low degree?

Pomponazzi is ready to accept as unavoidable a life of restlessness and disturbance as part of the human condition, for, 'in human happiness a steadfastness that cannot be destroyed is enough, although it may be disturbed somewhat'. But what will save man is his virtue, for 'nothing is more precious and more happy than virtue itself, it is above all things to be chosen' even if it brings about death. And 'Indeed the wise man would much prefer to be in extreme necessity and the greatest troubles rather than to be stupid, cowardly, and vicious under the opposite conditions.' Nor is the belief in immortality necessary for this virtue, for it is not true

> that one who sees immense labours, withdrawal from bodily pleasures, obscure knowledge of things, the easy loss of what has been acquired, would turn aside to vice and bodily things rather than be moved to acquire knowledge, if that man acts according to reason. For the slightest modicum of knowledge and virtue is to be preferred to all bodily delights. . . .[21]

This attitude of Pomponazzi seems to have more in common with the Stoics than with some of the ways that Aristotelian ethics was interpreted in the Renaissance, but it can be matched by similar statements by Morandi which were also of Peripatetic derivation, though Morandi clearly showed his admiration of the Stoic hero, Cato. As a matter of very interesting historical fact there seems to have been a relationship between Stoicism and Aristotelian moral theory in the Renaissance. It was possible to argue that the *verum bonum* of the Stoics and the *summum bonum* of the Aristotelians approximated each other, since each consisted in virtue, despite the Peripatetic admission and the Stoic exclusion of bodily and exterior goods. It was also possible to confuse Stoic insistence that true reason would disperse vice by proving its error with the Peripatetic doctrine of right reason as a guide in moral decision. Moreover humanists might have found some precedent for this combination in Cicero, who seems to have attempted a synthesis of Stoicism and Peripateticism, or at least refers to such an attempt on the part of his Middle-Academy teacher, Antiochus, at the beginning of Book I of *De natura deorum*.[22]

As is well known, Leonardo Bruni's *Isagogicon moralis disciplinae* is an attempt to synthesize or at least find a common ground in Stoic and Peripatetic moral doctrine, and in Epicurean as well. And it seems probable that this was the reason Lorenzo Valla made Bruni the spokesman for 'Stoicism' in the first version of his *De vero bono* [then called *De voluptate*].[23] Valla's opposition to Stoicism and to Aristotelianism, as we have shown above, was equally violent, and it seems very probable that he considered contemporary representatives of each school, both humanists and scholastic philosophers and theologians, guilty of the same crime. And what was this crime but to attempt to find an approximation to Christian morality in the classical exaltation of virtue as the highest or the only true value in human life, whereas virtue was only a means to the end of beatitude or else a manifestation of a certain organisation and direction of human affects. And man's actions could lead to his heavenly beatitude only if he was divinely elected. Petrarch, as is also well known, had a less clear or a less constant position and frequently brought together not only Stoic and Peripatetic but Platonic and Christian moral conceptions, as well.[24] Valla's position was that, apart from grace and final beatitude, all human actions were equally voluptuarian and sinful, even the so-called virtues. It is interesting that his protégé Giovanni Garzoni seems to take a similar position with less clarity and emphasis, and that to some extent Ficino seems to argue that without immortality of the soul, the life of animals who attain a fulfilment of their vegetative, nutritive and sensitive natures was happier than that of men striving to be virtuous and learned with continuous disturbance and in vain.

Thus Pomponazzi's Stoical Aristotelianism acquires a new significance against this background, because he is the first to come out and say (and as far as we have any evidence the first to think), that if man is mortal, the moral life (whether viewed Stoically or Peripatetically) represents his greatest happiness and his highest achievement, and not because it will lead him to future bliss but because it will make the collective life of man here and now a richer, more harmonious, more dignified one. I should like to continue the comparison of Pomponazzi with the humanistic Aristotelian, Morandi, going into greater detail on their notions of free will and virtue, since Morandi did not venture the doctrine of the mortality of the soul. But first it will be interesting to look at Pomponazzi's attitude towards virtue as its own reward and vice as its own punishment, which he sets forth in answer to the charge that providence and divine justice, rewarding good and punishing evil, would be destroyed if immortality is denied. In answer Pomponazzi quotes Plato in the *Crito*, 'To the good man neither alive nor dead can evil happen', and adds himself, 'But it is the opposite with vice. For the punishment of the vicious is vice itself, than which nothing can be more miserable, nothing more unhappy.' And, 'no evil remains in essence unpunished, nor any good in essence unrewarded'.[25]

He not only finds his way back to the understanding of the ancient position, upheld in several schools, that virtue as an autonomous goal upholds the noblest vision of man and the universe, apart from considerations of reward. But he grasped the need of his own time, and of the modern age generally, for once again a morality of personal responsibility, in other words an autonomous one in which each individual of his own rational choice takes on the duty of conducting himself as a component part of human society in such a way that he will contribute most to the well-being of that society. For external sanctions of juridical reward and punishment, as well as religious sanctions in terms of an other-worldly destiny, diminish the value of the moral action or increase the evil of a vicious one. Thus,

> accidental reward is far more imperfect than essential reward, for gold is more imperfect than virtue. And accidental punishment is far less than essential punishment; for accidental punishment is the punishment of a penalty, but essential, that of guilt. But the punishment of guilt is far worse than the punishment of a penalty.[26]

Pomponazzi realises a psychological and moral truth that might go far in explaining the rule of conscience in the Puritan epoch that was to succeed the Renaissance in at least northern Europe and America, and which has puzzled very many in their attempts to reconcile it with the Calvinistic doctrine of predestination. We shall, also, look briefly at Pomponazzi's own more Stoic fatalism, but we must continue the present analysis. He adds, with an insight that is surprisingly comparable with Valla's rejection[27] of the meritoriousness of actions in conformity to the bond of a religious oath,

> when good is accidentally rewarded, essential good seems to be diminished, nor does it remain in its perfection. For example, if one man acts virtuously

without hope of reward, and another with hope of reward, the act of the second is not considered as virtuous as that of the first. . . . Likewise, he who acts viciously and is punished accidentally, seems to be punished less than he who is not punished accidentally; for the punishment of guilt is greater and worse than the punishment of a penalty; and when the punishment of a penalty is added to guilt, it diminishes the guilt.[28]

Later in this same chapter he repeats essentially the same idea and adds:

Wherefore those who claim that the soul is mortal seem better to save the grounds of virtue than those who claim it to be immortal. For the hope of reward and the fear of punishment seem to suggest a certain servility, which is contrary to the grounds of virtue.[29]

The fact that he published those words a year before Luther nailed his theses on that church door in Wittenberg cannot possibly imply that Pomponazzi's ideas had anything to do with the Reformation, for they would most likely have been anathema to most of the Reformers. But what he says does suggest a comparison with the Lutheran effort to detach religious faith from merits and works and considerations of human morality, since to Luther also good works performed out of fear or greed indicated a kind of servility in comparison with the Christian liberty which expressed an inner love through outer good works without concern for reward or punishment. And Pomponazzi's doctrine, although it embraces the very classical moralities he abhorred, does agree with Valla's notions that truly moral actions were manifestations of spontaneous charitableness. However, as we shall see, there is a greater element of rational deliberation and choice involved in Pomponazzi's conception of human morality than in Luther's or Valla's.

A major question in Pomponazzi's, and in any Renaissance conception of man, is the degree to which a freedom or a capacity to transcend and go beyond the naturally determining forces of internal and external nature is recognised. Pomponazzi wrote a lengthy work on this question which he finished in 1520, four years after the *De immortalitate animae* and shortly after the publication of his *Apologia* in 1518 and his *Defensorium* in 1519 in support of the same ideas. In the *De immortalitate animae*, he expressed himself on the question of whether man was truly a microcosm or whether he had the power of becoming whatever level of being he wished, as Ficino and Pico had declared in testifying to the dignity of man. Man, says Pomponazzi, 'is the most perfect of animals' because he is a mean between the material and the immaterial, and thus participates in the properties of both extremes, although he is neither.[30]

> Wherefore also the human soul has some of the properties of the Intelligences and some of the properties of all material things; whence it is that when it performs functions through which it agrees with the Intelligences, it is said to be divine and to be changed into a God; but when it performs the functions of beasts, it is said to be changed into a beast; for because of malice it is said to be a serpent or a fox, because of cruelty a tiger, and so on. For there is nothing in the world which because of some property cannot agree with man himself; wherefore man is not undeservedly called a microcosm, or little world. Therefore some have said that man is a great marvel, [Ficino? Pico?] since he is the whole world and can change into every nature, since to him is given the power to follow whatever property of things he may prefer. Therefore the ancients were telling the right fable when they said that some men had been made into gods, some into lions, some into wolves, some into eagles, some into fish, some into plants, some into stones, and so on. . . . For we must know that however much man thus participates in the material and the immaterial, yet he is properly said to participate in the immaterial, because he lacks much of immateriality; but he is not properly said to participate in the brute and the vegetable, but rather to contain them, for he is below the immaterial and above the material. Wherefore he cannot arrive at the perfection of the immaterial, whence men are not to be called gods, but godlike or divine. But man cannot only make himself equal to the beast, nay [he can] exceed the beast.[31]

Thus while Pomponazzi is ready to use the same image of man as a cosmic chameleon, he considers it only as a metaphor as far as any movement upward towards divinity is concerned, but man can truly decline into a beast. And thus it is his emphasis to distinguish the human from the animal rather than to identify the human with the divine.

Benedetto Morandi comes to the question of free will in refuting Garzoni's charge that the scholar easily fell or was impelled into vice. To Morandi this was impossible if he was already a man of virtue, as he necessarily had to be if a scholar.

> But if he is not possessed of virtue, how do you want him to be impelled from a virtue which he does not have towards wickedness, as a terminus from which this movement might begin is lacking in this change from

> virtue to vice? Moreover if a man is impelled, the impulse comes from himself or from another. It is absurd to say it comes from another since each man has free will and it is even not permitted by custom, by law or by nature that choice and will in man is not free. Therefore such an impulse will come from him, himself, from one of the three qualities which are in the soul, namely, affect, potency, or habit.

It cannot be habit, since this is already one or the other, virtuous or vicious. Potency is merely an aptitude leading to habit, and the affects are made good or bad by habit. 'So it is certain that no man can be forced to embrace crimes except one who wills and wishes it after reason has been crushed.'[32] This argument is directed against the notion that Garzoni most likely derived from Valla that the will was the ultimate determinant of human behaviour, and was primarily affective, irrational, unpredictable and impulsive, so that the Aristotelian theory of the rationally built up *habitus* of virtue was simply unsound because it neglected the human psychological reality for abstract theories.

Pomponazzi in his extensive work on *Fate, Free Will and Predestination* also recognised that there was a human will, as well as a freedom of the will resting on an obvious observation of human experience. But his discussion makes clear that the inherent rationalism of the Peripatetic tradition was definitely inclined to down-grade the will, which, as we have seen, was given such a large scope in humanist thought under the influence of St. Augustine. Pomponazzi in fact properly distinguishes between 'free will' which he calls 'free choice', *liberum arbitrium*, and the will itself. It is a common opinion, to be found both in the *Nicomachean Ethics*, III, 1, and in Augustine's *De Trinitate*, VIII, 5–6, 'that free choice is perfected by two powers, namely the intellect and the will, but with the intellect as though subservient to the will and the will as though the true and principal mistress'.[33] The intellect may be viewed as ministering to the will in one of three ways, either it moves the will, or it shows what is to be done to the will as though a counsellor to a king, or both the intellect and the will partially concur in an action in which the intellect shows the will its object. But the will acts principally and the object attracts secondarily.[34] To Pomponazzi, however, the problem can be solved in a better way:

either the intellect and the will are one and the same power, or if they are diverse powers, the intellect is that in which an act of free choice properly resides, since it is in the intellect as the efficient cause, but in the will improperly and in the role of an executive, since the will merely passively agrees to that action. Liberty, moreover, consists more in action than in passion.[35]

Thus he seems to attach freedom of choice to the intellect rather than to the will.

But just how real and how much power does Pomponazzi wish to concede to the will? A crucial question was that of sin. As in the case of Morandi's reply to Garzoni, Pomponazzi considers whether a man in full possession of his reason can deliberately sin and again says 'no'. In fact he goes further, and skipping the analysis of habit, seems to take an outright Stoic position that sins of commission are due only to intellectual error. According to the Christian religion 'which I profess and for which I am ready to bear the cross and to die with Christ and for Christ', a man in full possession of his intellect can sin, and St. Augustine upheld this position vigorously against the Stoic and Platonic doctrine that knowledge was virtue. Christians hold that the intellect erring or not erring, the will

knowing and willing chooses evil. . . . Note however that where this is a sin of commission this cannot be conceded, but only in a sin of omission. For in a sin of commission evil is chosen because the will is shown by the intellect that it is good, therefore it is the intellect that sins since it shows something otherwise than it is, or it rejects the good because it is thought to be evil, since the intellect shows it to be such to the will. Therefore the error is in the intellect itself and is transferred to the will.[36]

On the other hand, Pomponazzi admits in strict logic that divine providence is compatible with free will. God is the cause of such an act in an absolute sense, since that act is known by God, but in a relative sense God is not the cause, since the act is not known in a determinate way but only conditionally and potentially.

Nor can God in every sense be the cause of a voluntary act if He wishes the act to be ours and free, since it would be unintelligible to say otherwise. Therefore in considering the nature of contingency and why something is indeterminate or determinate and that the acts are free and ours, it does not seem possible to me to speak otherwise.[37]

But despite its compatibility with divine providence, this freedom of the human will in a physical sense was very limited, since in so many things man stood within the network of natural causes through which God operated in the world, known as 'fate'. God's own freedom to operate outside of determined natural channels of cause and effect was also small.

> And I say, as I said before, that either Aristotle posited fate as the Stoics do, or he contradicts himself; because if we hold to free will, it stands that something always will be which yet is not necessary; this contradicts what he says in the first book of *De coelo*. Consequently I do not see both the possibility that virtues and vices exist by necessity and that yet they are in our power; nor do I see any incompatibility that no man sins, since God wishes the impossible when He would wish all men to be saved; just as there is no incompatibility that every man sins.[38]

If, as he is suggesting here, a consistent naturalistic conception of the universe would imply fatalism imposing operations inside established natural laws for God, and rendering man's freedom only an apparent one, then the consequences for man are seemingly far less noble and happy. He reverts to an earlier passage from his second book on *Fate* discussing the consequences for man of the fatality and inequality of the universe, so that it seems to be a game of the gods, like a game of ball among men. [Cf. Calvin's remark that God does not toss men about like tennis-balls.]

> Does it not also seem to be a game of the gods that [the universe] generates man in such great genius and equipment (for man is *organizatissimus*) and immediately after man has been made it destroys him? For does not God seem like an architect who has constructed a most beautiful palace with great labour and expense lacking in nothing and as soon as he has completed the palace ruins it? Wouldn't this be attributed to the insanity of the architect? It is no less unintelligible whether it is a game, or insanity, or folly to guide man to the highest summit and then as soon as he has attained the peak to eject him and cast him into the depths. And infinite numbers of examples could be adduced which seem to argue either insanity, or cruelty, or a game, or the like in God; yet all these [appearances] are saved since the nature of the universe requires them to be such. Therefore if the universe is good, all these things seem good.[39]

One must, it seems, recognise in Pomponazzi something of the pathos and sense of apparent irrationality that was being generated, historically, in so many of his contemporaries of the early Cinquecento. It was no longer easy to assume a bland and benign universe and deity and have an optimistic vision of man's fate. Things were much more like Pomponazzi described them. One may even compare what he is doing here with what Calvin hardly a generation later struggled to do, namely save the appearances of disorder, construct a new and more adequate theodicy. And it is striking that both these men turned to Stoicism for inspiration, and that Calvin's image of God, so different from Pomponazzi's, none the less stressed the orderliness of God's nature and His inclination to operate through natural processes.[40] Calvin's God, however, remained free to choose not to be bound, whereas Pomponazzi found it incomprehensible that God could resort to an arbitrary, volitional *potentia absoluta.* Or did he?

Pomponazzi immediately applies the same reasoning to the world of man, and produces an explanation of human inequality and injustice by stressing the same diversity of status of which man was capable that his humanist and Platonic predecessors had used to underline man's multi-potentiality. There could hardly be a more diverse use of the same *topos:*

> Then if anyone will consider human nature he will see that there must be described in human nature what is also said to be in the universe. For human nature is a kind of universe; for since it is in the middle between eternal things and the generable and corruptible ones, it ought to contain both natures. Consequently there ought to be some men who are like gods, such as we see prophets and the best men to be, indeed not in an absolute sense but in so far as their fragility and human nature allows; some are like innocent animals, some like serpents, some like tigers, some like lions, some like foxes, some like stones and so on in given individuals. Human nature requires this and no defect should be ascribed to God on account of it just as there should not be any defect in the universe itself although there seems to be very great diversity in the universe.[41]

Human inequality, which, as we have seen, is a continuous theme in Pomponazzi, is derived from nature which gives different men different physical, psychic and mental endowments, and from 'fortune' which causes some to be born in palaces and others in hovels. Like the modern deterministic psychologist and sociologist he leaves but the slightest room for man's free will. Man is in nature, not above nature as the Renaissance Christian exegesis of *Genesis* i had made him.

This was the passage to which he referred back from his fourth book after he has discussed divine providence. And he proceeds next to juxtapose the two conceptions of a fatalistic and a providential universe. Although the passage is long, it seems to be important. For he clearly rejects the optimistic Renaissance Christian vision of the creation of the world, providentially, for the sake of man and his use and enjoyment and happiness, both now and in the hereafter. It is the Renaissance Aristotelian philosopher, not the humanist or Platonist, who prefers the more pessimistic classical view.

> It was also said in the same chapter that the operation of worldly affairs seemed to be a kind of game, for if anyone examines all sublunary things he should either laugh or cry. To this it may be said that according to all other opinions except that of Christians it seems to be a game. For the world has a beginning and an end and all its operation is made on account of man, at least secondarily, so that he may enjoy beatitude; for God ordered all corporeal things for man that he might use them well and from their good use afterwards enjoy the Trinity eternally; whence nothing more beautiful or useful can be imagined.

In contrast to this comes the pagan view:

> But whatever the others say, it seems to be a game. Whence the Stoics and Peripatetics, who say God acts from necessity, have to say that the goodness of God requires that his essence be communicated as far as it can be communicated; and since it is communicable according to as many degrees and as many modes as we see in the universe, therefore it is communicated.

The world of generation and corruption is the lowest and seems to be nothing in comparison with the eternal. 'Therefore it seems worthy of little consideration and it seems to be a certain game in comparison to those supreme things.'[42]

At this point Pomponazzi adds what comfort he can, which is small comfort in comparison to the Christian and Renaissance Platonist image of man, but not so small as Pomponazzi in purely mortal terms regards it. And possibly it fits the mood of his own and the subsequent grimmer age quite well.

> But although these things are corruptible, nevertheless they include some perfection. Therefore since it is better to be than not to be, and whatever kind of existence may be God also makes it the best of possible ones, this is why God makes and conserves such things.

Then applying this reasoning to human life, he adds:

> Therefore although human life is as nothing in comparison with the eternal, nevertheless it is much in comparison with other generable things, just as

each generable thing is in comparison to not-being. Therefore since it is better to live for one year than never to live at all, life for one year is not to be spurned. . . . And so it ought not to be thought a game if there is such great variation in the universe, since the nature of the universe demands it.[42]

Where does Pomponazzi stand? If it is not a game he does not agree with Plato who said in the *Laws* that man should regard life as a game, nor with the other ancients. Neither does he agree with the poets who said 'It is best never to have been born, but next best is to die young.' Life is most definitely a value to him, and this life, and there is little doubt how he would resolve Hamlet's question, even though he does say elsewhere that the choice of virtue is to be preferred even if one consequence of it may be death. But it seems equally clear that he cannot intellectually follow the Christian vision either, though he is at pains to make this seem unclear.

Much also was said in the first book in defence of the Stoics which seems to be opposed to this opinion; for much [also] could be collected here which could be adduced against the opinion of the Christian religion. But, as I think, and also from what has been said in Book IV if the matter is well and carefully regarded, the solution to these things will appear easy and open; therefore I will personally abstain from that business.[42]

In the last chapter of the *De immortalitate animae*, Pomponazzi turns from philosophy to revelation to affirm that the soul is immortal.

But that the soul is immortal is an article of faith, as appears from the Apostles' Creed and the Athanasian Creed; hence it ought to be proved by what is proper to faith. But the means on which faith relies is revelation and canonical Scripture. Hence it is proved truly and properly only by them; but other reasons are foreign, and rely on a means that does not prove what is intended. Hence it is not surprising if philosophers disagree among themselves about the immortality of the soul, when they rely on arguments foreign to the conclusion and fallacious; but all followers of Christ agree, since they proceed by what is proper and infallible, since matters cannot be except in one way.[43]

And in his lectures on Aristotle's *De generatione et corruptione*, No. 85, he discussed the question of resurrection, which is a Christian item of faith, and not the same as the philosophical question of the immortality of the soul. Here he said,

And theologians generally hold that this union of the soul [to the body] is necessary, and thus it will be reunited to the body on account of the desire which it has to exist in the body. They say, nevertheless, that this union can be accomplished only by God, and that nature cannot do this. Nevertheless, you should know that with Aristotle that resurrection is impossible.[44]

It has been pointed out many times that Pomponazzi, in accord with the traditional practice of Renaissance natural philosophers, made a sharp distinction between philosophy and theology, between the truths to which natural reason led, and the image of the universe based on revelation. It has also been suggested that, as a good Christian, as he professed to be, he accepted the doctrine of resurrection on the basis of faith, but not that of the immortality of the soul, based on reason, or Aristotle. And he does so profess. Pomponazzi, however, also embraced the notion that side by side with philosophical truth which wise and learned men laboured to acquire, there was a more figurative truth prepared by priests or law-givers for the vulgar and ignorant. And he certainly implied very broadly that one could not accept a literal interpretation of the miracles of the Bible, although as we hope to show in another chapter this does not depart so far from traditional Christian positions and certainly not from the humanist desire to interpret the Scriptures allegorically as they did pagan poetry.[45] [However, Salutati, in advocating this, also insisted on the truth of the literal meaning.] Pomponazzi commented on Averroes' proem to his commentary on the third book of Aristotle's *Physics* where the Commentator set forth the doctrine of truth for the philosopher but fables for the masses.[46] Also in his own commentary on *De coelo* he questions the Biblical story that Joshua made the sun stand still. If the heavens stopped, so would life, which is impossible since then God would not exist.

I say that according to the philosophers it is impossible for God not to move the heavens, which theologians deny because they do not wish there to be an essential order between movement and God Himself, and they do not think that if the heavens stopped it implies a contradiction. What about it? Joshua made the sun stand still and so on. . . . At length a certain Jew said to me: you must believe that if what is said concerning Joshua making the sun stand still were true, infinite historians would have spoken of it, just as they have spoken of many other things, since there has not been much time since Joshua lived, for there are only two thousand years [?]. But only Jewish fables speak of this.[47]

And Pomponazzi, not hiding behind an anonymous Jew, also spoke of Galen believing that the immortality of the soul was an indemonstrable proposition, 'for he himself believed that the soul is mortal, and although he had no demonstration of the opposite, nevertheless he believed *quel che credeva la canaia per non esser lapidato*'[48] ['what the *canaille* believed in order not to be stoned'], lapsing into Italian. And on the other hand, in reference to the use of myths and fables for the purposes of moral instruction he repeats Averroes' explanation that Eve was said to be created by taking a rib from Adam's side in order to suggest the equality of the sexes, he added 'But the commentator is *ribaldissimus* and do not believe him.'[49] Despite this (possibly questionable) statement attributed to him, an essential ambiguity remained in Pomponazzi on the evidence of his writings – that is, it is not clear whether he had faith in a literal revelation. Though he was quite convinced about the mortality of man as an individual, he still seems to have wished to remain faithful to the Christian religion.

But he took great pride in his devotion to 'pure' truth as a philosopher, which he felt was a higher and nobler role than that of the priest, the law-giver, or the humanist, The men of the first age, speaking chronologically and not philosophically, were like iron, he said in reference to the Hesiodic myth.

> And on account of this the poetic art was invented that it might remove them from vices and lead to virtues. Afterwards came rhetoric which as a whole does not speak of things as they are but persuades. But philosophers alone are merely speaking truth. Thus poetry, rhetoric and philosophy are given for the instruction of men. Thus the Commentator in his *Poetics* says that laws are similar to poetry, since they do not say the true, for 'poets sing what is to be marvelled at not believed'. But they do this that they might lead men towards well-doing and for the instruction of men.[50]

Thus Pomponazzi finds himself on the opposite side of the argument that began with Petrarch's declaration that it is better to love the good than to know the truth, though Pomponazzi most certainly wished to love the good. But the road to the good, he felt, was only through truth, for then man did not deal in illusions, nor did he introduce sordid and commercial motives of reward and punishment into his well doing. His was a sparser, purer, perhaps more lonely conception of man and a no less fervent awe for his God for all of His not being imagined anthropomorphically and for being the centre of a vast rational machine.

Part IV. Studia Humanitatis and Studia Divinitatis: The Christian Renaissance in Italy

Introduction: Salutati's Programmatic Response to Giovanni Dominici

Thus far this book has been concerned primarily with the substance of Italian humanist thinking on the nature of man in relationship to man's divine origin and destiny. We have seen how Petrarch struggled with the problems of man's affective nature, prone to sin, harassed by vicissitudes, elated beyond measure by the smallest gratifications, divided within, unable to conform to the demands of his Maker, forced to turn at last to the ever-available divine mercy and grace. We have seen how the resources of classical moral thought, and especially of classical moral rhetoric, were utilised, evaluated, criticised, given a place within the Christian framework yet subject to the severest limitations. We have seen how Petrarch shaped for himself a coherent, though often confusing, complex, though emotionally simplified, vision of man and God; a vision but not a theology, a pious attitude, a religious mood and stance, but not a logical and systematic structure of religious thought.

We have seen how Salutati attempted to give the very theological structure that Petrarch had avoided, but one that comprehended the grasp and feeling for the deeply affective and voluntarist nature of man which Petrarch, the poet as well as the humanist, had expressed. And we stressed that despite Salutati's urge toward the restructuring in formal terms of the relationship of human destiny to divine providence there was in him a distrust of the logical and rational approaches to theology of the scholastics because they tended to look too objectively at the nature of the external world and insufficiently subjectively at man's truly emotive and will-driven soul. There was in Salutati an equal need and an equal reality of trust in God to reconcile the logical contradictions of man's devising in favour of the salvation and glorification of man. There was in him and in Petrarch a recognition that rhetoric and moral exhortation were the instruments in the hands of man whereby he might aid the process of divine providence, as well as impede or subvert it.

We have claimed in connection with this exposition, and we would claim, that the anti-dialectical and anti-metaphysical implications in their position were more than the professional assertions of leading representatives of the newly forming disciplines of the humanities. We assert and would assert that an essential historical motivation for the emergence of humanism itself is contained in this struggle to achieve a new synthesis between the traditional religious faith of medieval Europe and the new social, economic, political, geographical, sensual, secular experiences of the men of the fourteenth and fifteenth centuries, particularly the city-dwellers of north and central Italy, but also the middle and upper classes all over Europe. The emergence of the humanities, or rather their re-emergence and quickening, was, on the one hand, an irresistible movement towards the delights of contemplating, studying, describing, analysing and expressing human culture – towards literacy and conversation, towards poetry and epistolography, towards history and story, ancient and modern, towards oratory and polish in public life. On the other hand, it was an effort to devise new methods with which to deal with – not the practical material problems of life to which, outside of diplomacy and political display, humanism made and could make but a minimal contribution – but the spiritual, moral, cultural and intellectual problems. It was an effort to devise new methods in the face of the irrelevancy of the older methods to the spiritual and cultural needs of the laity. What were these older methods? As we stressed before, they were those logical and systematic and classificatory methodologies in which thirteenth-century scholastics, as professionals, revelled.

Scholars have learned, all of us, of the hazards of generalisation and oversimplification. But they have also learned that when they do have fundamental convictions, it is better to express them than to deny them in their work. I do believe that the following historical generalisations are valid, but I also know full well that others equally convinced of the very opposite can argue effectively on their own behalf. These are mine. Theology is not a science in the sense that physics is a science.

Theology may present its postulates in a systematic and logical form, but in the final analysis it rests on faith and persuasion. The great thirteenth-century scholastics all knew this. None the less, and doubtless for valid historical reasons, scholastic theology gradually was absorbed into becoming part of an organised system of studying and teaching which was more suited to promoting the ends of ecclesiastical bureaucracy or of the administration of ecclesiastical law than to inducing in mankind the motivation and behaviour that would presumably cure their souls for this life and lead them to salvation in the next.[1]

It was the very great intellectual and historical contribution of fourteenth-century nominalism to prove by the very same methods within the self-same establishment of universities and religious orders that not only the methodology but also the metaphysical content of their predecessors' thought was irrelevant for the basic goals of the Christian religion, salvation and life according to the Gospels. What can be said positively, and needs must be, is that these methods were more appropriate for the systematic understanding of the physical and material world and for its ultimate conquest with the aid of science four and five and six centuries later. These methods thrived in the medical faculties and among the natural philosophers. Without being held to state just how it happened, I do believe that, despite the baggage of ancient errors as well as their own, these procedures evolved, together with the contributions of their nominalist critics, into the modern science of the seventeenth century.[2] There is more in common between the mode of discourse of natural science today and that of thirteenth-century scholasticism than there ever was or could be between either of them and the humanities.[3]

But the subject is religion and the emergence of humanism. The early humanists Petrarch and Salutati were sincerely convinced that their studies contained the key to the moral and religious dilemmas of the men of their time. It was rhetoric and poetry and history and Christianly-conceived moral philosophy that could set mankind on the road to salvation by providing that clarification of the relationship of man and God that was obscured by both the falsely simple rationalism of scholastic theology and the esoteric, cryptic and private language in which their ideas were presented, by providing that deeper kind of inducement and persuasion that reaches the basic emotions and motivates men for faith and action.

With Valla we have also stressed the completeness and the radicalism of his anti-rationalism, of his deeply passional conception of human nature and of the heavenly and earthly ends of man. It was perhaps even more his conviction that the older methodologies were worthless since they were based on false assumptions about human and the divine nature. Even though he does not entirely abandon the categories of traditional metaphysics, still retaining the notion of substances, his great emphasis was on the qualities and actions which by far outweighed and dwarfed in significance the substances which they modified and activated. And for him rhetoric and poetry, not to mention grammar or the philological study of language, were the human instruments for manipulating and responding to the qualities and actions which derived from the human will. There was in his mind no separation of the content of human thought about man's nature and his relationship to God and the methods whereby he dealt with them. Humanist methodology and disciplines followed from conceiving man, God and the world as he conceived them, and he arrived at these convictions through these methods.

Our second part, on the humanists' treatment of the human condition, laid no stress at all on method or explanation, as our first part necessarily did, but simply presented their vision of the status of man in relation to his divine creation 'in the image of God', and his subsequent life according to that image, broken by the Fall, or restored by the Incarnation, in this world and the next. It needs no further comment here, since its difference from what we are about to examine in Part IV is patent.

Part III, in its turn, has attempted to show the impact of humanist discussions of the nature and condition of man, and of his divine origin and destiny on the thought of Ficino, Pico, Egidio da Viterbo and Pomponazzi, men who must be considered more as 'philosophers' than 'humanists', and Pomponazzi, certainly, humanist in no sense at all. Recognising Kristeller's insistent distinction between these disciplines, we have none the less stressed their continuity and interdependence. Part III links these later thinkers with the humanist writings of both Part I and Part II, and again content, rather than methodology, was at issue, assuming that Renaissance philosophers, both the new Platonists as well as the Aristotelians, were professionally committed to differing disciplines.

What we are about to examine is the more specific application of the humanist disciplines or methodologies to some of the traditional religious activities, studies and procedures which evolved in antiquity and through the Middle Ages and were alive and omnipresent in the fourteenth and fifteenth centuries. Although basic conceptions and assumptions, such as we examined in Part I, are present or implied, they are for the most part not overtly discussed, more or less being taken for granted. We shall first of all deal with the Italian humanists' Biblical scholarship and with their interpretative and literary treatment of the Scriptures. The importance and appropriateness of this as an inevitable application of humanism to religion is obvious. What is not obvious is the extent of their Biblical studies, which were, in fact, far greater than has usually been assumed,[4] and thus an inevitable outcome of humanism as such beginning in Quattrocento Italy and not something dependent on the appearance of a so-called Christian humanism in northern Europe in the sixteenth century.

Biblical studies involved the grammatical and rhetorical interests of the humanists. Although not in consecutive order, we shall also look at their conception of the relation of poetry to religion in a chapter which seeks to show how some of the leading ideas of *theologia platonica* were derived from earlier humanist conceptions of *theologia poetica.* We shall move into the field of humanist moral thought in two chapters on humanist treatises on the sacraments and on the status of the religious (the life according to vows of the religious orders). We shall refer to humanist ventures into religious history and biography, such as the most important treatise of Valla on the Donation of Constantine, but we shall not give them special treatment. Neither shall we study the most important question of humanist translations of the Greek Church Fathers because this is primarily a question of methodology and influence. The latter, certainly, is relevant to our purposes but it is beyond our power at this point to control since it involves collecting and examining citations of the Fathers in their translations. We are primarily interested, in all of this Part IV, in humanist thought and in their attitudes towards what they were doing rather than in the level of technical competence which they displayed. The significance of their work, it seems to me, does lie in the religious and scholarly attitudes motivating it and deriving from it, since in sheer technique they were both dependent on Patristic or medieval predecessors and were soon surpassed by more modern scholarship, as was the case with their secular scholarship as well. This should not obscure, however, the very great historical importance of their pioneer efforts.

The spirit of this section of the book, as well as the title, is derived from Coluccio Salutati's reply to Giovanni Dominici's *Lucula Noctis* where the Blessed Dominican Father presented his condemnation of the study of pagan philosophy or literature by Christians, in the form of a direct attack on Salutati. We cited above Salutati's personal affirmation of his faith and piety.[5] His answer to the charges, first that he placed the will above the intellect and second that he promoted the study of pagan letters, was to postpone his answer to the first (and death intervened), but to defend the liberal arts as essential to religion. This treatise (for so it was, though it is printed by Novati in his *Epistolario*) was far more than a defense, however, but rather a programmatic conception of the tasks of humanism with regard to religion. Speaking of grammar, he asks 'How can anyone who is ignorant of letters [*illiterate*] gain any knowledge of the Holy Scriptures?' But grammar alone does not suffice. It is important to him to conceive of a good Christian as an educated, even a learned man, although certainly simple faith is possible.

> I confess sincerity of faith can be achieved without literacy, but neither the Scriptures nor the expositions and teachings of the doctors can be known, which men of letters are scarcely able to understand, and not only those simply educated in grammar but also those who sweat in dialectics and rhetoric. And even grammar itself for the most part cannot be known without knowledge of content and the ways in which essences vary and the assistance of all the sciences, besides the necessary knowledge of terms.

He then avers, almost as a slogan, 'The *studia humanitatis* and the *studia divinitatis* are so interconnected that true and complete knowledge of the one cannot be had without the other', and adds –

> But whatever ease or difficulty there is in learning grammar, what will the situation be if you consider the doctrines of faith? A Christian is scarcely

able to know what should be believed; and if anyone in his simplicity is opposed with the authority of the Holy Scriptures or even feeble reason, he will not know what he ought to reply and he will begin to vacillate over the truth of faith. O how many and how great are the things we daily see which cannot be explained by illiterate and uncultured holy rusticity![6]

It is interesting that Salutati, although he uses the term *studia humanitatis*, projects here the relationship between the traditional division of the *trivium* and *quadrivium*, the seven liberal arts. He feels called upon, although there may be irony in directing this to a Dominican who did not at all repudiate the learning of his own doctors, to explain the importance of dialectic to sacred studies.

Who can deny, since dialectic is the investigation of truth, which is the only end of all the liberal arts as well as the sciences, that this is necessary for Christians to learn. . . . Therefore it is essential for neophytes to learn along with faith, the reason by which they are able to defend it.[7]

It is interesting and also evident here that, regarding the will as more important than the intellect, and religion based on faith as more profound than a rationally conceived one, he defends dialectic essentially negatively, as a supplement to faith, in case of doubts raised by the attacks of reason, not as the road itself to the knowledge of religious truth. In fact he reaffirms his commitment to the *potentia absoluta* of God, which goes beyond reason.

But if nature does not reveal some truths, natural ones namely, but hides them in profundity, what must be thought of that infinite power which is such by nature that it meritedly ought to be called supernatural, especially since the first kind of truths are finite, but these it is necessary to confess are infinite.[8]

He has more confidence in the value of rhetoric. 'But now enough has been said about logic which captures and forces the intellect by its reasons, and we come to rhetoric which argues with the will.'[9] He begins by quoting the entire third paragraph [cap. II] of the fourth book of Augustine's *De doctrina Christiana* which ends,

While the faculty of eloquence, which is of great value in urging either evil or justice, is in itself indifferent, why should it not be learned for the uses of the good in the service of truth if the evil usurp it for the winning of perverse and vain causes in defence of iniquity and error.[10]

And after this ambivalent tribute to rhetoric as a weapon that could be used on both sides [an important admission for a humanist to have made], Salutati strengthens his argument by using Augustine as an example of a Christian rhetor, not fearing the pagan weapon inherited from Cicero. Citing Augustine's praise of Cicero's *Hortensius* in his *Confessions*, III, iv, he offers this as evidence of the great fruit God can draw from the sweepings and filth of the pagans; thus Augustine 'remembered what they were, through the grace of God, for his own salvation, and knew they were not only an instrument but a collection of many truths which nourish the investigation of truth. . . .[11]

Dealing with the *quadrivium*, Salutati offers a curiously conservative justification of the knowledge of mathematics for the purpose of understanding the mystical meanings of numbers in the Scriptures. This, of course, is closer to the traditional allegorical exegesis of Holy Writ, and Salutati comes to this, as the last part of his reply.[12] Poetry occupies a special position above and outside of the liberal arts. He had not yet integrated it with the new division of the *studia humanitatis*. Since we shall deal more fully with these ideas in the chapter on *theologia poetica*, we shall not discuss this section here. But the Scriptures he regarded as 'nothing other than poetry, although, most learned man, you seem to be horrified at that name. For what are the Holy Scriptures either in terms or even in subject but figures of speech?'[13]

For Salutati there was no problem about a Christian using classical pagan writers, because one could not be both a good Christian and an ignorant one – at least not for very long, since ignorance would expose one to error and leave one helpless in the complexities of exegesis and tradition. Christianity was a 'religion of the book', and Salutati recognised that this made it also a learned one. But Christian learning was inherited from the pagans and to reject all pagan writing would be to reject all learning. Therefore the position of Giovanni Dominici amounted to a rejection of the most ancient Christian traditions and the putting forth of a modern obscurantism. The liberal arts were necessarily to be put in the service of Christianity, although they could also serve its enemies. They were then necessary as a weapon of defence.

XII. Italian Humanism and the Scriptures

1. Petrarch, Salutati and the Figural Tradition

This chapter is a study not so much of the Biblical scholarship of the humanists as of their attitudes towards the Bible and of their approaches to its study. Since I cannot qualify as a Biblical scholar, and my knowledge of Greek is rudimentary, of Hebrew non-existent, it will be my purpose, therefore, while attempting to avoid the problems for which the competence of a modern Biblical scholar is desirable, to contribute where I can do so to the understanding of the importance of Italian humanism for the historical emergence of modern Biblical studies.[1]

Attitudes towards the Bible are of the greatest importance in this connection, because they are the key to exegesis and hermeneutics. Moreover, they are involved in the most central items of Christian faith. The Bible is held to be the Word of God. It is the instrument through which God communicated His wishes directly to mankind and educated them with His revelation of divine truth. Therefore a Christian scholar cannot turn to the study of the Bible without in some way resolving the question of the relationship of divine and human authorship – whether this scholar is a humanistic philologian or anyone else.

Moreover, the Divine Word was held to be the Incarnate Son, the second person of the Trinity, the Wisdom of God. This doctrine endowed the Scriptures with more than the oracular quality of being documents of divine revelation; it gave them the status of divinity itself. How far and how legitimate, then, was it for mere man to subject the Divine Word to human investigation? Could he engage in such study at all if he was not considered to be a chosen instrument for further revelation? Was it possible in any sense to regard the Scriptures from the standpoint of a literary critic, or of a historian, or to analyse them from a grammatical and linguistic point of view?

Furthermore, the relationship of Christian doctrine revealed in the Scriptures to subsequent doctrine elaborated within the history and tradition of the Church was a poignant one. Did revelation cease beyond the bounds of the sacred canon? If not, were the Scriptures but the first of a lengthening series of divine oracles codified in the decrees of the Councils, the writings of the Fathers, the declarations of the Popes? Or, on the other hand, was the more moderate view the correct one, that Christian truth and doctrine revealed or issued subsequent to the Scriptures was in perfect harmony with everything revealed therein and had to be regarded as mere elucidation and clarification, as a bringing of the latent truths of the divine text out into relevant application?[2]

Since this last was the more prevalent view of the relationship of tradition and Scripture in the fourteenth and fifteenth centuries – as in a less explicit way it had been for many earlier centuries – there was a necessarily two-fold result. For all pronouncements of Christian truth, for all theological declarations and argumentation there had to be a constant buttressing by Biblical citation in order to prove the conformity of the statement with orthodoxy. This was, of course, one of the reasons why Christianity necessarily had to have a learned clergy. The other result, conversely, was the squaring of the meaning of the Scriptures with what was currently held to be the eternal verity. Since verity encountered variety at least in its external form, it was necessary to engage in constant interpretation and exegesis of Holy Writ to prove the correspondence of its truth to less sanctified statements thereof in subsequent hands. This led, of course, to the development of the allegorical and of the four-fold modes of exegesis of the Middle Ages and to its continuation in the Renaissance.[3]

The humanists' attitudes towards, and treatment of the Scriptures fall into two types, and to some extent into two temporal phases, although there was much overlapping in both respects. Moreover, both types derived in a certain way from their commitment to the *studia humanitatis*, to, in other words, grammar, rhetoric, poetry and history (not to mention moral philosophy). The Bible was plainly a written text, but it was also indubitably Holy. The first impulse of the humanists was to assimilate it to their own study of secular, and pagan-classical and patristic texts by combining the old tradition that the Bible was poetry' and that its meanings were concealed in metaphors and figures of speech – what Curtius has called 'Biblical Poetics'[4] – with the conception of 'true' poetry outside of the Bible, whether Christian or pagan, regarding both as divinely inspired. This was primarily the attitude of Petrarch, Boccaccio and Salutati towards poetry, and we shall deal with it in our chapter on *Theologia Poetica.*[5] But when it came to the direct treatment of the Biblical text, itself, this approach to it meant, on the one hand, the traditional drawing forth of relevant Biblical passages as evidence in support of a position being argued. Salutati's *De seculo et religione* is an excellent example of this authoritarian use of the Scriptures.[6] Incidentally, this was also in largest part the kind of usage that the humanists made of classical, non-Christian literary texts – utilising appropriate and apposite quotations to prove or clarify their points, or to add the authority of Cicero, Seneca, Vergil, Livy to their own point of view. By far the greatest usage of Biblical and classical literature was for this purpose. And it was essentially rhetorical in nature. On the other hand, the conception of the Bible as poetry, apart from the value of this notion as a defence of all poetry, pagan as well as Christian, led the humanists to look directly at the literary and poetic merits of the Scriptures.

It is this consequence of the traditional view of the Bible as poetry as it occurred in humanist hands that represents something new. Since the allegorical view of poetry in general has itself certain ambiguities and regards poetry both as the embodiment of concealed truth and as also (and particularly among humanists) a highly charged literary statement capable of moving and inspiring the reader, it could be approached analytically and argumentatively for doctrinal purposes as indicated above, or appreciatively for the pleasure of its beauty and for its inspiration towards goodness and towards faith, hope and charity.

Representative of this view is the passage that Petrarch piously devoted to the Scriptures at the end of his *De otio religioso.* After counselling the monks, in whatever time was left them from their devotions and the necessities of nature, to study the Scriptures, he quoted St. Jerome's letter to Paulinus.

> And so as he to him, so I say to you, brothers, 'pray that you live with these, meditate upon them, know of nothing else, and seek nothing else'; nor should the 'simplicity' of the Holy Scriptures disturb you and the 'vileness

as it were of the words which, as the same one said, 'are so gotten out either by the badness of the translators or on purpose that they more easily instruct a rustic assembly, and what a learned man hears, an illiterate in the same sentence hears differently'.

This semi-apology reveals that it seemed normal to Petrarch to regard the Scriptures as a poor product from a literary point of view, surely a difficult point to sustain in view of their sanctity. Hence he quickly adds, 'But whatever they seem to be superficially, nothing is sweeter than the marrow, nothing smoother, and nothing more healthful.' And then he adds a personal tribute to the Scriptures and a confession of his belated discovery of their delights.

Therefore this is undoubtedly the Queen of all literature, although the envious are consumed and the arrogant are puffed up and sick hearts do not understand the truth. . . . And certainly what I now assert, not many years ago, and perhaps silently, I would have denied. Thanks be to Him who opened my eyes that I might see something that in the face of great danger I did not see, and who will now, I hope, purge my clouded eyes that I may see the rest which with damnable lateness I did not see. What has been the case with me up to now I wonder at the less when I hear Jerome confessing about himself that, absorbed in the books of the pagans, when he turned first to sacred eloquence he 'was horrified by its uncultured language'. If this could happen to such a man who was most practiced in the holy books from adolescence, what couldn't happen to me, a sinner, I do not say learned in secular letters, I would not lie, but delighted in them from infancy, who did not have teachers such as Gregory of Nazianzen as he did, or someone at least who if not of high genius was of faithful and devoted soul, but those rather who laughed at the Psalter of David, which is the most pregnant writing of all, and at every text of the divine pages as old wives' tales.[7]

Then, telling again of his own return to sacred studies through the influence of St. Augustine's *Confessions* and thence to Ambrose, Jerome, Gregory, Chrysostom and Lactantius he comments,

Thus through this beautiful company I reverently entered the confines of the Holy Scriptures which previously I had despised and found everything otherwise than I had believed. There came the opportune necessity of celebrating the daily office of divine praises, which I had poorly done, and because of this I was often compelled to run through the Psalter itself of David; from these sources I longed to drink not that I might become wiser from them, but, if I was able, better, and not that I might depart a more able disputant but a lesser sinner.[8]

Then counselling the monks to cultivate the Scriptures which they had before them from the beginning, whereas he came to them late as a stranger, he comments on their sanctity, and antiquity, and beauty, beyond that of all other literature.

> If it is asked concerning their authority, they have been published by the Holy Spirit and confirmed by the mouth of Christ; if concerning their antiquity, they went forth before all secular literature – before Cadmus the founder of the Greeks, before Isis of the Egyptians, before Carmentis the inventress of the Latins was born, these celebrated writings were abroad in the world; or if virtue is expected – and 'they are sharp arrows' and ardent ones which bring those to life in whose hearts they were affixed; if profit is sought, the reward of other things is either a brief gain, a transitory joy, or a false favour, the end of these is eternal life and true happiness; or if perchance beauty is demanded, though much can be said on this score, yet the sum of it all is that certain other writings are superficially comelier, none is more beautiful.[9]

Petrarch's treatise on the *Retirement of the Religious*, from which these passages are taken, is itself a commentary on Psalm 45. But his treatment is not philological or analytical, but, as said above, eulogistic and inspirational. There is here, however, a new recognition of the Scriptures as literature and, if far superior to other literature in every respect, as he just said, still subject to comparison. Moreover, if the most ancient, still this gave the Bible a place in the history of letters. This is as far as Petrarch's humanism took him in viewing the Scriptures.

His letter to Francesco Nelli, Prior of Santi Apostoli, is a similar declaration of the personal value to him of the Scriptures. Again he states his turn to sacred studies in terms of a comparison which brings the Bible (and the Church Fathers) into the context of letters. But at the same time, he here makes a distinction between secular writing, to which he is devoted for its aesthetic qualities, and sacred writings, from which he profits.

> I confess I have loved Cicero and Vergil so much that I have been delighted with their style and talent beyond all others. . . . I have similarly loved Plato and Homer from the Greeks, whose genius when compared to ours often made me dubious of my judgement. But now I am stirred by a greater matter, and the concern for salvation is greater than that for eloquence. I have read what delighted, I read what profits.[10]

Thus he echoes Horace's dictum that poets profit and delight, but only to separate the classics from sacred text according to these functions.

> And now my orators were Ambrose, Augustine, Jerome and Gregory; my philosopher Paul, my poet David. . . . Nor because I prefer these do I reject the others, as it seems to me Jerome said he did, approving, rather than following, their style. I seem able to love both at the same time, only I am not unaware that I prefer the first as a model in words, the other in content. For what, I ask, prevents one from becoming rich in both silver and gold when you so know the value of each that you are not able to be deceived in either one, especially since those ancients require nothing more from me than that they do not fall into oblivion and content with their preliminary study cede all time now to their betters. For style, if the occasion demands I use Vergil and Cicero, and do not blush to borrow from Greece if Latium seems to lack anything. But for life, although I knew many useful things among the ancients, nevertheless I use those counsellors and leaders of salvation of whose faith and doctrine there is no suspicion of error. Among these David always was deservedly the greatest to me, more beautiful, (in that in which he is less polished), more learned and discreet (in that in which he is purer). I wish to have his Psalter always in my hands and before my eyes while awake, and when asleep or dying, lying under my head.[11]

Clearly he still feels that the pagans are the better writers.

Turning to Salutati – as we have seen, he regarded the Bible as poetry in the sense that it concealed a deeper and more eternal meaning within its metaphors and figures of speech that had to be elicited by allegorical interpretation. Unless this was acceptable one would have to criticise the efforts of various earlier Christian writers to paraphrase the Scriptures in verse – certain of whom Dominici had praised. He had just finished affirming that poetry, which by its images aroused the reader to desire or horror, was not contrary to Christianity. Whereupon he proceeds:

> Juvencus and Sedulius would have done badly and less Christianly; they, we know, set the evangelical histories in the elegance of divine verse; Arator would have acted stupidly when he set forth the deeds of the most holy apostles with the lights of allegorical exposition and grandly in verse. Also Peter of Riga would have laboured damnably when he renewed the body of the Old and New Testaments in indifferent verses, even allegorising much of it. Alain [of Lille] and John, who is also called Architrenius, would

have sinned most seriously because they edited their books in poetic figures and verses. Also many others whom it would be tedious to mention would have sinned, who followed the poets in invention and song, men such as Prudentius and Prosper and Father Ambrose who wrote many hymns in various kinds of metres.[12]

Salutati therefore reveals the complete acceptability of considering and treating the Scriptures as literature by citing these examples of versification or allegorisation of the Bible by medieval or late classical authors of undoubted orthodoxy. Yet as we shall immediately see his own treatment of Scripture was exceedingly traditional.

Although he argues in this unfinished treatise [in reply to Giovanni Dominici] that poetry should be acceptable to Christians because the Bible is poetic, his demonstration that this was so also took on the usual medieval approach to the Scriptures in general. It will not be out of place to indicate this in a little detail in order to emphasise how sharply later humanists departed from it – some of them, that is.

Are not the Holy Scriptures the word and speech of God? And what is there in the entire body of the sacred volume of the Old Testament (which according to the number of Hebrew letters is divided into twenty-four books) or even of the New, which the first contains in foreshadowed language (and which is dispersed in four Gospels, the canonic Epistles, the *Acts of the Apostles* and the *Apocalypse* remote from understanding), which, is not to be read allegorically, and which does not also contain beneath the skin something other than it shows, and which cannot rightly be called and should be called bilingual? What seems to be less allegorical than the beginning of *Genesis* and the work of the six days? But did not Adamantius Origen, of whom it is written that what he said well no one said better, and what badly no one worse, leading all back to mystical understanding, expound it in miraculous allegorical senses and piously and laudably adapt it to our customs and the capacities of our minds? Regard the Judaic histories, look at *Kings* and the rest which follows, are they not all reduced to allegorical comprehension? Pray suggest any passage of the Old Testament which the most sacred doctors do not expound in the hidden mystery of its meaning. What is more poetic and with a song more amatory and lascivious than *The Song of Songs*? What more mysterious and more poetic than the book and story of *Job*, whose secrets the most holy prelate Gregory, better than all the many others who had done so, treated in multifold senses? It is written concerning the secrets of the most recent prophecy that it contains as many sacraments as words. This book is of such great profundity that it drives many almost to madness lifting them beyond themselves in ecstasy. Finally is not the entire Old Testament believed to be the figure and idea of the New?[13]

Salutati's ideas are in complete harmony with the long patristic and medieval traditions of 'figural' interpretation. One need not question whether his desire to prove the value of 'poetry' to religious studies lent him greater zeal in this argument, for it is fully consistent with his own practice and declarations in *De seculo et religione.* Rather, as we shall see, his devotion to poetry reinforces his conception of the Scriptures as a tissue of concealed mystical meanings, of what were called *sacramenta,* in each word.

He offers examples of this type of interpretation, beginning with Psalm 21.

> Thus it happens that whatever in divine Scripture departs from its proper and natural meaning, and whatever predicts 'figurally' concerning another is wholly poetic and such that it entirely represents what it intends obliquely, not directly. Wherefore, when the Psalmist sings of Christ, 'But I am a worm and no man', he calls Christ a worm for this reason, just as a worm is not born by seminal generation, so Christ was conceived by no man's semen. That he also said, 'and no man', he either said because of divinity, for He alone was no man, or because He was so generated as a man that in His beginning He was wholly subject to no sin, which does not happen at all to any man, whereas a boy is not without sin for even a single day, as though he said 'and not a man' since all men are sinners, but I indeed not. There are two worms, namely not born from sexual conception: first Adam, of whom it is written 'And therefore God formed man from the mud of the earth and breathed into his face the breath of life and man was made into a living soul.' We wish not only to explain why, in this naming of man, Eva is also included, concerning whom Moses now said, 'God created man in his own image, in the image of God created He him, male and female created He them', since Adam is also interpreted as earthly man or red earth. For it is said that among the Hebrews this name Adam meant the same as this word man among us in which both man and woman are signified. Moreover the other worm was our Lord, Jesus Christ, who was not born from the flow of seed but who, as Holy Church dogmatises, we firmly believe, piously and orthodoxly confess, is the only born Son of God, born of the Father before all ages, God from God, light from light, true God from true God, generated not made, consubstantial with the Father, through whom all is done, who on account of us men and our salvation descended from heaven and was incarnated of the Holy Spirit from the Virgin Mary, and was made man, and the rest which follows. Neither have I said this that I might explain His origin, who hides his carnal nativity and

surpasses all knowledge no less than his divine generation, so that the Prophet well said, 'who shall declare his generation?'[14]

With this example of his mode of Biblical exegesis we may pass over the others he offers, in dependence on Peter Damiani,[15] namely how Christ is a lion, a pelican and an owl. As he repeats, 'all is mystical, all is reduced to allegorical understanding. Nothing is in them which is not bilingual, which does not bear one meaning on the surface and another within and which cannot be expounded and summarised according to various senses of the Holy Spirit.'[16]

2. Valla and Manetti, and the Greek New Testament

If, as frequently happened, Petrarch in his highly personal approach was nevertheless more prophetic of later developments in humanism than Salutati, the latter, despite his fervent reaffirmations of tradition, led in more practical ways towards the development of the typical skills of humanistic scholarship and pointed towards some of the attitudes that might be in keeping with them. And out of the momentum generated by Salutati came the practical step of the appointment of Chrysoloras, and the ensuing group of younger humanists who engaged themselves busily in translation from the Greek. Of these men, two in the Florentine ambience were outstanding, Leonardo Bruni and Ambrogio Traversari. As we have indicated, we shall not make a study here of the translations of the Greek fathers, in which Traversari played such an important role. Perhaps equally important was the Camaldulensian Prior's venture into secular translation with the first Latin version of Diogenes Laertius' *Lives of the Philosophers.* So also Bruni, with his most important translations of Aristotle's *Nicomachean Ethics*, *Politics*, and the *Economics*, several dialogues of Plato, Demosthenes, assorted Greek historians, and others, included one work of a Church Father, Basil's letter defending the study of secular letters. But as far as Biblical studies were concerned, it was perhaps Traversari who, through his influence at least on his pupil, Giannozzo Manetti, had the greater importance. Moreover Bruni, despite his assertive defence of his own kind of translation of Aristotle in *De recta interpretatione* was also traditional in his attitude towards the Scriptural text. If, as historians of humanism and the Reformation have assumed, the application of humanistic norms of scholarship and translation to the Bible was to have a revolutionary consequence in the relationship of Holy Writ to Holy Church, neither this application nor this consequence occurred with Bruni.

We shall presently examine Bruni's actual attitudes towards the study of Scripture and particularly of Hebrew in connection with our study of Manetti. More immediately relevant is Bruni's most famous pupil, Lorenzo Valla, who, to be sure, seems to have repudiated the alleged viewpoint of his master in his first surviving work, the *De voluptate*, as we have seen above. Without any doubt Valla acquired special fame among the northern humanists and the Reformers of the sixteenth century for his *Adnotationes in Novum Testamentum*,[17] found by Erasmus, and published by him in 1505 with a laudatory preface. Valla wrote this work, apparently, around 1449 or 1450, after he had left Naples for the Rome of Nicholas V. It is difficult to determine very much about Valla's motivations for undertaking this study of the Vulgate version of the New Testament in the light of the Greek text from any general statements in his work itself. But certainly some of his ideas concerning the nature of the Scriptures do emerge in it. Valla, it must be recalled, strongly emphasised in all his methodological writings, such as the *Elegantiae* and the *Dialecticae*, that the evidence for the nature of thought is to be found in the language or the words in which it is expressed. When it came to the Bible, he regarded this as the available evidence to mankind of the purposes and actions of God. The Word of God, expressed through men by the Holy Spirit, thus had a similar status to the word of man in secular texts. In both cases he rejected involved abstract speculation that removed the question from the context of life, will and action. Gianni Zippel has called attention to a passage in Valla's *Repastinatio dialecticae et philosophiae*, which we also have cited in our chapter on Valla above, that makes his position clear. In the midst of his discussion of the nature of the Trinity, where he has argued that the three natures of the three Persons were three 'qualities' of the one 'substance' or 'consubstance' of God, he cites Quintilian to the effect that 'nature' and 'quality' are words conveying the same meaning. Then he adds,

> For every question of this sort in which philosophers and theologians torture themselves in their disputing is concerned with a name [*de vocabulo est*]. But it seems otiose to me when the thing is known to grow old while inquiring

into and misrepresenting names which especially rest on the solid authority of no one. This perhaps is not to inquire after the word [*de voce*] which is action in God.[18]

Thus Valla at least had a point of view ten years previously in which the Word of God, substantiated by the written text, carried far greater weight than philosophical and theological disputations, since it was divine enactment. We shall deal with his work on the New Testament but briefly, adducing a few examples of his procedure that reveal something of the range of his interests. These seem to have been three: *grammatical* in the strict sense of the accuracy of translation of words and syntax from one language to the other, *stylistic* in the realisation in Latin of the rhetorical or poetic power of the Greek, and *substantive* or *philosophical* in the true rendering of doctrines expressed in the original language into the other.[19]

Perhaps six or eight years after Valla wrote this work, somewhere between 1455 and 1458, Giannozzo Manetti made a new translation of the New Testament from a Greek text.[20] In this work, of course, he does not reveal the basis of the changes he introduces but merely presents them as a finished product. We shall compare Manetti's rendering with the specific passages of Valla's *Adnotationes* we have selected for illustration. All of them are drawn from Paul's *Epistles* to the *Romans* and to the *Corinthians* [both I and II].

We shall begin with two examples of a strictly grammatical nature:

(1) On *Romans*, i:20: Invisibilia enim ipsius a creatura mundi per ea quae facta sunt, intellecta conspiciuntur. 'The Greek word which is translated here as *creatura*, κτίσεως, can be translated *creatione*. . . . Nor are there five Greek words *per ea quae facta sunt*, but one, *operibus* or *factis* τοῖς ποιήμασιν. Also I would have said *cernuntur* rather than *conspiciuntur*.'[21] Manetti seems to agree with Valla on the two first accounts but not on the third. The first, *creatura* rather than *creatione* is merely awkward; the second involves circumlocution but only slight change of meaning, and the third seems to be entirely a matter of taste. Manetti reads: Invisibilia enim *eius* a *creatione* mundi *ex operibus factis* intellecta conspiciuntur. Italics indicate his changes.[22]

(2) On II *Corinthians*, iii:6: Qui et idoneos nos fecit ministros novi testamenti, non littera, sed spiritu. 'What does he intend by Fecit nos ministros non littera, that is, *per litteram*? For who is made minister

through the letter? Certainly no one. Therefore it should be said, Qui fecit nos ministros non *litterae*, that which is the Old Testament, sed *spiritus*, which is the New Testament, whereas the letter of the Old Testament kills, but the spirit of that one which is the New Testament gives life.'[23] Manetti comes to the same conclusion: 'Sed sufficientia nostra ex Deo est [verse 5 b] qui et *sufficientes* nos fecit ministros novi testamenti non *litterae* sed *spiritus*. . . .' Manetti also changes *idoneos* to *sufficientes*.[24] Both men seek only grammatical clarification.

We now offer one example of Valla's stylistic criticism of the Vulgate.

(3) On II *Corinthians*, vi:8–10: . . . Ut seductores, et veraces; sicut qui ignoti, et cogniti; quasi morientes, et ecce vivimus; ut castigati, et non mortificati; quasi tristes, semper autem gaudentes; sicut egentes, multum autem locupletantes; tanquam nihil habentes, et omnia possidentes. 'Learned men say that there is more majesty in the simplicity of Homer than grace in the festivity of Vergil, where the one lists the Greek princes and peoples, the other the Italian. Thus in this place the festivity of this translator varying the diction so that now he says *quasi*, now *tanquam*, now *sicut*, now *ut*, does not seem to me to have as much beauty as that very Greek simplicity, that is, the sublime and urgent Pauline language repeating the same word in the beginning of the sentence in this way: Ut seductores, et veraces; ut ignoti, et cogniti; ut morientes, et vivimus; ut castigati, et non mortificati; ut tristes, sed semper gaudentes; ut egentes, multas tamen locupletantes; ut nihil habentes et omnia possidentes.'[25]

Manetti, however, does not vary from the standard Latin translation.[26] Here it is, of course, a matter of taste. But Valla, in addition to seeing how the stylistic power of one language may be different from that of another and yet can be captured, also certainly sees the written text of the Scriptures as subject to human variation by the author through which the Holy Spirit speaks, and by the translator as well. This comment is also notable, in contrast to Petrarch's rather grudging acceptance of beauty in the Biblical text, which offered salvation more than style to him.

But what was essentially radical in Valla's textual criticism was his grasp of the theological implications, or of the support that could be offered or removed from particular doctrines by 'correct' or 'incorrect' philology. Our first example is not of any great significance in challenging existing doctrine; Valla simply indicates how, if taken seriously, it makes no sense theologically, whereas the Greek does.

(4) On I *Corinthians* ii:13 [cited by Zippel, but incorrectly as II *Cor.* 13]: Non in doctis humanae sapientiae verbis, sed in doctrina spiritus, spiritualia comparantes. 'Why do the translators vary the Greek word? for it reads thus in Greek: Non in doctis humanae sapientes verbis sive sermonibus, sed in doctis spiritus sancti, as if words are in human wisdom, doctrine moreover in the Holy Spirit, which is not so.'[27]

Manetti found the same error and corrected it to 'Non in *docibilibus* humanae sapientie sed in *docibilibus* spiritus sancti verbis, spiritualibus spiritualia comparantes'; a still more radical correction.[28]

The next example has most definite theological content, for in it Valla attacks the notion of cooperative or creative grace, and asserts that there is a Biblical basis in St. Paul only for attributing acts of grace totally to God – a position that became critical in the Reformation.

(5) On I *Corinthians*, xv:10: Non autem ego, sed gratia Dei mecum. 'How not I if the grace of God with me? Therefore it should be said the grace of God which is with me [Gratia Dei quae est mecum] ἀλλ' ἡ χάρις τοῦ θεοῦ ἡ σὺν ἐμοί. so that they say nothing who call this cooperating grace of God [qui hanc vocant gratiam Dei cooperantem], for Paul did not attribute this to himself but referred all received to God.'[29] Manetti, however, makes no change in this passage.[30]

The next passage selected also reveals Valla as insisting on eternal predestination, so that a single act of the will should not be called a 'destined will'.

(6) On II *Corinthians*, viii: 19: In hac gratia quae ministratura vobis [*sic*] ad gloriam Domini, et destinatam voluntatem vestram [*sic*]. [Vulgate today reads *nobis* and *nostram*] 'Indeed [it should be] for your readiness or alacrity [ad promptitudinem, seu alacritatem vestram] in rendering προθυμίαν for the will is ready, προθυνία. They expound this place ridiculously "destinate will, predestined from God" [Destinatam voluntatem praedestinatam a Deo], Who has predestinated you from eternity to have such a will.'[31] Manetti makes the same correction, translating 'in hac gratia quae ministratur a nobis ad domini gloriam et *promptitudinem* vestram'.[32]

Our final example is one that has been cited by Gianni Zippel,[33] who also points out that Luther cited it as justification for his rejection of any Scriptural basis for the Catholic sacrament of penance.

(7) On II *Corinthians* vii:10: Quae enim secundum Deum tristitia est, poenitentiam in salutem stabilem operatur. '*Stabilem* does not refer to *salutem* but to *poenitentiam* because in Greek it is said *Impoenitibilem* ἀμεταμέλητον, although the two Greek words μετάνοια and μεταμέλησια differ from ours. For *poenitentia* is derived from *poenitet*, which is "it is boring", or "it disgusts", as in Vergil:

Nec te poenitet calamo trivisse labellum.

Aulus Gellius disputes about this word on the side of Cicero against Asinius Pollio. The Greek words mean "withdrawing from sense" and changing cares into something better; a more elegant mode of diction than ours, as Lactantius said. And so in our language the meaning is "sadness experienced", in Greek, "correction of mind". Therefore those who dispute over this passage say nothing if sadness is the same as penitence; they say penitence is three-fold: one part which is contrition, a second which is confession, a third which is satisfaction. This sentence, since it is false, does nothing in explaining the meaning of Paul.'[34] Manetti made no change in his translation.[35] For all his elaborate linguistic argument Valla did not change the translation substantially. What he did do was indicate that there was no basis in the text for reading into it the fully formed and complex notion of the Latin sacrament of penance. This was a commentary on the exegesis of the text more than on the text itself.[36]

Lorenzo Valla was not only a gifted stylist, a grammatical theoretician, as well as a sharp historical critic, but a man who had grappled with some of the fundamentals of Christian theology and ethics in an effort to produce an original synthesis more adequate to his experience of human existence. I think it is evident that a textual commentary on the New Testament by such a humanist would have shown a constant awareness of the doctrinal implications of the Scriptural text and of the alleged misuse of it for questionable theological disputation – questionable to Valla and others of a similar mind, that is. Such a study of the Scriptures would not have been merely philological and grammatical and stylistic, although the historical importance of this, too, should not be minimised, and it is true that the bulk of the *Adnotationes* is of this character. To Valla must go the credit, if it is regarded as credit, of having been the first to realise what a potent instrument for religious controversy and for reformation the textual study of the Bible could be. And this surely must have reinforced the conviction that the fundamentals of Christianity were to be discovered in this manner rather than in the theological disputation and the citation of ecclesiastical authority that had become the prevailing method. It accounts for the enthusiasm of Erasmus and, for more controversial reasons, of Luther, as well as for the suspiciousness of Bellarmine towards this and other ventures of Valla into the field of religious controversy. However, we must recall our own words in our chapter on Valla's views of the nature of man and God, that Valla's radical individualism and almost libidinal conception of spiritual substances, divine, angelic and human, must ultimately put him beyond the bounds of even a reformed Christianity that clung to the bureaucratic reality of an *ecclesia*. His ideas were grist to the mills of radical spiritual reformers within Catholicism and of passing use to the later northern Reformation, Lutheran and Calvinist, but in the final analysis unviable.

Giannozzo Manetti was a different kind of man. We shall not, as we can not, make the kind of careful comparison of his rendering of the Greek text of the New Testament with the linguistic choices and gambits of his predecessors and successors. The little we have shown in relation to Valla's criticisms reveals him to have been independent in his judgements. I am unable to prove that he was influenced by Valla, though, of course, he may have been. Although Manetti was in Rome as Apostolic Secretary from 1453–55, contemporaneously with Valla, we do not know, even, whether he was aware of the existence of Valla's work, much less had seen or used it. But at the same time it is of interest that he comes to some of the same alterations of the Vulgate text that Valla came to, whether more or less literally, *ad verbum*, only the careful comparison with the Greek texts that a Biblical scholar can control can lead to such judgements. Unfortunately, Father Garofalo's promised edition of twenty years ago – of Valla's *Adnotationes* as well as of Manetti's Biblical translations – has not materialised.[37] Historically Manetti had far less influence than Valla on New

Testament studies, if it can even be established that he had any. Erasmus apparently did not know that he had him for a predecessor in translating the New Testament. Yet the fact that Manetti anticipated Erasmus in this is the clearest kind of proof that the tendencies let loose by the development of Italian humanism were bound to lead to translations of even Holy Writ, and even if St. Jerome and his translations enjoyed exceptional prestige among the humanists as the Church Father who was in many respects most like them in his own activities.

3. The Beginnings of Hebraic Studies: Bruni versus Manetti

But Manetti's truly great importance was in the field of his Hebrew studies and Old Testament scholarship, where he was without any question a pioneer in the history of European culture. It is at this place that Leonardo Bruni's views of this question may properly be cited, for they reveal just how amazingly far Manetti was able to go in a new and courageous attitude in contrast with the prejudices that even so enlightened a humanist as Leonardo Bruni was not ashamed to affirm. His views are in a letter to Giovanni Cirignani of uncertain date, summarised by Mehus as 'He shows that Hebrew letters are useless, Greek, indeed, and Latin most useful.'[38] Everything worthwhile is already translated, an ironic statement in view of Bruni's new translation of Aristotle and his defence of this. But he comes to this question himself. He does not consider it, he says at first, a wicked or reprehensible thing to know Hebrew but useless and vain. It is not necessary for attaining the *summum bonum* or for the knowledge of God.

> For neither Augustine, nor Basil, nor very many others among ours and the Greeks, who did not know Hebrew, would have known God, if the knowledge of God is not possible without knowledge of the Hebrew language. On the other hand, we see Jews who are most expert in the Hebrew language who nevertheless have no knowledge of the highest good and of the true God but are the worst enemies of religion and the faith.[39]

Of course this argument was a complete *non sequitur* and the exact opposite of the one Bruni and his mentor Salutati had used to defend the study of pagan classics despite their non-Christian authorship. And Bruni turns immediately to answer this argument from his correspondent.

> But Jerome damned the fables of the poets and the cleverness of the orators. What of it? For I do not call you to fables of poets nor to contentions in the forum, but if any effort is to be made in philosophy and the liberal arts, if men are to be imbued with discipline and morals, . . . I say this can be done much more readily and fully with Latin and Greek literature than with Jewish barbarism.

If these studies are neglected and the contemplation of God is declining, knowledge of Hebrew is not a necessary remedy, since many who are most learned in it are the most perfidious enemies of our religion.[40]

Bruni then switches to argue against the claim that 'the foundations of right faith derive from the books of the Jews, which, even if they are translated, it is much better to follow their sources than their tributaries'. 'But I say, if we are Christians, the sources are among us and not with the Jews.' He comes close to reading the Old Testament out of the Bible, as some of the ancient Gnostics did. 'For the entire New Testament is ours, as I would say, not the Jews'.' Only one evangelist wrote in Hebrew, only one of Paul's Epistles was in Hebrew; all the rest are in Greek. 'But if these seem to be streams to you and not sources, then add the many and so outstanding doctors of the Christian faith, how many there were who had Latin and Greek.' He names Dionysius the Areopagite, Gregory Nazianzen, Basil, Chrysostom, and many other excellent Greeks; Augustine, Jerome, Cyprian, Ambrose, Gregory, Thomas Aquinas and many other Latins. 'Therefore, if you wish to have a perfect knowledge of the Christian faith, and not a vulgar one, I ask you to read these men and know them, to whom you can find nothing similar among the Hebrews.'[41] The moment when the veneration of the Hebrew prophets as the prefigurers of Christianity was to revive in Renaissance art and humanist thought had not yet come for Bruni. (Though Krautheimer's study of the Ghiberti Gates of Paradise seems to suggest that Ambrogio Traversari, or some other contemporary, was more up to date than Bruni in this respect.)[42]

Bruni seems to endorse the post-Biblical tradition of the Church as perhaps a more important source than the Scriptures, certainly than the Hebrew Scriptures. He turns to the councils.

> What of the Councils? in which very many heresies and various quarrels of Christians were entirely extirpated. Were they not entirely composed of

Latins and Greeks and not at all of Hebrews? The Lateran, the Nicaean, the Chalcedonian? What then do you seek among the Hebrews? The foundations of the Christian faith? Certainly they are with us. Disputations of doctors and determinations of doubts? But these are found with us, not with them.[43]

The Old Testament, however, remains. His opponent argued that much can be learned for confirmation of the faith from the Prophets and other books of the Hebrews. But these are already translated by many most learned men, so that there is no greater profit in reading them in Hebrew than in Latin: 'Unless perhaps you distrust Jerome, a most holy and most learned man, and are confident that you yourself can know better than he knew.'[44]

Again he comes to the rescue of Greek from similar charges that it can be known through translation and therefore its study is similarly useless. But what was true for Jerome was not true for the translators of Aristotle. 'For if the Greek language had had such translators as Jerome was, it would have freed me and others of much labour. But they who translated the books of Aristotle render them barbarian rather than Latin.' This moves him to an encomium of Greek culture and a denunciation of Hebrew learning.

> Then what does the erudition of the Greeks have in common with the rudeness of the Jews? For the Greek tongue adds the grace of philosophy and other disciplines. It confers a perfection of literature on Latins. Certainly it seems to have the same origin, the same structure and almost the same figures of speech. But there can be no such attraction to the Hebrews. For no philosophers, no poets, no orators are found among them. Their language and the forms of their letters are so abhorrent to ours that even in writing they begin in the opposite direction from which we begin. What commerce can you have with this tongue whose letters cannot be companions of ours, when ours begin to the right, theirs flee to the left?[45]

Bruni comes back to defend humanist eloquence which his correspondent apparently is criticising along with his inquiry about Hebrew studies, and Bruni alleges the eloquence and use of oratory by St. Paul, and its value in conciliating differences in public life so that it was considered by the Stoics as among the greatest virtues. One should not be deterred by Jerome's remarks that on Judgement-day many rustics, ignorant of letters and oratory, would be preferred. But,

> What prevents me from saying about theology what he said about learning and oratory, 'O how many rustics and illiterates will be happier than many

> who have time for the knowledge of sacred letters.' Thus the Arians and Manicheans and Sabellians and other heretics who were learned in sacred letters and believed perversely about God were damned to eternal fire. You now have my judgement about the study of Hebrew letters.[46]

Perhaps the fact that Bruni ventured so little into the area of religious speculation and commentary, in comparison with other humanists, may find some explanation in the attitude he just expressed, which condemns not only Hebrew studies but the study of the Scriptures and theology in general as unsafe, presumably, for the layman. In this respect he was among the more conservative of the humanists.

Although in contrast to their contemporary, Bruni, Poggio Bracciolini at least thought about studying Hebrew as early as the Council of Constance and Ambrogio Traversari seems to have had some knowledge of the language and to have possessed Hebrew manusscripts,[47] the real beginning of Hebraism in the age of Hellenism came with Giannozzo Manetti's decision, very probably influenced by Traversari, to take up the study of Hebrew. Dates cannot be set for this. But if it began around 1435, Manetti would have been about forty years old. At any rate it is known that he took into his house as a tutor and member of his family, a young Jewish scholar, whom he eventually converted to Christianity, and who became known as Gianfrancesco di Messer Giannozzo Manetti. He also studied with a 'Manuello', who, Cassuto thinks, was Immanuel ben Abraham da San Miniato who paid a tax in Florence in 1437. In return for lessons in philosophy, Manetti read through the Old Testament twice with Manuello, beginning this for the first time on 11 November 1442. He then read medieval Hebrew Biblical commentaries with him.[48] In the course of these studies Manetti assembled a small library of Hebrew manuscripts, most of which have survived with his library to become an important section of the Fondo Palatino of the Biblioteca Vaticana. His Hebrew manuscripts, now in the Fondo Vaticano Ebraico, form the nucleus of that collection. They include the Hebrew Old Testament with various collections of commentaries by David Qimhi, Abraham ibn Ezra, Salomon Isaaci, Levi Gersonid; Maimonides' *Directorium in Theologiam*; Josippon's *Commentaries on Jewish History*; a Hebrew merchant's account-book that strayed into his collection by oversight. One volume also was owned by Ambrogio Traversari and seems to have been borrowed by Manetti but never returned.[49] Manetti not only used this study and the competence developed in it to undertake his translation from the Old Testament of the Psalter, but seems to have developed an active interest in Hebrew and Jewish affairs. We will discuss below certain interesting judgements on ancient and later Hebrew culture that he makes in his *Contra Iudeos et Gentes.* Besides converting his tutor, Cassuto reports him as being present at a disputation with all the learned Hebrews of Rimini and certain Christian scholars that Sigismondo Malatesta arranged in Rimini in 1447. He also helped Cardinal Giuliano Cesarini convert a Spanish Jewish physician residing at Florence, a man known as Giovanni Agnolo.[50]

With all this preparation and interest, he wrote his *Contra Iudeos et Gentes* in 1454, a work which he considered unfinished and which has survived in a single Urbino manuscript but has disappeared from his own library. In this he seeks to show the Jews where they erred in their own past and how the New Testament demonstrates that Christ is the true Son of God.[51] Two years previously he had finished his *De dignitate hominis,* which we have discussed above.[52] Meanwhile he had been forced to leave Florence. After he had served Nicholas V for two years in Rome, in 1455 King Alfonso of Naples took him into his royal council, made him president of the court of the *Sommaria,* gave him a palace and a large secretarial staff. Manetti went to work and in three year's time completed his translation of the New Testament, translated Aristotle's *Magna Moralia, Nicomachean Ethics* and *Eudemian Ethics*; wrote a work on *Earthquakes* at the request of the king, revised and enlarged his *Contra Iudeos et Gentes.* During this same period he undertook his translation of the Old Testament, but completed only the Psalter, which he dedicated to Alfonso, together with his *Apologeticus* (*Adversus suae novae Psalterii traductionis obtrectatores apologetici libri V*).[53]

Manetti's motives for undertaking this task are difficult to determine despite his lengthy explanations. He states in his preface to the king that he wished to undertake 'literary labours that were greater and weightier and more appropriate certainly to these your new abilities', since the king had put aside his earlier involvement 'with poets, orators and historians and other *studia humanitatis* of this type' and 'turned to the study of philosophy and divine wisdom' which is called theology. But then he adds, for his own part,

For since the true and solid foundations of both [ancient] and modern theology (as I would call it), by the agreement of all learned men, are contained only in the books of the Old and New Testaments, and I daily hear both of them, as translated from the true sources of the Hebrews and the Greeks into the Latin language by those from whom we have received them, criticised and torn to shreds, I have no longer been able to bear and tolerate this peaceably according to my strength. Especially influenced by this reason I have recently undertaken not improperly the labour of a new translation of both Testaments, although, whatever else it is, it is certainly a great and arduous task. . . .

He hopes for the aid of God and that he will not be thought arrogant. He does not cite specific criticisms of the older versions, but we may assume their existence. Perhaps weighing heavier with him is the fear of his own efforts being criticised for arrogance, but we shall see immediately how he answered his own critics when we turn to his *Apologeticus*.[54]

The preface makes it quite clear that he is offering only a part of what he hoped to complete, as he refers to other matters he will discuss in future prefaces, if, aided by divine favour, he is able to complete the entire translation of the Old Testament. So that the king may judge the merits of his own translation of the *Psalms*, he placed it alongside of Jerome's two versions, the one from the Greek of the Septuagint – 'that is, the one which the Roman Church is accustomed to use in its prayers from the beginning up to our own time' – and the other which bears the title *De Hebraica veritate*. In the Palatine Latin manuscripts, 40 and 41, which came from Manetti's own library, the three versions are indeed copied in three columns, with Manetti's labelled *pene ad verbum*, 'almost literal'. The Urbino manuscript (Bibl. Vat., Urb. lat. 5) copied only Manetti's own version, which made a more beautiful and more handsomely decorated, but less interesting page. Since the King died in July of 1458, there is some doubt as to whether he ever had his copy delivered to him. One in Manetti's possession seems to have been this dedication copy (Pal. lat. 41). Manetti himself died the very next year, and as a consequence never completed his translation of the entire Old Testament. On the other hand, in his *Apologeticus* he speaks of a year having elapsed since he completed his translation of the Psalter. And there would have to be some circulation of the work in order for there to be criticisms of it for him to meet. The *Apologeticus* is contained along with his translation in the following manuscripts: Pal. lat. 40 and 41, and in Urb. lat. 5; but not in Pal. lat. 42 or 43 or in Brussels, Bibl. Royale, Ms. 10745. Marucelliana C 336 goes only through Psalm 36 and also does not contain the *Apologeticus*. It is copied in double column with only Jerome's *De Hebraica veritate*, and Manetti's.[55]

We shall not enter into details on the character of Manetti's translation since this requires its edition. To make a close analysis of Manetti's linguistic judgements and decisions would also be out of place and beyond my competence. Our purpose is to examine his ideas and attitudes towards such an undertaking rather than to evaluate it philologically and technically. Therefore we shall be concerned now with his *Apologeticus* primarily.

He had stated in his preface that he was induced to make his new translation by the constant criticism of the traditional text, as we have seen. And he also hoped that his work would not be judged useless by learned men if he was enabled by it to respond to the critics of the Latin text and 'even enjoin and induce them to perpetual silence'.[56] In his *Apology* he begins by speaking of his critics, whose main charge, as we have also seen in the case of Bruni, was that it was useless and arrogant to make a new translation after that of Jerome. But his critics, he claims, were both Christians and Jews. And his *Apology* develops into essentially a defence of Jerome's translating activities, especially from the Hebrew, in order to meet, as Jerome also said in the preface to his translation of the Psalter, the charge of the Jews that their sacred text had been mistranslated into Greek or Latin, and that this mistranslation hence was a cause of the religious errors of the Christians. Now an interesting question arises, and that is how much did Manetti try to hide behind the saintly figure of Jerome by arguing that he was merely doing what Jerome had done before him? But the question still remained, if Jerome had successfully met the criticisms of the Jews and others by his translation, why was it now necessary for Manetti to make a new one? Manetti never once criticises Jerome's translations, but, as we shall see, there is no doubt that he thought he had either corrected or improved upon them even though he never directly says so.[57]

His first book is called *On Different Detractors of All Authors*,[58] and it is indeed a catalogue of criticisms and of philosophical and literary controversy. He believes that in view of this rather expected consequence of authorship he can bear his criticisms equably, despite the fact that he thought he should have received commendation instead 'for my many and great and pious and devout labours and night-studies in defence of the Holy Scriptures of the Latins against some false accusations and calumnies of Hebrew men about our books.'[59] He especially marvels that 'professors of divine letters and certain Christian and most religious men' could not avoid imitating the ancient writers in their quarrels and controversies.

> Thus Augustine and Rufinus violently criticised Jerome in many places of the Scriptures and did not hesitate to damn his entire translation of the Old Testament as unnecessary and superfluous and useless, subject to perpetual infamy, after he had published it.

And Jerome, of course, did not fear to reply to them in his prefaces and in some of his letters and he repeated it in his book *On the Right Kind of Translation*. And if Aristotle did not fear to defend himself against Thales and Socrates and even his master Plato, 'what should we Christian men do for the defence of the Catholic faith and the conservation of divine and sacred truth?'[60]

Manetti then enters upon his defence, but it is not a defence at all in the ordinary sense of the word. Cutting through and ignoring the point of view which held the Scriptures as untouchable and undiscussable, he plunges into a history of their composition and of their various translations, and of the controversies that developed over them. It is a survey of Biblical criticism from the Hebrew traditions, through the question of the Septuagint translation, the later Greek translations, the early Latin translations, to the activities and role of St. Jerome.[61]

He begins with an explanation of the major division of the Old Testament, the twenty-four books, their supposed authors, the Hebrew names of the parts of the Old Testament, the lives and historical circumstances of the various prophets.[62] He brings in information from his own Hebrew studies such as that it is generally believed that the seventy translators of the Septuagint wrote the *Paralipomenon* [*Chronicles*], but this work, called *Diureagianum* in Hebrew, was written by Esdra according to Rabbi Salomon.[63] *Job* was written by Moses, according to Hebrew tradition, and

It made known certain true and express doctrines concerning divine providence, about which ancient philosophers had doubted enough and bitterly disagreed with each other and quarrelled among themselves, for the use of all mankind; yet some of our Catholic and sacred doctors seem to feel far otherwise about the author of this aforementioned book and believe that the disputation of the aforesaid dialogue was written just as it actually happened by a certain Job not of Hebrew origin but a Gentile and a proselyte.[64]

He next takes up the Psalter of David, which is the specific object of his Apology. Four questions are raised: whether it is divided into more than one book? whether it is written as poetry or prose? whether there are one hundred and fifty Psalms, no more, no less, and whether David is author of all of them? His treatment of the first question is of interest because he sides with Hebraic tradition against Jerome. All Hebrew commentators say it is divided into five books, because it is so found in both ancient and in emended codices, because it was so divided in Esdra's canonical division of the Old Testament, and because it is confirmed in the traditions of the ancient Hebrews. Jerome opposed this, as he says in his preface to Sophronius before his translation *De Hebraica veritate*, because the old Hebrews and the Apostles, as is shown in the New Testament, speak of the book of *Psalms*, because the old Latin translation spoke of a *Liber hymnorum*.[65]

Nevertheless in our translation we have preferred to follow and imitate the common opinion of all the Hebrew scholars as it is found in all their volumes, and we are forced to do so by a certain, true and sincere law of translation, since we find it thus written expressly in that language from which we profess to translate into Latin eloquence, although in that celebrated translation into Greek by the seventy-two interpreters it exists in only one book.[66]

On the second question all agree that it is poetry, and he is able to quote Jerome at length. The third question involves the difference in division between the Septuagint and, following it, the Vulgate versions, and the Hebrew and its translations. He simply and clearly explains that some Psalms are differently divided, or combined, so that both come out to one hundred and fifty, although the numbering for many does not correspond in the two traditions. Moreover, David is not the author of them all, since other names are used. He then explains how the name comes from the instrument by which the singers were accompanied in reciting the text, the psaltery.[67]

Although much of this material does not fall under his heading for Book I, on detractors of various authors, he continues with another very important subject for the tradition of sacred wisdom. As is well known, Ficino and Pico della Mirandola held as an important item of their conception of the mystical unity of Scriptural and Platonic thought, that Moses influenced the early Greek sages, as well as Plato. Manetti considers this question on the basis of Eusebius Pamphilius of Caesarea's assertion in *De preparatione evangelica.* Eusebius holds that Plato followed the Hebrew law in many respects which he knew through a Greek translation of the Old Testament made prior to Alexander, 'for the Mosaic volumes were translated before Alexander, king of Macedonia and his empire'. 'He dared to write that Plato is nothing else than Moses speaking in the Attic tongue.' But Manetti seems to have had a sounder capacity for historical judgement than his more philosophical successors, for he adds,

> This he could not at all have done since the ancient Greeks, because they were most avid about elegance of speech, entirely lacked a knowledge of Hebrew letters, for this language seemed to horrify them as though it was something barbarous and wild, far from any polished elegance, especially in those times in which the study of Greek eloquence first flourished and it alone was held in honour and valued.

Unless another translation had been made, they could have known nothing of Moses, and it is uncertain when such a translation could have been made, if it ever was made.[68]

Dividing his discourse at this point, he begins Book II, *On Various Translators of the Holy Scriptures.* He first takes up the Septuagint version, beginning with a brief explanation of the foundation of the Hellenistic kingdom of the Ptolemies after the death of Alexander. He claims to take this information from Arrian and Aristobulus, but his sources are not always certain. He describes the decision to build the great Alexandrian library which was put in charge of Aristobulus and Demetrius Phalerius, a disciple of Theophrastus. Then follows the story, based on Aristeas and other sources, of the king's desire to have the writings of all peoples, and especially the sacred books of the Jews, included in the library, of the negotiations between Ptolemy and Eleazar, of the sending of seventy-two Hebrew sages learned in Hebrew and Greek to Alexandria, where, seated in separate cells, they produced an identical translation of the Old Testament into Greek. It turns out, however, that Eusebius is Manetti's chief source, and all his references to Aristeas follow Eusebius' own citations.[69] But this does not mean that he had no first-hand knowledge of Aristeas; he may have possessed a Greek manuscript of Aristeas' story of *The Seventy-Two Translators.*[70] Manetti's erudition is frequently considerably deeper than he chooses to reveal in his pages. For one thing, whether out of modesty or pretentiousness, he likes to make very long excerpts of patristic and classical sources, as he may be seen to do in his *De dignitate hominis*. But our knowledge, in exceptional detail, of his library, which, though not preserved entirely intact, was held together in its great bulk by his sons and grandsons, shows the amazing range of his purchases in Hebrew, Greek and Latin, of classical, Patristic and medieval works.[71] Aristeas, incidentally, was translated into Latin by Matthias Palmieri of Pisa (not Matteo, the Florentine contemporary of Manetti), but his translation, dedicated to Paul II, seems to have been made after Manetti's death in 1459.[72] Bartolomeo della Fonte also made an Italian translation of this work presumably, from Palmieri's Latin, which enjoyed a certain limited diffusion.[73] What this indicates is that, beginning at least with Manetti, this question of the textual history of the Scriptures, including Aristeas' rather romantic contribution to it, began to evoke interest in humanist circles in Italy.

Manetti, also, is inclined to hide his own views behind the famous authors he quotes. This seems to be true in this instance. With his long citation of Eusebius he is only leading up to the controversy between St. Augustine and St. Jerome over the value of the Septuagint translation.[74] After recounting the Eusebian version, which, of course, followed Aristeas and completely accepted not only the dating but the legend of the intervention of the Holy Spirit to produce seventy-two identical translations, Manetti places it in what is to him its proper historical context by telling the story of Pisistratus assembling seventy-two learned Greeks to revise and establish the text of Homer. He cites Cicero's *De oratore* on the learning of Pisistratus, and brings forward Diogenes Laertius' attribution of the restoration of Homer to Solon. 'But if what we have recited above was true according as it was written, then certainly what was written by Eusebius about the seventy-two famous translators of the Scriptures, indeed, seems to be similar [to the story of Pisistratus].'[75] His capacity to confront given accounts with differing versions also came out in his interjecting the opinion of Aulus Gellius that the Alexandrian library had only 70,000 volumes in Greek rather than the 100,000 alleged by Aristeas.[76]

He then brings forth Augustine's views that the Scriptures are the authentic voice of the Holy Spirit in whatever version, the Hebrew or the Septuagint, but in this statement the Saint clearly seems to favour the notion of an additional prophetic intervention in the Septuagint version. Manetti quotes the entire chapters forty-three and forty-four of *De civitate Dei*, Lib. XVIII. He immediately follows it by introducing Jerome, who doubts the story and seeks in many places in his writings to refute it as false. The exact language of Jerome he selects, from the *Preface to the Pentateuch*,[77] is itself interesting, as Jerome rests his case on the contrary statements from Josephus, an author with whom Manetti was most familiar. Jerome begins:

> I do not know what author in his falsehood first constructed the seventy cells at Alexandria, divided into which they are supposed to have written. Since Aristeas, who was the *hyperaspistes* of the same Ptolemy, and Josephus (in a much later time) reported no such thing, gathered into one basilica, they wrote and did not prophecy. For a prophet is one thing and a translator is another. In one case the spirit predicts the future. In the other, by erudition and a supply of words a man translates what he knows by these means, unless perchance it is thought that Cicero was afflated with the rhetorical spirit when he translated the *Economics* of Xenophon, the *Protagoras* of Plato and the *Ctesiphonte* of Demosthenes.[78]

Manetti's position in regard to this difference is curious. He has actually cited the main patristic sources for the story of the Septuagint, using the passages that modern scholars also repeat in their accounts, though not coming to the conclusion that the dating of the Septuagint at the time of Ptolemy Philadelphus is itself uncertain. He refuses to commit himself to either Augustine or Jerome. His own translation, however, most clearly follows Jerome's precedent in returning to the Hebrew. The trouble of course was that the accepted Vulgate version of the Scriptures was based on Jerome's translation of the Septuagint and not *De Hebraica veritate*. He comments,

> Therefore this translation of the seventy interpreters in whatever way it was produced, either separately and apart, or simultaneously and conjointly,

> nevertheless was immediately held in such honour and was so prized that in a few years it had occupied almost all Greece,

because it was unique at that time, solemnly made, and enjoyed the dignity of Ptolemy's patronage and the seventy-two elders. Their names should have been recorded, and the fact that they have fallen into oblivion,

> we marvel at and bear with a certain annoyance, since it was a matter worthy of being perpetuated in literary monuments and should have been recorded in early annals.

They should be highly esteemed today, as some of the Apostles and Evangelists used their version.[79]

But he now wishes to introduce the question of subsequent translation that supports his own cause. So he adds,

> for these reasons it [the Septuagint] survived alone for a long time in the greatest esteem, until some other translators appeared who, indeed, since it was apparent that in the aforementioned translation of the elders there were many insertions, some omissions, and much differently translated, assumed the labours of certain other new translations in various times.[80]

His language here is significant because the types of defects enumerated correspond to the titles of his Books III and IV, where he lists the errors of the Septuagint, as we shall see below.

He now, however, enumerates the various ancient translations into Greek before the time of Jerome, giving the approximate dates of Aquila Ponticus as in the time of Hadrian, of Theodotion as under Commodus, of Symmachus as under Pertinax, of an anonymous fourth translation known as the Hieric version as under Caracalla, a fifth known as the common and vulgate edition, and then a sixth edition, all of which Origen compared with the Septuagint in his *Hexaplorum*, indicating the omissions with asterisks and the additions with daggers. Then Jerome began his own version from the Hebrew, not fearing to note the many differences between these translations, 'partly that he might reply to the Jews alleging against the Christians the falsity of their old translations of the Holy Scriptures and impose silence on them, partly also that he might remove such great and multifold variety of the different translations'.[81]

It would not at all be alien to his purposes to say a little about

Jerome's translation. Briefly describing his life and his study of Greek and theology at Constantinople with Gregory Nazianzen, he turns to Jerome's study of Hebrew, which he undertook for two reasons. 'The first was that that language abounded in figures of speech and metaphors within which great mysteries and secrets of divine matters seemed to be hidden, and which could not be translated into a foreign language with a proper expression of their meanings.' This, of course, spoke for the need of a knowledge of the Scriptures in Hebrew itself. The other reason was the great divergence of the different translations from each other which,

> to the limits of his strength he could not bear. Thence wishing to remove this [discrepancy], he thought it would be not only useful but necessary if through a certain new and whole translation from Hebrew into the Latin language, all ambiguity whatsoever due to the diverse translations of the Holy Scriptures might as far as possible be entirely taken away.

Jerome, of course, also hoped to meet the objections of the Jews to the falsities of the different translations from the Hebrew.[82]

Manetti's attitude towards this translation is interesting. He regards it, of course, as the most important single piece of writing for the Latin Christians because of its contribution to their salvation. But, as he very well knew, it was not Jerome's translation from the Hebrew Old Testament that gained currency as the Vulgate, but one of his translations of the Septuagint Greek text. Thus by praising Jerome's *De Hebraica veritate*, he is praising his own translation.

A large element of concern for Manetti was, naturally enough, the persistence of Judaism. No man in his century could have taken the courageous step of learning Hebrew without being hyper-conscious of the modern Jewish religious community and of its attitudes towards the Christian community, which, besides its persecutions and harsh treatments, had taken over its Holy Books and used them to support a faith in what was regarded as a false messiah and an impostor. Since Manetti's motivations in learning Hebrew – and from contemporary Jewish scholars – and in acquiring a library of Hebrew manuscripts necessarily also from Jewish copyists and booksellers, was basically religious, he could not help being aware of their attitudes. It was natural enough that he would see what he had to regard as their errors as well as their faults and weaknesses, just as it was natural that he should attempt to convert those Jews with whom he associated. At the same time there must have been a basic respect for the religious and Scriptural traditions of the Jews for him to enter as deeply into them as he did. Therefore, the emphasis which he placed in this *Apology* on the desire to meet Jewish objections to errors and discrepancies in the Christian translated versions of the Scriptures seems quite genuine. And though it certainly seems true that he would have translated the Psalter for the benefit of Christians and not for the Jews, and he would therefore be hiding to a certain extent behind the need to convince the Jews as a false justification for his undertaking, still the sense of proselytism was strong in him, and perhaps could not help manifesting itself. Certainly his treatise against the Jews, as we shall presently see, was directed primarily towards convincing them of the truth of the Christian revelation rather than towards convincing his contemporary Christians of his staunch support of the faith. Both elements are present in the following discussion of the Jews and the Bible in this *Apology*, as well, but the former seems the more important.

Despite Jerome's translation the Jews continued to speak 'of the falsity of our Scriptures and did not cease daily to insult and vilify Christians'.

> For in the first place they imitate their ancestors and hence they are incensed against Christians and hate all of them equally. Then they especially envy us the Scriptures whereas we have, both by Greek translations and especially this Latin one, snatched away from them that supply of HolyWritings, in which they alone were accustomed to glory when other people at first despised them, and we have vindicated them to ourselves. In addition none of the Jews, or at least very few, seem to have had any knowledge of Greek or Latin literature since Philo and Josephus, those two noble and celebrated Jews who were most learned in both the Hebrew and Greek languages.[83]

Manetti does not seem to be aware of the medieval Jewish translators who helped to bring Arabic and Greek works into Latin, but he feels that this lack of knowledge prevented the Jews from really knowing whether the Scriptures are rightly translated or not.

> Whence it happens that from this ignorance of foreign languages itself they not only cannot know that which is rightly and that which is wrongly contained, if such there are, in Christian translations, but they are unable perfectly to know and understand their own language and vernacular, as well. For it is never possible to perceive and know one language perfectly

as it is constituted in rules, canons and norms, without some, or at least a little, knowledge of excellent foreign idioms.

As a consequence the Jews

therefore, content with their own alone and seeking no other, have long lacked foreign languages, also know their own and its vernacular wrongly. For this reason they are deprived of the poets and historians and orators and mathematicians and dialecticians and natural philosophers and moral philosophers and metaphysicians and seem to have entirely lacked a certain knowledge of all the liberal arts. Thence long conditioned by a crass and supine ignorance of all things, they lie moribund, like unclean swine in mud, and in this way they are buried alive in their own perfidy as if in a sepulchre. . . .[84]

If the Jews had known Greek and Latin, they would have known that the Mosaic law was reduced to nothing.

Since they have not been able to learn and know the characters and patterns of Hebrew letters elsewhere than in the sacred books, (which they easily could have done if they had not in the first place protected themselves by providing such harsh punishments against any foolhardy transgressors of their traditions, and secondly, if they had not also so established the order of their points, which are used in place of the vowels of Greek and Latin among them, that they should be found only in the aforementioned sacred books, that is the vowels without which nothing can be read and no reading confirmed), as a consequence of this, whatever Hebrew literature they knew, they could read nothing outside of the sacred books on account of the lack of points, so that they are held to be and are 'schulers' [*scioli*] of the Holy Scriptures. Therefore, since from a certain crass ignorance of all things and also from the fact that, as we have said, from infancy and the cradle they are steeped in the Scriptures, afterward, advancing through different ages, they think our Scriptures false and our faith impious.[85]

And though they saw other Jews converted to Christianity, they remained obstinately in their perfidy, despite Jerome's translation. This in summary form is Manetti's views of the state of Jewish culture and its relationship to the text of the Scriptures. It strikes me that this image of self-encapsulation was an exceptionally perceptive one, despite his failure to take into account the way Christian hostility to the Jews had also contributed to bringing about such a 'ghetto-mentality'.

Manetti turns next to Jerome's translations of the Psalter. Seeing that the Septuagint version prevailed among the Greeks, and not wishing to disturb the primitive church with suspicious novelties, he first translated this into Latin. But not much later, in view of the discrepancies of the Septuagint from the Hebrew, and moved by the prayers and observations of Sophronius, Jerome began and completed the work whose title was *Psalterium secundum Hieronymum de Hebraica veritate*. This he wrote because of the many omissions, additions, and faulty renderings of the Septuagint, and of the succeeding Greek versions of Aquila, Symmachus and Theodotion. Manetti quotes, with a few omissions, Jerome's preface to Sophronius.[86]

Thus Jerome made two versions of the Psalter, 'although a third version has circulated among the people which is called the "Gallican" and is used among some. But what its origin was, or who its author was, is unknown to many and especially to those who contend that in some way or other it emanated from Jerome.'[87] Of course, many modern Biblical scholars do attribute this version also to Jerome, though there is no unanimity. Manetti strongly doubts it is Jerome's, because one such translation would suffice and, if he had made two, it would be mentioned somewhere in his writings. It should be noted that Manetti with this narrative and these observations is in fact writing an early history of the textual tradition of the Bible in Greek and Latin. What he does not do, and lacks the capacities to do, is to look into the history of the Hebrew text itself, which he takes for granted must have been the most ancient, although modern scholars are aware that it continued to evolve even after the time of the Septuagint translation.

He then speaks of the many differences between Jerome's two versions, not to mention the Gallican. If all were listed they would number over six thousand. He intends to deal with them in his next two books.[88] Book III is called *On the Many and Great Differences of the Two Most Celebrated Translations of the Entire Psalter*.[89] Book IV is called *On Wrong Translations together with the Different Titles of All the Psalms*.[90] In fact, he has sorted out the differences systematically into four categories. Book III deals first with 'additions' in the translation of the Septuagint of words, phrases and lines which do not occur in the translation *De Hebraica veritate*; then, secondly, it deals with 'omissions' in the Septuagint of words, phrases and lines which do occur in the version from the Hebrew. Book IV, as the title indicates, first lists what he judges to be faulty translations, then lists the ways in which the titles and attributions differ from the Hebrew version. He does this

Psalm by Psalm, following the numbering of the Hebrew version. Here is another example of the painstaking philological analysis by a humanist, comparable to that of Valla, except for the fact that Manetti does not give the Hebrew and discuss its meanings. He simply tabulates the Latin and gives his judgement and conclusions.

But, there is one large fact missing in what we have said, and in what he announced he was doing. Why should not any careful compiler simply take Jerome's two versions in Latin and make such a tabulation of all the differences? However, this is not what Manetti did. An examination shows that, in fact, he did not compare the two versions of Jerome as he said he was going to do, but instead he compared the Septuagint translation of Jerome with his own original translation from the Hebrew. Thus he does have the Hebrew basis for making the comparison. Anyone who studies these two books in the three columnar manuscripts giving the Septuagint and the *De Hebraica* versions of Jerome and then Manetti's version, to which the *Apologeticus* seems originally to have been attached, would very quickly become aware that he was in fact showing what he considered to be his own corrections of both versions of Jerome, although pretending only to compare Jerome's two versions.[91]

However, his own version is labelled *pene ad verbum*, which might suggest that he was only making it to show the superiority of Jerome's less literal rendering. What then are we to make of the fact that Book V, *Some Things Worth Saying on Right Translation*,[92] in effect defends Jerome's methods of translation, and then adds almost as an appendix an explanation and perhaps even a justification for the Church's preference for the Septuagint Psalter as found in the Vulgate edition of the Scriptures in its divine services? It looks as though he was leaning over backwards to avoid saying one overt word in defence of having made this new translation, hiding his own defence behind a carefully considered and detailed exposition of Jerome's virtues. He might thus meet by counter-attack (against a non-existent enemy, perhaps) the charge that he himself was criticising Jerome by wishing to make a new translation superseding the Saint's.

As to the literalism of Manetti's translation, I cannot judge without knowledge of Hebrew, but, as we shall see, he defends translation not *ad verbum* but *ad sensum*, though differentiating between the much stricter requirements of theology and philosophy and those of the humanities. He never returns to the once enunciated theme of the mysteries contained in the Hebrew metaphors which cannot be easily rendered in a foreign tongue. But judging his work solely by the Latin, it does not seem to me that Manetti made his version any less mellifluous than the traditional ones. Perhaps to call his own *pene ad verbum* must be interpreted to mean that he wished to be more accurate within the limit of rendering the sense rather than the letter.

Manetti's fifth book is both relevant for understanding his attitude towards Biblical translation and of general interest as a humanist statement on the art of translation. He does not mention Leonardo Bruni's short disquisition *De recta interpretatione*,[93] possibly because he was currently translating Aristotle's *Nicomachean Ethics* (and other ethical writings), himself. Bruni's translation of the *Ethics* formed the grounds for his discussion and criticism of medieval modes of translation. However, Manetti does refer to Bessarion's translation of Aristotle's *Metaphysics* and Traversari's translation of Pseudo-Dionysius the Areopagite and Diogenes Laertius as examples of contemporary translations improving upon older, more literal ones which lost the sense of the metaphors and figures of speech.[94] His criteria for translation are strictly humanistic. First of all a translator should have a knowledge of the foreign tongue which is not small and vulgar but based on minute and full and accurate and long reading of its poets, orators, historians, philosophers, and, if he is translating Scriptures, of its doctors [i.e. theologians and commentators]. Otherwise he will not know how to render the meaning of the figures of speech and metaphors, which, if they are translated as the words sound, it will be not only ridiculous and stupid but false. Secondly a translator must know his own language thoroughly, dominate it and have it in his power so that when he renders word for word he will not seem helpless or to be writing in a strange and foreign tongue. He should know the force and nature of words subtly and exactly, so that he will not use *modicum* for *parvum*. He should use figures of speech correctly and have a good ear.[95]

There are three kinds of translation: the literal or *ad verbum*, translation according to meaning or *ad sensum* and thirdly where for the sake of embellishment a translator omits certain words, adds others.[96] He follows this up by an extended discussion of the views of Cicero, Horace and Jerome and offers examples of different kinds of translation, including those mentioned above. He distinguished sharply between the kind of translation required for the humanistic disciplines of poetry, rhetoric and history, and that which is necessary for philosophy and theology.

> In the case of the three first mentioned it is fitting that in any translation the meanings are somehow shown to be served by being ornamented and illuminated according to the evident diversity and variety of the first author. The other two disciplines seem to demand a certain weightier and more severe translation.[97]

Offering examples of translations of humanistic works, he mentions, among many others, two recent translations of both Thucydides and Herodotus. One of them certainly was Valla's, and he also refers to translations of Josephus' works.

Turning to philosophy and theology, he completes his definition of proper translation in those fields as follows:

> But with regard to philosophy and theology, although we are unable to translate properly by being literal in any sort of translation, nevertheless it should not be too wide and diffuse and ample both in words and means, or polished also with lights and ornaments, but somewhat more compressed and weightier and more exact in these two fields than in the three previous fields. Certainly translation according to the gravity and the articulation of the meanings, in which both these faculties especially abound, is required, so that they are rendered in neither more nor fewer words, meanwhile, except in so far as a certain necessity of the figures of speech and the metaphors and sometimes too great obscurity of understanding seems to exact and demand, which we think and believe must be especially used, and rightly so, in the Holy Scriptures.[98]

After a brief discussion of Cicero's theories and practices as a translator, quoting his proem to *De finibus*, and wishing that he had indeed translated Plato and Aristotle [rather than expounded and paraphrased their ideas as he states in the proem],[99] Manetti comes again to his ideas of translating the Scriptures.

> For what should we feel about the translations of the sacred and Holy Scriptures, where all the meanings are sacred and divine and in them human salvation entirely or especially seems to consist and be concealed? Though this seems to be so, nevertheless excellent translators of the Holy Scriptures

> seem to be so horrified at literal translation that they think the meanings are obscured and perverted by it, so that they use in the middle of the sacred text, sometimes amplifications, at other times wrongly translated words.

Jerome did this in his translations of Eusebius. Manetti quotes his preface to the *De temporibus*, where he asserts the necessity for doing so in order to render the meaning.[100]

Manetti then quotes Jerome at great length, almost recapitulating his entire letter LVII to Pammachius, *De optimo genere interpretandi*.[101] This is important because in it Jerome runs through a number of clear errors and faulty attributions in the Gospels where the Old Testament is being cited. To this should be added the many examples Manetti himself gave in the preceding two books of additions, omissions and falsifications. 'Certainly the number of such discrepancies may be thought to be incredible and almost infinite.' Our ancient doctors were accustomed to note these by the use of asterisks and other conventional signs in their volumes.[102] Referring to Origen's *Hexaplorum*, he again describes how he arranged the Hebrew, the Septuagint and five other ancient translations in parallel columns, side by side, showing all of the differences.[103] Besides, Manetti adds, there are two excellent Chaldean [i.e. Aramaic] texts of the Old Testament, one called the *Chaldaic Targum* and the other going by the name of Jonathan ben Uziel.[104]

At last Manetti is ready to make a very faint-hearted justification of his own translation. In the view of the above wide-ranging differences there is a need for a stricter, though not absolutely literal, mode of translation.

> We recall that we have above fully and openly proved and confirmed by certain argument and by the authority also of many most outstanding men that no literal translation can be laudable and perfect, and we have demonstrated that there is great diversity between the translators of poets, orators and historians and the interpreters of philosophers and theologians and that manifestly there ought to be. For it is licit for these first converters of poets, or orators or historians to amplify the arid, meagre and thin for the sake of elegance and ornateness, and to omit the obscure and to translate more lucidly according to their will. But faithful translators of philosophers and theologians should not run about and wander around so freely and widely as their fancy chooses as though through a wide open field. But pressed within certain narrower laws of translating, and constricted within certain barriers, they are compelled to move and proceed more modestly

and seriously according to the certain severe norm of their profession, and not to wander too far away from their assumed purpose in translating. Nor adhering entirely even to the first authors, but holding to a middle and safe road, as it is said, they should conduct themselves so modestly that they will seem to decline and bend in neither direction. For they consider that this is how the burden of translating should be diligently and accurately assumed, especially in divine matters, leaving philosophers to one side. The authority of the Holy Scriptures, I say, is thought to demand and exact this from them in the first place, and not unjustly.[105]

Manetti is extremely cautious in affirming this move towards greater strictness, and he does not want it to be thought of as literalism which had come in for so much humanist scorn. On the other hand, he fears to criticise the Septuagint version, which in his eyes is so loose, because of its high esteem. But its translators are believed to have been permitted this wide licence justly,

> because they are thought to have known the divine mysteries of the Holy Scriptures with heavenly assistance. Indeed, illuminated by this revelation of abstruse matters they thus seemed able to translate as though they perceived what those first writers divinely had known and proclaimed, and for this reason alone they are excused, not without merit, for having departed so far from the right office of suitable and faithful translators.

In this he now sides with Augustine.[106]

Again, more emphatically and more specifically he says,

> For I feel as follows about all translators of other subjects into another language, that all writings of any other authors, excepting the Holy Scriptures alone, can and may be translated according to the free choice of their translators in a different way than it was written, serving only the meaning of the first writers. But the Holy Scriptures, because of their divine authority in all matters, which neither deceives nor is deceived, seem to exact and demand especially and chiefly a certain solemn and accurate, serious and studied translation; yet not so that the translation is made so literally that it does not recede from the letter for the sake of clarity and understanding, nor so wild and playful that it departs very far from it. And it should never add to it with new matter nor omit the old, nor be permitted to translate and express much in a different manner.[107]

Clearly he has in mind exactly the *super addicta*, the *omissa* and the *aliena* that he had tabulated in his third and fourth books. Clearly he did wish to justify his own translation, however timidly he was willing to say so. Clearly also he was putting forth a new, more scholarly, less rhetorical ideal of translation, at least where the Scriptures were concerned, for they contained the Word of God.

Manetti, however, remained cautious to the very end. He immediately declares after this fairly forthright statement of his own ideal, that Jerome both preached and practiced it, even though by implication he did not entirely do so in Manetti's eyes, and in fact in his own letter to Pammachius Jerome also took the same position that Augustine had, that oneness of spirit justified the various deviations from accuracy in the Evangelists' quotations of the Old Testament.[108] Jerome's own views, however, it must be conceded, were seen by Manetti as in essential harmony with his own scholarly notions of the ideal Biblical translator.

Moreover, Manetti felt that he must also justify the Church's preference for the Septuagint, despite his own notions of interpretative justice. 'Why does the Roman Church in its private and public prayers and in its long and universal practice seem to prefer the Septuagint translation of the Psalter over the other translation of Jerome *De Hebraica veritate*?' He asks this

> especially since in that prior and older one much has been added, more omitted, some translated in another way, as we have shown, one by one, in the above third and fourth books. In the other translation [Jerome's from the Hebrew], indeed, either nothing or very little of that sort of thing is to be found.

Having thought about the reasons for this astonishing and so mystifying fact, he has come up with four explanations. First it is the common opinion that the first translation appeared before the advent of Jesus Christ. Secondly, it was quoted by the Apostles and the Evangelists. Thirdly, it is commonly believed to have been translated by each of the elders in separate cells,

> so that it seemed one translation only and not many. Hence, since this could not be done by or derive from human powers, it is believed to have been made and published by the Holy Spirit. Finally it is preferred on account of the sonority of the poetry and the harmony of the verses. For that Septuagint translation seems, with the agreement of all, to contain more melodious and harmonious songs and ones that are more adapted to the singing and musical expression of the clergy.[109]

With all of his hesitations and what must have been genuine uncertainties and quite sincere and pious admiration for the work of St. Jerome and the venerable tradition of the Vulgate Scriptures and their basis in the Septuagint, Manetti undertook a very important pioneer work of Biblical scholarship, certainly earlier than in the histories of this field it is generally supposed it began, and definitely more significantly than most of those scholars who were aware of the existence of these works of Manetti have supposed. Certainly Father Garofalo has had a true appreciation of his importance, but for whatever reason his studies of Manetti are to remain unfinished and unpublished. For these reasons, if I am able to call attention to the necessity of studying this important and neglected humanist Biblical scholar, I shall have accomplished my purpose.

4. Brandolini's Defence of the Humanist as Biblical Scholar

It is an interesting historical coincidence that two of the Italian humanists who wrote in more enthusiastic terms of the dignity of man, emphasising his actions and satisfactions in this life, should also have engaged in the study of the Bible, and specifically the Old Testament within a humanistic frame of reference. For another contributor to these studies was the humanist Aurelio Brandolini whose works on the condition of man we have considered at some length in a previous part of this book.[110] Brandolini seems to have been attracted towards the Bible as a field for utilising his humanistic talents while he was at the papal curia either under Sixtus IV, or Innocent VII, for it was before he departed for Budapest and the court of Matthias Corvinus. His interest in the Old Testament, specifically, was reflected in a work, which he called *On the Sacred History of the Hebrews*. He dedicated this work to the Cardinal Francesco Piccolomini of Siena. The character of the work may be gathered from the second title with which he headed the work itself after a long and most interesting preface: 'Epitome on the Sacred History of the Jews from the Volume which they call the Bible and from Josephus, Most Faithful Historian.' It is, in other words, a re-writing of the historical portions of the Old Testament, supplemented from Josephus, in order to give a narrative history of the ancient Hebrews.[111]

Although the scholarly value of this effort is slight, it is perhaps of more interest from a literary point of view, for Brandolini certainly had it in mind to use the rhetorical or literary skills of humanism to make at least the historical sections of the Old Testament more easily understandable. It was, to some extent, an effort to 'popularise' the Bible, to write as it were a Bible for the Common Reader, for the literate layman. Therefore the effort itself, however weakly executed, is of importance in the history of religion and certainly represents an effort to open up the Scriptures to the laity. It must be compared, also, to the illustrated retellings of Old Testament stories which began to circulate at this time and which, if Wind's theory is correct, had some influence on the iconography of Michelangelo's Sistine ceiling.[112]

As a matter of fact, as such a work it is not very impressive. Brandolini divided it into twenty-one books, corresponding almost entirely to the books of the Old Testament which he uses. For example, *Liber primus qui Genesis appellatur*.[113] Moreover, the books are divided into chapters which correspond very closely to the chapter divisions of the Bible. Sometimes he omits one or two chapters or condenses two into one. He gives the chapters titles which are based on the content of the material, for instance chapter I, of Book II, *Qui Exodus Dicitur* is called 'On the Servitude and Calamities of the Hebrews'.[114]

He makes no judgements or critical comments whatsoever, but piously and faithfully simplifies and explains what he finds. He draws very sparingly on Josephus. He follows the order of Old Testament books from *Genesis*, *Exodus*, *Leviticus*, *Numbers*, to *Deuteronomy*, which he decides to compress somewhat, since it is the second law; then follow in proper order *Joshua*, *Judges*, *Ruth*. *Samuel* he calls *First Kings* also, but *Second Samuel* he simply calls *Second Kings*; *Third* and *Fourth Kings* follow without incident. *First* and *Second Paralipomenon*, or *Chronicles*, he skips; then come *First Esdra* and *Nehemiah*.[115] He next inserts what he calls *Second Esdra* and runs it up to chapter 5, where he says,

> Concerning the things contained in the following book – from here to the end of the book the same things are repeated on the return of the Jews and the restoration of the temple which are described in the first book; these easily induce me to believe that this book was not written by Esdra.

And after the chapter, he says, 'There follows the book of Esdra which is called second by some, third by others. Whereas this contains partly the quarrels of the times and partly the pronouncements of angels, it cannot be reduced to an epitome; therefore omitting this we proceed to the next.'[116] He then goes through *Tobias*, *Judith* and *Esther* without incident, bringing him to the end of the narrative books of the Old Testament. Book XIX covers all that he wishes to include from the prophets and the *Hagiographa*. He covers *Job* from 'the book of Jerome' in three chapters.[117] He then announces:

> The books of Solomon and the Prophets follow, which contain for the most part either precepts or prophecies and divine oracles. There is either no explanation of events in them or the minimum. And so we, omitting precepts and oracles which belong to religion, will follow what is historical in the individual books, consulting our own judgement.[118]

Thus he follows *Jeremiah*, chapters 36 to 44, because it throws light on the captivity of the Jews; chapters 1 to 6 of the *Book of Daniel*, the *History of Susannah*, and the *History of Bel and the Dragon*. His last two books correspond to *First* and *Second Maccabees*.[119] Clearly Brandolini is making an important distinction between the historical and the oracular parts of the Old Testament with the former subject to the literary treatment of a humanist and the latter reserved for the theologian. We shall shortly examine his defence of his procedure. It should be noted, however, that from the allegorical or 'figural' point of view, even the historical narratives had oracular significance. Thus Brandolini's distinction is a significant innovation in Biblical criticism, departing even from earlier humanist tendencies to re-emphasise that it is poetry and hence contains a hidden meaning.

I have followed two Vatican manuscripts of this work: Ottoboniano latino 121 is clearly his autograph working copy with many lines crossed out, insertions in the top and bottom margins and between the lines. It is defective, however, missing the first sheet with the title, as well as most of the last book, breaking off in the middle of chapter four of *Second Maccabees'* fifteen chapters, about six sheets from the end. The other, also an Ottoboniano manuscript, latino 438, may possibly be the dedication copy; it is prepared carefully on quality paper with the crest at the bottom of the title page and it follows out all of the very disorderly and scrawling corrections of the other manuscript. There are a few corrections in the hand of the first manuscript, which hardly could be anyone's but Brandolini's. Incidentally some of the corrections and revisions in 121 are so tiny and yet neat and clear that it is hard to think of the writer's having bad eyesight; perhaps he had very powerful spectacles. I know of no other manuscripts, which might suggest an absence of diffusion, but this is a question we shall come to below in relationship to his proem.

Far more important than the work itself is the introduction that Brandolini wrote to it: 'in which he states the reasons for writing this work and defends himself against the calumniators of his action.'[120] His reasons are patent, for nothing is worthier or better for man than the contemplation and study of divine matters. Since all our hope lies in the one God, so by such studies we advance our intellect towards His knowledge and our will towards His love. Therefore since in recent years he had been involved in a more accurate reading of the volume of sacred histories of the Hebrews, which we now call the Bible, he wished to carry away some fruit from his labours.[121] But immediately a mixture of motives presents itself, for the Bible, which was written by 'those most ancient Jewish authors in a certain plebeian simplicity and inelegant style and afterwards translated by our writers as was necessary for the sake of the vulgar, I would like to set forth clearly as though collected into one book, both briefly and elegantly'.[122]

In other words, he wished to simplify and make easy and at the same time to apply a kind of rhetorical polish to the Bible,

> for as they wrote it, it does not seem possible for it either to be read freely or easily retained in the memory. Indeed they deterred many from its reading because of its length and called away many on account of its inelegance. Anyone who reads it through once can neither remember everything on account of the multitude of its contents nor be able to read it again because of the tedium and labour of reading it.

Therefore,

> I have wished to attempt whether I can add some light to most beautiful things by means of elegance and beauty of speech; and I have made from that universal history which is contained in the sacred volume a kind of epitome which is both suited for retention in the memory on account of its brevity and for pleasure in reading because of the not unpleasing grace of its style.[123]

Actually Brandolini was trying to write a popularisation of the Old Testament story of the Hebrews, but felt compelled both to repudiate 'plebeian simplicity' and proclaim the humanistic polish he wished to add. Moreover, he fully intended to walk carefully in this for he wants to skip those parts which contain either the prophecies of prophets or precepts of life, as we see he did, 'which indeed since they have mystical meanings in the individual words, cannot be spoken otherwise'.[124] And he also does not wish to judge where Josephus seems to differ from the sacred writers and

> yet always bases himself on their authority; I, who am not able to discriminate between them and judge the truth, so that fuller and more perfect knowledge of all things may be had and the authors entirely trusted, have given both opinions in doubtful cases, hoping that these our labours will profit many and that they can offend and displease no one.[125]

All his caution and seeming simplicity of motivation, however, was of no avail, since he apparently was violently attacked before he had even completed the work. It is his report of this and his defence of his right to compose such an epitome of the Scriptures that lends a certain significance to an otherwise trivial and not very distinguished production. Attributing it to the hatred for humanism on the part of those who wished to retain the study of Scripture for themselves, he reports that they tried to enlist the authority of the pope and that they included three cardinals and sought to destroy what was at that time already written,

> shouting with anger that a new Bible was made and the old one neglected because of it, that it was wicked to change the words of Jerome, and that it was not permitted to anyone who had not received the badge and insignia of doctors in theology to write anything at all on sacred matters.[126]

The affair was quashed with the blessing of the pope and the intervention of Cardinal Piccolomini, to whom he dedicates it.[127]

But he has now decided to respond to his critics in writing and the Cardinal shall be the judge.[128] His reply is in effect an assertion of the right of the layman as well as the humanist to engage in theological and religious writing and scholarship. Specifically, there were three charges, as we have already suggested. The first was that no one should engage in sacred studies who was not a doctor of theology, 'For this is their proper function and they alone have the right to write; others do not.'[129] Secondly, if outsiders are permitted to write on other things, they are especially not allowed to deal with the Bible,

> in which all the mysteries of our religion are contained; it is wicked to use any other words than those in which it is written, or to write in any other

style or to change it in any way whatsoever. For the mysteries are contained not in the matter itself, only, but in the individual words also. Moreover, in this way the old Bible is perverted and a new one made, rather than stories being excerpted or more briefly explained.[130]

Finally sacred matters are not to be written in more elegant style or more cultured speech. Certainly they pertain not only to learned men but to the uneducated and plebeian as well and to every age and sex. Moreover the salvation of all is involved, so that it is necessary for it to be known by all. If they had desired a splendour and elegance of style, Jerome, a lover of Cicero almost to a vice, by whom it was translated, would have done that best, and willingly would have done it.[131]

Brandolini answers the first claim – that only doctors of theology should deal with religious questions and the Scriptures – with the following arguments. How can they say this when the city is full of ignorant and uneducated men who daily pray and deal with the most sacred matters in writing and disputation and are held in the highest praise? What about those ancients whose writings we hold in the highest veneration, Hilary, Cyprian, Lactantius, Chrysostom, Origen, Eusebius and innumerable others? Were they subject to licensing? What about those we consider the leading doctors of the Church, Jerome, Gregory, Ambrose and Augustine, did they ever receive or seek the insignia of office? All of this argument is intended to show the narrowness and formalism of the defenders of the degree. Do they believe that if someone has the title he is able to write but is not able if he doesn't? Today the degree is conferred promiscuously on princes and others who are uneducated.[132]

This capacity for writing ought not to be more that of the doctor than of the *doctus*. But is it the property of theologians and not that of orators to write on divine matters? I however ask you first whether this subject is more properly that of the theologians than of the orators, since orators must have all divine and human things subject to them for speaking?

This is to refer to the claim of the orator or the poet to know all matters, especially philosophy, since he must speak on them. But Brandolini carries it one significant step further.

Then what prohibits me from being both an orator and a theologian? For all disciplines are so connected with each other and related that whoever wishes to master one of them absolutely is compelled in a certain way to attain to and draw all of them to himself.

From wishing to draw the lines narrowly between the disciplines and professions, the argument has moved to a recognition of their necessary interdependence. But this is not simply a debate between humanist and theologian, for it involves the question of the layman, whether he can pronounce on religious matters. Brandolini does not fail to assert this claim as well.

> Finally how do you suspect that I am not a theologian when you know that I am a Christian, and that I not only speak not unlearnedly about God, which makes the name of theologian, but also you see that I do not write ignorantly?[133]

His reply to the argument that the Bible should not be used as the basis for writing because each word contains a mystery is of greater religious and historical substance. In place of a view of the Scriptures as narrowly restricted to a group of authorised experts, Brandolini expresses the notion that the benefits of contact with the Bible should be as widespread as possible. No object is more appropriate for writing or better for a Christian or more worthy than that which contains all the foundations of our religion and salvation. 'Shouldn't this be published and diffused in every way by every author, in all languages, so that it will reach unto all nations far and wide?' Whoever does this should not be damned but highly commended.[134]

He then considers the question of changing the words and losing their mystical sense. But the mystical sense is in the meanings and content, not in the individual words. This is not changed when one word is replaced by another with the same meaning whether in the same or a different language. And it is not even changed when words are replaced by metaphorical equivalents, 'as if for "bread" one says "wheat".' Where has he written anything that did not express the former meaning to a hair?

> If, moreover, you criticise me in that I have explained the sacred histories in other style and speech than they were written, and you call that changing or reforming the Bible, why do you not also reprehend Jerome and the other translators who not only expressed the same things in a different style but also in a different language? But you say they used the same words in a different language. I have used the same meanings in the same language for if it is not permitted to change the style it is not permitted to change the language even.[135]

How could the Apostles spread the Gospels into the entire world if they were not permitted to change the language or the style? Do all nations use the same language, or different kinds of men the same style? See if it is not a greater vice not to know how to change the speech than not to wish to.[136]

We may recall Salutati's argument that the Bible could be interpreted poetically if it was not wrong to paraphrase the Scriptures or put them into verse as a number of early medieval writers had done. Brandolini, also, in defence of his position, alleges some of the very examples that Salutati used: Prudentius, Juvencus, Arator, who put the Gospels, the Epistles and the Old Testament in verse. If they could keep the same meaning in verse, 'why can't I do so, confined to no necessity of metres and syllables?'

> And they, indeed, executed it with all the actions of Christ, all the precepts, in which our salvation and the universal faith is contained. I have not wished to touch the predictions of the prophets which contain a mystical sense, nor the precepts of Solomon. . . .

If they are universally praised, why should my attempt be rejected? 'If you approve of their writings, I plainly wish that you approve of mine also. For I prefer to err with such great authors than to feel rightly with you.' We then who have explained the sacred histories in cultured and lucid language are said to be reforming the Bible, while you

> who corrupt it with barbaric commentaries, leave it intact and unviolated! We who illumine the events in the splendour and clarity of oration render the Bible obscure; you who envelop all in the fog of barbarism and in a multitude of opinion and obscurity, in your judgement clarify and illuminate it. Beware I ask, beware, lest that rather is to corrupt and change the sacred books; that you rather, who daily add new and inane opinions to the ancient writings, deprave the sacred volumes.[137]

Although with his rhetorical desire to improve the style and language of the Scriptures, one could hardly think of Brandolini as a literalist, still his argument against the imposition of theological innovation by an exegesis moulded by the theological schools was a cry raised by the Bibliolatrists of the sixteenth century.

> You in your ignorance confound sacred things, you, I say, in your barbarity not only dirty and pervert the Bible but all theology as well. Thus the Bible

is said to be changed by us by our style, only it turns out to be depraved and corrupted by you and your petty little commentaries. It may certainly be that we act to renew the Bible, but you should know that you destroy and abolish it.[138]

It is interesting to note that Brandolini does have a new attitude towards the Scriptures, which approaches the desire of the reformers to clear away the obscurities of scholastic theology. His innovation, however, is a partial and a limited one. For him the word of God conveyed through the prophets retains its mystico-poetic character and he prefers not to touch it, but as for the rest, he is ready to treat it as history and as literature, though its content is sacred and its authorship divine. And Brandolini wishes to apply the norms of literature and style rather than the strictness of philosophy to its interpretation.

This assimilation of the Bible to the cultural frame of reference of humanism and to the particular disciplines of humanism is further articulated in his much lengthier reply to the third objection – that sacred matters do not need elegance of style. 'For it is necessary that what is written for all can also be understood by all, as if, indeed, these things cannot be understood by all, or that men are prohibited from reading them.' Thus his first argument had to do specifically with the popularity and diffusion of the Bible. We have already spoken of his mixture of motives, wishing to abbreviate and clarify, and at the same time to beautify and polish. Here the same ambivalence appears. For he seems to want to bring the Bible out into public circulation, but at the same time make it such that a humanistically educated layman would particularly benefit from it. Who are his critics to say that his treatment of sacred history will not be read and understood broadly? They assume that unless something is similar to their writings it can't be understood. 'For you judge others according to yourselves, and you credit all that is similar to you, so that what you do not understand will not be understood.' Moreover Brandolini assures them that he is quite native and so is his language – Latin. 'Is not this Latin, is it not our own, are not these the customary words? What about us, are we not all born under this sky and educated in this language?' We are not Germans or Scythians, but even they eagerly read and thoroughly learn this language. 'But no wonder that you, as you are horrified at our customs, are especially horrified at our language, and you think others are likewise horrified.'[139]

But having argued that his humanistic Latin was really a common coinage open to all readers – and his text is indeed a most simple and unelaborate piece of writing – he feels the need to make a separation between the reading habits of the crowd and that of the educated laity.

> But the crowd may not be able to understand our version! Who, I pray, forces anyone to read this version or not to read the other? The crowd has its own means of learning through which it delights in sacred things and is filled with joy by reading them. It should leave this one to the more educated and cultured, for as the crowd cannot understand these more refined matters, so the learned cannot read these simpler and lengthier matters.[140]

This connects with his complaint that the Bible was too simple and too long, so that it had to be re-treated for the benefit of the more cultured reader. Thus he seeks on the one hand to make it more available, and on the other to limit its availability specifically to the educated laity.

Their fear that 'those more ancient and holy volumes will be neglected for these' he has made is a poor argument, for if they are, then his work cannot be a bad one, since what is admitted to be the best of all is neglected for his. But who will neglect them for his, since his does not contain all things 'but only those which seem to be capable of being woven into a history; whoever wants the others must get them from those archetypes'. And, as they confess, his will not be understood by everyone.[141]

He comes to the more ticklish question of whether the inherently splendid Scriptures need any rhetorical polish. He replies with a defence of beautification in general, and all the efforts of antiquity to achieve it.

> If there is any dignity present in these activities, any beauty which men ought to seek and marvel at, that certainly ought to be universally contributed to divine matters to which all honour and effort of mortals is owed.

It cannot be said that because the Scriptures are beautiful they need no further embellishment, because the human figure is beautiful, yet beautiful garments are sought, gems are beautiful, yet they are set in gold. Thus the other liberal arts are nude and plain without rhetoric, but become beautiful when it is added;

> only if at length these ornaments are added can they sufficiently show and retain that beauty which they naturally have. Are not sacred matters thought to be brightened and refined by these arts and without them they cannot be announced and expressed?[142]

But decoration and beautification are not the only things that rhetoric has to offer, though it is sometimes forgotten how important this aesthetic side of it was in humanist thought and Renaissance taste. Brandolini moves right to the other capacity of rhetoric – persuasion. 'Who is either so beast-like and so inhuman by nature, or such an enemy to this faculty and so hostile that he will not admit that he is moved by it and in a certain way compelled to every emotion?'[143]

These powers of arousal, as well as of sedation, lead him to a statement of what we have been calling *theologia rhetorica*, the humanist thesis that since matters of faith cannot be proved by logic, they must be induced by rhetoric – the word of man in the service of the Word of God. The humanist can inculcate faith, whereas the scholastic theologian with his dialectic cannot.

> Certainly the end of [rhetoric] is to persuade and its art lies in speaking aptly for the sake of persuasion, and nothing is so incredible that (as Cicero said) it cannot be made probable by speaking. Indeed, I do not see how divine matters, which not only exceed all our faith but our thinking also, can be written or pronounced so that they are approved by the people without the greatest power and eloquence of speech. For who has such facility of mind that, when he hears either that a man was born of a virgin without sexual intercourse, or that the entire body of Christ is enclosed in the tiny figure of the host, or that there are three persons in one substance, which are all positions of our dogma, he can easily be induced to believe? The greatest rhetorical power and infinite eloquence is needed for persuading of this, which indeed cannot be done without eloquence.[144]

Again Brandolini has said in a sharper and more outspoken way what many humanists before him were suggesting in more muted tones. Indeed, the very examples of Christian articles of faith he selects seem to reflect the continuing influence of Valla's thought in Roman humanist circles, for two of these were dogmas which Valla had himself dealt with [the Eucharist and the Trinity], and Valla had, of course, stressed that the weakness of dialectic in matters of faith left no alternative but recourse to sacred rhetoric.[145]

Brandolini continues his defence of *theologia rhetorica*, now answering the charge that the ancient theologians rejected rhetoric by reference to the rhetorical powers of Paul and the other Apostles, and of the Greek and Latin Fathers. Moreover, he finds sacred eloquence in daily use in the prayers and sacraments of the Church.

> What of the hymns, prayers, readings and other types which we daily use everywhere in divine services, are they not all most elegant, and written by the most eloquent men? Indeed, if we consider the truth more accurately, nothing is found in these which is not terse and elegant, unless it has been added by you and men like you afterwards with the greatest audacity, so that it clearly appears that whatever in divine matters is corrupt has been corrupted by your barbarism and ignorance.[146]

Thus Brandolini, leaving aside the doctrinal validity of his assertions, has grasped the fact that beauty and beautification and the arts of persuasion were a necessary and traditional part of the life of the Church. But one thing in his defence of rhetorically supported Christianity bothered him, and it was central, of course, to his entire endeavour. The Bible seemed plain and unadorned. He, of course, was professing to adorn it, whether effectively or not does not matter. But how account for that eloquent Christian rhetorician, Jerome, leaving the Bible so plain when he translated it?

> Since, moreover, in that time very many everywhere fought against the truth itself, and for that reason numerous sects opposed to our religion rose up interpreting the Bible according to their own wishes, it was necessary both that the alien interpretation could be refuted and that ours could be confirmed, that the Bible sound in Latin as it sounded in Greek and Hebrew, and that our individual words correspond to their individual words in their own order. Thus Jerome in that translation which he desired to be absolutely literal did not hesitate to transgress the laws and boundaries of grammar itself. But what it was then necessary to do in refuting the adversaries and clearing up our doubts, in our time, since they have been removed and its status confirmed, should not be used. For if the cause is removed the effect and its traces also are taken away.[147]

This finishes his argument, and what remains is his exhortation to his enemies to stop their criticism and to let his re-writing of sacred history circulate. But this latter question was one he wished to place in the hands of the Cardinal Piccolomini for final judgement and decision. He knows that he will not let it pass into the hands of men unemended.[148] 'Indeed I have promised the supreme pontiff that I would not publish this work except on the advice of the most learned men.'

So the Cardinal should either suppress or release the work.[149] Whether it circulated beyond this copy he seems to have had prepared for Piccolomini, we do not know. But, as we can see, it involved an interesting question of ecclesiastical policy and of doctrine, as well. But his statement in defence of re-working the Scriptures from a literary and historical point of view demonstrates that the natural impetus of humanism was towards a freer treatment of the Scriptures, and a wider circulation of them, since they were the written Word, the word of man as well as that of God. One must also observe from this effort of Brandolini that the rhetorical and literary interests of the humanists might set some of them on the road to embellishment of the Scriptures while the grammatical and philological and linguistic interests of others might lead to the demand for a stricter rendering from the Hebrew and the Greek. And both impulses had doctrinal and theological implications, as became manifest in the age of reformation which soon followed. But again it is important to stress, with this further example of Brandolini's effort to rewrite the sacred history, that these were impulses that manifested themselves already in the middle and late Quattrocento among the Italian humanists.

5. Return to Allegory: Ficino and Pico

With the development of Renaissance Platonism in Florence in the late Quattrocento, humanist interest in the Bible took a new turn, or rather a return to an older mode of Biblical interpretation with a new content. Marsilio Ficino and Giovanni Pico della Mirandola, the two leading representatives of Platonism, each wrote an important commentary on the Scriptures: Ficino on Paul's *Epistle to the Romans* and Pico on a number of the *Psalms* (No. 6, 10, 11, 15, 17, 18, 47 and 50) as well as his *Heptaplus*, his commentary on *Genesis* discussed above. Since Ficino utilised the *Epistle* as an occasion to discuss and compare the pre-Christian moral, religious and philosophical ideas of the Jews and of the pagans, and to establish their relationship and difference from Christian revelation, we shall discuss this along with his *De religione Christiana* and Manetti's *Contra Iudeos et Gentes* in a later chapter.[150] It was essentially an attempt to show how Paul's statements corresponded with and fitted into his own philosophy, and it did not represent in any way an attempt to interpret the text philologically.

Pico's *Commentaries* had a more mixed character. They have been described and considered in relation to his other works and ideas by Eugenio Garin, who said of them: 'the Biblical text is nothing but the point of departure for digressions of every type'. On the other hand, as Garin indicates, some of them begin with 'a philological examination of the Hebrew, Greek and Latin texts' [*Ps.* 11, as also 47].[151]

Pico, who, as is well known, followed up Manetti's beginning with a very thorough study of Hebrew and the Hebrew exegetical traditions as well as the Cabala, also applied his familiarity with such commentators as Solomon ben Isaac and Abraham Ibn Esdra (whose works were in Manetti's library) to the interpretation of the Psalms. Much of Pico's interest was in the moral exhortation of the Psalms, but perhaps most important were the allegorical interpretations which took him into the metaphysics of the mind, the celestial hierarchies, the structure of the cosmos and especially the condition and dignity of man and his place in the universe conceived in comparable terms to his *Oration on the Dignity of Man* and his *Heptaplus*.[152] There was a deliberate return to the fourfold modes of interpretation that flourished in the Middle Ages and were vigorously maintained by early humanists such as Salutati. But both Pico and Ficino discovered in this formally traditional method of treatment a new freedom of philosophical exploration that offered possibilities of expounding their Christian-Platonist philosophies in intimate contact with the sacred text. Theirs was a more fluid treatment of both philosophy and the language and statements of the Scriptures than occurred or could ocur in medieval theological discussion. But with all their superiority of scholarship and mastery of languages, with their philosophical sophistication and profundity, their attitude towards the Bible was fundamentally closer to the medieval one which looked for the concealed allegorical sense than to the other new humanist tendencies to seek an accurate and literal or historical nd literary analysis of the Scriptures, both as document and as Word of God behind which man could not penetrate.

Both of these approaches to the Scriptures – the survival and renewal of allegorical interpretation, and the application of scholarly, literary and historical norms to the written page – represented complementary efforts to bring the documents of divine revelation into the context and under the control of man's own efforts to interpret himself and his world.

XIII. Humanists on the Sacraments

The Sacraments of the Roman Catholic Church were traditionally and canonically the preserve of the ordained clergy of the Church. Nor was there any lack of learned Churchmen, priests, doctors of sacred laws who were available, well able, and disposed to explain and defend the sacramental traditions and practices of the Church. Nevertheless, the Italian humanists also ventured to write and to speak within this area that was seemingly a clerical monopoly. They did not, for the most part, do so in the role of critics and reformers but much more as apologists and exegetes, as, what they imagined themselves to be, eloquent spokesmen. It was a kind of sacred rhetoric in the hands of laymen, for those who wrote on this subject were for the most part the lay humanists rather than those who had taken sacred orders. They considered themselves as translators and transmitters to the laity of an understanding and an appreciation of the sacred ceremonies and religious acts of their church.[1]

Yet, in so doing, it must be recognised that something new was involved. On the one hand, it was another evidence of the manner in which this new profession of writers and speakers extended their activities into every field of human discourse. On the other hand, there is the suggestion of, again, an over-technicality on the part of the clergy who held aloof from such explanations and writings. But there is the question of levels. The popular preacher no doubt did not neglect to dwell upon and praise the divine virtues of the high religious moments of the faith. But between the exhortations of the masses and the technical discussions of the doctors, there was a gap. No one was reaching the educated layman of the middle and upper classes in a form that was congenial to his taste. Moreover something that is special to the point of view of the humanist or the educated laity comes through in these writings. Just how much we shall see.

This chapter is not an attempt to survey this entire field but to make rather a few salient samplings in an area where the secular eloquence of the humanists ran remarkably free on sacred subjects. We wish to establish its existence and its nature but not its entire extent.

1. On Penance

Sicco Polenton, 1376–1447, a Trentine humanist, active in Padua during the first half of the Quattrocento, a Chancellor of the commune, the author of the first humanist history of Latin letters and of stylistic analyses of Cicero,[2] also was engaged in writing a well-known ribald comedy, the *Catinia*, as well as lives of saints. In 1437 he wrote the *Life and Miracles of Saint Anthony, the Confessor of Padua*; in 1434 he had written the *Lives and Miracles of the Blessed Anthony the Pilgrim and Helen the Nun.*[3] And in 1435 or 36, nearly in his sixtieth year, he wrote four books *On Christian Confession*, dedicated to Pietro Donato, Bishop of Padua from 1428–47. Although we shall use the Vatican manuscript of the work [Vat. lat. 7781], it exists in at least five other fifteenth-century manuscripts, presumably of north Italian provenance.[4]

Polenton's work is thoroughly orthodox, literally dependent on unnamed, but apparently several, handbooks of confessors. Some traces of such earlier medieval works as St. Bernard's *Steps of Pride* are evident. He cites by name Saints Augustine, Ambrose and Gregory.

Polenton, addressing the bishop, and asking him to be his censor, expresses his awareness that this is an unusual field for a humanist.

> But I am not unaware that this is a difficult and wide province which pertains to me in no professional sense but to the greatest doctors of pontifical law and to distinguished theologians and has been dealt with by many of them most fully and learnedly. But although it is doubtless proper to them, nevertheless I hope this will turn out to be as though a collection of flowers from a flourishing meadow made by us from them, and written according to law and with moderation. . . . For I have selected and used nothing from my own head, as the saying is, but only what the holy fathers, what the popes, what the leading theologians felt, but recalled in my own words and order.

In doing this he certainly could not have picked a subject that would be more pleasing to God, better for Christians or more useful to himself, for what better is there than this sacrament which opens the road by which we who are sinners are able both to avoid the harsh punishments of hell and to gain the eternal life we desire? Indeed by confession the sinner is purged of filth if it is done with perfect integrity and the supreme and just God is inclined to mercy.[5]

Moreover he formally states that 'the type of writing will be in the form of a dialogue',[6] and then proceeds to set up a conversation between *Peccator*, a sinner, and *Sacerdos*, his priest, in a Church in carnival time while festivities are proceeding without. Though the form as a dialogue is humanistic it actually has much in common with the Magister-Idiota form of so many medieval textbooks. *Peccator* has very little to say throughout except to ask formal questions and acknowledge satisfaction after he has received a suitable lecture. The dialogue is in four books spread over four days, and the programme is pre-announced at the very beginning. The first day will cover what is confession, why, how and by whom it was first established, how many kinds of confession there are, how much is the force of confession and other things of this sort that ought to persuade one to confession. The second day's 'sermon' will tell how many and what are the mandates of divine law, how many and what are the articles of faith and such; thence what are venial sins and in what ways mortal sins are distinguished from venial. The third day will deal with mortal sins and what their genera and species are. The fourth day, which will be at the end of Carnival, will speak of penance and its parts: contrition of heart, confession of mouth, satisfaction of action. 'For thus you will know both in what things man sins and by what remedies he is freed from sin. And if you observe carefully you will see that in these two consists the entire reason for confessing.'[7]

This work in its literal recapitulation of ecclesiastical formulae and canonical practice stands in somewhat strange relationship to the extent and concentration of general humanist concern with moral philosophy. We have shown in the first part of this book how much Petrarch and Salutati, not to mention Valla, tended to step aside from the formalities and examine primarily the psychological involvements and motivations of individual souls, drawn towards the pettily inane or grossly corrupting activities of this world, seeking to find cleansing and forgiveness in an ever-present divine mercy and grace, as in Petrarch's case; or how in particular Salutati sought to encourage a manful morality despite a lack of any certainty whatsoever that it could lead a Christian to salvation in which he had to trust entirely in divine providence. It is striking to find how little there is of this attempt to get at the actuality of human experience and divine aspiration in Sicco Polenton, and how almost unconcerned he is with the relationship that might exist between a Christianly conceived human existence and the various classical moralities. Yet withal, he is not entirely without the concern with psychology and motivation that is regularly encountered in other early humanists, but it cannot be denied that this is derived as much from his medieval Christian sources as from any other possible ones.

He starts off by a reference to Augustine's definition of repentance in *De poenitentia*, a secret disease of the soul opened up in hope of forgiveness.[8] But he immediately formalises it:

> For he knew that sin is a secret disease of the soul which he opens up to the priest and he gives him hope of forgiveness, which when canonically done, is confession. Indeed this formula is held in a double way, one implicit and general, the other explicit and particular. The priest frequently uses the former especially when he is celebrating mass at the altar and wipes out those sins which are minimal and called venial. The other sin is considered mortal. When the sinner commits mortal sins he should confess these to the Confessor privately and canonically. Certainly both kinds are good and should be understood, but what extinguishes mortal sin is weightier and should be more accurately and diligently considered.[9]

The source of all sin is human pride, and he expands upon this theme, beginning with the revolt of Lucifer and the disobedience of the first parents. Pride persuades men to undertake all sorts of crimes and especially induces them not to fear God by whom they were made out of nothing, not fearing Him, to despise Him, despising, not to worship Him, not worshipping to offend and in offending to sin a hundred times. 'The gates of heaven were long closed to mankind whom God formed in his own image out of his goodness and made almost equal to the holy angels', and they were so tightly closed that no one, not even a good man or a prophet, could enter and had to remain in limbo until the Advent of Christ.[10] The Incarnation and Crucifixion opened the gates of heaven to those in limbo, and Christ entrusted the keys, from then on, to the Apostle Peter for future generations of good men. Christ it was who purged men of their sins and founded confessions.[11]

Peccator inquires whether there was confession among the Hebrews. *Sacerdos* tells him yes: David in the *Psalms*, Moses in *Genesis* and *Leviticus*, and *Job*. He had hoped to spare him details meant only for theologians, but he will go into the origin of confession. The doctors of the Church recognise three kinds: natural, figural, and that of grace. Natural confession was the oldest, lasting from the first parents until Moses. These rude men, living under no law, but guided by the light of nature, silently confessed to themselves in the court of their heart. By the light of reason given to him by God man knew when he had sinned and felt by the light of reason and nature what was fitting, what evil and what was virtuous. The second kind of confession from Moses to Christ was called figural because it prefigured the future kind under Christ. The third kind which is now in use was founded by Christ. 'Certainly if you should hear all things of this sort which are many and infinitely disputed privately among theologians you would perchance become more learned', but he will pass over these details and stick to the general aspects of confession.[12]

Examples from the Gospels and Epistles of Christ and John the Baptist and St. James urging repentance are reviewed. The Fathers of the Church all urged confession. The Church says that all of both sexes should confess at least once a year to their own priest and fulfil the penance enjoined upon them, and abstain from communion if they do not. He does not see why so easy a thing, which saves souls from damnation, should be passed up. 'Certainly the Lord gave this road to all by which any Christian, purged of sins, can ascend to heaven and attain eternal glory, if only he worships Him rightly, knows and believes in the articles of faith, is humble in heart.'

> For what is more easy than to repent of your sins? What more just, what more equitable, what more agreeable than to humiliate ourselves before God, than to obey the Lord and confess ourselves and repent of having sinned? Add the reward, and consider that eternal life is given to those confessing here, than which nothing better can be sought, nothing more wholesome given, nothing more precious had. ... In it you will see God sitting on his throne in highest majesty and you will see the most merciful mother of God, the immaculate virgin Mary, you will see the choruses of angels

and will avoid all the tortures of hell.[13]

The first book continues even further on the impediments to confession to the excommunicate, Jews, heretics, but the tone is, as in this citation, one that emphasises in a pragmatic Pelagianism of ritual conformity how simple and easy it is to rise above sin and attain eternal life. Polenton mixes the technicalities of the canonist in with the exhortations of the preacher.[14]

The second book deals with sins in a predominantly formalistic way. To sin is to violate the mandates of the divine laws or the articles of faith. The divine laws are the ten commandments. The first three apply to God, the next seven to one's neighbour, or fellow man. These are carefully explained and in legalistic detail. Polenton follows through here the casuistic approach that was developed in late medieval canon law without raising a single doubt concerning the multiplication of external rules, but it would be unfair to say that he does not also show a constant awareness that behind them is the crucial question of the attitude of the Christian, whether pious toward God or just towards his fellow. The Articles of Faith are defined as the *Symbolum*, the Seven Sacraments and the rules pertaining to these, the Gifts of the Holy Spirit: Wisdom, Intellect, Council, Fortitude, Knowledge, Piety and Fear of God. Each of these is explained.[15]

Then the theological and moral virtues are reviewed, and the mercies, corporal and spiritual. Sins are then divided into original and actual. Baptism removes original sin, so the actual are of greater importance to a Christian.

> Sin which is actual they consider to be what we ourselves do, not by the guilt of our first parents but when we sin by our own vice and free will. Certainly all sin is voluntary.

There are two kinds of evil, guilt and punishment. Today venial sins will be discussed and tomorrow the mortal. Venial sins are such things as eating too much, using vain words, speaking too much or too little, arriving late to Church, neglecting the poor, engaging in idle games. No man escapes venial sins and every man commits them daily.

> For no man is thought to be so prudent, so modest, so just, that he is able to avoid them. . . . For our life cannot be without sin, at least without venial sin. For certainly the weakness of mankind is too great and the Enemy snares us in too many traps.[16]

Sin is then discussed according to the scholastic distinctions of *suggestio, delectio, consensus* and *operatio*. If it stops with suggestion it is not sin, but if it goes as far as consent without act it can be a mortal sin.[17] He enters into such typical casuistic problems as the following; 'What if a man sins with no deliberation and no delight and no agreement of free will as happens when the cause is fortuitous or due to violence or a certain sudden impulse of the mind or ignorance or forgetfulness?' *Sacerdos* answers that distinctions must be made between mortal sins such as denying an article of faith, which nothing can excuse, but if it is something which cannot be ascribed to mortal sin by its own nature, then the sinner is only subject to venial sin. *Peccator* doubts if men really sin out of negligence or forgetfulness. *Sacerdos* explains that if the negligence arises from contempt it is a mortal sin, otherwise it is venial. Ignorance is no excuse. But really it requires those who are learned in theology to distinguish between mortal and venial sins on all occasions.

> Moreover man was created for worshipping God and for profiting and serving man. They sin venially who, though they desire riches and the goods of fortune do so with moderation and deliberation so that they do not yield nor desire the things of the world more than they worship, love and desire God.[18]

Conscience and the dictates of right reason are discussed. These are the same and to violate them is a mortal sin. But he takes a pretty strict line. To eat meat in Lent is sinful, even if done out of ignorance or when starving.[19] *Peccator* asks 'What if I do whatever is truly laudable and virtuous but I am doubtful in my mind whether it is virtuous or evil?' He is answered, 'You sin certainly if any turpitude seems present on account of that doubt.'[20] A later Post-Tridentine casuistry held that the presence of doubt relieved one of sin. On the other hand, it is not always sinful to act by deliberate will, for a monk who speaks when enjoined to silence sins mortally if it is deliberate, venially if he forgets.[21]

The third book on mortal sins first defines the seven deadly sins one by one.[22] Mortal sins are deliberate violations of divine law or deliberate neglect. All are grave but there are degrees of gravity. The gravest sins are those against the Holy Spirit; those who labour in obstinacy of mind and in despite of truth, who trust too much in divine mercy or despair entirely of it and die without repentance are guilty of it. Those who oppose the patent truth, or who envy fraternal charity, or who promote discord also sin against the Holy Spirit and so displease God that their sins are irremediable in this world and the next.[23] The graver sins are those against nature. The simply grave are the original seven.[24] He goes into an exhaustive analysis of each of the seven sins according to their modes, their species, their affects and their degrees.[25]

Superbia is again considered the worst and may be taken as an example.[26] It is a mortal sin in six modes: arrogance if one thinks he is good but is not, lust for human praise or vain-glory, the attribution of one's virtues to oneself and not to God, boasting of false values, presumption or giving merit to self instead of God, singularity or thinking oneself better than others. The species of *superbia* are contempt of God which can be manifested in many ways but is a kind of elation or contempt of divine things; contempt of neighbour and elation at his misery; false sense of potency or abuse of powers; those who live magnificently and arrogantly. The effects of *superbia* are *excusatio* or not to accept or admit one's faults; *inobedientia* or to despise and defy divine and human law; *despectio* or to despise others and withhold honours from them; *ingratitudo* or to give all credit to oneself.

> For they do not consider that they are given so much wealth and so many gifts by God and by men; they do not consider that they, by the benefit, liberality and grace of God, were made something out of nothing and men not beasts; they do not consider that they were made Christians and not pagans or Jews by the bitter and hard passion and death of our Lord Jesus Christ and are redeemed from the power of demons and liberated from perpetual punishments of hell.[27]

He proceeds to the twelve degrees of *superbia*, which parallel St. Bernard's twelve steps of pride by which the sinner progresses to his downfall. These twelve steps are: *curiositas*, *levitas*, *vana leticia*, *iactancia*, *singularitas*, *arrogantia*, *presumptio*, *malitia*, *impatientia*, *rebellio*, *libertas peccandi*, and *consuetudo peccandi*.[28] Let us look at what he says about only one – *singularitas*, since this became something of a Renaissance virtue, or at least a supposedly admirable attribute of a man of the age in the view of Burckhardt and others, with ample confirmation from the statements of other humanists. Polenton states:

For these do not follow the common life but in all opinions, customs and rules of living are alien to others. Certainly they do not keep in the right way the vigils and festivals the priest indicates. They fast unordered, they sleep the whole day, they are active at night when sleep is ordained for others; they spurn the laws and practices proven by the experience of elders and the good customs of the city they reprove and injure; they introduce certain evil and ridiculous ways of living. What others confess to be good and praise, they openly deny and criticise. Nothing pleases them which is pleasing to others; they live by their own choice and so live that they seem as though they were born, educated and nourished under some foreign sky as alien wanderers in their own fatherland.[29]

What we have reported here in most abbreviated form of his treatment of *superbia* he repeats for each of the other seven sins, borrowing profusely from standard ecclesiastical sources, particularly the tendency to codify and endlessly subdivide into categories which repeat each other from aspect to aspect of a particular sin, and from sin to sin. His fourth book deals specifically with the three parts of penance: contrition, confession and satisfaction. The purpose of the sacrament is to avoid the repetition of the sin, otherwise it is of no avail. Therefore sin must be punished in the self. The three parts of penance correspond to the three parts of sin, contrition to delectation, confession to impudence, satisfaction to pride, and mutually oppose them.[30]

Taking up contrition, it is the true sorrow of the penitent at having sinned, containing in it the purpose of abstaining from further sin, confessing and giving satisfaction for what has been done. It induces: bitterness of mind and sorrow at sin; repentance and shame in heart and soul for offending God and neighbour; the wish to avoid and detect the wickedness of sin; the fear of damnation; the fear of losing the glory of paradise; the hope of forgiveness and grace and glory. To be truly contrite one must not be so lightly, but continuously, and not be content with mere sorrow about one's sin. Contrition has the effect of remission of the sin, purification, the opening of the doors of paradise. From all this it can be seen how formalistically he approaches this subject, and how it comes right out of one of the many Confessor's Manuals.[31]

He runs through all the rules and aspects of confession in a similarly formal way. It should be simple, humble, pure, faithful, frequent, bare, discrete, willing, truthful, whole, secret, tearful, rapid, strong, self-accusing and well-prepared. He discusses the meanings of each of these qualities at no little length showing the kind of moral-psychological considerations that medieval moral theology was so rich in elaborating.[32] Then he discusses the character of the Confessor. Starting from the doctrine of the keys, all clergy are true confessors though in case of necessity confession can be heard by a layman. The legalities are strictly stated here; but in addition the qualities of the man himself count. He should be a good, faithful, learned man, not a heretic, a schismatic, an ex-communicate, suspended, an apostate, an adulterer, a homicide, a drunkard, an Epicurean, live with a concubine, or have any other vices, or be rude or unlearned.[33] Confession best takes place in one's years of discretion which are defined as over seven. All men of all sorts and kinds are obligated to confess – popes, kings, emperors even. No man is without sin, and he cannot be absolved without a confessor. 'For no one lives with such great prudence, reason or sanctity that human fragility does not meanwhile lapse, and often he will offend a neighbour or even the high God.'[34]

The question of whether both venial and mortal sins should be confessed has raised no little controversy among the learned. Some say that communion, the Lord's prayer, episcopal blessing, fasting or charity can eliminate venial sins. Others argue with St. Augustine that all must be confessed. Hostiensis distinguishes three kinds of venial sins. Those of long standing such as drunkenness and lying ought to be confessed because they may become mortal; the other two are removed by the general confession of the Mass. One confession of a sin should suffice. Confession should be at least once a year. It is safest to confess right after sinning. Lent is the best time because it is a time of abstinence, composed mind and religiosity.[35]

The manner of confession is important. It should be in a calm mind after the sinner has carefully thought over in advance and recalled his sins and their circumstances. The circumstances, as is inherent in a casuistic system such as medieval canon law had evolved, were of crucial importance for telling when a sin was truly serious and how much satisfaction should be demanded. Polenton also stresses circumstances and summarises them in the proverbial jingle: *Quis, quid, ubi, per, quos, quotiens, cur, quoniam, quando.*

For the sins we commit should be kept in the memory with special diligence so that the confession may be made integrally, recalling both their nature and considering their degree. For they are large and far more and greater than we think. We go to a Confessor who is a Father and governor of Christian souls and acts as the agent of Christ on earth.

But I confess that God is merciful beyond this. And they do not deny that He is also just and I would say that it is true that those who easily recall their sins should rightly and canonically confess them, and they should have the same diligence in confessing them as they had in committing them, and as every Christian ought, they should desire celestial things more than terrestrial.[36]

This leads Polenton to, possibly, the one section of his work where he seems to look at the men and the world around him. And he enunciates a doctrine which is quite contrary to the theology of faith and grace that nominalism had made popular and was to come to the fore in the following century.

For there is the greatest zeal, the greatest alertness, the greatest care among mortals for increasing and retaining the riches of this world, but so many of them when they regard divine matters care for them little as though superfluous and vain and almost neglect them entirely, and they have the highest confidence in the mercy of God. And they hear that He is entirely pious and merciful and seeks life not death for the sinner. They think they satisfy the Church if they only go to the confessor and on bended knee they say those sins which either occur to them or the confessor inquires about.

Therefore, they should not rely on an easy access to grace, and confession should be undertaken with the greatest of seriousness and concern.[37]

It is inquired whether all arts are sinful. Although there are those whose purpose is the worship of God or the virtuous use of the life of man, nevertheless according to the place, time, mode, form, cause or person in which they are done, they are sinful and unvirtuous. Others invented for pleasure or lust, forbidden games, unjust wars are by nature sinful. All human crafts and professions are full of deceit, fraud, selfishness, whether the farmer, the merchant, the craftsman, the man of learning and profession. Lawyers, magistrates, prelates, rulers of all sorts mistreat their subject or cheat their clients. The rich and noble gamble and seek pomp and glory, and lascivious pleasures.[38] Polenton's complaints in this passage may be compared to Facio on the dissatisfactions of all walks of life in his *De felicitate vitae*, or to Poggio's views in his *De miseria*. In this rather extended description he seems more in the frame of mind of many of his contemporary or later humanists. It recalls Petrarch's *De remediis* also, of course.[39] But the purpose, here, is to assert the absolute necessity of the sacrament of penance with its important part of confession as the one, yet easily available, corrective to the universally sinful life of mankind. Therefore it is necessary for the one confessing to give all the circumstances to the Confessor so that the latter can judge adequately the gravity of the sin and give a penance properly adjusted to it.[40]

This brings him to the final part of penance, satisfaction, which he treats somewhat more briefly, speaking of the types of penalties imposed in the most general terms: fasting, charity, prayer. There are three kinds of abstinence: from food, from the affection causing the sin, from pleasure. Questions such as whether confession and satisfaction without contrition is valid are raised with the obvious negative answer. Or are lapsed sinners forgivable? Polenton leans towards severity here.[41] But as *Sacerdos* says on these matters:

> Little questions of this sort, which in my opinion we are now discussing, are a thousand thousand and almost innumerable, and if we continue to pursue them you will find them multiple and infinite. For the books of the most learned theologians are full of these questions. The reasons for confessing are indeed infinite, and every disputation and doctrine which exists in sacred letters can be dragged into it. And what many learned and serious men who have spoken accurately on this question have decided is true, since they have explained much and they think that nothing remains beyond what they have said, so that no one can say everything about this question on which they are found to have said so much.[42]

Thus even Polenton seems finally to have felt the excess of formal detail against which Erasmus and other humanists protested.

Bartolomeo della Fonte also wrote about the sacrament of penance some thirty or more years later than Sicco Polenton's dialogue.[43] This little work of Fontius presents some interesting contrasts with that of its predecessor, although more perhaps in the form of the argument than in the content. It, too, is a dialogue, but between himself and the eminent Florentine humanist-statesman Donato Acciaiuoli, rather than the *Peccator-Sacerdos* of Polenton. It is written in a much more elegant literary style and dedicated to Giuliano de' Medici. We shall discuss its content and the ways in which its argument differed from Polenton's presently.

It is of a certain interest, however, to note that this work passed through at least three versions before Fontius arrived at satisfaction with it. Probably the first version was written in 1468, or the winter of 1469, after he had returned briefly from a stay at the court of the Este at Ferrara.[44] It had originally been intended for Giovanni Vitez, Bishop of Strigonia [in Hungary] from 1456–72.[45] After his death, Fontius changed the dedication to Giuliano. But this earlier version circulated in three triplet humanist manuscripts retaining the old introduction and wording but also titled *Ad Julianum Medicem.*[46] In 1478, he prepared a version for printing and it appeared in its definitive version in three incunabula of Florence of that year. He also included it in his autographic manuscript of his works sent to Matthias Corvinus in 1489, and it is this version that we shall follow.[47]

However, there seems to have been still another earlier version contained in an Ashburnham manuscript owned by the Pandolfini family.[48] This has many corrections in Fontius' own hand, possibly added at a date posterior to the acquisition of the codex by the Pandolfinis. It corresponds to the earlier triplet version, but it also has two pages of text carefully crossed out [doubtless by Fontius] and four additional folios cut out of the manuscript between these two pages.[49] In other words, the work originally contained five folios or ten pages of text he wished later to eliminate. From what can be deciphered of the cancelled portion, and also from the fact that part of it corresponds verbally with a letter written by Fontius to Pietro Fannio 15th October 1472,[50] it is possible to determine that the missing passage contained a description of the tortures of the impenitent souls in Tartarus based on classical accounts of the underworld. His letter complains that some thought these *fabulosa dicta.*[51] At any rate he saw to it that this version did not circulate and removed the offending passage from the Pandolfini copy. Judging by the letter the passage also contained an argument on the immortality of the soul.

In his definitive version, the *Donatus seu de Poenitentia*, 'Fontius' comes to the house of 'Acciaiuoli' on the morning of Good Friday. The latter, surprised at his appearance when he should be at home mourning his sins, is asked to explain penance to his protégé. With some reluctance 'Donato' agrees. He starts with the opposite of penance, which is sin, just as Polenton also discussed sin. Sin is quickly summarised as venial and mortal. Venial sins are easily removed but mortal sins are the death of the soul, not the death of obliteration, for that never happens, but of separation from God. It is at this point that Fontius included the passage on the torments of the unrepentant in Hell which he later excised.[52]

Leaping quickly from this truncated treatment of sin to penance itself, he announces that he will speak of what it is and its qualities, and then of how necessary and useful, finally how distinguished. Penitence comes from having the punishment, *poenam tenere*, which one inflicts on oneself for having committed a sin. 'But if anyone is affected by this sorrow over errors, for which he should mourn not only lest they be committed in the future but also that he might acquire some greater grace by new merits, this man will always also act rightly.'[53] 'Fontius' will not pass over, but neither does he develop the traditional division into compunction, confession and satisfaction.

> Although also in the meantime if either the priest or the one to whom the injury must be recompensed is lacking, it still can rightly be done. For God does not require the work of lips or hands, if we are not able to perform them, but only the will. For it is in the judgement of the heart and the intention of the will and mind that true penance consists.[54]

This declaration of the essentially inward character of the sacrament, although it does not deny the propriety of any of the forms, is certainly a far different approach from Polenton's, and one that seems more consistent with the humanist tradition of moral thought with its emphasis on inwardness. Although this anti-formalism in some ways anticipates the Reformation attack on the sacrament, it differs from the Reformers in a way that, perhaps, should be considered representative of the humanist position, namely to leave the forms and doctrines standing but to shift the emphasis on to inwardness of feeling and the direction of the will.

After this dismissal of the necessity of the external forms, 'Fontius' is prompted to inquire whether there is any penance which is not true?

'Acciaiuoli' follows this up by a further attack on formalism, asserting that, yes, there are three kinds of penance, two false and one true: that which is out of fear, or out of ostentation, or out of love.

> But by far the worst of all are the simulators of penitence that they might seem most saintly to others. For these in order that they might be thought good men, depart far from their duties, pronounce their prayers with a clear voice in the temple, now bow their bared heads, now lift them up, quaver in voice and tremble so that under this appearance of virtue they may more easily deceive all. But indeed this is not penitence but a certain fraud for deceiving men that should be called contempt of God. For not such deceptive garb, not the scraggly beard, not short hair or eyebrows, not the eyes bowed towards the ground, not false tears, not artificial pallor but simplicity of heart, sincerity of soul constitute true penitence.[55]

This passage, of course, is an echo of the humanist criticisms of the hypocrisy of the clergy such as Bruni's and Poggio's and others, which we mention in our next chapter.[56] But this is also closer to the later Erasmian spirit of stressing true but unostentatious feeling rather than the externalities of canonical form.

Penance done out of fear is also condemned, but with less vehemence. For if it is done out of fear, it may in time grow into love. But if it does not so develop, it is inane and sterile and playful. 'For what proceeds from fear alone is strengthened by no faith, hope or charity. Therefore it does not clear the conscience, nor dissolve the crime, nor bring out any forgiveness.' For if the fear of penalty is taken away the sin is immediately resumed.[57]

The third kind, proceeding out of love of divine virtue with great zeal and emotion, is perfected by pure purpose of mind. It grows from faith, hope and charity and leads to eternal beatitude. The woman in the Gospel who kissed Christ's feet and washed them with her tears and dried them with her hair was intended to show the true contrition of heart and contempt of earthly things with which penance should be done. 'With mourning, therefore, and tears, and simplicity of heart and humility of mind and true confession of sins, and restoration of damages to God if we are not able to make them to men, true penance is to be performed.'[58]

Penance, moreover, is easier to acquire than other virtues which are gathered only over a long period with great trouble. For one act of fortitude does not for that reason make one called strong, nor one act of justice just, nor of modesty or prudence, modest and prudent. 'But has anyone once been truly converted? he is truly also called penitent. For this does not require an exterior action, but the will alone.'[59] On the other hand, forgiveness should speedily be sought for our sins. 'For God who promises forgiveness to the penitent does not permit a prolongation of time. Indeed nothing offends Him so much as if, when we sin, we are proud and elated and rigidly do not bend in order to seek forgiveness.'[60] And we should not wait for old age to set in before ending our sins, for who knows the hour of his death? Although he who lives a lifetime of sin can gain forgiveness from God in the moment of his death, this happens but rarely. Of thousands who live evilly but one good man emerges.[61]

In this manner the oration or humanist sermon proceeds with many of the stock themes urging the reader to penance. Although he had eliminated the passage on the tortures of hell, possibly because it was contradictory to the argument that penance should be out of love not fear, he puts back the same theme.

> Have before your eyes the perpetual tortures of hell and compare this time with them. We wish briefly to mourn that we may rejoice perpetually. Let us extinguish the flames of lusts with penitence that we may flee from eternal fires. . . . This present life is brief compared to eternity even if it lasts a thousand years. . . . What, I ask, do riches and pleasures now profit those who always live in evil gratifications and lusts? . . . Therefore let us not be delighted by the fragile and temporary goods of the body and fortune but by the perfect tears of penitence which surpass all in virtue. That you may more easily do this and seek the kingdom of God, God should always be kept in view and the earthly things, which are fleeting and changeable, despised, bending your entire soul towards heaven, nor caring greatly for life, but seeking beyond it for the truth, which is God, or for God, since necessity demands it. In the first place God's commandments are to be obeyed. . . . Moreover, who accepts His word more than he who corrects and mends himself? This is His true and proper word, so that whereas meanwhile we cannot not sin, when we fall, we may be raised up, and we recall ourselves from guilt.[62]

He is led to urge that the examples of holy men be followed, and these are to be found in the Scriptures, which tell of vices and virtues, duties, despising of death, punishment and reward, God and much else.

> But there are certain persons of such perverse custom that they wish to hear, read or approve of nothing unless it gratifies the ears with a smoother sound. To them the Lord will rightly say on that last day, Depart from me all who are Christians and have neglected to read the Scriptures. But, although divine writings ought to be bare and simple so that all may openly understand what is written for the salvation of all, nevertheless we have certain ones also whose language is not uncultivated and whose style is not unrefined. For, as I pass over others in silence, what greater elegance or ampler eloquence can be desired or found than in what is written by Jerome, Augustine, Ambrose and that most learned of Christians, Lactantius?[63]

Thus Fontius prefers the typically humanist Christian models of the Latin Fathers to the compilers of the handbooks and the scholastics that formed the meat of Polenton's dialogue – and if need be to the Bible.

He now considers that he has amply covered the question of the nature of repentence and passes to the second part of his dialogue: 'we now briefly expound the reason why we judge it to be far more necessary than the other virtues.'[64] This is immediately to put a sacrament of the Christian Church into the category of a discussion of the moral virtues, even though it is to be preferred to the others. Penance comes to be treated as a virtue rather than as a sacrament, and indeed with his emphasis on its depending solely on will and inwardness he has already so treated it.

Since the weakness of human nature is so great that we are unable to carry on life without sin, even in those most eagerly pursuing virtues, sin can be dissolved, not by gold, silver or gems, but only by penitence. 'For if anyone considers the reason of his faults, is sorry for having committed them, professes his iniquities, humbly seeks forgiveness, mends his error, corrects the guilt, all will immediately be forgiven him.' Our redeemer and saviour Christ said, 'Ask and it will be given you, seek and you will find, knock and it will be opened.' And He said 'I did not come to call the just to repentance but sinners.' 'And come to me all ye who labour and are heavily burdened and I will remake you.' Thus without penitence no one can be saved. Therefore it is the most necessary of virtues.[65]

It is also the most useful virtue, for that is most useful which brings the greatest reward to mankind. But what is richer or greater than salvation, and for this repentance is necessary. Expanding on this he comes to his final part.[66]

> Since therefore we see from these things that repentance is the cause of the salvation of souls, than which there is nothing better, or more desirable, or happier to be found, for this reason it certainly is to be judged without any dispute as better than any other virtue. But now we begin to argue what we promised would be re-asserted in the last place, that it excels all other virtues.

His point of view is quite simple. Repentance contains in itself all other virtues, therefore it excels them all. Just as the whole body of man is superior to the head, shoulder, back, hand and so on taken separately, 'thus the virtue in which all other virtues are conjoined excels all'. Certainly justice is in the penitent because he renders to each what is his due, and without the reparation of sins he would again fall into injustice. Prudence is in repentance 'because through recollection of past actions he wishes and does nothing but the right nor can he be again deflected into any vice'. Temperance is in it because he does not exceed the law of moderation and submits his desire to the yoke of reason. Fortitude also is in it because he excels in magnanimity, constancy, forebearance and firmness. For he can be compelled to sin by no force nor frightened by any iron, fire, torment, hunger, thirst, sickness of the body from his purpose of acting rightly.[67]

'Acciaiuoli', however, is willing to add more to his argument, as a liberal vendor adding something to the just measure.

> Any other men engaged in business or in leisure with great merit and praise have some vice joined to their virtue, so that, as Horace rightly held, the best can be thought to be he who is least pressed. The penitent alone is ornamented with the signs of all the virtues and excludes all vice from himself. For as I pass over other Christians who are innumerable, in what crime were either Peter or Paul contaminated after they had rightly done penance? For when were they afterwards bibulous as Cato, greedy as Aristotle, lascivious as Plato, ambitious as Cicero? O penitence, since you are all in one body and the school of all the virtues, what further can I say about you?

With this we can break off his much lengthier peroration.[68]

Certainly the character of Fontius' approach to this most central Christian sacrament is radically different from the still very legalistic treatment of Sicco Polenton, although even Polenton does grasp the centrality of penance as the key to the moral and spiritual life of man. But Fontius brings it much more clearly and sharply within the purview of humanism's concern with the moral virtues and with the responsibility of the individual for his moral destiny. What is notable about both these treatises, however, is their easy, almost blatant Pelagianism. All men are subject to sin, but it seems as though these sins are for the most part venial. But even where they are more serious, it is like choosing of one's own free will to repent. True, love is necessary, and faith, hope and charity. But none of the tremendous difficulties and doubts that fill the pages of Petrarch are present here. It seems all very simple and clear, and perhaps it necessarily was and had to be as an escape from the complex network of minute distinctions and casuistry with which they were surrounded in the moral theology of the canonists of their time. The external forum of conscience so characteristic of medieval Christianity has been abandoned both in Petrarch's and Fontius' discussions. Moreover, Fontius' work was hortatory. It was translated into the vernacular and there called a sermon.[69] And all sermonising has an implicit Pelagianism in it, otherwise to what avail the exhortation? But here the emphasis on freedom of will is central.

Accordingly, the typically humanist stress on the will, rather than on knowledge of the distinctions of theology and canon law, is also present in Fontius. Simplicity of heart, goodness of will – this is lay piety of the sort that we find in another and later lay sermon, Erasmus' *Handbook for a Christian Knight.* Much of the same elements are present such as the positive exhortations to piety, but not the sharpness of criticism that is in Erasmus. It is present but played down and mild. The casting of Donato Acciaiuoli in the role of the lay counsellor is also important, as this figure had the utmost respect of his generation as a man of the greatest moral solidity, and he was a leading humanist Aristotelian withal. He was indeed Fontius' mentor, as a long letter citing a private sermon to him, which I have quoted elsewhere, makes very plain.[70] Whether or not the lay piety of Erasmus was derived from Italian humanism, its prevalence in Italy from the beginnings of the humanist movement may not be denied.

2. On the Eucharist

One of the most remarkable religious statements of the Renaissance was the brief sermon of Lorenzo Valla on *The Mystery of the Eucharist.*[71] For the occasion was one where rhetoric might alone have filled the need of the day. Yet Valla attempted instead, not a metaphysical, but an epistemological analysis of the doctrines involved in the Transubstantiation of bread and wine into the flesh and blood of the Saviour, so that man's faith in the sacrament might be vindicated. And he did this not by arguing, as some Protestants later did, that this miraculous action was merely symbolical, but demonstrated rather that it had fully as much basis for human acceptance and belief as any of the most central aspects of the Christian faith, or indeed of some aspects of ordinary human experience.

It is a short and tightly argued piece, and we shall follow it in close detail, without literally translating it, but offering our own commentary. It is completely consistent with the notions he developed in his *Reconstruction of Philosophy and Dialectic*,[72] depending on a close and literal observation of human experience to prove the necessity of a separation of rational philosophy and theology from faith. Mystery is equally involved in the small and in the large.

Venerable fathers and distinguished citizens speaking in this place have many times held this sacrament in admiration while they attempted to explain and show how much divinity and how great a miracle it is that 'the bread which is baked by us from wheat by the force of the divine words pronounced by the mouth of priests is transformed not only into a man but, what seems to surpass all intellect, into God'. He too will praise this as all who can ought, but to investigate it and render the reason for it is reserved to the most few wise men. If he can give no probable explanation why the bread is converted into God, he should not be thought to be lacking in religion or divine knowledge. For this is not a matter of knowledge but of faith. And we believe God, by faith, in the same way as we believe a friend whose truth we have previously known and explored. In other words, faith in God and faith in friends are analogous, but even more their basis is the same because in each case it rests on previous experience and trust rather than knowledge. 'Whence it is written "Blessed are they who did not see and believed", as though they did not know and believed. For what does anyone see that is hoped for? For he does not believe another but in his very self.' When it was said of Abraham that he had believed in hope beyond hope, it meant that Abraham believed in God and trusted that this would be counted for him for justice, 'thus it will be counted by us for justice if we will have faith beyond faith'.

Therefore the first attitude that was necessary towards the sacrament was a faith in it that was a trust in God that carried forward also in hope.[73]

But he feels he can offer a more specific reason for having this faith. It does not seem so incredible that the bread is converted into God, 'although I don't know whether it is bread into God or God into bread, God, nevertheless, existing'. If God exists and one has faith, then this is not incredible. For it does not differ from our faith that the Word was made flesh, which it is said, but not that the flesh was made Word. Elsewhere Christ said 'I am the bread of life which descends from heaven.' 'Now before the sacrament of the Eucharist He called Himself bread as though He would convert himself into bread. That is He will give himself for bread.' How should this be interpreted? 'The Son of God coming into the world assumed from the most immaculate body of the Virgin, I do not know if I should say, "flesh".' For the body comes from the flowering of flesh rather than is itself flesh. But flesh is made out of food, and from what food, certainly from bread. And since it is not to be believed that the most holy Virgin lived on flesh, 'Thus it happened that first it was bread, thence it was flesh that the Lord was derived from while he was Incarnate. In this way by the soul He animated men and likewise filled them with divinity.' The miracle of the Incarnation was bread become the flesh of the Lord which is paralleled by the miracle of the animation or life of mankind, and, thus, man's divinisation. The next step of his reasoning towards the explanation of the Eucharist becomes immediately obvious.

> By the same process He converts the bread of the sacrosanct altar into His own flesh, that is, He infuses man and God. Therefore I do not see that this incarnation in the altar rather than that transformation in the womb of the Virgin is more difficult of belief or more miraculous.[74]

He turns immediately to a further problem. The Incarnation happened once but the Transubstantiation happens many times in many places and even simultaneously. But this, he says, is a different question and does not apply only to the Eucharist. How could Christ appear both with the Apostles in Jerusalem and with the Disciples on the road? How is He both in heaven and among men? He does not try to answer this as he does not wish to fly beyond his powers but offers more moderate examples. Why is his voice simultaneously in all your ears? How do the rays of the sun strike both the roof and the floor of a house? How is it we can see the sun reflected both on the roof and in a jar of water at our feet? Likewise you cannot affirm that what will be done will happen. 'Who does not know that one man cannot see in different directions at the same time? Likewise we may believe in a picture which is an image of a man and nothing can happen in it which does not happen in the man, but still it may be seen in many pictures.'

> There are many things of this sort to be wondered at in human and corporeal things. How much more marvellous things we should think there are in spiritual and divine matters? Will we ignore, with reason dictating, that God is everywhere and all is in God? Nor is it possible that all things which are in Him do not persist through Him through Whom they exist. Therefore whoever has any doubts about the advent of God in the mystery of the bread seems to be considering not the divine nature but the weakness of man. Therefore God must be thought, felt and spoken about with greater courage than we do if we call His omnipotence into doubt.[75]

This argument is not just the usual appeal to the feebleness of man but rather one that questions the possibility of going beyond the literalness of both words and factual observation, in the manner in which Valla has also shown he wished the Scriptures to be interpreted. To him miracles are no more of a problem for rational explanation than human knowledge itself.

Having shown what he is able concerning the transformation of God into bread or of bread into God, he will now make the praises of God he had promised. But again this does not turn out to be an ordinary rhetorical exercise but is further laden with doctrine. What greater gift can God give us than Himself, and that before we have reached paradise? Did He not wish to be called 'Emanuel' which is God with us? If He is with us, where else would we wish to go? But He does not present Himself to us as manifest divinity, since we are not yet capable of contemplating the divine majesty – as we shall later in paradise. So although we see Him now through a mirror as in an enigma, yet we have Him for certain as defender, elder and protector, and not with us only but within us. 'Can anything more desirable be said or thought than that God is touched by the hands of men, or placed in the mouth, or stored away in the depths of the breast? And He will remain there, a pure and mundane guest of our house as long as we serve Him.' Thus he turns the symbolism of remembrance into the literal image of the physical possession of God within ourselves, as far as in this world it is possible, and in this way gives the utmost spiritual meaning to the Eucharist. Jesus Christ established this sacrament with His disciples when he promised to be with them always at His last supper with them before His death, and He promised that nevertheless He would never leave them, and if they substituted this sacrament in His place, He would always be present. He not only by His ascension gave Himself to the angels in heaven, but remains here with us.

> O ineffable, not only mystery, but gift given to mortals for although we are equal with the angels in that we and they possess Jesus Christ, yet in this we ought to be considered superior, because out of our own mouth, which is not permitted to the angels, this sacrament and mystery is wrought.[76]

He continues here to develop the humanist theme of the ascent of man above the angels, which has its beginning in man's possession of the sacrament of the Eucharist which it has been given to him to perform.

> He is truly called Emanuel, God with us, since He is more with us than with the angels. Nor only from this fact, namely that He is also more similar to us than to the angels, but from this it may also be known, which God shows among pious and not disbelieving minds, that just as He transforms that bread, so he transforms us in the day of judgement into God.

We are His members, as He is the head of the whole body. 'What shall I call man, who, nourished from bread, made from dust, ascends beyond the heavens and becomes God?' This is demonstrated and promised in the Eucharist, a Greek word, called the host by the Latins. What does the action of grace of this sacrament truly signify? Either that Christ, received with the bread in our hand, asks thanks or that we in receiving Him must give thanks to Him. Therefore by daily giving thanks with this sacrament we shall one day give thanks to the Father along with Jesus Christ, to Whom we owe thanks for all the graces among which is the gift of His Son.[77]

Remarkable in the tightness of his argumentation, Valla has managed in this statement to turn the problem into a consideration of the subjective elements of faith in the Eucharist. This is something that Valla consistently does when he deals with religious questions. For him there is no possible transition or connection between a rational demonstration and an act of faith. Doubtless any, and other, statements on the Transubstantiation which take the form of a sermon must make their appeal on a subjective basis to the faith of the congregation and to the benefits that they must believe it confers. And Valla is not unique in grasping this inherently rhetorical aspect of the situation. But what gives his statement its peculiar distinction and also makes it characteristic of his mode of argumentation is the discussion of the logic of faith, of the subjective logic that is involved in faith. Thus he avoids ecstatic emotional appeal by presenting a quiet conviction and an intellectual statement that lifts the audience to an acceptance of this miracle if they are to accept any miracle, and the acceptance of this particular miracle because it is shown by Valla to be so centrally appropriate to the daily commemoration of the essence of the Christian faith, which is the Incarnation. He manages further to elevate the listener into an identification with the very miracle he is observing, and in communing with God through the Eucharist to gain the sense of not the host alône becoming God, but of man becoming God, so that man, himself, is the ultimate miracle in whose presence and whose future life, Valla urges, he must have faith.

There were many other humanist sermons on various religious subjects, some of which have come down in scattered sources. We know of the importance of the lay religious associations, such as that presided over by Ficino, described by Kristeller,[78] and in Florence there was active humanist participation in these sodalities or confraternities. Perhaps it was not an unusual thing for a layman to preach a sermon to such an association, but certainly the gathering of so many humanist sermons in the two manuscripts already described by Kristeller is exceptional. Among these sermons in the Riccardiana and Strozzi manuscripts there are several by humanists on the Eucharist, the Lord's Supper and the *Corpo del Cristo*, including ones by Cristoforo Landino, Donato Acciaiuoli, Alemanno Rinuccini and by that indefatigable spokesman of the humanism of the younger generation, prophet and follower of Savonarola, Giovanni Nesi, whose sermons in these collections outnumber all the others, and were delivered when he was a very young man indeed.[79]

The sermon of Cristoforo Landino 'in commemoration of the body of Christ and recited in the Company of the Magi' contained in the Riccardiana manuscript is undated.[80] Although his purpose is essentially homiletic and rhetorical, Landino had some compilation of theological judgements and interpretations of the Eucharist close by and gives, himself, an abbreviated exposition of doctrine in addition to exhortation. This renders his sermon more loquacious and possibly less effective than that of Donato Acciaiuoli on which we shall also comment. This sacrament, he begins, gives man the chance to flee arrogance and to gain Christian humility. It has been established to enable us to put aside the cares of the world and gain a contrite and humbled heart. It offers us, through its reminder of Christ, the unique example of humility that his sacrifice for us was, and it comforts, exhorts, commands and constrains us not only to humiliate ourselves but to become prisoners. 'It informs our minds that putting aside any investigation which seeks a demonstration and knowledge of things through syllogistic arguments we should submit to faith alone with sincere and ardent charity.' In contemplating this sacred mystery of the descent of the true and holy body of Christ into the consecrate bread, not by natural but by supernatural means, sincere, undoubting and constant faith should be our guide.[81]

But in turning towards an affirmation of faith, Landino cannot resist reporting the discussions of the *fidelissimi doctori delle sacre lettere*. These are divided into two principal parts: what is the essence of the sacrament, and in what way it is sacred. The first part is subdivided into three parts: what it is, by whom it is received, and whether it contains the essence of the species in the accident of the bread. They again divide the question into the dignity of the sacrament, its institution or origin, its integrity and perfection. Its dignity is demonstrated through its efficacy. Its institution establishes in what hour and form Christ established the sacrament, but also 'why the Church in celebrating it does not observe this hour'. The third is really the proper ritual procedure of the sacrament.[82]

The second major heading – in what way it is sacred – is also subdivided into the questions of how it was instituted, what happens, and what is its form. Its institution raises the question of whether the bread and wine was consecrated under both the Old and the New Covenants, or if it was fittingly pre-figured in the Old Testament, and if it was fittingly established. Because of the brevity of his time he will discuss only three questions himself: first the *grandezza* of the gift in itself, secondly the miraculous effects it has on us, thirdly how the abuse of it leads to damnation.[83]

With this rather formal introduction, which pays a surprising degree of attention to the doctrinal discussions he professes to pass over in favour of an exhortation to faith, he is ready to offer his own exposition. The not-so-much liberty, as the charity of the Creator towards His creature, was so immense that we are not only unable to express it but even to conceive it in our minds. The sublimity of the descent of divinity into this vile species of animal is even more striking when we consider how rare it is for mortals to spend their riches on a friend and that it is almost without example for them to sacrifice their own life.

> Indeed I say that if you wished to die for a friend you do not first become a horse or a goat but in the human species in which you were created you go to your death without degenerating into a viler species which is not human. Now look within your own breast and recalling your mind as much as you are able from visible to invisible things, consider how inexpressible it is and how much sublimity there is in the divine majesty, and see that it is so much more noble than the separate substances and the angelic natures that no comparison can be made, because between the infinite and the finite there is no measure.

The angelic nature is immortal, free of disease, discomfort and pain; it lives without perturbations of soul in perpetual felicity without the least pang of misery. Yet Christ descended beyond this into a man. 'He not only became a man with the so miserable conditions of humanity, but He even chose the lowest status of human life, deprived of treasure, poor, lacking in friends and laborious.' He was tempted, maligned, mocked, tried and condemned to death by the envy of princes and priests, and what a death! He suffered bitterly for hours between two thieves.[84]

> It did not suffice for the infinite clemency and charity to expose His most precious body to death for us most ungrateful sinners a single time. From that time He continued to do so through the unique remedy for our salvation by deigning through four little words spoken by any vile priest to descend into the host.

He made of it a food and nourishment which alone maintains the spiritual life of the soul. But it cannot be considered by natural reason and requires firm faith to believe what Paul the Apostle saw when he was raised up to the third heaven.[85]

After this general plea and reminder that the communion was the perpetuation of the Incarnation and Atonement, Landino returns to a more technical discussion derived from the theologians. In the bread of the host, the food is its substance while the taste, shape and quantity are its accidents. After the words *Hoc est corpus meum* are pronounced by the priest, the substance becomes the true body of Christ, but the accidents remain the same and do not change. Although he has told us that the divine mind is inscrutable, he proceeds to explain God's reasons for this procedure and the nature of the sacrament. First, if Christ returned to us in His own form we should be deprived of the merit of faith. Second, no one presumes in this life to see the glory of Christ. Third, although this argument would seem to deny the possibility of the original Incarnation, he holds that our unworthiness makes it unfitting for Christ to come in such a form as his own. Fourth, Christ glorified is so splendid that we would be blinded as by the sun. Fifth, we could not eat such a human body without error and caprice of soul. Therefore the substance changes in an instant without any succession of time and the accidents remain. We observe that Landino has retained the type of medieval theological argument that deals in literal and logical deduction from basic doctrine rather than engaging in the more subjectivistic discussion of the nature of faith in the miracle of Transubstantiation that Valla offered, which to a modern reader, at least, seems to avoid the naïveté displayed by Landino and to be more rhetorically effective. But Landino proceeds, echoing the metaphysicians, to argue that the instantaneity of the transubstantiation is not nullified by the Aristotelian-Averroist metaphysics of change.

> Moreover every interval of time which is in the transformation of one thing into another proceeds as Averroes says in the *Metaphysics* either from the resistance which the thing being changed makes or from the distance between the thing changed and the one who changes it. But nothing can make resistance to God, nothing can be far from Him. Therefore the change made by Him is without interval of time.

The most happy Christian has merited this admirable gift although unmerited. None of the fathers of the Old Testament foresaw this great mercy but it was prefigured by Melchizedech's sacrifice of bread and wine, in the paschal lamb, and in the manna of the exodus.[86]

Thus in presenting the first part of his own exposition – on the greatness of the sacrament – Landino has given at least equal emphasis to a reassertion of scholastic theological arguments in the midst of not overly-forceful rhetorical pleas, and this despite his assertion that faith, not syllogistic reason, was essential. His second part on the benefits to man of the excellence of this sacrament follows more usual humanistic lines in stressing the goal of human fulfilment and happiness which cannot take place in this life and which requires this sacrament to assure it for the next. The proper and first office of man is to investigate how to gain the *summum bonum* in which lies happiness. But nothing leads to the highest good besides this most holy sacrament. Therefore there is nothing more useful to man. Persuading more by argument than exhortation he proceeds to point out that we are made of body and soul, one is mortal and the other is immortal. It is easy to prove that happiness does not lie in the body. Because the body loses its being, it is the sum of misery, not happiness. Therefore happiness is in the soul, 'which is then happy when it returns to the highest which created it, contemplating His majesty, and in contemplating gains fruition, and in its fruition feels ineffable and eternal joy'. He proceeds to dwell on the uncertainties and sufferings of this life.

> And certainly not having in this mortal life a stable city or certain domicile, we are in continual pilgrimage and journey in order to arrive in the celestial fatherland in which, as the Apostle said, we are not strangers but citizens with the saints and members of the household of God.

Thus our souls without the divine food of the ineffable sacrament cannot be conducted to the desired goal if they are not strengthened by it through the mediation of divine grace. The word *Eucharist* is Greek and means good grace. Original sin in man is wiped out by the sacrament of Baptism. But as every generated animal needs food, so our regenerated soul needs this divine food of the Eucharist. This comparison inspires him to carry it even farther; Baptism, Confirmation and the Eucharist are comparable to the three powers of the vegetative soul: namely the generative, the augmentative and the nutritive.[87] It is apparent that Landino cannot resist bringing into his sermon all sorts of fragments that he had collected from scholastic and clerical sermon sources, as either a kind of intellectual pretentiousness or else as a manifestation of a certain lack of discrimination and rhetorical sensitivity.

His third part on the abuse of the sacraments seems also to fall at times into triviality. He makes the generally known point that the communicant should approach the sacrament in a purified and purged state of soul – presumably after Confession. No one of us, he says, is of such rude habits and 'so alien to any urbanity' that he would invite even his most vile friends to dine with him without his house being clean and neat, the table laid in linen, the tableware clean and polished, so that whoever comes will feel no offense. Thus our souls must also be clean as they are to be the receptacle and vessel of the One who made us. Those who throw the host into unclean souls sin more than those who would throw the host into the mud.[88]

None of the patriarchs, who in many other ways possessed the Holy Spirit, had the benefits of this sacrament, which is reserved to you Christians alone, since Christ Who created you died to dissolve your sins.

> Thence O unheard of clemency, O ineffable charity, if a thousand times a day He dies on account of your sins, rescuing you by the mediation of this sacrament, truly it is by the *Eucharist*, that is good grace. This recalls to the memory the passion of Christ. This confirms our faith. This increases hope. This inflames charity from which we may acquire all the other virtues. This gives grace to life. . . . This, taken with penitent and contrite soul, purges our mind and frees it from all human passions and places it in such a condition that while it passes through this valley so full of calamity and misery it lives always joyously. No other means such as the abundance of present earthly goods makes such enjoyment as this possible. . . . He is not afflicted who finds himself in calamity. And finally he does not grow arrogant through prosperity, nor does he despair through adversity. But established in perfect mediocrity he lives the better part and renders praise to God. And then having arrived at the end of his mortal body he passes on to eternal glory towards which He who created you, who then died in order to create you once again, through his infinite mercy, leads you and me. Amen.[89]

Notable as it may seem to find another leading humanist engaging in a sermon or disquisition on the Eucharist, though actually this seems to have been fairly common, it is perhaps the doctrine that Landino puts forth that rather requires comment. Valla's sermon was a reasoned plea for faith, and a demonstration of the congruity and centrality of this sacrament within the Christian life and outlook. Landino's statement is more diffuse, less focused and concentrated, but none the less, he

13—IOIAL II

seems to stress in contrast to Valla the objective, magical, though incomprehensible, aspects of the sacrament which seem in a more literal way to sustain a man of faith and humility in a state of earthly joy and heavenly fulfilment. Landino, with his recapitulation of the traditional theological arguments, but even more as he reveals it in his own statements and rhetoric, holds to the more traditional view of the sacrament as ever objectively there and available for salvation, as almost facilely to be seized upon.

Donato Acciaiuoli preached his sermon on the Eucharist before the Company of the Magi on 13th April 1468.[90] Whether he preceded or followed Landino, it is impossible to say. The structure of his sermon, however, to some extent parallels that of Landino. Acciaiuoli eschews any kind of doctrinal treatment of the sacrament, and wishes to make it a statement expressive of his own piety and moving for his audience. And unlike Landino, he keeps his word in this. But he does present two parts, the praise of the dignity and excellence of the sacrament and the statement of its benefits – apparently a standard mode of treatment. He omits Landino's third theme of the abusers of the sacrament, and instead ends with a prayer.

Acciaiuoli, however, differs markedly in the tone and in the forceful, yet smoothly flowing, concentration of his disquisition. He possesses all the rhetorical virtues that Landino seems to lack, and in possessing them gives a sense of clarity and deep conviction. He does not dwell on the aspect of the faith that is necessary for this sacrament, although he refers to it, but rather he convinces by manifesting it. In beginning he says that if he could speak with every part of his body as though it were a tongue he could not express the least part of this most sacred mystery, therefore he prays for the aid of grace to give him sufficient *ingegno* to be able to satisfy his audience's desire for consolation. The sacrament represents to him the most important mode by which Christ reinforces faith in His doctrine, as it is a commemoration of the divine Incarnation by which and through which Christ became the great teacher of mankind.[91]

> Our saviour Jesus Christ, my beloved Fathers, having so greatly benefited human nature by first assuming this our flesh and then through all the course of His life in teaching the people and spreading his doctrines among readers,

in freeing the weak and raising the dead, in removing sins and in most holy works gave Himself as a most singular example of every kind of virtue.

Christ as the teacher and exemplar was a conception of Christ that was most congenial to humanists and is reminiscent of the conceptions of the northern Brothers of the Common Life and their most famous students Thomas à Kempis and Erasmus. Acciaiuoli continues,

Finally approaching towards the hour of His passion, as a benign teacher, he wished to leave to his disciples and to faithful Christians a memorial full of every charity, full of such great delight, that there is no intellect which can sufficiently consider this; and if it is said to be a most grand sign of friendship when friends consider all their things to be in common, how great an indication of love and benevolence did our Lord show in sharing not only His possessions but even Himself according to the truth of his saying: 'Who eats my flesh and drinks my blood remains in me and I in him.'[92]

Thus Acciaiuoli takes the sacrament back to its evangelical origin as a love feast, and a memorial and a manifestation of the magnitude of divine charity.

He knows, however, that beyond the Scriptural events there has been much analysis, but this he leaves aside. We know there have been

many subtle investigations which the doctors have made concerning its matter, its form, its efficient cause and its final cause, and how the substance of the bread and the wine is transformed into the most true body of Christ, and how the accidents remain without the subject, and many other speculations which the most subtle theologians have come to investigate.

Leaving these aside he will be concerned only with the two themes mentioned above, its dignity and its benefits, as more fitting to the occasion.[93]

Again he invokes divine aid in speaking of the excellence of this sacrament 'which increases the force of human genius'. Jerome's saying about the Apocalypse that all praise is inadequate is appropriate here.

Moreover, considering the marvellous works which are in the universe and turning the eyes towards the heavens and thinking of the beauty of the sun and the moon and the stars and all the superior bodies, and running through the earth to consider the variety of things both animate and inanimate, of rational and irrational animals, of their perfections in their degree, there is no one who does not remain stupefied. But this admiration ought to turn much more towards considering the supreme excellence of this sacrament which exceeds the creation and surpasses all created things. For in speaking of this sacrament it should be understood that here is the most true body and soul and divinity according to the truth of the Scriptures which say it.[94]

This argument is a *topos* used effectively by St. Augustine who argued that the miracle of the world and man himself made other greater miracles comprehensible; it is not unlike Valla's argument for faith in the Eucharist if there is faith in Christ and the Incarnation. Acciaiuoli develops this by quoting the New Testament – 'What once He assumed He never puts aside.' 'Humanity and divinity being together, that is Christ Himself, what excellence can be conceived or imagined that can be compared to that.' Then he quotes St. Augustine directly, 'Who among the faithful can have any doubt that in the very hour of sacrifice at the voice of the priest the heavens open and in that mystery of Jesus Christ the choruses of angels are present.'[95]

He adds also the same argument that Landino used, concerning the overwhelming glory of Christ that needs the commoner form of the Eucharist to be received by man, but he does so with a different and more persuasive turn to his word.

If it were possible, beloved Fathers and Brothers, that through divine grace there might be manifested the splendour of that most Holy body and the glory of the Saviour as most faithfully we must believe is in that sacrament, what sense would not remain confused? In contemplating the height of divine counsel and of this most worthy sacrament, it is therefore necessary to approach it with faith and with the intellect.

Space does not permit him to dwell longer on this the most excellent of all the sacraments.[96]

As for the benefits of the Eucharist, he lists the various ways in which it has been named: *communion* in respect to the faithful present together communicating in Christ; *viaticum* as the road towards man's future fruition; *eucharist* which means 'good grace' either for the future or because it really contains Christ who is full of grace; *oblation*, victim, host, sacrifice in respect to the most sacred passion in which the immaculate lamb offered Himself as a sacrifice for our salvation; *memorial* since it is a commemoration by which we show our gratitude for the great benefit of our salvation. Singling out no one of these, but showing how the name itself implies the doctrine in a philological rather than theological approach, he says,

> All these names have the signification of the gracious effects in which faithful Christians may come to participate if they are well-prepared to receive this most worthy sacrament. Therefore this is the fountain of graces, those which give strength to our souls, which sustain life and render it victorious over vices and sins, which render souls quiet and tranquil; and if in this life there is any happiness, it makes them happy and gives almost a foretaste of the strongest beatitude.

But ultimately it is the daily return of Christ to man in the sacrament that he stresses, quoting 'What is man that Thou remembrest him.' Our ancestors of the Old Testament never had these given except by means of similitude and figure. He lists the commonly cited prefigurations in Melchizedech's sacrifice, the manna of the desert, the paschal lamb. 'This is what is called the food of angels. O most happy Christians who are made similar to the angelic hierarchy. . . .'[97]

He turns at last to deliver a beautiful prayer for light in men's intellect, contrition in their heart, love in their will so that they might participate in the eternal benefits of the sacrament and arrive at last at the supernal glory of rejoicing in eternal happiness and beatitude.[98] One cannot doubt the depth and sincerity of Donato's own faith which he was able to render public in this elegantly wrought sermon, with its coherence, restraint, rationality and piety. Here is without doubt an example of an Italian *devotio moderna*, fully in the spirit of the humanistic studies towards which Acciaiuoli was equally devoted. Moreover, the doctrinal content is essentially evangelical and pious, rather than doctrinal, metaphysical, or theological. And yet he was, as is known, an Aristotelian and spokesman, perhaps, of Argyropoulos' interpretation of the Stagirite, shown recently by Garin to have shared certain attitudes also expressed through Ficino's Platonism.[99]

As I stated in beginning this chapter, the above are but samplings of a large literature, possibly as diversified and unwieldy as the corpus of medieval and Renaissance ecclesiastical sermons. To these disquisitions on the sacraments, whether offered in the more literate form of a dialogue or delivered directly as a sermon – *theologia rhetorica* in the most direct and literal meaning of the term – there should be added the considerable number of saints' lives written by humanists, to some of which we have already made reference.[100] Moreover, to this employment of the humanist historical skills in sacred, as well as secular, biography, there may also be mentioned such meditative works on religious themes of great contemporary popularity as Mafeo Vegio's *Meditations on the Four Last States of Man: Death, Judgement, Inferno and Paradise*.[101] Our next chapter will deal with the humanists' treatments of the condition of being a member of a religious order, and Mafeo Vegio also wrote a large work in that category,[102] though I do not discuss it. This figure, who became a Canon Regular of St. Augustine at St. Peter's in Rome, is a case in point. The works just named were possibly more literate repetitions of conventional religious themes, but intended to be inspirational, rather than technical. We have seen how our selected works on the sacraments tended to move towards a recapitulation of the technical analysis of the sacrament and the hortatory, and we shall in a moment return to discuss the significance of this. Mafeo Vegio, however, a friend of Lorenzo Valla, also employed his talents in a rather unique endeavour to elevate the cult of St. Augustine and his mother, St. Monica, by writing sacramental commemorative services. He also did the same for San Nicolò Tolentino, Celestine V, and San Bernardino of Siena. Thus he created an additional genre of religious literature supported by his humanistic scholarship and sense of literary form.[103]

Humanist writing on the sacraments and related sacred subjects may be regarded in two ways: first it was the entirely expected entry of a new class of professional writers and scholars into an area that was an important and normal part of the contemporary culture. In turning to these themes they might be expected to add a certain literary grace and cultivated elegance to subjects that had long been dominated either by the ecclesiastical technicians or had been developed as part of the popular sermon literature by preachers and religious leaders. And the humanists borrowed freely from the analyses and arguments of both these categories of their predecessors. Doubtless the two works of Sicco Polenton and Cristoforo Landino that we have discussed illustrate this aspect.

But there was a second and more important aspect that has come out in the other contributions we have examined. The very fact of their commitment to rhetoric, philology and the language arts led some of them to a new kind of religious emphasis. Since they were less interested in establishing technical theological niceties or the objective sacred significance of the sacraments than they were in moving their readers and listeners to a receptive and believing state of mind, they were led to stress in the very content of their dialogues and sermons this personal, subjective and psychological aspect of the meaning and importance of the sacraments. Thus we have seen that they emphasised the will, faith and the credibility of the miraculous nature and effects of these established sacred rituals. In the case of Fontius on the subject of penance, the external and fixed rules of procedure are accepted as valid but then dismissed as unessential. Penance is regarded as a state of mind, and, where it is psychologically valid, as springing from love rather than from fear or ostentation, it is also religiously valid and effective. He brings it, moreover, into the context of humanist moral philosophy by discussing it as the greatest of the virtues since it includes all others and yields the greatest reward, namely salvation.

What was true in his case seems also to have been true of Valla and Acciaiuoli; along with an emphasis on the importance of the will [or the will to believe] went at least a rhetorical Pelagianism which regarded the will as free or easily swayable by their writings and arguments. Grace lies within the sacrament of the Eucharist and is freely available to all who approach it in charity. Thus there is the paradox of their position which relates them on the one hand to the Reformers, and particularly Luther, who regarded the subjective as religiously central, but on the other hand to the sacramental revivalism of late medieval catholicism which shared in the inherent Pelagianism of the Ockhamists. In fact this dual stress on inwardness and free will must be interpreted as the unique characteristic of their special approach to religion. It clearly differentiates them both from the common ecclesiastical culture of their time concerning which their approach was implicitly critical and from those future Reformation views which regarded the individual as needing to be subjectively related to religious verity through faith yet at the same time regarded the process as tightly determined by the over-powering divine will.

The humanists were anthropocentric in their approach to the miracle of the sacraments rather than theocentric in either the nominalist way of God's *potentia absoluta*, or in the Lutheran or Calvinist ways. In their approach to the sacraments, as in their approach to other *studia divinitatis*, their employment of the *studia humanitatis* predisposed them to positions which corresponded to their predominant conceptions of man as voluntaristic and active and to their consistent and persistent concern with the moral conditions of man and his place and status within the universe. As the latter flowed, as we have sought to show, from their reiteration and renewal of the traditional exegesis of *Genesis* which stressed the centrality of man's position in the creation and the restoration of his dignity with the Incarnation, so in these two sacraments of penance and the Eucharist the role of man in the recovery of his dignity through the varieties of grace that was inherent in their establishment as consequence of the Incarnation again comes to the fore. It is difficult and essentially arbitrary either to separate the humanists' views of human nature from their peculiar approaches to religion, or on the other hand to do the reverse.

XIV. Humanists on the Status of the Professional Religious*

Not only have we seen how the Italian humanists, deeply religious in their outlooks, (though undoubtedly there were some who could not be so described), were of the conviction expressed apologetically by Salutati that the *studia humanitatis* had a vital contribution to make to the *studia divinitatis*, but we have also examined their actual ventures into two of these fields of religion that were formerly the almost exclusive preserve of the clergy – that of Biblical studies, and that of disquisitions on and exhortations towards faith in the sacraments. Some of them entered these areas hesitantly and others (always Valla) boldly; but hesitantly or boldly in their manner, the consequences were revolutionary in the two senses that laymen had invaded the traditionally sacrosanct area that was the responsibility of the clergy alone as the arm of Mother Church, and that as humanists these laymen gave a new form and a new content to the ways in which these fields were previously treated. Moreover, as (for the most part) lay men of learning committed to the rhetorical tradition newly redefined as the five *studia humanitatis*, the humanists had found it essential to incorporate their more humanly centred approach to learning, which sprang both from the nature of their arts and from the concerns of ancient classical moral philosophy in which they were steeped, into their completely Christian vision of life.

We have seen, therefore, in Part I the attempted reconciliation of human existence as they themselves experienced it – as primarily

* The following chapter reprints with slight modifications my earlier paper: 'Humanist Treatises on the Status of the Religious: Petrarch, Salutati, Valla', from *Studies in the Renaissance*, XI (1964), pp. 7–45, with the kind permission of the Editors.

sensuous, affective and voluntaristic – with the two intellectual traditions which were of meaningful concern to them – the classical and the Christian. Not only were these intellectual traditions, but in both the emphasis was on the superiority of the intellect as a faculty of human nature. Thus Petrarch, Salutati and Valla among the early humanists polemicised against both classical and scholastic intellectualism and found as their primary support in their argumentation the earlier patristic Christian tradition, especially the will-centred theology of St. Augustine. Thus I have argued for the centrality of a Christian conception of man in humanist moral theology (as I have called it). This Christian conception, essentially Augustinian and generally patristic, they found harmonised more readily with their own experience of human life and history and with classical moral philosophy as it was expressed by the great representatives of the philosophically-minded Latin rhetorical tradition – Cicero and Seneca principally. But one of these three humanists, namely Valla, found ancient philosophy, even when embedded in the rhetorical tradition, as distasteful as its presence in medieval theology among the scholastics. Moreover, as we have seen, both Petrarch and Salutati as well found themselves at certain moments at odds with classical philosophical thought.

Moreover Part II has demonstrated, I believe, that humanist anthropocentrism, whether exalting the dignity or bemoaning the misery of the human state, found expression in two corresponding literary genres – the *Dignitas hominis* and the *Miseria humanae conditionis*. In these they revived a Christian exegesis of the creation and the Fall of man which in its patristic origins was also heavily influenced by an ancient amalgam of Platonic and Stoic thought. We have claimed, possibly rashly, that this humanist tradition formed the essential background and cultural conditioning for the more philosophical assertion of the theme of the dignity of man and the discussions of man's place in the universe by the Platonic philosophers of the late Quattrocento and even in some respects for the rebellious Neo-Stoic representative of Paduan Aristotelianism, Pietro Pomponazzi. But we do not claim that the centrality of a patristic Christian conception of man in humanist moral philosophy excluded them from dealing with many other peculiarly secular aspects of moral thought; nor do we claim to be the first or only scholar to have examined the ideas of the humanists within a religious context.

Due attention has long been given to *philosophia moralis*, claimed as the fifth *studia humanitatis* by Italian humanists from the early fifteenth century, and as such a subject properly theirs. Scholars have been interested in 'The Moral Thought of Renaissance Humanism'[1] (as Professor Kristeller entitled his recent survey) primarily for the special attitudes of humanists toward 'man',[2] toward 'nobility',[3] toward 'wisdom',[4] toward 'happiness',[5] toward 'civic'[6] activity and good citizenship. They have paid attention to attempts the humanists made to reconcile ancient philosophies with Christianity, principally those stemming from Florentine Neoplatonism. They have emphasized the scholarly activities of the humanists in editing and translating patristic writing – Latin and especially Greek. Less interest seems to have been shown in those humanist treatises that dealt directly with traditional medieval problems of ecclesiastical morality or with questions of Christian religious thought – not to call it 'theology' – or in the devotional writings and lay sermons of the humanists. In saying this, I am not forgetting the many contributions such as Garin's short but penetrating surveys (published in 1948 and in 1952 and reprinted in 1961 in *La cultura filosofica del rinascimento italiano*[7]), or Kristeller's judicious summary in the fourth lecture of his *Classics and Renaissance Thought*.[8] Nor am I unfamiliar with the sweeping interpretation of humanism as essentially a chapter in the history of Christianity made by Toffanin and his followers. The contributions of Angelieri, Buck, and Seidlmayer are also of importance.[9]

The present chapter is an attempt to discuss in greater detail than is usual the content of three of the more important humanist treatises on the question of the position of special sanctity or meritoriousness granted emphatically and traditionally to the members of religious orders during the middle ages. These three authors, whose philosophies of man and God were the subject of Part I above, – Francesco Petrarca, Coluccio Salutati, and Lorenzo Valla – were, moreover, certainly among the more important and influential – I hesitate to add representative – humanists. But whatever the impact of their authors, these treatises do illustrate how much the question of the value of their kind of secular existence and scholarly activities in comparison to the life of the religious, so generally granted superior value, was a matter of persistent concern to the humanists. As will also become evident, they illustrate the variety of ways in which the life and status of the regular clergy could be viewed by humanists with, at the same time, perfect consistency with their humanistic or classical allegiances.

1. Petrarch's Advice to the Brothers

One rightly starts with Petrarch's *De otio religioso.*[10] In many respects this work is extremely traditional in its view of the status of the regular clergy. It does not in any way suggest that the monastic life was defective or inferior or even simply of equal value to life in the world. The status of the monk is regarded as both easier than that of the layman, because its objectives were more clear and it was more sheltered, and at the same time more strenuous, since the 'retirement of the religious' was a withdrawal from the world in order to do battle. Petrarch several times called the monks *militia Christi*, a notion that might be contrasted with Erasmus' criticism of monastic formalism in his *Enchiridion militis Christiani* written for a definitely secular Christian knight.

As in so many of Petrarch's writings, his meanings and intentions are revealed in his comments on his own relationship to the situation. This treatise was intended as a 'thank-you-note' to the Carthusian monks of Montrieux (Provence) with whom he stayed in January 1347 on a visit to his brother Gerardo, a member of this house.[11] Because at that time he had hurriedly passed over what this visit was to mean to him, he hoped to pay the tongue's debt with his fingers, if not more graciously, at least more durably. And to avoid the disease common to preachers of being both loquacious and deaf, he proposed so to modify his style that it would be a sermon to his present self and a letter to the absent monks, 'although, as I will confess it, in the most and greater part I am present'.[12] Thus, as in his *Secret*,[13] he again sets forth an ideal to which he subscribes but to which in his own life he does not or cannot conform. 'Listen', he tells them, 'rather to what I am saying than examine how I am living.'[14]

Although there is no evidence that he was ordained as a priest, Petrarch enjoyed the living of a number of benefices granted to him as a kind of ecclesiastical patronage of his literary career. But he never actively filled the priestly office. As Wilkins has shown,[15] in most respects he thought and acted as a layman. In this treatise, however, he took the opportunity afforded to preach, not so much to himself, as he proposed, but to the Carthusian brothers he addressed. Passing quickly from the troubles and perils of life in this world, introduced by citation of the penitential Psalm xlvi, he dwelt at first upon the theme *Vacate*, rest ye, retire, withdraw, urged on the brothers as having for its goal, not war, but eternal peace. Unlike the Aristotelian teaching that one labours for the sake of rest, here one rests for the sake of rest.[16] 'Among others labour is sought for the sake of labour, among you quiet for the sake of quiet.'[17] He develops this opening theme rhetorically with many urgings and warnings against the temptations of life.[18] 'Love not the world and those things which are in it, for all is lust of the flesh, lust of the eyes, and worldly ambition; therefore Augustine [cf. *Confessions*, bk. 10] warns and informs us of these; but there are infinite other sayings of this kind for the counsel and consolation of souls.'[19] He repeats a great many of these. Then he turns to the traditional list of admonitions drawn from so many medieval pastoral works such as Gregory I's *Book of Pastoral Care:* let it be said to the greedy; let it be said to the lustful . . .; let it be said to the melancholy . . .; etc. 'Let it be said to the penitent, "Joy will be in heaven over one sinner doing penance" ',[20] and many more. Each of the individual counsels appropriate to the particular sin or sinner is drawn from the Scriptures. He advises the brothers to avoid all danger and not to test their own powers of resistance, for they are arts of the adversary. One step follows the other upward or downward; in this he follows St. Benedict and St. Bernard. 'Have your profession before your eyes, keep your vow, fulfill the rule; if you do this easily, it is sufficient.'[21] Each brother should know and beware of his own special weakness. 'Anger tortured this one, lust this, pride elevated another, *accidia* depressed that one.' Just because you are in the camp of Christ and under the best leader, do not think you are safe. Avoid especially the three great enemies: the snares of the world, the enticement of the flesh, the artifices of demons. Thus for twelve long pages in Rotondi's edition he has clung to the traditional hortatory formulae.[22]

Reference to the enemies of the monks leads to their war with Satan and the need not to flee from the victor to the vanquished. Here the humanist and historian of the illustrious men of Rome can add something special. 'We read in secular histories', Petrarch says, 'of the mockery of Labienus, who leaving the victorious Caesar crossed over to Pompey. . . . How much more justly should he be laughed at who, deserting Christ the most victorious king, flees to'[23] Satan? Then pointing out that military commanders try their troops in battle in order to know their qualities, so our Commander also tries us, although He knows us, that we may come to know ourselves and not, blind and ungrateful, attribute to ourselves powers that are His. To support this thought he quotes Cicero, 'O immortal gods, for I attribute to you what are yours. . . .' This gave him the opportunity to insert in a long parenthesis one of his apologies for Cicero's use of the plural 'gods' and a statement of his admiration and hope for Cicero, despite his paganism, because 'he had taught how the invisible things of God are seen through those which are made'.[24]

He then requotes the Ciceronian passage in a paraphrase after quoting a passage on the dangers of servitude to demons in St. Augustine's *De vera religione*, a work which Petrarch had been constantly citing, though following only somewhat freely. ('Et Augustinus in eo libro quem sepe hodie in testimonium arcesso – loquenti enim de otio religioso, quid opportunius quam *Vere religionis* liber astipuletur?)[25] Cicero can offer great consolation in keeping up the struggle against the powers of darkness.[26] And the great insecurity of life came not only from the threat of spiritual powers but from unforeseen calamities and the unexpected deaths of temporal existence. Therefore, he urges the brothers to constant vigilance, to avoid the enjoyment of peace, to 'choose war, not indeed for its own sake but for Christ's glory and eternal peace' (this time agreeing with the Aristotelian saying he earlier spurned). And he urges them to this by 'an example drawn from the gentiles' where not only Cato but Appius Claudius and Quintus Metellus warned lest 'security, *otium*, and quiet overturn what fear, *negotium*, and trouble kept in full vigour'.[27]

Next the enemies are dealt with, and this leads him away from the traditional temptations of the world, the flesh, and the demons to the realm of faith and doctrine. Men do not worship ivory, wood, or golden images of God.

> Nevertheless, in our own age, we see so many believe in them, that . . . the gold and silver gods, whom ancient kings, instructed by the words of holy priests, tore down out of reverence to Christ, are eagerly renovated today in

injury to Christ by our kings and prelates. If indeed this is so, although they do not worship silver and gold as gods, . . . nevertheless, gold and silver are cultivated with as much reverence as Christ Himself is not, and often the live God is despised out of admiration for inanimate metals.

And it is no better to succumb to the madness of worshipping Hercules the furious, the homicide Mars, the adulterer Jove, or the thief Mercury.[28] A careful reader of the writings of their worshippers can discover for himself what the greatest prophets and the *Institutes* of Lactantius[29] tell us, that these gods are demons. Nor should we listen to those who have no faith in Christ and still expect a future Messiah. The destruction of Jerusalem, described by Josephus, should convince us of the justice of God's punishment of the Jews for their impiety and lack of gratitude.

Enough on the Jews. What more? should we listen to the dolorous fables of Mahomet, or the quarrels and inscrutable ambiguities of the philosophers, or the poison of the insolent Averroes, . . . or, perchance, the sacrileges of Fotinus, the trifles of the Manichaeans, or the blasphemies of Arius? And if all those things are far away from wholesome hearts, if neither the most miserable error of the pagans, the obstinate blindness of the Jews, the hateful madness of the Saracens, the windy sophisms of the false philosophers, nor the devious and exotic dogmas of the heretics touch or delight souls or offer scarcely any hope, what should we regard, what do, what port should we seek in the shipwreck of this life except Christ in Whom all cast the anchor of their hope.[30]

And thus the monks are exhorted to renewed faith in the infinite mercy of God Who sent Christ His Son to dwell among us.

This leads to the discussion of the Advent, predicted both by Isaiah and the Erythraean sybil. Both Lactantius and Augustine testified to the agreement of the Biblical prophecies and the sybilline. And the great age of the sybils – dating back to the time of Romulus and to even before the Trojan Wars – cannot be doubted.[31] Then citing the well-known passages from Vergil – *Eclogue* IV, 6, 7 and *Aeneid* VI, 789–800 – he added:

This, indeed, religious and pious reader, although spoken of Caesar, rather concerned the Celestial Emperor, whose advent was preceded by signs in all the world. Hearing these, the poet, not aspiring higher, applied them to the advent of the Roman emperor, than whom he knew none greater; if the true light had flooded his eyes, no doubt he would have applied them to the other. Now indeed to us, thanks to Him who even so undeservedly loved us, all these things are clear without any external witnesses, and the rays of divine light so overflow the eyes of the faithful that there is no blind man who does not see in his mind the sun of justice, Christ, and although by truth itself, it has been most truthfully said: 'Blessed are the eyes which see what you see.'[32]

Those who knew Christ in the flesh are next compared with the subsequent generations who must know Him by faith, and he gratefully follows the books of St. Augustine, 'that standard-bearer of the City of God', in refuting the doubters and the enemies of the faith.[33] Thus in his own day rustics are seen firmer in faith than the apostle St. Thomas and not demanding to see the nail holes and the wound. And on the other hand, considering the condition of mankind, it is a blessing that 'although the Son of God punishes as a judge he also shows mercy like a father'.

Behold our weakness is before our eyes always and we do nothing which does not warn us of the human condition and misery. Some have written whole books and others fine treatises concerning this. Pliny in the seventh of his *Natural History* briefly touched on this but in excellent style and a florid richness of sentences. And Augustine dealt more widely with it in the *City of God*. Concerning it Cicero above all filled the book of his consolation. There was also some impulse in me to say something about this.[34]

From all this faith lifts us. 'Therefore rejoice, human nature, from the extremes of misery made happier than you could become by [your own] nature alone.'[35]

In this Petrarch subscribes to the Christian-Augustinian view of history as occurring within the context of divine providence and the salvation of mankind in the fulness of time. How does this view relate to the new secular conception of the succession of antiquity, dark ages, and modern times, which the late Professor Mommsen found adumbrated in Petrarch's *De viris illustribus*?[36] That Petrarch was himself aware of this question is shown by the fact that in continuing the passage just quoted he makes use of the occasion to differentiate between the kind of knowledge that antiquity affords and what can come only from Christian faith.

Heed this, O men of literary talent, listen, Plato, Aristotle, Pythagoras; not that ridiculous circuit of souls and vain metempsychosis, but rather the secret of true salvation is hidden here.

Varro, Cicero, Demosthenes, Vergil, and Homer are also thus addressed.

> You have left us much concerning clouds, rain-storms, lightning, winds, ice, snow, tempers, hail, much on the nature of animals, the power of herbs, the qualities of things, much, finally, concerning the heaving of the sea, the quaking of the earth, the motions of the heavens and the stars, sharply disputed and subtly treated. But in what ways heaven may be joined and united with earth, this alone of all you did not see. . . . Between heaven and earth, certainly the distance, I confess, is great but finite, between God and man infinite. . . . Certainly it is well known that in some of your books God is preached and His Word, and much about the highest point of faith and the co-eternal persons of Father and Son, which is in agreement with the evangelical Scriptures, according to Augustine, namely, that, 'In the beginning was the Word, and the Word was with God, and the Word was God.' And that all was done through Him, and without Him nothing was done. But how that Word became flesh, how joined to the earth it dwelt in us, this the learned Plato did not know, as Jerome said, of this the eloquent Demosthenes was ignorant.

The real point of difference was over the incarnation. Plato is alleged to have said, 'No God is mingled with men', but Seneca spoke better who said, 'God comes to men, no mind is good without God'. But neither knew that the one true conjunction of divinity and humanity was the incarnation.[37]

After a brief discussion of the exact nature of the incarnation and a warning against the possibilities of heresy latent in a faulty understanding of it,[38] Petrarch returns to addressing the monks. Ending his digression concerning the enemies within the world, he now warns them against the enemies within their walls. There is the danger of diffidence and of their resolution breaking down over particular arguments. He discusses how these should be met.[39] It is important to have models for behaviour, and as Jerome said, every group has its own sort of princes.

> The Romans may imitate as leaders the Camilluses, the Fabriciuses, the Reguluses, the Scipios. Philosophers may propose to themselves Pythagoras, Socrates, Plato, and Aristotle. Poets may emulate Homer, Vergil, Menander, Terence; historians Thucydides, Sallust, Herodotus, Livy; orators Lysias, the Gracchi, Demosthenes, Tully. And now we come to our own: the bishops and priests may have as an example the apostles and men of apostolic times. . . . We, moreover, have provided as our princes Paul, Antony, Julian,

> Hilary, Macarius, and, as we return to the truth of the Scriptures, our prince is Elijah, is Elisha, our leaders the sons of the prophets! Thus, brothers, those who were Jerome's leaders are your leaders; further we have Jerome, himself, and Augustine and Gregory, and all those anywhere who for love of Christ, by leading a solitary and eremitical life have been known to have been distinguished by religious leisure.

Significant in these lists is the fact that the monastic heroes, both his own and those taken from Jerome, were all patristic or Biblical rather than the well-known medieval founders of monastic orders and the medieval saints. The monastic heroes are derived from antiquity just as those of the generals, philosophers, poets, historians, and orators were. However, he does refer to the fact that he discusses others in *De vita solitaria*,[40] and later in book II he makes a reference to the example of St. Francis' struggle against *voluptas*.[41] With five more pages of exhortation to the monks to follow these leaders and to have faith and not to need the evidence of miracles, the first book ends.[42]

We must even more hurriedly pass through Petrarch's second book. He first presents his version of the miseries and evils of worldly life and of contempt for the world. He dwells on the downfall of all past human greatness.[43] Where is Babylon? All is change and decay. 'As it may be said with Heraclitus, we enter the same and a different city at the same time. Into the same city twice we enter and do not enter.'[44] 'O mournful and unhappy transformation, all into worms and into serpents, all at length fell into nothingness.'[45] It is salutary to watch funerals and to open recent graves with rotting corpses. He takes full advantage of an opportunity to quote Cicero, Seneca, and other ancients on the miseries of life and the evils of sensuality. He carefully avoids quoting any of his numerous medieval predecessors on this theme – as if he wished deliberately to show the value of the classics for such strictly religious rhetoric.[46]

The late Professor Mommsen in another brilliant study showed how Petrarch was the first to restate the ancient choice between paths of virtue and vice as illustrated by Prodicus's story of Hercules at the parting of the ways (transmitted by Xenophon and quoted by Cicero, Petrarch's source). Professor Mommsen points out that this passage was unique and that elsewhere Petrarch considered virtue as coming from divine grace rather than within man's choice.[47] This is true of this treatise also, for here he argues that all paths to happiness are false except trust in the strong right arm of God. ' "Blessed are all who trust in Him." Indeed true confidence does not arise except from virtue. . . . And by knowing that "the salvation of man is vain, in God we shall do virtue, and he will reduce our enemies to nothing"; this is our salvation, our virtue, this our security, this our unique remedy against the anger of God – to retire, to hope, to fear, to pray "lest in His fury he condemn us, lest His anger accuse us".'[48]

For present purposes this most limited exposition must suffice. Petrarch here views the monastic life not so much as separated from the life of the worldly but as the safer and more fully religious way. He apparently felt no friction between his own way and that of the monks, only admiration and a few regrets. His treatment is fundamentally hortatory and rhetorical, perhaps showing that the classicist's rhetoric could outdo the medieval preacher's, though Petrarch also uses much of the latter. It is in his second book, which I have treated so lightly, that the classical models for bewailing the mutability and fragility of human affairs – the life outside the monastery in the world – show their mettle. Yet even in Book I, where the state of life and the conflicts within the monastery walls are the main stress of his sermonizing, he falls back mainly on the classical Christians for support – on Augustine, Lactantius, and Jerome. Moreover, he shows little sense of any distinction between asserting the truth of the Christian vision on the basis of faith and revelation and exhorting the monks to stand firm in their religion. To be religious seems to mean quite simply to be a religious; this appears to be in this treatise as true for Petrarch as it was a commonplace of the medieval outlook.

On the other hand, Petrarch's concern for a release from the responsibilities and distractions of worldly existence for the sake of peace of soul and literary productivity, as set forth in *De vita solitaria*, is well known. In *De otio religioso* Petrarch called *De vita solitaria* cognate in purpose[49] though there is no direct allusion to an *otium literatum*. It should not be forgotten, however, that he writes his treatise from without the walls and from without the order, if not as a layman technically (since he was a non-serving member of the secular clergy), at least in the spirit of a layman. And it would thus seem that he accomplished what he set out to do, to write a sermon to himself, so that he could well be religious without being a religious. If this distinction between having faith and leading the life of a member of the regular clergy tends to be blurred, it could mean either that only the professional 'religious' was a true Christian and man of the faith or, on the other hand, that the layman could be just as much a man of faith except more exposed to the world's dangers and distractions. This would seem to be implied in Petrarch's attitude expressed in this treatise, and it would mean that the privileged and special position of sanctity and merit granted to the religious in medieval Catholicism was being diluted and that the difference between layman and regular clergy was becoming one of degree, or lesser degree. It did not occur to Petrarch to allude to the special sanctity and greater merit of the religious because he was not prepared in any sense to attack or to ridicule them (as later humanists were to do), but by the very fact of not alluding to this or affirming their special status except in admiring the comparative safety and serenity of their conditions of life he was contributing to an eventual challenge to the notion that the professional religious were inherently more meritorious or more pious than lay Christians.

2. Salutati's Humanistic Apologia for the Religious Vocation

Another important humanist treatise on the life of the regular clergy was Salutati's *De seculo et religione*.[50] This is a lengthier and more systematic treatise, one that was more traditional than Petrarch's in its explicit exposition and acceptance of the doctrine of the higher degree of sanctity and merit in the life of the religious. Book I of thirty-seven chapters runs to eighty-seven pages in Ullman's edition and deals with the dangers of secular life. Book II of fifteen chapters runs to seventy-nine pages and stresses the advantages of the religious. Much of it seems, as Ullman at one time apparently felt,[51] conventional and rhetorical, a good example of how a humanist could turn his talents to any mode of eloquence with relative indifference to the subject matter or the point of view. Salutati was so important and influential a figure in firmly establishing the new humanistic disciplines in Florence that historians seem to demand that his ideas conform to those of some of his famous protégés, or at least show more apparent consistency.[52] Where they do not, sometimes an effort is made to discount or explain away those that do not fit. Even though this work was relatively early (Ullman dates it c.

1381), let us bear in mind the precedent of Petrarch's contradictory writings and not be too hasty to give Salutati a split personality or to disbelieve his sincerity when inconsistency is encountered. It is not exclusively medieval to be religious, and Salutati's religious notions may well be regarded as perfectly consonant with his humanism. His ideas from work to work and even within the confines of a single work may very well also be inconsistent. This is not a completely unheard of occurrence in the history of thought. On the other hand, the fact that a man is a humanist i.e., a rhetorician, doesn't necessarily mean that he is not serious about the ideas he presents, although, of course, on occasions he may not be.

Let us look first at some of what may be called the humanistic sides of this work. Referring to his citations of Cicero, Vergil, Juvenal, Sallust, Livy, Aristotle, Homer, and Propertius, Ullman states, 'Etsi vestigia litterarum renascentium in hoc opera pauca sunt, non tamen plane desunt.' And since, he says, except for Papias medieval writers are cited 'fere nunquam', besides Augustine the fathers are 'vix' cited, Ullman adds, 'Hoc ergo sensu opus Colucii inter opera humanistica poni potest.'[53] In fact, Walafrid Strabo is cited indirectly, Thomas Aquinas is paraphrased without acknowledgement, and other medieval writers are cited; Gregory the Great, Justin, and Jerome are further fathers cited; Macrobius, Servius, Isidore of Seville, and Boethius are late classical, early medieval figures cited more than once; Balbus, Florus, Horace, Lucan, Ovid, Persius, Pliny, and Valerius Maximus are additional Roman writers cited, the last one four times.[54] Of course, classical citations, as such, do not make a Renaissance humanist, as they were about as common in the middle ages. Moreover, Salutati, like Petrarch, antedated the great additions to the works of Latin writers and the translations from the Greek which came predominantly in the Quattrocento. Furthermore, the bulk of his references in this work are overwhelmingly scriptural. It is rather the kind of use made of classical references that distinguished the Renaissance humanist from his medieval predecessor.

What has puzzled Ullman and others about this work is that, while written by a successful worldly man of letters who had already attained fame and influence in civic affairs through his position as the first humanist chancellor of the Florentine state, this treatise was, nevertheless, so outspoken in its condemnation of secular life. Apart from the very effective eloquence employed to deter Niccolò da Uzzano, recently entered into the Camaldulensian Cloister of S. Maria degli Angeli, from regretting his decision (and to benefit other readers also to whom Coluccio alludes), it is possible to find a clear and consistent position toward the secular world in this treatise.

Chapter 35 of Book I is titled 'That the world is the minister of necessities'.[55] It is well known that both St. Augustine and St. Thomas Aquinas found a place for this world in their writings (although in crucially different ways), and it would be no shock doctrinally to find amidst all the other sharply negative chapters on the world in Salutati's treatise, which by their titles as well as their contents are outspokenly condemnatory of secular life, a recognition of the importance, notwithstanding, of worldly civilization for the sustenance of life, but subordinated to the higher religious function of the church, namely, the salvation of souls. Salutati, however, does not confirm this expectation. Instead he surprises us in this chapter by making use of one of the classical conceptions of the early life of mankind to strengthen the devotion and resolve of his friend Niccolò to lead a severely ascetic existence within his cell. 'Indeed the world provides things necessary to us, necessary certainly for passing through this corruptible life.'[56] The conception is Augustinian and not neo-Aristotelian, clearly. But Coluccio is unwilling to permit even the degree of worldliness Augustine had allowed in book XIX of the *City of God* (well-known and heavily cited here by Salutati). His limits are more drastic. Consulting the barest necessity of nature, he would permit only that and nothing of civilization. 'For nature desires hunger to be repressed, thirst extinguished, rain and cold repelled, the force of winds and heat to be driven off. Anything beyond this is from evil.'[57]

He then adds a remarkable passage which utilizes for his own purposes the ancient conception of a harsh primitive life (to be distinguished, as Lovejoy and Boas have shown,[58] from the other classical conception of a soft primitivism in a golden age). It is, of course, the moral purity and simplicity of the primitive life that should induce the modern man, who cannot go back to the primitive age, to seek the equivalent in the monastery.

> How easy it is to satisfy these necessities the first age teaches, which, as is read, satisfied hunger with acorns, conquered thirst from brooks, drove off cold with skins, avoided rain, wind and heat through caves and grottoes. This is that most innocent age which the poets, extolling in many praises, called golden, then Saturnine. O happy acorns, O health-giving rivers. The poisons of delicate food did not then excite lust by their heat; nor did languid drunkenness insanely tempt the brain; there was no arguing with neighbours over boundaries or over government. All things were in common. Grass provided beds, caves homes, not guarded, not closed, but open to all. Hidden then, indeed not yet invented, were those two quarrelsome words which disturb the peace of mortals, and which bar to men the road to heaven, which are inciters of avarice and authors of contentions, namely, '*meum*' and '*tuum*'. . . . But now we are so worldly and given to delights that, in comparing that age to our customs, indeed, not customs but abuses and crimes, we think it fabulous and not historical, and we say it is impossible for the fragile life of our own times to return to that harshness. I admit it is more fragile because more vicious, and as the fomenter of vices more pleasure-loving. Certainly it seems impossible to return to the frugality and mutuality (*communionem*) of early times.[59]

The classical sources of this notion are plural. Juvenal, Vergil, and Boethius[60] are either echoed or quoted directly in this passage. Perhaps it is better not to try to designate Salutati's point of view as Stoic or as that of any of the other possible classical schools. As will be seen, it is consistent with another argument later in this treatise in Book II. This conception of the primitive austerity bears, perhaps, the same relationship to his specific views on the life of the religious as Petrarch's praise of the life of solitude bore to his admiration of monastic retirement – except that Salutati makes the connection much more explicit. Indeed, he continues in a most interesting way. He does not agree that men of his day are too delicate to withstand the rigors of a primitive life. Men can submit to monastic discipline.

> Take away greed, wretched man, depose riches, renounce the world, lead your life according to the precepts, attempt to fulfil the counsels, subdue your will to the divine will, . . . begin to love God, hate the world, love poverty, hate riches. You cannot leave these things unless you hate them, you cannot go over to the others unless you love them. Do not accuse our age of weakness. Our body is potent to undergo all hardships. I do not refer you to Daniel and his companions turning to a diet of herbs from the delights of the royal table. I do not propose to you as the greatest example that precursor of the Lord among men born to women; nor the anchorites of whose miracles

> we read in the *Vita patrum*; nor the hermits even of our times; nor the monks, many of whom we see choose poverty, love fasting, flee all pleasure. For I know that when I mention these the lover of the world will reply that they both now can and then were able to do this only while filled with the grace of the Holy Spirit, and that the spirit inspires when, where and how it wills, and that this does not depend on our own free will.[61]

Therefore, he proposes two natural examples drawn from contemporary secular life: the harsh existence of the Carinthian mountaineers, compelled to live in this severe way, and the despicable condition of sailors on the ships sailing out into the Atlantic to England, an adventure undertaken for the smallest of rewards.[62] 'Indeed we are able to abandon the world and subjugate our bodies to that extreme necessity of nature.'[63]

Another classical *topos* used by Salutati in this work also has to do with the admirable nature of abstinence. Chapter 9 of book II deals with 'The Vow of Poverty'.[64] Among other observations on the evil of wealth, he remarks in a vein similar to the one discussed above, 'Nor do we wretched mortals think it contrary to nature that through avarice we appropriate those things created for the use of all to the dominion of our own property, and although they ought to serve our life we make them instruments of our crimes, pleasures and other wickedness.' Worldly goods, he states, fall into the Stoic class of *media* or indifferent things, 'and thus are only good if we use them well, for they are bad for those using them poorly'.[65] After further condemnation of riches, citing Jesus, Paul, and Ecclesiastes, he turns to a consideration of the lesson of history.

> If we would recall that altogether there were and there are two cities destined for mortals, one spiritual which we call 'of God' and the other, indeed, carnal which we may call 'of the world'; and if to one or the other of them we commit our loves and the goal of our actions; it will occur to us that each city was established by paupers and ruined and corrupted by the rich. And first, if you will, we will examine what authors this mundane city had. Although I easily could, I do not wish to discuss all kingdoms but I shall investigate that one which was greatest and strongest of all and which still retains the principate, at least in name, specifically that of the Romans.[66]

Salutati then devotes the next four pages (in Ullman's edition) to a review of Roman history, utilizing Florus' epitome, Pliny, Juvenal, Eutropius, Cicero, but mainly Livy, Valerius Maximus, and Sallust as his sources. Here is the standard classical view of the poor, moral, and abstemious early Romans, who brought about the rise of Rome to world dominion only to encounter its downfall after the age of Scipio and Cato in the hands of men of great wealth.[67]

What more [can be said] when the books of all the historians are full of the poverty, moderation and abstinence of the Romans? These paupers founded so great an empire that, as a noble and truly great historian [Sallust] said, 'afterward, when riches began to be honoured, and glory, empire and power followed them, virtue began to fade, poverty to be held shameful,' rich successors brought it to ruin. . . . For the Republic of the Romans, which the pauper Romulus founded and the poorest princes raised to such greatness that its empire was bounded by the ocean and its glory, indeed, by the stars, and from the rising to the setting of the sun all, tamed by arms, obeyed only them, this the rich men, cruel Sulla, ferocious Cinna and ambitious Marius shook to its foundations, and the even richer men Crassus, Pompey the Great, and Gaius Caesar the son of Lucius utterly destroyed. Thus in the memory of these events, as in a kind of mirror, mankind can see that for establishing, increasing and conserving this earthly city, poor men excel rich.[68]

There has recently been a flurry of interest on the part of historians in the possible political influence of Florence's humanist chancellors. It is worth noting that Salutati wrote these lines in 1381 during the rule of the *popolo minuto*, after the rise of the Ciompi, and prior to the overthrow of this regime by the oligarchy in the very next year. Perhaps his views do have some contemporary significance, but perhaps more reflective than determinative. It should also interest Hans Baron that these republican sentiments were uttered in the middle of such a 'medieval' book as *De seculo*, and a considerable time before Salutati wrote his *De tyranno*, the pro-imperialist, 'medieval' sentiments of which Baron finds so hard to explain.[69]

Our interest in this chapter does not stop with Salutati's essay on the public benefits of poverty in the 'city of the world'. He deals in parallel fashion with the experience of the Catholic Church as the 'City of God'. 'Moreover, what may I say of that city which looks toward heavenly Jerusalem?'[70] Was not Christ, its founder, a pauper who said when he entered Jerusalem, 'Foxes have holes and the birds of the air have nests, but the Son of Man has nowhere to lay his head'?[71] What of Cephas, what of Paul, what of Peter, what of Ananias and Saphyra?

> Thus it is manifest that all those first founders of the heavenly city and the Catholic Church in the renewal of time either were paupers or sold all that they had and chose voluntary poverty by sharing in common. . . . These poor and humble men, by infinite martyrdoms through two hundred and thirty and more years, from Nero, the first persecutor of Christians, to the emperors Diocletian and Maximus [*sic*], in whose time the tenth plague of persecution boiled up, founded the Catholic Church. After Constantine, who did not endow so much as enrich the Church and hand to it the proud ornaments of the imperial height (as may be said with everybody's permission), these our prelates, in whom just as in the case of those other leaders of the earthly kingdom first the love of money and then of empire increased, after they had likewise dined on honey and oil, become bejewelled with gold and silver, dressed in linen and damask robes of many colours, become excessively elegant, and proceeded to rule—these prelates rendered that glorious city abominable. Now (what is most to be lamented) although they see the Christian faith, once diffused throughout the world, has lost so many lands to the Saracenic abomination, although they see the old schism of the *Graeculi* separate so many peoples, so many cities and so many once opulent kingdoms from the unity of Holy Mother Church, just as if it were too large a mass and there were too great a multitude of faithful, by electing two supreme pontiffs at various times (if they can still be called elections which hatred or ambition or the other turbid passions of human minds extort and which are not celebrated in zeal of faith and for the building of celestial Jerusalem), they have created the most pernicious schism. Thus, just as those princes and founders of both cities, while they loved poverty, in laying the foundations of those two cities not only perfected them into a huge work of the greatest size but enlarged them by miraculous increases with labour and blood, so these rich men, with wealth corrupting minds and good customs, destroyed almost all with their glorious wealth of all things. This being so, unless we rejoice in being fools, if we wish to serve the heavenly or earthly city, if we wish to show ourselves useful to both or either one, who does not see that riches, which so corrupt and defile their possessors, ought to be cast away?[72]

Notable here is the direct undiscriminating parallelism between the two cities and the equality of their corruption and the absence of any clearly stated subordination of the one to the other. Adhering to the monastic vow of poverty apparently offers the only substitute for a return to the pristine days of the Roman republic or the early centuries of the apostolic church.

It is apparent that Salutati managed to combine a classical Roman interpretation of history with the Augustinian–Christian conception of the two cities, and to utilize this, in addition, to express his views of the contemporary state of the church as well as to confirm his monastic reader in his vow of poverty. A further application of a humanistic interest to a Christian religious practice may be seen in chapter II of Book II, *De oratione*, 'On Prayer'.[73] This is the longest chapter in the book, nineteen pages when most chapters run to two or three pages in Ullman's edition. It is a humanist discussion of the rhetoric of sacred discourse – the Christian addressing himself to his God. First of all, the proper psychological attitude must be present in the person praying; therefore a discussion of the three theological virtues and the four cardinal virtues ensues. Many interesting topics are taken up in connection with these. Under charity he takes up the question of what is legitimate self-love as the measure of our love for our neighbour and inveighs against love of our bodies from which all the civilized arts, which he lengthily enumerates, flow.[74] He feels called upon to explain away the Old Testament injunctions to destroy one's enemies and offers his own principles of exegesis; 'whatever sprinkling of maledictions is found within the oracle of the Holy Scriptures certainly ought to be referred to the rule of true charity or the divine justice by some mystery of exposition, or it should be expounded in such a way in the light of a higher sense that love of God and of neighbour are in no way contradicted, since a specially wide way is open to expositors . . .'[75] His discussion of prudence leads to a direct assertion of rhetorical principles;[76] justice involves him in a discussion of free will and divine providence, since it is unjust to pray for what has not already been provided for by God.[77] The relationship of oral spoken prayer to inner spiritual meditation is considered. Although true prayer is of the heart and not of the mouth, vocal prayer should not be neglected. Through it we serve God in body as well as spirit, and a sluggish spirit can be aroused by voices.[78]

In considering prayer Salutati required the presence of the separate virtues, theological and moral. In the previous chapter 10, 'On the Vow of Obedience',[79] he had included an astounding passage on the motivations of virtue. The reference to Professor Mommsen's paper on Petrarch and the choice of Hercules will be recalled.[80] In the *De otio religioso* Petrarch did not manifest the new classical conception of virtue as the choice of a path in life but made virtue depend, traditionally, on divine grace. Mommsen's discussion was an elaboration and correction of an earlier paper by Erwin Panofsky,[81] who had credited Salutati with the first non-medieval account of virtue in his *De laboribus Herculis*[82] and in the letter to Giovanni da Siena on which it was based,[83] Salutati, in these later pieces, had not endorsed the pagan conception but had only stated it. In the passage that follows from the *De seculo et religione*, II, 10 he sharply attacks what he takes to be the pagan approach to virtue as both desirable for its own sake and for the enjoyment of a clear conscience. By the way he begins, he seems to want to be taken quite seriously.

> I don't know if I speak truly, still most devoutly I dare to assert that all those who do something virtuous in any way other than obedience to divine majesty not only do not acquire merit but act badly. And all those who, for example, do frequent acts of fortitude or temperance only for the reason that they might be brave or temperate (and not merely that they might seem so) —all such not only are wise after the flesh but also do not differ from the philosophers of the Gentiles. (For I omit the Romans who sought mundane glory for themselves as the end of all their [virtuous] actions). Do not those philosophers who wish virtue to be the goal of all goods (which was especially the opinion of the Stoics; I dismiss the others of vainer opinions), contenting themselves with themselves, as they say, require nothing further from their actions except the secret of conscience and that they can become virtuous and enjoy the acquisition of virtue? In what way would we say a Christian differs from these pagans who, forgetting the command of God and losing the *habitus* of this virtue [of obedience], acts not that he might please or obey God but only that he might do some good!? Certainly, securely I will say that he is so much the worse if he has been established in grace by the regeneration of baptism and taught the truth in the Gospel, and yet neither does as he ought nor practices virtues themselves in the proper way. Indeed, he tries against reason, to joy in virtues, and by joying in them he is more truly said to abuse them.

Even grace is not a sufficient cause of virtue. As he stresses here and in the next chapter (already discussed), it should be one's free will to fulfill the eternal commands of God in voluntary devotion – a thoroughly Augustinian position. 'Let us therefore not know earthly things, but, since we are forced by the necessity of nature to nothing, let us faithfully obey God, to whom we have promised faith, in the liberty conceded to us in our will.'[84]

Based on similar reasoning is Salutati's affirmation in chapter 6 that superior merits are due those who live bound by vows – the technical criterion of the religious.[85] Instead of totally rejecting the secular way of life, or blurring the differences between it and the religious (as Petrarch seemed at times to do), Salutati reverts to the conception common in medieval moral theology of a spiritual hierarchy leading upward from ordinary lay Christians, through the secular clergy, to the religious, with each status differing in the corresponding degree of its religious perfection and therefore meriting higher or lower rewards. The reason for the highest merits being conferred on the religious is stated by Salutati as follows:

> For you, upon entering religion, have dedicated yourself, your will and your work to God. . . . This is truly a *holocaust*, that is, a total consumption and burning up in which all that we are and can be we commit to God and leave nothing in our own power. This they do not do who without the vow offer only works. And on this account it is not right that they should merit as much in the benefits of God as those who are indebted by vows. For who merits more of grace, he who would give only the fruits of the tree to a superior in such a way that he is held to give them only as much as he pleases, or he who gives both tree and fruit under such conditions that after the gift he is unable to revoke it? No one would doubt that he who gives more merits more. . . .[86] Moreover, whoever does good out of free will, as happens in one free of a vow, does a single good; but whoever vows and also does good while he obligates himself by a vow, deserves and does a good. In making a vow, even though he creates a debt, nevertheless he does good. For they should not be heard who madly attempt to assert that goods which are done without a vow are greater than those we do out of obedience to a vow, adducing that we are more obligated to the one giving by free will than to one paying a debt (as if because by vowing one is made a debtor he does not proceed from free will), and that we owe nothing to someone freely promising something because he promised. . . . Certainly they err. For in far greater charity, which is the end of the precept, it is vowed and perfected than if we simply offer something.[87]

As can be seen from this passage, Salutati preserves and defends the basic medieval conception of the superior perfection of the life of the professional religious, that is, those who by vowing or professing constituted the professional.

This notion of degrees of perfection, together with its essential counterpart – the notion of the total sacrifice of the individual's will to the divine will (we should become '*non actores sed sola instrumenta*')[88]

– must already in his time have encountered criticism of the sort we shall shortly consider in Lorenzo Valla (below), judging by his reference to 'those who madly attempt to assert'.

How central these ideas were to his conception of the relationship of the laity, the clergy, and the religious may be seen in their exposition in his closing exhortation:

> When we were born in succession to the first parents, to whom we all are heirs and sons, we were born vessels of wrath. And soon by the establishment of Holy Mother Church, through the purification of baptism, we are renewed in grace. Indeed, the first and true religion, in which receiving the signature of Christianity one renounces the devil and his works, is our faith, and if properly observed is indeed fully the way of perfection to God. Yet by perverse custom it is so mixed with temporal affairs that, unless the mercy of God overcomes our injustice, although many are called, few will attain to the benefits of election. Perfection, however, is fuller when by daily service of divine majesty, though still in abundance of things, we bind ourselves outside the world through the clerical order. Indeed the fullest perfection in this life is when we not only follow God, shunning the devil, when we not only give ourselves in service of God, relinquishing the world (for a cleric ought not to involve himself in secular affairs), but also when we offer ourselves to God through a vow of chastity, obedience and poverty, and consecrate ourselves as a true holocaust on the altar of religion. Thus not improperly it can be said, as I indicated above, that to all Christians sowing in good soil a thirty-fold fruit is reserved, to clerics a sixty-fold, to the religious, indeed, a hundred-fold.[89]

Although this discussion of the treatise will end on this very traditional and, doctrinally, completely orthodox note, it should not be forgotten that in my selective analysis he was shown to be effectively humanist in the service he was able to render his argument on behalf of the monastic life through the new disciplines and points of view. These were his discussion of the classical legend of the hard primitive life of the golden age as an inducement to monastic asceticism, his adoption of the classical Roman interpretation of history attributing Roman greatness to poverty and the parallel lesson of the decline of the church through affluence, his interest in the rhetorical and moral philosophical nature of prayer. Although he showed little restraint in his graphic depiction of the dangers and temptations and evil consequences of secular life in his highly rhetorical first book, it is quite clear that he did not reject his own status of a layman. This is no inconsistency brought about by a purely rhetorical endorsement of the religious life on behalf of his friend Niccolò da Uzzano, as Ullman and Garin have suggested. The layman, according to his very explicit argument, could lead a moral and religious life, but one of lesser perfection and merit than the cleric's, and still less than that of the religious. There was no contradiction in Salutati's mind between humanism and his inherited religious faith and practices (called his 'medievalism' by von Martin and by Ullman); nor was there any inconsistency in being a lay Christian and regarding the status of the religious as spiritually superior. As he said in his reply to Giovanni Dominici:

> connexa sunt humanitatis studia; connexa sunt et studia divinitatis, ut unius rei sine alia vera completaque scientia non possit haberi.[90]

Salutati's two most famous protégés, Leonardo Bruni and Poggio Bracciolini, both wrote works that in a less direct way than the ones we are considering here dealt with the religious orders. Each of these works, Bruni's *Oratio in hypocritas*[91] of 1417 and Poggio's *Dialogus contra hypocritas*[92] of 1447–8, was primarily rhetorical in character, expressing a sharp hostility to principally the friars, admitting that their impugning of the motives of the religious did not apply to all, conceding that hypocrisy was also present among the laity.[93] They are of far more social than doctrinal importance, since neither one of them so much as considers the question of the validity of the status of the religious to either affirm it or to question it. Bruni's oration is short, compact, rhetorically effective and ends with an affirmation of the importance of conscience as a monitor of religious and moral integrity.

> For indeed the good man is joyful and gay from good conscience of his deeds and from good hope which no fear of punishments disturbs. On the other hand their misdeeds burn the hypocrites and may be observed as furies before their eyes. For it is necessary for them, although they are evil, to think sometimes about themselves and their errors. For each man is constituted as a right and perpetual judge of himself and his actions. This is certainly a most sure and true judgement which can not be deceived or seduced or circumvented in any way. For it is not believed because of witnesses, nor is the accused censured by means of documents, nor is he defended by a patron through favour or eloquence. This judge knows all, was present at every crime, and one is not judged once only but often and frequently. The condemnation of this internal judge forces tears from you and compels you to weep among

> sacred things. But believe me, . . . this is a game and a joke compared with that eternal and ineffable judgement of God which awaits you after death.[94]

It is difficult to consider these works as having very much theoretical or doctrinal importance, although they certainly reveal the growth of hostility toward the clergy in some humanist circles. At any rate they do not contribute to the problem of this chapter.[95]

3. Valla's Case for the Equality of Merits

When in c. 1441, sixty years later than Salutati's treatise, Lorenzo Valla wrote his dialogue on *The Profession of the Religious* (*De professione religiosorum*),[96] it was as if he wished to reply directly to his predecessor, so opposite is it in viewpoint. A more likely target, however, was such a work as San Bernardino's *De Christiana religione*[97] or Girolamo Aliotti d'Arezzo's *De felici statu religionis monasticae*.[98] The participants in the dialogue are simply 'Frater' and 'Lorenzo'. This is not a subtle or cautious work, but bold and outspoken in challenging the fundamental doctrinal basis of the privileged position of the religious. He starts right in as follows: 'I ask before all . . . why . . . you will receive greater remuneration from God. . . . When the layman and the religious differ and depart from each other in no quality of mind or body, and to both all things are equal which happen extrinsically to men, and both are engaged in the same actions of life, is nevertheless greater remuneration owed by God to him who has professed that sect which you call "religion" and hence call yourselves "religious" than to him who has professed no sect, neither yours nor the monks?'[99] Valla's attack is partly philological, questioning the propriety of the language, but this rests on the more fundamental questioning of the religious assumption. He proceeds to defend his use of the word 'sect' rather than 'religious order', which the friar had protested against. 'Still I prefer to call this, about which you wonder, a sect rather than a religion, not only for reasons of style but also out of necessity. For since I do not think as much ought to be attributed to this your life as you attribute, it seems too much that you impose on it such a sacred and venerable name as "religion". Otherwise there is no reason why we should be arguing. For if you alone are "religious", it must be conceded that you are the best of all men. That this, as I believe, is not so, I am about to dispute.'[100]

He goes on to suggest that the differences between various religious orders are comparable to the difference between philosophical sects.

Valla anticipates the Reformation position here, which denied any special status or vocation to the clergy or to the members of religious orders, considering each Christian equal in status as far as externals were concerned. Valla resumed his argument by asking whether a priest or a pope was 'religious' or whether none other than the friar could be. This position was not so much arrogant with respect to members of religious orders as contemptuous of other persons. 'For what greater praise can be given me than to be called "religious" and what greater vituperation than to be called "irreligious"? For what else is it to be religious than to be a Christian? . . . Religion is the same thing as faith, and "religious" the same as "faithful", faithful, I say, not as though dead without works, but with works in the way in which one can be called a true Christian.'[101] Refusing to acknowledge the traditional degrees of perfection distinguishing the different stages of holiness, Valla proceeds to argue that if the friar's position is accepted, all others must be condemned as not religious. 'And so since you would make you only religious who have professed, and you would deny that others are truly religious, what else do you admit but that you alone are Christians, you alone good, you alone pure and sinless; moreover the others you would damn, despise, hurl into Tartarus. . . Since this is so I do not act ungenerously toward you if I hesitate to call you "religious" when many others also, who have not professed that sect or rule, ought to be called "religious" since they lead most saintly lives, and many of your brothers ought not to be called "religious" because they live most iniquitously.'[102]

After further argument on this proposition that the religious and the lay Christians can be equal in magnitude of virtue but unequal in kind, the question is raised: granting that some Christians live subject to rules and vows, why should they acquire greater merit with God for this? The friar gives the following reasons: first, they promise and always observe poverty, chastity, and obedience. Secondly, they are in this way restricted more than other men. Thirdly, if they lapse they will suffer greater punishment. Thus they should receive a greater reward if they keep their rule. In reply Valla engages in a dialectical disputation attempting to turn the friars' words back on themselves. These claims seem to mean that the greatest of our virtues can be increased by taking a vow and for this reason our reward should be greater. But is not a man who is exposed to the greater danger and overcomes it deserving of the greater reward? And should not the man who lives in a more tranquil and sheltered situation and fails to do his duty receive a greater punishment? When he gets the friar to admit this, he says that the first is the situation of the lay Christian in the world, who, exposed to greater peril, merits more for his goodness, while the second, the taker of vows, should be more severely punished for his lapses. The friar protests: 'You drive me almost to insanity with your words; you weaken our virtues, you almost take away our rewards, you increase our vices, you multiply our penalties, religions and all religious, truly as you have said, you hurl into the mire.'[103]

The argument turns to whether a vow has any merit in it *per se*. Again, Valla, the humanist, indulges in an extended discussion of the meanings of words. 'Vow' means both prayerful wish and devout promise. How does *votum* differ from *sponsio* (pledge) or *iusiurandum* (oath)? After a lengthy analysis of their meanings, Valla concedes that 'you do make an oath or promise, but I do not concede the vow'.[104] If a pledge to observe poverty, chastity, and obedience is valid, what need is there for an oath? If it is invalid, you have promised nothing. The friar replies that a pledge is valid, but an oath makes it more valid. Valla asks how health can be healthier, the full fuller, the perfect more perfect. His argument comes down to claiming that an oath does not make a virtuous life any more virtuous, that the real test for divine mercy is the inner attitude and not the outer form. 'Profession is not a *votum* but a *devotio*. For it is to devote, *devovere*, to speak briefly, as *dicare* or *dedicare*.'[105]

Turning to the contents of the vow, obedience, poverty, and chastity, Lorenzo concedes that they confer merit but apart from profession. But, he adds, 'These are not necessary to every one.'[106] On the specific pledge of obedience to superiors Valla asks why, if with baptism one promises God future obedience to his commandments, need one pledge obedience to men? How can you give what you already have given? The friar replies: 'I do not retract my pledge, nor do I give to a man what I have given to God, nor do I promise to God what I previously promised. But in those things in which I have a choice while serving God such as in dressing, eating, going, acting, lying, sleeping, remaining awake, and finally speaking, the liberty of doing these things, and as I said, the choice, I hand over to another.'[107] Valla questions the validity of thus trying to have another ruler besides Christ. He cites *Hebrews* xi. 37–8 depicting the sacrifices of the faithful to show that the religious cannot be compared 'to those retaining their own liberty' in degree of sanctity.[108] What then of kings, pontiffs, and other rulers, must they be bound to obedience? To the friar's statement that rulers are granted merit if they rule well, we, if we obey well, Valla asks:

> Is there thus no middle ground so that we only either have servants or serve? . . . Not all are lords and not all are servants, and not all are teachers and not all are disciples; they do not obtain a lesser degree of merit who are in the middle. And, as desirable as it is to belong to the status of prelates and preceptors, just as miserable is it to be in the number of subjects and disciples. Certainly this is of far less dignity than to be, as I have said, in the middle and for one to be able to be without a lord and to live and know without a master. I do not venture to say that it is a sign of an abject and ignorant soul to commit oneself to the charge of a tutor in the manner of a boy and to the care of a preceptor. But if he is able to admonish, teach and rule others, why does he subject himself especially to others who, as frequently happens, are ignorant and unworthy. . . . A greater reward is given to those who rule well than to those who obey well . . . thus your pledge of obedience is a kind of servitude. . . . While I would prefer to be the master rather than a servant of others, I certainly prefer to be master of myself.[109]

With this affirmation of individualism applied to the monastic vow of obedience, Valla concludes his attack on it by saying, 'To obey the rule is to obey God, not man, which we also do. Nor can another rule be held better than the one handed down by Christ and the apostles.'[110]

Thus in this discussion, too, Valla takes a position that is firmly opposed to a basic medieval Catholic conception, namely, that of the authority that inheres in sacredotal and abbatial office. Obedience had a place only between the Christian and God, without the intervention of man, except in a tutorial relation. Obviously this attack on the moral and juridical aspects of the religious life involved more than a simple question of the superior merit a monk might gain by adherence to his vow of obedience, and it contrasts notably with the passage cited above from Salutati which found virtue solely in submission to divine command.

In discussing the vow of poverty Valla made an equally fundamental attack on another favoured medieval value, though a value that could also be cherished from a Renaissance humanist point of view, as the case of Salutati's discussion of the primitive life and Roman virtue shows. Nor does Valla launch into the kind of satiric invective so easy to indulge in at that time and best illustrated by Poggio's *Contra hypocritas* and his *De avaritia*, showing the great wealth of the religious. Rather he questioned the whole notion of poverty as being in any way valuable except as a token of humility. Is it poverty to live as you do lacking nothing essential, not even wine? You are poor men in desire, but your virtue is no greater than that of others who have not professed poverty. Is it necessary to embrace poverty if I can live innocently with wealth? The poor in spirit, not in goods, are praised, and the rich are disapproved only in spirit. 'What do you ask? If you and I differ not at all in living temperately and frugally, how can it be that you are a pauper and I a rich man . . .?' The friar suggests that he might sell all and give it to the poor. Valla replies: 'should I also sell all my books and distribute the proceeds? Is it the precept for the apostles and for those to whom it was granted to reply to princes to be without books, without learning, without premeditation? Codices are necessary to me and also not a little money with which I may buy many codices and other needs of life. For what would be more perverse than to give your possessions to beggars and become a beggar afterward yourself? . . . So it is sufficient if I do not revel and delight in riches and renounce them not in fact but in spirit.' The friar answers: 'Then you concede that we are like the apostles who renounce riches in spirit and so in fact.' To which Lorenzo: 'Nothing less. I said money is necessary to me to buy codices. You, if you do otherwise and hand it to paupers, are stupid and do not love yourself as your neighbour.'[111] The monks and friars deserve little for their poverty because they are relieved of destitution and care. 'You give up the hope of acquisition but also the solicitude. You will not have better things but will not suffer worse things either.' I hope to please God as readily as you do but without renunciation. '*Non exterior homo sed interior placet Deo.*'[112] If he lavished all his wealth on the poor, he would lack necessities and be unable to defend religion. He might become impious and unable to care for an old or sick parent or wife and child.[113] There are Aristotelian and Ciceronian (rather than Epicurean) overtones in this emphasis on the need for wealth to do good deeds. But the more fundamental argument of Valla against the ideal of poverty was that it should be a spiritual attitude, not a literal act.

On the vow of continence he seems to turn as much on the priest as on the regular clergy. And again his is an argument for the acceptance of a moderated sensual life as well as against the notion that sexual abstinence by itself is of any value. 'It is much better to be safe in the middle than on high with danger of ruin. O that bishops, presbyters, deacons were husbands of one wife and not rather, forgive the saying, lovers of more than one whore. . . . Yet priests will not merit on account of chastity more than I will merit. For in this respect women would be in a worse condition since they cannot be priests, and yet with God there is neither Greek nor barbarian, master nor slave, neither male nor female. . . .'[114]

The general conclusion of his dialogue is that submission to a rule, the religious life, is motivated by fear rather than love, and hence is an inferior kind of Christianity to his own lay existence. It is not that individual monks and friars are evil or hypocrites, though he concedes many are, but that the whole basis of considering their life more perfect in sanctity is a false one.

> You obey: I assume the care of others. You live poor and continent; I lead a life equal to yours. You have bound yourself for keeping this, I have not thought that servitude necessary. You do rightly by necessity, I by choice; you out of fear of God, I out of love; perfect charity drives away fear. If you had not feared that otherwise you could not please God, certainly you never would have bound yourself. For what else induced you to make your profession . . . except that no cause should deflect you from the worship of God through free will. Thus you see hardly anyone entering your company unless wicked, criminal, poor, destitute and who otherwise despairs of serving either God or his own body well. . . . And so all the way of the vow, all imposition of a fast, all oath and finally all law (your profession is a certain law) was invented on account of fear, that is, as I speak more openly, on account of bad people. . . . Did not Paul say, The Law is imposed on account of transgression? . . . Thus I don't know what else you can ask of God except the fruit of obedience, poverty, and continence. But you are not content with this and demand that you be placed above others on account of danger.

> But if you consider the danger of punishment among you, consider in my case the danger of sinning more easily, who am bound by no anchor of fear. This makes the same act of virtue greater in me than in you.[115]

He apparently is ready to broaden his attack to include the secular clergy as well as the religious.

> Therefore let us make both you and us equal in the manner of Paul, who of those eating and not eating said, 'each observes in his own sense,' and conclude: Thus profession does not render men better, such as deaconhood, priesthood, episcopacy and papacy. You are not better because you have been consecrated a deacon or priest, but you wished to be consecrated that you might become better; nor because you have sworn do you for that reason merit much, but you have sworn that you might merit much; nor are you good because penalties have been proposed for you, for you are able to be evil, but in order that you may be good you undergo the danger of punishment.[116]

Various holy men have not been inferior for not having professed religion or been a bishop or priest. He is aware of how meritorious the founders of convents have been, although their followers depart from goodness. He offers, finally, as evidence that he is not the enemy of the friars a peroration of praise, which is in some ways even less than faint.[117]

There is no doubt in my mind that Valla moved far in this treatise toward a repudiation of the entire medieval conception of a sacerdotal hierarchy and a special profession of those leading a more perfectly religious life – the religious. And the basis of his attack was evangelical and primarily Pauline. It was more than a defense of the religiosity of the laity; it was a reassertion of the universality and multiplicity and equality of the ways to salvation open to all who are Christian in spirit. It was built on a more literal and historical interpretation of Paul's attack on the special sanctity of adherence to the Hebrew law.

This treatise, first edited by Vahlen on the basis of a unique manuscript (Bibl. Vat., Cod. Urb. Lat. 595), was not published in his *Opera omnia* and was probably hardly known at all in the sixteenth century. If it had achieved a wider circulation it would undoubtedly have been given a strongly favourable reception by the reformers, more so than that which his much more ambiguous *De libero arbitrio* received.[118]

Perhaps, if it had then been known, we would be calling Valla a 'Pre-reformer' today. However, it is quite clear that he had no intention of attacking the historical authority of the church, even though in his *Apology*[119] he does not retract the ideas expressed in this treatise but reaffirms them. Undoubtedly he could not have recognized the significance and the interpretation I have just given to this treatise, since it requires historical hindsight to do so. It would be unhistorical, then, to claim him and his thought as part of the Reformation, since no man then knew it was to occur within eighty years. Yet the resemblance of his ideas to those of the reformers is none the less striking.

A more relevant question is the relation of these ideas to his humanism. My analysis of Petrarch and Salutati has made clear that there is no single necessary one, because they took such opposite positions. To my mind the connection in all three lies in the effort to define the relation of the lay Christian to the professional religious. The humanists' claim to the field of moral philosophy could not be isolated from religion, so that they became lay preachers and religious counsellors as well. Such were Petrarch and Salutati. Valla seems to have drawn a logical conclusion from this situation – two generations ahead of the Erasmian Christian humanists,[120] and no less emphatically.

For all three of these influential humanists the problem of the religious life was internal and subjective, concerned with the relations of the individual, of all individuals, to God. Where Salutati was the most conservative in preserving the conception of degrees of religiosity and therefore of sanctity in retaining the triple categories of lay Christian, priest, and religious, still the stress within his treatise is frequently on the inwardness of prayer and devotion. For Petrarch the psychological aspects of the devotion of monks and laity alike are his central concern, as we have also emphasised in more general form in Part I, Chapter I, above. Valla, in perfect consistency with his views of human nature expressed in *De vero bono* and his *Repastinatio dialecticae et philosophiae* went beyond all in making religion a matter flowing from an internally determined emotional direction and in rejecting the externals.

In this they were as one with the other humanist critics of the clergy who stressed the hypocrisy that was especially manifested by the friars – Bruni and Poggio, Fontius, Acciaiuoli among others. Certainly here they were feeling their way towards positions that had a certain consistency with their role as humanists and which were more specific to them than to the laity in general. Thus it is not enough to state that the humanists upheld the religious birthrights of the laity. In each instance in a special way their views reflect their humanism as such. And while there was certainly a wide variety of viewpoints among the humanists, they had their humanism in common.

This meant a belief in language, in the *word*, as the expression of the inwardness of the individual, as well as the means of reaching the inwardness of other individuals. The rhetorical relationship was an interpersonal relationship. It reflected and it modulated the state of the wills of the inter-related persons. Hypocrisy was the falsified external manifestation of an inward state. The external manifestation was labile and instrumental. Rhetoric taught them this. But rhetoric was only effective when it was affective, when it carried conviction of the genuineness of the speaker's feelings. Objective external manifestations of sacral and religious validity, if they still in some instance recognised their existence, increasingly became for the humanists a peripheral, and even dispensable, aspect of a truly internal harmonisation of wills externally mediated by words and by prayer.

This also was to be seen in their relationships to divinity. The relationship of man and God became not so much the ritualistically precise performance of established sacred norms as an inner response of the human will to the divine love and will manifested towards him by grace. Only Valla came close to spelling out the implications of this new religious relationship inherent in humanism, but all moved towards it in varying degree. By implication all individuals were accessible to divine grace for the inner perfection of their wills, and hence no special status of those who were professionally devout was needed for the full attainment of the goals of religion. Valla makes it clear that he believes this. Moreover, as we saw in our previous chapter on the sacraments, more important than the mediating ministry of the priest was the inner faith of the communicant, and even in penance, as Fontius suggested, the sinner with genuine repentance could, if need be, make his peace directly with God.

XV. From *Theologia Poetica* to *Theologia Platonica*

1. The Place of Poetry and Allegory in Humanist Thought

The dominant tendency of recent interpretations of Renaissance humanism has been to stress the rhetorical and political aspects of this movement, regarding it as essentially a response to, if not an involvement in, the struggle for political and social dominance in the urban republics of the Renaissance and in the princely despotisms that accompanied and succeeded them. There is a sense in which it is correct to say, as a scholar recently has said, that 'in large part, the force of humanism in the Florentine community was the disguised force of the ruling class itself'.[1] Although we shall be very much concerned with 'disguised' meanings in this chapter of humanist poetic interpretation, we are not concerned with their connection with the 'ruling class' or even whether the humanists were part thereof. We wish rather to stress the poetical and theological aspects of humanist thought, and in so doing we shall be regarding the humanists as more important as part of a cultural and intellectual movement than of a political or social one. Clearly the pressures of old institutions and new economic and political opportunities for personal advancement were powerfully present in the Renaissance, still the process of attempted resolutions of the contradictory experiences of life, particularly the resolution of the old and the new values, seems to have been an equally potent historical force in the Renaissance. The attempt to attain such resolution in the area of intellectual, aesthetic, moral and religious attitudes seems to have been the particular vocation the humanists assigned to themselves.

Poetry is inherently less susceptible to employment for political and mundane purposes than rhetoric, and by professional inheritance and historical origin the humanists were equally dedicated to poetry and rhetoric. The fact that Petrarch was a most gifted and accomplished poet has often seemed to be only accidentally connected with the fact that he was the most potently formative individual in the evolution of the humanist movement. It was not accidental, however. And though he was in many respects a very ambivalent and inconsistent man, he regarded his poetry as an inseparable part of his profession and of his vocation. But he did not call himself a 'humanist' since he lived before that word was coined. Yet we, today, do have that word, and 'humanism' as well, and legitimately apply them to him since he engaged in literary activities that comprehended the whole of 'humanism' in its later distinguished parts of rhetoric, history, poetry and moral philosophy. Only grammar, which he recognised as a necessary base, and which as far as his command of Latin and knowledge of literature was concerned he had more than 'mastered', can be less clearly distinguished and labelled as among his areas of cultural productivity. Yet even here his activity as a discoverer and critic of texts gives him a place as a grammarian. As for his own consciousness of these divisions of humanism, we can recognise that he clearly distinguished only between poetry and rhetoric, with philosophy contained in both but primarily as a part of poetry. He viewed history as part of rhetoric, but called himself *historicus* in his coronation diploma. Others called him *philosophus moralis*. Yet all of these distinctions can possibly be taken overseriously and so become a modern scholar's game.[2]

Today we regard poetry as the only one of the five *studia humanitatis* that can be called 'art', yet in the Renaissance all five *studia* were considered 'arts', since some of them had been part of the *artes liberales* and came to be called by Salutati's term of *studia humanitatis* [if he really was the first humanist to use that term, as he seems to have been]. It is possible to argue that it is we who are ambiguous when we say 'art', not the humanists who used it in the traditional Greek, Roman and medieval sense of a traditional mode of doing something together with the *facultas* or capacity to do it whether acquired by nature or training. And these modes of doing things were divided between the mechanical and the liberal. Thus the liberal or 'intellectual and verbal' arts (which also included music among the mathematical arts of the *quadrivium*) borrowed the term and its meaning from its original application to the shaping of the materials of nature for the use or enjoyment of man – *techne* in its original Greek meaning. It was recognised in the Renaissance, however, that the individual working in an art could be gifted with a capacity for superlative accomplishment beyond that of the ordinary practitioner, something frequently called *ingenium*, but this quality could be present or absent in any of the particular arts. Thus they classified what we today call the 'fine' arts, without distinction, either, in the case of poetry, as among the liberal arts or the *studia humanitatis* [the 'humanities'], or, in the case of musical composition as in the *quadrivium* or mathematical disciplines, or, as in the case of the visual arts, as among the mechanical arts.[3]

Poetry, however, was something special. In the Middle Ages it was frequently classified as one of two or three modes of composition within rhetoric, and so had no special place of its own in the *trivium*, but was a component of the *ars dictaminis* – rhetoric as a profession.[4] In the Renaissance poetry, both in the vernacular and in Latin, quite suddenly acquired an enormous new prestige – despite the circumstance that there had been innumerable medieval versifiers, a number of very good poets, and many admirers of Vergil. I believe that, although poetry would probably because of its own charms have acquired this new prestige anyhow, it is difficult to separate its new status from the enormous impact that Dante's *Divina Commedia* had in the fourteenth century within a generation of his death, and continued to have. Of course, Petrarch only rather grudgingly also recognised the greatness of Dante, but it is also fair to say that Petrarch became a great lyricist quite independently. And Petrarch, too, contributed to poetry's prestige, possibly over-valuing his Latin epic, *Africa*, and under-valuing his Italian lyrics.

Two theoretical problems immediately were apparent. How should poetry be fitted into the other liberal arts, and how was it possible to account for its unmistakable greatness which none of these other arts even mildly shared? The solution to each of these problems contributed to the other. The powerfully moving quality of such poetry as Dante's [and Petrarch's] could only be explained by the accession of some super-human quality, or divine inspiration, and the subject matter of their poetry, even where as in Petrarch's case it dealt with love, was essentially theological. Hence poetry could not be considered as one other of the liberal arts but had to be seen as standing above them and supported by them – as we have already seen Salutati classified it.[5]

And in this it was aided by the analogy of the scholastic conception of theology as the Queen of the sciences, standing above the others, and especially the liberal arts which were at the bottom of the pyramid. But the notion of poetry as specially concerned with philosophical and theological subject matters was also a traditional one, so that this idea is certainly not a Renaissance invention.[6] Rather it received a powerful new reinforcement, and even revival, among the humanists of the fourteenth century.

The concern with poetry in the early Renaissance was theological in another sense also. Dante and Petrarch could seek to express a spiritualised conception of human love, which in Dante's case could lift his Beatrice into the role of his guide in Paradise. There was a specifically Christian and specifically late medieval and early Renaissance mingling of earthly and other-worldly passion, an etherealisation of the erotic in their poetry – not that there was to be no frankly and joyfully sensual poetry in the Renaissance. But as J. A. Symonds, and others who have wished to stress a Renaissance 'paganism' have explained, there was also a greatly expanded interest in classical poetry. How could classical poetry that, on the one hand, reflected the wholly accepted and 'natural' sensuality of antiquity, and, on the other hand, either made constant and innumerable allusions to pagan deities and religious practices, or chose as its theme and content the myths and tales of the gods and heroes, be regarded by the men of these fervently Christian centuries? Of course, in many different ways. But which ways were to be considered legitimate and preferable? There was therefore an inescapable problem of interpretation of the classical images of the divine and human inherent in all but the one alternative of prohibition.

Prohibition, however, was unthinkable, except to those puritanical guides to men's consciences, the zealots among the Mendicants. The men of the Middle Ages had read those of the Latin classical poets whose texts were generally available, and the humanists' rediscoveries of those that were not available were rediscoveries of even earlier medieval manusscripts. How the poets were read and interpreted in the Middle Ages, however, is another question, outside our scope, yet certainly discussed in a very illuminating way by E. R. Curtius, among others.[7] And indeed there was a surprisingly wide range of attitudes. But the predominant mode of interpretation was to allegorise the myths of the gods and the stories of lust into illustrations of Christian religious doctrine and morality.[8] This sort of interpretation was ready-made for the humanists who sought to answer the attacks of Giovanni Dominici and the others. Curtius was right in suggesting that the early humanist defences of poetry were motivated by the desire to protect their own literary activities and interest from these unjustified persecutions.[9]

But I do believe that he misses the main point in not emphasising that the point of view of Mussatto, Petrarch, Boccaccio and Salutati was also a positive one which they fully accepted rather than a merely negative defensive warding-off of a narrow-minded zeal that could well arouse popular and inquisitorial antagonism against them. They were also explaining to themselves why it was legitimate to read the classical poets, since they also had Christian consciences. And classical poetry was a great delight, an object of enormous admiration, and a very definite model and inspiration for these lovers of literature. Moreover, it was not simply a question of finding a *modus vivendi* for a limited circle of aesthetes who were charmed by the artistry of the ancients but also trembled at the peril to their immortal souls. Reading the classical poets, the Latins first, and later the Greeks, meant the discovery and exploration of a marvellous world of human thought, feeling and action. In it they found images and narrations that corresponded closely to their own widened and deepened vision of the nature of man and the possibilities of human life in the here-and-now. But these were features of classical poetry that could appeal to increasingly wide sections of the educated upper and middle classes, those very sections of Renaissance society who so eagerly sought to have their children educated by the humanists so that this great world of classical imagination, thought, and experience could be opened to them.

Those historians of the nineteenth century who concocted the myth that many men of the Renaissance were converted to paganism by reading the classics were right in at least one sense. It was a serious problem for the Renaissance reader of the classics to relate the polytheistic and erotic content of what he read to his Christian faith. But the humanists who introduced him to the classics also provided him with ways of interpreting that literature and reconciling its contents with Christianity. One way would have been the rather scholarly approach which would more or less ignore the incompatible elements as products of a pre-Christian age, easily explained away on the assumption that these great authors, if they had only known Christ, could easily have adapted their ideas to Christianity. There are certain similarities between this gambit and the way moderns read the literatures of the world – from a non-religious point of view, however, but assuming the necessity of understanding the religious conceptions and references of the author in order to interpret and appreciate his meaning and artistry. But this sort of nascent cultural relativism was difficult to sustain in an age which regarded faith in and knowledge of religious truth as one of the essentials in avoiding eternal damnation. To read the classics was to read the literature of the damned. They could not be read with the kind of detachment towards their religious content that is now possible. This content had to be viewed as at least containing some of the generalities of Christian doctrine, if not the specifics, which came from the revelation of the Scriptures and the history and tradition of the sacred events and the Church. But generalities were much more readily to be seen in the philosophers such as Aristotle, Seneca, Cicero and Plato and the Neoplatonists in so far as they were known. The poets when they referred to religious matters made specific references to specific pagan deities and religious rites and beliefs.

In order to meet this problem the humanists resorted to the well-established medieval practice of allegorical interpretation. The point I am making here is that allegory is exactly a mode of interpretation which discovers the general concealed in the specific; it is a conversion of the literal poetic image into a moral, or a natural-philosophical, or a theological truth, which is a statement in general terms. It is the reverse interpretive procedure to that which finds in Christian practice the concrete application of a general truth stated by a philosopher or theologian (whether pagan or Christian). Certain assumptions had, of course, to be made about the mentality or purpose of the pagan author whose poetry was subject to such discovery of moral or religious truth concealed beneath the surface. These, as we shall see, were either that he deliberately and consciously buried his general meanings beneath an apparent surface meaning, or that, unconsciously and with divine inspiration, a sacred meaning was infused into his work. The poet, therefore, had still to be regarded as something of a prophet, since his utterances were oracular and needed interpretation to reveal their concealed meanings. In this way, the *theologia poetica*, as it was called, paralleled 'Biblical Poetics', which, as we saw above in Salutati's re-utterance of the medieval hunt for spiritual and figural meanings in the Scriptures,[10] sought to move, not from the concrete image to the generalisation, but from the concrete image to the specific religious revelation.

Theologia poetica has an important place in the context of this book because it was one of the dominant ways in which the men of the Renaissance, through the humanists, moved towards the acceptance of a widened and deepened vision of human life and yet were able to discover in this movement a re-affirmation of their traditional Christian faith. It is important because it led towards a greater universality in the conception of human culture by finding a means of bringing the vast world of ancient paganism within the frame of a Christian image of God and His works. *Theologia poetica* was one of the chief procedures by which the wide varieties of human experience and human culture could be regarded as corresponding to one universal conception of man which was at that time identified with the Christian. A true understanding of the Christian vision of life would reveal it as, necessarily, the true universal vision of man. At the same time, men of all religions and traditions, in so far as one could discover the universal elements contained within the concrete images and forms, could be brought into relationship with the universal and Christian vision. The inner nature and meaning of human life everywhere could be embraced, since human universality was Christian, provided the outer shell or husk was regarded as merely the symbolic vehicle in which the truth was concealed. This is the aspect of humanist discussions of the theological character of poetry that we shall now examine through certain selected examples in a limited survey, and we shall then look at the ways in which Renaissance Platonism also sought a universal truth in a diversity of theological forms and consider the possible connections between the *theologia poetica* and *theologia platonica*.

2. *Theologia Poetica* and the *Prisci Poetae* in Petrarch and Boccaccio

A classic statement of the *theologia poetica* was made by Petrarch in one of his letters to his brother Gerardo [*Rerum familiarium* X, 4]. 'Poetic is not at all opposed to theology.' In the first place the Scriptures show that theology is poetry about God. What is it but poetry when Christ is spoken of as a lion, as a lamb, as a worm? He repeats Peter Damiani's exegesis as Salutati also did. There are a thousand such examples in the Scriptures. What are the parables but tales whose meaning is alien to the language? These he would call *alieniloquium* rather than the more usual Greek term, 'allegory'. But what about poetry that has a secular subject matter? The Scriptures are about God and divine things, secular literature deals with gods and men. And we read in Aristotle that the first poets were 'theologisers' [*theologisantes*].[11]

What is the origin of the poet and his name? The best belief is that

> when at one time rude men, but burning with that desire which is innate in man for knowing the truth and for discovering the divine, began to think that there was some higher power by which mortals are ruled, they considered that power worthy to be venerated by a more than human ceremony and in an awesome ritual.

Therefore they erected ample temples, established priests and ministers, provided golden vessels and purple vestments, and

> lest these should be silent honours, it was decided to please the divinity with high-sounding words and to confer a sacred praise to the higher powers by a style of speaking that was far from anything vulgar and plebeian, and confined to metres in which charm is present and boredom avoided. It was certainly necessary to create this not in a vulgar form but in a certain new and exquisite and highly artful way. Because in the Greek language this was called poetic, those who used it were called poets.[12]

His source for this account was Isidore of Seville's *Etymologies*, VIII, 7, *De poetis*, which was based on Varro and Suetonius, who wrote lost lives of the poets. But many of the authors of the Old Testament also wrote in heroic and other kinds of verse. As we saw above, David was a particular favourite of Petrarch, who here calls him the 'poet of the Christians'. Moreover Ambrose, Augustine and Jerome wrote sacred poetry, and Prudentius, Prosper of Aquitaine and Sedulius also wrote sacred verse.[13] Thus, he emphasises the essentially religious character of poetry to his mind, both the pagan and the Christian. The poet is an inspired oracle of divine truth. Petrarch then proceeds to analyse one of his own Eclogues showing his brother the theological meaning contained in it.

In his *Invectives Against a Certain Doctor*, he offers another defence of the poet along with the humanist in general.[14] Here he deals more explicitly with the problem of the paganism of the classical poets, and he even more specifically develops the theme of the theological origins of poetry among the Greeks.

> You belch forth imprecations against the poets as though they were enemies of the true faith to be avoided by the faithful and driven away by the Church; what do you think of Ambrose, Augustine and Jerome, what of Cyprian, Victorinus the martyr, what of Lactantius and the other catholic writers, among whom almost nothing is written without the traces of the poets, while on the contrary almost none of the heretics has inserted something poetic in his little works either because of his ignorance or because there was nothing in harmony with his errors among the poets. For although many mention the names of the gods (which it must be believed they did on account of the nature of the times and the culture of those peoples rather than because they followed their own judgements, and which the very philosophers also did who, as we may read in the rhetorical books, did not think the gods existed), nevertheless the very greatest of the poets have declared in their works that they believed in one omnipotent God, the creator, ruler and maker of everything.[15]

He was, however, aware that this declaration of the poets' monotheism was insufficient, since there was much other evidence to the contrary. He therefore claims that they should be allowed the same margin of error as the philosophers. And one should not wonder if they fell into errors before the advent of the truth when so many catholic men have departed from the right road and the truth has never been so bitterly fought as by these.[16] As for their obscurity, he offers both the obscurity of philosophers and the praise of obscurity by Christian writers, even that of the Scriptures. But here is the standard point where recourse to an allegorical interpretation is upheld. Petrarch only hints at it, but nevertheless, he justifies under the cover of the delight of unravelling the mysteries concealed in the poets' obscurity their offensive attribution of envy, fraud, wars and lusts to the gods.[17] Moreover their very portrayal of the gods proves they did not think them gods but men:

> For who but a madman would worship adulterers and deceivers as gods? Or who would really believe those were gods concerning whom he heard of such crimes as he would not consider tolerable among men? Besides who

> can doubt that sins, which snatch away their very humanity from men, in the same way but much more remove the deity from such gods? Homer and Vergil made mutual belligerents of the gods, and for that reason Homer was held to be mad by the Athenians, as Cornelius Nepos reports. I believe this was too easily believed by the mob, but learned men know that if there are many gods and if they can quarrel and make war among themselves, it is necessary that one is the victor and another the vanquished, and so they are neither immortal nor omnipotent and consequently not even a god; therefore there is one God and not many; the vulgar, however, are deceived.[18]

It is essential to see in this attitude a new confidence in the rational judgement of the intelligent and learned man. Pagan poetry, he is saying, is no threat to the intelligent Christian because he can easily see through the theological absurdities and superficialities of mythology. This is, of course, a more enlightened response than the insistence on the hidden allegorical meaning. But Petrarch clung to both views, and so exemplified the fact that the humanist attitude towards pagan mythology was and continued to be an amalgam of new scholarly insights that could hold old error at a distance, as error, and the need simultaneously to find a unity of truth beneath the surface divergences.

It is in keeping with the latter motive that Petrarch reaffirms the old theory of the *prisci poetae* as also being theologians – the same figures who in Renaissance Platonist thought were called the *prisci theologi*:

> The greatest philosophers testify and the authority of the saints confirms, that the first theologians among the gentiles certainly were the poets, and, if you do not know it, the name of poet itself indicates it. Among these Orpheus was especially ennobled, whom Augustine mentions in the eighteenth book of the *City of God*. 'But they failed to arrive at the destination they sought' someone has said. I admit it, for perfect knowledge of the true God is the consequence not of human study but of heavenly grace. Nevertheless the spirit of these most studious men should be praised, because, by what roads they could, they drew near to the desired heights of truth so that they preceded the philosophers in this very great and necessary inquest. It should be believed also that these most ardent investigators did at least reach as far as they were able to go by human powers, so that, according to that principle of the Apostle stated above, invisible things having been known and seen from those things which are made, they attained to some sort of knowledge of the first cause and of the one God; and thus they successively acted in all ways so that, what they did not dare do publicly because the living truth had not yet illumined the world, they might secretly persuade – that the gods were false whom the deluded people worshipped.[19]

Thus the affirmation of the existence of a secret tradition differing from the manifest meaning of their writings, in which the divine truth was known by inspired ancient pagan bards – poets or theologians – was clearly made by Petrarch. It is this theory of the ancient *theologia poetica* which is again taken up by the Platonists of the late Quattrocento as an essential part of their conception of a *theologia platonica.*

Giovanni Boccaccio's *De genealogia deorum* was one of the most influential early humanist works in laying out a pattern of arguments both about the antique gods and about poetic theology. While, as Seznec has shown,[20] it is essentially dependent on his late classical, patristic and medieval predecessors, Boccacio's was a recapitulation of the legends about the gods that enjoyed enormous popularity until displaced in the mid-sixteenth century by more recent compilations. As we shall show, it was not without successors in the fourteenth century (principally Salutati's *De laboribus Herculis*) and in the fifteenth century, but it remained the major humanist work in this genre.

He waits until he has completed his exposition and allegorical interpretations of the ancient gods to supply his explanation and justification for what he has done in his last two books [the XIVth and XVth). He fears that

> there are certain pietists who, in reading my words, will be moved by holy zeal to charge me with an injury to the most sacrosanct Christian religion; for I allege that the pagan poets are theologians – a distinction which Christians grant only to those instructed in sacred literature.

But if they will only recall St. Augustine's *City of God* there they would find him citing Varro concerning the three kinds of theology contained in the poets – the mythical, the physical and the civil. The physical is the most important since it deals with the nature of the cosmos and of man. And since the greatest of poets dealt with the gods in hymns of praise and with their powers and nature, Aristotle and other ancients called them theologians.[21]

Today Christian theologians call themselves doctors of theology to distinguish themselves from the mythological ones and any others,

> Such distinction admits no possible exception as implying an injury to the name of Christianity. Do we not speak of all mortals who have bodies and rational souls as men? Some may be Gentiles, some Israelites, some Agarenes,

some Christians, and some so depraved as to deserve the name of gross beasts, not men. Yet we do not wrong our Saviour by calling them men, though with his Godhead He is known to have been literally human. No more is there any harm in speaking of the old poets as theologians.

Such poets were not 'sacred' theologians.

Yet the old theology can sometimes be employed in the service of Catholic truth, if the fashioner of myths should choose. I have observed this in the case of more than one orthodox poet in whose investiture of fiction the sacred teachings were closed. Nor let my pious critics be offended to hear the poets sometimes called even sacred theologians.[22]

One of the most important aspects of these discussions of 'Poetic Theology' was the question of the origin of poetry, which was closely linked with the question of the origin of religion, or of theology. Now, of course, there was no question as to the divine origin of the Hebrew religion as the preparation for the Advent of Christ. But sometime later the various pagan cults took their rise. Boccaccio speaks of how tremendously widespread paganism was, rising among the descendants of Noah, as tradition had it, but already of considerable dimension by the time of Abraham. Poetry, on the other hand, was thought to have arisen either first among the Hebrews, or among the Chaldeans or among the Greeks. Boccaccio, of course, accepts the first: 'So it seems that poetry had its origin among the Hebrews not earlier than Moses, leader of the Israelites.' He cannot believe that it first arose among people as barbarous as the Chaldeans. The claim of the Greeks was more probable.[23]

He sets forth this view of the early history of poetry in detail giving an exposition of the concept of *prisci poetae*, those poet theologians who 'began to wonder at the works of their mother nature; and as they meditated they came gradually to believe in some one Being by whose operation and command all visible things are governed and ordered. Him they named God.' As Petrarch also had put it, they erected temples, fashioned gold vessels, appointed priests who at last developed a mode of addressing and praising the Deity in a language that was finer than that used for ordinary discourse and appropriate to the divinities.[24]

Some of these, though few – and among them, it is thought, were Musaeus, Linus and Orpheus – under the prompting stimulus of the Divine Mind, invented strange songs in regular time and measure, designed for the praise

> of God. To strengthen the authority of these songs, they enclosed the high mysteries of divine things in a covering of words, with the intention that the adorable majesty of such things should not become the object of too common knowledge, and thus fall into contempt.[25]

This practice of course got to be called poetry. After debating various theories as to the time and person of its invention, whether Musaeus or Linus or an older or more recent Orpheus was the inventor, he concludes,

> I cannot believe that the sublime effects of this great art were first bestowed upon Musaeus, or Linus, or Orpheus, however ancient, unless, as some say, Moses and Musaeus were one and the same. Of the beast Nimrod [of the Chaldeans] I take no account. Rather it was instilled into most sacred prophets dedicated to God. For we read that Moses, impelled by what I take to be this poetic longing, at dictation of the Holy Ghost, wrote the largest part of the Pentateuch not in prose but in heroic verse. In like manner others have set forth the great works of God in the metrical garments of letters, which we call poetic. And I think the poets of the Gentiles in their poetry – not perhaps without understanding – followed in the steps of these prophets. . . .[26]

Here, of course, is a restatement of the theory of the *prisci poetae*. It had its origin among the ancients who attempted to account for the origin of poetry by it and it was taken up and propagated by such Fathers of the Church as St. Augustine and was repeated by Cassiodorus and Isidore of Seville. It thus became a central conception of early medieval thought until it was displaced by the general downgrading of poetry by the scholastic theologians.[27] Petrarch, and even more Boccaccio, revived this theory and gave it once again the currency which it had lost after the twelfth century. The form of the argument is important, for Boccaccio adds to Petrarch's version the theory that Moses was the *priscus poeta* and that the Greeks followed after him and the other Biblical prophets. We shall recur to this argument in showing its strange parallelism to the Renaissance Platonist's theories of the *prisci theologi*.[28] But if it became accepted that the early Greek poet-theologians, though not inspired by the Holy Spirit, followed in the footsteps of the prophets, and also concealed deeper mysteries beneath their outward images, then a long step had been taken towards the naturalisation of paganism, and the universalisation of the multiple human traditions.

St. Augustine's recognition of 'the poets, who were also called theologues, because they made hymns about the gods', was tempered by his recognition of their polytheism:

> And if, among much that is vain and false, they sang anything of the true God, yet, by worshipping him along with others who are not gods, and showing them the service which is due to Him alone, they did not serve Him at all rightly; and even such poets as Orpheus, Musaeus and Linus were unable to abstain from dishonouring their gods by fables. But yet these theologues worshipped the gods.[29]

For Boccaccio, as for Petrarch, and, as we shortly shall see, for Salutati, the poets were not necessarily polytheists but rather masked their more philosophical view of divinity behind the polytheistic myths. Said Boccaccio,

> Yet without question poets do say in their works that there are many gods, when there is but one. But they should not therefore be charged with falsehood, since they neither believe nor assert it as a fact, but only as a myth or fiction, according to their wont. Who is witless enough to suppose that a man deeply versed in philosophy hasn't any more sense than to accept polytheism? As sensible men we must easily admit that the learned have been most devoted investigators of the truth, and have gone as far as the human mind can explore; thus they know beyond any shadow of doubt that there is but one God. As for poets their own works clearly show that they have attained to such knowledge. Read Vergil and you will find the prayer: 'If any vows, Almighty Jove, can bend Thy will – ' an epithet you will never see applied to another god. The multitude of other gods, they looked upon not as gods, but as members or functions of the Divinity; such was Plato's opinion, and we call him a theologian. But to those functions they gave a name in comformity with Deity because of their veneration for the particular function in each instance.[30]

This very latitudinarian kind of interpretation did not really invite Christians to follow the pagan practices and manners of speaking but rather it brought the pagan poets within the circle of permissible toleration. Moreover Boccaccio was careful to admit that even beneath the surface they frequently erred. 'Of course I do not doubt that pagan poets had an imperfect sense of the true God, and so sometimes wrote of Him what was not altogether true.' He also excuses the pagan poets on the ground that they lived too soon to know Christ and were excluded by the Jews from their pre-Christian revelations. One cannot be blamed for ignorance.

Such are the pagan poets who . . . could not know the truth of Christianity; for that light of the eternal truth which lighteth every man that cometh into the world had not yet shone forth upon the nations. Not yet had these servants gone throughout the earth bidding every man to the supper of the Lamb. To the Israelites alone had this gift been granted of knowing God aright, and truly worshipping Him. But they never invited anyone to share the great feast with them, nor admitted any of the Gentiles at their doors. And if pagan poets wrote not the whole truth concerning the true God, though they thought they did, such ignorance is an acceptable excuse. . . .[31]

3. Concept and Practice of *Theologia Poetica* in Salutati

Salutati, as we have seen above,[32] was deeply concerned with the interrelationships of the different sciences of learning and expression and particularly emphasised to Fra Giovanni Dominici that the humanities were essential for the divinities. He thought he knew from having worked so long in the past on his ambitious *Four Books on the Labours of Hercules*[33] in which the resources of the liberal arts were first utilised for an understanding of the poetry of the classical accounts of the legendary demi-God, and then philosophy, moral and natural, and theology were called upon to aid in interpreting the hidden mystical meanings of these myths. Salutati's work has not yet received the analysis it deserves as a mirror of a late-medieval early Renaissance mind, and we shall not attempt to give it here. For this short discussion will not deal with his hero, Hercules, but only with Salutati's conception of the theological character of pagan poetry and his notion of its basic content when subjected to allegorical analysis – not as applied to Hercules but to Jupiter and Juno. His first book, which is also methodological on the relationships of poetry and the liberal arts, and which elevates poetry over the liberal arts in an analogous position to theology, we also pass over, since we have already discussed his ideas on these questions in connection with his reply to Giovanni Dominici.[34] It is perhaps worth mentioning that he does not yet speak of the 'humanities', the *studia humanitatis*, here, although the term does occur in his *De fato* written before 1396.[35]

Chapter one of the second book of his *De laboribus Herculis* is called 'When and from what sources did the practice of deifying men and idols originate.' And he begins, 'Since poetry, because it seems to me to be most similar, had its beginnings with the worship of idols, I believe we must investigate how and at what time so great an error invaded the world.'[36] He finds the origin of idolatry in the *Book of Wisdom*, chapter 14, which describes how the practice began when a mourning father made an image of his dead son and compelled his servants to worship it. This practice caught on and had great appeal for a number of reasons, among them the very beauty of the simulated men and the right of asylum in temple precincts.[37] He turns for confirmation to the Hermetic text attributed to Hermes Trismegistus, the *Asclepius*, which he also used in his *De fato*, 'For of all the miracles this one wins in astonishment, that man is able to invent the divine nature and produce it.' Not being able to make souls also to reside in the image of the gods, they called down the souls of angels and demons to inhabit them, thus giving them powers of doing good or evil.[38]

The poets also had their origin at this time because they began to write about these false gods, concealing from the public their true nature beneath a veil of myths, fearing the public wrath if they wrote openly concerning the vanity and falsity of this kind of worship. And these poets were 'far greater friends and public witnesses of the truth than the very philosophers who gloried in being professors of truth itself.'[39] Salutati also discusses whether paganism first began in Egypt, Babylonia or Greece. He resolves it in favour of the worship of Bel, or Baal, at the time of Ninus, using the chronological tables of Eusebius and Jerome as a guide. But poetry actually began earlier, with the worship of the true God in the time of Enoch, the grandson of Noah,

> since it is written that Enoch began to invoke the name of the Lord; but it is impossible to speak properly of God by words of human invention, since He is entirely infinite and inexpressible, and cannot be explained by us; therefore that invocation was undoubtedly by means of figurative words signifying something else than Him; thus from this time it may be said that our poetry, which we are discussing, began. For also many Hebrews thought the image of God itself was invented for which depreciatory words were spread.[40]

His second chapter of the foundations of poetry wishes to show in connection with the concealed inner meaning of poetry both the source from which and the end to which it moves. And he will not do this with the true or Scriptural poetry but with the secular. For, just as the Holy Scriptures have the love of God and of neighbour out of which it is composed and into which whatever that is composed in it is resolved, so the secular, as I would call it, and human poetry has the creator and the creature into whom or into whose actions whatever is concealed may be reduced.

The central content of the concealed mystical meaning of secular poetry, therefore, is a discussion of the nature and relations of God and man. Hence it is truly theological, as well as 'anthropological'.[41] Salutati immediately supplies examples.

Indeed our poetry deals with God both in terms of Himself and His intrinsic actions, and in terms of the effects which proceed [from Him] into the outside world. For when our poet [Vergil] says, 'For my virtues and my great power are born only from the supreme Father who despises the weapons of Typheus,' if you piously understand, it is a statement of the secrets of divine majesty, namely concerning the unity of essence and multiplicity of persons. And although the mystery of the true God and the profundity of the Trinity was hidden from Vergil and the other pagan poets, nevertheless much that they said about their own gods, while they struggled to lift them to the majesty of deity, applied not to those gods, indeed, which certainly are nothing, but was in conformity with the true God.[42]

Again he urges,

Therefore beneath the words which the poet speaks about Jupiter, and which are entirely unfitting, there is expressed in a certain way the condition of the true God, that He not only knows Himself but through His will He rules the spiritual creatures, which he calls by the name of gods, and also the affairs of men, namely actions and volitions, which He alone is able to direct who was also able to create.[43]

He quotes Valerius Soranus out of St. Augustine that *Jupiter omnipotens* was the genitor of all gods and the one God, and Macrobius' *Saturnalia* that

all gods and goddesses by the imitation of rites, by similarity of statues, by the authority of oracles, by the identity of effects, by the same meaning of names, by the order of ceremonies, and by many other arguments, are none other than Apollo. Therefore, unless I am wrong, it was thought that the poets did not believe in any other than one god in that crowd of their gods. For . . . presupposing that all that multiplicity of gods had one essence but a variety of powers and actions, they called it by diverse names so that the names, which indeed are different from the facts, signified not many things but the multiform powers, actions and effects of the same thing.

Therefore,

> I say that everything which seems fabulous in the poets must necessarily be reduced by due exposition to God or to creatures or to something pertaining to them. And since a mystical interpretation opens up the secrets of the poets and adapts them to God, nature or the customs of individuals, thus, although not contrived by the author, it may doubtless be so regarded that what he invented may be said to have fallen into an acceptable opinion. For if it is possible to modify the scheme of proper names into what he really meant, I boldly assert that this without controversy has elicited the true meaning of the author, or if perchance it is not his meaning, and does not come near to that name which the author intended, still it is a far more appropriate meaning than the one the author thought he had invented.[44]

Salutati seems astonishingly naïve, here, for he is saying that the Christian interpreter can find the true meanings of the pagan poets, or at any rate better meanings, than they intended, which he assuredly could do. But this endorsement of arbitrary interpretation does not in its turn mean that Salutati would countenance any but an exegesis that seemed close to the possibilities of analogy contained in the text. Moreover, in an earlier work he had also granted that such methods were useful in finding the desired meanings in the Scriptures as well.[45] And he has a supreme confidence that he is able to find the meaning that God Himself wished to be found. For he adds, 'This is not to be wondered at, for mortals plan many things for some particular purpose which God the Director of things guides to another outcome. Thus we daily see inconceivable events happening.' Secular poetry was also under the aegis of divine providence, but it differed from the sacred oracle of the Scriptures,

> since the latter are totally true whether you consider the letter or contemplate the hidden meaning; but the others grasp the truth whenever it is under the outer surface, while the exterior, though it may resemble the truth, is always definitely fictitious.

Man cannot interpret the Scriptures in any other way than God intended, but human literature can have a meaning given by God which the author did not intend. 'But whereas the analogies of things are infinite, they can, not unfittingly, be drawn to other meanings at which they arrive who seem to marvel at many expositions.'[46]

Salutati proceeds to expound the many ways in which Jupiter and

Juno could be interpreted, following Cicero, *On the Nature of the Gods*, Lactantius, *On the Divine Institutes*, Hyginus, *On the Images of the Heavens*, and especially Giovanni Boccaccio *On the Genealogies of the Gods* in whom is to be found composed and digested not only what may be read with the others, 'but what cannot be read elsewhere'.[47] First of all, he assures us, they are human beings and so 'express the condition of man'.[48] But they are sometimes presented with the qualities of the one true God. Sometimes the quarrels of the gods must be taken for the conflicting influences of the stars over human life, sometimes for the elements such as fire or ether. They operate as a general supercelestial influence or as the reason and will of God and sometimes even as 'fortune'.[49]

His fifth chapter, 'That Jupiter sometimes is taken for a supernatural agent and that then Juno is used for the will of God and sometimes for fortune', shows him working out the complexities of his own ideas of the interrelationship of divine providence, human free will, fate and fortune, as he also did in his *De fato* which we discussed earlier.[50] He finds the poetic discussions particularly consoling because they seem to correspond in their complications to his own notions. In fact it is very useful to divide the deity into several gods in order to explain and interrelate all of His aspects.

> But perchance someone will be moved to think it inconvenient that there are in the poets the imagined conversations of the gods since the one God who is called Jupiter is all gods. And if Juno, as has just now been assumed, is known as the disposition or will of Jupiter, which is nothing else than Jupiter willing or disposing, so that they do not see how that will can differ from Jupiter himself and indeed, as many wish, it should not be called anything except the same essence with Jupiter willing, then the poets most incongruously represent Jupiter speaking to Juno as though to another person. And although in God, who is the supreme simplicity, the will is His own essence, and this is the same in the souls of men, as the image and vestige of the Trinity can be expressly assigned to us, nevertheless some hold and affirm that, because there is one principle of the divine will and another of God willing, and likewise of the angel or of the willing soul, this sort of conversation is not ineptly to be found among the poets, since we daily experience how we differ within ourselves about various things. And the authority of the Scriptures may be added to this explanation: do we not say it is incongruously written about God 'And He said, "Let us make man in our own image and similitude"'? Nevertheless the unity of the essence was

expressed when it was said 'He said' and the mystery of His Trinity when it was added, 'Let us make' and the pronoun 'our' which connotes the plurality not of the essence but of the person.[51]

What does this explanation of Salutati's methods of poetic exposition demonstrate? First of all that he considered it legitimate to use an almost arbitrary freedom in interpretation. From it came the possibility of using an exposition of classical poetry, and of literature in general, as a series of concrete images which expressed certain general ideas by analogy. And as he himself said, the similitudes of things are almost infinite, so it was quite possible for him, or any such expositor, to project his entire theology and philosophy of man on to an arbitrary interpretation. In the second place, although he refers to the physical and astrological analogies in dealing with the gods, his own interests were almost entirely in finding a metaphorical expression of the interplay of human motivations and actions with the supernatural power of the divine will. But however much and however easy it was in this age of astrological naturalism to equate the planets with the gods of the pantheon, Salutati's own conception of a fundamentally voluntaristic Deity acting providentially, and of a man dominated by will, certainly found a much closer approximation to the narrative and dramatic character of pagan poetry. Thus his arbitrariness was itself limited by the appropriate correspondence between a voluntaristic philosophy of man and God, and the character of the poetry itself. From the concrete events of the tales he could draw specific generalisations about man and God because he conceived of man and God in terms of the very principles and relationships which seemed to be concretely illustrated in poetry. In the third place his claim would seem to have a certain justification, namely, that the poets were committed to a false religious philosophy but nevertheless revealed more of the actuality and truth about life than they were conscious of doing. In the fourth place, it should perhaps be recognised that modern literary criticism, in so far as it seeks to discuss the content and general meaning of a work and is not primarily formal and stylistic, must necessarily resort to the same principles that Salutati upheld, *magari* with more precise methods and greater controls. There is thus also a certain justification in the claim that it was an event of great cultural and human significance for Salutati to turn to the exposition of Hercules as a mirror of human life.[52]

Perhaps it needs to be added that from Salutati's own point of view he could legitimately do this only insofar as he also sought to find concealed in the poets those true Christian insights about the nature of God which might confirm and establish the validity of his insights about man.

Thus in greatly expanding the application of the allegorical method of interpretation to the pagan poets he was simultaneously staying within an old and Christian tradition of Biblical and literary exegesis and opening it up to include the necessary and expanded vision of human life. Thus also he fulfils the need that was at that time felt to relate the wide world of the poets' imagination to the Christian world of the Renaissance, to show that not only Dante and Petrarch composed poetry with Christian meaning, but that, if Christian meaning was also human meaning, this legitimately could and should be sought in Homer and Vergil as well. It meant a movement towards a universalising, not only of literature – a conception of the possibility of a world literature where a Christian Dante could stand beside a pagan Homer – but towards a universalising of human experience, so that a Renaissance Christian might understand the experience of an ancient pagan and also find in it elements that were comparable to his own. Therefore the principle and practice of allegorical interpretation in the Renaissance was not a mere vestige and prolongation of the Middle Ages but an instrument of innovation. It suggests, moreover, that works of poetic interpretation, such as this of Salutati, are important for the content of logical, philosophical and moral ideas that he presents through his allegorical interpretations and not simply for their illustration of a particular methodology.

Salutati had begun the second book of *The Labours of Hercules* with a disquisition on the interdependence of dialectic and rhetoric, and on the infinite yearning of the will to knowledge which could never be satisfied with one science alone but quickly discovered that all were connected and all had to be mastered.

> No one ever learned as much as he wanted, nor was entirely able to arrive at the end of any art whatsoever or to have perceived it in its completeness. Nor can perfection of any one art be had (they are so tied together and the one depends on the other) unless the others are learned.[53]

Truly a Faustian declaration to be compared with Ficino's description of man's insatiable passion for infinite knowledge. The pursuit of a *theologia poetica* by Salutati may also be considered part of a humanist's desire to demonstrate that the content of philosophy and theology might be discovered in poetry. Thus there was in the development of this traditional mode of interpretation in the Renaissance an effort to arrive at two kinds of conciliation: between Christian theological doctrine and the pagan poetic vision of divinity, and between humanism and scholastic philosophy or theology.

4. *Theologia Poetica* in the Mid-Quattrocento: Giovanni Caldiera's *Concordantia*

This motif is uppermost in another work of this genre of interpreting the classical myths written by a Venetian scholar of the Quattrocento who managed [surprisingly early in the century for this] to combine the careers of physician and humanist. Giovanni Caldiera [or Latin, Calderia] was born, probably, somewhere around 1400, or slightly earlier, since he is listed as a professor of medicine at the University of Padua in 1424[54] [but also delivered an inaugural oration in 1423]. He was much in demand at the university as an orator on formal occasions, and also developed an apparently successful medical practice in Venice. His known writings also span the two fields. He dedicated a *Book on the Canons of Astrology as well as a Description of the Whole World*[55] to King Alfonso of Naples. He wrote an *Exposition of Cato*[56] for the education of his daughter, which is apparently the same as his treatise *On the Moral and Theological Virtues.*[57] He wrote on *The Venetian Economy*[58] and a work on *The Excellence of the Venetian Republic and on the Arts Cultivated in it both Mechanical and Liberal and of the Virtues which are Especially Due to the Venetian Republic*, in five books, 1473.[59] He tried his hand at religious works,[60] also, composing an *Exposition of the Psalms.*[61] In addition he wrote the work that we are about to discuss. He died in 1474 after a lengthy career.

Sometime between 1447 and 1455, he completed his two books *On the Concord of the Poets, Philosophers and Theologians.* After the end he wrote as a heading for a table of contents:

> This *summa* [*sic*] contains two books. In the first we expound the poems of all the pagans, naturally, morally and spiritually. In the second book we

> expound all the sciences, arts and crafts as well as the Church militant and triumphant, poetically, naturally, morally and spiritually.[62]

This work is significant not only as an attempt to unite the disciplines of the humanist and the natural philosopher, but is also a striking venture of a layman into the precincts of theology. The first book, which is his *theologia poetica*, is by far the longest. It gives a panoramic view of Christian doctrine derived from a very ingenious allegorical exposition, but also offers moralistic and astrological interpretations of the myths, and disquisitions on the nature and differences of the arts. The second book is more directly concerned with the intellectual and practical disciplines and the greatness of the Venetians in them, and is probably the basis on which he elaborated his later laudation of the Venetian republic. It attained some diffusion in the fifteenth century. A copy was prepared for the library of Federigo da Montefeltro, the Duke of Urbino, and Giannozzo Manetti had acquired a manuscript of it for his library, written in the more highly abbreviated fifteenth-century university text-book hand, but apparently more accurately than the Urbino manuscript. A third manuscript of the fifteenth century is in the Biblioteca Civica of Fossombrone. There is also an extraordinarily defective edition of Venice, 1557 [and possible one of 1547, although this may be an erroneous listing of the 1557 edition].[63]

In his proemial chapter he seeks to show that God was known by poets, philosophers and theologians before His advent. Distinguished and pious men have long wondered about the first philosophers who dealt with gods and men in beautiful poetry. Their gods were thought to be completely alien to any true divinity. Yet the Stoics and the Peripatetics found a divine basis for goodness and truth, and they thought, for that reason, that intelligence, perfect knowledge of truth, and love of the good must be grafted into all men. But these more ancient bards were less learned and uneducated and they worshipped gods who were frequently accustomed to deceive men and seduce them from good morals. Indeed they permitted such rites as were fitting neither to gods nor to human dignity and excellence.

> Wherefore most beloved daughter if you neglect, abhor and are frequently in the practice of condemning the morals and teachings of the poets and the first philosophers, I certainly do not at all wonder, since all morals are most divine in your view. You are so practiced in the establishments of the

eminent Christ, you so admire the life of the most divine virgin that you consider all men who too little resemble them as alien from religion and the dignity of man.[64]

But she should think otherwise. 'For all men, indeed all things, have an innate divinity, although many also hold to divine things on the basis of false knowledge.' All being, knowledge and love descends from the first cause.

> Therefore the perfections of all things are from God, and if they are secretly usurped by men and other entities, they cease to exist. Therefore our existence is divine, similarly our life, knowledge and love are from God, and these qualities are contained in other entities according to their own perfection. . . . Therefore the primeval men observed many effects produced by nature but were ignorant of their causes. Later certain would-be philosophers more studiously observing the first causes of things, some thought it fire, others air, still others water, or earth, and certain of them many elements composing the beginning of all things. Therefore the poets following their teaching assigned the principle of divinity to the prime elements and they thought that there were certain divine men who surpassed the others in talent, virtue and learning.[65]

This was the first or philosophical mode of knowledge of divinity. On it was based the poetic.

In the second place is the prophetic mode of knowledge.

> But besides this natural kind of knowledge there is another mode in which the divine light is infused into our minds so that we may see future things just as prophets and certain most ancient sibyls who foreknew the affairs of gods and men at a most distant age from their own. These foretold the advent of the great God and the hope of a future life by certain parables and a shadowy kind of teaching. Afterwards they transmitted these predictions to us in writing, when the Son of God had assumed human flesh and protected a secret divinity under the veil of humanity so that he might fully complete the mystery of the passion and redeem lost mankind.[66]
>
> Therefore, we received much from the instruction of Christ, which taught a knowledge of most divine and especially of secret things, whereas the human intellect is most distant from the perfection of God and could not understand either the first cause or the separate forms. He therefore professed his entire divinity by certain distinguished examples and sometimes in the custom of the prophets and sometimes by miracles. Moreover we have received from His teaching the complete explanation of the Father, Son and Holy Spirit. When indeed our souls are separated from the body and attain a merited glory we shall see the eternal God with perfect vision in

which we shall know the present, the past and the future in their different natures. For everything which the travellers have received in faith will be established in the first and certain vision of God.[67]

Therefore man proceeds from observation and poetic myth-making, through inspired prophecy, to revelation in the Incarnation and finally to direct and final vision of God, in four levels of knowledge of divinity. The first three of these are earthly and correspond to the non-Scriptural philosophic and poetic modes of knowledge and to theological insight through the prophets and sybils, and through the Incarnation. He will therefore try to show how these three levels of knowledge, the philosophical, the poetic and the theological, may be united in an exposition of the poets.

Taking one of the first of his attempts as an example of his method, we shall look at his exposition of the 'Mystery of the Trinity which the ancient poets obscurely transmitted'.[68] Although the Gentiles knew it through the poets, the Jews through the prophets and the Christians by the testimony of individual saints, nevertheless our knowledge of the Trinity is very foggy. The Gentiles saw that splendour entirely through a cloud. The Jews beyond the cloud saw divinity but did not distinguish the three persons. The Christians are contained within the cloud and therefore distinguish divinity and Trinity. But unless the fog is dispelled, the human intellect cannot see it perfectly. 'But certain men who are closer to divinity dissolve the cloud as though they were living in heaven and see divinity and the mystery of the entire Trinity clearly and everything such as we hold by faith they know by certain knowledge.'[69]

He then proceeds to tell the tale of Zeus' attempted union with Thetis, of his warning, of her marriage with Peleus, the quarrels of Athene, Hera and Aphrodite at the wedding and of the Judgement of Paris.[70] He then gives his first 'moral exposition'. Thetis the water nymph represents water and Zeus fire. If fire is joined to water it loses all its strength. Peleus is earth so the resulting offspring of water and earth is mud.

If therefore from Peleus and Thetis man is generated whom we have defined as the most perfect of all mixtures in our books of natural philosophy, it is necessary that many influences and many ordinances of the heavens agree for the generation of man. . . . After man is born and the age of reason comes to him, the three goddesses because they represent three modes of living are

> offered to men. In one we choose Pallas because we follow wisdom. In another Juno because we intensely desire riches and dignities. In the third we take Venus because we are easily forced into every kind of pleasure. And we consult Jupiter, who is God, as to which of these three goddesses we ought to pursue. God refuses his judgement since he has granted intellect to men in which perfect discretion and right choice is contained. For, for their merits and demerits, men receive rewards or punishments; therefore man, ignorant of his own life, passes up the judgement of reason and pursues the subject of his choice, preferring Venus in which everything voluptuous is promised. But we imitate the wisdom of Pallas by long labours, vigils and abstentions, and we gain the riches of Juno by the greatest dangers and anxieties.[71]

In this explanation there may be recognised the famous threefold choice of a way of life that went back at least to Macrobius' *Dream of Scipio*, and was thought to have a basis in the *Ethics* of Aristotle as well as in Plato's threefold division of the soul and their corresponding ways of life. It may be seen represented in Raphael's 'Dream of Scipio', and was applied to the Judgement of Paris in Fulgentius' *Mythologiae* [II, 1]. It was also the subject of a little treatise by Ficino.[72]

Giovanni Caldiera, however, is not content to let this interpretation stand and proceeds to offer a second moral interpretation.

> For Thetis we may understand honours of the body, for Peleus man's flesh, for Jove the soul which composes and forms a part of the body, for the three goddesses the three kinds of learning in which men are involved. For some devote their minds entirely to the speculative sciences, others to the practical and others to the operative arts. The Stoics place all happiness and perfection of virtue in the intellectual habit only. . . . Also certain most Christian men pursue God and the glory of the future age by speculations in soul and reason. But the Peripatetics arrive at virtue and happiness more principally by operation than by habit since those who have suffered are crowned and not those who have the habit of virtue; certain of the most Christian borrow their doctrine, imitating Christ not by prayers alone but by actions. The third sect of the philosophers departs far from virtue, since it considers the human soul as corruptible and prefers everything which adds to the pleasure of the body thus dignifying Venus. But those imitating the Peripatetics prefer Juno and those imitating the Stoics place Pallas before all others.

Thus, although he has separated the three classical sects, he has in substance made Aristotle's distinction of the three types of arts and virtues correspond to the three kinds of life.[73]

But Caldiera's third, 'Spiritual and Christian interpretation', is more unusual. For he interprets the three goddesses as the Christian Trinity and the theological virtues.

> For Proteus we know God the Father, for Jove, Christ, for Peleus the Christian people, for Thetis the holy Catholic Church which Christ vehemently loved, but He did not remain joined to it corporeally but spiritually and sacramentally, for if He had always remained with us corporeally we would not be saved by our own merits but Christ's.

Here, as earlier, Caldiera's Pelagianism seems blatantly naïve. He continues:

> For the three goddesses we know the three theological virtues; through Juno, the goddess of power, we arrive at the knowledge of the Father through virtue whereas power is attributed to the Father, and the saints will dwell in the kingdom of paradise through faith and they will know the omnipotence of God the Father. For Pallas the goddess of wisdom we may know true hope. For wisdom speaks concerning itself. Therefore in many ways through hope of beauty, love, fear and holy hope we are led to the wisdom of the Son and we know [His] generation into divine things, for wisdom is attributed to the Son. Through Venus, the goddess of love, we know charity which manifests the emanation of the Holy Spirit into our minds. For the will is attributed to [The Spirit] in which reason is contained through the affects of love in it. Therefore these three goddesses are invited to the eternal banquet where no discord and no quarrel can exist because the saints rejoice in peace alone. But the devil of discords when he was excluded from the divine company by God, perverted Adam, our parent, from the commandments of God especially because it was his work to throw the golden apple made by marvellous artistry, because He is God made man, into the middle of the goddesses, and by this apple, the human intellect judges all the goddesses according to the well-merited excellence of Christians. But because one ought rightly to be preferred, therefore Mercury, since he is human intellect, by a resounding pipe, which is the language of wisdom, carried a dubious sentence for the dignity of the goddesses and therefore conducted them to Paris, which is to the Apostle Paul, so that he might judge which is more beautiful, who since he saw them nude and without any veil gave the judgement in favour of charity, and since he had placed her ahead, awarded her the golden apple, because the greatest of all is charity. Therefore we best follow the principle of all the precepts through love of God and neighbour because on these two the law of Christ and all the prophets is founded. Therefore if we compare the powers of the soul, charity is found in the will, faith in the intellect, hope in the memory. And since we know the perfection of powers from the

perfection of their objects, therefore we prefer first the will, second, the intellect, and last memory. But you should most studiously pay attention to all of these.[74]

Apart from the fact that he seems to have switched his identifications of faith with memory, or the Father, and of hope with intellect, or the Son, this interpretation, which identifies the Apostle Paul with Paris, manages to turn the usual rejection of *amor* and pleasure upside down with its preference for Venus as charity. It is suggestive that his presumed Aristotelianism finds itself preferring love and the will to the intellect. In this way of interpretation, Caldiera truly anticipates the Platonic philosophy of love that came with Landino, Ficino, Pico, and Leone Ebreo in the next generation. The fact that a manuscript of his work was possessed by Manetti, a Florentine humanist, suggests that his influence was not confined to the Venetian area, but there is no traceable connection with Florentine Platonism.

His exposition of the goddess Venus later in the book is also interesting in this connection, because, like the Platonists, he expounds both a heavenly and an earthly Venus. The Epicureans embrace the earthly Venus, and the Stoics reject both, but the Peripatetics believe that Venus comes to all because love and pleasure is innate in all things in order for them to pursue their natural objects; even all mixed, inanimate beings have a certain natural appetite by which they are moved towards their object. And animate beings are more perfectly moved by the sensitive soul and carried towards the object known.

But the most perfect of living beings, such as men, pursue their objects after knowledge and after election; through these three appetites, therefore, we distinguish three kinds of loves, according to which the first is natural, the second sensitive, and the third intellective.[75]

The heavenly Venus is then analysed in terms of astrology and the effects of conjunctions of Venus with other planets on human life. If Venus joins Jupiter there is a good effect, but if to Mars or Bacchus, there is not much evil.

For the better is effected from good things rather than wicked from evil. All these things the famous and most erudite bard Vergil has explained to us. For when Aeneas saw Jupiter with Venus in the high heaven, after a few days he received part of the kingdom from his wife. Moreover when Venus appeared to Aeneas very sad, Dido perished by her own hand. Moreover when Mercury was sent by Jupiter to the low place of Lybia, that signified to Aeneas that if he would have friendships, they would not last a long time. But when Venus appeared to Aeneas as a virgin that meant that when he kept the men in their virginity, he made them merciful and mild.[76]

The exposition of the terrestrial Venus is full of exceptionally interesting allusions and connections. For instance he comments on the Three Graces who are nude and always assist Venus, 'whereas Graces ought to be without any covering'. The first is called Pasithea because she is attracting, the second Heriale because she is caressing, the third Heuprosine because she is retaining. He also speaks of the three kinds of love that come from Venus: from the union of Venus and Jupiter virtuous love, from Venus and Mars useful love, from Venus and Bacchus delectable love. 'In the eighth book of the *Ethics* Aristotle clearly distinguishes the first as stable and perfect from the others which are fallen and erroneous.'[77] He also has many details on the cult of Venus and on erotic practices in Cyprus and a remarkably wide-ranging knowledge of mythological detail.[78]

These are only two of the topics from his very extensive attempt to link the allegorical interpretation of the pagan poets with precepts of ancient philosophy and with Christian doctrine. Although his book certainly had nothing like the influence of Boccaccio's, it is not only a mid-Quattrocento example of a genre that was supposed not to be represented between the fourteenth and the sixteenth centuries,[79] but it is one that reveals the rich and more detailed kind of knowledge of ancient practices that was an inevitable accompaniment of the more advanced classical scholarship of fifteenth-century humanism. It is an important step towards the efforts at mythological exegesis within the framework of Ficino's Platonism which came a generation later, although, as we have said, a direct link may be difficult to establish.

Brief mention should be made of another, and a lesser work, in the same genre by the Neoplatonist and 'Hermetic-Christian' poet, Lodovico Lazzarelli. Some time after he was made 'Poet-Laureate' by Frederick III in 1469, twin manuscripts of his two books on *The Images of the Gentile Gods*[80] were prepared for the library of Federigo of Urbino. These consist of short expositions, largely astrological and iconographical, of the planetary gods and the nine muses and those

Olympians who had been excluded from the celestial spheres by lack of satellites. The remarkably executed illustrations of these twenty-seven odd figures with all of their proper symbolic accompaniments is perhaps of greater interest to the history of art. Lazzarelli's work represents, however, another indication of the continuing interest in the Quattrocento in compilations and expositions of the pagan divinities, and connects Boccaccio and Salutati in the fourteenth with Cartari and Gyraldi in the sixteenth century.

5. *Theologia Poetica* into *Theologia Platonica* in Cristoforo Landino

Cristoforo Landino, Florentine humanist and protagonist of Ficino's Platonic philosophy, brought the development of the humanist Poetic Theology to a culmination with his famous commentaries on Vergil's *Aeneid* and Dante's *Divina Commedia*. As we shall see, he fused the earlier humanist emphasis on the voluntarist character of man with the Renaissance Platonist theories of *eros*. He picked up and elaborated the conception of the two Venuses, an earthly libidinal and a heavenly contemplative one. He utilised the same notion of the threefold life of pleasure, honour and wisdom that Caldiera had expounded, but now it was developed into a central scheme of interpretation for the epic works of both Dante and Vergil. Although he has been little appreciated by literary critics and historians of philosophy because his ideas were quite patently borrowed, his work is of the utmost historical importance because it reveals and illuminates both the interrelationship of earlier humanist thought and Ficino's Platonism and the transformation of the one into the other. Moreover he also accomplished, at the same time, a transformation and fusion of certain not completely assimilated classical elements of earlier humanist speculation with an Augustinian-Christian vision of life and of man. It is true, of course, that this can also be said about the work of Ficino himself, and that Ficino probably showed him the way. But what Ficino did for the reconciliation and 'Christianisation' [in an Augustinian sense] of ancient Platonism and Neoplatonism, Landino did for the great Roman epic poem, the self-conscious mirror of the classical ideal of the hero-statesman, Aeneas-Augustas. For he transformed Vergil into a Platonist, and 'wandering' Aeneas into a Christian 'Everyman' engaged in an Augustinian pilgrim's progress. Moreover, specifically with Landino, *theologia poetica* becomes *theologia platonica.*

In the first place, if we follow his prologue to his exposition of Vergil's *Aeneid,*[81] which is an expansion of a similar passage in his *Camaldulensian Disputations* and parallels his introduction to his commentary on Dante, we see that he stresses much more firmly and explicitly than had Boccaccio or Salutati that the poet is divinely inspired. He had, of course, the much better known Platonic dicta in the *Ion* and the *Phaedrus* to back him up, and Ficino, too, had pronounced on this. Earlier in the century Leonardo Bruni, having just translated the *Phaedrus,* also wrote concerning divinely inspired poets, although he did not regard Dante as one.[82] Landino regarded the poet as somewhere between man and God because he created partly with material and partly out of his own mind, whereas man always created with material and God created out of nothing.

> Therefore those who are affected by a power of this sort [of divine inspiration] the Greeks called poets because they both ascend above men and yet are not able to become gods. For God produces what He wishes out of nothing, which we call to create. True man, on the contrary, is able to bring about nothing except from material available to him. But the poet, although not entirely without material, constructs a poem (for Vergil chose for himself the wanderings and wars of Aeneas as a subject to sing about, and yet, besides this outline through which the whole work runs in its proper order, he included the most profound kinds of meanings drawn almost out of nothing and hidden and concealed in that argument in which, if anyone comprehends them, he will at length know in what way man, born for praise, little by little overcoming his stupidity and various errors, is able to arrive at the *summum bonum*). . . . For God produced heaven and earth out of nothing.

Quoting this opening verse of *Genesis* in Greek, he shows that it uses the verb *poiein.*

> Therefore you see where the Greeks derived the name of 'poet'. But the Latins also do not seem to be ignorant of the divinity of the poet, for they call him *vates* from that which is the greatest of all in man, *mentis vis,* force of mind. Therefore these poets [*vates*] are divine.[83]

The semi-divine and divinely inspired poet would, of course, have access to or express certain truths about divinity concealed from other men. The poet was therefore also a theologian. 'For the great and true poet is nothing other than a theologian, which not only the authority and testimony of so great a philosopher as Aristotle shows, but also their own writings most openly teach.' Here he introduces the concept of the *prisca theologia*, borrowed from Ficino, which is identical in Landino's mind with what earlier humanists and the long tradition before them had called the *theologia poetica*, first written by the *prisci poetae*.

> For theology is two-fold. There is one which they call *prisca*, whose fountain that man Mercury of the cognomen Trismegistus first opened. The other is ours, which is not only demonstrated to be truer, but so much the truest that no one can add to it or subtract anything from it. Therefore, was not Orpheus so involved in that *prisca* theology that he wrote much about God, much about angels, much about incorporeal minds, much about human souls?

Ficino had, of course, translated the *Orphic Hymns* and given a content to the legendary poetic writings of Orpheus. Landino adds:

> For he showed that God is one, and that He is the same everywhere, and that he is circumscribed and limited to no places or times. He does all, He uses all, He works through all, and whatever He does, He does it through that which He himself is. And He knows Himself first, and then individuals. Likewise He knows the infinite. He added to this that God has will, and through it carries out everything outside Himself; and that will is at the same time necessary and free so that by means of it He acts in complete freedom. And He so acts that supreme love is in it and the highest providence towards all things. Linus and Musaeus sang almost the same things as I judge must be believed from what we see others have written about both of them. Also Homer did so if we diligently read those hymns that have been written by him.[84]

Vergil also must count as a *Priscus Theologus-Poeta*, 'for by an admirable and almost divine artistry he demonstrates to us that the *summum bonum* of man consists in the contemplation of divine things, and he shows the most difficult path which leads to it', as Landino himself sought to show in the last two books of his *Camaldulensian Disputations*. Then, of course, there are the great theological poets of the Bible: David, Solomon, the author of *Deuteronomy*, Isaiah and Moses. Biblical Poetics is combined with *theologia poetica* and *theologia platonica* in essential union, for, as Ficino and Pico held, the divine insights of Moses and the prophets were transmitted to the *prisci* pagan theologians and from them to Plato. Then he refers to Dante's long poetic journey through the other worlds, which, of course, by no historical accident, is genuinely closer to the Scriptural origin.[85]

Landino, who in this commentary on the *Aeneid* promises to deal only with its grammatical and rhetorical aspects, now points to the two levels of interpretation in all theological poetry, the manifest and the latent. Those who see only the poet's page do not suspect what lies hidden. But the manifest meaning is given an interesting exegesis here, for it contains the depiction of the civic virtues of the active life. Landino's roots go back to the period when civic humanism was flourishing in Florence. Thus he urges that both the active and the contemplative life receive their support in poetry and in Vergil, the former out of the manifest, the latter out of the latent meaning.

> But, as we recognise this in Vergil, there are accordingly two modes of living among men, of which one consists in speculation, and the other is placed in action. So also in this poet, as he informs us about the whole man, you will apprehend a double meaning. For if you judge that which appears to be extrinsic from a knowledge of the words, it is concerned entirely with civil life and right actions and from these the perfect actions which are concerned with life and the moral virtues; so you will find it not only described but also depicted, so that he not only teaches these things by his very clear doctrine but also draws you to it by his marvellous smoothness of speech and also when necessary incites and drives you towards it by the vehemence and force of his style.[86]

One might well argue that this is the true Vergil which literary historians might today recognise. And it is significant that the humanist, Landino, filled with the values of the rhetorician, the historian and the civil moral philosopher grants it a place and will devote this commentary in part to it.

But the would-be philosopher, Landino, and the poet, both of which were traditional and legitimate aspirations of the humanists, also sees the other side:

> If, however, it is permitted to look into his most intimate *penetralia*, how much, immortal God, how great, how admirable, and finally how salutary for us you will find it. For, since he knew both by himself from his own great wisdom and also learned from the divine Plato, that men are so created by the supreme God that we are eager to be of value not only to ourselves but to all others, as far as it can be done, he decided to compose this poem

> in such a way that it would teach us where and what is the final good, and what other goods are to be sought on account of it, and also by what methods we might be carried there as though by a certain and indubitable road. And he proposed to write about this not by the more vulgar practice of many philosophers but in the rare and poetic way.[87]

Landino developed the same theme in his earlier work, emphasising Vergil's dependence on Plato. It is much more divine and much more difficult to investigate the hidden philosophy of a poet than to elucidate the historical and literary elements of the *Aeneid*. It was Plato's view of Homer that

> all arts either divine or human flow together as though in their own receptacle in one poem of Homer. Vergil observed, therefore, that all the learning of that man absorbed from the fountains of the Egyptian priests had most similar principles to those of the Platonists, of whom he himself was a very great student, and he so greatly admired him that he wished to create the same kind of work with his Aeneas as Homer had previously created in the *Odyssey*. . . .

And Vergil when he learned from Plato that the *summum bonum* consisted in the contemplation of divine things decided that while he would not pass over that part of philosophy called ethics he would also enter the more laborious but more divine business 'in which one is rendered happy and at the same time wise and is joined to God'.[88]

Landino then declared that there are four methods of interpreting a poem and opening the mind of a poet: the first which looks at what happens is the historical, the second which inquires for what reason something is done is the ethical, or *aethimologia*; the third which tries to reconcile incompatible statements he calls *analogia*. The fourth, which is the one he intends to follow, is that of allegory, which is concerned not with what the words mean but with what is hidden under a figure of speech.[89]

He begins his interpretation by affirming love as a central force in human life. In his elaboration, human action follows from man's volition which occurs because of an erotic attachment to the object of his action. At an early age he chooses between love of self, which is pleasure, or love of higher things, which is virtue. Thus he combines the legend of the choice of Hercules with Neoplatonism. In his exposition of the Venuses we are brought back to the tendency of early humanist thought, as we examined it from Petrarch, through Salutati to Valla, to emphasise the volitional, and in Valla's case to identify love with passionate attachment and pleasure, but to distinguish between an earthly *eros* and one which aimed at a heavenly fruition.[90]

Landino interprets Paris and Aeneas, representing the two kinds of *eros*, as follows:

> But the one, whereas he put Venus before Pallas, that is pleasure before virtue, had by necessity to perish together with Troy. The other, however, guided by Mother Venus saved himself from the great conflagration. How else may we understand this than that those who inflamed by a great love are impelled towards the knowledge of truth are able easily to achieve anything? Therefore we may rightly interpret Venus as divine love.[91]

This is stated by 'Alberti', who represents Landino's point of view in the dialogue. Against this 'Lorenzo' is made to object,

> I wonder therefore that you interpret Venus as love, especially as that love which is not only chaste but also divine. For I see that Venus, not only among poets but also with other writers is assumed to be of such a character that through her they wish to signify nothing except the conjunction of man and woman. . . . For I do not see why, if Venus is good, Paris is harmed, if evil, that Aeneas is aided.[92]

But 'Alberti' brushes aside his further suggestion of an astrological conjunction such as Caldiera had given of Venus and Jupiter, and he also passes over historical explanations, 'since all our disputation has no historical basis, but attempts to express entirely what the Greek word allegory covers. . . .[93] Vergil might have exercised the poets' arbitrary power not only to invent but to pervert, add and subtract, and pay no attention to history. But Vergil respected the tradition on which his poem was based, and so retained Venus as the mother of Aeneas. 'He was certainly a wonderful man who composed his work, not from arbitrarily chosen materials but from those given, so that although he departed hardly at all from history, yet through it expressed human happiness in incredible disguise.' That Venus could well be considered divine love he proceeded to argue by quoting Plato in the *Phaedrus* and in the speech of Pausanias in the *Symposium*.[94]

But Landino did not mind departing from Vergil in order to set forth a conception of human nature that might correspond to his interpretation of the two kinds of love, or Venuses.

Moreover our soul since it also has certain similar powers of knowing and generating is likewise said to have two Venuses which are accompanied by two Cupids. For when bodily beauty is placed as an object before our eyes, our mind, which is the first Venus, marvels at it, not because it is corporeal but because it is an image of divine beauty, and it loves it and is elevated by it as though it was a certain road to heaven. Moreover the force of generation, which is the second Venus, desires to generate a form similar to this. Therefore both are rightly called love [*amor*] as it is the desire of the one to contemplate and of the other to generate beauty. Therefore no one, unless he is totally without reason, will dare to damn those two *amores*, since both are very necessary to human nature.[95]

I believe the resemblance of this doctrine to some of the statements of Valla that we presented above is remarkably clear, without at the same requiring us to conclude that Landino [or Ficino] was an 'Epicurean' or that Valla was a Platonist. I believe, however, that there was a broad common ground running through the thought of humanists of various schools on the basis of which they stressed the centrality of will, conceived as a love-like attachment, in the nature and behaviour of man. This was also evident in a nominal 'Aristotelian' such as Caldiera whom we have just discussed. It was a central element in Salutati's thought, and in his conception of poetry, as well. But in all these cases [except Valla's] some element of rational control, such as 'right reason', was assumed to be necessary to inform the will. And even in Valla's case the will needed and used the intellect, although it could not be swayed from its 'love' by it. We shall presently see how 'reason' also entered into Landino's thought.

Landino has now accepted the two kinds of love, or Venuses, as a necessary part of human nature and of human life. Why then was Paris harmed by the earthly love? Because 'he was more avid for generating than right reason advised, and more occupied in it than he needed to be, he was plunged into bodily pleasure alone'.[96] Moreover, Aeneas also had to learn the lessons of reason through hard experience when he reached true wisdom through many wanderings and sweat and toil. But he only arrived at his goal because he was aroused and carried by love.

For true love, as the speech of Eryximachus in the same work of Plato shows, is the creator of all natural things and their preserver. For all similar things are drawn to the things which are similar to themselves in eternal concord.

> Love is likewise the master of all the greatest arts. For no one ever invented an art or added to one invented by another unless the delight of investigation and the lust for learning incited him. And if our Vergil does not overtly show this, he does it nevertheless more obscurely, as is the custom with poets.[97]

However, the divine love is what lifts man to his true goal. Yet it meditates, is moved and labours for nothing else than that it be seized of bodily beauty.

> For while our souls are submerged in corporeal darkness, they do not recognise the divine except in the shadows and in certain images which are placed before our senses. Not only the *prisci* philosophers of Greece expressed this idea, among whom I can name Pythagoras, Empedocles, Heraclitus and above all Plato, but also Christians do not in the least depart from that opinion. For both Paul and he who was an auditor of Paul, Dionysius the Areopagite, held that celestial and divine things which do not fall under the senses might be seen through those things which are perceived by the senses. This therefore is that true Venus which lifts our mind to divinity.[98]

Combining the humanist theme of the evolution of primitive undisciplined human society to a condition where men learned to live together in reason[99] with his Platonist theme of the two loves, he argues that Troy represented the first age of mankind when men were irrational and did not know divine things. And they sought their happiness through a voluptuary life. But little by little they discovered how weak and passing such pleasures are. Then he reverts to the need for a transformation of passion from earthly to divine things. True love has such force that it stirs up the mind and makes it the master of anything it wishes.

> Thence since it thinks that nothing is difficult, provided only it possesses the loved object, it bears all labours, and overcomes all difficulties. This is that Venus which is not of the vulgar which has the power of generation mixed with matter, but that celestial one which is remote from all matter, which is from our mind and excites the mind itself. . . .[100]

Having worked through the exposition of the two Venuses and the two kinds of love in the human soul, he presents a further Platonist theme, that of the obscuration of the mind by the forces of matter in the body. Our souls are created by God in such a way that they may easily attain all truth by their own nature. But from corporeal material all evil arises. For it makes the mind slavish and disturbs it and obscures it with darkness. And from this ignorance all vice comes. For this reason Chrysippus and the other Stoics said all perturbations arose from false opinions. If vice comes from ignorance, and ignorance from the blindness of the body, then, as Plato thought, all vice will be from the body. Vergil represents this notion through Aeneas being the offspring of Anchises, who stands for the mortal body, and Venus, the immortal soul. There is in Aeneas and between them a struggle of spirit and flesh. Thus Anchises wishes to remain in Troy for he wishes to perish with the senses rather than be deprived of pleasure. But he changes his mind and is carried away by Aeneas. Then Lucifer, the star of Venus, represents the love of discovery of truth and rises in him who abandons a life of pleasure.[101] 'For such love excites reason and illuminated by its light we are able to know the true. Moreover it appears from Mount Ida, that is from beauty, for *eidos* means form in Greek. Moreover love in Plato is defined as desire for beauty.' Aeneas is an exile because he knows the *summum bonum* is not in pleasure but has not yet discovered what it is. He is borne across the sea because our soul wherever it goes is moved by nothing except appetite.[102]

This reference to appetite introduces a new discussion of human nature. One kind of appetite arises from the force of knowing and judging what is good and evil.

> If, moreover, that same force of knowing is illuminated by the light of saving reason and directed by its rules, it does not judge that to be good in which the senses are gratified but what right reason dictates. . . . Since, therefore, this kind of force decides that this is good and that is evil, it arouses in us another force which urges towards acquiring the good and declining the evil; moreover all call this appetite. But this also is necessarily two-fold, one, which does everything by that judgement which is from sense alone, is always in suspense and seeks nothing with reason, and another, which follows nothing at all unless reason first commands it. We call the first one lust and this second one the will.[103]

This interpretation, which is taken from Ficino's concept of 'natural appetite', he illustrates by the example of the black and white horses and the charioteer in the *Phaedrus*. Reverting to the *Aeneid*, he repeats that appetite is like the sea which bears Aeneas because it can be turbulent or calm. It is lustful when disturbed and reasonable when calm.[104]

This is but a small yet a typical sample of Landino's exegesis as he follows Aeneas in his wanderings and wars. The work is of genuine value in its own right as a statement of Landino's views on human nature and ethics and religion, as a continuation of the first books of the *Camaldulensian Disputations* where the relative merits of the active and contemplative lives and the *summum bonum* were discussed. It is of perhaps less value in the history of Vergil criticism, since it so overtly imposes Landino's own philosophical ideas on Vergil. His more philological and rhetorical analysis in his *Commentary* is no doubt of greater interest from the point of view of literary criticism.[105]

Nevertheless, these two books of the *Disputationes* are of major importance in the history of humanist thought. They were completed shortly after Ficino's *Commentary on Plato's Symposium* had begun to circulate, although Ficino may well have known their contents previously. In eliciting from Vergil meanings that clearly corresponded to and were derived from Ficino's philosophy of love, Landino filled the role of linking these notions with certain traditional mythological themes that were, indeed, susceptible to this kind of exegesis, especially the Hesiodic myth of the two Aphrodites. Certainly Venus was given the role of a goddess of fruition and achievement by Vergil, and it was perhaps important to establish a clear basis for Christian acceptance and identification with her. Caldiera had recognised the theological virtue of *caritas* in her, but provided no elaboration of a philosophy of will, appetite, passion, love, fruition. He was certainly aware that these had positive and not only negative values. It was Landino, however, who, by combining the exegesis of Aeneas' patron-goddess with a higher heavenly love directed towards the contemplation of divinity, helped to establish the iconographical treatment of love in late Quattrocento and Cinquecento art and literature. Moreover, he gave this imagery, by which a synthesis of mythological and Christian values might be expressed, a status within philosophy as well by his identification of the old theme of the *prisci poetae* who were philosophers and theologians with the new Renaissance-Platonist historical myth of the transmission of divine revelation from the Hebrews into and among the Gentiles through the *prisci theologi*, some of whom were identical figures with the *prisci poetae*.

XVI. Accommodation and Separation in the Destiny of Mankind: Manetti, Ficino and Pico on Christians, Jews and Gentiles

The following and final chapter is a direct continuation of the preceding one, for it takes up the question of the relationship of Christian history and philosophy with that of the Hebrews and the Pagan Classical traditions. Actually, through this poetic and mythologic exegesis just discussed, an attempt was being made to arrive at an intellectual and religious accommodation of the rival and false religious traditions to Latin Christian culture, to forge a retrospective reconciliation of Christians, Jews and Gentiles. And we have seen how, by the device of allegorical interpretation with its roots deep not only in medieval practice but in antique precedent, the events and statements of the Old Testament could be made to pre-figure the Christian drama of Incarnation, Atonement and Salvation of the New. By a similar use of allegory within the theory of the *theologia poetica* the rampantly polytheistic and amoral mythology of Greek and Latin poetry could be made to reveal an inner core of proto-Christian orthodoxy beneath an outer cortex of amorous and litigious heroes and deities. But now some new statement of the universal history of mankind was necessary – one that would stress the underlying unity and harmony of meanings and religious insights, on the one hand, as well as account in an adequate way for both the surface differences and the drifting apart of the rival and erroneous traditions from the true, on the other. In this process the *studia humanitatis*, taking their contents to comprise the works of their learning and culture, were being transformed into *studia divinitatis*, just as simultaneously the *studia divinitatis* were being subjected to the methods and disciplines of the *studia humanitatis*.

Almost from the first the humanists, and after them other philosophers of the Renaissance, were reaching out to these rival traditions and religions. The conciliar movement had itself begun as a conciliation movement in an effort to end the schism in the western Church. The abortive Councils of Ferrara and Florence were both a direct effort to come to terms with the schismatic Greek Church and an effort to meet the strong impetus towards conciliation that was coming from the rival Council of Basel with its threat to papal supremacy. There were also the Jews and the Moslems. But greater perhaps than the problem and challenge of the contemporary rival religions and Churches was the question of the rival traditions. Not only the Christian but the Hebrew and the pagan traditions had the stamp of divinity upon them. The Jews were the people of the divine oracles of the Old Testament. It was the ancient Hebraic tradition in the Scriptures and the medieval Jewish Biblical scholarship and moral-philosophical speculation that needed to be grasped, evaluated, the valuable elements separated from the harmful. It was the influence of ideas and scholarship rather than any real religious competition from contemporary Judaism that faced this Renaissance movement of intellectual reaching-out and expansion. The great value of classical philosophy and letters had been recognised by the very Fathers of the Church who had to put forth a firm theological foundation for the new faith in the face of the old established philosophical schools. There was Aristotle's enormous influence on scholastic thought and the increasing humanist and Renaissance interest in him. There was the tradition of pre-Renaissance Platonism. There were the Stoics such as Seneca and such well-intentioned good men as Cicero, a Stoic? an Academic? an Eclectic? It was hard to tell. With the greatly increased knowledge of these ancient philosophies, and even a reformed knowledge of Aristotle, and with the great increase in the clarity of understanding of what these men actually thought [a vast improvement over medieval standards, though certainly defective by ours], some new basis for the acceptance of these traditions which simultaneously would screen out the unacceptable elements was a prime need.

This need, however, was not simply an expression of scholarly and intellectual and artistic respect for men who had been so fruitful and productive in their intellectual labours. This need also sprang from a decline in sectarianism and suspicion and hostility to the strange and the different that accompanied the rise of secularism. The fourteenth-century world was a cosmopolitan one and the fifteenth and sixteenth centuries were even more so. But possibly more even than the direct contacts with men of a different culture and religion, the reading of their literature, especially the literature of the ancients, their philosophies, their moral thought, the curiosity about and increasing sensitivity to the nature and values of ancient art fed a recognition that mankind was a world-wide species with universal qualities, that the various branches of humanity were more striking in their similarities than in their differences. It was difficult to engage in so much speculation and comment on the status of man without seeing that this condition of life, miserable or noble, must include the men of the other traditions and religions, contemporary and of the historical past.

The new sense of the nature of man also involved a new historical sense, a recognition that the features of human life that made up man's culture were gradually and historically acquired especially through the great educational and civilising work of the early poets, philosophers, prophets, moralists and teachers. These were the men with whom the humanists identified their own origin. The fact that they distinguished themselves from the vulgar made them aware that they should be the educators and civilisers in their own day. All of this underlined a sense that men had a basic core of similarity and universality to which tradition and, in particular, the history of culture itself had added their present and particular customs, attitudes and intellectual and artistic capacities and predilections.

The most important train of history to them was, of course, the development of religion. Scholars have shown how the humanist's veneration for antiquity led them, as early as Petrarch, to divide history into antiquity, a dark ages, and a present age with potentialities for progress or decline.[1] Other humanists, as we have seen, stressed man's material and intellectual progress as a consequence of his great intelligence and capacity to will and act. But both of these secular conceptions of historical pattern could not overthrow the long tradition of providential historical thought that sprang from Augustine, Orosius and others in antiquity and had been nourished throughout the Middle Ages.[2] Only now the Sacred History of the creation of mankind, the Fall, the deluge, the revelation of the Law, the prophecies and preparations for the Messiah and the Evangel, the Advent and Incarnation and Redemption, the Apostolic Age, the rise and consolidation of the Church, the wars with pagans, the perfidy of the Jews, the threat of the Moslem infidels, the schism between Eastern and Western Churches, the western schism – all of these unexpungible elements of a Christian-providential view of man's past had to be brought into relationship with the new historical sense of man himself – as a practical and concrete manifestation of the great powers of will and intelligence attributed to him by the humanists – making history. And they had to be brought into relationship with the new secular schemas of history which stressed human civilisation and the greatness of the ancients in achieving this, the barbarism that ensued, the obscurantism of many churchmen towards learning and culture.

One way that the providential and the secular views of mankind could be brought into relationship was through the identification of Christian values as contained within and beneath the surface of pagan thought and expression. This we have seen happening. It could go remarkably far. Around 1491, in his *Poetics*, Bartolomeo della Fonte almost casually remarked that the pagan poets always believed that God was unique and one only, the best and eternal. This, as we have seen, Boccaccio and Salutati also argued. Fontius adds,

> Moreover, besides Him, whose son the Gentiles call Jove, we Christ, the Asiatics and Libyans Mahomet, and other peoples by other names, there were and today are and always will be among mortals other minor deities, called heroes or saints; this I do not doubt. And I affirm that good poets are acceptable to this highest God, the ruler of the universe, the genitor of the other gods and men, and to the minor gods also, according to the variety of places, times and religions.[3]

Certainly this was a far-going expression of the urge to synthesis that could see Christ and Jove as the same, except for their names.

1. Manetti's Humanist Version of Sacred History: His *Contra Iudeos et Gentes*

But the humanists also recognised and sought to understand and identify the differences, and they sought to explain why paganism, Judaism and Moslemism are inferior in their values to Christianity, or harmful and dangerous. Works of this sort belong together with those which seek a new kind of literary-philosophical syncretism beneath the claim of an underlying universal religious insight. We have spoken above of Giannozzo Manetti's Hebrew and Biblical studies and of his treatise *Against the Jews and Gentiles*.[4] Its relevance to his efforts to attain a more authentic version of the Old and New Testaments has been pointed out. But we have reserved a discussion of this work for this chapter, even though it does not deal with poetry, because it does deal fundamentally with the question of how Gentiles and Hebrews, and modern-day Jews, are to be fitted into the course of providential history that was an essential part of his Christian religious outlook. Manetti was also the humanist, it may be recalled, who had one of the most exalted notions of the human condition and went so far as to claim that the Incarnation would have occurred for the glorification of man, even if it had not been necessary for his redemption. His treatise on the *Dignity and Excellence of Man* was written between 1451 and 1453. (though there seems to have been a version of 1449 or earlier). The *Contra Iudeos et Gentes* was written the very next year, 1454, although never fully completed before his death in 1459, as he intended to add other books of biographies.[5]

The work is divided into two clearly distinct parts: the first four books covering the history of man from the creation to the advent, and the life, teachings and death of Christ, the ensuing six books which are collections of biographies of Christian writers, confessors, martyrs and virgins. His treatment of the pagans and Jews is contained in the first part, and we shall deal, therefore, only with the first four books.[6]

Manetti's treatise is a serious venture into the interpretation of sacred history as well as being a sober attempt to demonstrate the superiority of Christianity over its two great historically superseded rivals, paganism and ancient Judaism. Unfortunately (from the subsequent Christian standpoint) Judaism survived the Advent of Jesus and therefore also remained as a living rival of Christianity; and certainly much of

Manetti's purpose in writing is to address contemporary Jews and convince them that their ancestors had made a colossal mistake. His outlook, therefore, is fundamentally evangelical, and at the same time, as we shall indicate, he reveals a propensity to deal with the ancient history of the Hebrews and with the Gospel story with the methods and conceptions of history that he has acquired as a humanist. As in the classical rhetorical view of history, in Manetti's hands history becomes an instrument of persuasion both of belief and of morality.

His first book runs rapidly through the creation of man, conceived in accord with this theme of man's dignity residing in his position of having been modelled on the image of God. God created man last,

> so that he himself might be considered as worthier and more excellent than [God's] other works. For this reason when God established the angelic spirits and incorporeal intelligences a little before, He wished to create another nature that would be both corporeal and capable of intelligence for the sake of a certain greater beauty and harmony of the entire universe; composed of body and soul, He called him Adam in Hebrew, which in Latin means man. Therefore when He had wonderfully adorned him with every gift of the soul and the body, He decided and decreed that he should command and rule over all His works that had now been created. But in order that he would be able to govern and rule these creations better and by this means convert what he wisely governed and benignly ruled into his own use, man was given a right clever and sagacious mind.[7]

But man with all his great gifts and natural capacities was subjected to a law within the Paradise of pleasures, in order to prevent his lapse. Nevertheless, out of human frailty, ambition, or diabolic temptation, Adam transgressed the law, and mankind became miserably damned and cursed. There followed after a long interval the flood and the survial of Noah and his family, still later the circumcision taught Abraham the source of salvation, and at the time of Moses God added the Ten Commandments 'both to the first law of nature [i.e. Adam's] and also to the new mandates which had been revealed to Noah and Abraham, those two aforementioned just and pious men'. But none of these mandates were heeded until the time of Christ.[8]

Meanwhile in the aftermath of the flood, there occurred the episode of the Tower of Babel and the confusion of tongues and the dispersion of the peoples. This was the occasion of the origin of paganism and the rise of many different theologies and moral conceptions. At this point

Manetti introduces his consideration of the pagans. He first reviews their conceptions of natural philosophy, dividing them into schools according to whether they taught the eternity of the world or creation, providence (as Aristotle and Plato) or chance (as Democritus and Epicurus), one or several or many universes. He gives a short sketch of Greek philosophy beginning with the Italic and Ionian schools led by Pythagoras and Thales, their successors up to Socrates, then the differences of Plato and Aristotle. He next reviews the way philosophers divided on the nature of the soul, whether it was mortal or immortal, and on the *summum bonum* and the virtues, sketching the positions of the Stoics, Academics, Peripatetics and Epicureans. Cicero is quite obviously his principal source, here, although he was also familiar, as we know, with his own teacher Ambrogio Traversari's translation of Diogenes Laertius' *Lives of the Philosophers.* He then passes in review the pagan religions: Isis and Osiris, the worship of sun and moon, of rocks, plants and animals, the cult of Cybele, the legend of Cadmus as the founder of Greek religion and of the birth of Dionysius to Semele and Zeus, the gods and goddesses of the Roman religion. He stresses their diversity and contrariety and cites Cicero's *De natura deorum* on the competing religious ideas of the philosophers.[9]

There is evident in him here the same desire to give a clear, objective straightforward account that is evident in his other writings. If his views sometimes seem a little summary and superficial, there was also a caution and conscientiousness in him and perhaps too great respect for sources that we today know are not always definitive. But there is evidence from his library that his reading may well have been wider and deeper than what he reveals by these historical sketches. He does seem inclined to trust the judgement of Cicero over more obscure men.

His polemic against the pagans immediately follows his history of their thought and religions. Ancient philosophy and ethics, as well as philosophical theology, are spared. Following Lactantius' *Institutiones divinae,* he singles out the obscenity, sensuality and cruelty of their religious practices for criticism. In this he continually contrasts them with the ancient Hebrews, as we shall see, suggesting that he may have been influenced in his approach to this by his association with Jewish scholars. Cicero showed how the gods were based on the human figure with a quasi-body and quasi-blood. What bothers him most is that sexuality is attributed to them. For how could they need sexual reproduction if they were immortal? But all the pagans seemed to practice offensive excesses in their religious rites. If the Romans, who were more prudent than other nations, also did so, what wonder that the others were even worse. 'Therefore all peoples excepting only the Hebrews, for whom alone was reserved the task of worshipping the true and pious and omnipotent God, were converted to idolatry.'[10] He reviews the tales of divine lust as the poets and historians revealed them – those of Hercules, Apollo, Mars, Pluto, Mercury, Neptune and Jupiter. Ovid's *Metamorphoses* and Terence were his chief sources. But all peoples had horrible rites, the Egyptians, the Phrygians, the Rhodians, Salamis, Chios, Sparta, Crete, Latium, Carthage, Laodicea, the Arabs: all seem to practice human sacrifice. He dwells on phallic worship at Rome under the god Liber, the various Bacchanalia, the cult of Priapus. Men have surpassed the ferocity of wild beasts in their sacrifices of infants, youths, men of all ages at the anniversary rites of the gods.[11]

There was clearly no temptation on Manetti's part to identify the pagan gods with aspects of the Christian deity (as through the use of allegorical interpretation certain humanists did). But there was also a clear effort to distinguish between the pagan cults and the thought of the philosophers and moralists living under paganism. But since he is approaching these questions within the framework of sacred history, he turns next to the ancient Hebrews. In contrast with the pagan tendency to deify all material things and forces in the universe the Hebrews knew they were simply composed of elements, and they held that the sun, moon, planets and other stars were not gods but were insensate and inanimate.

> And since they saw the whole world filled with animals of different kinds, they knew that that could not have happened without providence, and from the greatness and beauty of creatures and because of their purity of mind, they knew that the creator of all was himself immortal and invisible.

Whence they agreed with that famous saying of Paul, that the invisible things of the world are known from the visible.

> They also thought that man was a certain individual particle of the whole universe, and they considered the soul, the true, interior man, as a special

> part of him, and the body as a kind of clothing of man. Hence they took so much greater care for the cultivation of souls than of bodies that they despised bodies. Indeed, because souls were created in the likeness of God, they magnified them so greatly, that they thought the highest good of man was the knowledge of God.[12]

The Hebrews established a special tribe of priests for the worship of the highest god, and many of them, armed by this pious and immaculate cult, attained the pinnacle of the virtues and experienced a vision of angels and divine oracles without having to resort to syllogisms, conjectures and other human arguments. And filled with divine grace they saw the future as if it were present. And all this happened,

> before the name of the Greeks was in the earth and even before Moses, and before there was a nation of Jews these things miraculously became known to the *prisci* Hebrews, those true and pious worshippers of omnipotent God. For the Jews were called such after the time of Moses from *Judah*, but the Hebrews were named from *Heber*, from whom Abraham descended.

This was an interesting and important distinction for Manetti to have drawn, and allowed him to shower his quite genuine admiration on the old 'Hebrew' patriarchs and to reserve his criticism for the later less admirable ways of the 'Jews'. The ancient Hebrews

> guided finally by this piety, aided by this grace of the Lord, lived piously and in a holy way for many ages before Moses without any written law, and without the teachings of the divine laws, which were not yet given to them, they miraculously understood by oracles alone and sharpness of mind the certain pure truth of the highest matters.[13]

At this point in his discussion of the Hebrews Manetti turns to Moses, who, inspired by the divine spirit, ordered his thoughts to be set down in letters. Adhering to the tradition that Moses was the author of *Genesis* and *Exodus*, Manetti now casts him in the role of a humanist historian, for, he says, Moses before he transmitted the Laws to the people wished to impress on the living as well as on posterity the morality he was proposing and to reinforce it with examples of *prisci viri*, lest the precepts of the laws prove too difficult to follow. Whereupon Manetti himself takes over Moses' role and presents a series of sketches of illustrious men for historical and moral exemplification drawn from the Scriptures. It is interesting that he does this at this point, because the last six books of this work are also dedicated to defending the truth of Christianity by presenting a series of sketches of the lives of those men and women who best exemplified the Christian life. As we shall see, his treatment of Christ is also a variant on this method. Thus he covers Enos, Enoch, Noah, Melchizedech.[14]

When he comes to Abraham he again comments on the name Hebrew. These men were not called Jews, as their posterity, nor Gentiles, since they did not believe in a plurality of gods, as the Gentiles did.

> But we call them Hebrews rather and more exactly either from *Heber* as has been said, or we more truly call them this because the name means *transituri* or 'they who will cross over' in Hebrew. Certainly only the Hebrews were able, by natural reason and by law that was not written but innate, to cross over from the creatures to the knowledge of the true God, and despising the pleasures of the body arrive at the right road for living.

Abraham thus reached the perfection of his justice not by the Mosaic Law but by the knowledge of God and sincere faith.[15]

Esau he omits as unworthy of imitation 'in this catalogue of holy men'. But he includes: Isaac and his twelve sons, the patriarchs who founded the twelve tribes, followed by Aaron, the first priest of the Hebrews and founder of the Levite clan, and finally, in a lengthy treatment, Moses.[16]

Manetti clearly recognises Moses, not only as the Lawgiver, but as the true founder of the Jewish religion, and makes a break in the historical record between 'Hebrews' and 'Jews' with him. The Law of the Ten Commandments he respects, since it contains in it, without any doubt, the Christian law of love of God and neighbour, but he regards the Jewish Law in general as defective for three interesting reasons. First of all it offers no rewards or punishments for good and evil deeds, except 'weak, momentaneous and earthly ones'. 'For the Jews, although they sacrifice and pray to the one and only and omnipotent God, expect, however, only temporal and visible goods from Him.' Secondly, they practiced many impure, frivolous or even bloody sacrifices. He cites many examples from the Old Testament. In the third place he objects to the dietary laws because some of their prohibitions 'seem servile and not worthy of a free man'.[17] Thus the ancient Hebrews worship God with pious prayers and devout words as the Christians do, but 'religion is to be sought neither in the confusion of the pagans whom we frequently call by other words Gentiles, nor in the blindness and obstinacy of the Jews, . . . but among those only who are called Christians'.[18]

This leads him to consider the signs of the coming of Christ in the Old Testament. The Old Law foreshadowed the New and was, in Paul's words, *noster pedagogus*. Fifteen hundred years after Moses Christ came in the fullness of time, which the Greeks more precisely call *eukairia*. But Christ's teachings and commandments are so full of authority and dignity that they have abolished all the Old Law entirely and filled the world with glory and majesty. This leads him to inquire how such different demands could be made by the same God. But the same head of a family treats different members of it differently according to their needs and natures. 'Thus divine providence, although it is entirely unchangeable, nevertheless aids and supports changeable creatures in variable ways and according to the diversity of the diseases suffered orders or forbids different things to different persons.'[19]

But the problem is also one of the traditions and relationships of the Old and New Covenant. It was important for the humanist to establish an acceptable historical relationship between the different manifestations of truth in different epochs. The problem is similar to that of the relationship of pagan philosophic truth to Christian. His answer, of course, is dependent on Paul's analysis in the *Epistle to the Romans*, and on those patristic ones derived from him such as St. Augustine's in the *City of God*. We shall soon see how Ficino also devotes especial attention to this question in his *Commentary* on the *Epistle to the Romans*. In Manetti's words,

> Men seem to be divided into two kinds as regards the present question, in one of which is the mob of the impious, namely of the old exterior and earthy man. In the other, indeed, there is contained a multitude of the pious, namely of the interior, new and celestial man. But ecclesiastical history describes the life and customs of earthy man from Adam to John the Baptist, whose history indeed, published in the name of the Old Testament, is thus named and called as if of one promising an earthly kingdom. All of it is nothing else than a certain mystical image of a new people and an open shadow of the New Testament, promising without any doubt the eternal kingdom of heaven; indeed the life of this people begins from the most blessed advent of our Lord in a certain high and admirable humility and it extends to the final day of the general judgement.[20]

Thus he adheres to the providential and eschatological notion of history as divided into the age of preparation and the age of the evangel. But at the same time the motifs of humanist historical thought are woven into this older ecclesiastical pattern of history.

The new historical and literary treatment of the Scriptures is evident in Manetti's next three books. These are based narrowly on the four Gospels, but the problem of Christ is analysed into three separate aspects, corresponding to these three books. In the first he tells the life of Christ with great emphasis on the nativity and all of the evidence of its divinity and truth. He bases his account on the miracles that accompanied Christ's birth and the correspondence of the prophecies in the Old Testament to it. He is especially impressed with the coming of the barbarian Magi from a distance to worship Christ when the Jews ignored all of these miracles. The book continues with other miracles performed by Christ. It is, in other words, devoted to the evidence of the miracles.[21] The second book, instead, separates out all of the sayings and parables of Jesus to compile what he calls the 'doctrine' or teachings of Christ.[22] The third book deals with the death of Christ, and is basically a narrative of the passion story. It dwells also on the perfidy of Judas, who is compared to the youth who burned down the temple of Diana at Ephesus, but his purpose seems to be more to persuade the Jews of their mistake than to condemn them for their blindness.[23] He is straightforward and evangelical in these three books, in keeping with the approach to the Scriptures he manifested in justifying his translation of the Psalter, as we saw above.[24]

But his acceptance of a kind of literalism as far as the scriptural text was concerned, which was similar to the way he frequently accepted the authority of classical historians and philosophers, did not stand in the way of his acceptance of the miraculous. Though he does not go into many details about the mystical foreshadowing of the New Testament by the Old, he professes and accepts it. But when he deals with the contents of either, he tends to be literal and historical rather than allegorical in his exegesis. He therefore anticipates something of the coming religious tendency to use the literal evidence of sacred history as a reinforcement of faith in the miraculous and the divine.

On the other hand, it would be wrong to seek any kind of theological depth in Manetti, or any psychologically involved analysis of the contrast between a religion based on the Law and the new dispensation of

Grace. He sees Christ naïvely and simply as both the divinity manifested by his miracles and as the best and wisest of men. Yet his criticism of post-Mosaic Judaism was sharp and penetrating in his rejection of externality and temporalism.

This work of Manetti's has a certain importance also in his placing together in juxtaposition both the Jewish and the pagan religious beliefs, out of which Christianity in his own day had evolved, rejecting them, but putting them into a comprehensible historical perspective. In the case of both of these ancestral traditions he clearly makes a distinction between the part that is to be rejected and the part that can be admired. In the case of the pagans their extravagant, bloody and lustful religious practices are rejected, but value is seen in certain of the ancient philosophies, such as Plato's, Aristotle's and Cicero's. In the case of the Jews, the Hebrews are carefully distinguished from the Jews and given an extraordinary degree of admiration for their sobriety, piety and inwardness. As we suggested in a previous chapter, Manetti must be recognised as one of the first to see the western Christian tradition as nurtured by both a Hellenism and a Hebraism.

2. Ficino's Vindication of the Christian Religion and Design for the Providential History of Mankind

Manetti, prompted by his need to come to terms with the very Judaic religious tradition with which his humanistic study of Hebrew confronted him, composed his defence of Christianity and critique of paganism and Judaism in the 1440s and '50s. Roughly twenty years later (*ca.* 1476) Marsilio Ficino wrote his work *On the Christian Religion*,[25] prompted, perhaps also, by the need to settle in his own mind the relationship of the ideas he had encountered in Plato and the Neoplatonists with Christianity and his own Christian faith. Although he had entitled his great work on the immortality of the soul, *Theologia platonica*, and professed not to recognise a distinction between theology and philosophy, he did see that there was a difference between *sapientia* and *religio*, and between the philosopher and the priest. Although he entitled the proem to this work 'That there is the greatest kinship between Wisdom and Religion',[26] this does not imply identity. The two mental states derived from the distinction within the human soul between intellect and will by which the soul as it pleases our Plato can, as though by two wings (that is by intellect and will) fly back to the heavenly Father and fatherland, and the philosopher relies on the intellect and the priest especially leans on the will, the intellect illumines the will and the will kindles the intellect, . . .[27]

The wise and holy men of all nations were philosophers and priests. The Hebrew prophets undertook both roles; the Persian philosophers were also Magi and priests. The Egyptian priests were also mathematicians and metaphysicians. The Hindu Brahmins gave counsel both on nature and on purgation. 'The same custom prevailed in Greece under Linus, Orpheus, Musaeus, Eumolpus, Aglaophemus and Pythagoras.' Thus he linked together the early Greek sages and poets, combining the traditions of *prisci poetae* and *prisci theologi*. The Celts, Romans and the *prisci* Christian bishops also united the roles of philosopher and priest.[28]

He bemoans the fact that they have become separated:

O much too unhappy ages, when the separation and divorce of Pallas and Themis (that is wisdom and virtue) miserably occurred. For learning has for the most part been passed down to the profane with whom it has for the most part become an instrument of iniquity and lust, and it should be called malice rather than science. [Cf. Valla.] The most precious pearls of religion, on the other hand, are often handled by the ignorant and are trampled by them as if they were swine. For the inert ministry of the ignorant and lazy ought to be called supersition rather than religion, it seems. Thus on the one hand those who are learned do not know the truth sincerely as something divine that might lighten the eyes of the pious alone. On the other hand the clergy, entirely ignorant of divine and human things, do not worship God and administer sacred things rightly as far as they are able. How long must we sustain this hard and miserable fate of the iron age?[29]

This is Ficino's judgement on the relation of secular and religious truth and roles, in his own day, and a certain suggestion of his personal motivation and hope that a Platonic theology might simultaneously purify and elevate the clergy and return the philosophers to the service of the cure of souls. One can see in this a persistence of the same motivation that led Petrarch to condemn the Aristotelians of his day and put his trust in Ciceronian rhetoric and a revival of Plato – sight unseen. Ficino, however, as a humanist-turned-philosopher, did not despise all the help he could get from the scholastic philosophic and theological traditions. But he wished to transform religious thought so that it would enlighten the clergy and the minds of the Christians through his new philosophy. And he found his own purposes close to the humanistic conception of a poetic theology, so that those men who were praised as *prisci poetae* in the one tradition, in their role of bards and prophets, were taken over by Ficino as *prisci theologi*, or founders and early participants in a divinely inspired philosophical-religious tradition.

Ficino's *De religione Christiana* is, like Manetti's *Contra Iudeos et Gentes*, an apologetic work which seeks, on the one hand, to establish the supremacy and truth of Christianity over its rivals, which for Ficino included the Moslems as well as the Jews and Gentiles. On the other hand, it is a work which also seeks to establish the relationships and points of contact within the total plan of divine providence between the non-Christian religions and Christianity – the extent to which the pagans and infidel shared in revealed truth and the modes and sources of the transmission of the truth.

In keeping with his entire philosophy, this work is also centred about man though it deals with religion. But, as he titles chapter one, 'Religion is especially proper and genuine to man,'[30] as he had argued in *Theologia platonica*, it was man's restless pursuit of infinity and immortality that most sharply separated him from the mortal animals,[31] so here he reaffirms that while animals share many human talents, man alone is religious. Again it is as proper for us to raise our minds to the King of heaven as it is to walk erectly. If men do sometimes pay honours to animals as though they were divine [e.g. in Egypt, etc.] these men are either ignorant or the animals are disguised celestial beings. Man is the most perfect animal by that quality which most sharply distinguishes him from the lower animals and joins him to divinity. Man alone abstains from temporal goods for the sake of divine worship and celestial goods.

> Add that the sting of conscience constantly pricks us alone and the fear of divine jealousy of lower beings sharply vexes us. Therefore if religion is vain, as we have argued, there is no animal more insane or unhappy than man.

Here he repeats the opening statement of the *Theologia platonica*. If man's religious faith is illusory he is the most imperfect of all, if true the most perfect. He must be most perfect since God, the highest truth and goodness, would not deceive his own progeny, mankind.[32]

Moreover, his second chapter continues this demonstration and reiteration of the universality of religion. As Plato emphasised in the *Protagoras*, man alone participates in divinity by recognising God, for 'God without God is not known'. The soul is raised to God in so far as it is flooded with divine light. Man, in fact, is completely preoccupied with God. 'The human mind is constantly agitated about God, the heart daily burns with God, the breast sighs over God, the tongue sings Him, head, hand and knee adore Him, the works of man refer to Him.' If God was ignorant or deaf to these things He would be an ingrate. But the supreme wisdom and charity can be neither ignorant nor ungrateful. If the human mind attains to the divine mind, it is necessary that the human be understood and governed by divinity.[33]

This means that religion is a universal and admirable characteristic of man. The problem then is how to discriminate between the true and the false, the good and the bad. How can one move from a philosophical view of man and God to a specifically revealed religion, in particular to Christianity? Ficino must devise an argument that all religions are true and all religions are good, but one is truer and better than the others. Indeed, he must show that it alone is specifically true and good. The first step in this dialectic occurs in chapter four, 'Every religion has some good, provided it is directed to God Himself, the Creator of all things, but the Christian is sincere.'[34] Divine providence solves the problem for Ficino, in the traditional sense that providence is shown to have permitted a universal but partial revelation to all men, true and perfect revelation to a chosen few, all as a part of a design for the opening of ultimate revelation and the possibility of salvation to all.

But the details of the design, as Ficino reads it, are his own and necessarily related to his admiration of Plato and the Neoplatonists and to his need to place them in acceptable historical relationship to the sacred history of the Scriptures. Therefore 'divine providence did not permit there to be in any time any region of the world entirely without any religion; however, it permitted different rites of worship to be observed in different times and places.' God 'prefers to be worshipped, though it be ineptly or humanly, to not being worshipped at all due to human pride.' But in this universality of religion, only those who worship God by goodness of actions, truth of speech, clarity of mind and charity of spirit are truly sincere. These are those who who adore God in the manner Christ and His disciples taught.[35]

This introduces a defence of the truth of Christianity by the human evidence of a demonstration of its 'sincerity' as manifested in the spirit and sacrifices of the disciples and apostles.[36] These used none of the methods of persuasion of Demosthenes or Cicero and nevertheless they won the hearts of mankind. This could only have happened if the religion that inspired them was founded on divine power, wisdom and hope. Moreover, the Scriptures themselves were of the greatest aid to these men, and indeed are a further demonstration of Christian truth because of their intrinsic power and sincerity.

> For in them there is a new force, singular in its simplicity, sobriety, ardour, gravity, profundity and majesty. . . . These writers have an indescribable something pious and awesome, and there is something marvellous common to them all, not in the least shared with any others.[37]

The next succeeding chapters supply further arguments to prove the divine authority of Christ, and the miraculous character of His mission. His advent was not predicted by astrologers but by prophets of the Hebrews and pagan sibyls. The moment of His death was accompanied by an eclipse and other celestial phenomena that have been widely attested.[38] Though there are reports of contemporary miracles, there is no need to ask for new miracles to prove the divinity of Christ as some do.[39] Many pagan rulers, writers and philosophers after the time of Christ testified to His divinity even when they did not discard their other beliefs. Some of the Neoplatonists engaged in bitter attacks on Christianity, which was defended by the Fathers, but others thought of it as something to imitate.[40] The Moslems, as the Koran shows, thought of Jesus as divine, born of a virgin, the last of the prophets and the most sublime, the first of all men, as Mary was the first of all women. But they held to two errors: one that Christ was divine but of a lesser substance than the Father, which they derived from the Arians; and the other that Christ was snatched up to heaven and a substitute crucified in his place, which they learned from the Manichaeans.[41] Thus the Gentiles, the Jews and the Moslems all agree that the Christian law is the best, though they all cling to their own heresy. They prefer Christianity to all other religions except their own.

From this rhetorical defence of Christianity by the attestation of human experience and human testimony Ficino turns to a philosophical defence which is intended to show that, just as representatives of other faiths admitted their admiration for the partial acceptance of Christian authority, so the philosophers gave a partial recognition to the same truths on which Christianity had to rest. Thus the Son is generated by God by an act of divine thought. The *prisci theologi* Orpheus, Plato, Hermes Trismegistus and Zoroaster all believe in the divine birth of the *logos*. 'They said, of course, what they were able, and that with the aid of God. Moreover God alone knows this and those to whom He wished to reveal it.' But they all agreed, that

> In God, because essence and knowledge are the same, knowledge, which is God always knowing Himself, always generates as though a most exact image of Himself; and what is generated has the same essence as He who generated, although by a certain marvellous relationship as though the generated is distinguished from the generating.

Thus in a rough way they had a knowledge of the Trinity.[42]

But there is need to go beyond these approximations to the more precise doctrine which Ficino proceeds to elucidate in the succeeding chapters. After outlining the hierarchies of the heavens,[43] he moves towards and concentrates on the specifically Christian doctrine of the Incarnation. For the Incarnation is the revealed Christian form of the unification of the divine and the human, which he found in a general way in the Gentile philosophers, particularly in the so-called *prisci theologi*, and the later Platonists. Thus by this exposition he both demonstrates the superiority and preciseness of Christianity (as well as its supreme truth and authority), and establishes the grounds for partial contact with the Gentiles. The creation of individual men is itself a kind of incarnation, since by divine will a rational soul is joined to a fleshly foetus.[44] This Platonic doctrine must, of course, be contrasted with a view such as Pomponazzi's which sees the human soul in an inseparable organic relationship with corporeal physiology. For Ficino the Platonic notion of the soul, not as the form of the body, but as the temporary inhabitant and animator, has obvious advantages, since it makes possible this analogy between human incarnation and the divine Incarnation.

The divine Incarnation occurred in time when not the nature of God, but the person of the Son, or Word, was united, not to the person of Jesus but to the human nature of Jesus. In this there is another analogy, for the Word become flesh is like a human thought which is insensible while in the mind but which becomes sensible when spoken or written. The divine Word, similarly, remained invisible in God from eternity, but was made visible with its assumption of humanity.[45] Moreover, 'the divine sublimity was not depressed to the human as if through some defect, but the human rather was elevated to Him; and the infinite light of the divine sun never can become anything less by the union with man, but man is always illumined and perfected by it'.[46] This idea of the Christian Incarnation as the specific way in which man can find his much sought-after immortality, which Ficino had lengthily discussed philosophically in the *Theologia platonica*, is developed here as the central demonstration of the Christian truth. Man as the composite of all powers, in the body, as he had proved in the other work, 'is the most harmonious image of heaven. Moreover it was fitting for a universal creature to be joined to God, the common leader of all. . . . Therefore it was necessary for God to be united to human nature in which are all qualities.' 'Moreover God in man renders man divine.'[47]

The consequences of the Incarnation are then presented. Man's defects were reformed. It was not less for God, the effecter of all, to perfect what was defective, just as to be well is not less than simply to be. Divine power, wisdom and benevolence manifested themselves in the union also.

> Therefore God so declared and acted that nothing would be deformed in the world, nothing wholly contemptible, since the earthly was joined to the king of heaven and in such way that it was made equal to the celestial. . . . And there is no more apt way for this to have happened than that God should become man, so that man, who was made of the corporeal in corporeal things, might now desire God in a certain way and so that he would more clearly recognise the corporeal and human and more ardently love God and also more easily and diligently imitate Him and become blessed. Finally man could not be perfectly cured unless he recovered the innocence of mind and friendship of God and his own excellence, which he had when he was subject to God alone according to his nature at the beginning.[48]

Besides the recovery of the lost perfection and the repair of the defect in man, there was added the new virtues of faith, hope and charity.

We could not have faith if God had not become man, since it rises from a foundation of knowledge. Revelation and the Incarnation itself, then, were essential for faith to confirm philosophical speculation. The Incarnation also gave man the hope of being himself joined to God, of deification. Love which is the bliss of divine contemplation is impossible without faith and hope.

> Therefore let men cease now to doubt their own divinity, on account of which doubt they drown themselves in mortal things. They should revere themselves as though divine beings, and hope that they can ascend to God, since in a certain way it was worthy enough for divine majesty to descend to them.[49]

Christ's Incarnation removed the burden and sufferings of sin,[50] and Christ was a teacher sent to instruct man in virtue by His example of perfectly filling all offices. 'For actions are much more moving than words, especially in moral discipline whose most proper end is involved in action.'[51] Christ also expelled all the errors that were rampant in the universe and manifested in the worship of demons and materialistic and obscene religious cults. Christ, not Hercules, conquered these foul monsters. In the centuries after Christ these horrible cults which raged everywhere were put down solely by the power of the Christian inspired by the virtue of Christ.[52]

He is at this point concerned to show how Christ was the fulfilment of all which lacked in the Gentile philosophers, however great, as well as how these latter were able to come at all close to the insights that mankind received by the manifestation of Christ. 'What else was Christ but a certain living book of moral and divine philosophy, sent from heaven and manifesting the divine idea itself of the virtues to human eyes.'[53] But some of these things were known through the Sibyls and the Hebrew prophets, and by the *prisci theologi*.[54] But if they possessed any such knowledge before the time of Christ, it was usurped from the Hebrew Scriptures as very many pagan writers testify and prove.

> From this it appears that the Gentiles, as Clement of Alexandria, Atticus the Platonist, Eusebius and Aristobulus have proved, if they had any outstanding dogmas and mysteries, had usurped them from the Jews, but whatever was contained among the latter as simple history was transformed by the former into poetic fables. . . . Plato imitated the Jews so far that Numenius the Pythagorean said he was nothing but Moses speaking in the Attic tongue.[55]

Plato attributed the knowledge of science itself to a certain barbarian from Syria, Judea or Galilee was always part of Syria and called Phoenicia by the ancients. Thus when Proclus revered Phoenician theology before all and Pliny called the Phoenicians the inventors of letters and astrology, they were referring to the Hebrews. When the Chaldeans are praised, these also were the Jews who, as Lactantius proved, were often called Chaldeans. When Orpheus said God was known solely by a certain Chaldean, he meant Enoch or Abraham or Moses. Zoroaster, according to Dydimus, was the son of Chan or Canham who lived at the time of Abraham. The Jews also mingled with the Egyptians and passed their gifts on to them. He adds many more examples of this rather outrageous misreading of history, but they are significant of his efforts not only to claim priority for the Scriptural tradition but to prove a Biblical origin for pagan philosophy. Even more specifically he believes that the Pentateuch was translated into Greek before the time of the Persian empire, and that at the time of Ptolemy Philadelphus the Septuagint translation made possible the further dissemination of the pre-Advent revelation of Christian truth.[56]

But the *prisca theologia*, which began Gentile philosophy on the basis of Hebrew prophecy and revelation, led up to post-Advent Neoplatonism which could borrow even more directly from the knowledge of Christ himself as spread by the Apostles.

> The *prisca theologia* of the Gentiles, in which Zoroaster, Mercury, Orpheus, Aglaophemus, Pythagoras agree, was all contained in the books of our Plato. Plato predicted in his letters that these mysteries could at length become manifest to men after many centuries. This, indeed, happened, for in the times of Philo and Numenius the mind of the *prisci theologi* first began to be understood in the pages of the Platonists, namely immediately after the preaching and writing of the Apostles and apostolic Disciples. For the Platonists used the divine light of the Christians for interpreting the divine Plato. This is what Basil the Great and Augustine have proved, the Platonists have usurped the mysteries of John the Evangelist for themselves. I certainly have found that especially the mysteries of Numenius, Philo, Plotinus, Iamblichus and Proclus were received from John, Paul, Hierotheus and Dionysius the Areopagite. For whatever they have said concerning the divine mind, and the angels and other things pertaining to theology, however magnificently, they manifestly usurped from them.[57]

Having settled in this way the relationship of the manifestation of divine truth in the person of Christ and in the Biblical tradition to that pagan tradition which to his mind contained the closest approximation to the same truth, Ficino turned to meet the question of Judaism. First of all he shows in two long exegetical chapters how ample prefiguration of the coming of Christ and of the sacred events may be found by a careful reading of the Old Testament.[58] To this the Jews are blind, as they were blind to Christ himself.[59] Then he turns to the books of Jewish writers for confirmation of Christian truth, just as he had done with the Gentiles.[60]

Ficino was, along with Manetti and his own disciple Pico, a student of Jewish theology and Biblical commentary. He was not an accomplished Hebraist as Manetti was, and his knowledge of medieval Jewish theology and of the Cabalistic tradition was far more limited than that of Pico. None the less it is of interest that he shows some knowledge here of writers other than Josephus, whom he could read in Latin or Greek. Using translations and compendia he cited the *Targumin*, the *Seder 'Olam*, the *Talmud*, the *Midrashim*, the Bible Commentaries of Rashi, Nachmanide, Levi ben Gereshom, the *Book of Things to Believe* of Sa'adia, Maimonides' *Directorium*, and *Letter to the Africans*, and the Cabalistic *Lucidus*. According to Umberto Cassuto his references are very inexact and his names are quite mixed up and approximate. Later he acquired a somewhat more direct knowledge of Hebrew scholarship through Pico. But in general Ficino's scholarship in Hebrew studies was limited.[61]

Like Manetti, Ficino compares the Mosaic Law and the Christian Law. The former is civil and moral and the latter purgative, purifying the soul by the example of heavenly virtues and enabling it to move towards immortality. The Mosaic Law is vain in comparison to the Christian, but superior to all others. It is a preparation for the Christian. However, he also distinguishes between the moral and ritual aspects of the Mosaic Law, as Manetti did. The latter are superseded.[62]

By far the greatest proportion of his polemic is directed against the Jews, who interpreted the same text of the Old Testament [in their own Hebrew version, of course, with certain variants] in terms of a very different theology, and without the necessity of viewing it as a prefiguration of the New Testament. His polemic against the pagans consisted mostly in trying to show that they were not original, and erroneous in clinging to the old gods.[63] He has correspondingly little to say against the Moslems, mainly repeating what we reported earlier in the two short chapters near the end of his work.[64]

This book, which is so clearly of a parallel character to Manetti's *Contra Iudeos et Gentes*, was not Ficino's only effort to render an account of Christianity in relation to the Gentile and Hebrew traditions. We spoke earlier of his exegetical work on Paul's *Epistle to the Romans*.[65] And its contents require that we discuss it in the present context. The occasion of the *Epistle*, he holds,[66] was the need to counter the rival claims of Jewish and Gentile Christians at Rome to spiritual pre-eminence by pointing out the faults of both. Ficino approached the actual text, however, by first providing a theological explanation of Christianity which runs parallel to that of the *De religione Christiana*. Paul was called to bring all men to Christ, and it is the missionary role of Paul that is in the centre of Ficino's interest – as an instrument of divine providence, not as a fervent preacher. The Old and New Testaments respectively deal with the human and divine natures of Christ, as Christ was descended from David through the Jews.[67] He must therefore briefly explain the Trinity. The divine nature cannot be double, so that Father and Son are of one nature, but in the relative opposition of the generating and generated, they may be seen as twin persons, not natures. Thus if any human mind knows perfectly and loves itself strongly, it has a sharper image of the Trinity.[68]

Why also was there an Incarnation? Again, he answered, that it was necessary to overcome the limitations of human sense by providing a living figure of God that could be seen by human eyes.[69] The sum of the *Epistle* is therefore to convince Jews and Greeks both that they are called by Grace alone, and not by either the Old Law of the Jews or the science of the Gentiles, both of which are superseded.[70] Salvation is offered to the Jews first, not because there is any distinction or separation of persons with God, but, because the Jews had the privilege of having the Prophets and Christ, they ought to come to salvation first as an example to the others. The Greeks, on the other hand, represent and stand for all idolators.[71]

Paul says that the just live by faith, and the justice of God is revealed in faith. This means that a double faith is necessary, in the prophets and in Christ and His apostles. And it must be a faith sustained by works as well as words, because accompanied by charity. So the justice of God does not rest on the external ceremonies and rules of the Jews but in Evangelical spiritual truth. He compares the Mosaic Law with its limited worldly provisions and the Greek philosophical conception of justice of rendering each his due. Plato made justice the harmony of all parts of the soul, which is closer to the Evangelic justice of Paul.

> This justice neither the Gentiles nor the Mosaic Law fully achieved. For while the Gentiles' was promulgated according to the opinions of men, the Mosaic was according to the nature and custom of the people. But the Evangelic law leads on to justice, that is universal virtue, not civil only, but purgatory and even that of the soul already purged.

So in this way Ficino accommodates his exposition to his own conception of the virtue that leads to purification and immortality.[72]

He is again establishing a parallelism between the religious thought of the Jews and Greeks as preparatory to but short of Evangelical truth, which does correspond to Paul's argumentation. But he finds in Plato and Socrates a critical vision of the fault of the Greeks which allows him to place them almost on the same level as St. Paul. They, like the Lord in the Gospel, criticised the Greeks' vindictive conception of justice, which was similar to the Jews' insistence on punishment by equality of injury, as may be seen in *Crito*, *Gorgias*, *The Republic* and Plato's letters.[73]

When Paul speaks of the virtue of God, Ficino interprets this as meaning that the Evangel is the virtue of God, which is Christ, the Word of God, dressed in humanity, sanctified by the Spirit. Here he unites the word of man religiously uttered with inspiration of the Spirit, with the Divine word. This is a passage of especial importance because it gives an almost sacramental character not only to the Scriptures, but to the religious speech and oratory and prayer of man, so that, almost like the Eucharist, Ficino says, the language of the Gospel bears in itself the Divine Word, or Son.

> The Evangel also, either in meditation, or in voice, or in writing, is the Word of God, delivered indeed by the inspiring Spirit, but dressed in human meditation, or voice, or writing; moreover the linking in this way of the Divine Word with the body seems to have existed not only in the Apostles but in the Prophets from the beginning, so that the entire Holy Scriptures speaking of Christ through the Holy Spirit, is as if it is Christ Himself,

living everywhere and breathing into all who ever reads, hears, meditates by a more powerful affection. Therefore Paul seems secretly to warn that we should approach the Evangel with the highest reverence, almost as if to the Eucharist.[74]

It was one thing for God to condemn the Jews, who possessed the oracles and prophecies, for their perfidy, but it was more difficult to argue that the Gentiles were inexcusable. And as Paul speaks of the anger of God towards all, Ficino engages in a long explanation of how the Greeks possessed a far-reaching natural knowledge of God but worshipped Him wrongly. Moreover, they had been shown the truth by Plato in the seventh book of the *Republic*. 'God manifested Himself through a common knowledge of divine things, just as He revealed Himself to the Jews through the Prophets so He made Himself manifest to the Gentiles through the Philosophers.'[75]

This leads to a long exposition of *Romans*, I, 20. *Invisibilia enim ipsius a creatura mundi, per ea quae facta sunt, intellecta, conspicuuntur*. The invisibles of God are the intellectual substances created *ex nihilo*. From these ideas all visible things are made, as by exemplars. There are two ages, eternity and time. The Word, or divine reason, made this world so that temporal things depend on eternal things, and reflect the eternal brightness. As Paul says, the things of the intellect are seen. We do not need to follow through this long recapitulation of his Platonic philosophy which he finds so fitting to this verse. It has the purpose here of affirming how the Gentile philosophers had every opportunity to know the divine truth and know it well, and that in fact the Platonists did so.

> Indeed, the philosophers, especially the Platonists, considering the forms in the matter of the world, knew they were likenesses of the ideas, just as men through the images in a mirror, if only they are in a mirror, notice that they are entirely inverted. Turning their contenance towards those ideas which are in the other life, as Paul said, in deep awareness, they will contemplate them face to face.[76]

But since they knew God and did not worship Him, they are, as Paul says in the next verse, 'inexcusable'. The Gentiles through their laws and philosophy fully knew 'one God, Creator of all, provident of individuals, the beginning and end of all things', yet they neglected His worship deliberately or through a disturbance of the mind. Therefore Paul condemns four types of impiety when they transferred the glory due to God to another as though it were God or divine. 'Moreover the soul which first attempts to find rest in itself, on account of this injustice [of the neglect of God], does not seek God nor enjoy itself, because it lacks the true idea of what the soul is and in which the soul is formed.'[77] Paul had said [*Romans* i:23] 'and they changed the glory of the incorruptible God into the likeness of the image of corruptible man'. Ficino comments:

> For the Platonists and Homer as well as Vergil called our body the image of the soul. The Apostle, alluding to this, condemns the Gentiles because they did not worship the soul of man, nor even at least the animated body of man which is called the image of the soul, but the likeness of the body, that is, they honoured a sculpture and a painting.[78]

Covering the remainder of Paul's first chapter in his next two, Ficino dwells on the many sins of the Gentiles and even suggests that Plato disapproved of unnatural love in the *Phaedrus*. He believes that Paul touched upon the three types of pagan theology that Augustine named following Varro: the civil, the poetic and the philosophic. When Paul says they did 'not have God in knowledge' rather than had no knowledge of God, it means that the pagans lacked the love and enjoyment of God that Paul also enjoined and that comes with the theological virtues.[79]

But man, subject to his own sins, forgets them and judges the sins of others, when it is God's mercy that should lead him to repentance. Ficino interprets this statement of Paul [*Rom.* ii:1–4] as indicating that the Jews judged the Gentiles for being without the Law and for worshipping idols, whereas the Gentiles judged the Jews for having possessed the true God but having failed to live up to their gift and for being ingrates. But each shared the other's defects, and they condemn each other not for the sake of amendment but out of their own pride. When Plato says in the *Timaeus* that true knowledge is proper to God but opinion to men, it refers to this situation, where men constitute themselves judges over others, but judgement is divine and inescapable.[80] Paul's next verses [*Rom.* ii:5–6] refer to the divine wrath in the day of judgement when men are judged according to their deeds. Ficino relates this to the Platonic accounts of a final judgement in the myths in *Gorgias* and the tenth book of the *Republic*, and in the *Orphic Hymns*.[81]

Here he takes up the question that later disturbed Pico, as to whether sins of a finite nature deserve infinite punishment. There are both eternal punishments and daily judgements of Christ. But sins correspond to the three aspects of the Trinity; those against the paternal power, those against the wisdom of the Son, and those against the benignity of the Spirit. Guilty through impotence or through ignorance, the first two are more easily forgiven than those through malice against the Spirit. It is also proper for Christ to judge men, since men judged Him.

> Finally if we consider it seems horrible to concede the attributes of judgement to the paternal power, lest a more rigid sentence be expected, to attribute too much to the clemency of the Spirit is to stand in confidence of indulgence. Therefore Christ judges justly according to wisdom and at the same time seems to regard things with equity.[82]

The Jews also will be judged more severely, just as they were to be rewarded as first in divine privileges and offices.[83] Nevertheless, there is no acceptance of persons in God; as Paul says, 'God damns Jews and Gentiles equally, although the ones without the Law, the others sinned with it.' Similarly there is equality of reward and promise to Jews and Gentiles. On the other hand, Ficino finds it necessary to argue that the Jews will be more heavily punished.

> The guilt of the Jews is indeed graver because they were divinely given the Mosaic Law which does not permit the Jews ever to have the excuse of ignorance, and He rendered them subject to a narrower bond. Therefore sinners among the Gentiles who were neither instructed in the Mosaic Law nor bound by it will be more lightly punished.[84]

But the Gentiles 'were a Law unto themselves', and knew by conscience all that was revealed by prophecy to the Jews [*Rom.* ii:14–16]. According to Ficino the Jews received a double law from Moses, the Decalogue, comprehensive and enduring forever, to which the Gentiles also are subject, and the ceremonial laws, valid up until the time of the Gospel, to which the Gentiles are not subject. As we saw before, Manetti criticised the second law even before the time of Christ, and Ficino himself made the same distinction in *De religione Christiana*. The first part of the Mosaic Law corresponds to natural law, and only its works are subject to the Last Judgement. 'Yet no law, either natural, or written, has efficacy for justice and salvation, unless divine grace, beyond the intellect, moves the affections also and so moves them that the precepts of the law are obeyed for the sake of God Himself.' In all of this discussion, which may seem to fall into a kind of legalism, as indeed it also seems to do in Paul himself, if the context is removed, Ficino does not forget Paul's stress, and his own, on grace.

As to the Pauline statement that the Gentiles 'are a law unto themselves' – this to Ficino is conscience. 'Certainly that true light illumining all men coming into this world infuses the light of truth into the mind.' This light, 'like a judge, sits in the soul and takes the place of God in man.' Through it all knowledge of right and wrong, both in doing and not doing, of the good, of the virtuous, of the fitting, of the just is made known internally to man. All of this should lead as an innate light to the worship of God, just as in his *Theologia platonica*, he showed the Platonic reasons for thinking so.[85]

Ficino's comments on conscience have a special importance, apart from the Pauline context, which he proceeds to develop here. Although the question of grace is not cast aside by Ficino, he, like certain of the humanists, placed a significantly greater emphasis on human moral autonomy as implemented through the conscience than on the external formalities. We need to hear him here at slightly greater length. The conscience acts as a judge within, weighing the evidence for and against the soul. It has of course a close connection with the human will, but it sits in judgement over the will both before and after action.

> Now indeed the power of the conscience considering the case for the soul and against the soul in the heart by an internal light, as though a judge holding court, produces witnesses, thoughts, and frequent memories, which sometimes accuse us, objecting by a certain reason against something badly done. . . . And so often by a mutual kind of alternation, while recognising that these are matters under judgement, the conscience is divided. But accusation and defence and judgement cannot take place without a certain knowledge of the law. Through these therefore it is confirmed that a moral law is impressed into our minds. Through this some more prudent and temperate men carry on a just life in a certain way without any written laws. Written laws seem to be additional armaments for compelling the imprudent and the unwise who neglect the internal laws.[86]

There thus seems to be in Ficino, also, the rejection of the formal, external modes of solving the problems of conscience which, as we saw above,[87] Bruni and Valla rejected in the procedures of the regular clergy. We shall see how this leads him to a further deprecation of the legalistic formalism of Judaism.

The action of conscience, he claims, meant in Paul's argument the preparation of the soul in the daily forum for the two days of judgement at the moment of death, and the final judgement, when a total decision was made. The daily forum of the conscience considers doubts and alternations take place. These present self-judgements, Paul means, prove that in the next life souls will be damned by their own judgement; just as sick eyes avoid light, sick souls flee into evil and hide in its darkness. As Plato said in the Laws, 'The wicked by their own inclination seek a place suitable to their merits, just as fire is born upwards by a certain levity and earth downwards.'[88]

That Ficino does regard the Jews more severely than the Gentiles because the Jews sought to live by a formal morality seems to appear from a comment to Paul's succeeding verses on the arrogance of the Jews in seeking to teach the Gentiles when they sin themselves. Ficino says, 'and he generally means that they are some way worse than the Gentiles. And, as it seems to me, he interrogates them with a certain indignation and rejects them almost with a certain invective.'[89] And to Paul's invective against both Jews and Gentiles in iii:9–20, Ficino says, 'Therefore both seem to be blamed by the Apostle but especially the Jews.' But because he believes so strongly in the natural knowledge of good and evil, he interprets Paul's 'for by the law is the knowledge of sin' [*Rom.* iii:20] to mean that with the law we sin in a certain more serious damnation, rather than that by means of the imposition of external constraints of law, whether Mosaic or political, man develops the inner awareness of conscience. Ficino's ethical and philosophical naturalism is prominent here, as would follow from his Platonism.[90]

But Ficino's naturalism does not carry so far that he believes man can be saved by his innate knowledge of righteousness without the aid of grace. His great emphasis on the Incarnation, as we saw it above, should make that plain. So he again alludes to his previous discussion that original sin must be removed by some infinite power given by God.[91] 'Not through the merit of legal works but through Christian faith is the Gentile made just and saved as likewise the Jew.' Grace meant that the Jews were equally guilty and the Gentiles equally saveable. There is one law of works, the Mosaic, which is intended for disposing of external actions rather than removing the perturbations of the soul. The other law of faith, the Evangelic law, not only disposes actions but moderates and removes the disturbances of the soul.

> Faith certainly living, and operating through charity, revealed in Christ, brings about perfect justice to whomever believes in it even if he was not involved in the works of the law. Nevertheless it is necessary that the believer perform legitimate works so that faith will not be judged dead without works.[92]

Moreover,

> From external works civil and human justice is acquired, giving glory among men indeed, but nothing similar with God, because external glory does not make man worthy unless a great affection of faith and charity, given by divine grace, is added to it and precedes it.[93]

Indeed, his anti-nomianism goes so far that he seems predisposed to think the Gentiles had the greater possibility of salvation,[94] depending on grace alone.

Grace, also, contrary to some interpreters who, like Anders Nygren,[95] seek to impute an *eros* derived from man's own soul, rather than a charity infused from above in Ficino's 'pagan' thinking, was clearly descended from God in Ficino's thought. Faith, to him, was not the cause of grace but a gift of grace from which follows charity, joy and glory.

> For if our charity towards God has its beginning from the charity itself of God towards us, truly what is also necessary to charity, namely faith and hope, proceed from the same divinity. . . . That moreover the instinct towards the divine in us proceeds from divinity itself is also confirmed because everything mortal connected with the soul in earthly things generates the contrary instinct in us so that the soul is not able to be detached from the mortal things except through divinity.[96]

Charity is kindled in us from the flame of divine charity as fire from a spark. The Apostle proves the firmness of our hope by a double argument. In the present life it is a gift to us from the Holy Spirit; in the future by the death of Christ.

> Meanwhile he touches both kinds of charity, that in the sense that God loves us and that in which we love God, and he shows that both are impressed into our wills through the Holy Spirit. We, moreover, as we speak with our Thomas, expound as follows: the Holy Spirit, which is the love of the Father

> and the Son, is given to us in order to lead us to the participation in His love which certainly is His Holy Spirit, and by this participation we are made into lovers of God Himself. Now indeed from the fact that we love Him, we have the proof that He loves us. Not as though we first loved God, but because He first loved us.[97]

I have quoted this passage more fully specifically because it so patently contradicts not only Nygren's distorted Lutheran desire to misinterpret Ficino but also because it seems to be the exact opposite of Walter Dress' statement in *Die Mystik des Marsilio Ficinos*.[98] Dress says,

> Indeed the love which draws man into the realm of the Seraphim is not once thought of as the work of the Holy Spirit; on the contrary the Spirit rather follows the love-instinct. It is identified with the knowledge of God which comes out of love – thus it is apparent how little Ficino understood Christian ways of thinking.[99]

We need not carry this very far. Dress claims that Ficino has no understanding of Paul and treats him as on the same level as a pagan philosopher. I would not, on the contrary, want to argue that Ficino was a forerunner of Luther, which might perhaps be what Nygren and Dress would demand of him. What does seem quite clear is that a careful reading of Paul's *Epistle* did give Ficino a certain confirmation of his previously developed ideas that among certain pagan *prisci theologi*, and particularly in Plato, there was a grasp of the religious [or metaphysical] limitations of the civil law prevailing in their times. Ficino by no means claimed that man could attain through philosophy alone to salvation, although salvation was the goal of his philosophy, at least the demonstration of the immortality of the soul.

He was, however, too deeply immersed in the medieval Christian tradition, and especially in Augustinianism, from which Luther also derived much, to leave himself subject to the charge of 'paganism'. Nor would he, on the other hand, exclude the great insights of the Greek philosophers, and particularly those of Plato and the Neoplatonists, from the work of divine providence. He was an enlightened Christian, and despite his efforts to develop a 'spiritual magic', not an obscurantist. He was, it is true, by no stretch of the imagination a Lutheran of the sort, at least, that the early twentieth century sometimes produced. But in his concentration on the nature of the human soul and its strivings, he also gave an emphasis to the subjective side of philosophy and of man, as Luther in his own quite different way was to do. These remarks are in fact quite irrelevant to my purposes and necessary only because certain scholars seem to have found that the reaching towards greater universality in man's intellectual and religious traditions was a great crime in the Renaissance, and have seen in Marsilio Ficino one of its principal perpetrators.

3. Pico's Pursuit of Theological Concord

But that overlooks his student and follower Giovanni Pico della Mirandola. In the second part of his *Oration*[100] inviting the learned doctors of theology to dispute his nine hundred theses, which has been mislabelled *On the Dignity of Man*, Pico puts forth a plea for and a conception of philosophical and theological peace. If we are to ascend to the highest of all levels, we must transcend the disunity of Osiris torn to pieces and seek to arrive at a restored unity such as Job said God required. He uses Empedocles as the expounder of Job, Empedocles who taught the two principles of love and strife, which to Pico symbolise the higher and lower natures of which man is capable.

> Surely, Fathers, there is in us a discord many times as great; we have at hand wars grievous and more than civil, wars of the spirit which, if we dislike them, if we aspire to that peace which may so raise us to the sublime that we shall be established among the exalted of the Lord, only philosophy will entirely allay and subdue us.[101]

He wishes to transcend the possible civil peace of moral philosophy, and the possibility of logical agreement inherent in dialectic, and even the peace of science or natural philosophy on which men of all nations, traditions, religions and schools might conceivably agree. What he wishes is a concord between theologies and metaphysics to find the truth that all identically contain. And this is like the mystic unity of the pagan mysteries. Again using a metaphor he suggests this is shown to us by Bacchus the leader of the muses who,

> by showing in his mysteries, that is, in the visible signs of nature, the invisible things of God to us who study philosophy, will intoxicate us with the fullness of God's house, in which, if we prove faithful, like Moses, hallowed theology shall come and inspire us with a double frenzy. For, exalted to her lofty height, we shall measure therefrom all things that are and shall be and have been in indivisible eternity; and admiring their original beauty, like the

seers of Phoebus, we shall become her own winged lovers. And at last, roused by ineffable love as by a sting, like burning Seraphim rapt from ourselves, full of divine power we shall no longer be ourselves but shall become He Himself Who made us.[102]

Thus aspiring towards the same deification that has been expressed by so many humanists, he proceeds to enumerate the philosophies and schools that can be brought to unity. And though he makes only a few references to a *Poetic Theology*[103] which he promised to write but did not, his method and assumption has a remarkable analogy to that of the humanist and earlier medieval interpreters of Christian truths as contained within the kernel of pagan verse. Only for Pico it is also the philosophers, mystics and theologians who, besides the poets, wrap a hidden esoteric meaning within a manifest public meaning.

Beginning 'with the men of our faith' he lists and characterises those who meant most to him among the scholastics: Duns Scotus, Thomas, Aegidius Romanus, Franciscus de Mayronis, Albertus Magnus, Henry of Ghent, who to be sure differed much among themselves. But as Pico said, 'there is in each school something distinctive that is not common to the others'. After the western scholastics come the Arabs: Averroes, Avempace, Alfarabi, Avicenna. Then the Greeks: the Peripatetics, Simplicius, Themistius, Theophrastus, Alexander of Aphrodisias and Ammonius, followed by the lesser Platonists Porphyry, Iamblichus, Plotinus [not so minor], Proclus, Olympiodorus, Hermias, Damascius. It is his purpose that

that light of truth Plato mentions in his *Epistles* through this comparison of several sects and this discussion of manifold philosophies might dawn more brightly on our minds, like the sun rising from the deep. What were the gain if only the philosophy of the Latins were investigated . . . if the Greek and Arabian philosophers were left out – since all wisdom has flowed from the East to the Greeks and from the Greeks to us?[104]

But he wishes to bring his own mind to bear on all this as something more than sayings drawn from a notebook,

as if the discoveries of our predecessors had closed the way to our own industry and the power of nature were exhausted in us, to produce nothing from ourselves which, if it does not actually demonstrate the truth, at least intimates it from afar.

Thus he has not been content 'to add to the tenets held in common many teachings taken from the ancient theology [*prisca theologia*] of Hermes Trismegistus, many from the doctrines of the Chaldaeans and of Pythagoras, and many from the occult mysteries of the Hebrews'.[105] He wishes, as is well known, to demonstrate, what others have only promised, the harmony between Plato and Aristotle. 'I have moreover brought to bear several passages in which I maintain that the opinion of Scotus and Thomas, and several in which I hold that those of Averroes and Avicenna, which are considered to be contradictory, are in agreement.' He wishes to revive the 'method of philosophising through numbers', which is not mere bookkeeping, and prophetic of the sixteenth-century fascination with a Pythagorean metaphysics.[106]

But the most seriously intended of his purposed innovations has to do with a kind of theological 'magic' to be distinguished from the ordinary commerce with demons which he condemns and abhors. This second kind of magic is the same as the *prisca theologia*. Pythagoras, Empedocles, Democritus and Plato all sought it and thought it was possessed by Zamolxis and Zoroaster.

> If we ask Plato what the magic of both these men was, he will reply, in his *Alcibiades*, that the magic of Zoroaster was none other than the science of the Divine in which the kings of Persia instructed their sons, to the end that they might be taught to rule their own commonwealth by the example of the commonwealth of the world. He will answer, in the *Charmides*, that the magic of Zamolxis was that medicine of the soul through which temperance is brought to the soul as through temperance health is brought to the body. In their footsteps Charondas, Damigeron, Apollonius, Osthanes and Dardanus thereafter persevered. Homer persevered, whom I shall sometime prove in my *Poetic Theology* to have concealed this philosophy in the wanderings of his Ulysses, just as he has concealed all others.

The latter magic,

> abounding in the loftiest mysteries, embraces the deepest contemplation of the most secret things, and at last the knowledge of all nature. The latter, in calling forth into the light as if from their hiding-places the powers scattered and sown in the world by the loving-kindness of God, does not so much work wonders as diligently serve a wonder-working nature. The latter, having more searchingly examined into the harmony of the universe . . . brings forth into the open the miracles concealed in the recesses of the world, in the depths of nature, and in the storehouses and mysteries of God, just as

20—IOIAL II • •

if she herself were their maker; . . . the latter arouses him to the admiration of God's works which is the most certain condition of a willing faith, hope and love. For nothing moves one to religion and to the worship of God more than the diligent contemplation of the wonders of God. . . .[107]

Parallel to this secret knowledge of divine mysteries among the *prisci theologi* were 'the things I have elicited from the ancient mysteries of the Hebrews and have cited for the confirmation of the inviolable Catholic faith'. How mysterious, divine and necessary they are for confuting the falsifications of the modern Hebrews.

Not only the famous doctors of the Hebrews, but also, from among men of our opinion, Esdras, Hilary, and Origen write that Moses on the mount received from God not only the Law, which he left to posterity written down in five books, but also a true and more occult explanation of the Law.

He was commanded to commit the Law to writing but to keep the mysterious interpretation as an oral tradition to be passed down by word of mouth through the priests.

It was enough through the guileless story to recognise now the power of God, now His wrath against the wicked, his mercy to the righteous, his justice to all; and through divine and beneficial precepts to be brought to a good and happy way of life and the worship of true religion.[108]

Thus Pico agrees with Manetti and Ficino in considering the Mosaic revelation limited and essentially civil, with a certain external religious content. But like the poetic critics who saw a secret meaning hidden beneath the word of the Scriptures and of poetry, Pico, too, puts forth a doctrine of the necessarily mysterious meaning of the Scriptures but now makes it into something much more deliberately commanded and provided by God Himself.

But to make public the occult mysteries, the secrets of the supreme Godhead hidden beneath the shell of the Law and under a clumsy show of words – what else were this than to give a holy thing to dogs and to cast pearls before swine? Therefore to keep hidden from the people the things to be shared by the initiate, among whom alone, Paul says, he spoke wisdom, was not the part of human deliberation but of divine command.[109]

There was precedent for this among the Pythagoreans, the Platonists and the Peripatetics.

What further? Origen asserts that Jesus Christ, the Teacher of Life, made many revelations to his disciples, which they were unwilling to write down

> lest they should become commonplaces to the rabble. This is in the highest degree confirmed by Dionysius the Areopagite, who says that the occult mysteries were conveyed by the founders of our religion . . . from mind to mind, without writing, through the medium of speech.[110]

Such being his view, Pico was far from Evangelical in his interpretation of the New Testament, for behind the simplest sayings of Christ great mysteries were hidden. The contrast to the other humanist tendency to greater literalism and a more historical approach, as we saw it in Manetti, should be remarked. But Pico is, in fact, reverting to the older medieval and early Renaissance tradition of a mystical allegorical interpretation with his own special doctrinal justification of it.

Pico, on the other hand, must be accorded an equal recognition as a Hebrew scholar to that due Manetti; and Pico's Hebrew guides were philosophers and theologians and not simply obscure exegetes.[111] Through them he came into contact not only with a mystical version of Averroism but with the mystical tradition of the Cabala, with which he became so fascinated. The true interpretation of the Law handed down to Moses by God, to be kept as an oral mystery, was called according to the tradition, the 'Cabala'. But knowledge of it became so scattered that it was in danger of disappearance. Therefore Esdras, after the editing of the Old Testament

> decided that those of the elders then surviving should be called together and that each should impart to the gathering whatever he possessed by personal recollection concerning the mysteries of the Law and that scribes should be employed to collect them into seventy volumes.[112]

This story is like that of the seventy-two elders who mystically translated the Old Testament into the Septuagint version. So the Cabala was held to be not an oral but a written tradition in Pico's days, whenever it was written. Pico declares that in it is contained 'the ineffable theology of this supersubstantial deity; the fountain of wisdom, that is the exact metaphysic of the intellectual and angelic forms; and the stream of knowledge, that is, the most steadfast philosophy of natural things'. Pope Sixtus IV, he points out, sought to have a Latin translation made. Pico saw in it

> not so much the Mosaic as the Christian religion. There is the mystery of the Trinity, there the Incarnation of the Word, there the divinity of the Messiah; there I have read about original sin, its expiation through Christ,

> the heavenly Jerusalem, the fall of the devils, the orders of the angels, purgatory, and the punishments of hell, the same things we read daily in Paul and Dionysius, in Jerome and Augustine.[113]

Apart from the syncretistic desire to find unity with Christian doctrine, and particularly the mystically revealed parts of Christian belief, this does not suggest that the content is so esoteric as Pico wished it to seem.

His motive is, it seems, the unity of Hebrew, Greek and Christian tradition, by finding a beneath-the-surface mystical interpretation that will make them all come out properly orthodox.

> But in those parts which concern philosophy you really seem to hear Pythagoras and Plato, whose principles are so closely related to the Christian faith that our Augustine gives immeasurable thanks to God that the books of the Platonists have come into his hands. Taken together there is absolutely no controversy between ourselves and the Hebrews on any matter, with regard to which they cannot be refuted and gainsaid out of the cabalistic books, so that there will not even be a corner left in which they may hide themselves.

Like Manetti called upon to convert the Jewish elders of Rimini by Sigismondo Malatesta, Pico tells how he heard at a banquet, 'Dactylus, a Hebrew trained in this lore, with all his heart agree entirely to the Christian idea of the Trinity.'[114]

But beyond the early theological magic and the mystical interpretation of the Scriptures Pico wishes to add Orphic theology and the doctrines [of the *Chaldaean Oracles*] atributed to Zoroaster – both familiar to the circle of Ficino.

> Now to pass over Zoroaster, the frequent mention of whom among the Platonists is never without the greatest respect, Jamblichus of Chalcis writes that Pythagoras followed the Orphic theology as the model on which he fashioned and built his own philosophy. Nay furthermore, they say that the maxims of Pythagoras are alone called holy, because he proceeded from the principles of Orpheus; and that the secret doctrine of numbers and whatever Greek philosophy has of the great or the sublime has flowed from thence as its first fount. But as was the practice of the ancient theologians, even so did Orpheus protect the mysteries of his dogmas with the coverings of fables, and conceal them with a poetic veil, so that whoever should read his hymns would suppose there was nothing beneath them beyond idle tales and perfectly unadulterated trifles.[115]

And so this brings Pico back to the poetic legend of the beginning of wisdom with the *prisci poetae* who were also *theologi* who concealed their insights from the common mass of men behind poetic veils, and who were the true founders of philosophy. So we have proceeded from the *theologia poetica* to the *theologia platonica*, with pagan mythology and Hebrew doctrine reconciled in many roundabout and devious ways with the Christian. But in this process, which prolonged the mystagogic thinking of antiquity and the Middle Ages, we need to see the emergence of a new and wider dimension and perspective in which humanity with its variegated cultures and religions could be grasped and accepted.

If Manetti with his greater emphasis on textual literalism moved towards a scholarly accommodation of Gentile philosophy and Hebraism with the Christian tradition, Ficino employed his considerable talents as a philosopher to find the many points of contact between Christian doctrine and the Neoplatonic tradition. Since Christian theology had itself been shaped under the influence of the same ancient movements of thought that influenced Ficino in his interpretation of Plato, it was not too difficult to find the common ground. Possibly more than anything else he is asserting in these exegetical works that Christianity has more in common with the more meditative and subjectively interested Platonic tradition than it had with Aristotelian naturalism, however much of the latter he had absorbed into his own thought. Certainly also he is eager to prove that the Gentiles in the Platonic tradition were more receptive to the Gospel than the perfidious Jews.

Pico, however, stands on broader ground, for his embrace included the Jews through the Cabala, which he insisted, if properly understood, contained the Christian truths. But in another sense Pico narrowed the issue, for he was looking not only for a universal, but for an esoteric tradition, limited to a chosen few on whom the light of secret revelation had shown. It strikes me that this brings his position, as Nardi has suggested,[116] possibly closer to the Averroist doctrine of a higher intellect not shared by mankind, which was immortal and separable, and universal, and trans-individual. Moreover it would not be hard to harmonise Pico's views [he was after all the master of harmonisations] of a universal revelation to an élite of all nations with that other Averroist position that reserved true philosophy for a small élite and regarded civil laws and fables of poetry and religion as suited to the needs of the masses. But this would be an error, for the parallelism can reach only so far, and Pico certainly stressed man's freedom in finding his metaphysical level of existence. Nevertheless, the resemblance is strangely compelling and suggests that when the great freedom of choice is between hierarchical levels, once the choice has been made, the hierarchy becomes again deterministic. Must we see then in Pico's doctrine of an esoteric universal revelation a tendency that to some degree counters his other view of man's ontological freedom?

But in this simultaneous movement towards an effort to embrace a wider segment of mankind both through a scholarly study of the Christian and rival traditions and in the application of the methods of poetic theology in the search for hidden concordances, it is possible to see an effort to conceive of man, of Christian man, under a universal aspect, *sub specie aeternitatis*, thus making overt a latent universality in the Evangelical and Pauline conceptions of religion and of man. This may be said despite Wind's most perceptive comment on the potential conflict between the scholarly and the allegorical:

> By that time (1520) the growth of biblical philology and literalism had spread distrust of any search for hidden concordances. It was one of those distressing cases in which intolerance was bred by enlightenment.[117]

And this remark may be taken as suggestive of the coming intolerance and conflict within the Christian world itself.

Unity and Plurality in the Humanist Visions of Man and God—an Appraisal

I have tried in this book to look at the men and ideas of the Renaissance and of the Humanist movement as a central part thereof as much as possible in terms of their own problems and preconceptions. Now the time has come to inquire whether certain common characteristics truly emerge. My assumption has been that this period we have examined is an autonomous period of history, and therefore should not be strictly medieval, nor modern, nor even that hybrid conception of a transition between the two, but something clearly and definitely its own.

But in looking for the general quality and trying in a tentative way to formulate it here, a word of caution is in order. The Renaissance was a complex civilisation and full of individual variation. If individuals alone were regarded, a disconnected episodic chaos would emerge. But this is true of all but the simplest primitive societies. The historian's duty is to discover interpretative abstractions that make sense of the evidence he has uncovered, arranged and reported. Never mind that his selection of what to uncover, and his arranging and reporting, already impose an organisation and pattern. This is unavoidable and not necessarily arbitrary beyond endurance; the available evidence itself can frequently show him the way. Therefore, whatever the situation, the following is my version of the unity of discoverable humanist ideas of human nature and divinity amidst a plurality we all know is there.

It is obvious that the humanists were religious and Christian; the religious ideas and practices they knew were those that awaited them when they were born, and were guarded, promulgated, promoted and operated by a well-organised international body of professional administrators or 'ministers' of religion and a numerous body or bodies of men professionally dedicated to leading a religious life, the 'religious', monks and friars. It is equally obvious that no humanist was born a humanist, but had to become one by encountering the ideas and practices of a pre-existing group of men who, if at one point they were not 'humanists' were rapidly becoming humanists. As humanists they were involved through their writings with the moral problems and religious outlooks of their contemporaries, and were imbued with a knowledge of ancient moral thought. As a consequence of this situation, which varied greatly according to whether it was early or late fourteenth century, early, middle, or late fifteenth century, and so on, a task of self-justification of their literary activities and mode of life in relation to the religious establishment was inescapably imposed on the humanists.

Now this self-justification has often been regarded as directed primarily towards the natural philosophers, or the physicians, or the lawyers (though more ambivalently because of certain professional interrelationships). It has also at times been regarded as directed in a critical way against the clergy generally, or in a more limited way towards some group such as the Fraticelli or the Observant Franciscans. Because the humanists have been so obviously part of a secular, if not an entirely lay, movement, less attention has been focused on their theological notions, or on their turning of their humanistic skills towards religious tasks. But, as we have amply demonstrated, a significant number of the more influential humanists entered the realm of religious thought and counselling both as an inseparable part of their general activities and in works of a specifically religious character. Obviously there was competition between these humanists and theologians, and many statements have been cited of their awareness that they were treading on forbidden ground, and of their attempted justification of their so doing.

The humanists may have felt that they could handle the religious theme well because of their skill in writing, their rhetorical or poetic talents; or they might use it as a convenient and popular subject on which to discourse in a letter or dialogue, or on an appropriate oratorical occasion, such as in a funeral oration, or in a speech of consolation; or as something they could do effectively by dressing up ideas that were taken over completely from popular and established sources. In plain fact this unthinking conventional utilisation of religious notions was certainly apparent in many of the instances that we have studied. The frequency, however, with which certain points of view have come to the fore and the peculiarly, though not exclusively, humanist quality of these views suggests at the same time that they tried also to say something on their own account and of a special nature about man and his relationship to God, if not to their contemporaries, at least to themselves. That the form and content of humanist anthropological and religious thought was itself characteristic and important is, in short, an inescapable conclusion.

I have found in looking at the humanists' ideas of human nature in conjunction with their religious ideas that it is practically impossible to separate the two areas. Even where they are not completely integrated and identical, whenever the humanists single out certain theories as having a secular, or a pagan, or a philosophical or a rhetorical character separate from either religion or Christianity, they are immediately at pains to establish between the two what should be to their mind the proper relationship. Those ideas that seem clearly opposed to religion, or to Christianity, they sincerely reject. Or else they find by a process of reinterpretation either the common ground between the two spheres or the hidden harmony in the pagan or secular with the true faith.

Now this practice, or rather state of mind, seems to be a definite characteristic of the Renaissance, or of Renaissance humanism. It was not medieval, although in some ways resembling medieval practices, because it was far more self-conscious than the medieval procedures, where medieval writers sometimes even accept the pagan images and ideas wholesale and naïvely, unaware of the possible discrepancy. Such seems to have been the attitude of Bernard Sylvester in his *De universitate mundi*, as Curtius interprets him. Certain representatives of scholastic thought, on the other hand, were far more confident of the extent to which classical metaphysics and natural philosophy could be integrated into Christian doctrine than many of the humanists cared for. At least the humanists, and also the Renaissance Platonist, Ficino, while they of course sought to draw upon and find bases of fusion of classical and Christian ideas, did so with a much greater historical sophistication.

At the same time, this attitude and practice could by no means be called modern, or it would not have made so many modern historians, Catholic, Protestant, non-religious alike, uncomfortable and apologetic.

It is indeed the source of much of the confusion and controversy about the Renaissance. From a religious point of view – modern Protestant or Catholic – the humanists and Platonists went much too far in secularising, classicising, stressing the oneness of spirit of the Christian traditions and revelation with the pagan and secular traditions and ideas. From the non-religious, or even anti-clerical and anti-religious point of view, which has been fairly endemic among modern historians, the humanists obviously did not go far enough in rejecting the peculiarly and traditionally Christian and revelational. In my last chapter I wrote about 'Accommodation and Separation' of the traditions. Renaissance thinkers, and particularly humanists and Platonists predominantly stressed the accommodation. The succeeding world of the Reformation and Counter-Reformation and the triumph of secularism tended more to stress the separation and uniqueness of the traditions, wanting any kind of universality to be strictly in their own terms, completely Catholic, completely Evangelical, completely secular. This was not the Renaissance outlook, which sought unity within plurality.

Possibly today when the slogans of 'Ecumenism' have so much support, a look at what the humanists and Platonists were trying to do in this respect would be helpful, for it seems quite clear that the ideal of the brotherhood of mankind, if it can ever become concrete, cannot become so if the vast cultural and historical divergences among the peoples of the world are compressed into one homogeneous totalitarian mass, but due recognition must be given to a unity in the midst of plurality. One cannot forget in this connection the influence of the Conciliar movement in the Renaissance which, though it might have staved off the Protestant schism, certainly failed to do so, and which certainly surrendered the ideal of unity within plurality to the curial centralists. The relationships between humanists and clergy in the history of the conciliar movement and its demise needs a major historical study.

A further question is that of the specific influence of the humanist movement on subsequent religious developments both Protestant and Catholic. It is certainly true that the tendency towards philological exactness of the Italian humanists greatly furthered, through their northern and German humanist successors, an Evangelical literalism which was ahistorical in its attempts to purge itself of the excrescences of tradition. Valla is the humanist who went farthest in this respect. Some of his ideas may have contributed to a new rigorism of historical and Scriptural interpretation limiting the movement towards universality amid plurality. Valla, however, despite his fiery polemics aimed sharply against the historical misinterpretations embedded in ecclesiastical tradition, including the Donation of Constantine, the interpretation of the Creed and the translation of the New Testament, must be recognised as a staunch Catholic and a Romanist. He is very much distrusted by Catholic scholars today, and Father Garofalo is a good example. Yet he did not wish for a Protestantism, but a more historically responsible and at the same time liberal Catholicism under the leadership of the Roman curia and the Pope. I believe neither that he was cynical in his labours for Nicholas V or Calixtus IV, nor that they were naïve in supporting him.

Valla had many ideas which in the light of Post-Tridentine Catholicism were alien and even dangerous, but he was a Romanist before all. Believing in the sanctity of the Word and in the sacred trust with which the human word, embodied in the Latin language should be regarded, he looked upon the Roman Church as the providentially appointed guardian of human civilisation embodied in the great Latin tradition of European culture. His inaugural oration in the last year of his life makes this clear. Thus, though he was probably a very irritating and unorthodox Catholic, and even at one point knowingly supported a heretical dogma of the schismatic Greek Church on the procession of the Holy Spirit, he was basically a Roman Christian who found the rhetorical and philological values of Roman civilisation embodied in the Roman Church. It needed to be purged of philosophy, particularly the alien Greek Aristotelianism and Stoicism, and this judgement obviously created for him an automatic opposition from the Scholastic establishment. But Protestant he cannot be imagined.

Valla represents the extreme of a humanist statement of position both on religion and human nature. But in his extremity much is revealed about humanism generally. Valla's positivism and philologism points up most sharply the affinity that the humanists felt between a rhetorical, anti-metaphysical approach to the world and the tradition of a Scriptural, revelational approach to the Christian religion. It was inevitable, and it would seem inevitable once it is realised how central was the concern of the humanists with rhetorical force and philological precision, that they would seek to unify the secular with the religious, historical and literary traditions. But again they wished to do this with a sharp eye for historical and textual accuracy. This would lead to the new Biblical studies of which we have written.

Manetti also belongs to the literalist school of interpretation, perhaps making up in erudition for his total inability to compete in analytical acuteness with Valla. Yet Manetti was an equally pious Catholic, just as bold as Valla in his actual literary activities but as timid in the way he talked and thought about what he was doing as Valla was defiant and boastful. Then there was Aurelio Brandolini, who challenged the doctors of theology but ended up as an Augustinian Hermit; Poggio, whose attacks on the Observants did not lessen his religious orthodoxy and conservatism; and the fervently pious and loyal Salutati who looked for new ways to interpret man's actual and desirable freedom of will in relation to the providence and power of God; and the indescribably subtle Petrarch who bared the depths of his religious feeling.

All of these men, and the others, were a challenge to the old order of considerable significance and proportion, and if their influence had become dominant, there is no doubt that at least the tone and manner of the practice of the Christian religion would have changed drastically. But none of these men were reformers in the sense of the Protestant Reformers. They represent a certain ideal of human life within a Christian framework in the age of the Renaissance. The outlook that they expressed became a characteristic of the Renaissance, but they were not reformers, nor even 'Pre-Reformers', nor do they succeed in changing the course of events in the history of religion.

This suggests that the humanists were lost in the Renaissance in some in-between or truly 'middle' age that was overwhelmed by a far more powerful course of events. But this would be an exaggeration, or rather a minimisation, of their influence, which was more truly in the area of this book's concern. If it was not to be their destiny to shape the major events of European history, they nevertheless did contribute markedly to a new view of human nature and a new attitude towards man's place in the world.

Thus the major historical role of the humanist movement was in the shaping of the values of European culture rather than in their impact on economic and political events and institutions or on ecclesiastical history. They had far more to do with the civic attitudes and the religious attitudes of their contemporaries and of the succeeding centuries than they had to do with the behaviour of the rich, the powerful, the prestigious. Although I do not subscribe to the materialist interpretation of history, I am ready to concede the power of those who were in a position to manipulate wealth or authority or military force. But already with the humanists, if this had not been always true for the great mass of mankind, these activities were regarded almost like the intrusions of the weather, as meteorological events, as most truly those kinds of actions that were under the sway of the stars and out of the control of man, except as they could be interpreted as fulfilling God's divinely providential purpose in some way.

Yet paradoxically, the humanists offered through their writings a new affirmation of the possibility and value of human action. They presented a vision of man controlling and shaping his own life and the future course of his history and they stressed a new conception of human nature modelled on their own image of the Deity. There is no need to attempt here a condensed version of the medieval conception of human nature and man's role in the world, since this would result in caricature. In the closing medieval centuries, however, there was a great deal of frantic anxiety either present or deliberately inculcated by the popular literature and the arts concerning the minutiae of human behaviour which might determine one's destiny in the Last Judgement. The medieval God may have been a quiescent one, as Valla and later Calvin charged, but it is certain that to the scholastics and the canonists he was a finicky, hair-splitting one, intimately concerned with all the minute details of the circumstances, motivation, timing, internal attitudes, external manifestations of individual human behaviour. And a conviction was present among the scholastic theologians and the canonists of all schools that these infinite distinctions counted, were in fact crucial, that there was a one right way of interpreting religion and guiding human behaviour, even though there might be infinite disagreement as to what that way was.

I can agree with the Lutheran criticism of this procedure and attitude as a vain and fruitless producer of needless anxiety, whatever the merits of the doctrine of salvation *sola fide*. But it can also be seen how this great challenging insight of the Reformation was rather too quickly swamped in a new kind of scriptural literalism which insisted on the minutely accurate interpretation of the divine word, or in the more Calvinistic anxiety of a casuistic examination of one's conscience and behaviour in order to determine whether one had 'made his election'.

Coming from the rhetorical tradition, the humanists offered the first great challenge and the first great alternative to this fixation on the practical detail and on the over-refined distinction. This was a major historical contribution. It is true that they contributed in some way to the later Protestant casuistries and to the Counter-Reformational Jesuit ones too, but this was after their own day had passed and certain of their scholarly procedures had been taken up and misapplied in an exaggerated way.

Beginning with Petrarch, the humanists broke free from the bonds of religious externalism and objectivism that resulted from the application of the dialectical procedures of scholastic philosophy and theology to ordinary Christian life. The humanist turned back to man as a living, feeling subject. He found him frightened and overwhelmed with despair at the impossibility of believing that such a finicky deity could have any interest in the salvation of such a disorganised, loosely behaving, though well-intentioned Christian. It was Petrarch who grasped the psychological untenability of this version of man's relationship to God. There came from his writings, as we have seen, a vision of an all-merciful, loving Father who, far above and beyond the limits of our understanding and of our capacity to master-mind His judgements about our salvation or damnation, had offered His grace freely to all. Running consistently through all of his work was this new conception of man and of God.

Much too much time has been wasted wondering about Petrarch's doctrinal inconsistencies, his eclecticism and inclination to mix the philosophies from all the classical schools with each other and with Christianity. For the very point of his whole position was that these were merely diverse human ways of trying to make sense out of something that was too complicated and turbulent and constantly changing to be grasped for long by any one such point of view. God Himself had to be viewed by Petrarch as majestically free and moved more by his outpouring of love or anger than by any attempt to sit down and make precise calculations. And man in his image and likeness would share these qualities on a lesser and weaker scale, over-timorous and over-bold, needing to find the balance between elation and despair, aware of the limitations of his capacity and the strength of the vicissitudes with which his life was beset, but equally aware of his position within the creation and encouraged by it, created in the image and likeness of God, destined to be the master of all the world, and the replica in this of God and the universe.

Will comes to the fore with Petrarch, since intellect can be so betraying. But he does not dispense with intellect. Rather he feels it should not be misapplied to a vain attempt either to calculate man's own destiny or to manipulate the physical world in ways that are beyond man's capacity. Sometimes he sounds anti-intellectual, anti-scientific, but it is because he trusts to the insights of literature and poetry and history more than to those of dialectic and natural philosophy. The former reveal the actualities of human life and feeling, the latter deal in false abstractions. Moreover action, which is the consequence of the human word used in discourse to direct and influence the feelings of others, is more in keeping with the image of man dealing with his own human world and with the sub-human animal and vegetable and mineral worlds. Man's dignity lies in his acting in a providential way as he believed his God was doing, but not as though he were not a subordinate part of the divine providence itself and subject to it.

One can see how this stress on will continues through Salutati and Valla and influences many other humanists. One can also see the compatibility of such an image of man with the rhetorical approach to existence. We need to remind and to stress again just how far Salutati and Valla went in this, and how much more explicitly they applied it to a conception of man created in the image of God. But it is also necessary to be aware constantly that some of these statements of the humanists were exaggerations and that they did not abandon the intellect or reject the value of theory and philosophy altogether. Through the intellect man acquired the knowledge that was essential to his shaping of his affairs within the world. The intellect was, as Salutati and Valla as well as Petrarch claimed, the minister or agent of the will. Men did not and should not act blindly. It was not a case of 'Blind

Eros' as it was later depicted in classical Renaissance artistic treatments of the theme. Salutati strove valiantly to create a new synthesis of divine providence, natural physical order, and human free will. A philosopher might judge it as probably not very successful, although it has its merits. The point is, Salutati was fearful not of philosophy in general, but of the kind of philosophy and science that would by implication give man a false image of himself.

Man was by nature volitional and operative. He was involved in the world in managing his individual and his communal affairs through business, politics and family life. But he needed not to forget what his nature was in his pursuit of more and more efficient means of accomplishing subsidiary purposes. Both Petrarch and Salutati had a strong impulse to glorify man and his achievements, if not of their contemporaries, then of the ancients. But they never forgot the perils with which human life was beset and the danger that man, in his emulation of the providential activist, volitional deity, would imagine he was himself truly a god and not see that he had to wait for his deification in the next world. Man's triumph was to act as though he truly were made in the image and likeness of God, but not to act as though he was God and therefore lose his dignity. For man to be God meant for man to become beast-like to other men and to God's creation and find in himself the image of the beast and not of God.

All of these ideas came better from the pen of a humanist than from the sermons of a preacher, though the latter was not to be scorned. For the humanist might be able to help his contemporaries see the larger image. The humanist sought to join together the functions of the theoretical theologian and the practical preacher in what I have called *theologia rhetorica*. The one was far too above and the other too far below the spiritual needs and level of the educated ruling classes of the Renaissance cities. Salutati and Petrarch had many clerical friends and were most respectful of them, but never feared to disagree. The popular preacher and the scholastic theologian they both disliked. Humanism did not espouse a cause that was exclusively its own but one that was shared by contemporaries and certainly many members of the clergy, as the associations of the humanists make very clear.

Now Valla moved from the comparatively moderate vision of volitional and operational man to what I have called a 'passional' view of human nature. Regardless of the value of his epistemological and philosophical notions, of his construction of a philologically based 'non-philosophy' which was a philosophy, certainly this conception of human nature is remarkable in both its insight and its modernity. As I have suggested, its roots are Augustinian and patristic Christian, as were those of Petrarch and Salutati, but Valla went far beyond the bounds of previous speculation on the dynamics and power of the affects, of the will, of the emotions in human nature. Man became an emotional force, imbued with love and hate, fearless of the consequences in enacting his purposes, not completely blind, since he had the intellect at his disposal, but careless of the voice of the intellect when his passions were sufficiently powerful to sweep him beyond it. As a description of human behaviour as it can be observed in history, literature and experience, this is a profound and magnificent insight. Whether it is in the final analysis a true one, or one that does not need to be tempered by the realisation of the power of man's sheer fascination with the kinds of orderliness his mind leads him to perceive in the world, is another question. We are not examining its validity but only its historical significance, which to me seems enormous both for its early statement of a later romantic and twentieth-century psychological point of view and for its expressiveness of so much of the behaviour of individuals in the Renaissance. The Stendhalian, Burckhardtian, Nietzschean image of the Renaissance is epitomised in this theory.

But with it go his epistemology and his religious ideas. It was a psychology of man acting, impelled by the power of his loves and his hates, and these were mediated to him by the meanings he perceived through language and words. Words to Valla were quite literally actions since they pronounced a view of reality which helped to shape the direction of the passions. God revealed the world through his Word in the Scriptures, whereupon this became the reality with which man had to live and deal. And man, cast in the image and likeness of God, moved towards ultimate union with Him in the next world if powerful enough verbal images urged him on his way. Valla's 'Epicureanism' was all psychological and non-material. Man loved and hated, not according to material or physical realities, either the external or internal physiological ones. In fact the emotions could suppress physiological reactions and sensual perceptions easily. Man's loves and actions were according to his images mediated by the words he used to describe his perceptions. Man was, in fact, like God, constantly creating his own world through his words in literature and art and in personal life.

Manetti, influenced more by the civic tradition of Florence and the high estimation of Aristotle after Bruni's new translation, was none the less equally eclectic in his outlook, and equally emphatic in his emphasis on action. Will is important but not to the exclusion of the intellect. What seems most important in his thinking was his projection of the character of man's striving in the third book of his treatise on the *Dignity and Excellence of Man*. Man wishes to be, and this is a matter of will underlying his nature, or rather God wished to produce in man, who is made in His own image and likeness, the most beautiful, the most ingenious, the most wise, the most opulent and the most powerful of creatures. This image of the five qualities that men in the Renaissance seemed to strive after is central in Manetti's conception of man, along with his operative conception of the intellect.

Manetti's Aristotelianism is a functional and not a hieratic one. It is not necessary that there be complete doctrinal congruity between these thinkers, for us to see the kinship of these ideas to those of his predecessors. But close to Manetti in his operational Aristotelianism, and in his emphasis on the creative and inventive powers of human industry, and the goodness of human labours and even hardships and sufferings, not for the inheritance of a heavenly recompense but for their this-worldly advantages to the human species, was the Bolognese Benedetto Morandi. What is interesting is the way in which these humanist Aristotelians gave forth a far more optimistic and operational conception of man than Pomponazzi, even, did. The latter, despite his also operational Aristotelianism, could not help being overwhelmed by the pessimistic implication of the more Stoic, universal, natural determinism he saw everywhere. The humanist tradition, on the other hand, with its adherence to Providence and Revelation, had a larger vision of the possibility of man managing his affairs, and this was in good part the consequence of the rhetorical attitude of directing and influencing men as individuals and groups that stimulated this kind of thinking. Philosophic naturalism, hierarchical and static in its traditional aspects, as Pomponazzi well saw, tended also, even when viewed operationally, to paralyse by its commitment to a purely theoretical stance.

We have also found an underlying consistency between the humanists and the Platonists, particularly with Ficino, but with Pico as well in a more complicated way. The fashion of thinking of Ficinian Platonism as a departure from the civic and operational spirit of humanist Florence is an erroneous one to my mind. Ficino was a true Florentine, and in his yearnings for immortality did no more than Manetti did in describing the great earthly achievements of man as part of his striving towards immortality. If man did not have the possibility of becoming immortal it would be senseless for him so to strive in emulation of the qualities of God. Ficino also retained a stress on the superiority of the will, though more hesitantly than the earlier humanists, as Kristeller has demonstrated.

What significantly distinguishes Ficino from the humanists is his elaboration of a metaphysics. One cannot say whether a Valla would regard this with equal disdain to his contempt for scholastic metaphysics. But in general I believe it is wrong to interpret the hostility of many of the humanists towards the inherited metaphysical systems either of the natural philosophers or the theologians as an absolute hostility towards philosophy of all sorts. We have seen that Salutati, in fact, attempted to elaborate a philosophy in his *De fato*. And Valla, as a matter of fact, did also, though he preferred to think of it as its opposite. By and large the humanists did not wish to be sectarians and isolated from the mainstreams of intellectual life, which meant university learning. Their various efforts to elaborate theological ideas, as well as moral philosophies are evidence of this. Ficino was able to offer the humanists the kind of interpretation of the Platonic tradition that might seem compatible with their own emphasis on the internal, psychological side of man, on an emotional-moral dialectic, on will and love. It is ridiculous to argue as to whether Ficino was the philosophical fulfilment of humanism or not. The point is that contemporary humanists flocked to his ideas and his 'academy' with no hesitation and great approval, understanding his philosophy or not.

Thus, just as in their conception of the relation between the various parts of mankind and the various religious and intellectual traditions the humanists and the Renaissance Platonists sought a unity amidst plurality, so in their conceptions of man – manifesting in his own trinitarian nature of memory, intellect and will, the image and likeness of the divine Trinity – they reveal a remarkable degree of homogeneity in their ideas with a plurality of variations and borrowings from various schools of ancient and Christian moral philosophy and theology. In each instance there is an absence of any kind of doctrinal purity, an eclecticism among the humanists or an attempt at syncretism among the Platonists, allowing them to build out of a variety of sources and traditions a new homogeneous view of man knowing, willing and acting in the image and likeness of God.

Notes and References to Volume II

Notes to Part III, Chapter IX

1. Kristeller's studies of Ficino must form the basic guide to any treatment of this philosopher today. Cf. P. O. Kristeller, ed. *Supplementum Ficinianum*, 2 vols., Florence, 1937; his *The Philosophy of Marsilio Ficino*, New York, 1943, and the more fully documented Italian version, *Il pensiero filosofico di Marsilio Ficino*, Florence, 1953; his numerous shorter studies, many of which are assembled in his *Studies in Renaissance Thought and Letters*, Rome, 1956, II, 'Marsilio Ficino and His Circle'. Cf. in connection with Ficino's preparation and background as a philosopher, Kristeller, 'The Scholastic Background of Marsilio Ficino', *Studies*, 4, pp. 35–55, cf. especially his last sentence, p. 55. My dependence on Kristeller throughout this chapter is obvious. For the numerous other studies of Ficino, cf. Kristeller's bibliography, *Il pensiero*, pp. 443–8. Cf. also Giuseppe Saitta, *Marsilio Ficino e la filosofia dell'Umanesimo*, 3rd expanded ed., Bologna, 1954; Raymond Marcel, *Marsile Ficin*, Paris, 1958; M. Schiavone, *Problemi filosofici in Marsilio Ficino*, Milan, 1957; Sears Jayne, *John Colet and Marsilio Ficino*, London, 1963.
2. Cf. below Part IV, Chapter XIV, pp. 673–4, for Poggio's and Bruni's treatises.
3. The implication is that events and actions were getting out of hand, which was to some extent true but possibly not to the degree that the Italian wars after 1494 and the ensuing century and a half of religious wars induced a sense of helplessness and pessimism. Cf. Felix Gilbert's interpretation of Guicciardini, *Machiavelli and Guicciardini*, Princeton, 1965, pp. 284 ff.
4. Cf. note 1 above. While Kristeller's well-known and clear distinction between humanism and philosophy is salutary, and it is true that Ficino went beyond the humanists both in the rational form of his arguments and in their content, it is my contention that some of the problems to which he addressed himself in his philosophy, especially those involving thought and action, were derived from the humanists and that he favoured the same kinds of attitudes in solving them as the humanists had favoured. It is exactly because Ficino's concerns were so much in the mainstream of the humanists' concerns that he has been so frequently dealt with as the culmination of humanism. We must certainly maintain clarity about the nature of intellectual disciplines, but this is no reason to lose sight of the tremendous involvement of the humanist movement and Renaissance Platonism with each other.
5. It is a pleasure to be able to use Raymond Marcel's new edition of this work, *Marsile Ficin, Théologie Platonicienne de l'immortalité des âmes*, texte critique établi et traduit par Raymond Marcel, Vols. I and II, Paris, 1964. Vol. III, containing Books XV to XVIII, is to appear shortly. Marcel's text has benefited from Kristeller's scrutiny. I have, however, noted

places where the French translation seems strained or erroneous. The *Theologia platonica* is the source of this present chapter. I deal with Ficino's *De religione Christiana* in Part IV, Chapter XVI. References to Marcel will be indicated as *Theol.*, followed volume and page, and, where needed, by book and chapter, from Ficino.

6. *Theol.*, *Prohemium*, I, pp. 35–6, '... cum nihil usquam sive morale, sive dialecticum, aut mathematicum, aut physicum tractet, quin mox ad contemplationem cultumque Dei summa cum pietate reducat. Quoniam vero animum esse tamquam speculum arbitratur, in quo facile divini vultus imago reluceat, idcirco dum per vestigia singula Deum ipsum diligenter indagat, in animi speciem ubique divertit, intelligens oraculum illud "nosce te ipsum" id potissimum admonere, ut quicumque Deum optat agnoscere, seipsum ante cognoscat. Quamobrem quisquis Platonica, quae iamdiu omnia latina feci, diligentissime legerit, consequetur quidem cuncta, sed duo haec ex omnibus potissima, et pium cogniti Dei cultum, et animorum divinitatem. ...'
7. *Theol.*, ibid., I, p. 36, '... in quibus universa consistit rerum perceptio et omnis institutio vitae totaque felicitas. Presertim cum Plato de his ita sentiat, ut Aurelius Augustinus eum, tamquam christianae veritati omnium proximum, ex omni philosophorum numero elegerit imitandum, Platonicos asserueritque, mutatis paucis, christianos fore.'
8. Ibid., '... ut in ipsa creatae mentis divinitate, ceu speculo rerum omnium medio, creatoris ipsius tum opera speculemur, tum mentem contemplemur atque colamus ... quae soli divinae legis auctoritati haud facile cedunt, platonicis saltem rationibus religioni admodum suffragantibus acquiescant, et quicumque philosophiae studium impie nimium a sancta religione seiungunt, agnoscant aliquando se non aliter aberrare, quam si quis vel amorem sapientiae a sapientiae ipsius honore vel intelligentiam veram a recta voluntate disiunxerit.' Although Ficino argues here, in the tradition of the humanists, against the isolation of philosophy from religion in the contemporary scholastic tradition, it is significant of the difference between a philosophical and a humanist approach to the dignity of man that Ficino warns against the very separation of wisdom and will that Valla insisted upon. Cf. above, pp. 104–5, 126–7.
9. Cf. 'Lay Religious Traditions and Florentine Platonism', *Studies*, op. cit., pp. 99–122.
10. Cf. Oberman's article, op. cit.
11. Kristeller has reviewed the entire question of Ficino's changing positions on the relationship of will and intellect in two recent studies: 'A Thomist Critique of Marsilio Ficino's Theory of Will and Intellect', *Harry A. Wolfson Jubilee Volume*, Jerusalem, 1965, pp. 463–94, espec. 474–6; *Le Thomisme et la pensée italienne de la Renaissance*, Montréal and Paris, 1967, pp. 109–11. The latter study edits Vincenzo Bandello's critique

of Ficino's position on the will from a Thomist point of view, pp. 195–278.

12. *Theol.*, I, pp. 225–6, Lib. VI, cap. 2, p. 226, 'Habes igitur actionem naturalem, sensum, intelligentiam.' It is not noted by Marcel, nor does Kristeller cite it in *Il pensiero*, that Ficino's stages exactly parallel the first three stages of Augustine's seven in *De quantitate animae*, XXXXIII, 70–2, Migne, *P. L.* 32, 1073–5.
13. Cf. Lib. VI, chapters 3 to 12. It is interesting that, besides citations from Plato and Plotinus, the chief source overtly followed by Ficino is Avicenna, Lib. VI, *Naturalium*. The argument does, however, parallel that of Augustine, *De quantitate animae* in its anti-corporealism, and Marcel makes reference to this work, finally, on p. 234, n. 1. Ficino's review of the problem may be compared to Manetti's attack on corporealism in Book II of the *De dignitate*, (cf. above, pp. 234–6) and Landino's in Book I of *De anima*.
14. *Theol.*, I, 224 (VI, 1), 'quorum vestigia sequitur plurimum physicus Aristoteles.'
15. Cf. above, pp. 234–6.
16. Ibid., pp. 226–7. Cit. p. 226, 'tribus his praeceptoribus tamquam sophistis omnino dimissis.'
17. Ibid., p. 227, 'Mens protinus respondebit non incorporalem esse animam solummodo, sed divinam. Magnum quiddam es, o anima, si te parva non implent; optimum quoque, si displicent tibi mala; pulcherrimum, si horres turpia; sempiternum, si temporalia parvipendis. Postquam talis es, si invenire te cupis, quaere, obsecro, ibi teipsum ubi sunt talia. Magna vero ibi sunt solum, ubi nullum locus imponit limite finem. Optima, ubi nihil contingit adversi. Pulcherrima, ubi nihil est dissonum. Sempiterna, ubi defectus est nullus. Quaere te igitur extra mundum. Verum ut et quaeras te et invenias extra, extra vola. Immo extra respice. Es enim extra, dum mundum ipsa complecteris.'
18. Cf. Plato, *Theatetus*, 152 A, as well as the entire dialogue. Ficino, *Theol.*, I, pp. 227–8 (VI, 2), 'Sed esse te putas in infimo loco mundi, quia teipsam quidem non cernis super aethera pervolantem, sed umbram tuam corpus vides in infimo. Perinde ac si puer aliquis super puteum constitutus esse se in fundo putei arbitretur, dum in seipsum aciem non convertit, sed suam quasi in fundo prospicit umbram. Aut si avis in aere volans credat se in terra volare, dum umbram suam videt in terra. Ergo relictis umbrae huius angustiis, revertere in teipsum. Sic enim reverteris in amplum. Immensam esse scito in spiritu amplitudinem, in corpore vero infinitam, ut ita loquar, angustiam. Quod ex hoc licet perspicere, quod numeri, qui spiritali naturae propinquant, cum et situ careant, et metiantur numerentque secundum formam tam corporea quam incorporea et nihil aliud sint quam quaedam unitatis ipsius replicationes, unitas autem sit incorporea, quia omne corporale sit multiplex. Numeri, inquam, qui

spirituales sunt, sine fine crescunt, non tamen sine fine decrescunt. Magnitudo contra, terminum quidem habet augmenti quamvis non habeat terminum decrementi.'

19. Ibid., pp. 228–9, 'Sensuum errata quis corrigit? Ratio. Nobilius autem quod emendat et perficit quam quod perficitur. . . . Nihilominus ratio, cunctos redarguens, esse etiam aliquid incorporale vaticinatur, et vere vaticinatur, et multo verius quam sensus qui et a se invicem damnantur et redarguuntur ab illa. Quid enim stultius est quam concedere nos bestiis ratione praestare atque ea quae sensu percipimus existere aliquid confiteri, quae etiam bestiae acutius sentiunt; id autem quod rationis ocule intuemur, nihil esse contendere?'

20. Ibid., pp. 230–1, 'Animadvertant aliquando ex diuturna cum corpore consuetudine se factos esse usque adeo corporales ut merito nihil noverint nisi corpus, aut rem corpore natam. Puri fiant, et pura percipient. Experiantur aliquando in seipsis, (possunt enim, modo velint) quod iamdiu in universo desiderant. Percipiunt certe composita, percipiunt et formas plurimas in compositis. Formas insuper desiderant aliquas extra composita segregatas. Ipsi ex anima et corpore compositi sunt. Habent vitam ab anima corpori traditam; habent et vitam animae ipsius in seipsa vigentem. Illam ergo despiciant, hanc aspiciant. Vitam intellectualem agant a corpore separatam; separati statim separatas formas attingent Socraticamque mox sententiam re ipsa probabunt super formas quae in subjectis formatis iacent, quoniam imperfectae sunt, esse formas in seipsis atque perfectas, unde informia subiecta formentur; atque unicam ad incorporea non attingenda solum sed etiam possidenda viam esse, seipsum videlicet incorporeum reddere, hoc est mentem a motu, sensu, affectu, imaginatione corporali pro viribus sevocare. Sic enim experientia ipsa constabit, primo quidem qualis sit purus animus, id est ratio secum ipsa vivens, seque circa ipsum veritatis lumen avide versans. Secundo qualis angelus, id est intellectus purus, infuso iam veritatis lumine gaudens. Tertio, quando animus ipse tamquam angelus pleno veritatis gaudebit lumine, Deum esse persentiet tum veritatem ipsam seipsa lucentem atque gaudentem, tum ipsam lucem veritate gaudentem propria, tum ipsum gaudium veritate propria lucens.'

21. Cf. Kristeller, *Il pensiero*, Parte II, Cap. I, 'L'esperienza interiore', pp. 218–45.

22. Cf. above, pp. 65–6.

23. *Theol.*, I, p. 231 (VI, 2), 'Esse vero plebeiorum errorem a corporea consuetudine natum, nosse incipiemus aliquantum, si saltem contrariam illius educationem aliquam cogitemus. . . .'

24. Ibid., pp. 231–4.

25. Ibid. II, pp. 59–60 (X, 2), 'Sed numquid humanum corpus ea est dignitate donatum ut mentem perpetuam excipere hospitem mereatur? Proculdubio. . . . Non enim voluit delicatam aequalitatem nostri corporis

deformare, neque potuit infinitis actionibus hominis, quae infinitam sequuntur cogitationem, innumerabilia vel propugnacula vel instrumenta suppeditare, sed, ut inquit Aristoteles, dum mentem manumque dedit, artes omnes atque omnia instrumenta concessit. . . . tum propter figuram erectam, non humi sed superne spectantem et caelum quasi patriam suam proprius agnoscentem, tum propter membrorum variorum decorem omnino mirabilem, tum quia ignis et aer elementa purissima in nobis valent quamplurimum, quod etiam indicat agilitas corporis, procerus habitus et erectus aspectus. Maxime vero propter complexionem temperatissimam, quae significatur ex delicata, leni, firma et nitida carnis mollitie, quae non fit nisi exactissima elementorum temperatione.'

26. Ibid., p. 60.
27. Ibid., pp. 61–2, 'Concludamus igitur hominem ad contemplandum esse natum, ut Anaxagoras inquit, postquam ita in eo tam cerebrum quam reliquum corpus constitutum est, ut continuo contemplationis officio serviat, quod et cerebri requirat mollitiem et complexionem corporis temperatam. . . . Cum vero tanta sit et tam sublimis nostri corporis moderatio ut caeli temperantiam imitetur, nihil mirum est si caelestis animus hanc ad tempus aedem habitat caelo simillimam. . . . Ac merito immortalis anima per immortale corpus illud aeterium mortalibus corporibus iungitur. Perpetuum quidem illud colit semper, haec ad breve tempus mortalia, ut merito appellari animus debeat Deus quidam, sive stella circumfusa nube, sive daemon, non incola terrae, sed hospes.'
28. *Theol.*, II, p. 196 ff. Lib. XIII, cap. 1, 'Quantum anima corpori dominatur a multis ostenditur signis, ac primum ab affectibus phantasiae.'
29. Ibid., p. 206 (XIII, 2), 'Tres rerum ordines ad humanam animam pertinere videntur: providentia, fatum, natura. Providentia est series mentium, fatum series animarum, natura series corporum.'
30. Ibid., p. 207 et seq. passim.
31. Ibid., p. 209, 'Anima igitur per mentem est supra fatum in solo providentiae ordine tamquam superna imitans et inferiora una cum illis gubernans. Ipsa enim tamquam providentiae particeps ad divinae gubernationis exemplar regit se, domum, civitatem, artes et animalia. Per idolum est in ordine fati similiter, non sub fato. Siquidem animae nostrae idolum natura sua cum supernis idolis concurrit ad formandum corpus atque movendum. Per naturam quidem corpus est sub fato; anima in fato naturam suam, corpus; mens super fatum in providentia est; idolum in fato super naturam, natura sub fato supra corpus. Sic anima in providentiae, fati, naturae legibus, non ut patiens modo ponitur, sed ut agens. . . . Cum vero ex tribus illis partibus astringamur partim rerum ordini, partim non astringamur, ex quarta praecipue solvimur nostrique sumus omnino. Haec ratio est, quam inter mentem animae caput et idolum animae pedem mediam collocamus.' We retain the Latin *idolum*, rather

than translating it as 'imagination', because as the part of the soul that indudes imagination among its faculties it has the literally image-forming character sometimes called the *sensus communis* within the quasi-physiological level of perception rather than the poetic creation of images that is ordinarily associated with the English word, 'imagination'. Cf. Plotinus, *Enneada*, II, iv, 5 and iv, 3, 10. For Ficino it is semi-organic in function.

32. Ibid., pp. 210–11, 'Mens enim animae inest non quantum anima proprie est, sed quantum angelica et a supernis mentibus occupata. Idolum quoque illud animae, id est rectrix potentia corporis, non est animae purae officium, sed animae iam vergentis ad corpus. Verum ratio interponitur, vis quaedam verarum propria animarum, per quam in universali conceptu a principiis rerum ad conclusiones temporali successione discurrunt effectus resolvunt in causas, causas iterum in effectus deducunt, discurrunt etiam conceptu particulari ad discursionis universalis exemplar. . . . ['Ac merito post mentem hanc animae stabilem angelos imitantem sequitur ratio mobilis animae propria. Huius pedissequae sunt vires illae sentiendi brutae, quae sunt in idolo, phantasia scilicet confusa, quae instinctum sequitur naturalem, imaginatioque quinque sensuum congregatrix. Idoli pedissequa est natura'. I insert this passage in the middle of the one in the text because it clarifies Ficino's conception of the soul's divisions.] . . . Atque ut ad vim revertar rationalem, saepe eam aiunt ita se ad mentem habere, ut sermonem ad animam se habere videmus, et in motu perpetuo liberoque versari. Denique facultas illa rationalis, quae propria est animae verae natura, non est ad aliquid unum determinata, nam libero motu sursum deorsumque vagatur. . . . Quamobrem licet per mentem, idolum, naturam quodammodo communi rerum ordini subnectamur, per mentem providentiae, per idolum fato, per naturam singularem universae naturae, tamen per rationem nostri iuris sumus omnino, et tamquam soluti, modo has partes, modo illas sectamur. Quandoque ratio menti cohaeret, ubi surgit in providentiam, quandoque idolo obsequitur et naturae, ubi fatum suo quodam subit amore, dum sensibus confisa huc et illuc rerum sensibilium occursu distrahitur, quandoque omissis aliis in seipsam se recipit, ubi aut res alias perquirit argumentando, aut indagat semetipsam. Usque adeo vis haec media propriaque animae, et libera est, et inquieta. Et quando aliquid in nostra incurrit extrema, puta in mentem, idolum vel naturam, fieri quidem potest ut anima statim illud quoquomodo percipiat, non tamen prius animadvertit se illud percipere, quam in potentiam transeat mediam. Cum enim potentia media sit, per quam nos homines sumus, immo et quod ipsi sumus, quod pertinet ad eam, evidentissime ad homines pertinet.' Cf. Plotinus, *Enneada*, II, 9, 1; III, 9, 1.

33. Cf. Garin, *L'Umanesimo italiano*, op. cit., p. 124; P. O. Kristeller, *Eight Philosophers of the Italian Renaissance*, Stanford, 1964, pp. 66–7. Kristeller

comments: 'Unlike Pico, Ficino retains man (including *ratio*) as a part of the universal hierarchy.'

34. *Theol.*, II, pp. 197–8 (Lib. XIII, Cap. I, Quantum anima corpori dominatur a multis ostenditur signis, ac primum ab affectibus phantasiae), p. 198, 'Quamobrem affectus illi quatuor corpori penitus dominantur, cum illud undique mutent. Sunt autem hi motus ipsius animi. Nam quantum animus bonum quippiam iudicat aut malum, tantum cupit, gaudet, timet et dolet. Unde sequitur naturam corporis animae motibus penitus subiici. ... [Plato] addit etiam animi potentissimi motiones proprium corpus et resolvere et dissolvere. Quod non in affectu solum, verumetiam in speculationis intentione contingat.'
35. Ibid., pp. 199–200, 'Profecto, quando per animi affectum motus aliqui in corpus redundant, non per vim corporis, sed per animi imperium in corpus videntur descendere. Corpus enim vim non habet agendi atque accipit subito motus illatos ab animo, nulla intercedente mora. ... Sentire et iudicare actus est animi. Itaque per suum actum proprie, non per corporis violentiam, animus perturbatur, ideoque seipsum movet, non movetur a corpore. Quod ex hoc plane conspicitur, quia ex vehementiore cogitatione animi et affectu semper agitatur et corpus, neque potest illi corpus obsistere; ex passione vero et cruciatu corporis non necessario animus de suo statu deiicitur.' These passages may be compared with the statements of Salutati and Valla on the power of the emotions over perception, above, pp. 64, 67 and pp. 158–9.
36. Ibid., Lib. XIII, Cap. II is devoted to the passions of the intellect classified into these four types. The idea generally parallels Plato's four types of madness and his ensuing discussion in *Phaedrus*, 244–9, although he draws examples from a wide range of sources.
37. Ibid., II, pp. 201–3, '... animi aciem quodammodo ab alienis ad propria revocant sistuntque in contemplando et ad centram rerum conferunt penetranda. Neque tamen planetae et humores eiusmodi tamquam efficientes causae id operantur, sed vel praebent occasionem vel impedimenta repellunt, animus autem ipse et invitatus et expeditus talia perficit. Magnum certe est mentis imperium, quae virtute sua a compedibus corporis solvitur. Ingens opulentia mentis, quae quotiens pretiosos Dei et naturae cupit thesauros, non ex terrae visceribus, sed ex proprio eruit sinu.'
38. Ibid., II, pp. 203–4.
39. Ibid., II, pp. 204–5, 'Sacerdotes multos ante horum tempora instinctu daemonum solitos debacchari et mirabilia quaedam effari omnis testatur antiquitas.'
40. Ibid., II, pp. 205–14, 'De Faticidis et Prophetis.' We have cited considerable portions of this section above, pp. 476–9. Ibid., II, pp. 214–222, 'Septem vacationis genera.'
41. Ibid., II, p. 213, 'Quando mentium ille influxus rationem nostram sortitur

otiosam sive menti vacantem, ipsi aliquid ostendit eorum, quae ad universalem aeternarum rerum cognitionem seu mundi gubernationem pertinent, ut vel Dei legem et ordines angelorum vel saeculorum restitutiones et regnorum mutationes praevideat. Quando idolorum naturarumque instinctus rationem omnino et phantasiam offendit vacuam, aliquid sibi portendit eorum quae ad temporum vicissitudines elementorumque turbationes attinent, ut futuram praevideat pluviam, terrae motus atque similia.'

42. Ibid., II, pp. 215–16, 'Sunt et multi voluptuosae vitae contemptatores, rerum tamen civilium studiosi vel imperii et gloriae cupidi. In his dormientibus consopitur interdum etiam phantasia, et ratio tunc privata et publica tractat negotia, et iis plurimum occupatur. Sunt nonnulli tam voluptatum quam humanae gloriae contemptatores, sed indagationi rerum divinarum et naturalium dediti. Horum in somno cessat aliquando non phantasia solum sed rationis etiam activae anxia consultatio. Resurgit autem consueta illa rationis speculatricis investigatio, ut vel metiri caelum videamur, vel elementa partiri, vel animalium species numerare. Nullis eorum quos numeravimus communiter convenit vaticinium, licet postremi ii philosophantes vere ratiocinentur etiam dormientes, immo et inveniant quandoque quae diu quaesita non invenerant vigilantes, quia ratio est tranquillior.'

43. Ibid., II, p. 216, 'Neque desunt aliqui, licet perpauci tales reperiantur, qui domitis voluptatibus civilibusque rebus neglectis ita suam vitam instituant, ut veritatis quidem assequendae flagrent cupiditate, eam tamen humanis vestigiis, quibus ambigua mens naturalium philosophorum plerumque solet confidere, investigari posse diffidant. Itaque Deo ita se dedunt, ipsi moliuntur nihil. Apertis et purgatis oculis, quid maxime divinitus ostendatur expectant, quod et praecepisse dicitur Socrates et facisse. Hi pii homines et religiosi vocantur. Horum animus in vigilia vacat prae caeteris, vacat in somnis omnino. Quapropter supernus impulsus ab eo facile animadvertitur.'

44. Ibid., II, p. 223 (Lib. XIII, Cap. III, pp. 223–9), 'Caetera animalia vel absque arte vivunt, vel singula una quadam arte, ad cuius usum non ipsa se conferunt, sed fatali lege trahuntur. Cuius signum quod ad operis fabricandi industriam nihil proficiunt tempore. Contra homines artium innumerabilium inventores sunt, quas suo exsequuntur arbitrio. Quod significatur ex eo quod singuli multas exercent artes, mutant, et diuturno usu fiunt solertiores, et quod mirabile est, humanae artes fabricant per seipsas quaecumque fabricat ipsa natura, quas non servi simus naturae, sed aemuli. . . . Denique homo omnia divinae naturae opera imitatur et naturae inferioris opera perficit, corrigit et emendat.' Cf. above, pp. 247–8 for Manetti's vision of man as a second creator.

45. Ibid., II, pp. 224–5, 'Similis ergo ferme vis hominis est naturae divinae, quandoquidem homo per seipsum, id est per suum consilium atque

artem regit seipsum a corporalibus naturae limitibus minime circumscriptum, et singula naturae altioris opera aemulatur. Et tanto minus quam bruta naturae inferioris eget subsidio, quanto pauciora corporis munimenta sortitus est a natura quam bruta, sed ipsemet illa sua copia construit alimenta, vestes, stramenta, habitacula, suppellectilia, arma. Ideo cum ipse sua facultate se fulciat, fulcit uberius quam bestias ipsa natura. Hinc proficiscitur inenarrabilis varietas voluptatum hos quinque sensus corporis oblectantium, quas ipsimet nobis proprio ingenio machinamur. Bruta brevissimis naturae claustris concluduntur. Non solum ad corporis necessitatem noster animus respicit, sicut bestiae naturae imperio mancipatae, sed ad oblectamenta sensuum varia, quasi quaedam pabula phantasiae. Neque solum per varia blandimenta ipsi phantasiae animus adulatur, dum quasi per iocum diversis ludis delinit quotidie phantasiam, verumetiam agit interdum cogitatrix ratio serius, et suae prolis propagandae cupida emicat foras, et quanto polleat ingenio, evidenter ostentat per variam lanificiorum sericique texturam, picturas, sculpturas et aedificia. In quibus componendis saepe nullum corporis respicit commodum, nullum sensuum blandimentum, cum aliquando sponte ex iis incommodum et molestiam patiatur, sed fecundae [Text: facundiae] suae amplificationem appropbationemque virtutis.

'In iis artificiis animadvertere licet, quemadmodum homo et omnes et undique tractat mundi materias, quasi homini omnes subiiciantur. Tractat, inquam, elementa, lapides, metalla, plantas et animalia, et in multas traducit formas atque figuras; quod numquam bestiae faciunt. Neque uno est elemento contentus aut quibusdam ut bruta, sed utitur omnibus, quasi sit omnium dominus. Terram calcat, sulcat aquam, altissimis turribus conscendit in aerem, ut pennas Daedali vel Icari pretermittam. Accendit ignem et foco familiariter utitur et delectatur praecipue ipse solus. Merito caelesti elemento solum caeleste animal delectatur. Caelesti virtute ascendit caelum atque metitur. Supercaelesti mente transcendit caelum. Nec utitur tantum elementis homo, sed ornat; quod nullum facit brutorum. Quam mirabilis per omnem orbem terrae cultura! Quam stupenda aedificiorum structura et urbium! Irrigatio aquarum quam artificiosa! Vicem gerit Dei qui omnia elementa habitat colitque omnia, et terrae praesens non abest ab aethere. Atqui non modo elementis, verumetiam elementorum animalibus utitur omnibus, terrenis, aquatalibus, volatilibus ad escam, commoditatem et voluptatem, supernis caelestibusque ad doctrinam magicaeque miracula. Nec utitur brutis solum, sed et imperat. Fieri quidem potest, ut armis quibusdam a natura acceptis bruta nonnulla quandoque vel impetum in hominem faciant vel hominis effugiant impetum, homo autem acceptis a seipso armis et vitat ferarum impetus, et fugat et domat. Quis vidit umquam homines ullos sub bestiarum imperio detineri, quemadmodum ubique videmus tam immanissimarum ferarum quam mitium armenta per omnem vitam parere hominibus? Non imperat bestiis homo crudeliter tantum, sed gubernat etiam illas, fovet et docet. Universalis providentia Dei, qui est universalis causa, propria est. Homo igitur qui universaliter cunctis et viventibus et non viventibus providet est quidam deus. Deus est proculdubio animalium qui utitur omnibus, imperat cunctis, instruit plurima. Deum quoque esse constitit elementorum qui habitat colitque omnia. Deum denique omnium materiarum qui tractat omnes, vertit et format. Qui tot tantisque in rebus corpori dominatur et immortalis Dei gerit vicem est proculdubio immortalis.' Cf. above, pp. 193–4 and pp. 240, 246–8 for Petrarch's and Manetti's less fulsome remarks on this theme.

46. Ibid., II, pp. 225–6, 'Sed artes huiusmodi, licet materiam mundi figurent et animalibus imperent, atque ita Deum naturae artificem imitentur, sunt tamen artibus illis inferiores, quae regnum imitatae divinum humanae gubernationis suscipiunt curam. Singula bruta vix ad sui ipsius vel brevem natorum curam sufficiunt; homo autem unus tanta abundat perfectione, ut sibiipsi imperet primum, quod bestiae nullae faciunt, gubernet deinde familiam, administret rempublicam, regat gentes et toti imperat orbi. Et quasi qui ad regnandum sit natus est omnino servitutis impatiens. Adde quod boni publici gratia subit mortem, quod bruta non agunt, utpote qui singula haec mortalia despicit bona, communis aeternique boni firmitati confisus.'

47. Ibid., II, p. 226, 'Caeterum ad praesentem vitam artes huiusmodi pertinere alicui forsitan videbuntur, quamvis non sit tanta cura ad vitam praesentem necessaria, sed spectet potius ad divinitatis providentiam imitandam. Consideremus igitur artes illas, quae non modo corporali victui necessariae non sunt, sed plurimum noxiae, quales sunt omnes scientiae liberales, quarum studia corpus enervant et vitae impediunt commoda. Subtilis computatio numerorum, figurarum curiosa descriptio, linearum obscurissimi motus, superstitiosa musicae consonantia, astrorum observatio diuturna, naturalium inquisitio causarum, diuturnorum investigatio, oratorum facundia poetarumque furores. In iis omnibus animus hominis corporis despicit ministerium, utpote qui quandoque possit et iam incipiat sine corporis auxilio vivere.'

48. Ibid., II, p. 226, 'Cum igitur homo caelorum ordinem unde moveantur, quo progrediantur et quibus mensuris, quidve pariant, viderit, quis neget eum esse ingenio, ut ita loquar, pene eodem quo et auctor ille caelorum, ac posse quodammodo caelos facere, si instrumenta nactus fuerit materiamque caelestem, postquam facit eos nunc, licet ex alia materia, tamen persimiles ordine?'

49. Ibid., II, pp. 227–8, 'Postremo loquendi usus atque scribendi homini proprius divinam quamdam indicat nobis inesse mentem, qua careant bestiae. Absque sermone ita nos possemus vivere, sicut et bestiae et homines muti. Ideo ad excellentius aliquod opus est nobis sermo tributus,

videlicet tamquam mentis interpres, infinitorum inventorum praeco et nuntius infinitus.'

50. Ibid., II, pp. 228–9, 'Verum mens hominis infinitarum distinctarumque inventrix rerum usu sermonis innumerabilis suffulta est, quasi quodam digno eius interprete, manibus quoque munita tamquam aptissimis instrumentis ad inventa mentis innumerabilia fabricanda, quae quidem instrumenta natura eadem dedisset et bestiis, si illis inesset artifex idem interior talibus instrumentis usurus. Ergo tot concipit mens in seipsa intelligendo, quot Deus intelligendo facit in mundo. Totidem loquendo exprimit in aere. Totidem calamo scribit in chartis. Totidem fabricando in materia mundi figurat. Quapropter dementem esse illum constat, qui negaverit animam, quae in artibus et gubernationibus est aemula Dei, esse divinam.' Cf. Cicero, *De nat. deorum*, II, 59–60, speech and hands as instruments of the mind.

51. Ibid., II, p. 229 (Lib. XIII, Cap. IV, Quartum signum, Ab effectu miraculorum), 'Non solum vero in formanda et figuranda per rationem artis materia, sicut diximus, mens humana ius sibi divinum vendicat, verumetiam in speciebus rerum per imperium transmutandis, quod quidem opus miraculum appellatur, non quia praeter naturam sit nostrae animae, quando Dei fit instrumentum, sed quia cum magnum quiddam sit et fiat raro parit admirationem. Hinc admiramur quod animae hominum Deo deditae imperent elementis, citent ventos, nubes cogent in pluvias, nebulas pellant, humanorum corporum curent morbos et reliqua. Quae palam facta fuisse quibusdam saeculis apud varias nationes poetae canunt, narrant historici, non negant excellentissimi quique philosophi nostri, praesertim Platonici, testantur theologi veteres, Mercurius in primis et Orpheus, posteriores quoque theologi verbo et opere comprobarunt.'

52. Cf. below, pp. 498–503 for a more extended discussion of Yates' and Walker's interpretation of the Hermetic influence on Ficino. Cf. Frances Yates, *Giordano Bruno and the Hermetic Tradition*, London and Chicago, 1964, Chapter IV, 'Ficino's Natural Magic', pp. 62–83; D. P. Walker, *Spiritual and Demonic Magic from Ficino to Campanella*, London, 1958, Chapter II, 'Ficino's Magic', pp. 30–59.

53. *Theol.*, II, p. 246 (Lib. XIV, Cap. I, Quod anima nitatur Deus fieri, ostendimus signis duodecim secundum duodecim Dei dotes).

54. Ibid., p. 247, 'Totus igitur animae nostrae conatus est, ut Deus efficiatur. Conatus talis naturalis est hominibus non minus quam conatus avibus ad volandum. Inest enim hominibus semper ubique. Ideo non contingentem alicuius hominis qualitatem, sed naturam ipsam sequitur speciei. . . . Potest igitur quandoque nixus humanus in Deum intentus expleri. Nam quis hunc inseruit animis nostris, nisi idem ipse Deus, quem petimus, qui cum solus [Text: solius] sit auctor specierum, proprium speciebus inserit appetitum?' Cf. Kristeller, *Pensiero*, op. cit., Parte

Prima, Cap. VIII, 'Teoria dell' "Appetitus Naturalis" '; cf. also p. 365 where this passage is cited as a central argument within Cap. V of Parte Seconda, 'Immortalità dell'Anima'.

55. *Theol.*, II, p. 249, 'Quod si mens quanto altius ad contemplanda spiritalia elevatur, tanto longius discedit a corporalibus, supremus autem terminus, quem attingere potest intelligentia, est ipsa Dei substantia, sequitur ut tunc demum mens divinam subire substantiam valeat, quando fuerit a mortalibus sensibus penitus aliena. Igitur anima ab huius corporis vinculis exempta puraque decedens, certa quadam ratione fit Deus. Deus autem ac Dei aeternitas idem. Igitur ratione simili fit aeternitas multoque magis fit aeterna. Quem quidem statum Ioannes theologus appellat Deo similem fieri, Paulus autem in Dei imaginem transformari.'

56. Ibid., II, p. 250 (Lib. XIV, Cap. II, Quintum immortalitatis signum ab eo quod anima petit primum verum et primum bonum), 'Ergo Deum ipsum appetimus. Sed quid in eo potissimum affectamus. Illi similes fieri. . . . Finis ergo noster est per intellectum Deum videre, per voluntatem viso Deo frui, quia summum bonum nostrum est summae potentiae nostrae obiectum summum sive actus perfectissimus circa ipsum.'

57. Ibid., II, pp. 251–3, 'Comedere quidem raro corpus exigit, rarius vero coire. Verum autem bonumque singulis optamus momentis. Semper enim novarum rerum imaginationumque et rationum cupidi sumus. Semper oculos patefacimus ad quaelibet occurrentia et longissimo amplissimoque prospectu nimium delectamur, immo solo contenti sumus immenso. Semper arrigimus aures ad quaelibet audienda, quod infantes faciunt et adulti, gnari pariter et ignari, atque omnes in arte qualibet artifices, duce natura. Adde quod domari potest coitus libido, edendi voracitas minui, veri autem bonique voluntas minime. Immo vero decrescunt illa aetate, haec augetur. Adde insuper, quod illa corporalia propter aliud appetuntur, haec autem gratia sui. Quanto igitur naturalior est veri bonique quam cibi coitusque cupiditas, tanto magis a naturae duce provisum est ut finem suum prorsus adipiscatur.'

58. Ibid., II, pp. 253–4. For Pomponazzi see below, Part III, Chapter XI.

59. Ibid., II, pp. 256–8, (Lib. XIV, Cap. III, Sextum signum. Quia animus conatur omnia fieri), pp. 256–7, 'Vitam siquidem agit plantae, quatenus saginando indulget corpori. Vitam bruti, quatenus sensibus adulatur. Vitam hominis, prout de humanis negotiis ratione consultat. Vitam heroum, quantum naturalia investigat. Vitam daemonum, prout mathematica speculatur. Vitam angelorum, prout divina inquirit mysteria. Vitam Dei, quantum Dei gratia omnia operatur. Omnis hominis anima haec in se cuncta quodammodo experitur, licet aliter aliae, atque ita genus humanum contendit omnia fieri, cum omnium agat vitas. Quod admiratus Mercurius Trimegistus inquit: "Magnum miraculum esse hominem, animal venerandum et adorandum, qui genus daemonum noverit quasi natura cognatum, quive in Deum transeat, quasi ipse sit

deus."' p. 258, '... cum intellectus quaerat res omnes intelligere et intelligendo formis earum penitus vestiatur, consequens est ut quaerat res omnes effici, unde nititur Deus fieri, in quo sunt omnia, dum nititur omnia fieri.'

60. Ibid., II, pp. 258–9, 'Utraque enim fiunt quidem omnia, intellectus omnia vera, voluntas omnia bona, sed intellectus res in seipsum transferendo illis unitur, voluntas contra in res transferendo seipsam.' Cf. above, pp. 64–5 and pp. 163–4.

61. Ibid., II, p. 260 (Lib. XIV, Cap. IV, Septimum signum et octavum. Quoniam animus conatur facere omnia atque item omnia superare), 'Qui etiam si servire cogatur, odit dominum, utpote qui serviat contra naturam. Superare autem obnixe qualibet in re contendit, pudetque vel in rebus minimis ludisque levissimis superari, tamquam id sit contra naturalem hominis dignitatem, et omnino pudoris verecundiaeque affectus humano generi proprius nescio quid augustum latere in nobis significat, quod nefas sit temerari, quodve sit veneratione dignissimum.... Sed quantum pertinet ad victoriae cupiditatem, immensam animi nostri magnificentiam ex hoc manifeste licet perspicere, quod non satis illi futurum sit mundi huius imperium, si hoc subacto alium resciverit superesse mundum, quem nondum subegerit. ... Ita nec superiorem vult homo neque parem, neque patitur superesse aliquid ab imperio eius exclusum. Solius Dei hic status est. Statum igitur quaerit divinum.' For Valla and Manetti, cf. above, pp. 160–1 and p. 252.

62. Ibid., II, p. 261 (Lib. XIV, Cap. V, Nonum signum et decimum. Quod homo affectat unique esse atque item esse semper), 'Deus praeterea ubique est et semper. Cupit autem homo ubique esse. Quatuor enim elementis utitur, sicut diximus. Terram metitur et caelum ac profundas Tartari latebras perscrutatur. Non illi caelum videtur altissimum, ut Mercurii verbis utar, non centrum terrae profundum. Non temporum locorumve intervalla impediunt quin per omnia percurrat quaecumque sunt in quibuscumque temporibus et locis. Nullus paries eius aut obtundit aut retundit intuitum. Nulli fines sibi sunt satis. Ubique studet imperare, ubique laudari. Atque ita conatur esse, ut Deus, ubique.' Cf. Burckhardt's Part IV, 'The Discovery of the World and of Man', op. cit.; Cassirer, op. cit., Chapter 4, 'The Subject-Object Problem in the Philosophy of the Renaissance'.

63. Ibid., II, pp. 261–2, 'Primo quod per omne futurum tempus in ore hominum restare contendit, doletque neque potuisse etiam in omnibus praeteritis saeculis celebrari, neque posse in futuris ab omnibus tum hominum nationibus tum brutorum generibus honorari. Id omnes tam adolescentes quam adulti, tam rudes quam eruditi omni ope studioque nituntur, et tanto affectant ardentius quanto magis excellunt ingenio. Quod autem omnes appetunt homines, maxime vero praestantiores, hoc ab illis naturali lege tamquam bonum desideratur. ... Non prodest laus

quae non sentitur. Quapropter species humana vaticinatur se in saeculis futuris sensu non carituram, cum saepe etiam praesentem contemnat vitam ut a posteris celebretur.' On the widespread stress on 'duration' in the Renaissance, see Alberto Tenenti, *Il senso della morte e l'amore della vita nel Rinascimento*, Turin, 1957, Chapter II, 'Il senso della durata'.

64. Ibid., II, p. 264, 'Temperavit autem naturae artifex cum essentia cognitionem, cum cognitione appetitum, cum appetitu finis adeptionem. Ergo sicut brutum esse tantum temporale cognoscit pro naturae suae capacitate ac secundum naturam esse appetit temporale, ita noster animus naturae suae magnificentia sempiternum esse cognoscit et naturaliter appetit.'

65. Ibid., II, pp. 266–8, (Lib. XIV, Cap. VI, Signum XI, XII, XIII, XIV: Quod cupimus quatuor Dei virtutes assequi), p. 268, 'Deus qui virtus ipsa exemplaris est, animae humanae speciem afficit ab initio seminibus quibusdam incitamentisque virtutum, per quae humanis virtutibus, id est civilibus, purgatoriis, purgati animi ad exemplares divinasque virtutes commode praeparamur.'

66. Ibid., II, pp. 269–73 (Lib. XIV, Cap. VII, Decimumquintum signum: Quod animus summam expetit opulentiam et voluptatem), p. 269, 'Accedit quod vitam Dei opulentissimam et iocundissimam posuimus. Nam solus ille summa est opulantia summaque voluptas, qui fons est bonorum omnium, nullis egenus. Si ergo summam opulentiam et voluptatem summam omnes expetunt homines, dii expetunt fieri.'

67. Ibid., II, pp. 269–70, '. . . sed paulum quid in iis adeptum se putat, donec restat aliquid vel minimum acquirendum. . . . Non corpori serviunt isti, sed obsunt, neque damni corporalis ignari non corpori obsequuntur, sed divinae felicitatis invidi immensam sibi illius copiam tam rerum quam voluptatum usurpare contendunt. . . . At interim vel ratio intellectualis rerum inquirit causas studiose et anxie de rebus consultat agendis, vel ratio cogitatrix novas fingit et postulat voluptates. Stimulatur paenitentia, suspicione sollicitatur. Anxietas huiusmodi hominis ipsius est propria, siquidem a viribus animi homini propriis oritur, non elementorum corporalium, non bestiae viribus, quae in nobis sat habent, ut diximus. Quamobrem homo solus in praesenti hoc vivendi habitu quiescit numquam, solus hoc loco non est contentus. Solus igitur homo in regionibus his peregrinatur, et in ipso itinere non potest quiescere, dum ad patriam aspirat caelestem, quam petimus omnes, quamvis propter varietatem opinionis atque consilii diverso calle proficiscamur.'

68. Ibid., II, pp. 270–2, 'Porro, quod mirabile est, quotiens otiosi sumus totiens tamquam exules incidimus in moerorem, quamvis moeroris nostri causam aut nesciamus aut certe non cogitemus. Ex quo factum est, ut homo nequeat solus vivere. Nam caeterorum hominum societate ac insuper multiplici oblectamentorum varietate latentem perpetuamque moestitiam expellere posse putamus. Sed fallimur heu nimium. Sane

in mediis voluptatum ludis suspiramus nonnumquam, ac ludis peractis discedimus tristiores. . . . Nos quoque menti nectar, id est visionis paternae gaudium sitienti offerimus lethales Lethaei fluminis aquas, dum umbratiles adhibemus ludos corporalium voluptatum quae falsae voluptates sunt, non solum quia brevissimae ac plenae solicitudinis, sed quia mixtae dolori, siquidem appetitio indiga dolor quidam est. . . . Merito igitur oblectamenta terrena non implent animum sed titillant.' p. 273, '. . . non iniuria Euripides hanc vitam umbrae somnium appellaverit.'

69. Ibid., II, pp. 273–9 (Lib. XIV, Cap. VIII, Decimum sextum signum: Quod colimus nos ipsos ac Deum), pp. 273–4, '. . . quod omnes non modo, ut caetera faciunt cuncta, se diligunt et tuentur, verumetiam colunt seipsos magnopere et quasi quaedam numina venerantur. . . . Augustam quoque suae mentis maiestatem velut divinam statuam vilibus cogitationibus terrenisque sordibus temerare nefas existimant. Quae quidem notio naturalis humano generi pudorem verecundiamque ingenuit, ut non modo aliorum hominum conspectum quasi divinorum, verumetiam propriae mentis conscientiam, quod praecepit Pythagoras, tamquam Dei faciem vereamur. . . . Cuncti denique homines excellentissimos animos atque optime de humano genere meritos in hac vita ut divinos honorant, solutos a corporibus adorant, ut deos quosdam Deo summo charissimos, quos prisci heroas nominaverunt.'

70. Ibid., II, 274, 'Quod Plato in *Protagora* maximum esse vult nostrae divinitatis indicium, quod soli nos tamquam sortis divinae participes ob cognationem quamdam Deum agnoscimus et cupimus tamquam auctorem, invocamus et amamus ut patrem, ut regem veneramur, timemus ut dominum.'

71. Ibid., II, p. 276, 'Divinus hic agricola colit pampinos, capreolos et radices. . . . Numquid solos despicit homines, qui soli in terris divinam non despiciunt maiestatem? Absit. Immo vero si Deus nullas omnino vel minimas mundi negligit partes, profecto non despicit genus humanum, quod est mundi pars adeo pretiosa ut media sit temporalium rerum et aeternarum, quantum aeterna capit, ordinat temporalia; adeo Deo proxima ut sese divinae mentis arcanis insinuans opus hoc Dei, ordinem scilicet mundi cognoscat. Mundani ordini intelligentia eo ipso ordine est excellentior, siquidem ordo huiusmodi per intelligentiam est factus et regitur. Si per cognitionem animus noster est mundo praestantior, per vitam quoque praestantior erit. Cuius virtute a corpore separabili idipsum habet, ut per operationem possit a corpore separari, ipsumque mundum vitae, ut ita dixerim, supermundanae virtute transcendere.'

72. Ibid., II, p. 272, 'Si Deum sentit animus, cur non et Deus sentiat animum, praesertim cum Deus hanc ipsam vim actionemque sentiendi animo dederit, et servet, et ducat? . . . Praeterea, si animus ad Deum ascendit, cur non descendat quodammodo Deus ad animum? . . . Itaque homines multi omnia, omnes certe quam plurima vitae commoda temporalis

abiiciunt Dei amore vel suspicione vel metu. Deus igitur debet pro temporalibus aeterna tribuere. Nullum vero animalium reliquorum praesentibus abstinet bonis propter futurorum aviditatem. Quo fit ut homo stultissimus sit animalium omnium atque miserrimus, si neque praesenti fruitur vita neque futura.' Cf. Valla's arguments above, pp. 133–6; also Manetti, pp. 240–1.

73. Cf. above, pp. 481–6.

74. Ibid., II, pp. 279–83 (Lib. XIV, Cap. IX, Religionem esse humano generi maxime omnium propriam et verdicam), pp. 279–80, 'Hominem esse brutis praestantiorem opera eius evidentissimo testimonio sunt, quod ostendit duodecimo libro Animalium Aristoteles, Quaeramus igitur qua praecipue dote sit praestantissimus. Videtur sane praestare artium et gubernationis ingenio, praesertim quia, ut alias declaravimus, homines variant artificia, utpote qui ipsi artifices sint, non alterius artificis instrumenta. Bestiae veri non variant, quia artificiosae naturae instrumenta sint potius quam artem ipsae possideant. Verum licet artis et gubernationis ingenio caeteris animalibus praecellamus, communis tamen haec nobis est cum brutis industria. Oportet autem humanam speciem, postquam a brutis distincta est, distinctam aliquam propriamque habere perfectionem, cuius non sint bestiae ullae ullo modo participes. Num sermo hic erit? At nutu, clamore et cantu sermonem bestiae imitantur. Num ratio? Ratio certe. Non omnis tamen operatio rationis, nam ratio quidem activa habet et in bestiis vestigia quaedam per artium et gubernationis indicia. Ratio quoque rerum naturalium speculatrix habere videtur nonnihil in bestiis imaginarium. Nam et ipsae morbis suis ciborum remediorumque quorundam electione medentur, et quasi futurarum tempestatum providae argumenta praeferunt futurorum mutantque loca, ut ventura temporum vitent discrimina, quamvis ad hoc ducantur potius natura quam ducunt. Quid ergo reliquum est, quod omnino solius sit hominis? Contemplatio divinorum. Nullum enim bruta prae se ferunt religionis indicium, ut propria nobis sit mentis in Deum caeli regem erectio sicut corporis in caelum erectio propria. Cultusque divinus ita ferme hominibus est naturalis, sicut equis hinnitus canibusve latratus.' Cf. Aristotle, *De partibus animalium*, II, X, 4.

75. Cf. D. P. Walker, op. cit.; Frances Yates, op. cit.; Garin's interest in the Hermetic tradition is evident in 'La "Dignitas Hominis" etc.', op. cit. of 1938. Since then he has published a series of articles on Hermetism and magic: Cf. in *Medioevo e Rinascimento*, Bari, 1954, pp. 150–69, 170–91; in *La cultura filosofica*, op. cit., 'Nota sull'Ermetismo', pp. 143–58; 'Le "Elezioni" e il problema dell'astrologia', in *Umanesimo e esoterismo*, ed. E. Castelli, Padua, 1960, pp. 7 ff; among others. C. Vasoli, 'Temi e fonte della tradizione ermetica in uno scritto di Symphorien Champier', *Umanesimo e esoterismo*, op. cit., pp. 235–89; François Secret, on the 'Emithologie' of Guillaume Postel, pp. 381–437 of *Umanesimo e esoterismo*;

also 'L'hermeneutique de Guillaume Postel', in *Umanesimo e ermeneutica*, ed. E. Castelli, Padua, 1963, pp. 91–145, most recently *Les Kabbalistes chrétiens de la Renaissance*, Paris, 1964. Kristeller, who made a fundamental contribution to the history of Hermetism in the Renaissance (cf. 'Marsilio Ficino e Lodovico Lazzarelli: Contributo alla diffusione delle idee ermetiche nel Rinascimento', *Studies*, op. cit., pp. 221–48), indicates the doctrinal points where Ficino seems influenced by the Hermetics but lays no special stress on Hermetic influences on Ficino. Cf. *Il pensiero*, passim.

76. Op. cit., p. 155.
77. Ibid., pp. 155–6.
78. Ibid., p. 156.
79. Ibid.
80. Cf. section 2 of her Chapter IX, 'Against Magic . . . (2) The Humanist Tradition', pp. 159–68. Miss Yates separates a 'Latin' humanism of the early Renaissance which was scholarly, sober and anti-magical, from a 'Greek' humanism of the Quattrocento of which Pico is her chief example. But among the Latin humanists she cites are some – Valla and Poggio – who were also Greek scholars. Her distinctions do not seem viable. I do recognise, of course, a trend towards a strict scholarly approach among the humanists, but there was also a more speculative trend that antedated the Platonists and later joined in with them. Ficino and Pico were also both scholars and humanists as well as philosophers more sympathetic to the scholastic tradition, but selectively sympathetic. As we have shown, some of the humanists were not as isolated and contemptuous of medieval philosophy as has sometimes been claimed.
81. Cf. below, Part IV, Chapter XV, 'From *Theologia Poetica* to *Theologia Platonica*'.

Notes to Part III, Chapter X

1. Cf. Umberto Cassuto, *Gli Ebrei a Firenze*, Florence, 1918, pp. 277–81.
2. Ibid., pp. 275–7.
3. Cf. below, pp. 586–7 and pp. 726–34.
4. Cassuto, op. cit., pp. 281–323.
5. The recent bio-bibliographical study of P. O. Kristeller is indispensable, 'Giovanni Pico della Mirandola and His Sources', pp. 35–133, *L'opera e il pensiero di Giovanni Pico della Mirandola nella storia dell'Umanesimo*, Florence, 1965, including a tentative list of Pico manuscripts and an updated bibliography. E. Garin, *Giovanni Pico della Mirandola*, Florence, 1937, remains the fundamental study of his philosophy. Cf. also the recent studies by Garin listed by Kristeller, and the papers reprinted in *La cultura filosofica*, op. cit., Parte seconda, 'Ricerche su Giovanni Pico della Mirandola', pp. 231–89. Garin has also edited Pico's most important

works, *Opere*, Vol. I, *De hominis dignitate, Heptaplus, De ente et uno, e scritti vari* (which we shall use below), Florence, 1942, Vols. II and III, *Disputationes adversus astrologiam divinatricem*, Florence, 1946, 1952. Garin's edition of Pico's commentary on the *Psalms* is promised. Two essential recent works on Pico's religious thought are: Engelbert Monnerjahn, *Giovanni Pico della Mirandola, Ein Beitrag zur philosophischen Theologie des italienischen Humanismus*, Wiesbaden, 1960; Giovanni di Napoli, *Giovanni Pico della Mirandola e la problematica dottrinale del suo tempo*, Rome, 1965. On Pico and the Cabbala, cf. Cassuto, above; J. L. Blau, *The Christian Interpretation of the Cabala in the Renaissance*, New York, 1944, and more recently: G. Scholem, 'Zur Geschichte der Anfänge der christlichen Kabbala', *Essays Presented to L. Baeck*, London, 1954; François Secret, 'Pico della Mirandola e gli inizi della cabala cristiana', *Convivium*, I (1957). The last two items are supplied from Frances Yates' important study on Hermetism, op. cit., p. 94, n. 1, cf. her Chapter V, 'Pico della Mirandola and Cabalist Magic', pp. 84–116. Cf. also F. Secret, *Le Zôhar chez les kabbalistes chrétiens de la Renaissance* op. cit.

6. Cf. Cassuto, op. cit., pp. 282–99, on Elia del Medigo and Pico; cf. also Bruno Nardi, 'La mistica averroistica e Pico della Mirandola', *Umanesimo e Machiavellismo*, ed. E. Castelli, Padua, 1949, pp. 55–74; also in Nardi's *L'Aristotelismo Padovano*, Florence, 1955, pp. 127–46.
7. Cf. Garin's edition, op. cit., pp. 102–65 (Latin and Italian on facing pages) section on dignity of man, pp. 102–10 (i.e. 4), on sources and traditions, pp. 110 *ad finem* (i.e. 27). Cf. Part IV, Chapter XVI below, pp. 753–8 for discussion of this section of the *Oration* in its proper context.
8. Ibid., pp. 102–10.
9. Cf. above, pp. 477–8 and pp. 281–2.
10. Cf. above, pp. 240–3 and pp. 204–9.
11. Cit. above, pp. 181–2. Cf. Migne, *Patr. lat.*, 32, cols. 1073–77.
12. Cf. above, pp. 185–8 and pp. 395–6. It is interesting that Pico, speaking of Greek Fathers who have commented on *Genesis*, mentions 'Philo', Origen, Basil, Theodoretus, Apollinarius, Didymus, Diodorus, Severus, Eusebius, Josephus, Gennadius, Chrysostomus, but not Gregory or, Nemesius. Cf. *Heptaplus*, ed. Garin, p. 178.
13. Cf. above, pp. 184–5 and pp. 395–6.
14. The circumstances of its composition and its reception are described in Di Napoli, *Pico*, op. cit., Cap. IV, *Contemplator*, espec. pp. 200 ff.
15. Umberto Cassuto pointed this out in 1918, op. cit., p. 323.
16. Cf. above, pp. 476–8.
17. Kristeller, for instance, in, *Eight Philosophers of the Italian Renaissance*, op. cit., although he does not use the word 'microcosm', suggests this with respect to both the *Oration* and *Heptaplus*, p. 67. Monnerjahn, op. cit., p. 27, suggests there is no contradiction in these views, 'Hier

wird deutlich, warum der Mensch, obwohl Mikrokosmos, keineswegs seine Freiheit an die Welt verliert, sondern das freiste unter allen Geschöpfen ist.' Ed. Garin., p. 192, 'Est autem, praeter tres quos narravimus, quartus alius mundus in quo et ea omnia inveniantur quae sunt in reliquis. Hic ipse est homo qui et propterea, ut catholici dicunt doctores, in Evangelio omnis creaturae appellatione censetur, cum praedicandum hominibus Evangelium, non autem brutis et angelis, praedicandum tamen omni creaturae a Christo demandatur. Tritum in scholis verbum est, esse hominem minorem mundum, in quo mixtum ex elementis corpus et caelestis spiritus et plantarum anima vegetalis et brutorum sensus et ratio et angelica mens et Dei similitudo conspicitur.'

18. Kristeller, *Pensiero*, op. cit., Parte prima, Cap. VII, pp. 153–79; *Heptaplus*, ed. Garin, p. 220, 'Quemadmodum autem inferiorum omnium absoluta consummatio est homo, ita omnium hominum absoluta est consummatio Christus; quod si, ut dicunt philosophi, ab eo quod unaquoque in genere est perfectissimum ad ceteros eiusdem ordinis quasi a fonte omnis perfectio derivatur, dubium nemini a Christo homine in omnes homines totius bonitatis perfectionem derivari; illi scilicet uni datus non ad mensuram, ut de plenitudine eius omnes acciperemus. Vide quam haud dubie haec ei praerogativa debeatur Deo et homini, quae etiam, qua homo, est peculiaris ei et legitimo privilegio convenit.'

19. Ibid., 'Supremus omnium et princeps homo, quo mundi corruptibilis natura progressa sistit pedem et receptui canit.'

20. Ibid., p. 240, 'Hactenus de corporea caelorum natura. Nunc praedita ea animo rationali declaraturus, allegorice hominis meminit, non utique illius qui est caducus et terreus et quem videmus, sed a quo ut inquit Plotinus, is regitur homo qui videtur. . . . Astipulantur nostrae expositioni litterae sacrae, in quibus saepe angelica omnis natura et rationalis per hominem designatur. . . . Adiecit igitur Deus caelesti machinae vivam substantiam et rationalem, participem intellectus, ideoque ad imaginem et similitudinem suam hanc voluit praeesse his, de quibus paulo ante diximus, animantibus, idest sidereis omnibus signis et planetis, quae illius ita nutu versantur, ita dicto oboediunt, ut nulla mora, nulla sit contumacia.'

21. Ibid., pp. 242–4, 'Nobilis haec creatura et nobis suspicienda et celebranda: sed, si vel platonicae sententiae, ut theologos taceam, cuius modo meminimus, non sumus obliti, temperatos animos nostros ab opifice Deo in eodem cratere ex iisdemque elementis cum caelestibus animis, videamus ne nos illorum servos velimus, quos nos fratres esse natura voluit. Neque nostram conditionem de hoc infirmo corpore metiamur; neque enim homo, ut scriptum in *Alcibiade*, hoc quod videmus fragile et terrenum, sed animus est, sed intellectus, qui omnem ambitum caeli, omnem decursum temporis excedit. . . . Illum igitur timeamus, amemus et veneremur in quo, ut inquit Paulus, creata sunt omnia, sive visibilia

sive invisibilia; quod est principium in quo fecit Deus caelum et terram: hoc autem est Christus. . . . Quare neque stellarum imagines in metallis, sed illius, idest Verbi Dei imaginem in nostris animis reformemus. . . .'

22. Ibid., pp. 246–8, 'Denique quicquid alienum ab evangelica veritate deprehendemus confutabimus pro virili, quicquid sanctum et verum, a synagoga, ut ab iniusto possessore ad nos, legitimos Israelitas transferemus.'
23. Ibid., capp. 1–3.
24. Ibid., cap. 4; Cf. above, p. 221 and p. 249, for Facio and Manetti.
25. Ibid., p. 258, 'Haud aliter est nobis de his angelis intelligendum qui sublunaria curant. Diversis enim diversi corporalibus rebus aliisque ab homine praesunt, quoniam, quemadmodum Platonici, ita et nostri crediderunt variis mundi huius corruptibilis rebus varias spiritales substantias a Deo praefectas. Quocirca et Augustinus nullam esse visibilem rem apud nos, cui non praesit angelica potestas et corpora omnia per rationalem spiritum vitae regi constanter asseruit. . . . Verum, quemadmodum haec omnia infra hominem ad hominem referuntur, ita et omnis circa haec angelorum cura illi potissimum subancillatur et servit opere et studio, ut curent humana et nostrae auxiliantes imbecillitati efficiant quantum quidem patimur ipsi, ut pie atque feliciter vitam vivamus.'
26. Ibid., p. 262, 'Purgant igitur terram nostram aquae inferiores, unde et nitida sub aspectum venit; purgatam caelestes illuminant; supercaelestes igneo quodam rare atque vivifico perficiunt et fecundant ad tantam saepe felicitatem, ut non salutares iam herbas, sed ipsum germinet Salvatorem, et non una virtus, sed Christus, plenitudo omnium virtutum, formetur in nobis.'
27. Ibid., pp. 264–6, 'Postremo hominis meminit, non quia homo sit angelus, sed quia angelici mundi finis et terminus, quemadmodum et de natura corruptibili agens hominem etiam attulit illius naturae non partem sed principium et caput; quo fit ut ad tres mundos tractatus hominis pertineat, ad eum qui sibi est proprium et ad utrumque extremum, incorporeum scilicet et elementarem quorum ita est medius ut alterius finis, alterius principium statuatur. Sed video paratum laqueum nostrae expositioni, cum subiiciatur praeesse hominem piscibus maris, avibus et brutis. Nam si illa nobis naturam angelicam significant, quo pacto verum erit quod scribitur praeesse hominem illis, quem deminutum ab angelis et sciunt philosophi et Propheta testatur? Adsit Ille nobis et laqueum conterat, qui et contrivit Sathanam sub nostris pedibus, Iesus Christus primogenitus omnis creaturae; hic laqueum profecto conterit et nodum omnem solvit et abrumpit, quoniam non solum in eo in quo tota divinitas corporaliter habitavit adeo sublimata est natura humana, ut homo Christus, qua homo est, si credimus Dionysio, angelos doceat, illuminet et perficiat, tanto, ut inquit Paulus, melior angelis effectus, quanto differentius prae illis nomen hereditavit, sed et nos omnes, quibus

data potestas filios Dei fieri per gratiam cuius dator est Christus, supra angelicam dignitatem evehi possumus.'

28. Cf. above, pp. 190–1 for Petrarch, pp. 252–3 for Manetti, pp. 487–8 for Ficino, and below, pp. 636–7 for Valla.

29. Cf. above, pp. 188–90. See also the discussion of Egidio of Viterbo further on in this chapter.

30. Ed. Garin, pp. 266–8, 'Postquam de omnibus mundi partibus deque omni natura caelesti, angelica et corruptibili, tractatum satis a Propheta ostendimus, reliquum (si promissi memores sumus) totam iterum lectionem de homine interpretari, hoc re ipsa comprobaturi: nullam esse in universo hoc opere orationem, quae uti de tribus mundis, de quibus actum superius, ita de hominis etiam natura reconditos sensus et veritates altissimas non complectatur ... et profecto improbum et temerarium illius studium, qui adhuc sui ignarus adhuc nescius an scire aliquid possit, rerum tamen quae tam procul ab ipso sunt cognitionem sic audacter affectat.'

31. Ibid., Caput primum, pp. 270–2, 'Constat homo ex corpore et anima rationali. Rationalis animus caelum dicitur; nam et caelum animal a se ipso moto vocat Aristoteles, et animus noster (ut probant Platonici) substantia est se ipsam movens. ... Caelum in orbem movetur; animus rationalis, a causis ad effectus se transferens, rursusque ab effectibus recurrens in causas, ratiocinationis orbe circumvolvitur. ... Corpus dicitur terra, quoniam terrosa et gravis substantia est. Quare et de humo factum, ut scribit Moses homini dedit appellationem. Verum inter terrenum corpus et caelestem animi substantiam opus fuit medio vinculo, quod tam distantes naturas invicem copularet; huic muneri delegatum illud tenue et spiritale corpusculum, quod et medici et philosophi spiritum vocant, quem et diviniore esse natura quam elementa et caelo proportione respondere Aristoteles scribit; hic lux nuncupatur, quae cognominatio convenire magis non posset philosophorum sententientiae medicorum, quorum omnium communis est consensus esse illum substantia maxime lucida et nulla re magis quam luce gaudere, foveri, et recreari. Descendamus iam ad verba Prophetae, apud quem primum videmus creari caelum et terram, extrema scilicet nostrae substantiae, vim rationalem et corpus terrenum, quae postremum cum fit lux, idest lucidus accedit spiritus, sic uniuntur ut ex vespere et mane, idest ex corporis nocturna et mattutina animi natura, unus sit homo; et quoniam (ut ostendimus) per hanc lucem omnis vitalis sensualisque virtus ad terram nostram descendit, merito ante lucis natale terra fuit inanis et vacua, cui vitae motusque beneficia nisi per internuntium lumen participare suum caelum non poterat. Quare et statim causam adiunxit inanitatis, quia scilicet super eam adhuc tenebrae erant, luce nondum exorta.'

32. Ibid., Caput secundum, pp. 272–6, 'Intellectum enim, qui est in nobis, illustrat maior atque adeo divinus intellectus sive sit Deus (ut quidam

volunt), sive proxima homini et cognata mens, ut fere omnes Graeci, ut Arabes, ut Hebraeorum plurimi volunt. . . . Nec factum sine causa ut, priusquam hominem ex animo et corpore vinculo lucis constituisset, huius rei meminerit, ne forte crederemus non adesse spiritum hunc nostro intellectui, nisi cum esset corpori copulatus.'

33. Ibid., Caput tertium, pp. 276–8, 'Nam sensitivae omnes virtutes ad sensum quem ex re ipsa vocamus communem (hic autem si Aristotelem sequimur est in corde), uti flumina ad mare confluunt. Nec absurde dixerimus ab eo mari quinque corporis sensus quos videmus: auditum, visum, gustum, tactum, olfactum, quasi quinque maria mediterranea diffusos intrare corporis continentem . . . recte post illam aquarum congregationem, terram inducit statim viridem et florescentem. Praestiti enim a natura sensus omnibus mortalibus ad vitam corpori salutemque procurandam, ut per eos cognoscant quae sibi noxia, quae salutaria; tum cognita per appetentiam sensibus annexam, illa respuant, haec desiderent; postremo, per coniugem potestatem motricem, fugiant mala, utilia prosequantur. Videt oculus cibum, olfaciunt nares, accedunt pedes, capiunt manus, palatum experitur. Quae omnia ideo dicimus, ut cognoscamus apte coniunctam stabilimento aquarum, idest sensitivarum virium, terrae, quae iamdiu nobis corpus significat, uberem felicitatem.'

34. Ibid., Caput quartum, pp. 278–80, 'At vero cum multis rationalis natura et viribus et potentiis distinguatur, de nuda eius substantia supra est dictum. Nunc de ornatu et, ut ita dixerim, regia eius suppellectile dicendum . . . et quidem philosophi iuniores solem intellectum qui actu est, lunam eum qui est potentia forte interpretarentur; sed quoniam nobis magna de hac re cum illis controversia, nos interim sic exponamus ut qua parte ad aquas superiores, ad Domini Spiritum animus vergit, propterea quod totus lucet, sol nuncupetur; qua vero aquas inferiores, idest sensuales potentias respicit, unde infectionis aliquam contrahit maculam, lunae habeat appellationem. . . . Quoniam autem, dum a patria peregrinamur et in hac vitae praesentis nocte et tenebris vivimus, ea parte plurimum utimur quae ad sensus deflectitur, unde et plura opinamur quam scimus, cum vero dies futurae vitae illuxerit, alieni a sensibus ad divina conversi, superiori alia parte intelligemus, recte est dictum hunc nostrum solem praeesse diei, lunam autem praeesse nocti.'

35. Ibid., Caput quintum, pp. 280–4, 'Has per bestias designat et irrationale genus viventium, quia sunt nobis cum bestiis communes et, quod est infelicius, ad brutalem saepe nos vitam impellunt. . . . Ad aquas autem, idest sensum imaginationis, affectiones illas referamus, quae spiritales magis et nostrae potius cogitationis quam carnis soboles dici possunt; quod genus sunt quae ad honores, ad iram, ad ultionem, et cognatas his reliquas affectiones nos vocant; necessaria haec et utilia modice utentibus: irascendum enim, sed intra modum; et ultio saepe opus iustitiae, et sua unicuique tuenda dignitas nec recusandi honores qui honestis artibus

comparantur. Quod ideo dico, ne cum haec bruta, quae sensuales appetentias indicant, Deus creaverit creatisque benedixerit, si sint mala ex sua natura, credamus cum Manicheis a malo principio et non a bono potius Deo condita fuisse. Bona igitur illa omnia et homini necessaria, sed nos inde ad ambitionem, furorem, excandescentiam superbiamque excedentes, mala facimus nostra culpa quae Ille optimus optima instituerat.'

36. Ibid., Caput sextum, p. 284, '. . . et quidem de homine iam supra disputabamus, sed nunc primum in eo Dei imaginem intelligimus, unde illi in bruta dictio et imperium. Sic etenim a natura institutus homo, ut ratio sensibus dominaretur, frenareturque illius lege omnis tum irae tum libidinis furor et appetentia, sed obliterata imagine Dei per maculam peccati, coepimus miseri et infelices servire bestiis nostris et cum rege Chaldaeo diversari inter illas, humi procumbere, cupidi terrenorum, obliti patriae, obliti Patris, obliti regni et datae nobis in privilegium pristinae dignitatis. Scilicet homo cum in honore esset non intellexit sed comparatus est iumentis insipientibus et similis factus est illis.'

37. Ibid., Caput septimum, p. 286, 'Verum sicut omnes in primo Adam, qui oboedivit Sathanae magis quam Deo cuius filii secundum carnem, deformati ab homine degeneramus ad brutum, ita in Adam novissimo Iesu Christo qui Voluntatem Patris implevit et suo sanguine debellavit nequitias spiritales, cuius filii omnes secundum spiritum, reformati per gratiam regeneramur ab homine in adoptione filiorum Dei, si modo ut in illo ita in nobis princeps tenebrarum et mundi huius nihil invenerit.'

38. Ibid., pp. 300–2, 'Hactenus de tribus mundis supercaelesti, caelesti et sublunari. Nunc agendum de homine, de quo est scriptum: "Faciamus hominem ad imaginem nostram", qui non tam quartus est mundus, quasi nova aliqua creatura, quam trium quos diximus complexus et colligatio. . . . Haud aliter principem omnium Deum fecisse videmus, qui tota mundi machina constructa postremum omnium hominem in medio illius statuit ad imaginem suam et similitudinem formatum.'

39. Ibid., p. 302, 'Nos autem peculiare aliquid in homine quaerimus, unde et dignitas ei propria et imago divinae substantiae cum nulla sibi creatura communis comperiatur. Id quid esse aliud potest quam quod hominis substantia (ut Graeci etiam aliqui interpretes innuunt) omnium in se naturarum substantias et totius universitatis plenitudinem re ipsa complectitur? Dico autem re ipsa, quia et angeli et quaecumque creatura intelligens in se quodammodo continet omnia, dum plena formis et rationibus omnium rerum omnia cognoscit. At vero quemadmodum Deus non solum ob id quod omnia intelligit, sed quia in seipso verae rerum substantiae perfectionem totam unit et colligit, ita et homo (quamquam aliter, ut ostendemus, alioquin non Dei imago, sed Deus esset) ad integritatem suae substantiae omnes totius mundi naturas

corrogat et counit. Quod de nulla alia creatura, sive angelica, sive caelesti, sive sensibili, dicere possumus.'

40. Ibid., pp. 302–4, 'Est autem haec diversitas inter Deum et hominem, quod Deus in se omnia continet uti omnium principium, homo autem in se omnia continet uti omnium medium; quo fit ut in Deo sint omnia meliore nota quam in seipsis, in homine inferiora nobiliore sint conditione, superiora autem degenerant. ... Est harum omnium simul in unum confluentium naturarum vere divina possessio, ut libeat exclamare illud Mercurii: "Magnum, o Asclepi, miraculum est homo." Hoc praecipue nomine gloriari humana conditio potest, quo etiam factum ut servire illi nulla creata substantia dedignetur. Huic terra et elementa, huic bruta sunt praesto et famulantur, huic militat caelum, huic salutem bonumque procurant angelicae mentes, siquidem verum est quod scribit Paulus, esse omnes administratorios spiritus in ministerium missos propter eos qui hereditati salutis sunt destinati. Nec mirum alicui videri debet amari illum ab omnibus in quo omnia suum aliquid, immo se tota et sua omnia agnoscunt.' The first part of this passage and the end of the previous are cited by Monnerjahn, op. cit., p. 30.
41. Cf. Yates, op. cit., pp. 111 and 116. It is true that she emphasises the closeness of Pico's magic to religion and calls it *gnosis*, but she also stresses man as 'operator', p. 111, and 'man as Magus using both Magia and Cabala to act upon the world, to control his destiny by science', p. 116.
42. Cf. Chapters XV and XVI of Part IV below.
43. Edgar Wind, *Pagan Mysteries in the Renaissance*, London, 1958, now revised and expanded (Peregrine Books) 1967, espec. Introd. and Chap. I, 'Poetic Theology'. On Bernard Silvestris cf. E. R. Curtius, *European Literature and the Latin Middle Ages*, New York, 1953, pp. 108–13. Curtius shows Bernard's extensive use of the *Asclepius*. Cf. Curtius, passim on medieval *theologia poetica*.
44. Ed. Garin, op. cit., pp. 304–6, '... quia et caelestium et terrestrium vinculum [Text: vinculus] et nodus est, nec possunt utraque haec non habere cum eo pacem, si modo ipse secum pacem habuerit, qui illorum in se ipso pacem et foedera sancit. At caveamus, quaeso, ne in tanta dignitate constituti non intelligamus, verum illud ante oculos semper animi habeamus, uti et certam, exploratam et indubiam veritatem, sicuti favent omnia nobis eam legem servantibus quae nobis est data, ita si per peccatum, per legis praevaricationem deorbita defecerimus, omnia adversa infesta inimicaque habituros. Rationabile enim ut quemadmodum non modo nobis, sed universo quod in nobis complectimur, sed auctori ipsius mundi omnipotenti Deo iniuriam facimus, experiamur etiam omnia quae in mundo sunt, et Deum in primis, potentissimos vindices et acceptae iniuriae gravissimos ultores.'
45. Ibid., p. 306, 'Rei sunt enim violatae universitatis et laesae maiestatis divinae, cuius imaginem foedissima iniquitatis macula deturparunt....

Et omino omnem insaniam superat adduci ut credamus, cuipiam in civitate aliqua posito, decorato summis honoribus, licere in principem, in universam rempublicam de se optime meritam impune delinquere, ac non potius dari illum torquendum statim et cruciandum lictoribus et carnifici, aut totius populi consensu lapidibus obruendum.'

46. Ibid., p. 308, ' "Si paenituit peccator exultare laetitia omnes angelos" [I *Cor.* v:5]; hinc mysterii illius aperta ratio, quod absconditum fuit a saeculis, ut corrupta in primo Adam et deturpata de suo statu natura nostra per Christi crucem instauraretur. Nam et congruum fuit ut qui est imago Dei invisibilis, primogenitus omnis creaturae, in quo condita sunt universa, illi copularetur unione ineffabili qui ad imaginem factus est Dei, qui vinculum est omnis creaturae, in quo conclusa sunt universa. Nec erat, si cum homine tota natura periclitabatur, eius iactura aut negligenda aut reparanda per alium quam per quem tota fuerat instituta natura.'

47. Ibid., pp. 322–4, 'Ita nos animo proponamus extremorum copulam non nisi per eam naturam fieri posse quae, media extremorum cum sit, utrumque in se complexa ideo illa, idest extrema, inter se commode unit, quia in se ipsa illa per proprietatem suae naturae prius univit. . . . non posse hominem Deo coniungi nisi per eum qui, cum in se ipso hominem Deo coniunxerit, verus mediator effectus, potest ita homines Deo annectere ut, sicut in eo filius Dei hominem induit, ita per eum homines Dei filii fiant.'

48. Ibid., p. 372, '. . . reformarentur ad imaginem Dei. Nam si Baptismus Dei filios facit, filius autem imago Patris, nonne totius Trinitatis virtus operans in Baptismo illa est quae dicit: "Faciamus hominem ad imaginem nostram"? Si igitur sumus ad imaginem Dei, sumus et Filii. Si filii et heredes sumus, heredes Dei, coheredes Christi. Sed qui sunt filii? Scriptum a Paulo est, clamare nos *abba* (pater) in Spiritu Sancto. [*Rom.* viii:15; *Galat.* iv:6] Qui igitur Spiritu vivunt, ii sunt filii Dei, ii Christi fratres, ii destinati aeternae hereditati, quam mercedem et fidei et bene actae vitae in caelesti Hierusalem feliciter possidebunt.'

49. See below, Part IV, Chapters XV and XVI.

50. See above, Vol. I, pp. 183–4.

51. Cf. pp. 498–503.

52. Cf. pp. 188–90.

53. Cf. Giuseppe Signorelli, *Il Cardinale Egidio da Viterbo, Agostiniano, umanista e riformatore*, Florence, 1929, cap. 1 and passim. Giovanni Gioviano Pontano immortalised Egidio by naming one of his dialogues after him, 'Aegidius', pp. 245–84, *I dialoghi*, ed. Previtera, Florence, 1943. It includes a sermon in what purports to be the elegant and erudite style of Egidio, pp. 249–52. Cf. Francesco Fiorentino, 'Egidio da Viterbo ed i Pontaniani di Napoli', *Atti dell'Accademia Pontaniana*, XVI, I, pp. 249–71. Cf. Egidio's letter to Ficino, *Supplementum Ficinianum*, ed. Kristeller,

Florence, 1937, II, pp. 301–2. Cf. the following recent studies of Egidio: Francis X. Martin, 'The Problem of Giles of Viterbo: A Historiographical Survey'; *Augustiniana*, IX (1959), pp. 357–79, X (1960), pp. 43–60; John W. O'Malley, 'Giles of Viterbo: A Sixteenth Century Text on Doctrinal Development', *Traditio* XXII (1966), pp. 445–50; ibid., 'Giles of Viterbo: A Reformer's Thought on Renaissance Rome', *Renaissance Quarterly*, XX (1967), pp. 1–11.

54. Eugenio Massa, 'L'anima e l'uomo in Egidio da Viterbo e nella fonti classiche e medievali', in *Testi umanistici inediti sul 'De Anima'*, ed. Garin, series ed. E. Castelli, Rome, 1951: *I fondamenti metafisici della 'Dignitas hominis' e testi inediti di Egidio da Viterbo*, Turin, 1954. I have examined Vat. lat. 6325, which contains Egidio's text (among other MSS of it), but will follow the latter publication of Massa; cf. pp. 49–53 for his discussion of the text. Cf. also his critical study of Egidio, 'Egidio da Viterbo e la metodologia del sapere nel cinquecento', in *Pensée humaniste et tradition chrétienne*, Paris, 1950, pp. 189–94. There is need for a full publication of this work, as well as of Egidio's *Historia XX saeculorum*. Because of his taste for the Cabala, Egidio has attracted recent interest. Cf. François Secret's edition of *Scechina e Libellus de litteris hebraicis*, Rome, 1959, Edizione nazionale dei classici del pensiero italiano. Serie II, Nos. 10, 11.

55. Pp. 63–7, III (55), 'Hominem et Animam Imaginem Esse. Quid Homo Sit Conciliatioque.'

56. Ibid., p. 64, 'Alii, contra, haec omnia everterunt: primo quidem hominem non totum, sed animam solam esse credidere, corpus vero hominis organum, non partem fecerunt. Cuius quidem sententiae Plato princeps fuit. . . . Qui itaque cum Platone sentiat, hominem totum (ita enim vocat animam) ad Dei imaginem genitum putabit, facietque ut divinus sermo et recte et proprie dixerit hominem ad imaginem Dei factum esse, quod alii defendere non possunt, nisi ratione formae id dictum intelligant, quod cum dicunt, Moisem non proprie loquutum dicant necesse est.'

57. V (57), 'Imago in Angelis Praestantior Hominis Imagine est.' p. 70, '. . . humana conditio, non modo aequare, verum etiam superare videtur deorum naturas. Si vero non ea, quae homini accidunt, sed naturam ipsam humanam deorum caelestium naturae comparabimus, nemo non videt et Deos hominibus et deorum imaginem humanae imagini longe esse anteponendam . . . cum puri simplicesque actus sint, ut in *Metaphysicis* demonstratum est; quae quidem homini convenire non possunt.' pp. 70–1, 'Neque ad rem faciunt, quae supra contradicunt: nam de natura sermo, non de unico naturae accidente est institutus; cum enim comparantur aliqua, naturae comparantur, aut illae naturarum affectiones, quae ex internis naturae initiis proficiscuntur. Quod vero homo factus sit Deus, non ex interna affectione naturae, sed ex externa Dei misericordia dimanavit.'

58. Ibid., VI (58), 'Imago in Homine Potior Quam in Angelo Est Modo Quodam', pp. 71–4.
59. Ibid., pp. 71–2.
60. Ibid., p. 73, 'In his vero, quae ad divinam amicitiam et beatam faciunt vitam, nemo dubitat Diis immortalibus homines fuisse praelatos. Peccata enim hominum veniam impetrant, Deorum coelo cadentium nunquam impetrant. . . . Nam et Plato primo *De republica* pastores omnes non sibi, sed gregibus dare operam docet; at decimo *Legum* libro Deos pastores hominum facit; qua in re nobis ut inferiores sint necesse est; semper enim deteriora melioribus serviunt, ut in *Gorgia* disseruit Plato.'
61. Ibid., pp. 73–4, 'Dii denique in beata vita, qua perpetuo fruentur, unum tantum habebunt, quo nuda beatitudine fruentur, nudam solamque mentem: nos praeter mentis opes, corporis quoque laetabimur divinis beatisque deliciis, quales decebunt cives sanctissimae beatissimae civitatis. Accedent laborum et meritorum praemia; quorum omnium ratio habenda est: horum nihil sperari a Diis potest, qui vel laborare, vel reipublicae aut principis vitam exponere, mortem appetere, corpus periculis obiectare non possunt. Quare quibus certare datum non est, victoria triumphusque negatus est. Quibus ex rebus satis constare potest, si naturae partes concedantur Diis, quam plurima esse, in quibus Dii mortalibus cedant necesse est, quantoque nobis illi altiores natura sunt, tanto nos illis multis in rebus esse potiores.'
62. Edgar Wind, 'Michelangelo's Prophets and Sibyls', *Proceedings of the British Academy*, LI (1967), pp. 47–84; cf. pp. 82–3 and n. 1, p. 83.

Notes to Part III, Chapter XI

1. Again, as with Ficino and Pico, my treatment of Pomponazzi must defer to the historians of philosophy who have made fundamental studies: most important for Pomponazzi's general significance and for his ideas of man is, of course, J. H. Randall, Jr., 'The Place of Pomponazzi in the Padua Tradition', *The School of Padua and the Emergence of Modern Science*, Padua, 1961, pp. 69–114. Cf. his footnotes for the standard works on the Paduan Aristotelian tradition, espec. p. 70, n. 1; on Pomponazzi, p. 87, n. 31. This paper is a slightly revised version with Latin footnotes of Randall's *Introduction* to W. H. Hay II's translation of Pomponazzi's *De immortalitate animae*, in Cassirer, Kristeller, Randall, *The Renaissance Philosophy of Man*, op. cit., pp. 257–79 (Introduction) and pp. 280–381 (Text), which we shall cite in Hay's translation. Randall does not include references to many of the important studies of Bruno Nardi on both Paduan Aristotelianism and on Pomponazzi, now collected in *Saggi sull'Aristotelismo padovano dal secolo XIV al XVI*, Florence, 1958, and *Studi su Pietro Pomponazzi*, Florence, 1965. We have found both of these works of great value.

2. Cf. Randall, op. cit., pp. 86–9, for his general evaluation of Pomponazzi's place in the history of philosophy.
3. Cf. Part II, Chapter VII above.
4. Valla also declared that pagan 'Epicurean' ethics were valid before the advent of Christ for natural man but regarded Stoicism and the Aristotelianism he knew as representing contaminations of Christianity and paganism. [Cf. above, pp. 133–6.] Morandi represents an interesting move towards a natural morality that was Stoic and Aristotelian and certainly anticipates Pomponazzi in this, although the key to both men taking this position lies in the separation of philosophy and theology in the tradition and practice of university natural philosophy. For Morandi, cf. above, pp. 286–9.
5. Morandi, *Secunda reluctatio*, op. cit., Cod. Urb. lat. 1245, ff. 62r–3r, 'Analogum quidem verbum est felicitas, et gradus habet, nec in indivisibili uno consistit, sed connumerata, ut inquit Aristoteles, hoc est addito vel minimo bono fit maior. Solus Deus habet supremam, infinitam, incomprehensibilem ineffabilemque beatitudinem. Non ideo tamen angelorum felicitas nulla est, ita nec magnitudo felicitatis angelicae tollit humanam cuius est homo capax. Propius accedit mortalium felicitas ei quae est angelorum quam angelica divinae quia finiti ad infinitum proportio esse nequeat, quoniam hae limites habent et proportionantur. Sic numeri et magnitudines comparantur non ut se invicem tollant sed quia vel maiores vel minores dicuntur. Sic divinae simplicitas substantiae se habet ad intelligentias separatas quorum substantia comparatur eodem modo ad eam quae est animae humanae, sicut de felicitate dicimus. Aut prestabit ponere sicut in linea predicamentali, cuius supremum genus speties esse nullo modo potest. Media vero collata superioribus, vim generis amittunt, que si comparentur inferioribus, abneget nemo esse genera. Nulla erit itaque angelorum felicitas, eius respectu quae Dei est, collata vero cum felicitate hominis eam supprimet. At si hominem ad animantia reliqua comparaveris, sua, hoc est humana, nec ipse felicitate carebit propter dignitatem intellectus, et quia natura constantia omnia sibi usui sunt, suaeque subiacent dictioni, atque, ut inquit Aristoteles rerum physicorum homo finis est quod eius causa illa produxit natura.'
6. *De immortalitate* [trans. Hay, *Ren. Phil. of Man*, op. cit.] Chap. IX, p. 326.
7. Cf. above, pp. 493, 496, for Ficino; pp. 219, 223 for Facio.
8. *De immortalitate*, op. cit., Chap. XIII, p. 346. The reference is to Ficino, *Theol. Platon.*, I. 1, 'Si animus non esset immortalis nullum animal esset infelicius homine.'
9. Facio, of course, best illustrates the first position, whereas Manetti emphasises both immortality and earthly achievement. Brandolini fluctuated from the latter position to the former but compositely in both treatises.
10. Cf. above, pp. 482–4.

11. Cf. Part II, Chap. VII above.
12. *De immortalitate*, op. cit., Chap. XII, pp. 340–1.
13. Ibid., Chap. XIV, p. 351. Cf. below, p. 543, for his reference to Pico's position that man is a chameleon.
14. Ibid., pp. 351–2.
15. *S.C.G.* III, 113.
16. *De immortalitate*, op. cit., p. 353.
17. Ibid., pp. 353–5.
18. Ibid., pp. 355–6.
19. Ibid., pp. 356–7.
20. Cf. Werner Jaeger's discussion of Sophist humanism in *Paideia*, Vol. I, Bk. II, Chapter 3; and Mario Untersteiner, *The Sophists*, op. cit., pp.64–70.
21. Ficino, cit. sup., *De immortalitate*, op. cit., Chap. XIV, pp. 357–9.
22. Cf. above, pp. 283–5, for Morandi. For Cicero, *De nat. deor.* 1, 7.
23. Bruni, ed. Baron, op. cit.; cf. on Valla, Part I, Chapter III, above, pp. 116–26.
24. Cf. above, Part I, Chapter I, pp. 42–3, and Heitmann, op. cit., pp. 249–59.
25. *De immortalitate*, op. cit., p. 362.
26. Ibid., pp. 362–3.
27. Cf. below, Part IV, Chapter XIV, pp. 676–80.
28. Op. cit. p. 363.
29. Ibid., p. 375.
30. Ibid., pp. 375–6.
31. Ibid., pp. 376–7.
32. Urb. lat. 1245, ff. 75v–6r, '. . . At si non est virtutis compos, quomodo eum a virtute quam non habet ad scelera vis impelli, ut huic mutationi quae discessus est a virtute ad vitiam desit terminus a quo talis incepit motus. Adde quod si homo impellitur, aut a se aut ab alio is fit impulsus. Absurdum est ab alio dici, cum sit unicuique libera voluntas, quia etiam nec consuetudine, nec lege, nec natura permittitur quod in homine optio et voluntas non sit libera. Erit ergo a se ipso talis impulsus ex aliquo trium quae in animo fiunt, videlicet affectu, potentia, habitu. . . . certum est nulli vim afferri ut scelera complectatur, nisi volenti cupientique ultro calcata ratione.'
33. Pietro Pomponazzi, *Libri quinque de fato, de libero arbitrio et de praedestinatione*, ed. Richard LeMay, Lugano, 1957 [Thesaurus Mundi], Lib. III, cap. 2, p. 225, 'sic itaque secundum hos, duobus potentiis perficitur liberum arbitrium, intellectu scilicet et voluntate, sed intellectu tanquam subserviente voluntati, et voluntate tanquam vere et principaliter domina.'
34. Ibid., pp. 226–7.
35. Ibid., cap. 4, pp. 237–8, '. . . aut quod intellectus et voluntas sint una et eadem potentia, aut quod si sint diversae potentiae, intellectus est ille in quo proprie consistit actus liberi arbitrii, quoniam in eo tanquam in efficiente, in voluntate vero improprie et executive, quoniam mere

passive concurrit ad istos actus. Libertas autem magis consistit in agere quam in pati.'

36. Ibid., Lib. III, cap. 10, p. 227, '... quam ego profiteor et pro qua paratus sum tollere crucem et cum Christo et pro Christo mori ... quare sciens et volens elegit prava. ... Advertas tamen quod ubi esset peccatum commissionis, hoc non potest concedi, sed tantum in peccato omissionis. In peccato enim commissionis elegitur malum quod voluntati per intellectum ostenditur esse bonum, quare intellectus peccat quoniam ostendit aliter quam est, aut reiicitur bonum quod existimatur esse malum quoniam intellectus sic ostendit voluntati. Unde est error in ipso intellectu et transfertur voluntati.'

37. Ibid., Lib. III, cap. 12, pp. 299–300, 'Sed iam multotiens dictum est quod Deus illius actus simpliciter est causa et secundum quid non est causa, quare qua Deus est causa simpliciter huius actus, iste actus a Deo cognoscitur, qua vero secundum quid Deus non est huius actus causa, non cognoscitur determinate a Deo sed tantum sub conditione, ut est actus ille extra suas causas; veluti neque cognoscitur ut indeterminatus nisi quatenus actus ille est in potentia. ... Neque Deus secundum omnem modum potest esse causa actus voluntarii si vult actus esse nostros et liberos, quoniam aliter dicere est sermo unintelligibilis. Considerando igitur naturam contingentis, et unde habet indeterminationem et determinationem, et quod actus sint liberi et nostri, aliter videre meo dici non potest.'

38. Ibid., Lib. IV, cap. 6, pp. 384–5, 'Et dico, ut prius dixi, quod aut Aristoteles tenuit fatum ut Stoici, aut sibi contradixit; quoniam si tenemus voluntatem liberam, stat quod aliquod semper erit quod tamen non est necessarium, quod contradicit ipsi in I *De Coelo*. Unde quod virtutes et vitia sint necessaria esse et tamen sint in potestate nostra, non video compossibilitatem; neque video repugnantiam aliquam quod nullus homo peccet, quoniam Deus vellet impossibile cum vult omnes homines salvos fieri; sicuti nulla est repugnantia quod omnis homo peccet.'

39. Ibid., p. 385, 'Dicebatur et in eodem capitulo quod operatio mundanorum videtur esse quidam ludus. ...' Passage cited in text is from Lib. II, cap. 7, pp. 195–6, 'Nonne etiam ludus deorum videtur quod tanto ingenio et tot adminiculis generet hominem (est enim organizatissimus homo) et statim facto homine aliquando corrumpat? Nonne enim Deus videtur similis architecto qui multa opera et impensa construxisset aliquod paulatum pulcherrimum in nullo deficiens et statim confecto palatio rueret ipsum? Nonne hoc ascriberetur insaniae architecti? Non minus et unintelligibile videtur an sit ludus, an insania, an insipientia hominem perducere ad summum culmen, et quam primum limen attigerit ipsum eiicere et in profundum emittere. Et infinita possent adduci quae aut insaniam aut crudelitatem aut ludum aut simile in Deo arguere videntur; quae tamen omnia salvantur quoniam sic exigit universi natura. Quare si universum bonum est, omnia haec videntur

bona.' On Calvin, cf. *Institutio Christianae religionis*, I, xvii, 1, 'Iam et hoc addendum est, quamvis aut paternus Dei favor et beneficentia, aut iudicii severitas saepe in toto providentiae cursu reluceat, interdum tamen eorum quae accidunt occultas esse causas, ut obrepat cogitatio, caeco fortunae impetu volvi et rotari res humanas; vel ad obloquendum nos caro sollicitet, ac si Deus homines quasi pilas iactando, ludum exerceret.' See my 'Renaissance Problems in Calvin's Theology', *Studies in the Renaissance*, I (1954), pp. 59–80, p. 65 and n. 14.

40. My Calvin study, ibid., pp. 68 ff. Comparison with Salutati's *De Fato*, above Part I, Chapter II, pp. 80–92, is also relevant.

41. *De fato*, op. cit., Lib. II, cap. 7, p. 196, 'Unde si quis et humanam naturam consideraverit, videbit talia dicenda esse in natura humana quae et in universo dicuntur. Humana enim naturam est quoddam universa; cum enim media sit inter aeterna et generabilia et corruptibilia utramque naturam debet continere. Unde debent esse aliqui homines veluti Dii, quales videmus prophetas et viros optimos; non quidem simpliciter sed secundum quod substinent fragilitas et natura humana: aliqui velut animalia innocentia, aliqui velut serpentes, aliqui velut tigres, aliqui velut leones, aliqui velut vulpes, aliqui ut lapides et sic de singulis. Hoc igitur exigit natura humana, neque propter hoc defectus aliquis est Deo ascribendus, sicut neque in ipso universo, quanquam tanta videatur esse diversitas in ipso universo.'

42. Ibid., Lib. IV, cap. 6, pp. 385–6. Although it is broken up in the text, the whole passage, as follows, was cited: 'Dicebatur et in eodem capitulo quod operatio mundanorum videtur esse quidam ludus, si quis enim inspiceret omnia sublunaria, aut rideret aut fleret. Huic dicitur quod ludus videtur secundum omnes alias opiniones praeterquam secundum opinionem Christianorum. Nam mundus habet principium et habet finem, et tota ista operatio facta est propter hominem, saltem secundario, ut beatitudine fruatur; omnia enim corporalia Deus ordinavit in hominem ut eis bene uteretur, ex quorum bono usu postea frueretur Trinitate in aeternum; unde nihil pulchrius, nihil utilius excogitari potest.

'Ast quicquid dicant alii, ludus videtur. Unde Stoici et Peripatetici, qui dicunt Deum de necessitate agere, habent dicere hoc exigere Dei bonitatem ut suum esse communicet quantum est communicabile; et quoniam communicabilis est secundum tot gradus quot videmus in universo et tot modos ideo communicat. Generabilia autem et corruptibilia in ordine ad aeternum videntur fimus et nihil, quare videntur parvae existimationis, et videtur quidam ludus in comparatione ad illa suprema.

'Verum quanquam corruptibilia talia sint, aliquam tamen perfectionem includunt; quare cum esse melius sit quam non esse, quodcunque esse sit, et Deus de possibilibus facit quod melius est, hinc est quod Deus talia facit et conservat.

'Licet igitur vita humana in ordine ad aeterna quasi nihil sit, est tamen multum in ordine ad alia generabilia; et unumquodque generabile per comparationem ad non ens. Quare cum melius sit per unum annum quam nunquam vivere, non igitur vita unius anni spernenda est, cum semper appetitus feratur in bonum et in maius bonum.

'Non itaque ludus debet existimari si sit tanta variatio in universo; quoniam hoc exigit natura universi. Et sic de isto capitulo.

'Multa etiam dicta sunt in primo libro in defensionem Stoicorum quae huic opinioni adversari videntur; nam multa hinc colligi possent quae adduci possent adversus opinionem religionis Christianae. Verum, ut existimo, et his quae in quarto hoc volumine dicta sunt, si bene et attente perspecta sint, ad ea facilis et aperta apparebit solutio; quare ab eo negocio me abstineo.' Cf. *Laws*, VII, 803b–d.

43. *De immortalitate*, op. cit., p. 379.
44. Cf. Nardi, *Studi su P. Pomponazzi*, op. cit., p. 276, 'Et theologi aliqualiter tenent hoc, quod sit ista unio necessaria animae, et sic reunietur corpori propter desiderium quod habet de esse in corpore. Dicunt tamen quod solum haec unio potest fieri a Deo, et quod natura non potest hoc facere. Tamen sciatis, quod apud Aristotelem illa resurrectio est impossibilis.'
45. Cf. below, Part IV, Chapter XV.
46. Printed by Nardi, op. cit., pp. 143–8, from Paris, MS lat. 6533, but he also cites it from Arezzo, Bibl. della Fraternità de' Laici, Cod. 389.
47. Nardi, op. cit., p. 141, from Paris, MS lat. 6534, f. 139r–v, 'Dico quod secundum philosophos impossibile est deum non movere celum, quod theologi negant quia nolunt quod sit ordo essentialis inter motum et ipsum Deum, et quod celum quiescere non implicat contradictionem. Quid? Iosue fecit firmare solem et cetera. Negant hoc philosophi. Demum dixit mihi Hebreus, "Credis quod, si fuisset verum illud quod dicitur de Iosue faciente firmare solem, infinite historie dixissent, sicut dixerunt de aliis multis rebus, quoniam non est multum tempus quod fuit Iosue; sunt enim tantum duo millia anni. Sed hoc non dicunt nisi fabule iudaice".'
48. Nardi, op. cit., p. 137, from Paris, MS lat. 6534, f. 32r, '. . . credebat enim ipse quod anima esset mortalis, licet non haberet demonstrationem in oppositum; tamen quod credebat quel che credeva la canaia per non esser lapidato.'
49. Nardi, op. cit., p. 140, from Paris 6534, f. 111r–v, 'Sed Commentator est ribaldissimus et non credatis illi.'
50. Nardi, op. cit., p. 139, from Paris 6534, ff. 110v–111r, '. . . et propter hoc ars poetica facta ut removeret a vitiis et duceret ad virtutes. Post venit rhetorica que ex toto non dicit res ut sunt, sed persuadet. Sed soli philosophi sunt mere dicentes veritatem. Unde poësis, rhetorica et phylosophia date sunt ad instructionem hominum. Unde Commentator in sua *Poësi* dicit quod leges sunt similes poetis (MS poësi) quo non dicunt

verum, nam "miranda canunt, sed non credenda poete". Sed faciunt sic ut ducant homines ad bene faciendum et ad instructionem hominum.'

Notes to Part IV, Introduction

1. I am quite aware of the complexity of late medieval ecclesiastical history, and would agree that a generalisation such as this needs many kinds of modification. What I am saying amounts to claiming that the theologians were subordinated to the canonists, although neither functioned without the concern and influence of the others. It was the perennial dissidence within the Church between those who insisted on the correct path and those who felt that the spirit must be aroused – the popular preachers, the Tertiaries, the Franciscans, always on the edge of the heretical. But when we suggest that the humanists stepped into this gap, it must be clear that this lay piety was not at all for the masses but for the educated and the pillars of the social order.
2. I do not underestimate the revolutionary character or importance of the new insights of Copernicus, Kepler and Galileo. And though the procedures of the last were very different, the mode of thinking involved orderly, step by step, reasoning such as was the essence of the scholastic method.
3. Surely an outrageous statement to some. But I obviously refer not to the contents of science, or even to experimental methodology, but to the 'rhetoric' of science, which has a remarkable resemblance to the 'rhetoric' of scholastic philosophy and theology. But what both also have in common is organised, systematic thinking with elimination of all conceivable objections – the object to demonstrate, not persuade or cajole.
4. This is true despite Father S. Garofalo's fine article, 'Gli umansti italiani del secolo XV e la Bibbia', *La Bibbia e il concilio di Trento, Scripta Pontifici Instituti Biblici*, No. 96, Rome, 1947, pp. 338–75. Although I shall review much of the same material as Garofalo used, it will be in some respects more detailed and certainly presented within a quite different historical perspective.
5. Cf. Part I, Chapter 2, p. 55.
6. Novati, op. cit., IV, pp. 215–16, 'Quomodo potest enim Scripture sacre noticiam sumere qui litteras ignoravit? Potest sine litteris fidei sinceritas percipi fateor, sed non divina Scriptura, non doctorum expositiones atque traditiones intelligi, quas vix capere valeant litterati, et nedum simpliciter docti grammaticam, sed etiam qui dialecticis et rhetoricis insudarunt. Et eadem ipsa grammatica sine noticia rerum et quibus modis rerum essentia variatur et omnium scientiarum concursu preter necessitatem noticie terminorum maxima ex parte sciri non potest. Connexa sunt humanitatis studia, connexa sunt et studia divinitatis, ut unium rei sine alia vera completaque scientia non possit haberi. Sed quicquid sit de

grammatico facilitate vel eiusdem asperitate discendi, quid erit si doctrinam fidei respexeris? Christianus vix scire poterit quid credendum; et si quis, vel auctoritate divine Scripture vel quavis debili etiam licet ratione sue simplicitati obstiterit, quid respondere debeat ignorabit incipietque de veritate fidei vacillare. O quot et quanta quotidie videmus que non possit ruditas vel sancta rusticitas, cum careat litteris, explicare!'

7. Ibid., p. 222, 'Quis negare potest, cum dialectica sit inquisitiva veritatis, que sola fines est omnium liberalium artium et quaruncunque scientiarum, quod hanc necesse sit discere Christianos.' p. 223, 'Nunc autem que sola fide teneamus talia sunt, quod ad ea naturalis ratio non pertingat, ut facile sit sola fide fundatum alicuius humane rationis apparentia loco quem teneruit demovere. Quare necessarium est neophitis cum fide simul addiscere qua ratione valeant se tueri.'
8. Ibid., p. 223, 'Ut si natura veritates: naturales scilicet, alias quidem non norit; in profundum abstruxit, quid putandum est de illa infinita potentia, que sic natura est, quod merito recteque supra naturam debeat appellari, presertim cum illa finita sit, hanc autem infinitum oporteat confiteri?'
9. Ibid., 'Sed iam satis de logica dictum sit, que quidem capit cogitque suis rationibus intellectum et ad rhetoricam, que cum voluntate congreditur veneamus.'
10. Ibid., p. 224; Aug. *De doct. Christ.*, IV, ii.
11. Novati, op. cit., IV, pp. 224–5, '. . . ut quas per Dei gratiam sibi fuisse meminerat ad salutem, quas sciebat nedum instrumentum esse, sed collectionem etiam plurimum veritatum, quasque norat indaginem veritatis, . . .'
12. Ibid., pp. 224–230.
13. Ibid., p. 234, 'Certum sit ipsam divinam Scripturam nichil aliud esse quam poeticam; licet tu videaris, doctissime vir, nomen istud abhorrere. Sacra namque Scriptura quid est vel in terminis vel etiam rebus nisi figura?'

Notes to Part IV, Chapter XII

1. Reference was made (in note 4 to the Introduction to Part IV) to the article of Garofalo and to the fact that I must inevitably parallel it in my treatment, however independently I have proceeded. It is regrettable that further studies under his direction have not emanated from the Pontifical Biblical Institute with which many outstanding Biblical scholars are associated. It is also curious that so little attention has been paid by Protestant Biblical scholars to the Italian contribution or initiation of the Biblical studies that were to be so prominent a phase of the Reformation.
2. Cf. Heiko Oberman's discussion of the problem of the Scriptures and tradition in his *The Harvest of Medieval Theology*, Cambridge, 1963,

Chapter II, 'Holy Writ and Holy Church', pp. 361–422, espec. pp. 365–93.

3. Despite the enormous dimensions and critical importance of medieval and Renaissance exegesis comprehensive histories are rare; cf. however, C. Spicq, O.P., *Esquisse d'une histoire de l'exégèse latine au moyen âge*, Paris, 1944. Beryl Smalley, *The Study of the Bible in the Middle Ages*, 2nd ed., Oxford, 1952; Henri de Lubac, *Exégèse médiévale*, 4 vols., Paris, 1959–64.
4. Curtius, op. cit., passim and espec. pp. 40–1 and Excursus IV. In general Curtius' contribution to the understanding of medieval Biblical studies in relationship to the history of literature is of very great value. He is hardly concerned with it, however, as part of the history of ideas or of the history of religious doctrine.
5. Cf. below, Chapter XV.
6. Cf. below in Chapter XIV, pp. 662–5. As we show there Salutati does not hesitate to utilise classical texts for the support of his somewhat conservative views of the religious status. But this work, as Ullman remarked, is the great demonstration of his minute familiarity with the Scriptures and his adeptness in utilising this familiarity.
7. Op. cit., p. 103, 'Itaque, ut ille eum, sic ego vos, fratres, "oro inter hec vivere, ista meditari, nichil aliud nosse nichilque aliud querere"; neque vos moveat sacrarum "simplicitas" Scripturarum et quasi "vilitas" verborum que, ut ait idem, "vel vitio interpretum vel de industria sic prolate sunt, ut rusticam contionem facilius instruerunt et in una eadem sententia aliter doctus, aliter sentiret indoctus"; qualiscunque quidem superficies sit, medulla nichil est dulcius, nichil suavius nichiloque salubrius. Itaque scripturarum omnium hec hauddubie regina est, tabescunt licet invidi tumeantque superbi, nec verum egre aures capiant, quotiens indiffinitum scripture nomen audierimus hanc solam intelligimus, per eam quam anthonomasiam vocant Greci. Et sane quod nunc assero ante non multos annos forte vel tacite negassem: Illi gratias qui michi oculos aperuit ut aliquando viderem quod cum magno discrimine non videbam, quemque nunc etiam caligantes oculos purgaturum spero ad reliqua que damnosa tarditate nondum video, quam in me hactenus minus miror, cum Ieronimum ipsum de se fatentem audiam, quod sibi in libris gentilium occupato cum se ad sacra vertisset eloquia, ut verbo eius utar, "sermo horrebat incultus". Quod si tali viro et in libris sacris ab adolescentia exercitatissimo potuit evenire, quid non potuit michi peccatori literis secularibus non dicam erudito, ne mentiar, sed ab infantia delectato, qui magistros habui non Gregorium Nazanzenum, ut ille, seu quempiam et si non alti ingenii at fidelis saltem devotique animi, sed eos qui psalterium daviticum, qua nulla pregnantior scriptura est, et omnem divine textum pagine non aliter quam aniles fabulas irriderent?'
8. Ibid., p. 104, '. . . ita hoc pulcerrimo comitatu Scripturarum sacrarum

fines quos ante despexeram venerabundus ingredior et invenio cunta se aliter habere quam credideram. Accessit opportuna necessitas divinas laudes atque officium quotidianum, quod male distuleram, celebrandi, quam ob causam psalterium ipsum daviticum sepe percurrere sum coactus, e quibus fontibus haurire studui non unde disertior fierem, sed melior, si possem, neque unde evaderem disputator maior, sed peccator minor.'

9. Ibid., p. 105, 'Quarum si autoritas queritur, et a Spiritu Sancto prolate et Cristi ore firmate sunt, sive antiquitas, et omnes omnino seculares literas antecedunt – antequam Cadmus grecarum repertor, antequam Ysis egiptiarum, antequam Carmentis latinarum inventrix nasceretur, he litere celebres erant in orbe terrarum, sive virtus attenditur – et "sagitte sunt acute" et ardentes, que quibus infixe fuerint corda vivificant, sive fructus optatur, et certe cum ceterarum merces aut breve lucrum aut aura volatilis et falsus favor, harum finis vita eterna est et vera felicitas, sive forsitan ornatus exigitur, et quamvis multa de hoc dici possunt, hec tamen omnium summa est, quasdam forte superficietenus comptiores, pulcriorem nullam.'

10. *Ep. fam.*, XXII, 10, ed. Rossi, IV, pp. 126–8, ed. Fracassetti, vol. III, pp. 147–9, Cit. p. 127 and p. 148, 'Amavi ego Ciceronem fateor, et Virgilium amavi usque adeo quidem stilo delectatus et ingenio, ut nihil supra.... Amavi similiter Platonem ex Graecis atque Homerum, quorum ingenia nostris admota, saepe iudicii dubium me fecere. Sed iam nunc maius agitur negotium, maiorque salutis quam eloquentiae cura est. Legi quae delectabunt, lego quae prosint.'

11. Ibid., pp. 127–8 and 148–9, 'Iamque oratores mei fuerint Ambrosius, Augustinus, Hieronymus et Gregorius; philosophus meus Paulus, poeta David, ... Neque ideo quia hos praetulerim, illos abiicio, quod se fecisse Hieronymus scribere potius quam sequenti stilo approbare visus est mihi. Ego utrosque simul amare posse videor, modo quos in verborum, quos in rerum consilio praeferam non ignorem. Nam quid, oro te, prohibet ... et argenti simul et auri divitem fieri, cum utriusque pretium sic noveris ne in alterutro falli queas, presertim cum veteres illi nil aliud a me requirant, nisi non oblivione deleantur, et primitiis studiorum contenti, omne iam melioribus tempus cedant? Ad orationem, si res poscat, utar Marone vel Tullio, nec pudebit a Graecia mutari siquid Latio deesse videbitur; ad vitam vero, etsi multa apud illos utilia noverim, utar tamen iis consultoribus atque iis ducibus ad salutem, quorum fidei ac doctrinae nulla suspicio sit erroris. Quos inter merito mihi maximus David semper fuerit, eo formosior quo incomptior, eo doctior disertiorque quo purior. Huius ego Psalterium et vigilanti semper in manibus semperque sub oculis, et dormienti simul ac morienti sub capite situm velim.'

12. Novati, op. cit., IV, pp. 231–3, 'Male quidem minusque Christiane

fecissent Juvencus atque Sedulius, quos scimus historias evangelicas divini carmini elegantia cecinisse; stulte fecisset Arator, qui gesta sanctissimorum apostolorum cum expositionis allegorice luminibus grandiloque versibus allegavit. Petrus etiam de Riga damnabiliter laborasset, qui versibus inequalibus veteris et novi Testamenti corpus allegorizans etiam plurima, renovavit. Peccaverunt graviter Alanus atque Johannes, qui et Architrenius dictus est, quod libros suos figmentis poeticis et versibus ediderunt. Peccaverunt et alia plures quos tedium est referre, qui poetas inventione et carmine secuti sunt, ut Prudentius atque Prosper et Pater Ambrosius, qui plurimos hymnorum variis metrorum generibus expedevit.'

13. Ibid., pp. 235–6, 'Divina Scriptura nonne sermo et locutio Dei est? Et quid est in toto corpore sacri voluminis veteris Testamenti, quod iuxta litterarum Hebraicarum numerum in libros viginti duo sectum est; vel etiam novum quod primum illud adumbratis sermonibus continebat, quod in quatuor Evangelia, canonicas Epistolas, Actus apostolorum et remotam ab intellectibus Apocalypsim dispertitum est, quod allegorice non legatur, quod non etiam aliud sub cortice teneat quam ostendat; quod bilingue iure non possit et debeat appellari? Quid minus allegoricam esse videtur quam principium Geneseos et opera sex dierum? Nonne Adamantius Origines, de quo scriptum est quod ubi bene dixit, nemo melius, ubi male, nemo peius; cuncta reducens ad mysticum intellectum, mirabilis allegorice sensibus exposuit et ad mores nostros animeque nostre potentias pie et laudabiliter adaptavit? Vide Iudicum historias; vide Regum et reliqua quae sequuntur; nonne cuncta reducuntur ad allegoricum intellectum? Adduc precor passum aliquem veteris Instrumentum, quem sanctissimi doctores sensus occulti mysterio non exponunt. Quid magis poeticum et iuxta canticem magis amatorium et lascivium quam Cantica Canticorum? Quid mysteriosius, quidque magis poeticum quam liber et historia Iob, cuius occulta cum alii plures tum sanctissimus antistes Gregorius super omnes, multiplicatis sensibus, pertractavit? Scribitur de novissime prophetie secretis quod ipsa continent tot sacramenta quot verba. Qui liber tante profunditatis est quod supra se multos in extasim elevans pene coegerit insanire. Denique totum vetus testamentum nonne novi figura creditur et idea?'

14. Ibid., pp. 236–8, 'Quo fit ut quicquid in divina Scriptura a propria naturalique significatione discedit quicquidque figuraliter de alio predicatur, totum sit poeticum et prorsus tale quod oblique, non proprie, quod intenditur representet. Quare cum de Christum cecinit Psalmigraphus, "ego autem sum vermis et non homo", [*Psalms* xxi:7] vermem Christum dixit ex eo quod, sicut vermis non nascitur seminali generatione, sic et Christus de nullius viri semine productus est. Quod autem dixit: "et non homo", vel propter divinitatem dixit, solus enim homo non fuit, vel quia sic homo generatus est quod in illa principio nulli

peccato prorsus fuerit obnoxius, quod nulli quidem homini penitus non contingat, quoniam peccato puer non caret, etiam unius diei; quasi dicat: "et non homo", cum omnes sint homines peccatores, ego vero non. Duo sunt vermes, non nati scilicet de concubitu: primus Adam, de quo scriptum est, "formavit igitur Deus hominem de limo terre et inspiravit in faciem eius spiraculum vite et factus est homo in animam viventem". Nec id modo volumus explicare nunquid hominis appellatione hoc loco contineatur et Eva, de quibus iam dixerat Moyses: "et creavit Deus hominem ad imaginem suam, ad imaginem Dei creavit illum, masculum et feminam creavit eos", cum et Adam interpretur homo terrenus vel terra rubra. Dicitur enim apud Hebreos tantum volere hoc Adam quantum apud nos hoc vocabulum homo, quo tam masculus quam femina significatur. Alter autem vermis fuit dominus noster Jesus Christus, qui de fluxu seminis natus non est, sed quem, ut sancta dogmatizat Ecclesia, firmiter credimus, pie et catholice confitemur "Filium Dei unigenitum, ex patre natum ante omnia secula, Deum de Deo, lumen de lumine, Deum verum de Deo vero, genitum, non factum, consubstantialem patri; per quem omnia facta sunt; qui propter nos homines et propter nostram salutem descendit de celis et incarnatus est de Spiritu Sancto ex Maria virgine, et homo factus est," et reliqua que sequuntur [from Nicene and Constantinopolitan creeds]. Nec hec dixerim, ut explicem eius exortum, qui non minus latet et superat omnem intellectum nativitate carnali quam generatione divina, ut merito Propheta dixerit: "generationem eius quis ennarabit?" '

15. Petri Damiani, *De bono religiosi status et variorum animantium tropologia*, cap iii, 'De natura leonis'.
16. Novati, IV, p. 238, 'Sed cur per ista trahor? Quid est enim in tota divina Scriptura quod non habeat mysticum intellectum, sive verba sive hystorias, sive prophetias sive sapientie precepta consideres? Totum est mysticum, totum reducitur ad allegoricum intellectum. Nichil est in illis quod bilingue non est, quod non unum in cortice pre se ferat et aliud intrinsecus non intendat et secum varios Spiritus Sancti sensus exponi non valeat et sumi.'
17. I use the Basel, 1541, edition in the copy in the Biblioteca Apost. Vaticana.
18. Cf. above, Part I, Chapter III, pp. 154–5 and nn. 122 and 123; Zippel, op. cit., p. 326, n. 4. Cf. Valla's *Repastinatio* in Urb. lat. 1207, f. 67v, 'Omnis enim huiusmodi quaestio qua se philosophi theologique disputando torquent de vocabulo est. Sed ociosum mihi videtur re intellecta in disquirendis calumniandisque vocibus consenescere quae praesertim nullius solida auctoritate nituntur. Illud fortasse non de voce quaeritur quae sit in Deo actio, quam ullam esse non placebit iis qui Deum quiescere volunt.'
19. Cf. Garofalo's lengthier discussion, op. cit., pp. 343–53.
20. I will use the text of Bibl. Vaticana, Urb. lat. 6. Another MS: Pal. lat. 45.

21. Valla, op. cit., f. 133r–v, 'Quod autem Graecum hoc nomen, quod hic transferitur *Creatura*, κτίσεως, possit transferri *creatione*. . . . Nec quinque vocabula sunt Graece *per ea quae facta sunt*, sed unum, *operibus* seu *factis*, τοῖς ποιήμασιν. Etiam cernuntur dixissem potius quam conspiciuntur.'
22. Manetti, op. cit., f. 114v.
23. Valla, op. cit., f. 171v, 'Quid sibi vult, *Fecit nos ministros non littera*, hoc est, per literam? Quis enim minister factus est, per literam? certe nemo. Ergo dicendum, *Qui fecit nos ministros non litterae*, quod est Vetus Testamentum, *sed spiritus*, quod est Novum Testamentum, quia littera veteris testamenti occidebat, spiritus eiusdem, quod est novum testamentum, vivificat.'
24. Manetti, Urb. lat. 6, f. 141v.
25. Valla, op. cit., f. 175r–v, 'Aiunt quidam docti plus inesse maiestatis in illa Homeri simplicitate quam gratiae in illa Vergilii festivitate, ubi ille Graecos Principes populosque hic Italos enumerat. Ita hoc loco mihi videtur festivitas haec interpretis in variandis dictionibus, ut nunc dicat *Quasi*, nunc *tanquam*, nunc *sicut*, nunc *ut*, non tantum decoris habere quantum Graeca ipsa simplicitas, id est, Paulina oratio sublimis, atque urgens eiusdem dictionis repetitione in principio sententiarum, hoc modo:' etc.
26. Manetti, Urb. lat. 6, f. 143v.
27. Valla, op. cit., f. 149r–v, '. . . Cur variant interpres quaecum vocabulum? nam sic legitur graece: *Non in doctis humanae sapientiae verbis sive sermonibus*, sed in doctis spiritus sancti, quasi in humana sapientia sint verba, in spiritu autem sancto doctrina, quod non ita est.' Zippel, op. cit., p. 328 in note 4 to p. 326. Conceivably Valla could have stressed the difference between divine *Verba* and *doctrina* [human?] consistently with other statements. But he merely states it here.
28. Manetti, Urb. lat. 6, f. 28v.
29. Valla, op. cit., ff. 165v–6r, '. . . Quomodo non ego, si gratia Dei mecum? Igitur dicendum est, *Gratia Dei quae est mecum*, ἀλλ' ἡ χάρις τοῦ θεοῦ ἡ σὺν ἐμοί, ut nihil dicant qui hanc vocant gratiam Dei cooperantem. Paulus enim sibi non tribuit, sed totum Deo refert acceptum.' It may also be recalled that according to Leff, *Gregory of Rimini*, op. cit., pp. 186–7, *Bradwardine and the Pelagians*, op. cit., Part II, passim, the Ockhamists rejected natural and cooperative Grace.
30. Manetti, Urb. lat. 6, f. 138r.
31. Valla, op. cit., f. 176r, '. . . Immo ad *promptitudinem*, seu *alacritatem* vestrem in dando προθυμίαν . . . enim voluntas prompta est, προθυνία. Hanc locum ridicule quidam exponunt, *destinatam voluntatem* predestinatam a Deo, qui predestinavit ab aeterno vos talem voluntatem habere.'
32. Manetti, Urb. lat. 6, f. 145r.
33. Zippel, op. cit., 'La "Defensio . . ." ' etc., p. 326, n. 4.
34. Valla, op. cit., f. 176r, '. . . Non referatur stabilem ad salutem, sed ad

poenitentiam, quod Graece dicitur *impoenitibilem* ἀμεταμέλητον, quanquam duo vocabula graeca μετάνοια et μεταμέληια differunt a nostro. Nam poenitentia dicta est a poenitet, quod est taedet, vel piget, ut apud Vergilium

Nec te poeniteat calamo trivisse labellum

De quo vocabulo Aulus Gellius pro M. Tullio contra Asinium Pollionem disputat, Graeca vocabula dicta sunt a sensu retractando et cura in melius mutanda; elegantior dictio, ut ait Lactantius, quam nostra. Itaque in nostro verbo significatio est, *tristitia commissi*, in Graecis, *mentis emendatio*. Quare nihil dicunt qui super hanc locum disputantes, an tristitia idem sit quod poenitentia; aiunt triplicem esse poenitentiam, unam quae est contritio, alteram quae est confessio, tertiam quae est satisfactio. Quae sententia cum falsa sit, tum nihil ad explanandam sententiam Pauli faciens.'

35. Manetti, Urb. lat. 6, f. 144r.

36. Garofalo, op. cit., pp. 352–3, comments on Valla's exegetical efforts [and those of humanism in general] as follows: 'In realtà Lorenzo ha rosicchiato la corteccia del testo biblico: Tommaso [d'Aquinate] ne ha addentato e gustato il frutto. L'Umanesimo e il Rinascimento possono superare il Medio Evo nella critica filologica, ma gli sono nettamente inferiori nel campo esegetico. Il Valla sa di essere uno spulciatore di sillabe al quale manca il nerbo per affrontare una intepretazione solida e compiuta; l'esegesi non è pane per i suoi denti, e nei rarissimi casi in cui vi si avventura, se ne ritrae prontamente perchè non lo accusi di non credere alla Bibbia.' However, Zippel is readier to grant the exegetical implications of some of Valla's comments, and points out that in our last instance cited he provided a precedent for Luther's rejection of the Catholic interpretation of penance, citing Valla. In reality it depends on one's doctrinal point of view whether Valla's exegesis may be thought to have a certain potency. And certainly he was pointing the way towards an exegesis that was more dependent on accurate rendering of the sacred text, possibly a unity of philology and hermeneutics Garofalo would not permit himself to recognise.

37. Garofalo, op. cit., p. 354, n. 6, speaks of 'mia introduzione ed alla edizione critica delle sue traduzioni *di prossima publicazione*' [1947]. However I have been informed by Professor Kristeller [in 1967] that, according to Monsignor Michele Maccarrone, Garofalo has abandoned this project. Garofalo discusses Manetti's translation of the New Testament very briefly, p. 364.

38. Leon. Bruni, *Epistolarum libri VIII*, ed. L. Mehus, Florence, 1741, Vol. II, pp. 160–4, p. 160, 'Hebraicas literas inutiles, Graecas vero Latinasque utilissimas esse ostendit.'

39. Ibid., pp. 160–1, cit. p. 161, 'Neque enim Augustinus, neque Basilius,

neque alii permulti ex nostris ac Graecis, qui hebraice nesciverunt, Deum cognovissent, si absque litteris hebraicis Dei cognitio haberi non possit. Quin et Iudeos videmus litteris hebraicis perquam optime instructos, eosdem tamen summi boni, ac veri Dei cognitionem nequaquam habere, sed inimicissimos esse Religionis et Fidei.'

40. Ibid., p. 161, 'At enim Hieronymus Poetarum fabulas et oratorum argutias damnat. Quid ad rem? Ego enim non te ad fabulas Poetarum, neque ad argutias fori voco, sed si Philosophiae ac liberalibus studiis opera danda est, si disciplina et moribus imbuendi sunt homines . . . multo commodius, et plenus latinis et graecis litteris fieri id posse dico quam Iudeorum barbarie.'

41. Ibid., pp. 161–2, 'At enim, inquis, fundamenta rectae Fidei a Iudaeorum libris existunt, qui etsi sint translata, melius tamen est fontes consectari quam rivos. Certe si Christiani, non autem Iudei, apud nos esse fontes dico, non apud illos. Novum enim Testamentum totum, ut ita dixerim, nostrum est, non Iudaeorum. . . . An ii rivi tibi videntur, an non fontes? Adde tamen multos ac tam praestantes Doctores Christianae Fidei, quot habet lingua latina et graeca. . . . Si igitur Christianae Fidei cognitionem perfectam, ac non vulgarem habere vis, hos lege quaeso, ac intellige, quorum nihil simile apud Hebreos reperire potes.'

42. Richard and Trude Krautheimer, *Lorenzo Ghiberti*, Princeton, 1956, Chapter XII, 'The Program', pp. 169–88, of particular value on the whole subject of this chapter.

43. Bruni, op. cit., p. 162, 'Quid Concilia, in quibus permultae haereses, ac variae Christianorum lites sunt penitus extirpatae? Nonne tota Latinorum et Graecorum sunt, Hebraeorum nulla? Lateranense, Nicaenum, Chalcedonense? Quid igitur apud Hebraeos quaeris? An Christiane Fidei fundamenta? Certe apud nos illa sunt, non apud eos. Disputationes doctorum, et determinationes dubietatum? At illae apud nos reperiuntur, non apud illos.'

44. Ibid., pp. 162–3, cit. p. 163, 'Nisi forsitan diffidis Hieronymo sanctissimo ac doctissimo viro, et tibi ipsi confidis melius intelligere posse quam ille intellexit.'

45. Ibid., p. 163, 'Si enim tales interpretes quales Hieronymus fuit Graeca lingua habuisset, labore me et ceteros liberasset. Sed qui libros Aristotelis transtulerunt, barbaros magis quam latinos illos effecerant. . . . Deinde quid simile habet Graecorum eruditio cum Iudaeorum ruditate? Graeca enim lingua Philosophiae caeterarumque disciplinarum gratia addiscitur. Confert latinis ad perfectionem litterarum. Eadem quippe origo videtur eademque institutio, ac eadem pene litterarum figurae. Apud Hebraeos autem nullum tale invitamentum esse potest. Nulli enim illis Philosophi, nulli Poetae, nulli Oratores reperiuntur; lingua vera ac figuris litterarum sic abhorrent a nostris ut etiam in scribendo contrariam viam incedant quam non incedamus. Cum hac lingua tibi quid commercii sit, cuius

litterae comites nostris esse non possunt, sed cum destrorsum incidunt nostrae, illae sinistrorsum aufugiunt?'

46. Ibid., pp. 163–4, cit., p. 164, 'Quid vetat ut ille de oratoribus et disertis, sic etiam me de theologis dicere: "O quot rustici et illiterari feliciores erunt multis qui sacrarum litterarum cognitioni vacant." Siquidem Ariani et Manichaei et Sabelliani ac ceteri haeretici qui in Litteris Sacris versati perverse de Deo opinati sunt, sempiterno igne damnantur. Habes nunc iudicium meum de Hebraeicis litteris.'
47. Umberto Cassuto, *Gli Ebrei a Firenze nell'età del Rinascimento*, Florence, 1918 [Reprinted 1965], p. 274.
48. Ibid., pp. 275–6.
49. Cf. S. E. Assemani, *Bibliothecae Apostolicae Vaticanae Codicum Manuscriptorum Catalogus*, Partes Primae, Tomus Primus, *Codices Ebraici et Samaritani*, Rome, 1756, pp. 8–9, 22, 51–2, 54, 225–7, 380–1; U. Cassuto, *I manoscritti palatini ebraici della Biblioteca Apost. Vaticana e la loro storia, Studi e Testi* 66, Città del Vaticano, 1935, pp. 44–7, 79–90; U. Cassuto, *Codices Vaticani Hebraica. Codices 1-115*, Città del Vaticano, 1956, Nos. 8, 26, 28, 38, 46, 47, 71, 75, 82, 95, 262, 408, 425. Cf. Cagni, op. cit.
50. Cassuto, *Gli Ebrei*, op. cit., p. 277.
51. Cf. below Part IV, Chapter XVI, for discussion of this work.
52. Cf. above, pp. 230–1, for question of dating and Part II, Chapter VI, for discussion of the work.
53. Cf. Vespasiano, *Commentario*, op. cit., pp. 176–8. The *Apologeticus* is attached to three manuscripts of his translation: Bibl. Vatic., Pal. lat. 40, 41 and Urb. lat. 5. Pal. lat. 41 is the copy dedicated to King Alfonso; Pal. lat. 40 is a copy made by his son Agnolo. We have consulted and followed both these manuscripts but we cite it from Urb. lat. 5. Cf. Cagni, op. cit. pp. 35 and 38 and Garofalo, op. cit., pp. 358–60. Pal. lat. 42 and 43 are copies of the translation of the Psalter, only, made by Agnolo. There is a fragmentary version of this translation in Florence, Biblioteca Marucelliana, Cod. C 336, and there is also a Belgian manuscript: Brussels, Bibl. Royale, Ms 10745, of a provenance unknown to me. Although these lack, also, the *Apologeticus*, their existence indicates that there was, at least, a small diffusion beyond the Manetti family library. The presence of Alfonso's copy in Manetti's library [Pal. lat. 41] is attributed by Garofalo to the fact that it was pawned in 1460 for 15 ducats (after Alfonso's death in 1458), and probably then acquired by Agnolo Manetti, p. 360. Garofalo describes the contents of the *Apologeticus*, pp. 361–3, and publishes five excerpts from Manetti's preface and from the apology as an appendix, pp. 367–73. We believe that our discussion, which follows, is the first detailed analysis of this important work. Presumably Garofalo also discusses it at greater length in the introduction to his promised edition, but as we have noted, this was

twenty years ago, and its publication has been abandoned. On the role of Agnolo Manetti in his father's work, and thereafter, cf. Luisa Banti, 'Agnolo Manetti e alcuni scribi a Napoli nel secolo XV', *Annali della Scuola Normale Superiore di Pisa,* Ser. II, 8 (1939), pp. 382–94.

54. Urb. lat. 5, f 7r–v, 'Nam cum poetis oratoribus et historicis et caeteris huiusmodi humanitatis studiis quibus in adolescentia assiduam operam navaveras penitus et omnino pretermissis te ad gymnasia philosophie ac divine sapientie que grece unico verbo theologia appellatur omnibus animi et corporis ceu dicitur viribus merito cum ob illius vere et non adumbratilis sapientie dignitatem quoque ob persone tue sublimitatem conversum fuisse intelligerem, ac plene aperteque conspicerem, nempe maioribus gravioribus dignioribus atque sane his novis facultatibus tuis accomodatioribus litterariis laboribus nostris quam antea tecum dum inter poetica versabamur ludere consueveram deinceps agere operarique decrevi. Cum enim vere ac solide utriusque et prisce et moderne, ut ita dixerim, theologie fundamenta in cunctis veteris et novi testamenti codicibus tantum modo omnium doctorum hominum consensu iaciantur atque ambo illa a veris Hebreorum ac Grecorum fontibus in Latinam linguam traducta ab ipsis a quibus ea suscepimus quotidie carpi lacerarique acciperem pro virili mea ulterius equo animo ferre ac tollerare non potui. Quo circa hae precipua causa adductus laborem nove amborum testamentorum traductionis non iniuria nuper assumpsi, licet vero hoc quodcunque est opus magnum et arduam . . . si tamen Deus ut spero quando boni gratia hoc quodcunque laboris est magnanimiter aggredi atque libenter assumere voluerim adiutor noster erit optatos forsitan effectus quod si nobis divini ope patrocinioque suffutis evenire contingerit quicquid laboris in hac nostra translatione assumptum et exanclatum fuerit saltem ut sine arrogantia dictum velim ab omnibus doctis eruditis viris.'

55. Ibid., ff. 7v–8r, '. . . hec est illa qua romana ecclesia in orationibus suis iam pridem usque ad tempora nostra uti consuevit. Altera eiusdem Hieronimi perhibetur et est cuius titulus fertur *De Hebraica veritate.* Ac due dicte traductiones simul collate usque adeo ab invicem differunt diverseque cernuntur, ut mirabile quiddam videatur et sit. Atque hac comparatione diligenter et accurate habita, qualis hec nostra fuerit pro tua sapientia facile diiudicare poteris. Ceterum de ista nova Psalterii traductione hec impresentiarum dicta sufficiant, cum plura alia totius operis, si divino favore adiuti, ultimas ei manus tandem aliquando imponere valuerimus, prefatione non temere suis locis dicenda reserventur.' Cf. Cagni, op. cit., pp. 35 and 38; Garofalo, op. cit., pp. 358–60; Stornajolo, I, 8; Kristeller, *Iter,* I, 110; II, 389–90.

56. Urb. lat. 5, f. 7v, '. . . passim carpentibus et calumniantibus iure respondere ac etiam eis perpetuum silentium iniungere atque inducere valeamus.'

57. Ibid., Urb. lat. 5, f. 61r.
58. Ibid., f. 61r, 'De diversis cunctorum auctorum obtrectatoribus.'
59. Ibid., f. 61r–v, 'Nam cum pro multis et magnis et piis et devotis laboribus lucubrationibus meis ad defensionem sacrarum Latinarum literarum adversus nonnullas falsas Hebreorum virorum de codicibus nostris incusationes et calumnias dumtaxat conversas singularia quedam laudum et commendationum atque honorum premia deberemur. . . .'
60. Ibid., f. 63r–64r, '. . . et denique quot ceterorum omnium maximum et id quod iusta admiratione referctum videri debet, divinarum literarum professores et quidem Christiani ac religiosissimi homines huius vicissitudinarie emulationis nequaquam ex partes evasere. Si quidem Augustinus et Rufinus Hieronymum pluribus sacrarum litterarum locis vehementer reprehenderunt ac totam veteris testamenti translationem eius utpote non necessarium sed superfluam quandam ac inutilem perpetue quantum in ipsis fuit infamie postquam ediderat damnare non dubitarunt. Ante vero quam ediret amice exhortibuntur ne intra ducendis sacris veteribus litteris aliquatenus laboraret, quemadmodum duabus precipuis Augustini ad eum epistolis plane aperteque deprehenditur. Quibus quidem et aliis huiusmodi eius obrectatoribus ipse pluribus prefationum suarum locis acribus verbis et non sine ingenti quadam animi indignatione respondit, atque in epistolis quoque suis ab huiusmodi obtrectatoribus sese defendere non cessat. . . . et in libro de optimo genere interpretandi eadem repetit. . . . [64r]: Quid nos Christiani homines pro defensione catholice fidei ac sacre divineque veritatis conservatione facere debemus. . . .'
61. Ibid., ff. 64r–80v, comprising Books I and II.
62. Ibid., ff. 64r–67v.
63. Ibid., f. 66v.
64. Ibid., f. 67r, '. . . certa quedam et vera ac expressa de providentia divina de qua veteres philosophi satis dubitasse et ab invicem acriter contendisse ac inter se certasse creduntur sententia ad utilitatem totius humani generis innotesceret, licet nonnulli catholici sacrique doctores nostri longe aliter de commemorati libri auctore sentire videantur qui eam predicti dialogi disputationem a Iob quodam non Hebreo origine sed viro gentili ac proselito quemadmodum fuisse arbitrantur.'
65. Ibid., ff. 67v–8r.
66. Ibid., f. 68r, 'Et tamen in translatione nostra vulgatam omnium eruditorum Hebreorum opinionem ut in cunctis eorum codicibus reperitur sequi et imitari maluimus atque ut ita faceremus certa quadam vere sincereque interpretationis lege cogebamur, cum ita in ea lingua expresse scriptum comperiremus e qua in latinum eloquium traducere profitebamur, licet apud Grecos secundum celebratam illam septuagintaduorum intepretum traductionem unus duntaxat liber habeatur. . . .'
67. Ibid., ff. 68r–9r.
68. Ibid., f. 69r–v, '. . . Mosaica enim volumina ante Alexandrum Macedonie

regem eiusque imperium traducta fuere. . . . Qui nihil aliud esse Platonem quam Moysem Attica lingua loquentem scripsere ausus est. Quod efficere nequaquam potuisset cum prisci Greci ob elegantiam dicendi cuius avidissimi erant Hebrearum litterarum cognitione penitus caruissent que quidem lingua veluti barbara quedam et immanis ab omni politiori elegantia longe abhorrere illis presertim temporibus videbatur quibus Grece facundie studia apprime florebant, sola que in singulari honore ac precipuo pretio habebantur.'

69. Ibid., ff. 70r–3v. Eusebius, *De prep. evang.*, VIII, 2–5, Migne, *P. G.* XXI.
70. Cf. Pal. lat. 1916, ff. 530–51, for his Greek Mss. According to Pal. lat. 1916, f. 551, Pal. graec. 202, now another work, was 'substitutus loco Aristeae'; i.e. the original Fugger collection, built around Manetti's library, included Aristeas. Most likely this was Manetti's, although no direct evidence survives. Cf. Cagni, op. cit. p. 6, n. 3.
71. Cf. Cagni, op. cit., passim.
72. Cf. e.g. Urb. lat. 566, Aristeas, *De septuaginta interpretibus*, interprete Mathia Palmero, Praef. ad Paulum Secundum, ff. 1r–2r.
73. Cf. listings in Appendix II of my Fontius study, *Studies in the Renaissance*, VII, (1960), item No. 44, p. 131.
74. Cf. Manetti, op. cit., Urb. lat. 5, ff. 74v–6r.
75. Ibid., f. 74r, 'At si id verum fuit quod superius recitavimus quemadmodum scriptum legimus profecto illi quod de septuaginta duobus commemoratis sacrarum litterarum interpretibus ab Eusebio scribitur simile quiddam esse videbitur.' Cf. Cicero, *De oratore*, III, 137. *Noctes Atticae* VII, xvii, 3.
76. Ibid., f. 72r, Aulus Gellius, *Noctes Atticae*, VI.
77. Jerome, in Migne, *Patr. Lat.* 28, 181–2.
78. Manetti, op. cit., f. 76r, 'Nam quodam loco, "nescio" inquit "quis primus auctor septuaginta cellulas Alexandrie mendatio suo extruxit quibus divisi eadem scriptitarent. Cum Aristeas eiusdem Ptolemei yperaspistes et multo post tempore Iosephus nihil tale retulerint, sed in una basilica congregatos contulisse scribant non prophetasse. Aliud est enim vatem aliud esse interpretem. Ibi spiritus ventura predicit. Hic eruditio et verborum copia, ea quae intelligit, transfert: nisi forte putandus est Tullius *Economicum* Xenophontis et Platonis *Protagoram* et Demosthenis *Pro Ctesiphonte* orationem afflatus rhetorico spirito protulisse. . . ." '
79. Ibid., f. 76r–v, 'Huiusmodi igitur Septuaginta interpretum traductio quomodocunque sive seorsum et separatim sive simul et coniunctim celebrata fuerit tanto tamen in honore tantoque pretio primitus habita est ut paucis post annis totam pene Greciam occupaverit. . . et oblivia tradita et admiramur et non sine aliquali molestia tolleramus cum res perpetuis litterarum monumentis digna et priscis annalibus memoranda esset.'
80. Ibid., f. 76v, '. . . atque his de causis per multa tempora sola in maxima

quadam estimatione perseveravit, donec aliqui alii interpetes accesserunt qui quidem cum in predicta seniorum traductione multa superaddita, nonnulla omissa, pleraque aliter traducta conspicaretur, quarundam aliorum novarum translationum labores variis temporibus assumpserunt.'

81. Ibid., ff. 76v–7r, '... partim ut Iudeis Christianis hominibus divinarum scripturarum veterum falsitatem obicientibus responderet silentiumque post hac indiceret, partim etiam ut tantam ac tam multiplicem diversarum traductionum varietatem auferret....'

82. Ibid., ff. 77v–8r, 'Prima erat quedam troporum ac metaphorum copia quibus ea lingua vel maxime habundabat, ubi nonnulla ingentia divinarum rerum misteria interdum abstrusa latere videbantur, que quidem in alienam linguam cum tanta ac tam propria illarum sententiarum expressione transferri non poterant ... pro virili sua tollerare non potuit. Unde eam auferre cupiens non modo utile sed etiam et necessarium fore existimavit si per novam quandam et integram de Hebreo in Latinum eloquium traductionem omnis sacrarum scripturarum quecunque ex diversis traductionibus oriretur ambiguitas penitus et omnino et usque quaque tolleretur, atque his duabus, ut diximus, causis adductus ad cognitionem lingue Hebree ceteris posthabitis sese convertit....'

83. Ibid., f. 78r–v, '... de falsitate scripturarum nostrarum adversus Christianos quotidie insultare ac latrare non desinunt..... Primo namque maiores suos imitati atque ideo adversus Christianos insensi omnes passim uno ordine odio habent. Nobis deinde in sacris litteris vel maxime invident quoniam nos eam sacrorum scripturarum copiam, quibus soli ipsi vel maxime gloriari solebant cum cetere gentes illas apprime contemnerent tum Grecis interpretationibus, tum etiam hac presertim Latina ab illis arripuimus ac nobismetipsis vendicavimus. Ad hec accedit quod nulli Hebreorum vel certe admodum pauci ullam vel Grecarum vel Latinarum litterarum cognitionem post Philonem ac Iosephum duos illos nobiles celebresque Iudeos Hebree simul ac Grece lingue peritissimos habuisse videntur.'

84. Ibid., f. 78v, 'Unde factum est ut ex hac ipsa alienarum litterarum ignoratione non modo ea que recte ac etiam illa que perperam si qua fuissent in Christianis traductionibus contenta intelligere nequirent, sed propriam quoque et vernaculam linguam perfecte cognoscere callereque non possent. Fieri enim non potest ut una lingua presertim regulis canonibusque et normis instituta sine aliquali vel modica saltem alienorum excellentium idomatum cognitione ad unguem percipi perfecteque cognosci posset. ... suis ergo duntaxat contenti nec aliena querentes iam diu peregrinis linguis caruere, et propriam quoque ac vernaculam perperam intellexere. Quocirca et poetis et historicis et oratoribus et mathematicis et dialecticis et phisicis et moralibus et metaphisicis privati certa quadam omnium liberalium artium cognitione penitus ac omnino caruisse videntur. Proinde in crassa ac supina cunctarum rerum ignora-

tione diutius versati, quasi immunde sues in ceno moribundi iacent atque per hunc modum in eorum perfidia velut in sepulchro vivi sepeliuntur. . . .'

85. Ibid., f. 79r, 'Si deinde Hebraicarum litterarum caracteres ac documenta alibi quam in sacris codicibus discere intelligereque valerent, quod facile evenissent nisi et primum constitutis asperis adversus quoscunque temerarios transgressores penis ac suppliciis traditionibus suis severe admodum cavissent, et secundum quoque ordinationes punctorum suorum, que loco Grecarum et Latinarum vocalium apud eos habentur, ita instituissent ut in sacris duntaxat codicibus commemorata punta, hoc est vocales sine quibus ullatenus legi ac nequaquam ulla lectio fieri confirmarique potest, tantummodo reperiantur ex quo factum est ut quecunque Hebreas litteras noverunt cum alibi quam in sacris libris ob carentiam puntorum legere non potuerunt, divinarum scripturarum saltem scioli habeantur et sint. Quapropter cum ex crassa quadam cunctorum rerum ignorantia tum etiam quid ab infantia et cunabulis sacris litteris quemadmodum diximus imbuti et per diversas etates postea progressi, falsam, scripturam nostram et impiam fidem arbitrantur.' Translation changes Manetti's faulty syntax, also in Pal. lat. 41.
86. Ibid., ff. 79v–80r, Jerome's *Praefatium ad Sophronicum*, Migne *Patr. lat.*, 28, 1184–5.
87. Manetti, Urb. lat. 5, op. cit., f. 80v, '. . . tertia vulgato circumferatur quam Gallicanum dicunt et apud quosdam in usu habetur. Sed unde prodierit quisve auctor fuerit a plerisque ignoratur et presertim ab illis qui id qualecunque sit a Hieronymo emanasse contendunt.'
88. Ibid., f. 80v.
89. Ibid., f. 81r, 'De multis ac magnis duarum celeberrimarum totius Psalterii interpretationum differentiis.'
90. Ibid., f. 89v, 'De alienis interpretationibus una cum differentibus omnium psalmorum titulis.'
91. This is, in fact, what we have done, checked the errors against Manetti and Jerome.
92. Ibid., f. 100r, 'De interpretatione recta nonnulla memoratu digna.'
93. Ed., Baron, pp. 81–96, *Humanistich-philosophische Schriften*, op. cit.
94. Manetti, op. cit., Urb lat. 5, f. 104r.
95. Ibid., ff. 102r–3r.
96. Ibid., f. 103r–v.
97. Ibid., f. 104v, 'Tria enim illa antea posita in quavis conversione esse convenit ut sententia quodammodo servata cuncta alia secundum evidentem primorum auctorum diversitatem varietatemque ornata et illustrata fuisse ostendantur. Reliqua vero duo graviorem quandem et severiorem traductionem exigere et postulare videntur.'
98. Ibid., f. 105r, 'Ceterum de philosophis ac theologis, quamquam recte ut diximus in quibusvis interpretationibus ad verbum interpretari nequeamus, non ita tamen lata et vaga et ampla cum verborum tum sententiarum

quoque luminibus ornamentisque expolita, sed aliquanto pressior ac gravior et exactior in predictis duobus quam in tribus superioribus esse debet. Quippe ad gravitatem expressionemque sententiarum quibus utraque commemorata facultas vel maxime habundat in primis requiritur ut nec plura nec pauciora interdum verba reddantur nisi quantum certa troporum et figurarum et metaphorarum necessitas atque nonnunquam nimia intelligentie obscuritas exigere et postulare videatur, quod in sacris scripturis precipue maximeque servandum iure existimamus et credimus.'

99. Ibid., f. 105r–v.

100. Ibid., f. 105v, 'Quid nam de sacrarum divinarumque scripturarum conversionibus sentiemus ubi cuncti quique sententie sacre ac divine sunt, in quibus omnis duntaxat humana salus vel maxime consistere recondique videtur quod tam et si ita sit excellentes tamen sacrarum scripturarum interpretes usque adeo ab interpretatione ad verbum utpote ab illa quam et sententias obscurare et interdum pervertere arbitrantur abhoruisse videntur, ut in medio sacri textus, cum nonnunquam amplificationibus, tam alienis quoque interpretationibus utantur. . . .'

101. Migne, *P.L.* 22, 568–79. Manetti, op. cit., ff. 105v–6v.

102. Manetti, op. cit. [Urb. lat. 5], f. 106v, 'Profecto talium discrepantiarum numerus pene incredibilis et quasi infinitus putaretur. Hanc tantam et tam ingentem varietatem antiqui doctores nostri evidentibus signis in codicibus suis per hunc modum notare consueverant.'

103. Ibid., ff. 106v–7r; cf. Origen, *Hexaplorum quae supersunt*, Migne, *P.G.* V, VI, 1, 2, 3.

104. Ibid., f. 107r.

105. Ibid., f. 107r–v, 'Nullam ad verbum factam traductionem laudabilem ac perfectam esse posse quibusdam rationibus plurimisque etiam prestantissimorum virorum auctoritatibus plane et aperte superius probasse atque confirmasse meminimus ac magnam quoque inter poetarum, oratorum ac historicorum traductores et inter philosophorum ac theologorum interpretes diversitatem esse fierique oportere manifestissime demonstravimus. Nam illis primis sive poetarum sive oratorum sive historicorum ut ita dixerim conversoribus nonnunquam elegantie et ornatus gratia arida ieiunaque et exilia amplificare et obscura pretermittere et interdum pro sua voluntate dilucidius interpretari licet. Fidi vero philosophorum theologorumque interpretes non ita pro suo arbitrio vagi ac liberi quasi per latos et apertos campos hinc idem discurrere et pervagari debent. Sed artioribus quibusdam interpretandi legibus pressi et quasi certis cancellis astrictis modestius graviusque iuxta severam quandam professionis sue normam incedere progredique coguntur nec ab incepto convertendi proposito longius evagantes. Nec primis etiam auctoribus omnino ac penitus ad verbum adherentes sed medium et tutum ut dicitur iter tenentes inter interpretendum ita se mediocriter habere decet ut

neutrum in partem declinare ac propendere videantur. Hac enim ab eis si diligenter et accurate quale et quantum sit hoc ipsum interpretendi onus consideraverint divina presertim omissis philosophis. Hac inquam ab eis sacrarum scripturarum auctoritas in primis non iniuria exigere et postulare existimabitur.'

106. Ibid., f. 107v, '... quod divina sacrarum scripturarum misteria illis celitus innotuisse putentur. Qua quidem abstrusarum rerum revelatione illustrati ita interpretari posse videbantur, ut primos scriptores divinitus intellexisse et enuntiasse perceperant atque ob hanc solam causam a recto idoneorum fidorumque interpretum offitio tam procul recesisse non immerito excusantur.'

107. Ibid., ff. 107v–8r, 'Ego enim de cunctis aliarum rerum in alia idiomata interpretibus ita sentio ut cuncta queque aliorum auctorum scripta, sacris litteris duntaxat exceptis, pro libero voluntatis suorum interpretum arbitrio primorum scriptorum sensu tantummodo servato diversimode tamen ut dictum est traduci possent et valeant. Ceterum sacra scriptura ob divinam eius in omnibus auctoritatem que nec fallit nec fallitur solemnem quandam et accuratam, gravem atque affectatam, interpretationem vel maxime et in primis exigere et postulare videtur. Non tamen ita ad verbum fit conversio ut exinde declarationis et intelligentie gratia plerumque non recedat, nec ita vaga ac lasciva sit oportet ut procul abesse videatur, atque nunquam cum nova addat tum vetera pretermittat nec plura alia diversimode libuerit intepretur et exprimat....'

108. Jerome, op. cit., col. 576, 'Ex quibus universis perspicuum est, Apostolos et Evangelistas in interpretatione veterum Scripturarum, sensum quaesisse, non verba: nec magnopere de ordine sermonibusque curasse, dum intellectui res pateret.'

109. Manetti, op. cit. [Urb. lat. 5], f. 108r–v, 'Cur ecclesia Romana in orationibus privatis et publicis Septuaginta Psalterii interpretationem in diuturno et universali usu alterius Hieronymi de Hebraica veritate traductioni usque adeo pretulisse videtur? ... presertim cum in priori illa ac vetustiori multa addita, plurima omissa, nonnulla aliter conversa, certa quemadmodum supra tertio et quarto libro singillatim ostendimus. In altero vero vel nihil vel pauci huiusmodi reperiantur ... ut una sola et non plures interpretatio videretur. Unde cum hoc humanis viribus fieri et provenire non potuerit, a spiritu sancto facta et celebrata fuisse creditur. Ultimo propter carminum sonoritatem versuum concinnitatem. Illa enim septuaginta interpretatio carminum sonantiora ac concinniora et ecclesiasticis cantibus ac symphoniis accomodatiora quam altera Hieronymi consensu omnium continere videtur.'

110. Cf. above, Part II, Chapter VIII. Of course, Ficino and Pico also wrote Biblical commentaries and were known for their emphasis on the dignity of man.

111. Bibl. Vatic., Cod. Ottob. lat. 438, ff. 1–178v, and Cod. Ottob. lat. 121,

ff. 2r–241v [defective at beginning and end], *In sacram Hebreorum historiam.* Ott. lat. 438, f. 9r, [Ott. lat. 121, f. 11r, numeration of cod. 121 will be given from now on in brackets], Lippi Brandolini Epithomas In Sacram Judeorum Historiam ex volumine quam bibliam appellant et Josephe Historico Fidelissimo, Ad Reverendissimum patrem et dominum: D. Franciscum Picolomineum Cardinalem Senensem. Kristeller, *Iter* II, p. 425, on Ott. lat. 438, 'Probably the dedication copy'.

112. Cf. E. Wind, 'Maccabean Histories in the Sistine Ceiling', *Italian Renaissance Studies* (ed. E. F. Jacob), London, 1960, pp. 312–17.
113. Ottob. lat. 438, f. 9v [121:11r].
114. Ibid., f. 27v [36r], 'De servitute et calamitatibus Hebreorum Capitulum I.'
115. I will not recapitulate the table of contents. The books listed run from f. 9v to f. 139r [11r–198r].
116. Esdra, f. 141v [201r]; 143r [202v]: Cap. V, 'De his qui seguente libro continentur – Hinc usque ad libri finem eadem repetuntur. De reditu Iudeorum et templi restitutione: quae libro primo descripta sunt. Quae quidem facile me adducunt ut credam hunc librum ab Esdra scriptum non esse. . . . Sequitur liber Esdrae que ab aliis secundus ab aliis tertius appellatur. Qui quoniam partim querelas templorum, partim collucationes angelicas continet; redigi in epithoma non potest. Eo igitur omisso ad proxima descendimus.'
117. Ibid., f. 143r–53r [202v–12r].
118. Ibid., f. 153r [213r], 'Sequuntur libri Salomonis et prophetarum qui magna ex parte vel precepta vitae vel vaticinia et oracula divina continent. Rerum gestarum explicatio in illis aut nulla aut exigua est. Nos itaque preceptis oraculisque omissis, quae mutari religio est, quod in singulis est historiae persequemur, rerum notitiae consulentes.'
119. Ibid., ff. 153r–78v [ff. 213r–41v in middle of cap. 4 of II Macchabees, remainder of MS is missing].
120. Ibid., f. 2r [121 first folium missing] '. . . prefatio: In qua huius operis scribendi causas commemorat: seque adversus eius rei criminatores defendit.'
121. Ibid., f. 2r.
122. Ibid., f. 2v, 'me facturum putavi, si ea que erant ab antiquissimis illis Iudeis auctoribus plebeia quadam simplicitate et in concinna verborum copia ante conscripta, et a nostris postea ita ut erant vulgi gratia necessaria translata. Ego in unum quasi corpus collecta et brevius et ornatus explicarem. . . .'
123. Ibid., f. 2v, '. . . que enim ita posita erant, neque ab omnibus libenter legi, neque memoria facile retineri posse videbantur. Immo multas ab sui lectione partim propter longitudinem deterrebant, partim propter inconcinnitatem avocabant. Qui vero ea semel legerant, neque repetere propter lectionis tedium laboremque volebant. Itaque quum scirem nihil esse tam orridum tamque incultum (ut inquit Cicero) quod non

splendesceret oratione et tanquam excoleretur, tentare volui an addere aliquam pulcherrimis rebus lucem ornata et venustate orationis possem; effecique ex universa illa quae in sacro volumine continetur historia quoddam quasi epithoma, quod esset et ad res memoria retinendas propter brevitatem accommoditatum, et ad legentium voluptatem propter orationis gratiam non iniocundam.'

124. Ibid., f. 2v, 'Ea vero quibus vel vaticinia prophetarum, vel vitae precepta continebantur, que quidem quum in singulis verbis misticos sensus haberent aliter dici poterant omnino non attigi.'

125. Ibid., f. 2v, '. . . et tamen illorum semper auctoritate nitebatur, Ego, qui discernere inter eos et iudicare verum non possem, ut plenior perfectiorque haberetur omnium rerum noticia et fides penes auctores esset, utramque in dubiis rebus opinionem posui, ratus hos labores nostros prodesse multis, nemini obesse aut displicere posse.'

126. Ibid., ff. 2v–3r [121 begins in media, f. 2r], 'Verum mihi multo aliter quam putabam evenit, nonnulla enim ex eorum genere hominum que et sacrarum sibi rerum scientiam vendicant [Ott. lat. 121 begins here] et a litteris nostris abhorrent, ubi me hoc opus inchoasse audierunt invidia pariter arrogantiaque adducti, magno in nos impetu atque ardore in surrexere modisque omnibus nostrum hoc studium summi etiam pontificis auctoritate addita impedire, et ea que ad id tempus scripta fuerant abolere conati sunt, novam fieri Bibliam, veteremque ob id neglectum iri clamitantes, Ieronimi verba immutari nefas esse, neque licere eum qui in Theologia doctorum ornamenta atque insignia non accepisset quiquam omnino sacrarum rerum conscribere. Neque vero extreme sortis homines sed trium summorum ordinum principes haec dictitabant.'

127. My only evidence is the following passage with which he continues ibid.: 'Sed repressa tandem est improborum hominum invidiorumque perversitas cum mansuetudine atque equitate Pontificis maximi, tum vero tua, Francisce doctissime tuorumque collegarum prudentia atque doctrina. Cognitaque huius operis utilitate mihi scribendi quicquid videretur potestas est facta. Absolvi itaque primo quoque tempore quam inchoaveram invitis obtrectatoribus rerum ebrearum historiam, tuoque sacratissima nomini dedicavi quem quidem et harum rerum doctissimum et nostri amantissimum esse sciebam.'

128. Ibid., f. 3r [f. 2r–v].

129. Ibid., f. 3r [f. 2v], 'Dicunt igitur primum nobis qui Theologie (ut ipsi appellant) doctores non simus in sacris rebus quiquam non licere. Hoc enim proprium munus esse eorum atque ipsis tantum scribendi ius esse, aliis non esse.'

130. Ibid., f. 3r–v [f. 2v], 'Deinde si cetera scribere maxime liceat, sacrum tamen Biblie volumen in quo omnia nostre religionis misteria contineantur, aliis quam sit scriptum verbis, aut alio stilo scribi aut omnino mutari

nefas esse. Misteria enim non in rebus ipsis tantum, sed in singulis quoque verbis contineri. Hoc autem modo perverti veterem Bibliam novamque fieri, non excerpi historias, aut brevius eadem explicari.'

131. Ibid., f. 3v [2v], 'Postremo res sacras elegantiori stilo aut cultiora oratione scribendas non esse. Quippe quae non ad doctos modo viros sed ad imperitam etiam plebem atque adeo ad omnem aetatem sexumque pertineant. Que autem omnium salutis intersint, ab omnibus quoque intelligi oportere. Quod si ea splendorem orationis elegantiamque desiderassent, Jeronimum Ciceronis usque ad vitium amatorem a quo ea essent translata, id et facere optime potuisse et libentissime fuisse facturum.' Brandolini, it is evident, was taking quite a different position from Manetti's defence of himself and Jerome as translators *pene ad verbum*. Brandolini is in fact arguing for a literary not a literal Bible.

132. Ibid., f. 4r–v [ff. 2v–3v].

133. Ibid., ff. 4v–5r [f. 3v], 'Non debet hec scribendi vis magis doctoris esse quam docti. At est theologorum non oratorum proprium de divinis rebus perscribere? Ego vero a vobis primum quero qui magis haec materia theologorum quam oratorum sit propria, quum oratores divina et humana omnia sibi subiecta ad dicendum habeant, et ut queque latissime patent ita maxime oratori conveniant? Deinde quid prohibeat me et oratorem et theologum esse? Discipline enim omnes inter se coniuncte et cognate sunt adeo ut qui unam quampiam absolute consequi velit, omnes quoddammodo attingere atque ad se attrahere compellatur. Postremo qui suspicemini me non esse Theologum quum sciatis me Christianum esse, et de Deo non modo loqui non imperite, quod theologi nomen efficit, verum etiam non inscite scribere videatis?'

134. Ibid., f. 5r [f. 6r], 'Quae enim materia per immortalem Deum potest esse ad scribendum aptior, que Christiano homini melior, que Christiano dignior quam ea quae omnia nostrae religionis, nostrae salutis continet fundamenta? Nonne haec omnibus modis, omnibus auctoribus, omnibus linghuis, ut longe lateque ad omnes nationes perveniat, vulganda et diffundenda est? Quis in hac re potest, non dico ulla ex parte damnari sed non etiam summopere commendari?'

135. Ibid., f. 5r–v [f. 6r–v], '. . . ut si pro pane triticum. . . . Si autem vos in eo me reprehenditis quod sacras historias alio quam sunt scriptae stilo atque oratione explicaverim, idque mutari aut innovari Bibliam appellatis, cur potius Ieronimum et alios interpretes non reprehenditis, qui non modo alia oratione sed alia quoque lingua haec eadem expresserunt? At illi in diversa lingua eadem verba servaverunt. Ego in eadem lingua sententias easdem servavi, quod si mutare orationem non licet, ne linguam quidem licet.'

136. Ibid., f. 5v [f. 6v].

137. Ibid., ff. 5v–6r [Ott. lat. 121 has leaf out of order here: f. 6v–5r], 'Ego cur idem facere non possim nulla numerorum aut sillabarum necessitate

astrictus? aut si hoc illis facere versu licuit, cur mihi soluta oratione non liceat? Atque illi quidem omnes Christi res gestas, omnia precepta, in quibus nostra salus universa fidesque continetur prosecuti sunt. Ego neque vatum predicationes quae misticos sensus continent, neque Salomonis precepta que privata quoddammodo scripta sunt, attingere volui, quod si illorum scripta non modo non rejiciuntur, sed ab omnibus quoque summa cum auctorum laude expetuntur nostra cur hac nomine repudiari possint non video. Si vos illorum scripta improbatis, nostra quoque improbetis plane volo. Malo enim tantis auctoribus errare quam vobiscum bene sentire. Nos igitur qui sacras historias et culta et dilucida oratione explicamus Bibliam innovamus: vos qui eam barbaris commentationibus corrumpitis, intactam inviolatamque servatis. Nos qui res gestas orationis splendore et claritate illustramus, Bibliam obscuram reddimus; vos qui omnia barbarie caligine et opinionum multitudine atque obscuritate involuitis, ea vestro iudicio declaratis atque illustratis. Videte queso, videte ne istud potius sacra volumina corrumpere atque immutare sit; vos potius qui novas quotidie atque inanes veteribus scriptis opiniones astrictis, sacra volumina depravatis.' Cf. above, pp. 568–70 and this chapter n. 12.

138. Ibid., f. 6r [121: f. 5r–v], 'Vos vestra ignorantia res sacras confunditis, vos inquam vestra barbaria non modo Bibliam sed universam quoque theologiam foedatis atque pervertitis. Proinde a nobis Biblia nostra oratione immutata dicatur, modo eam a vobis vestris commentatiunculis constet esse depravatam atque corruptam. Sit sane id quod nos agimus Bibliam innovare, modo sciatis vos eam perdere atque abolere.'

139. Ibid., f. 6r–v [f. 5v–7r, skipping f. 6r–v] 'Sacre inquunt res nitore orationis non egent. Que enim omnibus scripta sunt, ab omnibus quoque intelligi posse necesse est. Quasi vero aut hec intelligi ab omnibus non possunt, aut illa legere homines prohibeantur. O summam atque intolerabilem hominum ignorantiam ne dicam? An ne invidiam? An ne utranque? Quis obsecro futurus est qui haec nostra non intelligat preter vos, qui nisi quae a vestra similibus scripta sunt, aliud omnino nihil intelligitis? Nam alios ex vobis iudicatis, vestrique omnes quam simillimos esse creditis, ut quae vos non intelligitis, ipsi quoque intellecturi non sunt? Nonne haec Latina, nonne propria nonne usitata verba sunt? Quid nos? nonne sub hoc caelo, in hac lingua, nati omnes et educati sumus? Quid obsecro cui vis facilius esse debet quam linguam patriam intelligere? Quid gratius quam eam omni tempore atque in omni disciplina posse lecitare? An expectamus ut Germani eam Scitheque intelligant? quamquam ipsi quoque illam hodie (si diis placet) et studiosius legunt et frequentius accuratiusque perdiscunt. Latina igitur scripta a nostris potissimum et legenda et intelligenda sunt. Sed nimirum vos ut a nostris moribus, ita a lingua maxime aborretis, aliosque item aborrere existimatis.'

140. Ibid., f. 6v [f. 7r], 'Sed esto vulgus nostra non intelligat. Quis obsecro

cogit quemquam ut hec legat, vel illa non legat? Habet vulgus qua erudiatur, qua delectetur in sacris rebus lectione illa perfruatur. Hanc eruditioribus cultioribusque relinquat, ut enim vulgus intelligere haec cultiora non potest, ita eruditi simpliciora illa legere et longiora non possunt.'

141. Ibid., f. 6v [f. 7r], 'At negligentur pro istis vetustiora illa et sanctiora volumina. Primum quidem si verum istud esset haberem ipse quod cuperem, ut mala nostra scripta non essent. Nam si illa quae optima esse nemo dubitat nostrarum gratia negligerentur, mala profecto nostra non essent; mala enim bonis si modo sanus est prefert nemo. Deinde qui possunt illa pro nostri omitti, quum haec neque omnia (ut vos ipsi fatemini) intelligantur, neque omnia quae sunt in illis scripta contineant.' Reverting to sentence preceding this passage, 'Huc accedit, quod nos non omnia complexi sumus sed ea tantum quae historiam texere posse videbantur, cetera qui volet ab illis archetypis accipiat necesse est.'

142. Ibid., f. 7r–v [ff. 7v–8r], 'Sin aliqua inest huic rei dignitas, aliquod ornamentum, quod homines expetere aut admirari debeant, id profecto universum in res divinas quibus omnis mortalium honos studiumque debetur conferendum est . . . immo nonnisi his demum adhibitis ornamentis eam quam habent a natura pulchritudinem aut ostendere aut retinere satis possunt; nonne illis divinae res illustrari atque excoli; immo sine illis enuntiari atque efferri non posse existimande sunt?'

143. Ibid., f. 7v [f. 8r–v], 'Vis autem in persuadendo quanto sit orationis, neminem dubitare arbitror. Quis est enim tam hebeti tamque obtuso ingenio, qui non animum his eloquentiae viribus in omnes flecti partes atque his tanquam frenis parere intelligat? Quis est vel natura tam ferreus tamque inhumanus, vel huic facultati tam inimicus tamque infensus qui non se ab ea ad omnes affectus moveri et quodammodo compelli fateatur?'

144. Ibid., ff. 7v–8r [f. 8v], 'Quippe cuius finis persuadere et officium apte dicere ad persuadendum sit, nihilque sit tam incredibile quod dicendo (ut ait Cicero) non fiat probabile. Divinae vero res quae nostram omnem non modo fidem verum etiam cogitationem excedunt, quo pacto sine summa vi dicendi et copia orationis vel scribi vel pronuntiari queant ut populo probentur non video. Quis enim est tanta animi facilitate qui cum audit vel hominem sine coitu natum de virgine, vel totum Christi corpus in exiguis hostie figuris conclusum esse, vel tres in una substantia esse personas, et quae nostri dogmatis positiones sunt, facile adduci possit ut credat? Summa profecto vi dicendi et infinita quadam orationis copia ad haec persuadendo opus est, quam quidem prestare nisi eloquentia non potest. Est igitur (ut videtis) eloquentia cum ob eam quam affert rebus dignitatem ac speciem tum ob eam quam habet in persuadendo vim divinis rebus vel maxime necessaria.'

145. Cf. Valla's discussion of the Trinity in his *Repastinatio*, above, Part I,

Chapter III, pp. 154–5, and his discussion of the Eucharist below, Chapter XIII, pp. 633–8.

146. Brandolini, op. cit., f. 8r [f. 9r], 'Quid himni, orationes, lectiones, et caetera quibus hodie in universa re divina utimur; nonne et omnia pene elegantissima sunt, et a dissertissimis viris conscripta? Immo (si verum accuratius discutiamus) nihil in illis non tersum et elegans reperitur, nisi quod a vobis et vestris similibus postea per summam audaciam atque importunitatem est additum, adeo ut liquido appareat quicquid in rebus divinis corruptum est, a vestra barbaria et ignorantia esse corruptum.'

147. Ibid., f. 8r–v [f. 9r], 'Cur igitur Bibliam transtulit sine ullo verborum lepore ornatuque Ieronimus? nempe quia sic apud Hebreos scriptam reperiebat. Quum autem eo tempore permulti verum ipsum omnia ex parte oppugnarent, eaque de causa frequentes adversus religionem nostram secte uno quoque Bibliam suo arbitratu interpretante insurgerent, necesse fuit cum ut aliena confutari, tum ut nostra confirmari possent; ita Latinae sonare Bibliam, ut Grece Ebreiceque sonabat, verbaque nostra singula singulis illorum verbis suo ordine respondere, adeo ut in ea interpretatione Jeronimus qui ad linguem omnia cupiebat exprimere, ipsius etiam grammatices leges ac fines egredi non dubitaret. Sed quod tunc instantibus adversariis dubiisque rebus nostris necessario faciendum fuit, nunc sublatis illis, statuque confirmato, servandum non est. Causa enim sublata effectus quoque ipse e vestigio tollitur.' Thus, again, he seems to come forth with opposite arguments to Manetti's plea for a new literalism.

148. Ibid., ff. 8v–9r [ff. 9r–10r].

149. Ibid., f. 9r [f. 10r], 'Ego vero pontifici maximo promisissem me hoc opus nonnisi ex doctissimorum virorum consilio publicaturum.'

150. Cf. Chapter XVI below, and Part III, Chapter X above [for discussion of Pico's *Heptaplus*].

151. Eugenio Garin, 'Ricerche su Giovanni Pico della Mirandola, II, Il commento ai Salmi', *La cultura filosofica*, op. cit., pp. 241–53, p. 246.

152. Garin, ibid. Cf. also Cassuto, *Gli Ebrei*, op. cit., pp. 282–323. Cf. also Garin's notes to his edition of the *Heptaplus*, op. cit. On Pico in general cf. Part III, Chapter X, n. 5 above, pp. 793–4.

Notes to Part IV, Chapter XIII

1. Reliably reviewed and summarised in *Dictionnaire de Théologie Catholique*, s.v. 'Confession', III, Paris, 1923, cols. 828–974; 'Penitence', XII, Paris, 1933, cols. 722–1138; 'Eucharistie', T. V., Paris, 1924, cols. 989–1368. We shall deal only with these two sacraments.

2. B. L. Ullman, ed., Sicco Polenton, *Scriptorum illustrium latinae linguae*, Rome, 1928.

3. Cf. Arnaldo Segarizzi, *La Catinia, le Orazioni e le Epistole di Sicco Polenton, umanista Trentino del secolo XV*, Bergamo, 1899, p. xliii.
4. Segarizzi, p. xvii, gives his birth as *ca.* 1376. He states in his preface that he wrote this work in his sixtieth year [f. 1r]. *De confessione Christiana*, Bibl. Vat. lat. 7781. Donato's dates as bishop of Padua, Segarizzi, p. xlvi. Segarizzi lists, p. lxxxiv, the following other mansucripts of this work: Bibl. Antoniana di Padova, scaff. XXII, 565; Modena, Bibl. Estense, Cod. Est. lat. VII F 17; Venice, Bibl. Marciana, Marc. lat. cl. III, 81, (2772); Marc. lat. cl. III, 82, (2773); Marc. lat. cl. III, 137 (2239) (cf. Kristeller, *Iter*, II, 218). Kristeller, *Iter*, I, p. 373, also lists Modena, Bibl. Est. Cod. 914 (Alpha S 9 14). I do not know if this is a different MS from the Estense listed by Segarizzi. References, as stated will be to Vat. lat., 7781 (cf. Kristeller, *Iter*, II, 343): f. 1r Siconis Polentoni *Liber Confessionis Christianae* Primus Incipit Ad Patrem Reverendissimum Dominum Petrum Donatum Episcopum Padovanum, Inc. 'Levavi oculos meos in montes'; Expl. f. 76v, 'dominus custodiat te, dominus protectio tua super manum dexteram tuam. Amen.'
5. Ibid., f. 2r–v, 'Neque vero sum nescius provinciam hanc et difficilem et amplam esse candemque ad me nullo professionis voce verum summos ad doctores pontificie legis et claros ad theologos pertinem atque ipsorum a multis copiose ac doctissime pertractatam. Sed quanquam sit eorum sine dubio propria, futurum tamen spero quod erit a nobis ipsorum quasi virentissimo e prato floribus recollectis ea cum lege ac moderatione scripta. . . . Nihil enim nostro ut dici solet e capite sed quae sancti patres quae pontifices summi quae magni theologi senciunt me opte arbitrio disposui atque uti sunt, nostris modo verbis et ordine memoravi . . . quae patefaciunt viam, qua possimus qui peccatores sumus et acerbas inferni devitare poenas, et quam desideramus quisque vitam assequi sempiternam? Confessione quidem si omni sit cum integritate perfecta et qui est peccator peccati mundatur sorde et qui Deus est summe iustus, ad misericordiam inclinatur. . . .'
6. Ibid., ff. 2v–3r, '. . . dicendi autem genus dialogi forma erit.'
7. Ibid., f. 5r, 'Sic enim et quibus in rebus peccet homo et quibus remediis liberetur a peccato cognosces. His namque in duobus, si animadvertis plane, consistit omnis ratio confitendi.'
8. Aug. *De poenitentia*, his *Sermo de poenitentia*, Migne, *P.L.* 39, col. 2215, seems to be reasonably close to this reference.
9. Vat. lat. 7781, ff. 6v–7r, 'Peccatum enim quod esse morbum animae occultum intelligit aperit sacerdoti datque veniae spem quae fit canonice facta confessio. Huius vero formula duplex habetur, una implicita est ac generalis, altera explicita et singularis. Superiori utitur Sacerdos saepe presertim cum est celebraturus ad altare missam delet ista quae peccata sunt minima et venalia appellantur. Altera peccatum mortale fugat. Cum peccator quae mortalia egit peccata Confessori singulatim et

canonice confitetur. Quippe bona utraque atque scienda, sed quae mortale peccatum extinguit ea ponderatius est accuratiusque ac diligentius observanda.'

10. Ibid., f. 8r, 'Hominum autem generi quod Dei benignitatis ad imaginem formavit suam inque prope sanctis Angelis adaequavit caeli fuit porta per diu clausa atque ita clausa quod nemo omnium quamvis bonus vir ac propheta sanctus caelos intraret.'
11. Ibid., ff. 9r–10r.
12. Ibid., ff. 10v–12v, cit. f. 12v, 'Nempe si audires huiusmodi omnia que multa et infinita sunt ac privatos inter theologos disputantur doctior fortasse inde caeteras ad res. . . .'
13. Ibid., ff. 12v–14v, cit. f. 14r–v, 'Quippe viam hanc Dominus dedit universis qua mundati peccatis ascendere ad caelos eternam assequi gloriam possit Christianus quisque si modo rite colat eum fidei sciat ac credat articulos sit humilis corde. . . . Quid enim facilius quam te delicti poenitere tui? . . . Quid iustius, quid aequius, quid convenientius quam humiliare nos Deo? quam Domino obedire? quam nos confiteri ac poenitere pecasse? Adde premium atque considera quod vita hinc confitentibus datur eterna, qua nihil potest melius peti, nihil salubrius dari, nihil preciosius haberi. . . . In quo videas Deum summa in maiestate ac suo in trono sedentem, videas clementissimam Deigenitricem et immaculatam virginem Mariam, videas angelorum choros . . .'
14. Ibid., ff. 15r–17v.
15. Ibid., ff. 17v–25r.
16. Ibid., ff. 25v–9r, cit. f. 26v, 'Peccatum vero id esse actuale tradunt quod agimus ipsi, nec primi parentis culpa, sed nostro vitio ac libera voluntate peccamus. Quippe voluntarium est omne peccatum. . . .' Cit., ff. 28v–9r, 'Committimus enim ipsa quotidie nec hominum esse putatur quisque adeo prudens adeoque modestus et iustus quod ea devitare ita queat. . . . Vita enim nostra non esse sine peccato saltem venialia potest. Nempe tanta est generis humani fragilitas totque nobis insidiatur laqueis Inimicus.'
17. Ibid., ff. 29r–30r. Cf. *Dictionnaire de Théologie Catholique*, XII, Part I, s.v. 'Péché,' cols. 190–275, but it does not cover this distinction since it is a review of doctrine strictly from a Thomistic point of view.
18. Ibid., ff. 30r–2r, cit., f. 30r–v, 'Quid si nulla cum deliberatione nullaque cum delectatione nec libere voluntatis consensu sed ut fit quandoque causa fortuita aut violentia seu mentis exagitate quodam subitaneo impetu aut per ignorantiam vel oblivionem peccat homo?' Cit., ff. 31v–2r, 'Homo autem ad Deum colendum atque ut homo homini prosit ac serviat creatus est. Illi vero peccant venialiter qui quanquam opes ac fortunae bona desiderent, ea tamen moderatione et gravitate desiderent quod adeo non recedent nec quae sint mundi magis quam Deum colant, ament, desiderent.'

19. Ibid., ff. 32r–3v.
20. Ibid., f. 34r, 'Quid si ago quiquam quod vere laudabile sit ac honestam, sed utrum honestum sit an turpe mente sum dubius? – Peccas utique quod illam ob dubitationem inesse rei turpitudo aliqua videatur.'
21. Ibid., f. 34r–v.
22. Ibid., ff. 35r–9r. Cf. M. W. Bloomfield, *The Seven Deadly Sins*, 1952.
23. Ibid., f. 39r–v.
24. Ibid., f. 40r.
25. Ibid., ff. 40r–52v.
26. Ibid., ff. 40v–6v.
27. Ibid., ff. 42v–3r, 'Non enim considerant se tot opibus tanto donatu, ipso a Deo et hominibus donatos esse, non considerant se beneficia, liberalitate, gratia Dei, ex nihilo aliquid atque homines non beluas, Christianos non paganos, neque Iudeos factos esse, non considerant se merito amarissime passionis ac durae mortis nostri domini Jesu Christi perpetua et infernali poena liberatas ac demonum de potestate redemptas esse.'
28. Ibid., ff. 43v–6v.
29. Ibid., ff. 44v–5r, 'Hi namque communem non sequitur vitam, sed opinione moribus omni denique vivendi lege sunt a ceteris alieni. Quippe quas indicit vigilias ac festa sacerdos, nullo pacto custodiunt. Ieiuniant iniussi, diem totam dormiunt, noctem agunt in somnem que instituta sunt maiorum probatusque veterum leges, ac bonos civitatis mores spernunt, reprobant, lacerant, novos eosdemque pravos ac ridiculos inducunt vivendi ritus. Quae alii bona esse fatentur et laudant, ea fronte aperta hi negant atque vituperant. Nihil sibi quod aliis placet, suapte vivunt arbitrio, atque ita vivunt quod nati, educati, nutriti alio quodam sub celo alienique a peregrini sua in patria videantur.' Cf. S. Bernardi *De gradibus humilitatis*, Cap. XIV.
30. Op. cit., ff. 53v–4r.
31. Ibid., ff. 55v–6r.
32. Ibid., ff. 56v–60r.
33. Ibid., ff. 60v–1v.
34. Ibid. ff. 61v–3r, cit. 63r, 'Tanta enim cum prudentia ratione sanctitate vivit nemo, ut non interdum fragilitas humana labatur ac saepe proximum aliquando etiam Deum summum non offendat.'
35. Ibid., ff. 63v–4v.
36. Ibid., ff. 65r–6v, 'Enim vero quae egimus peccata, maxima sunt cum diligentia ad memoriam ut integer fiat confessio, reducenda, qualiaque et quanta sint consideranda. Multa enim et magna longeque plura et maiora quam putemus sunt. Adire vero Confessorem qui et Pater est ac gubernator animae Christianae et Dei vices in terris gerit. . . . Sed fatear ultro quod Deus sit misericors. Ipsi quoque non negabunt illum etiam iustum esse, atque illud dicam verum esse quod illi facile peccata recordantur sua riteque ac canonice confitentur, qui eandem in recendis

peccatis quam suis in faciendis diligentiam habent, atque ut debet Christianus quisque magis celestia quam terrena desiderant.'

37. Ibid., f. 66v–7r, 'Summum enim studium summa vigilantia summa cura ad opes hinc augendos inde retinendos inest mortalibus quae autem tanti facis ac rem divinam inspiciunt, ea veluti superflua et vana curant parum, ac prope negligunt prorsus qui summe confidant in misericordia Dei. Audiuntque ipsum summe pium ac misericordem esse eundemque vitam non mortem querere peccatoris. Ecclesiae vero satisfactum putant si confessorem adeunt modo et genu flexu quae aut occurrunt memoriar aut investigant Confessor peccata dicunt sua.'
38. Ibid., ff. 68r–70r.
39. Cf. above, pp. 200–2 ,pp. 262–9 and pp. 35, 195–6.
40. Op. cit., f. 72r–v.
41. Ibid., ff. 73r–5v.
42. Ibid., f. 75v, 'Questiunculas huiusmodi quod ut meapte arbitrio nunc loquar ita, mille milia centena ac pene innumerabiles sint, si perquisieris passim, multas ac infinitas invenies. Sunt enim doctissimorum theologum libri talium questionum pleni. Est quidem confitendi ratio infinita et ad eam trahi quae habetur sacris in litteris omnis disputatio ac doctrina possit. Atque illud esse verum constat quod plurique docti et graves viri qui hac de re sunt accurate locuti, cum se multa explicasse ac nihil sibi quod dicerent, superesse putarint, parum multum dixisse inventi sint quod amplissima de re omnia dicere possit nemo. Est quidem principium facile sed difficile exitum invenire.'
43. Cf. Appendix II, No. 9, of my 'A Humanist's Image of Humanism: The Inaugural Orations of Bartolommeo della Fonte', *Studies in the Renaissance*, VII (1960), pp. 128–9, for a listing of MSS and editions. Additional information on another MS below.
44. Cf. Concetto Marchesi, *Bartolommeo della Fonte*, Catania, 1900, p. 30.
45. Cf. opening of first version, Vat. lat. 13679, 'Iohannis histrigomensis archiepiscopi nuper crebris litteris et nuntiis invitatus ut ad se in Pannoniam profisceret cum aliquod munusculum deferre mecum statuissem, proximis diebus scripsi in dialogo de penitentia; librum unum . . .' [f. 270v]. Cf. P. B. Gams, *Series episcoporum ecclesiae catholicae*, Ratisbon, 1873, p. 380.
46. Oxford, Bodleian, D'Orville 59 (Western 16937), ff. 226v–35r; Perugia, Bibl. Communale, Cod. 706 (I 100), ff. 289v–301v; Bibl. Vatic., Vat. lat. 13679, ff. 270v–8v, fragmentary at end.
47. Hain, 7227, 7228, 7229; Wolfenbüttel, Cod. 43 Aug. Fol. ff. 118v–30v.
48. Bib. Laur. Cod. Ashb. 918 (849), ff. 95–115. The Pandolfini ownership is indicated on flyleaf.
49. The cancelled folios are f. 96v and 101r, leaving ff. 97, 98, 99 and 100 missing in between. There is evidence of the excision also.

50. Cf. Lad. Juhàsz, ed. *Bartholomei Fontii Epistolarum libri III*, Budapest, 1931, Ep. I, 19, pp. 18–22.
51. Ibid., 'Etsi eam peccatis onustam putem in Tartareos fluctus demergi ac perpetuo supplicio cruciari, quando, quae de inferis scripta sunt, ad nostram emendationem, ne cupiditatibus moveremur, fabulosa dicta nonulli putent.' I do not suggest that this letter contains the missing passage, but rather takes off from it, and echoes some of the decipherable lines crossed out at the beginning and end.
52. 43 Aug. Fol., ff. 118v–19v.
53. Ibid., f. 120r, 'Verum quisquis erratorum dolore hoc addicitur, non solum pro quibus dolendum sit in posterum non committere, sed ut novis meritis aliquam maiorem gratiam consequatur, recte quoque etiam semper aget.'
54. Ibid., f. 120r–v, 'Quae tamen quomodo a quibusdam aliis sit descripta et cuius modi esse debeat non me praeterit. Nam si quae debet fuerit poenitudo, omnis eas profecto partis, quas illi compunctionis, confessionis, satisfactionis, charitatis attribuunt, continebit. Quanquam etiam interdum, si aut sacerdos aut unde restituatur ablatum desit, ea recte quidem fieri possit. Deus enim non labiorum aut manuum opera, si non possumus, sed solum voluntatem requirit. In iudicio nanque cordis et intentione affectionis et mentis, quae vera poenitentia est, consistit.'
55. Ibid., ff. 120v–1r, 'Nam aut amore fit, aut metu, aut ostentatione. Sed omnium longe deterrimi sunt, ut aliis sanctissimi videantur, poeniteniam simulantes. Hi enim a quorum officio longe distant, boni viri existementur, clara oratione verba sua in templa pronuntiant, detecta capita nunc deprimunt, nunc attolunt, modo pectus et labia quatiunt, ut sub hac virtutis specie decipere facilius omnes queant. Verum enimvero non est haec poenitentia, sed fallacia quaedam ad homines capiendos et Dei contemptio nuncupanda. Non enim talis alludens toga, non barba promissa, non capilli supercilio breviores, non deiecti ad terram occuli, non fictae lachrymae, non ora arte pallentia, sed cordis simplicitas, animique sinceritas veram poenitentiam praestunt.'
56. Cf. below, Chapter XIV, pp. 673–4.
57. Op. cit., f. 121r, 'Nam quae solum a timore procedit, nulla fide, spe, charitate munitur. Quare neque conscientiam purgat, neque crimina diluit, neque ullam veniam consequitur.'
58. Ibid., ff. 121r–2r, cit. f. 122r, 'Cum gemitu ergo et lachrymis, simplicitateque cordis, humilitateque mentis ac vera peccatorum confessione, et ablati restitutione ad Deum, si non ad homines possumus, vera poenitentia est agenda.'
59. Ibid., f. 122r, 'At que vere semel conversus fuerit?, vere quoque poenitens appellatur. Nanque hic non exterior actus ullus sed voluntas sola requiritur.'
60. Ibid., f. 122v, 'Nam Deus qui poenitenti veniam pollicetur, dilationem

temporis non permittit. Quin immo nulla alia re tantum offenditur, quam si cum deliquerimus, superbiamus et elati ac rigidi ad petendam veniam non flectamur.'

61. Ibid., f. 123r–v.
62. Ibid., ff. 124v–5v, 'Habeamus prae oculis geennae perpetuos cruciatus, et haec tempora illis cum temporibus comparemus. Velimus brevi deflere, ut perpetuo gaudeamus. Cupiditatum flama poenitentia sedemus, ut aeternos ignes effugiamus. . . . Brevis est autem praesens haec vita, etiam si annorum milia vixerimus ad aeterna collata. . . . Quid quaeso nunc opes et delitiae prosunt iis qui semper in malis voluptatibus cupidinibusque vixerunt? . . . Non ergo fragilibus et caducis vel corporis vel fortunae bonis, sed quae virtutes omnes exuperat, perfectae poenitentiae lachrymis oblectemur. Quam ut facilius agere et regnum Dei quaerere valeas, spectandus tibi semper Deus est et contemptis rebus terrenis omnibus, quae fluxae ac labiles sunt, toto animo ad caelestia incumbendum, neque magnopere de vita curandum, sed ultro illi pro veritate quae Deus est, aut pro Deo cum necessitas postulet occurendum. Servanda quoque in primis Dei mandata sunt. . . . Quis autem magis accipit verba eius quam is qui se corrigit et emendat? Hoc est enim verum et proprium verbum eius, ut quoniam non interdum peccare non possumus, cum lapsi fuerimus, erigamur, nosque ipsos a culpa revocemus.'
63. Ibid., ff. 125v–6r, 'Verum sunt quidam ita perversis moribus ut nihil audire, nihil legere, nihil probare velint, nisi quod aures blandiore sono permulceat. Quibus iure dicetur a Domino ultima illa die: Discedite a me omnes qui Christiani fuistis et sacras litteras legere neglexistis. Sed quamquam divinae scripturae nudae ac simplices esse debent, ut omnes aperte intelligant quae ad omnium salutem scribuntur, quosdam tamen habemus, quorum neque sermo incultus, neque incompta oratio est. Nam, ut reliquos taceam, quid ad Hieronymo, Augustino, Ambrosio, et Christianorum disertissimo Lactantio scribitur, in quo aut maiorem elegantiam desideremus aut ampliorem copiam expectamus?'
64. Ibid., f. 126v, '. . . nunc brevibus causam exponemus cur eam magis necessariam quam virtutes reliquas iudicemus.'
65. Ibid., ff. 126v–7; 'Nam siquis erratorum suorum rationem subducat, commissa doleat, profiteatur iniquitates suas, veniam suppliciter petat, errorem emendet, culpam corrigat, omnia statim debita remittuntur.' Cf. *Mat.* vii:7; *Luke* xi:9; *Luke* v:32; *Mat.* xi:28.
66. Ibid., ff. 127v–8r.
67. Ibid., ff. 128r–9r, 'Cum igitur ex iis quae vidimus animarum salutis causa poenitentia sit, qua nihil melius, nihil optatius, nihil felicius reperitur, ea profecto sine ullus controversia omni alia virtute iudicatur melior. Sed iam quod nos ultimo loco reseraturos promisimus, caeteris eam virtutibus praestare aperiamus. Illa mihi quidem virtus videtur sublimior quae si cui inest, reliquae quoque omnes in eo insunt. Ut enim totum

hominis corpus praestantius est quam separatim caput, humeri, pectus, manus, sic ea cunctis praestabit virtus, cui virtutes caeterae coniunguntur. . . . Eodem quoque modo inest vera prudentia poenitenti, quod praeteritorum recordatione nihil praeter rectum vult et facit, ne in ullum deflendum vitium rursus recidat.'

68. Ibid., f. 129r–v, 'Quicunque alii homines aut in ocio aut in negocio magna cum laude versati sunt, aliquod iniunctum virtutibus vitium habuerunt, ita ut recte Flacci sententia optimus existimari potuerit is qui minimis urgeretur. Solus vere poenitens omnium virtutum insignibus decoratus quodcunque vitium a se excludit. Nam ut caeteros Christianos qui innumeri sunt pertranseam, quo vel Petrus vel Paulus crimine se unquam post rite factam poenitentiam inquinarunt? Quando enim ii postea vinosi ut Cato, ut Aristoteles cupidi, ut Plato lascivii, ambitiosi ut Cicero extiterunt? O poenitentia igitur cum corpus unum virtutum omnium ac gymnasium sis, quid amplius de te referam?'
69. Florence, Bibl. Naz., Cod. Magl. 35, 20, ff. lxv bis r–c v. It corresponds to the later, revised version, *Donatus*, rather than to the earlier *De Poenitentia*, which suggests that the work was originally written in Latin and that the translation was an indication of its popularity.
70. Cf. the new preface to the re-issue of my *Adversity's Noblemen*, New York, 1965, pp. xii–xiv, xxi–xxiii, which is a translation of *Epist*. I, 18, 15–18 [Juhàsz, op, cit.].
71. *Sermo Laurentiae Vallae de mysterio Eucharistiae*, printed in *Lactantii opera*, Venice, 1521, ff. 158v–9r.
72. Cf. above Part I, Chapter III, section 3.
73. Op. cit., f. 158v, 'Scio ego plerosque Venerandi patres et cives egregi, qui ex hoc loco dixerunt de mysterio Eucharistiae in admiratione tanti sacramenti fuisse immoratos, dum aperire student atque ostendere quanta divinitas, quantum miraculum sit ut panis qui per nos ex tritico conficitur vi divinorum verborum ex sacerdotis ore prolatorum convertatur non solum in hominem sed quod omnem intellectum supergredi videtur in Deum. Post quae reliquam oratiunculae meae partem in laudibus huius sacramenti consumabo. Nam divina laudare quivis et potest et debet; illa vero investigare et eorum rationem reddere paucissimorum est perfectaeque sapientum. Etenim quo panis convertatur in Deum si nulla ratione probabilius facere possemus, tamen nihil nobis vel ad religionem vel ad divinam scientiam deesse existimare debemus, scientes fidem esse proprie cum nos Deo credimus, sicuti amico cuipiam, cuius veritatem cognitam habemus atque exploratam. Unde scriptum est, "Beati qui non viderunt et crediderunt." Quasi non intelligunt et credunt. Nam quod quivis videt quid speratur? Non enim credit alteri, sed sibi ipsi. Propterea de Abraham dictum est quod in spem praeter spem credidisset. Credit Abraham Deo et reputatum est illi ad iustitiam, ita nos ad iustitiam reputabitur, si fidem praeter fidem habuerimus.'

74. Ibid., 'Verum ut rationem quoque reddam, non video cur quibusdam tantopere hoc videatur incredibile, panem converti in Deum, quamquam nescio an in Deum panis, an Deus convertatur in panem, Deus tamen existens? Dicitur enim "Verbum caro factum est." Non autem caro facta est verbum. Et alibi. "Ego sum panis vitae qui de caelo descendi." Iam ante Eucharistiae sacramentum se panem vocat, quasi seipsum conversurus in panem. Hoc est pro pane se daturus. Sed accipite quonam modi id sit intelligendum. Filius Dei in mundum veniens sumsit ex intemeratissimo Virginis corpore, nescio an dicam carnem? Nam caro proprie dicitur quae liquida non est, sed ex carne, ut sic dicam nitidissimum florem. Quid dicis? Nonne caro illa sanctissima ex cibo facta est? Ita opinor. Quo ex cibo? Nempe ex pane. Neque enim sanctissimam Virginem ex carne victitasse credibile est. Ita fit ut prius panis, deinde caro fuerit id quod Dominus dum incarnatus est, delibavit. Quomodo anima homines animavit pariter et divinitate implevit. Eadem ratione panem sacrosancti altaris in carnem convertens seipsum, idest hominem Deumque infundit. Ideoque non video quid plus haec in altari quam illa in utero Virginis incarnatio habeat in credendo difficultatis atque miraculi.'

75. Ibid., ff. 158v–9r, 'At illam inquies semel fuit, haec vero quotidie et eadem tempore et plurimis in locis. Haec altera quaestio est et quae non solum ad hoc sacramentum pertineret. Quomodo enim idem Jesus et cum Apostolis in Hierusalem, et cum discipulis in via loquebatur? Quomodo est in caelo et inter homines? Sed ne altius quam vires meae ferunt volare videar, afferam exempla de medio. Cur vox mea in vestris omnium auribus est tota? Quomodo radius solis eodem puncto non dico medium aerem et extremum caeli uno icto contingit, sed pavimentum et tectum? Cum negare non possimus si vas aquae plenum, ut inquit Virgilius, accepto sole summi feri et laquearia tecti, quin prius sol aquam verberarit, quam aqua suo splendore reverberaverit tectum. Sed tamen videmus utrumque pariter fieri id quod posterius est factum esse posterius affirmare non possis. . . . Quis nescit unum hominem diversas partes eodem tempore non posse intueri? Idem crederemus in pictura, quae est hominis imago usu evenire, nec in ea posse contingere quod in ipso homine non contingit, et tamen id in multis picturis licet intueri. Quod nisi inspiceres nequaquam ad credendum verbis aut ratione induceris. Multa sunt huiusmodi admiranda in rebus humanis atque corporeis. Quanto debemus existimare in spiritalibus atque divinis admirabiliora? An ignoramus praesertim ratione dictante Deum ubique esse, et omnia esse in Deo? Nec fieri posse quin omnia quae sunt in eo persistant per quem existunt. Quare qui de hoc Dei adventu in mysterio panis ambigit, non divinam naturam sed hominis fragilitatem videtur cogitare. Maiore igitur animo de Deo cogitandum, sentiendum, loquendum est, quam ut eius omnipotentiam revocemus in dubium.'

76. Ibid., f. 159r, 'Quod maius a Deo dari nobis donum potuit quam ut seipsum donaret? Nempe seipsum. Et antequam illuc pergamus nos paradiso afficit. An non ipse vocari se voluit Emanuel, in nobiscum Deus? Si nobiscum est Deus, ut certe est, quo alio tendere velimus? Verum enim non praebet se nobis ille quidem sed nondum patefacta divinitate quia nondum capaces sumus contemplandae divinae maiestatis. In quam intuemur per speculum in aenigmate, tum pro certo habemus quod nobiscum est Deus defensor, adiutor, protector. Nec nobiscum modo, verum etiam intra nos. Quid optabilius dici et excogitari potest quam Deum manibus hominum contrectari? Ori admoveri? atque in intima pectoris recondi? Tandiu mansurum, quam diu hospitium domus nostrae purum mundanumque servabimus. Hoc autem sacramentum dominus noster Jesus Christus cum patribus olim in figura ostendisset discipulisque suis aliquandiu promisset, hodie in ultima ante obitum coena instituit, ut discipulos suos, immo et homines relicturus, tamen eos non relinqueret, nisi substituto in sui locum hoc sacramento per quod semper advenit, semper adest. Per quod nunquam recedit, ut non plus praebuerit angelis ascensionis cum se illis in caelo donavit, donavit perpetuo mansurum, quam hominibus cum hunc in modum nobiscum permanerent. O ineffabilem non modo mysterium, sed donum mortalibus datum, angelis enim cum pares simus quidem Jesum Christum quemadmodum et illi possidemus, tamen in hoc superiores censeri debemus, quod ex ore nostro id quod angelis non licet mysterium hoc sacramentumque conficitur.'
77. Ibid., 'Vere dictus Emanuel, nobiscum Deus, quae magis nobiscum quam cum angelis est. Neque ab re. Quoniam nobis quam angelis est ipse similior. Ex quo illud quoque intelligi licet quod Deus apud pias neque incredulas mentes ostendit, sicut panem illum convertit, sic nos in die iudicii convertet in Deum. Nos enim membra eius erimus, ut sit caput totius corporis. Orem quae vere exciperat omnem sensum. Hominem quid dicam, ex pane alitum, ex limo factum, supra caelos ascendere et Deum effici? Hoc ergo demonstrat. Hoc promittit. Haec hostia vere credentibus quae nunc a Latinis vocatur Eucharistia graeco nomine. Quod proprie significat gratiarum actio? Vel quia Christus cum panem in manu accepit, gratias egit. Vel quia nos in eo accipiendo gratias illi agere oportet. Quamobrem ut iam finem faciam cum semper alias, tum praecipue hoc sacramento die uno cum Domino nostro Jesu Christo, qui patri gratias egit, agere debemus, cui sit gratiarum actio, et gloria in saecula saeculorum.'
78. P. O. Kristeller, 'Lay Religious Traditions and Florentine Platonism', *Studies in Renaissance Thought and Letters*, Rome, 1956, pp. 99–122.
79. Cf. Kristeller, op. cit., p. 105, n. 17: Florence, Bibl. Naz., Cod. Magl. Strozzi, XXXV, 211; Bibl. Riccardiana 2204.
80. Ricc. 2204, f. 173v–81r, 'Sermone di messer Christofano Landino fatto

in commemoratione del corpo di christo et recitato nella compagnia de' Magi.' [Following modern numbering.]

81. Ibid., f. 173v, 'Le nostre menti informa che posto da parte ogni inquisitione, la quale per sylogistici argumenti cerca la dimonstratione et scientia della cosa alla sola fide con sincera et ardente carita ci sotto mettiamo.'
82. Ibid., ff. 173v–4r, '... dipoi perche la chiesa in celebrarlo non observa quella hora.'
83. Ibid., f. 174r–v.
84. Ibid., ff. 174v–5v, 'Dico bene quando tu volessi per l'amico morire non fa mestieri che prima diventi cavallo o capra, ma nella spetie humana nel la quale fussi creato, vai a tal morte sanza degenerare in piu vile spetie che none l'humana. Hora rivolgete dentro a vostri pecti et rivocando la mente quanto piu si puo dalle cose visibili all invisibili. Considerate quanto sia indicibile et in quanta sublimita sia posta la maesta divina, et vedete essere tanto piu nobile che le substanze separate et angeliche che nulla comparatione se nepuo fare, perche fra llo infinito el finito nonne misura.... Non solamente divento huomo con si miserabili conditioni che etiam della vita humana elesse il piu infimo stato, privato di thesori, povero, d'amici invita, laboriosa.'
85. Ibid., ff. 175r–6v, 'Ne basto alla infinita clementia et carita una volta exporre el suo pretiosissimo corpo alla morte per noi ingratissimi peccatori che da quel tempo in qua del continovo per unico remedio della nostra salvatione si degna per quattro parolette da ogni vile sacerdote dette descendere nell'ostia....'
86. Ibid., ff. 176v–7r, 'Imperoche ogni intervallo di tempo che e nel mutare una cosa in un altra procede come dice Averois nella *Metaphysica* o dalla resistentia che fa la cosa che fa amutare o dalla distantia che ce tralla cosa mutata et chi la muta. Ma a dio niente puo fare resistentia, niente gli puro essere lontano. Adunque la mutatione facta dallui e sanza intervallo di tempo.'
87. Ibid., ff. 177v–8v, cit. f. 178r, '... elquale allora e felice quando ritornato all altesimo chello creo contemplando la sua maesta et contemplando la fruisce et della fruitione senta ineffabile et aeterno gaudio.... Et certamente non havendo noi in questa mortal vita cipta stabile o certo domicilio, siamo in continua peregrinatione et cammino per arrivare alla celeste patria nella quale come dice l'apostolo non siamo forestieri ma ciptadini de sancti et domestici di dio.'
88. Ibid., ff. 179r–80r, '... et si alieno da ogni urbanita....'
89. Ibid., ff. 180v–1r, 'Dipoi o inaudita clementia, o ineffabile carita se mille volte el giorno per tuoi peccatti morissi mille volte per voi mediante questo sacramento risucitare a veramente eucaristia cioe buona gratia. Questo ci riduce ad memoria la passione di cristo. Questo confirma la fede. Questo acresce la speranza. Questo infiamma la carita donde

acquistiamo poi tute l'altre virtu. Questo ci da la vita di gratia. ... Questo preso con animo penitente et contrito purga la mente nostra et libera la da tutte le passioni humane et collocala in tale stato che mentre passa per questa valle piena di calamita et di miserie vive sempre lieto: non lo fa altra misura rallegrare l'abondanza de presenti bene terreni. ... Non safligge nella calamita nelle quali si truova. Et finalmente ne per le cose prospere insuperbisce, ne per l'adverse si dispera. Ma constituito in perfecta mediocrita cioche segue ripiglia in miglior parti et adio rerende loda. Et dipoi arrivato al fine del suo mortale corpo passa nella aeterna gloria alla quale chi ci creo, chi dipoi mori dinuovo ciricreo per la sua infinita misericordia voi et me conduchi. Amen.'

90. Ricc. 2204, ff. 181r–4v (following modern numbering, one higher than old), f. 181r, 'Oratione del corpo di Christo da Donato Acciaiuoli et dal lui nella compagnia de Magi recitata die xii aprilis 1468.'

91. Ibid., f. 181r.

92. Ibid., f. 181r–v, 'El nostro salvatore Christo Jehsu dilectissimi Padri miei, havendo tanto beneficato la natura humana prima in assummere questa nostra carne, dipoi per tutto il processo della vita sua in amaestrare e popoli et seminare fra legenti la sua doctrina, in liberare gli infermi, risucitore e morti, rimettere e peccati et consanctissimo opere dare di se in ogni spetie di virtu singularissimo exemplo. Ultimamente appresandosi lora della sua passione, come benigno maestro volle lasciare a suoi discepoli et a fedeli cristiani uno memoriale pieno di tutta carita, pieno di tanta dilectatione che none intellecto alcuno che sufficientamente lopossa considerare; peroche e sidice cheglie grandissimo segno d'amicitia quando gli amici ogni cosa fra loro riputono essere communi, quanta significatione d'amore et di benivolentia cia mostro il salvatore in communicarci non solamente le cose sua ma etiam se medesimo secondo la verita del suo parlare. *Qui manducat meam carnem et bibit meum sanguinem in me manet et ego in eo.*'

93. Ibid., f. 181v, '... la saremo in drieto molte sottili investigationi che si fanno da farci doctori circa alla sua materia, alla sua forma, et circa la cagione efficiente et finale et come la substantia del pane et del vino si trasforma nel verissimo corpo di Christo et come gli accidenti rimangono sanza el subiecto et molte altre speculationi che vanno investigando e subtilissimi theologi et solamente pigliareme due contemplatione piu accomodate al nostro proposito alla nostra sufficientia.'

94. Ibid., ff. 182r–v, '... peroche considerando le mirabili opere che sono nello universo et volgendo gli occhi a questi cieli et pensando la bellezza del sole et della luna, delle stelle et di tutti e corpi superiori, et discorrendo per la terra a considerare la varieta delle cose animate et inanimate, degli animali rationali et irrationali, et nel loro grado laloro perfectione e nonne alcuno che non rimanga stupefacto; ma molto piu ci debbe intervenire questa admiratione a contemplare la suprema excellentia di

questo sacramento el quale tanto excede la creatura et quanto esopravanza tutte le cose create peroche parlando di questo sacramento sa a intendere che qui vi sia el verissimo corpo et l'anima et la divinita secondo la verita delle sacre lettere che dicono.'

95. Ibid., f. 182v, '*Quod semel assumpsit nunquam dimisit.* Quello che pro se una volta nona mai lasciato et essendo insieme la humanita et divinita cioe epso Christo che excellentia si puo pensare o immaginare che si possa comparare a quello. Et pero lo Aurelio Augustino parlando con grandissimo admiratione di questo sacramento dice; *Quis fidelium habere dubium potuit in ipsa imolationis hora ad sacerdotis vocem caelos aperiri et in illo Jesu Christi misterio angelorum coros adesse.*' Cf. for Valla above, pp. 634–5; I have not been able to locate this passage from Augustine.

96. Ibid., f. 182v, 'Et se fussi possibile amantissimi Padri et Fratelli che per divina gratia si manifestassi lo splendore de quello sanctissimo corpo et la gloria del Salvatore come fedelissamente habbiamo a credere essere in quello sacramento quale e quello senso che non rimanessi confuso? Bisogna adunque supplire colla fide et colo intelletto contemplando l'altezza del divino consiglio et di questo dignissimo sacramento.'

97. Ibid., ff. 183r–v, 'Tutti questi nomi hanno significationi di gratiosi effetti de quali vengono a participare e fedeli Cristiani che sono bene preparati a recevere questo dignissimo sacramento. Peroche lui e la fontana delle gratie, eglie quello che da vigore alle anime nostre che la vita et la sovione et falle victoriose contra e vitii et peccati, chelle fa quiete et tranquille et se in questa mortal vita cie felicita alcuna le fa essere felici et quasi da una arra della fortissima beatitudine. . . . Questo e quello che e detto cibo degli angioli. O felicissimi cristiani che siate fatti simili alle angeliche Ierarchie. . . .'

98. Ibid., f. 184r–v.

99. Cf. Garin's 'Il problema dell'anima e dell'immortalità etc.', *La cultura filosofica*, op. cit., pp. 102–8. Also see his lengthy study of 'Donato Acciaiuoli, Cittadino Fiorentino', *Medioevo e Rinascimento*, Bari, 1954, pp. 211–87.

100. Cf. above, pp. 559–60. On Giovanni Garzoni's activities as a writer of saints lives, cf. Bologna, Biblioteca Universitaria, Codices 738, 739, 741, 744, and 746, which contain at least fifteen different lives of saints and martyrs written by Garzoni; cf. Manfré, op. cit., pp. 34–7 and 40–1, for descriptions of these manuscripts. Cf. also the works of Mafeo Vegio listed below in note 103 which combine saints' lives into commemorative offices. Cf. this Chapter, above, p. 616, for Sicco Polenton's saints' lives.

101. *De quattuor hominis novissimis: morte, iudicio, inferno et paradiso meditationes*, in *Maxima Bibliotheca Veterum Patrum*, Vol. XXVI, Lyons, 1677, pp. 745–54. Also Paris, 1511.

102. *De perseverantia religionis libri sex*, [Romae Apud S. Petrum, Idibus Iunii, 1448], in *Max. Bibl. Vet. Patr.*, op. cit., XXVI, pp. 688–744.

103. Bibl. Vaticana, Cod. Ottob. lat. 1253, contains, along with other works of Vegio, ff. 52r–61v, *De vita et officio Beati Augustini Liber* . . . V Kal. Septembris in Vigilia Beati Augustini ad Vesperas etc.; ff. 62r–76v, *De Vita et Officio Beatae Monicae*; ff. 77r–85v, *De Vita et obitu atque Officio Beati Nicolai Tollentinatis*; ff. 86r–119r, *De vita et obitu beatae Monicae ex verbis Sancti Augustini libri tres*; ff. 119v–41r, *De vita et obitu Caelestini Quinti Libri Tres*, Ad sum. Pont. Eugenium Quartum; ff. 141r–81v, *De vita et obitu atque officio Beati Bernardini*. Cf. on Vegio: Bartolomeo Nogara, *I codici di Mafeo Vegio nella Biblioteca Vaticana*, Milan, 1903; Luigi Raffaele, *Mafeo Vegio, Elenco delle opere*, Bologna, 1909; Socrate Corvi, ed., *Studi su Mafeo Vegio*, Lodi, 1959; Bruno Vignati, *Mafeo Vegio, umanista cristiano* (1407–58), Bergamo, 1959. Mention should also be made here of Kristeller's study of a French humanist's sermon on St. Stephen which was accompanied by explicit rhetorical analysis of his own work. Guillaume Fichet's Sermon was delivered at Rome before Pope Sixtus IV and the cardinals in 1476. P. O. Kristeller, 'An Unknown Humanist Sermon on St. Stephen by Guillaume Fichet', op. cit.

Notes to Part IV, Chapter XIV

1. In his *Renaissance Thought II*, New York, 1965, pp. 20–68. Apart from this reference and those given in footnotes 2–6 I shall make no attempt to list any more of the enormous literature on humanist moral philosophy.
2. Giovanni Gentile, 'Il concetto dell'uomo nel Rinascimento', in *Il pensiero italiano del Rinascimento*, Firenze, 1940, pp. 47–113.
3. Cf. Aldo Vallone, *Cortesia e nobiltà nel Rinascimento*, Asti, 1955.
4. Eugene F. Rice, Jr., *The Renaissance Idea of Wisdom*, Cambridge, Mass., 1958.
5. Cf. my *Adversity's Noblemen: the Italian Humanists on Happiness*, New York, 1940, re-issued 1965.
6. Hans Baron, *The Crisis of the Early Italian Renaissance: Civic Humanism and Republican Liberty in an Age of Classicism and Tyranny*, Princeton, 1955; Eugenio Garin, *L'Umanesimo italiano; filosofia e vita civile nel Rinascimento*, Bari, 1952.
7. 'Desideri di riforma nell'oratoria del Quattrocento', *Contributi alla storia del concilio di Trento e della controriforma*, Florence, 1948, *Quaderni di 'Belfagor'* 1, and pp. 166–82 of *La cultura filosofica del Rinascimento Italiano*, Florence 1961; 'Problemi di religione e filosofia nella cultura fiorentina del Quattrocento', pp. 70–82 in *Mélanges Renaudet* (*Bibliothèque d'Humanisme et Renaissance* XIV), 1952, and pp. 127–42 of *La cultura filosofica*. See below notes 72, 95, 114 for a discussion of the relationship of Garin's discussion to the present one.

8. Cambridge, Mass., 1955, 'Paganism and Christianity', pp. 70–91 (reprinted in his *Renaissance Thought*, New York, 1961, pp. 70–91). In connection with the religious thought and activity of the humanists another notable paper of Kristeller's should be mentioned: 'Lay Religious Traditions and Florentine Platonism', *Studies in Renaissance Thought and Letters*, Rome, 1956, pp. 99–122.
9. Giuseppe Toffanin, *Storia dell'Umanesimo*, enlarged ed., Bologna, 1950; C. Angelieri, *Il problema religioso del Rinascimento*, Florence, 1952, a bibliography; A. Buck, 'Das Problem des christlichen Humanismus in der italienischen Renaissance', *Sodalitas Erasmiana I, Il valore universale dell'umanesimo*, Naples, 1950, pp. 181–92; N. Seidlmayer, 'Religiös-ethische Probleme des italienischen Humanismus', *Germanisch-Romanische Monatsschrift*, N.F. VIII, 1958, 105–26.
10. *De otio religioso*, not *De otio religiosorum*, as G. Rotondi effectively argues in his 'Le due redazioni del *De otio* del Petrarca' *Aevum* IX, 1935, 27–77; cf. pp. 32–3. Guido Martellotti carried to completion Rotondi's edition, *Il 'De otio religioso' di Francesco Petrarca*, Città del Vaticano, 1958, *Studi e Testi* 195. This edition, hereafter cited as 'Rotondi', while not definitive, is a vast improvement over the text of the Basel, 1581 *Opera omnia*, with which I first struggled. Martellotti, in his introduction, pp. x–xv, convincingly shows how defective and full of lacunae and corruptions the old printed editions are (and this corresponds to my more limited experience), so that they must now be regarded not as a first redaction but as poor and incomplete versions of the text edited by Rotondi. The latter is essentially that of Bibl. Vat., Cod. Urb. lat. 333. The necessary study of the manuscript tradition, and particularly of those manuscripts which diverged and apparently form the basis of the old printed editions, remains to be made. We have also utilised this treatise in Part I, Chapter I above, but we believe the over-lapping will be minimal. It dealt, in fact, with both of these divergent themes.
11. E. H. R. Tatham, *Francesco Petrarca, the First Modern Man of Letters*, London, 1926, II, 395–99; E. H. Wilkins, *Studies in the Life and Works of Petrarch*, Cambridge, Mass., 1955, p. 13; the same, *Life of Petrarch*, Chicago, 1961, pp. 58–9. Martellotti, op. cit., pp. xii–xiv, shows that Petrarch was still revising the work in 1357, but not after 1360.
12. Rotondi, p. 2: '. . . quamvis, ut quod est fatear, maiore et meliore mei parte sim presens.'
13. *De secreto conflictu curarum mearum*, pp. 22–215 (with Italian translation), in Francesco Petrarca, *Prose*, ed. G. Martellotti, P. G. Ricci, E. Carrara, E. Bianchi, Milan-Naples, 1955, La Letteratura Italiana Storia e Testi 7. Cf. p. 214: 'Adero michi ipse quantum potero, et sparsa anime fragmenta recolligam, moraborque mecum sedulo. Sane nunc, dum loquimur, multa me magnaque, quamvis adhuc mortalia, negotia expectant.' And p. 192: 'deque aliis scribens, tui ipsius oblivisceris.' Cf. my discussion of the

Secretum in 'Petrarch's Views on the Individual and his Society', *Osiris* XI, 1954, 168–98, especially pp. 181–2, and above, Chap. I, pp. 5–16.

14. Rotondi, p. 15: '. . . potius auditura quid loquar, quam inspectura quid vivam.' Cf. also the remarkable autobiographical statement on pp. 103–5, where he describes his own belated study and love of the Scriptures under the stimulus of Augustine's *Confessions*: 'Accessit oportuna necessitas divinas laudes atque officium quotidianum, quod male distuleram, celebrandi, quam ob causam psalterium ipsum daviticum sepe percurrere sum coactus, e quibus fontibus haurire studui non unde disertior fierem, sed melior, si possem, neque unde evaderem disputator maior, sed peccator minor. Has ergo Scripturas, quas ego advena necdum notas odore illectus adamavi, sero licet, vos velut indigene et in his a principio enutriti amate, colite, veneramini, frequentate; nunquam de manibus vestris, si possibile sit, certe de mentibus vestris, nunquam excidant.'
15. 'Petrarch's Ecclesiastical Career', *Studies in the Life and Works of Petrarch*, Chap. 1. Wilkins states (p. 3): '. . . and he decided very naturally to enter the clerical profession. He must, then, have taken the tonsure. There is no evidence, however, that he took even the minor orders; theoretically only one who had taken those orders could hold benefices, but in Petrarch's time this requirement was not enforced. He certainly never took the major orders. No one of the benefices he received involved the cure of souls.' The passage quoted in the previous footnote, however, does suggest that he at least participated in divine services, whether or not he was fully ordained as a priest and thus able to say masses.
16. Rotondi, p. 2; *Psalms* xlvi, 10 (Vulg. xlv, 10).
17. Ibid., p. 4: 'labore labor apud ceteros; apud vos autem quiete quies queritur.'
18. Ibid., pp. 4–10.
19. Ibid., pp. 9–10: ' ". . . Nolite diligere mundum, neque ea que in mundo sunt, quia omne quod in mundo est concupiscentia carnis est et concupiscentia oculorum et ambitio seculi." [Augustine, *De vera religione* 4.] Horum ergo commeminit nosque commonuit Augustinus, sed infinita sunt alia id genus ad consolationem animarum et consilium dicta.'
20. Ibid., p. 13: 'Dicitur penitenti: "Ita gaudium erit in celo super uno peccatore penitentiam agente . . ." ' (*Luke* xv. 7; Gregory, *Libri regulæ pastoralis*, especially III.)
21. Ibid., p. 14: 'Habetote ante oculos vestros professionem vestram: votum servate, implete regulam; id si lete facitis satis est.' (Benedict, *Regula monachorum*, cap. 7; Bernard of Clairvaux, *De gradibus humilitatis*, cap. 3–6, 9.)
22. Ibid., p. 14: '. . . hunc ira torquebat, hunc libido, hunc superbia extollebat, hunc deprimebat accidia . . .'
23. Ibid., pp. 16–17: 'In secularibus historiis irrisum legimus Labienum quod, relicto Cesare victore, ad Pompeium transiverit. . . . quanto iustius

irridendus qui Cristo victoriosissimo rege deserto ad illum [Sathanem] confugit . . .'

24. Ibid., pp. 17–18, ' "O dii . . . immortales, vobis enim tribuam que vestra sunt." . . . qua "invisibilia Dei per ea que facta sunt intellecta conspiciuntur" . . . didicisset.' (Cicero, *Pro Sulla* 40; *Romans* i. 20.) This brief discussion of the value of Cicero for Christian religious exhortation is repeated on Lactantius' authority later on (p. 86) and at much greater length in Petrarch's *De sui ipsius et multorum ignorantia* (*Opera omnia*, Basel, 1581, pp. 1035–59; cf. Nachod's translation in Cassirer, Kristeller and Randall, *The Renaissance Philosophy of Man*, Chicago, 1948, pp. 79–91.)
25. Rotondi, pp. 18–19; Augustine, *De vera religione*, III.
26. Ibid., p. 19: 'Hec ciceroniana, pro re paucissimis immutatis, in usus nostros sic vertere libuit, ut anime salutem et de invisibili hoste victoriam a Deo recognoscere tali etiam teste discamus.'
27. Ibid., p. 20: 'optate bellum, non quidem pro se, sed propter Cristi gloriam et eternam pacem.' '. . . quas metus et negotium et labor in suo vigore tenuerunt, everterunt securitas, otium et quies. . . .'
28. Ibid., pp. 21–2: 'Nostra tamen etate tam multos eis credere cernimus etiam ex nostris, ut pudor et stupor occupet cogitantem aureos et argenteos deos, quos prisci reges sanctorum pontificum verbis instructi propter Cristi reverentiam delevere, ad Cristi iniuriam certatim a nostris hodie regibus ac pontificibus renovari. Si bene est quoniam argentum et aurum non ut deos colunt . . . colitur tamen argentum et aurum tanto cultu quanto nec Cristus ipse colitur et sepe vivus Deus inanimati metalli desiderio atque admiratione contemnitur. . . .'
29. Lactantius, *Institutiones, divinae* II, 18; also *Epitome*, 28.
30. Rotondi, p. 24: 'Et de Iudeis quidem hactenus. Quid deinceps? An dolosas Maometi fabulas, an philosophorum dissonas et inextricabiles ambages ac temerarii virus Averrois . . . an forte potius de illo vel sacrilegia Photini, vel Manichei nugas, vel Arii blasphemias audiamus? Que si omnia procul absunt a pectoribus sanis, si neque miserabilis paganorum error, neque cervicosa et obstinata Iudeorum cecitas, neque odibilis Saracenorum furor, neque fallacium philosophorum ventosa sophismata, neque hereticorum devia atque exotica dogmata tangunt animos aut delectant, aut nullam penitus spem salutis ostendunt, quid circumspicimus, quid agimus, aut quem inter huius vite naufragia portum petimus, nisi Cristum in quo quisquis spei sue anchoram iecit. . . .'
31. Ibid., pp. 27–8: *Isaiah* vii. 14; Augustine, *De civitate Dei*, XVIII, 23, Lactantius, *Institutiones, divinae* IV, 18. Petrarch takes his reference to Lactantius from this chapter where Augustine claims to have recollected the scattered sayings of the sibyl from Lactantius. Petrarch also repeats Augustine on the great age of the Erythraean sibyl.
32. Ibid., p. 29: 'Que quidem religiosus et pius lector, quamvis de Cesare

dicta, ad celestem potius trahet imperatorem, cuius in adventum toto orbe signa precesserant, que audiens poeta neque altius aspirans ad imperatoris Romani, quo nil maius noverat, reflexit adventum, cuius si vera lux oculis affulsisset hauddubie ad alium reflexisset. Nobis vero iam, gratias illi qui usque adeo immeritos nos dilexit, hec omnia sine ullis externis testibus clara sunt et ita se oculis fidelium divine lucis radii infundunt, ut nemo tam cecus sit qui non "iustitie solem" Cristum mente perspiciat; et quamvis ab ipsa veritate verissimum dictum sit "Beati oculi qui vident que vos videtis" ' (*Luke* x. 23).

33. Ibid., p. 31: 'illum signiferum *Civitatis Dei*.' Petrarch paraphrases *De civitate Dei*, XVIII, 51–4, in this section.

34. Ibid., p. 38: '. . . quamvis enim [Dei filius] ut iudex puniat miseretur ut pater . . . En fragilitas nostra ante oculos nostros semper; nichil agimus quod non nos humane conditionis admoneat atque miserie, de qua quidem integros ediderunt libros, tractatus alii eximios, de qua Plinius Secundus VII *Naturalis historie* breviter attigit, sed stilo excellenti ac florida ubertate sententiarum, de qua et Augustinus latius agit libro *Civitatis Dei*, unde Cicero ante omnes librum sue *Consolationis* adimpleverat, de qua michi quoque nonnunquam fuit impetus loqui aliquid . . . .' Cf. Pliny VII, 6 ff.; Augustine, *De civitate Dei*, XXII, 22, 23; Cicero's *De consolatione*, a lost work, was known to Petrarch through quotations in Cicero's *Disputationes Tusculanae*. Petrarch's own 'something' may refer to this work, pp. 34–7, to his *Secretum*, written four or five years earlier, to his *De remediis utriusque fortunae*.

35. Ibid., p. 39: 'Gaude igitur, humana natura, de extremis miseriis facta felicior quam toto capere possis ingenio.'

36. Theodor E. Mommsen, 'Petrarch's Conception of the "Dark Ages" ', in his *Medieval and Renaissance Studies*, Ithaca, 1959, pp. 106–29, originally in *Speculum* XVII, 1942, 226–42.

37. Rotondi, pp. 39–40: 'Intendite, queso, huc ingenia literata, audite Plato, Aristotiles, Pithagoras: non hic ridiculus ille circuitus animarum et vana metempsicosis, sed maius quoddam vere salutis archanum latet. . . . Multa de nubibus, de imbribus, de fulminibus, de ventis, de glacie, de nive, de tempestate, de grandine, multa de animalium naturis, de potentiis herbarum, de qualitatibus rerum, multa denique de tumore pelagi, de tremore terrarum, de motu celi ac stellarum disputata acriter et tractata subtiliter reliquistis, at quibus modis terre celum iungeretur atque uniretur unum hoc ex omnibus non vidistis. . . . Inter celum nempe et terram distantia ingens, fateor, sed finita est, inter Deum vero et hominem infinita. . . . In quibusdam sane codicibus vestris predicari Deum et eius Verbum et multa, que circa summum fidei verticem et coeternam Patri Filii personam evangelicis apicibus conveniant Augustino testante notum est, quod scilicet "in principio erat Verbum et Verbum erat apud Deum et Deus erat Verbum", quodque "omnia per ipsum facta sunt et sine ipso

factum est nichil", at qualiter "Verbum" illud "caro factum sit", qualiter terre iunctum "habitarit in nobis" "hoc doctus Plato nescivit", ut ait Ieronimus, "hoc Demosthenes eloquens ignoravit" . . . "nullus Deus miscetur hominibus". . . . "Deus ad homines veniet, nulla sine Deo mens bona est".' Cf. Augustine, *De civitate Dei*, x, 29; *John* i. 1, 3, 14; Jerome, *Epist.* LIII, 4; Seneca, *Epist.* LXXIII, 16.

38. Ibid., pp. 41–2.
39. Ibid., pp. 43–7.
40. Ibid., p. 48: ' ". . . romani principes imitentur Camillos, Fabritios, Regulos, Scipiones; philosophi proponant sibi Pithagoram, Socratem, Platonem, Aristotilem; poete emulentur Homerum, Vergilium, Menandrum, Terrentium; historici Tuchididem, Salustium, Herodotum, Livium; oratores Lisiam, Graccos, Demosthenem, Tullium et, ut ad nostra veniamus, epyscopi et presbyteri habeant in exemplum apostolos et apostolicos viros . . . Nos autem habemus propositi nostri principes Paulum, Antonium, Iulianum, Hilarionem, Macharium et ut ad veritatem Scripturarum redeamus noster princeps Helias, noster Heliseus, nostri duces filii prophetarum"; equidem, fratres, hi sunt vestri duces, qui Ieronimi duces erant. Insuper et ipse Ieronimus et Augustinus et Gregorius et omnino quisquis aliquando hactenus pro Cristi amore solitariam atque heremeticam agens vitam religioso otio claruisse noscitur' (Jerome, *Epist.* LVII, 5, which Petrarch liberally quotes). Petrarch adds (pp. 48–9): 'Non est animus nominatim hic reliquos attingere, quorum nomina satis in secundum *Solitarie vite* partem congessisse videor.' Cf. *De vita solitaria*, II, iv–ix, in *Prose*, pp. 430–82.
41. Ibid., p. 74.
42. Ibid., pp. 49–54.
43. Ibid., pp. 55–8.
44. Ibid., p. 60: '. . . eandem simulque aliam civitatem ingressos, ut dicatis cum Heraclito: in eandem civitatem bis intramus et non intramus.'
45. Ibid., p. 63: 'O flebilis et infelix transmutatio! Omnia in vermes inque serpentes, omnia tandem in nichilum abiere.'
46. Ibid., pp. 63–76. But cf. p. 65 for mention of St. Bernard, p. 74 for St. Francis.
47. Theodor E. Mommsen, 'Petrarch and the Story of the Choice of Hercules', *Medieval and Renaissance Studies* (n. 36), pp. 175–96; originally in *Jour. of the Warburg & Courtauld Inst.* XVI, 1953, 175–96. Cf. in this connection p. 192 (*J.W.C.I.*, p. 189).
48. Rotondi, pp. 77–8, ' ". . . beati omnes qui confidunt in eo". Vera quidem confidentia nisi de virtute non nascitur . . . et scientes quia "vana salus hominis; in Deo faciemus virtutem et ipse ad nichilum deducet inimicos nostros". Hec est, non alia, salus nostra; hec nostra virtus, hec nostra securitas, hoc remedium unicum contra iram Domini: vacare,

timere, sperare et orare "ne in furore suo arguat nos neque in ira sua corripiat nos." ' (*Psalms* ii. 13, cvii, 13–14, vi. 2.)

49. Op. cit., 286–591. Cf. Jacob Zeitlin's excellent introduction to his English translation (Urbana, 1924). Cf. my 'Petrarch's Views' etc. (cited n. 13), pp. 183–96. Petrarch considered the works as paralleling each other. Cf. Rotondi, p. 6: 'Sileo que sequuntur, nam et ea me scripsisse recolo in eo libro, quem huic et materia et stilo valde cognatum *De solitaria vita* nuper edidi, qui hunc ut tempore, sic serie rerum preit, et omnia ad unum tendunt, ad notam scilicet mortalis insanie magis labore gaudentis quam laboris fructu.'

50. *Colucii Salutati De seculo et religione* ex codicibus manuscriptis primum edidit B. L. Ullman, Florence, 1957, Nuova Collezione di Testi Umanistici Inediti o Rari XII. Citations will refer to this as 'Ullman edition'.

51. Ibid., Praefatio, p. vi: 'Liber ergo Colucii non est speculum mentis auctoris sed demonstrat eius facultatem disputandi et scientiam divinarum scripturarum. Si res postulasset, contra vitam monasticam perinde disputare potuisset.' This statement provoked me to question whether 'Colucius homo esse mediaevalis, ut ita dicam, non modernus videtur' (p. v) in a review, *Renaissance News* XI, 1958, 216–18. Whereupon Giuseppe Toffanin took up the question of a possible conflict of medievalism and humanism in Salutati in a short article, *Rinascimento* IX, 1958, 3–10; reprinted in his *Ultimi saggi*, Bologna, 1960, pp. 149–57, 'Per Coluccio Salutati'. Toffanin chided Ullman for regarding this work as in any way exceptional. It was not rhetorical but a sincere facing of the relationship between a medieval outlook and the Stoic ethic of Cicero. In *Rivista critica di storia della filosofia* XV, 1960, 73–82, 'A proposto di Coluccio Salutati', Eugenio Garin emphasized the rhetorical character of this treatise in support of Ullman. Ullman has now replied in *The Humanism of Coluccio Salutati*, Padua, 1963. Although he reaffirms his feeling that the work is rhetorical, that Salutati also argued against another friend entering a monastery, and feels 'in almost complete accord' with Garin, he makes the following statement (p. 28): 'Perhaps what I have just said is sufficient to remove the misunderstanding of my brief and possibly ambiguous remarks in the introduction of my edition of the *De seculo et religione*. I certainly had no thought of questioning Coluccio's sincerity. He believed that a man should hold to his monastic vows, therefore he brought every argument and every rhetorical device to bear on his Camaldolese friend.' On the previous page he had said, in reference to Alfred von Martin's *Mittelalterliche Welt- und Lebensanschauung im Spiegel der Schriften Coluccio Salutatis* (Munich, 1913), 'Martin's thesis has been seized upon by those who do not believe in a Renaissance. . . . Coluccio in particular was a humanist in a state of evolution, with many medieval traits clinging to him. Martin goes too far in thinking that Coluccio

believed all he said, that he favoured monasticism under any circumstances. Coluccio was sincere in urging it upon the monk. . . . He accepted the institution of monasticism but did not himself become a monk.' He would have been just as sincere if called upon to argue against entering a monastery. Although in a footnote I cannot discuss in detail my reactions to Ullman's statements here and elsewhere in this book, I need to say, as I hope my analysis of this work of Salutati will make clear, that there is a compatibility between such a so-called 'medieval' point of view as a defense of monasticism and 'humanism'. Moreover, Salutati's very acceptance of the 'medieval' notion of the relation of lay, secular-clerical, and religious states was not in the least inconsistent with his remaining a layman and feeling himself a good Christian and admirer of monasticism.

52. The previous footnote touches on this question. The political inconsistency of Salutati's *De tyranno* with the views of Bruni has especially bothered Hans Baron, *The Crisis of the Early Italian Renaissance*, chap. 7. The methodological misconception which insists that historical developments must be consistent to be meaningful cannot be discussed here.
53. Ullman edition, 'Praefatio', p. vi.
54. Cf. Ullman's 'Index Auctorum et Nominum' and page references given. Of course, in this, as in other works, Salutati frequently makes use of a medieval work without naming it. Cf. Toffanin, op cit., pp. 156–7; also Walter Rüegg, 'Entstehung, Quellen und Ziele von Salutatis "*De Fato et Fortuna*" ', *Rinascimento*, V, 1954, 143–88.
55. Ullman edition, p. 80, 'Quod munds suit ministrator necessariorum'.
56. Ibid.: 'Ministrat equidem necessaria nobis mundus, necessaria quippe ad vitam hanc corruptibilem transigendam.'
57. Ibid.: '. . . famen enim reprimi, sitim extingui, imbres et frigora pelli, ventorumque et estuum vim arceri natura desiderat. Quicquid ultra est a malo est.'
58. *A Documentary History of Primitivism and Related Ideas*, eds. A. O. Lovejoy, G. Chinard, G. Boas, R. S. Crane, Baltimore, 1935, I, 9–11.
59. Ullman edition, pp. 80–1: 'Quam facile vero his necessitatibus satisfiat, docuit etas prima, que famem, ut legitur, glande replevit, sitim compressit undis, frigora depulit pellibus, imbres, ventos, et estus antris ac specubus evitavit. Hec est illa innocentissima etas quam poete multis laudibus extollentes tum auream, tum Saturniam vocaverunt. O felices glandes! O saluberrima flumina! Non excitavit tunc estuantium ciborum virus suo calore libidinem; non tentavit cerebrum insanie simillima marcens ebrietas; non fuit cum proximo de finibus controversia, non de regno. Omnia communia erant. Thoros herba, domos antra non custodita, non clausa, sed cunctis patula ministrabant. Sublata tunc erant, imo nondum reperta, illa duo litigiosa vocabula que mortalium pacem turbant queve claudunt hominibus viam in celum, que sunt avaricie fomites et contentionum autores, scilicet "meum" et "tuum". . . . Sed adeo mundo et deliciis dati

sumus quod illa nostris moribus, imo non moribus sed abusibus ac flagitiis, comparantes fabulosa, non hystorica, reputemus, dicimusque fragiliorem fore temporis nostri etatem ut ad asperitatem illam impossibile sit redire. Fragilior autem est, fateor, quia vitiosior et, quod vitiorum fomes est, quia delicatior. Impossibilis profecto videtur reditus ad frugalitatem et prisci temporis communionem. . . .'

60. Juvenal, VI, I seqq.; Vergil, *Eclogues* 4, 6, 9, etc.; Boethius, *Consolatio*, II, 5, 23–4, 25–6.

61. Ullman edition, pp. 81–2: 'Tolle cupidinem, miser homo, depone divitias, abrenuntia mundo, duc vitam tuam sub preceptis, coneris adimplere consilia, subde voluntatem tuam voluntati divine, . . . incipe diligere deum, odire mundum, amare paupertatem, horrere divitias. Non potes hec relinquere nisi odio habeas; non potes ad illa transire ni diligas. Nec iam etatis nostre fragilitatem accuses. Potens est enim corpus nostrum per omnes incommoditates transire. Non referam tibi Danielem et socios in legumina regie mense delicias commutantes. Non proponam tibi in exemplum maximum illum inter natos mulierum domini precursorem; non anachoritas, de quibus mirabilia legimus in vita patrum, non heremitas etiam nostri temporis; non cenobitas, quorum multos videmus eligere paupertatem, amare ieiunia, et omnem fugere voluptatem. Scio enim quod, cum istos obiecero, respondebit amator mundi illos spiritus sancti gratia suffultos hec facere nunc posse et hactenus potuisse, et spiritum spirare quando, quantum, et ubi vult hocque a nostre voluntatis arbitrio non pendere.'

62. Ibid., pp. 82–3.

63. Ibid., p. 83: 'Mundum quidem relinquere possumus et deo servientes ad extremam illam necessitatem nature nostra corpora subiugare.'

64. Ibid., pp. 121–31, 'De voto paupertatis'.

65. Ibid., p. 123: 'Nec cogitamus miseri mortales contra naturam esse quod illas ad usum omnium procreatas per avariciam in nostre proprietatis dominium vendicemus, cumque vite nostre debeant deservire, facimus illas nobis flagitiorum, voluptatum, et cunctorum scelerum instrumenta. . . . et ita tantum bona si illis utamur bene. Nam male utentibus mala sunt.'

66. Ibid., pp. 124–5: 'Quod si cogitaremus duas omnino fuisse et esse debitas mortalibus civitates, unam spiritualem quam dei dicimus, alteram vero carnalem quam mundi possumus appellare, et ad alterutram ipsarum affectus nostros et finem nostrorum operum statueremus, occurreret nobis utramque civitatem a pauperibus institutam, a divitibus vero dirutam et corruptam. Et prius, si placet de hac mundana civitate quos autores habuerit speculemur. Nolo, licet facile possem per cuncta regna discurrere, sed illud quod omnium maximum et fortissimum fuit et quod adhuc saltem nominis obtinet principatum, Romanorum videlicet, perquiramus.'

67. Ibid., pp. 125–8. Cf. Ullman's footnotes for Salutati's classical sources.

68. Ibid., pp. 127–8: 'Quid plura, cum pleni sint omnium hystoriarum libri de paupertate, moderatione, et abstinentia Romanorum? Hi pauperes tantum imperium fundaverunt quod, "postea quam", ut nobilis et veritate insignis hystoricus ait, "divitie honori esse ceperunt et eas gloria, imperium, et potentia sequebatur, hebescere virtus, paupertas probro haberi cepit", successores divites everterunt. . . . Rem enim publicam Romanorum, quam pauper fundavit Romulus et pauperrimi principes ad tantam magnitudinem evexerunt ut imperium occeano, astris vero gloriam terminaret et eis ad occasum ab ortu solis omnia domita armis parerent, divites, L. Silla crudelis, Cinna ferox, ambitiosusque Marius, labefactaverunt, et ditiores, M. Crassus, Gn. Pompeius Magnus, ac Gaius Cesar, Lucii Cesaris filius, funditus destruxerunt. Ut in hac rerum gestarum memoria quasi quodam in speculo videre possit mortalium genus ad hanc terrenam civitatem instituendam, augendam, atque conservandum pauperes divitibus prestitisse.'

69. Vide supra note 52. Hans Baron referred to the passage discussed without connecting it to the Florentine political situation in his earlier article: 'Franciscan Poverty and Civic Wealth as Factors in the Rise of Humanistic Thought', *Speculum* XIII, 1938, 16–17. However, Marvin B. Becker specifically connects this passage and the one cited below in note 72 with the doctrines of the *Fraticelli* and their active role in the uprising of the Ciompi: 'Florentine Politics and the Diffusion of Heresy in the Trecento: a Socioeconomic Inquiry', *Speculum* XXXIV, 1959, 74–5, note 88.

70. Ullman edition, p. 128: 'Quid autem de illa civitate que ad supernam spectat Ierusalem dicam?'

71. Ibid., pp. 128–9; *Matthew* viii, 20.

72. Ibid., pp. 129–31: 'Ut manifeste cunctis appareat illos primos in renovatione temporum celestis civitatis et ecclesie catholice fundatores aut pauperes extitisse aut venditis omnibus que habebant et in communi collatis paupertatem voluntariam elegisse. . . . Hi pauperes et humiles infinitis martiriis per ducentos treginta et amplius annos ab Nerone, primo Christianorum persecutore, usque in Dyoclitianum et Maximum imperatores, quorum tempore decima plaga Christiane persecutionis efferbuit, ecclesiam catholicam fundaverunt. Quam post Constantinum, qui non dotavit sed ditavit ecclesiam et superba sibi tradidit imperialis apicis ornamenta (pace cunctorum dictum sit), hi nostri presules, quibus sicut aliis illis ducibus terrene civitatis primo pecunie, deinde imperii cupido crevit, postquam simulam, mel, et oleum comederunt et ornati sunt auro et argento et vestiti sunt bysso et pollimito et multicoloribus et decori facti sunt vehementer nimis et demum profecerunt in regnum, illam civitatem gloriosam abominabilem reddiderunt. Nunc, quod summe deflendum est, cum videant Christianam fidem olim toto orbe diffusam abominatione Saracenica tot terrarum spacia perdidisse, cum videant antiquum Greculorum scisma tot populos, tot urbes, totque quondam opulentissima

regna ab unitate sancte matris ecclesie separasse, quasi adhuc nimia moles esset nimiaque fidelium multitudo, duos summos pontifices variis temporibus eligendo, si tamen electiones censende sunt quas vel odium vel ambitio vel alie mentium humanarum turbide passiones extorquent, non que in zelo fidei et in edificationem celestis Ierusalem celebrantur, scisma perniciosissimum pepererunt. Ut, sicut illi utriusque civitatis principes et autores, dum paupertatem dilexerunt, nedum fundamenta duarum illarum urbium iacientes in ingens maxime molis opificium profecerunt sed incrementis mirabilibus inter labores et sanguinem aucti sunt, ita isti divites corrumpente pecunia mentes et bonos mores pene cuncta cum sua gloriosa rerum omnium opulentia destruxerunt. Que cum ita sint, nisi desipere gaudeamus, si celestis vel terrene civitati servire, si nos utrique vel alterutri volumus utiles exhibere, quis non videt dimittendas esse divitias, que suos adeo corrumpant et attaminent possessores?'

Garin ('Desideri di reforma', cited above, p. 169) singled out this passage from Salutati in order to associate him with later humanist diatribes against the corruption of the clergy. But, curiously, he combined the phrase 'vestiti sunt bysso' cited just above with a phrase from Book I, chap. 21 (Ullman edition, p. 46), 'non religiosus sed potius Ciprica mulier videatur', and then quotes at length from this earlier passage, which satirizes the vanity of a friar and the false arts of his preaching to prove 'Quod mundus sit spectaculum delictorum'. Apart from his taking this passage out of its own context, it is interesting that Garin's concern with Salutati is confined to seeking evidence of anti-clericalism rather than examining Salutati's position on the status of the regular clergy.

73. Ibid., pp. 137–56.
74. Ibid., pp. 138–40.
75. Ibid., p. 141: '. . . quicquid execrationis sparsum inter divinarum scripturarum oracula reperitur aliquo sane expositionis misterio ad vere caritatis regulam aut divine iusticie desiderium referri debeat vel alicuius altioris sensus limine sit taliter exponendum quod caritati dei et proximi nullatenus contradict, cum maxime lata via expositoribus pateat. . . .'
76. Ibid., pp. 145–9. His discussion here includes a short exposition of the Lord's Prayer.
77. Ibid., pp. 149–52.
78. Ibid., pp. 154–5.
79. Ibid., pp. 131–7, 'De obedientie voto'.
80. Cf. supra note 47.
81. *Hercules am Scheidewege und andere antike Bildstoffe in der neueren Kunst*, Leipzig and Berlin, 1930, *Studien der Bibliothek Warburg* XVIII, p. 155.
82. *Coluccio Salutati De laboribus Herculis*, edidit B. L. Ullman, Zurich, 1951.
83. Printed by Ullman in *De laboribus Herculis*, pp. 585–635.
84. Ullman edition, pp. 134–5: 'Nescio si verum dicam, devotissime tamen ausim asserere cunctos qui citra divine maiestatis obedientiam virtuosum

aliquid operantur, nedum non mereri sed improbe facere, et omnes qui agunt verbi gratia frequentes actus fortitudinis vel temperantie ob hoc solum, ut fortes vel temperati sint, non etiam ut videantur, nedum carnaliter sapere sed etiam a gentilium philosophis non differre. Omittamus enim Romanos, qui cunctarum actionum suarum finem sibi mundanam gloriam proponebant. Nonne illi philosophi qui terminum bonorum omnium virtutem, ut ceteros vanioris sententie dimittam, esse volebant, que maxime Stoycorum opinio fuit, se ipsis, ut aiebant, contenti nichil ulterius de suis actionibus requirebant nisi conscientie secretum et ut virtuosi possent evadere secumque de virtutum acquisitione gaudere? Quid igitur ab istis differre dixerimus Christianum qui dei iubentis oblitus et huius virtutis habitum derelinquens, non ut deo placeat vel obediat, sed solum ut bonum aliquod faciat operatur? Certe secure dixerim tanto deteriorem quanto constitutus per baptismi regenerationem in gratia et in evangelio veritatem edoctus nec sic agit ut debet nec ipsis virtutibus utitur ut deceret, imo virtutibus contra rationem nititur frui, quibus sic fruendo verius dicatur abuti. Non igitur terrena sapiamus sed, cum ad nichil cogamur necessitate nature, deo, cui fidem promisimus in libertate nobis de nostra voluntate concessa, fideliter pareamus.'

Toffanin ('Per Coluccio Salutati', *Ultimi saggi*, pp. 155–7), I discovered subsequently to writing this chapter, selected this exact quotation to show, through the addition of one more sentence—'Pareamus quidem alacriter et in caritate, sine qua, sicut sentit apostolus, cuncta virtutis operatio nichil est'—Salutati's agreement with Bonaventura and his opposition to Cicero's view of virtue as an end in itself. Toffanin cites Bonaventura's *Hexameron*, '. . . virtutes informes et nudae sunt philosophorum, vestitae autem sunt nostrae . . .'. I am inclined to think that Salutati's stress, here, is on obedience, rather than on charity and grace. Either stress, however, is clearly antagonistic to the pagan view of virtue which Mommsen and Panofsky see emerging in the Renaissance around the story of the choice of Hercules.

85. Ullman edition, pp. 109–14, 'Semper habenda professionis sue memoria et quod maius sit meritum religiosorum quam eorum qui citra voti vinculum operantur.'

86. Ibid., p. 111: 'Tu enim te ipsum, voluntatem et opera tua deo religionem ingrediens dedicasti. . . . Hoc est vere holocaustum, id est totum exustum et incensum, in quo totum quod sumus et possumus deo committimus, et nichil in nostra relinquimus potestate. Hoc non faciunt qui sine voto solum operas offerunt, et ob id apud dei benignitatem non est dignum ipsos tantundem quantum votis obnoxios promereri. Quis enim plus gratie meretur, an qui solum fructus arboris sic superiori donaret quod ad illorum prestationem nisi quantum sibi placuerit non teneatur, an qui et arborem donat et fructus tali condicione quod etiam post donationem nequeat revocare? Nemini dubium illum qui plus donaverit plus

mereri . . .'. Cf. *Eadmeri Monachi* [*Cantuariensis*] *Liber de sancti Anselmi similitudinibus*, Migne, *P.L.*, 159, cap. LXXXIV, 'Similitudo inter monachum et arborem', col. 656: 'Cujus igitur horum obsequium domino illi magis videtur acceptum? An illius, qui, quando quantumque voluerit, dat ei de fructu propriae arboris, vel illius qui arborem et fructum totaliter offert? Imo magis illius qui arborem totam dat ei cum fructu.' This may not have been Salutati's source, but it unquestionably was a medieval commonplace.

87. Ullman edition, p. 112: 'Etenim qui bonum libera voluntate facit, sicut evenit in solutis a voto, unicum bonum facit; qui vero vovet et facit, dum voto se obligat, meretur et bonum facit. Dum autem vota reddit, licet faciat debitum, nichilominus bonum facit. Non enim audiendi sunt qui delirantes conantur asserere bona que sine voto fiunt his que ex obedientia voti facimus esse maiora, adducentes quod plus obligamur libera voluntate donanti quam debitum persolventi, quasi quod vovens debitor factus sit, non ex libera processerit voluntate, et quod aliquid libere promittenti nichil eo quod promiserit debeamus. . . . Errant hi profecto. Nam longe maiore caritate, que finis est precepti, vovetur atque perficitur quam si simpliciter aliquid prebeamus.'

88. Ibid., p. 113.

89. Ibid., p. 163: 'Quando nascimur successione primi parentis, cuius omnes heredes sumus et filii, nascimur ire vasa moxque institutione sancte matris, ecclesie, per baptismi lavacrum renovamur in gratia. Prima quidem et vera religio, in qua diabolo et suisque pompis caratherem Christianitatis accipiens abrenuntiat, fides est nostra, plene quidem, si rite servetur, via perfectionis ad deum, adeo tamen perversa consuetudine temporalibus permixta negociis quod, nisi dei benignitas superet iniusticiam nostram, licet multi vocentur, pauci tamen sunt ad electionis beneficium perventuri. Plenior autem est quando quotidianis divine maiestatis servitiis, in copia tamen rerum nos extra seculum per clericatus ordinem obligamus. Plenissima vero perfectio est in via cum non solum deum sequimur diabolum fugientes, non solum in dei servitio famulamur relinquentes mundum (non enim debet clericus secularibus se negociis permiscere), sed etiam nos ipsos per castitatis, obedientie, et paupertatis votum deo offerimus et verum holocaustum in religionis altario consecramus, ut non incongrue dici possit, quod et superius attigi, omnibus Christianis tanquam in terram bonam seminantibus trigesimum fructum, clericis sexagesimum, religiosis vero centesimum reservari.'

90. *Epistolario di Coluccio Salutati*, ed. F. Novati, Rome, 1891–1911, IV, 216. Excerpt in Garin, *Il pensiero pedagogico dell'Umanesimo*, Florence, 1958, p. 60. Cf. above, p. 560 where we have also cited this passage as central to the whole conception of the relationship of humanism and religion.

91. Florence, Biblioteca Medicea-Laurenziana, Pl. 52, Cod. 3, ff. 25–30

92. Edited and translated into Italian by Giulio Vallese (Naples, 1946), on the basis of *Poggii Florentini dialogus, et Leonardi Aretini oratio adversus hypocrisim* ad fidem MSS edita et emendata a Hieronymo Sincero Lotharingo, Lugduni, MDCLXXIX. This edition was reprinted in 1691 and 1699. The text is printed by Vallese pp. 79–112.
93. Bruni, op. cit., f. 28v: 'Nec ego solum de religiosis verum etiam de. secularibus loquor. Nam in utroque genere haec infanda reperitur pestis.'
94. Ibid., f. 30: 'Nam bonus quidem vir letus et alacris est, ex recte factorum conscientia et ex bona spe, quam nulla penarum formido conturbat. Hypocritas autem sua urunt facinora et quasi furiae ante oculos observantur. Necesse est enim illos quamvis sint improbi interdum de se ac de suis erratis cogitare. Est enim unusquisque recte ac perperam factorum iudex sibi ipsi constitutus. Hoc est certissimum profecto ac verax iudicium quod neque falli neque seduci neque circumveniri ullo modo potest. Non enim testibus creditur, neque tabulis arguitus reus, non a patrono per gratiam vel eloquentiam defenditur. Omnia scit iudex, omnibus interfuit, nec semel tantum quis sed saepe frequenterque iudicatur. Huius interni iudicis condemnatio, lacrimas illas tibi excutit et inter sacra plorare compellit. Sed crede mihi, . . . hic ludus et iocus est, ad sempiternum illud ineffabilemque dei iudicium, quod te post mortem expectat.'
95. Garin, 'Desideri di riforma' (n. 7), pp. 170–3, uses these two works along with other humanist diatribes against the corruption of the clergy, regular or secular, as part of his argument that there was a continuing humanist reform movement within the confines of Catholicism, culminating in Savonarola and Gianfrancesco Pico, which sought a purification of customs and a deepening spirituality. As should be clear, my concern here is not with humanist denunciation of clerical abuses but with their basic notions of the status and relations of laity, clergy, and religious.
96. Edited from an apparently unique manuscript, Biblioteca Apostolica Vaticana, Cod. Urb. Lat. 595, fols. 1r–25r, by J. Vahlen, *Sitzungsberichte der kaiserlichen Akademie der Wissenschaften*, Phil.-Hist. Klasse, Bd. 62, Vienna, 1869, pp. 99–134. Now photographically reprinted in Laurentius Valla, *Opera omnia*, Turin, 1962, Tomus alter, pp. 287–322. Cf. also Vahlen's *Laurentii Vallae Opuscula tria*, Bd. 61, pp, 9–15 (Turin *Opera*, pp. 135–41), 50–66 (176–92). The date is controversial. Vahlen limits it to after 1438 and before 1442, Giorgio Radetti, in a recent review of the calculations of Vahlen, Mancini, and Sadoleto, concludes that it must be 1442. Cf. his introduction, pp. xxvii–xxix, to Lorenzo Valla, *Scritti filosofici e religiosi*, Florence, 1953.
97. *Quadragesimale de Christiana religione*, Sermo XVI, *De sacra religione*, art. III, cap. III: 'Tertia ratio est quia homo in Religione premiatur copiosius, et maxime propter tria': '. . . ratio triplex est: primo, ratione praecep-

torum; secundo, ratione consiliorum; tertio, ratione votorum', *Opera omnia*, Florence-Quaracchi, 1950, 1, 189, ff.

98. In Hieronymus Aliottus, *Epistolae et opuscula*, Arezzo, 1769. Aliotti (Agliotti, or Jeronimo Aretino) was an interlocutor in Poggio's *Dialogus adversus hypocrisim* (n. 92).

99. Op. cit., p. 103: 'Quaero ante omnia, . . . numquid id, . . . plus te a deo remunerationis assecuturum, eam vim habeat, quod cum duo inter se nihil mentium corporumque qualitate differant assintque utripue paria omnia quae extrinsecus hominibus accidunt et in eisdem ambo actionibus vitae versentur, plus tamen remunerationis a deo debeatur huic qui professus est istam sectam, quam religionem et inde vos religiosos appellatis, quam illi non professo aliquam sectam nec vestram nec monachorum . . .'

100. Ibid., p. 104: 'Tamen hoc de quo miraris quod sectam malui dicere quam religionem, non modo venustatis a me habita est ratio sed etiam necessitatis. Cum enim ego non tantum isti vestrae vitae tribuendum putem, quantum vos tribuitis, nimium visum est, vos huic rei tam sacrum venerandumque nomen imponere. Aliter non est causa, cur disputemus. Namque si vos soli religiosi estis, concedendum erit, optimos eosdem omnium hominum esse. Quod ita non est, ut sentio, de quo disputaturus sum.'

101. Ibid., p. 105: 'Qua in re non tam arrogantes de vobis quam contumeliosi in ceteros videmini. Quae enim mihi laus contingere uberior potest aut e contrario maior vituperatio quam vel religiosum esse vel irreligiosum? Nam quid est aliud esse religiosum quam esse christianum et quidem vere christianum? . . . ut idem sit religio quod fides et religiosus quod fidelis, fidelis, inquam, non tamquam mortuus sine operibus sed cum operibus et qualis dici possit vere christianus.' Cf. *James* i. 26–7.

102. Ibid., p. 106: 'Itaque cum vos religiosos tantum modo facitis, qui professi estis, ceteros vero religiosos negatis, quid aliud quam vos solos christianos, vos solos bonos, vos solos mundos immaculatosque fatemini, alios autem damnatis, contemnitis, in tartarum abiicitis? . . . Quae cum ita sint, non feci illiberaliter in vos, quod religiosos appellare dubitarim, cum et multi aliorum, qui istam sive sectam sive regulam professi non sunt, religiosi vocari debeant, quia sanctissime vivunt, et multi vestrorum vocari non debeant, quia coinquinatissme.'

103. Ibid., pp. 106–11; p. 111: 'Ad insaniam paene me redigis verbis, virtutes nostras extenuas, remunerationes prope aufers, vitia auges, poenas multiplicas, religiones ac religiosos omnes vere ut dixisti in lutum praecipites agis.'

Liber de sancti Anselmi similitudinibus (n. 86), cap. LXXXI–LXXXII, may be compared with the interchange in Valla reported here; cols. 653–4: 'Sed dicet aliquis: Melius esset ut Deo sine professione serviret spontaneus quam in monasterio professione se alligans servire cogeretur invitus. Hic autem est respondendum quia tanta distantia est inter illum qui non vult facere Deo promissionem serviendi sibi, et eum qui libenter eam facit, quanta inter homines duos qui ambo ex debito debent servire domino uni. . . . Sic autem et Deus inter professum monachum et nolentem profiteri judicat, si eos contra eum pecasse poeniteat. Non solum autem professum mitius judicat non professo, sed etiam quolibet laico adhuc in saeculo constituto. Licet enim uterque idem peccatum committat, tamen si toto ex corde monachum poeniteat deliquisse, eumque ordinem, cui se subdidit, ferventi amore custodiat, majorem quam laicus misericordiam consequetur, quantumlibet ille poeniteat saecularibus adhuc detentus. Si vero poenitere noluerit, majori quam laicus damnationi subjacebit.'

San Bernardino, op. cit. (n. 97), p. 191, may also be compared: 'Ex iam dictis patere potest quod qui facit aliquid sine voto, dat ei solum quod facit propter eius amorem. Qui enim non solum facit, sed etiam vovet, non tantum dat ei quod facit, sed etiam potentiam qua illud facit; facit enim se non posse quin faciat quod prius non facere licite poterat. . . .

'Et his tribus rationibus clarescere potest quod qui ex voto aliquid operatur, plus Deo donat, plura bona multiplicat atque firmius in bono opere se confirmat, ceteris paribus plus meretur, et sic per consequens in caelesti gloria copiosius praemiatur. . . . Haec autem dixisse velim de Religione et religiosis servantibus professionem suam, non autem de dissolutis et sceleratis.'

104. Op. cit., pp. 113–15; p. 115: 'Quod vos facitis, iusiurandum sive promissionem esse concedo, votum non concedo.'

105. Ibid., pp. 116-18; p. 118: 'Non est professio votum sed devotio. Est enim devovere, ut brevissime dixerim, quasi dicare aut dedicare.'

106. Ibid., p. 119: 'Verum non omnibus ista necessaria sunt.'

107. Ibid., p. 121: 'Non retracto ego sponsionem meam, nec homini do, quod deo dederam, nec iterum deo promitto, quod ante promiseram. Sed in quibuscumque etiam deo serviens arbitrium habebam, ut vestiendi, vescendi, eundi, agendi, cubandi, dormiendi, vigilandi, postremo loquendi, horum omnium libertatem et ut dixi arbitrium a me in alterum transcribo . . .'

108. Ibid., p. 121: 'illis, libertatem suam retinentibus'.

109. Ibid., pp. 122–3: 'Ergo nihil est medium, nisi ut aut servos habeamus aut servitia simus . . .? Non sunt omnes domini nec omnes servi, non omnes praeceptores nec omnes discipuli: nec minorem gradum o[b]tinent qui in medio sunt. Atque ut optabile est assequi statum praelatorum praeceptorumque, ita miserum in numero subditorum discipulorumque esse, certe longe hoc minoris dignitatis quam ut dixi in medio esse et per te posse sine domino et sine magistro vivere et scire. Non ausim dicere, abjecti indoctique animi signum et sibi ipsi diffidentis, in morem pueri tutoris se praesidio ac praeceptoris tutelaeque committere. Nam si idoneus est, ut alios admoneat, doceat, regat, quid ita se aliis subiicit, praesertim, ut frequenter evenit, imperitis et indignis . . . maius praemium deberi iis qui optime praesunt, quam qui optime obediunt. . . . Itaque genus servitutis

est vestra ista obedientiae sponsio. . . . Ego tamen dominum me aliorum malim esse quam servum aut certe dominum mei.'

110. Ibid., p. 123: 'Parere regulae est deo parere, non homini, quod et nos facimus, neque alia melior tradi regula potest quam est tradita a Christo atque apostolis.'

111. Ibid., p. 124: 'Quid quaeris? Si nihil in vivendo temperate atque frugaliter ego et tu discrepamus, qui tandem fieri potest ut tu pauper sis, ego dives . . . ? . . . Etiamne libros vendam et erogabo? Apostolis praeceptum est hoc et illis quibus sine libris, sine studio, sine praemeditatione tributum erat ut principibus responderent? Mihi vero codices necessarii sunt et pecuniae eaeque non paucae, unde codices plurimos et cetera vitae praesidia coemam. Nam quid perversius quam tua mendicis dare ut postea ipse mendices. . . . Itaque satis est, si opibus non fruar, non oblecter, eisque non re sed animo renuntiem. . . . Nihil minus. Dixi mihi necessarias esse pecunias ut coemam codices. Tu si aliter facis tradisque illas pauperibus, stultus sis, qui non te ut proximum amas.'

112. Ibid., p. 125: '. . . deponis spem acquirendi, sed et sollicitudinem, non es habiturus meliora, sed nec peiora passurus.'

113. Ibid., p. 126.

114. Ibid., p. 127: '. . . praestatque multo tutos esse in medio quam in summo cum ruinae periculo. Utinam, utinam episcopi, presbyteri, diacones essent unius uxoris viri et non potius, venia sit dicto, non unius scorti amatores . . . Non tamen plus sacerdos ob continentiam quam ego merebitur. Nam hoc modo peiore essent condicione feminae, quae nequeunt esse sacerdotes, cum tamen apud deum non sit neque graecus neque barbarus, neque dominus neque servus, neque masculus neque femina.' (*Galatians* iii. 28.)

Garin, 'Desideri di riforma' (n. 7), pp. 172, 173, uses this work of Valla to emphasize his criticism of the corruption of the clergy, quoting the passage—'Utinam, utinam' etc.—just cited and the one on p. 125—'non exterior homo sed interior placet deo'. It should be clear, here also, that Valla goes beyond corruption to question the basic validity of the status of the religious. The latter is my chief concern in this paper.

115. Op. cit., pp. 130–2: 'Tu obedisti, ego curam aliorum gessi; tu pauperem egisti et continentem, ego parem tibi vitam egi; tu ad haec custodienda te alligasti, ego mihi istam necessariam servitutem non putavi; tu necessitate recte egisti, ego voluntate, tu timore dei, ego amore: perfecta caritas foras mittit timorem. Si non timuisses te aliter non posse deo placere, profecto numquam te alligasses. Nam quid aliud ad promittendum vos induxit . . . nisi ut nulla vos a cultu dei per libertatem arbitrii causa reflecteret. Ideoque non videas fere quempiam ad vestrum consortium se conferre, nisi sceleratum, nefarium, inopem, destitutum et qui aliter vel deo vel corpori suo bene servire posse desperet. . . . Etenim omnis ratio voti, omnis indictio ieiunii, omne iusiurandum, omnis denique lex, est autem

professio lex quaedam, propter metum inventa est, id est ut apertius loquar, propter malos. . . . Nonne inquit Paulus: *lex propter transgressionem posita est* [*Romans* xiii. 4] . . . Itaque non intelligo, quid aliud a deo possitis exigere, nisi fructum obedientiae, paupertatis, continentiae. At vos hoc non contenti ceteris anteferri postulatis periculi gratia. Quodsi in te periculum poenae consideras, considera et in me periculum peccandi facilius, qui nulla timoris ancora sum alligatus: quod facit eandem virtutis actionem in me quam in te esse maiorem.'

116. Ibid., p. 132–3: 'Ideoque et vos et nos, more Pauli, qui de manducantibus et non manducantibus inquit, *unusquisque in suo sensu abundet* [*Romans* xiv. 3, 5], faciamus pares concludamusque, ita professionem homines non reddere meliores, ut diaconium, ut presbyterium, ut episcopatus, ac papatus. Nec quia diaconio aut sacerdotio initiati, iccirco meliores estis, sed iccirco initiari voluistis, ut meliores essetis: nec quia iurastis, iccirco multum meremini, sed iccirco iurastis, ut multum mereremini: nec quia poena proponitur vobis, iccirco boni estis, potestis namque esse mali, sed ut boni essetis, periculum poenae subistis.'

117. Ibid., pp. 133–4. That the peroration was faint praise and meant to be is witnessed by the friar's reply: '. . . perorationem tamen tuam non probo, quae non tam laudum fraternarum, quam timoris tui testimonium fuit. Cum enim proprium esset institutae orationis in vituperatione fratrum finem facere, ut copiosissime poteras, tu tamen, ne odium tibi illorum concitares, in laudatione facere maluisti.'

118. Cf. my introduction to the English translation of *De libero arbitrio* in Cassirer, Kristeller and Randall, *The Renaissance Philosophy of Man*, p. 153. Cf. above, pp. 165–7.

119. The relevant portion of the *Apology* is printed by Vahlen, pp. 135–8. Cf. also Radetti's translation, op. cit., pp. 447–50.

120. Erasmus wrote his *Enchiridion militis Christiani* in 1501 and first published it at Louvain, 1503, roughly sixty years after the date of Valla's treatise. Although the religious spirit may be judged similar, Erasmus' comment on monasticism—which gained a place for this book on the Index—was a more cautious one, 'Monasticism is not piety but a way of living, either useful or useless in proportion to one's moral and physical disposition" Raymond Himelick's translation, Bloomington, Ind., 1963. *Desid. Erasmi Roterodami Opera omnia* v, Louvain, 1704, col. 65: 'Monachatus non est pietas, sed vitæ genus pro suo cuique corporis ingeniique habitu, vel utile, vel inutile. Ad quod equidem ut te non adhortor, ita ne dehortor quidem.' Cf. E. Reusch, *Die Indices Librorum Prohibitorum des sechzehnten Jahrhunderts*, Tübingen, 1886, photo-reprint Nieukoop, 1961, pp. 83, 100, 156, 185, 221, 477 etc. for condemnations of the work in various sixteenth century *indices*. Presumably ignorance of Valla's work in the sixteenth century accounts both for its absence from the *indices* and from praise by reformers.

Notes to Part IV, Chapter XV

1. Martines, op. cit., p. 270.
2. On this question of his classification of his own professional activities see Kristeller's 'Humanism and Scholasticism', op. cit., pp. 571–2 and nn. 53 and 54; and Seigal's articles, op. cit. passim. Cf. P. O. Kristeller, 'Il Petrarca, l'Umanesimo e la scolastica a Venezia', *La civiltà veneziana del Trecento*, Venice, n.d. [1956?], pp. 149–78. Petrarch designated as *philosophus moralis* on p. 151.
3. Cf. P. O. Kristeller, 'The Modern System of the Arts', *Journal of the History of Ideas*, XII (1951), pp. 496–527, XIII (1952) pp. 17–46; reprinted in his *Renaissance Thought II*, New York, 1965, pp. 163–227.
4. Cf. C. S. Baldwin, *Medieval Rhetoric and Poetic*, New York, 1928, pp. 191–5; Curtius, *European Literature and the Latin Middle Ages*, op. cit., pp. 148–52.
5. Cf. above, p. 562. On Renaissance poetic theory in general see my 'The Unknown Quattrocento Poetics of Bartolommeo della Fonte', *Studies in the Renaissance*, XIII [1966], pp. 40–95, and the literature cited in nn. 4 and 5. Among these August Buck, *Italienische Dichtungslehre vom Mittelalter bis zum Ausgang der Renaissance*, Tübingen, 1952, and Francesco Tateo, *'Retorica' e 'poetica' fra Medioevo e Rinascimento*, Bari, 1960, may be especially mentioned.
6. Cf. E. R. Curtius, *European Literature and the Latin Middle Ages*, op. cit. passim. This chapter is an attempt to follow up an idea which occurred to me while preparing my edition of Fontius' *Poetics*. Cf. my introduction, op. cit., pp. 59–60, and n. 86. Eugenio Garin has also dealt with this theme in his usual incisive way in 'Le favole antiche', *Medioevo e Rinascimento*, Bari, 1954 and 1961, pp. 66–89, first published in *Rassegna della Letteratura Italiana*, 1953, No. 4. Garin criticises Seznec's stress on the traditionalism of Renaissance treatments of pagan mythology [except for their greater historicity, conformity of form and content]. He emphasises the importance of analysing the humanist interpretations of classical mythology as well as the link between the *theologia poetica* of the fourteenth-century humanists and the *theologia platonica* of Ficino and Pico. More recently Francesco Tateo has followed up Garin's suggestions with three studies of the theological ideas of the late Quattrocento poets: Jacopo Sannazaro, Giannantonio Petruciis and Michele Marullo. Cf. his *Tradizione e realtà nell'Umanesimo italiano*, Bari, 1967, pp. 11–219. Our study in this chapter will deal with humanist interpretation of poetry and mythology only, and not with the poetry itself as Tateo has so admirably done. Moreover, I do not aim at comprehensiveness but wish merely to suggest the rationale of this mode of humanist thought and point the way to further studies.
7. Curtius, op. cit.

8. Cf. J. Seznec, *The Survival of the Pagan Gods*, New York, 1953, Chapter III, 'The Moral Tradition', pp. 84–121.
9. Curtius, op. cit., pp. 226–7.
10. Above, pp. 568–71.
11. *Epistolae rerum familiarium*, ed. Rossi, II, 301; ed. Fracassetti, II, pp. 82–3, 'Theologie quidem minime adversa poetica est. Miraris? Parum abest quin dicam, theologiam poeticam esse de Deo, Christum modo leonem, modo agnum, modo vermem dici, quid nisi poeticum est? Mille talia in Scripturis sacris invenies, quae persequi longum est. Quid vero aliud parabole Salvatoris in Evangelio sonant, nisi sermonem a sensibus alienum, sive, ut uno verbo exprimam, alieniloquium, quam allegoriam usitatiori vocabulo nuncipamus? Atqui ex huiusce sermonis genere poetica omnis intexta est. Sed subiectum aliud. Quis negat? Illic de Deo deque divinis, hic de diis hominibus tractatur; unde et apud Aristotelem primos theologizantes poetas legimus.'
12. Ibid., Rossi, II, 301–2; Fracassetti, II, 83, 'Quaesitum enim est unde poetae nomen descendat: et quanquam varia ferantur illa tamen clarior sententia est, quod cum olim rudes homines sed noscendi veri praecipueque vestigande divinitatis studio, quod naturaliter inest homini, flagrantes, cogitare coepissent esse superiorem aliquam potestatem per quam mortalia regerentur; dignum rati sunt, illam omni plusquam humano obsequio et cultu augustiore venerari. Itaque ut edes amplissimas meditati sunt, que templa dixerunt, et ministros sacros quos sacerdotes dici placuit, et magnificas statuas et vasa aurea et marmoreas mensas et purpureos amictus; ac, ne mutus honos fieret, visum est et verbis altisonis divinitatem placare, et procul ab omni plebeio ac publico loquendi stilo sacras superis inferre blanditias, numeris insuper adhibitis, quibus et amoenitas inesset et tedia pellerentur. Id sane non vulgari forma sed artificiosa quadam et exquisita et nova fleri oportuit: quae quoniam greco sermone poetes dicta est, eos quoque qui hac utebantur poetas dixerunt.'
13. Ibid., Rossi, II, 302–3; Fracassetti, II, 84.
14. Francesco Petrarca, *Invective contra medicum*, ed. Pier Giorgio Ricci, Rome, 1950; Petrarch's defence of the poet is mainly in Book III, pp. 58–80.
15. Ibid., pp. 58–9, '. . . ructaveris in poetas, quasi vere fidei adversos vitandosque fidelibus et ab Ecclesia relegatos: quid de Ambrosio, Augustino et Ieronimo, quid de Cypriano, Victorinoque martire, quid de Lactantio ceterisque catholicis scriptoribus sentias: apud quos nullum pene mansurum opus sine poetarum calce construitur, cum contra fere nullus hereticorum poeticum aliquid opusculis suis inseruit, seu ignorantia, seu quod ibi suis erroribus consonum nichil esset. Quamvis deorum nomina multa commemorent, quod temporum qualitatem gentiumque potius quam suum iudicium secutos fecisse credendum est, quod ipsum et philosophi fecerunt, qui, ut in *Rhetoricis* legimus, deos esse non arbitrantur,

tamen poetarum clarissimi unum omnipotentem, omnia creantem, omnia regentem, opificem rerum Deum in suis operibus sunt confessi.'

16. Ibid., p. 66.
17. Ibid., pp. 69–71.
18. Ibid., p. 72, 'Quis enim nisi amens adulteros aut fallaces veneraretur deos? Aut quis penitus crederet deos esse, quorum ea flagitia audiret, que nec in hominibus tolerabilia iudicaret? Cui preterea dubium esse posset, quin peccata que humanitatem ipsam hominibus ereptura essent, eadem multo magis diis talibus preriperent deitatem? Belligerantes deo invicem Homerus et Virgilius fecerunt; propter quod Athenis Homerum pro insano habitum Cornelius Nepos refert. Credo nimirum apud vulgus; docti autem intelligunt, si plures sunt dii, et discordare illos et bella inter eos esse posse, et necesse esse ut, altero victore, alter victus, atque ita nec sit immortalis nec omnipotens, consequenterque ne deus quidem; unum esse igitur Deum non plures; vulgus autem falli.'
19. Ibid., pp. 71–2, 'Primos nempe theologos apud gentes fuisse poetas et philosophorum maximi testantur, et sanctorum confirmat autoritas, et ipsum, si nescis, poete nomen indicat. In quibus maxime nobilitatus Orpheus, cuius decimoctavo civitatis eterne libro Augustinus meminit. "At nequiverunt quo destinaverant pervenire", dicet aliquis. Fatebor. Nam perfecta cognitio veri Dei, non humani studii, sed celestis est gratie. Laudandum tamen animus studiosissimorum hominum, qui certe quibus poterant viis ad optatam veri celsitudinem anhelabant, adeo ut ipsos quoque philosophos in hac tanta et tam necessaria inquisitione precederent. Credibile est etiam hos ardentissimos inquisitores veri ad id saltem pervenisse, quo humano perveniri poterat ingenio, ut – secundum illud Apostoli supra relatum – per ea que facta sunt, invisibilibus intellectis atque conspectis, prime cause et unius Dei qualemcunque notitiam sortirentur; atque ita deinceps omnibus modis id egisse, ut – quod publice non audebant, eo quod nondum viva veritas terris illuxerat – clam suaderent falsos deos esse, quos illusa plebs coleret.'
20. Cf. Seznec, op. cit., p. 221. We shall use Osgood's standard and reliable translation of books XIV and XV, Charles G. Osgood, *Boccaccio on Poetry*, Princeton, 1930 [Reprint, Library of Liberal Arts, 1956], which is entirely suitable for our purposes.
21. *De geneal. deorum*, XV, 8, tr. Osgood, p. 121.
22. Ibid., XV, 8, tr. Osgood, pp. 122–3.
23. Ibid., XIV, 8, tr. Osgood, pp. 42–3.
24. Ibid., tr. Osgood, pp. 43–4.
25. Ibid., tr. Osgood, p. 44.
26. Ibid., tr. Osgood, pp. 45–6.
27. Cf. Curtius, op. cit., pp. 217–19.
28. Cf. below, pp. 714–5, 719–21, 741–2, 755–60.
29. *De civ. Dei*, XVII, 14.

30. Boccaccio, op. cit., XIV, 13, tr. Osgood, p. 65.
31. Ibid., tr. Osgood, pp. 65–6.
32. Cf. above, pp. 560–2.
33. *De laboribus Herculis libri quattuor*, ed. B. L. Ullman, op. cit.
34. Cf. above, pp. 560–2.
35. *De fato*, op. cit.; Urb. lat. 201, f. 16r, 'Nam usque adeo pauci sunt qui studiis humanitatis indulgeant, licet illa commendentur ab omnibus, placeant multis, et aliqui delectentur in ipsis, qui rem tam perdite collapsam et in peius continue delabentem erigere prorsus nequeant et quin pereat funditus obviare.' This statement, dating before 1396, is possibly the first use of the term *studia humanitatis*. Cf. Ullman, *The Humanism of C.S.*, op. cit., pp. 21–3, for the complicated dating of *De laboribus Herculis*.
36. Ed., Ullman p. 76, 'Quando et unde venerit deificandorum hominum atque simulacrorum origo.' 'Quoniam, sicut michi vero simillimum esse videtur, poetica cum deorum simulacrorum cultu principium habuit, scrutandum censeo qualiter et quo tempore tantus error mundum invaserit.'
37. Ibid., p. 77; *Sap.*, 14, 15.
38. Ibid., p. 78, ' "Omnium enim mirabilium vincit admirationem quod homo divinam potuit invenire naturam eamque efficere" ', citing Apuleius, *Asclepius*, 37.
39. Ibid., pp. 78–9, '. . . longe magis amici et publici veritatis testes quam ipsi philosophi, qui se ipsius veritatis professores gloriabantur.'
40. Ibid., pp. 79–82, cit. p. 82, '. . . cum scriptum sit Enos incepisse vocare nomen domini, nec possibile sit propriis et humane inventionis vocabulis de deo loqui, quoniam, cum undique infinitus et inenarrabilis sit, a nobis explicari non possit, figuratis et aliud ab eo significantibus verbis proculdubio fuit illa vocatio; ut ex tunc fas sit dicere nostram de qua locuti sumus poeticam incepisse. Nam et plurimi Hebreorum putaverunt ipsum dei effigiem fuisse commentum, ad quam verba deprecatoria fundebantur.'
41. Ibid., p. 82, '. . . sicut habet divina scriptura dilectionem dei et proximi, qua componitur et in quam quicquid est in ipsa compositum resolvatur, sic secularis, ut ita dixerim, et humana poetica creatorem habet et creaturam, in quos aut in quorum actus quicquid obtegit redigatur.'
42. Ibid., pp. 82–3, 'Et de deo quidem poetica nostra pertractat tum secundum se et actus intrinsecos, tum secundum effectus qui procedunt ad extra. Nam quod inquit poeta noster "Nate, mee vires, mea magna potentia, solus, nate, patris summi qui tela Typhoea temnis", ex abditis divine maiestatis, unitate scilicet essentie et multiplicitate persone, si pie intelligas, dictum est. Etenim quamvis Maronem et alios gentiles poetas veri dei misterium et profunditas latuerit trinitatis, multa tamen de suis diis

loquentes, dum ipsos ad deitatis maiestatem extollere stagabant, non illis quidem diis, qui profecto nulli sunt, se vero deo congruentia protulerunt.'

43. Ibid., p. 84, 'Est igitur sub verbis, que Iovi, de quo poeta loquitur, omnino non conveniunt, veri dei expressa quodam modo condicio, ut non se solum intelligat sed, quod voluntatis est, regat spirituales creaturas, quas deorum nomine expressit, ac etiam res, actus scilicet et voluntates, hominum, quas ipse solus potest dirigere qui potuit et creare.'

44. Ibid., pp. 85–6, '... omnes deos atque deas tum sacrorum emulatione, tum statuarum similitudine, tum oraculorum autoritate, tum identitate effectuum, tum consignificatione nominum, tum ordine cerimoniarum, tum aliis pluribus argumentis nichil aliud quam Apolline, esse; et tunc, ni fallor, nullatenus arbitrabitur poetas aliud quam unum deum illa sua deorum turba sensisse. Nam ... sic omnem illam deorum numerositatem unam omnium presupponentes essentiam iuxta potentiarum varietatem et actuum diversis nominibus vocaverunt, ut nomina, que quidem aliud sunt a rebus, non res plures sed multiformes eiusdem rei potentias, actus, et effectus significarent ... omnia, inquam, que apud poetas fabulosa videntur, oportet vel ad deum vel ad creaturas aut ad aliquid ad hos pertinens debita expositione reduci. Cumque poetarum abdita misticus interpretes aperiet, et ad deum, naturam, vel mores singula referens adaptaverit, sine dubitatione reputet se, quamvis incogitatum ab autore dici queat id quod invenerit, in sententiam tolerabilem incidisse. Quod si ad illa que senserit adaptare poterit propriorum nominum rationem, audacter affirmem ipsum sine controversia veram auctoris elicuisse sententiam, aut si forsitan illa non fuerit, et ad id quod autor intendisset nomina non accedant, longe commodiorem sensum quam cogitaverit invenisse.'

45. Cf. above, Part IV, Chap. XIV, p. 669.

46. Ed. Ullman, op. cit., pp. 86–7, 'Nec mirum. Multa quidem mortales ad unum aliquid ordinant que rerum director deus ad alium parat effectum. Unde incogitatos videmus eventus quotidie provenire. ... Ceterum ut in hoc aliquando concludam, hoc precipue differunt spiritualis et divina poesis ab humana et seculari, quoniam illa tota vera est, sive litteram consideres sive sensus abditos contempleris; hec autem veritatem amplectitur quandoque sub cortice, exterius autem, licet possit esse verax, ferme tamen semper solet esse figmentum. ... Sed quia infinite sunt rerum similitudines, possunt non inconvenienter ad alia trahi, quo desinant qui plures expositiones viderint admirari.'

47. Ibid., pp. 87–8, '... non solum que cum aliis leguntur sed que alibi legi non possunt.'

48. Ibid., p. 88, '... sed hominis condicionem expressit. ...'

49. Ibid., pp. 88–97, covering capp. 3 and 4.

50. Cf. Part I, Chapter II, above. Op. cit., p. 97, 'Quod Iupiter aliquando

sumitur pro agente supernaturali, et quod tunc Iuno ponitur pro voluntate dei et aliquando pro fortuna.'

51. Ibid., p. 102, 'Sed forte movebitur aliquis et inconvenienter arbitrabitur fictas apud poetas deorum collucutiones postquam idem deus qui Iupiter dicitur est omnes dii. Et si Iuno, ut proxime sumpta est, intelligitur Iovis dispositio seu voluntas, que nichil sunt aliud quam ipse Iupiter volens seu disponens, queve adeo non videntur ab ipso Iove differre quod omnino ipsa voluntas dici non possit, imo, ut multi volunt, dici non debeat nisi eadem essentia cum Iove volente, incongruentissime finxerunt poete quod Iupiter Iunoni quasi cuidam alteri loquatur. Et quamvis in deo, qui summe simplex est, voluntas sit sua essentia, et hoc idem in animabus hominum, ut expressius assignari queat in nobis imago atque vestigium trinitatis, nonnulli teneant et affirment, nichilominus tamen, cum sit alia ratio voluntatis divine et alia volentis dei et pariter angeli vel anime volentis, non inepte reperiuntur apud poetas huiusmodi locutiones, cum quotidie nobiscum experiamur ut intra nosmet ipsos de rebus variis disceptemus. Accedat et huic rationi sacrarum litterarum autoritas – an dicemus de deo incongrue scriptum esse "Et ait: 'Faciamus hominem ad imaginem et similitudinem nostram' "? Cum tamen ibidem exprimatur in unitate essentie cum dicitur "ait", ipsius misterium trinitatis cum subditur "faciamus" et illud pronomen "nostram" que connotant pluralitatem non essentie sed persone.'
52. Cf. E. Panofsky, *Hercules am Scheidewege*, op. cit.
53. Ed. Ullman, op. cit., p. 74, '... neminem unquam tantum didicisse quantum voluerit, nec omnino posse artis cuiuspiam finem attingere aut eius plenitudinem percepisse. Quin etiam alicuius artis nequit haberi perfectio (adeo simul alligate sunt, unaque pendet ex alter), nisi cetere sint percepte.'
54. The following information about Giovanni Caldiera is based, rather inadequately, on Fra Giovanni degli Agostini, O.M.O., *Notizie istorico-critiche intorno le vite e le opere degli scrittori Veneziani*, Tom. II, Venice, 1754, pp. 411–19. It is supplemented, where indicated, by bibliographical information from P. O. Kristeller, *Iter Italicum*, Vol. I, London and Leiden, 1963, Vol. II, London and Leiden, 1967.
55. *Liber canonum astrologiae ac totius orbis descriptione ad Alphonsum ... Regem Aragonum*. This is Venice, Bibl. Marciana VIII, 72 (3273), Cf. Kristeller, *Iter*, II, p. 228, Giovanni degli Agostini, op. cit., p. 414, speaks of a Manuscript Collection 'in Libreria del già Apostolo Zeno' where most of the works were seen.
56. Ibid., p. 416, *Catonis expositio pro filia erudienda* in a MS of the Biblioteca del Seminario Vescovile of Padua No. 39 acc. to Kristeller, *Iter*, II, p. 7. Kristeller adds Modena, Bibl. Estense, Cod. 299 (Gamma N 8, 4, 8) [I, p. 388] and Naples, Biblioteca Governativa dei Gerolamini, Cart. 29 (XIV, IV) [I, p. 397].

57. Degli Agostini, p. 418, *De virtutibus moralibus et theologicis*, which he says is also in Cod. 846 of the Bodleian.
58. *De Veneta Oeconomio*, also said to be in Cod. 846 of the Bodleian by Degli Agostini, p. 418.
59. Degli Agostini, p. 418: *De praestantia Venetae Politiae, et artibus in eadem excultis, tam mechanicis quam liberalibus et de virtutibus quae maxime Respublicae Venetae debentur*, V Libri, A.D. 1473. Kristeller [I, p. 195] adds: Florence, Bibl. Ricc., 669, ff. 310–69v and [p. 195 and p. 229] Florence, Libreria Olschi, 24068. This MS was subsequently purchased by Mr. Laurence Witten, bookseller, of New Haven, Conn. Cf. Kristeller, II, p. 519.
60. Degli Agostini, p. 419, lists *De ecclesiastico interdicto*, MS at Monte Oliveto of Siena. But he confused Caldiera with Giovanni Calderini, a 14 c. canonist and author of this work.
61. Kristeller, I, p. 373, *Expositio in Psalmos*, Modena, Bibl. Estense, Cod. 1000 (Alpha K 3, 6).
62. Bibl. Vatic. Urb. lat. 1178, f. 2v [original numbering IV, library has renumbered one higher], 'In hoc codice continetur Opus Ioannis Calderiae Veneti Medici Clarissimi De Concordia Poetarum, Philosophorum et Theologorum'; f. 3r, 'Incipit liber Iohannis Calderie de Concordantia Poetarum, Philosophorum et Theologorum. In Prohemale Capitulo Demonstratur Deum a Poetis, Philosophis et Theologis Fuisse Precognitum.' F. 207v, 'Summa haec continet duos libros. In primo gentilium omnium poemata naturaliter, moraliter et spiritualiter exponemus. In secundo libro scientiarum omnium et artium et practicarum similiter militantis et triumphantis ecclesiae poetice, nauraliter, moraliter et spiritualiter exponemus.'
63. Urbino copy as above. Manetti's copy is Palatino lat. 985. The Fossombrone Ms is Bibl. Civica Passionei, IV, F, Cf. Kristeller, *Iter*, II, 520. The edition of 1557 is in the Bibl. Vaticana and I have examined it. Degli Agostini, op. cit., mentions the date 1547 [p. 413]. The work was completed sometime during the pontificate of Nicholas V, 1447–55, as the *explicit* indicates, f. 208v, 'Et a Nicolao pontifice maximo ipsum ac puellas summopere curandas iussit. Ad laudem Sanctae trinitatis.' Manetti could have had his copy made in Rome during his service under Nicholas V. Caldiera's work has no formal dedication, but is addressed to his daughter.
64. Urb. lat. 1178 will be followed in our exposition, occasionally corrected by a more accurate reading from Pal. lat. 985, which though a highly abbreviated, cursive, paper manuscript for a working scholar, and not an elegantly wrought vellum for a Duke, is, not surprisingly, more accurate. The printed edition constantly makes such misreadings as *diversitas* for *divinitas* and is worse than useless. Urb. lat. ff. 3r–v, 'Quare dilectissima filia si poetarum, si primorum philosophorum mores ac doctrinam

negligis abhorres ac frequentius culpare soleas minime profecto admiror quoniam omnes tibi mores divinissimi sunt. Ita Christi preclari institutionibus versaris ita divinissime virginis vitam admiraris ut omnes homines qui haec longius imitantur et a religione et ab hominum dignitate alienos facis.'

65. Ibid., ff. 3v–4r, 'Nam omnes homines immo res omnes insitam divinitatem habent quamvis tum res divinas plerique falsa cognitione ferantur. . . . Omnium igitur perfectiones a deo sunt quae si ab hominibus et ceteris entibus subriperentur, prorsus desinerent. Esse igitur nostrum divinum esset, similiter vita, cognitio et amor a Deo sunt quae tamen in caeteribus entibus secundum perfectionem illorum continentur . . . primevi itaque homines effectus multos a natura productos conspiciebant, eorum tamen causas ignorabant. Quidam postea philosophantes rerum primas causas studiosius animadvertentes ignem quidam, aerem nonnulli, aquam alii, terram et quidam plura helementa componentes rerum omnium principium oppinabuntur, quare poetae illorum doctrinam imitantes rationem divinitatis primis helementis tribuerunt, et quosdam divinos homines arbitrabantur qui caeteros ingenio virtute doctrina superabant.'

66. Ibid., f. 4r–v, 'Verumtamen praeter hos insitum cognitionis genus est alius modus quo divinum lumen mentibus nostris infunditur ut res futuras intueamur sicut prophetae et vetustissimae quaedam sibillae quae deorum et hominum res a sua aetate distantissimas praesciebant. Hii adventum magni Dei et spem futuri seculi quibusdam parabolis et umbrata quadam doctrina dicebant. Postea vero nobis litteris tradiderunt, cum autem Dei filius carnem accepisset humanam et occultam divinitatem sub humanitatis velamine tueretur ut passionis misterium omne perficeret et humanum genus perditum redimeret.'

67. Ibid., f. 4v, 'Ideo multa Christi eruditione accepimus quae divinissimarum rerum et maxime occultarum cognitionem prebuerunt quia intellectus humanus a Dei perfectione distantissimus neque primam causam neque separatas formas intelligere potuisset. Ideo praeclaris quibusdam exemplis et aliquando prophetarum more et aliquando miraculis divinitatem omnem profitebatur. Sua praeterea doctrina patris, filii et sancti spiritus omnem rationem accepimus. Cum vero animae a corporibus separabuntur et gloriam promerimus aeternum Deum perfecta conspiciemus, intuitu quo presentium, praeteritorum ac futurorum distinctae rationes cognoscemus. Nam omnia quae viatores fide accipiunt in prima certa Dei intuitione constabunt. Quattuor igitur cognitionum genera divisimus quibus res divinas intueri homines possunt.'

68. Ibid., ff. 6r–8v, Cap. III, 'De Misterio Trinitatis Quod Antiqui Obscura Poesi Tradiderunt.'

69. Ibid., f. 6r–v, 'Quidam vero divinitati propinquissimi nubem postegarunt sicut existentes in patria divinitatem et omne misterium trinitatis clare conspiciunt et omnia quasi fide tenemus certe cognitione intuentur.'

70. Ibid., ff. 6v–7r.

71. Ibid., f. 7r–v, 'Si ergo ex Peleo et Thetide homo generatur quem mixtorum omnium perfectissimum in nostris naturalibus libris diffinivimus, necesse ut influxus multi et multae coelorum ordinationes pro hominis generatione conveniant, quia sol et homo peripeticorum sententia hominem generant, quod si coeli dispositiones dissentiant non posset mixtum tam perfectum sicut homo generari, propterea supra celestes dii qui pro generatione conveniunt discordiam non admiserunt qui generatione prohiberet. Postea vero quam homo nascitur et illi tempus cognitionis advenerit tres dee quia tres vivendi modi hominibus offeruntur, unus quo Paladem quia sapientiam prosequimur. Alter quo Iunonem quia divitias et dignitates summopere curamus. Tertius quo Venerem nam ad omne genus voluptatis facile compellimur. Iovem que deum consulimus quam istarum trium dearum prosequi debeamus. Deus iudicium fere recusat cum hominibus intellectum tribuisset in quo perfecta discretio et recta electio continentur. Nam pro meritis et demeritis homines praemia sive suplicia ferunt quare homo suae vitae ignarus iudicium rationis obmittit et se usum electionem [subiectum electionis 1557] prosequitur, Venerem preferens quae voluptuosa omnia pollicetur. Sed longis laboribus vigilis et abstinentia sapientiam Paladis imitamur et maximis periculis, anxietatibus copias Iunonis prosequimur.'

72. Cf. Edgar Wind, *Pagan Mysteries in the Renaissance*, op. cit., rev. ed., Chapter V, 'Virtue Reconciled with Pleasure', pp. 81–96. Wind demonstrates the extent of interest in this theme among artists and writers, but he does not know of Caldiera.

73. Op. cit., Urb. lat. 1178, ff. 7v–8r, 'Alia moralis interpretatio: per Thetim honores corporis intelligamus, per Peleum hominis carnem, per Iovem animam quae corporis partem componit et format, per has tres deas tria doctrinarum genera circa quae homines versantur. Nam speculativis quidam scientis ingenium omne conferunt, quidam practicis et quidam artibus operativis. Stoici omnem foelicitatem et virtutis perfectionem in habitu intellectuali tantummodo posuerint. Hii quidem virtutem et foelicitatem animo et cogitatione solum modo prosequuntur. Etiam christianissimi quidam homines Deum et gloriam futuri seculi animo et cogitatione speculationibus prosequuntur. Sed Peripatetici ad virtutem et foelicitatem principalius operatione quam habitu pervenerunt quoniam agonizantes coronantur et non qui habitum virtutis habent, quorum doctrinam Christianissimi quidam mutantur, non solummodo orationibus sed operationibus Christum imitantes. Tertia philosophorum secta longius a veritate secessit, quia animam humanam corruptibilem facit et omnia prefert quae ad corporis voluptatem accedunt Venerem dignificantes. Sed Peripateticos imitantes Iunonem preferunt, et Stoicos imitantes Palladem omnibus anteponunt.'

74. Ibid., f. 8r–v, 'Spiritualis et Christiana interpretatio: Per Protheum deum

patrem intelligimus. Per Iovem Christum, Per Peleum populum Christianum. Per Tetim sanctam ecclesiam catholicam quam Christus vehementer adamavit non tamen illi corporaliter sed spiritualiter et sacramentaliter coniunctus manet. Si enim corporaliter semper manisset non nostris sed Christi meritis salvi facti essemus. Per has tres deas tres virtutes theologicas intelligimus: per Iunonem deam potentiae in cognitionem potentiae patris per virtutem devenimus quia potentia patri atrribuitur, et sancti per fidem regna paradisi viserunt et omnipotentiam Dei patris intellexerunt. Per Palladem deam sapientiae et veram spem intelligimus. Nam sapientia de ipsa loquitur. Ergo multipliciter pulchrae, dilectionis, timoris et sanctae spei per spem ad sapientiam filii ducimur et generationem in divinis cognoscimus sapientia enim filio attribuitur. Per Venerem Deam amoris intelligimus caritatem quae mentibus nostris emanationem sancti spiritus manifestat. Nam sibi voluntas attribuitur in qua ratio per affectis amoris continetur. Haec igitur tres dee ad eternum convivium invitantur ubi nulla discordia, nulla lis esse potest, quia sancti sola pace fruuntur. Sed diabolus discordiarum Deo cum a divino consortio excluderetur, Adam parentem nostram a mandatis Dei pervertit, propterea opus fuit ut pomum aureum mirabili artificio fabricatum quia Deum hominem factum in medio dearum proieceretur quo pomo deas omnes intellectus humanus pro excellentias Christianorum benemeritas iudicavit. Sed quia altera preferi iure debet, ideo Mercurius, quia intellectus humanus sonora fistula quia sapientis lingua dubiam pro dignitate dearum sententiam feri, ideo illas ad Paridem conduxit quia ad Apostolum Paulum, ut de pulchriore sententiam ferat qui cum eas nudas et sine ullo velamine intueretur pro caritate sententiam tulit cumque eam anteposuisset sibi pomum aureum adiudicavit, quia omnium maiorem est caritas. Rationem igitur preceptorum omnium per dilectionem Dei et proximi magis imitamur quoniam super hiis duobus lex Christi et prophetarum omnium fundatur. Quare si potentias anime comparaverimus in voluntate caritas, intellectu fides, in memoria spes locatur. Et quia perfectionem potentiarum a perfectione obiectorum cognoscimus ideo primo voluntatem, secundo intellectum, ultimo memoriam preferemus. Haec tamen omnia studiosius animadvertas.'

75. Ibid., ff. 108v–9r, 'Sed viventia perfectissima sicut homines post cognitionem, post electionem obiecta sequuntur; per hos igitur tres appetitus tria amorum genera distinguimus quia primus amor est naturalis, secundus sensitivus, et tertius intellectivus. Supercelestis ergo Venus celi filia immo sydus omne ex celo suam generationem accepit.'

76. Ibid., ff. 109v–10r, 'Nam a bonis melior efficitur quam a malis pravia. Hec omnia preclarus ac eruditissimus vates Virgilius nobis significat. Nam cum Eneas Iovem cum Venere in supremo celo intueretur, paucis post diebus partem regni ab uxore suscepit. Cum autem Venus Enee

tristior apparuisset Dido se gladio peremit. Cum autem Mercurius ad occasum et infima loca Libiae a Iove transmissus fuerit ut significaret Aeneae si amicitias habiturum non tamen longo tempore duraturas. Sed cum Venus tanquam virgo apparuisset ut significaret quod quando in virgine continetur homines mites ac misericordes facit.'

77. Ibid., f. 112v, '. . . quia gratiae sine ullo tegumento esse debent . . .' '. . . octavo Ethicorum Aristoteles clare distinguit primam stabilem et perpetuam facit, caeteras lapsas atque caducas.'
78. Ibid., ff. 111r–12v.
79. Cf. Seznec, op. cit., p. 224. My former student, Miss Margaret L. King, is preparing a doctoral dissertation on Caldiera under the supervision of Professor Lewis W. Spitz at Stanford University. Another example of a mid-fifteenth-century treatise on the ancient gods is Lorenzo Domenichi, *Libri delle antiche religione*, of which the first book only is contained in Florence, Bibl. Naz. Centr. Cod. Magl. 37, 319; f. 48v, 'Finisce il libro delle antiche religione composto di Lorenzo di Domenico et mandato al prestantissimo huomo Bernardo del Nero A di xvii di Settembre MCCCCLXXIII'.
80. On Lazzarelli cf. Kristeller, *Studies*, op. cit., pp. 224–5. The MSS of *De gentilium imaginibus* are Bibl. Vat., Urb. lat. 716 and 717; it also is in Florence, Bibl. Naz. Centr., Nuovi Acquisti 272.
81. We shall use Cod. Laur. 53, 37, 'In hoc volumine continentur interpretationes Christophori Landini in P. Vergilii Opera que in circulis sunt adnota ad Petrem Medicem Laurenti Filium.' His commentary on the *Bucolics*, ff. 1r–43r, on the *Georgics*, ff. 43v–123v, on the *Aeneid*, ff. 125r–451v. Each has a prologue but only that to the *Aeneid*, ff. 125r–7v, concerns our subject. For the *Disputationes Camaldulenses* we also use the Laurenziana copy, Laur. 53, 28, though we have examined the dedication copy, Bibl. Vat., Urb. lat. 508, dedicated to Federigo of Urbino. His Vergil commentary, Laur, 53, 37, is, of course, the dedication copy. His commentary on the Divine Comedy, which exists in several editions, needs to be studied for Landino's own projection of late Quattrocento theological and poetic ideas rather than viewed as part of the history of Dante criticism. Unfortunately, we must confine ourselves to his general ideas on Poetic Theology and his mode of interpreting Vergil.
82. In his letter to Marrasius Siculus. Cf. L. Mehus, *Leon. Bruni Epistolarum libri VIII*, op. cit., Vol. II, pp. 36–40 [Ep. VI, 1].
83. Laur. 53, 37, ff. 125v–6r, 'Huiuscemodi igitur vi qui affecti sunt eos quoniam et supra homines ascenderint, et deos tamen attingere non valuerint, poetas Graeci appellarunt, Deus enim ex nihilo quae vult producit, quod quidem creare dicimus. Homo verus contra nihil nisi ex sibi proposita materia efficere valet. At poeta quamvis non omnino sine materia poema texat, delegat enim sibi errores atque bella Aeneae quae canerit Virgilius, et tamen praeter illud argumentum quo opus totum

suo ordine decurrit, profundissimos quosdam sensus ex nihilo pene latenter dissimulanterque in eo argumento includit, quo qui eos actingunt, tandem intelligant qua via vir ad laudem natus, paulatim stultitiam variosque errores exuens, ad summum bonum valeat provenire. . . . Nam caelum et terram ex nulla materia produxit Deus. Vides igitur unde poetae nomen Graeci deducerunt. Sed neque Latini poetarum divinitatem ignorasse videntur, cum ob ea quae in hominibus omnium maxima est, mentis vi, vates appellaverunt. Hi igitur divini vates sunt.'

84. Ibid., f. 126v, 'Neque enim alius est magnus verusque poeta quam theologus, quod non solum Aristotelis tanti philosophi auctoritas testimoniumque ostendit, sed ipsorum quoque scripta apertissime docent. Duplex enim theologia est. Altera quam priscam vocant, cuius divinus ille vir Mercurius cognomine Trismegistus primus fontem aperuit. Altera nostra est quae non modo verior comprobatur, sed ita verissima, ut neque addi quicquam nece imminui inde possit. In prisca igitur nonne Orpheus ita versatur ut multa de Deo, multa de angelis, multa de incorporeis mentibus, multa de humanis animis describat. Is enim ostendit Deum unum esse, eundemque ubique, nullis locis aut temporibus circumscriptum esse. Omnia agere, omnia servare, in omnibus operari, ac quicquid agit, per id quod ipse est agere. Ac se ipsum primum, deinde singula intelligere. Intelligere itidem infinita. Addit ad haec Deum voluntatem habere, perque illam extra se cuncta efficere, eamque voluntatem necessariam simul ac liberam esse qua quidem ut libere omnino agit. Atque ita agit ut summus in ea amor sit et summa in rebus omnibus providentia. Eadem pene Linum ac Museum cecinisse ex iis que de utroque ab aliis scripta vidimus, credendum iudico. Nam Homerum si eos qui ab eo scripti sunt hymnos diligenter legamus.'

85. Ibid., ff. 126v–7r, '. . . admirabili ac pene divino artificio illum nobis demonstrare: summum hominis bonum in diviniarum rerum speculatione consistere, ac difficillimam quae illuc ferat viam ostendere.'

86. Ibid., f. 127r–v, 'Verum ut haec in nostro Marone cognoscamus, quemadmodum duo sunt apud homines vivendi genera, quorum alterum in speculatione, alterum in actione positum est. Ita et in hoc poeta, ut hominem nobis totum informaret, duplicem sensum deprehendes. Nam si ea quae extrinsecus apparent, ex verborum notione iudicabis, vitam omnino civilem, rectasque; et ab iis quae de vita et moribus sunt virtutibus profectas actiones; ita non descriptas solum verum etiam depictas invenies, ut non solum perspicere sua illas doctrina doceat, verum tum mira orationis suavitate ad illas alliciat, tum etiam, cum opus est dicendi, vehementia atque impetu promoveat atque impellat.'

87. Ibid., f. 127v, 'Sin autem in intima eius penetralia intrare licebit, quam multa immortalis Deus, quam magna, quam admiranda, quam denique nobis salutaria invenies. Nam cum homines ita a summo Deo productos, tum ex se per summam sapientiam cognosceret, tum a divino Platone

accepisset, ut non nobis solum, sed caeteris omnibus, quoad id fieri liceret, usui esse studeremus, id conscribere statuit, quo et quid sit ultimum, illud propter quod reliqua expetuntur, et qua etiam ratione, veluti certa et indubitata via eo feramur, nos doceret. Idque non vulgatiori multorum philosophorum instituto, sed raro poeticoque more sibi tractandum proposuit.'

88. *Disputationes Camaldulenses,* Lib. III, op. cit., Laur. 53, 28, ff. 96v–7r, 'Is igitur in eo quod de summo bono scripsit, omnes artes sive divinae sive humanae illa sint, in unum Homeri poema veluti in proprium receptaculum confluxisse affirmat. Quamobrem animadvertens Maro doctrinam huius hominis ex Aegyptiorum sacerdotum fontibus haustam simillimam cum Platonitis, quorum studiosissimus fuit, rationem habere, eam usque adeo admiratus est, ut idem in suo Aenea efficere voluerit quod ille antea in Ulyxe finxerat . . . quo uno foelix simul et sapiens efficatur Deoque iungatur.'

89. Ibid., f. 97r–v.

90. Ibid., f. 98r–v.

91. Ibid., f. 98v, 'Verum alter quoniam Venerem Palladi, idest virtuti voluptatem, anteponit, necesse est ut una cum Troia pereat. Alter autem duce matre Venere se ab omni incendi explicat. Quod quid aliud intelligamus nisi eos qui magno amore inflamati ad veri cognitionem impellantur omnia facile consequi posse? Quapropter Venerem divinum amorem recte interpretabimur.'

92. Ibid., f. 99r–v, 'Miror igitur tu Venerem amorem interpreteris, eum praesertim amorem qui non modo castus, verum etiam divinus sit. Ego enim Venerem non solum apud poetas sed etiam apud reliquos scriptores ita sumptam video ut per eam non nisi maris feminaeque coniunctionem significare velint. . . . Ego enim non video cur si bona sit Venus, Paridi noceat, si mala prosit Aeneae.'

93. Ibid., f. 100r–v, 'Verum cum omnis nostra disputatio nullam historiae rationem habeat, sed eam quam totiens graeco verbo allegoriam nomino exprimere conetur. . . .'

94. Ibid., f. 101r–v, 'Mirus profecto vir, qui non ex optatis sed ex datis ita opus intexat, ut cum historiam minime deserat, per eam tamen incredibili integumente humanam foelicitatem exprimat.'

95. Ibid., ff. 101v–2r, 'Animus autem noster cum et ipse similes quasdam vires habeat intelligendi atque gignendi, duas itidem Veneres habere dicitur quas gemini comitentur cupidines. Cum enim corporea pulchritudo oculis nostris obiicitur, mens nostrae quae prima Venus est eam non quia corporea sit, sed quia simulacrum divini decoris admiratur atque diligit, eaque veluti via quadam ad caelos effertur. Gignendi autem vis, quae secunda Venus est, formam gignere huic similem concupiscit. Quapropter uterque amor iure dicitur ut alter contemplandae alter gignendae pulchritudinis desiderium sit. Nemo igitur nisi totius rationis

expers sit, duos istos amores damnare audebit, cum uterque humanae naturae necessarius sit.'

96. Ibid., f. 102r, '... quia illa male usus est. Vir enim gignendi avidior quam recta ratio dictet, et in ea re plus quam oportet occupatus in solis corporeis voluptatibus mergitur.'

97. Ibid., f. 103r, 'Amor enim verus ut apud eundem Platonem ostendit Eriximachi oratio, omnium naturalium rerum creator est, atque servator. Eo enim similia omnia ad ea quae sibi similia sunt perenni concordia trahuntur. Est itidem omnium maximarum artium magister. Nemo enim aut artem invenit aut ab alio inventam addiscit, nisi investigationis oblectatio et discendi cupido incitet. Quam quidem rem, si non aperte ostendit, obscurius tamen ut poetarum mos est, significat noster Virgilius.'

98. Ibid., ff. 103v–4r, 'Divinus enim amor nil aliud meditatur, nil molitur, nulla alia in re laborat, nihil tentat, nihil nititur nisi ut iam corporeae pulchritudinis rapiat. Dum enim corporeis tenebris demersi sunt animi nostri, divina non recognavit, nisi umbris et simulacris quibusdam quae sese nostris sensibus obiiciunt. Quam quidem rem non solum expresserunt prisci ex Graecia philosophi, in quibus Pythagorem, Empedoclem, Heraclitum, sed longe ante alios Platonem enumerare possum. Sed et Christiani ab eadem sententia minime discedunt. Nam et Paulus et qui Pauli auditor fuit Dionysius Ariopagita caelestia ac divina, quae in sensus non cadunt per ea, quae sensibus percipiuntur cerni volunt. Haec est igitur illa vera Venus, quae mentem nostram ad divina erigit.'

99. Cf. Erwin Panofsky's discussion of this important theme in his study of Piero di Cosimo, *Studies in Iconology*, New York, 1939, II, 'The Early History of Man in Two Cycles of Paintings by Piero di Cosimo', pp. 33–67.

100. Laur. 53, 28, op. cit., f. 104r–v, 'Habet enim haec vim verus amor ut pauloante dixi, ut mentem vehementer exacuat, magisterque illi rerum inveniendarum paulatim sit ut nihil eam latere possit. ... Deinde cum nihil difficile putet, modo re amata potiatur omnes labores tolerat, omnes difficultates superat. Haec est Venus illa non vulgaris quae materiae admixta vim habet gignendi, sed illa caelestis ab omni materia remota, quae a mente nostra est, ipsamque mentem excitat, et lucem illi suam nobis hactenus incognitam in nocte, id enim est in nostra inscitia ostendit seque deam fatetur.' Cf. Valla's comments on the force of the affects, above, pp. 160–1.

101. Ibid., ff. 105r–7r.

102. Ibid., f. 107r, 'Nam rationem excitat talis amor cuius luce illustrati verum nosse valeamus. Apparet autem ex Ida monte, id est ex pulchritudine, *eidos* enim apud Graecos formam significat. Amor autem apud Platonem pulchritudinis desiderium diffinitur.'

103. Ibid., f. 107v, 'Si autem eadem cogitandi vis salutari rationis lumine illustretur, et eius norma dirigatur non id bonum esse iudicat quo sensus

demulcentur, sed quod recta dictat ratio. . . . Cum igitur huiuscemodi vis hoc bonum illud vero malum esse decreverit, excitatur in nobis alia quaedam vis, quae ad bonum asciscendum malumque declinandum insurgat, hunc autem appetitum omnes appellant. Sed et eum duplicem esse oportet, alterum qui ab eo iudicio quod solus sensus fecit semper pendeat, nihilque cum ratione expectat, alterum qui nihil omnino sequatur nisi quod ratio prius praeceperit: primum illum libidinem, hunc secundum voluntatem nuncupamus.' Cf. concept of natural appetite in Ficino, in P. O. Kristeller, *Il pensiero filosofico di Marsilio Ficino*, op. cit., Parte I, Cap. VIII, 5, '*Appetitus naturalis*.'

104. Laur. 53, 28, op. cit., f. 108r.
105. Landino stated in the proem to his *Commentary* on Vergil, Cod. Laur. 53, 37 [Proem to *Aeneid*], f. 127v, 'Nam quemadmodum in Camaldulensibus philosophi interpretis munus obivimus, sin in his commentariis grammatici rhetorisque vices praestabimus'.

Notes to Part IV, Chapter XVI

1. Cf. Mommsen's study, 'Petrarch's Conception of the "Dark Ages"', op. cit.
2. Felix Gilbert has shown how even with that most secular of humanist historians, Francesco Guicciardini, there was a stress on the ultimate determination of human events by divine providence, *Machiavelli and Guicciardini*, op. cit., pp. 284, ff.
3. Cf. my 'The Unknown Quattrocento Poetics of Bartolommeo della Fonte', *Studies in the Renaissance*, XIII (1966), pp. 40–122; text, p. 104, '. . . ego quidem unicum tantummodo esse Deum eundemque optimum atque aeternum existimo. Neque unquam aliter poetae gentium putaverunt. Praeter hunc autem cuius filium Iovem gentiles dicunt, nos Christum, Asiatici et Lybes Maumethem, aliae atque aliae gentes alios, fuerunt atque hodie sunt eruntque semper apud mortales alii dii minores, quos seu heroas seu sanctos vocites, nihil laboro.'
4. Cf. above, pp. 581–2.
5. Cf. Vespasiano, *Commentario*, op. cit., p. 178. Manetti's work is variously labelled *Contra Iudeos et Gentes* and *Adversus Iudeos et Gentes* in the unique manuscript copy, Bibl. Vat., Urb. lat. 154. The dating must be taken as tentative, as this was apparently a work on which he worked over many years with the full knowledge of his associates. For instance, Antonio da Barga mentions this work in 1449. Cf. above, Part II, Chapter VI, n. 3.
6. Urb. lat. 154, ff. 1r–84v.
7. Ibid., f. 1r, '. . . ut is ipse ceteris operibus suis dignior atque excellentior consideretur. Quocirca cum angelicos spiritus intelligentes incorporeosque paulo ante constituisset ad maiorem quandam totius universi pulcritudinem ac decorum aliam naturam corpoream intellectusque capacem

instituere atque condere voluit, quam ex corpore animaque compactam, Adam Hebraice appellavit, quod Latine hominem significat. Hunc igitur cum omnibus animi et corporis dotibus mirabiliter exornasset, cunctis operibus suis iam ante creatis preesse ac predominari disposuit decrevitque. Sed ut melius ea ipsa gubernare regereque ac per hunc modum probe gubernata beneque recta in utilitatem suam convertere valeret illi rectam callidam et sagacem mentem largitus.'

8. Ibid., ff. 1r–2r, '. . . ac naturali prime legi et novis quodque mandatis que Noe et Abrahe predictis iustis piisque hominibus exhibita fuerant. . . .'

9. Ibid., ff. 2v–6v.

10. Ibid., f. 7r–v, 'Omnes itaque gentes preter Hebreos dumtaxat opus quos solos verus et pius omnipotens Dei cultus idcirco reservabatur . . . ad ydolatriam convertebantur.'

11. Ibid., ff. 7v–10r.

12. Ibid., f. 10v, '. . . et cum totum mundum diversorum generum animalibus refertum viderent, id non absque providentia provenire potuisse intelligebant, atque a magnitudine et pulcritudine creaturarum ob puritatem mentis creatorem omnium immortalem ipsum atque invisibilem cognoscebant. . . . Hominem quoque singularem quandam totius universi particularam existimaverunt atque animam scilicet verum et interiorem hominem precipuam eius partem, corpus autem quasi hominis indumentum putaverunt. Unde tanto maiorem curam ad cultum animarum quam corporum attulerunt ut corpora contempnerunt. Animas vero quia ad similitudinem Dei create erant usque adeo magnificarunt ut summum hominis bonum Dei cognitionem arbitrarentur.'

13. Ibid., ff. 10v–11r, '. . . atque hec antequam Grecorum nomen esset in terris, immo vero etiam ante Moysen et ante Iudeorum gentem priscis illis Hebreis veris et piis omnipotentis Dei cultoribus celitus innotescebant. Iudei enim post Moysen a Iuda, Hebrei vero ab Hebere a quo Abraham originem traxit appellati fuere. Hac denique pietate ducti, hac dominica gratia adiuti multis ante Moysen seculis absque aliqua lege scripta pie sancteque vivebant et absque ulla divinarum legum que nondum late fuerant doctrina solis oraculis mentisque acumine puram altissimorum rerum veritatem mirabiliter consequebantur.'

14. Ibid., f. 11r–v.

15. Ibid., f. 11v, '. . . sed Hebreos potius et expressius nuncupamus aut ab Hebere ut dictum est aut sic verius appellamus quia id nomen Hebraice transituros significabat. Sole quippe Hebrei a creaturis naturali ratione ac lege non scripta sed nata ad cognitionem veri Dei transire potuerunt et voluptatibus corporis contemptis ad rectam vivendi viam pervenerunt. . . .'

16. Ibid., ff. 12r–15r (Esau to Aaron), ff. 15v–18v (Moses).

17. Ibid., ff. 19r–22v, '. . . nisi caducum, nisi momentaneum, nisi terrenum . . . Iudei enim quamvis uni et soli et omnipotenti Deo sacrificarent suppli-

carentque, sola tamen temporalia et visibilia bona ab Illo expectabant.' [f. 20v], 'servilia et non libero homine digna videantur . . .' [f. 19r].

18. Ibid., f. 22v, 'Cum ergo hec omnia ita sint, profecto neque in confusione paganorum quos aliis verbis plerumque gentiles appellamus, neque in cecitate et obstinatione Iudeorum querenda est religio, . . . sed apud eos solos qui Christiani nominantur.'
19. Ibid., f. 23r–v, '. . . ita divina providentia cum sit omnino incommutabilis mutabili tamen creature varie opitulatur et subvenit et pro diversitate morborum alis alia iubet aut vetat.'
20. Ibid., ff. 23v–4r, 'In dua enim genera quantum ad hoc presens propositum spectat homines distributi videntur in quorum uno turba est impiorum veteris scilicet exterioris ac terreni hominis. In altero vero multitudo piorum interioris videlicet novi ac celestis hominis continetur. Sed Adam primo homine usque ad Johannem Baptistam ecclesiastica historia terreni hominis vitam moresque describit cuius quidem historiam divulgato veteris testamento nomine quasi terrenum pollicentis regnum appellatur et dicitur. Que tota nichil est aliud quam quedam mystica novi populi ymago et aperta novi testamenti umbra sempiternum celorum regnum absque aliqua dubitatione pollicentis cuius quidem populi vita a felicissimo domini nostri adventu in summa quadam et admirabili humilitate incipit, et usque ad ultimum generalis iudicii diem extenditur.'
21. Ibid., Lib. II, 'De vita, moribus ac miraculis Christi', ff. 24v–51v.
22. Ibid., Lib. III, 'De doctrina Christi', ff. 51v–71v.
23. Ibid., Lib. IV, 'De morte Christi', ff. 71v–84v.
24. Above, Part IV, Chapter XII, pp. 596–9.
25. *De religione Christiana*, *Opera omnia*, Basel, 1576, I, pp. 1–77. We have used Cod. Laur. 21, 9, and the edition of Paris, 1559, which we cite. On Ficino, cf. above, Part III, Chapter IX, n. 1.
26. Paris, 1559, f. 1r, 'Quod inter Sapientiam Religionemque maxima cognatio est.'
27. Ibid., f. 1r–v, 'Nam cum animus ut Platoni nostro placet duabus tantum alis (id est intellectu et voluntate) possit ad caelestem Patrem et patriam revolare ac philosophus intellectu maxime, sacerdos voluntate nitatur, et intellectus voluntatem illuminet, voluntas intellectum accendat, . . .'
28. Ibid., f. 1v, 'Eadem in Graecia consuetudo fuit sub Lino, Orpheo, Museo, Eumolpo, Aglaophemo atque Pythagora.'
29. Ibid., ff. 1v–2r, 'O secula tandem nimium infelicia, quando Palladis Themidisque (id est, sapientiae et honestatis) separatio et divortium miserabile contigit! Pro nefas, sic datum est sanctum canibus lacerandum. Doctrina enim magna ex parte ad prophanos translata est, unde ut plurimum iniquitatis evasit [Laur. 21, 9; 1559: emersit] et lasciviae instrumentum, ac malitia dicenda est potiusquam scientia. Margaritae autem religionis pretiosissimae saepe tractantur ab ignorantibus, atque ab iis tanquam suibus conculcantur. Saepe enim iners ignorantum ignavo-

rumque cura superstitio potiusquam religio appellanda videtur. Ita neque illi sincere veritatem intelligunt quae tanquam divina solis piorum oculis illucescit; neque isti quantum in eis est recte vel Deum colunt vel sacra gubernant divinarum humanarumque rerum prorsus ignari. Quamdiu duram et miserabilem hanc ferrei seculi sortem substinebimus'? Cf. Valla's claim that *malitia* and *prudentia* were identical, above, pp. 157–8

30. Ibid., f. 2v, 'Religio homini maxime propria est et veridica.'

31. Cf. above, pp. 496–8.

32. Ibid., ff. 2v–3v, 'Adde quod conscientiae stimulus nos solos pungit assidue divinae vindictae inferorumque timor acerrime vexat. Si ergo religio, ut diximus, vana est, nullum est animal dementius et infoelicius homine.'

33. Ibid., f. 4r–v, '. . . ita neque Deus sine Deo cognoscitur. . . . Deum agitat mens humana, quotidie Deo ardet cor. Deum suspirat pectus, eundem cantat lingua, eundem caput, manusque adorant et genua, eundem referunt hominum artificia.'

34. Ibid., f. 5v, 'Omnis religio boni habet nonnihil, modo ad Deum ipsum creatorem omnium dirigatur, Christiana vero sincera est.'

35. Ibid., ff. 5v–6v, 'Idcirco divina providentia non permittit esse aliquo in tempore ullam mundi regionem omnis prorsus religionis expertem quamvis permittat variis locis atque temporibus ritus adorationis varios observari. . . . Coli mavult quoquo modo vel inepte, modo humane, quam per superbiam nullo modi coli.'

36. Ibid., Capp. V, VI, VII, ff. 6v–13v.

37. Ibid., Cap. VIII, 'Christiana religio in sola Dei virtute fundata est.' ff. 14r–15r, 'In illis enim nova vis est singularis quo simplicitas, sobrietasque, et ardor, gravitas, profunditas et maiestas. . . . Habent scriptores illi nescio quid pium et augustum atque id quod mirabile est inter se quidem commune a caeteris omnibus penitus alienum. . . .'

38. Ibid., Cap. IX, 'Auctoritas Christi non ab astris, sed a Deo est,' ff. 19r–20v.

39. Ibid., Cap. X, 'Christi auctoritas absque miraculis minime fuit,' ff. 21r–5r.

40. Ibid., Cap. XI, 'Christi auctoritas apud gentiles,' f. 25r–8r.

41. Ibid., Cap. XII, 'Christi auctoritas apud Mahumetenses,' ff. 28r–9r.

42. Ibid., Cap. XIII, 'De generatione filii Dei in aeternitate,' ff. 29r–30v, 'Dixerunt isti quidem quod potuerunt, et id quidem adiuvante Deo. Deus autem hoc solus intelligit et cui Deus voluerit revelare. . . . In Deo autem quia esse et intelligere idem sunt, notio quam Deus semper intelligendo se ipsum gignit semper tanquam exactissimum sui ipsius imaginem, idem essentia est atque ipse qui generat quamvis mira quadam relatione tanquam genita distinguitur a generante.' [f. 30r].

43. Ibid., Cap. XIV, 'Ordo caelorum, angelorum, animarum circa Trinitatem quasi sphaerarum circa centrum,' ff. 30v–2r.

44. Ibid., Cap. XV, 'Generatio Filii in aeternitate et declaratio in tempore,' ff. 32r–3r.
45. Ibid., Cap. XVII, 'Qualis coniunctio sit Dei et hominis,' ff. 35r–v.
46. Ibid., f. 33r, '. . . neque se ad humanam quasi per defectum deiecit divina sublimitas, sed humana ad se potius elevavit, neque infinita divini solis lux ex adiunctione hominis ullo modo infici unquam potuit, sed homo unde semper [*sic* Laur. 21, 9; 1559, super] illustrari ac perfici. . . .'
47. Ibid., Cap. XVI, 'Conveniens fuit Deum se homini iungere,' ff. 33r–5r, cit., ff. 33v–4r, 34v, 'Est igitur anima hominis quodammodo omnia quod in *Theologia* nostra latius disputavimus, praesertim cum in corpore ex omnium viribus composito celique instar temperatissimo. Decet autem Deo communi omnium duci universam creaturam quodammodo iungi. . . . Naturae igitur humanae Deus uniatur oportet in qua sunt omnia.' 'Deus autem in homine hominem reddit divinum.'
48. Ibid., Cap. XVIII, 'Quam decens Dei hominisque coniunctio,' ff. 35v–7r, cit., f. 36r–v, 'Sic ergo et declaravit et fecit ut nihil esset in mundo deforme, nihil penitus contemnendum, cum regi caelorum terrena coniunxit atque ea quodammodo caelestibus adaequavit. . . . Nullus ad hoc aptior modus quam quod Deus fieret homo, ut homo qui corporalis iam factus corporalibus inhiabat Deum iam quodammodo et corporalem et humanam clarius cognosceret, et amaret ardentius, facilius quoque et diligentius imitaretur fieretque beatus. Postremo homo curari perfecte non poterat nisi recuperaret mentis innocentiam, Dei amicitiam, suam excellentiam, quae soli subiecta Deo fuerat ab initio secundum naturam. . . .'
49. Ibid., Cap. XIX, 'Adventus Christi dat beatitudinem fide, spe, charitate,' f. 37r–v, 'Desinant igitur iam desinant homines suae divinitatis diffidere, ob quam diffidentiam moralibus se ipsos mergunt. Revereantur se ipsos tanquam divinos, sperentque se posse ad Deum ascendere, quandoquidem ad eos dignata est quodammodo maiestas divina descendere.'
50. Ibid., Cap. XX, 'Adventus Christi ad peccati gravitatem levandam utilis fuit,' ff. 37v–8v.
51. Ibid., Cap. XXI, 'Christus perfectum instructionis genus implevit,' ff. 38v–9v, cit., f. 38v, 'Opera enim multo magis quam verba movent in disciplina praesertim morali cuius finis proprius versatur in actione.'
52. Ibid., Cap. XXII, 'Christus errores expulit, veritatem aperuit,' ff. 39v–42r.
53. Ibid., Cap. XXIII, 'Christus est idea et exemplar virtutum,' ff. 42r–3v, cit., f. 42r, 'Quid aliud Christus fuit nisi liber quidam moralis immo divinae philosophiae vivens, de caelo missus et divina ipsa idea virtutum humanis oculis manifesta.'
54. Ibid., Cap. XXIV, 'Auctoritas Sybillarum,' ff. 43v–6r; Cap. XXV, 'Testimonia Sibyllarum de Christo,' ff. 46r–7v; Cap. XXVI, 'De auctoritate prophetarum, nobilitate veteris testamenti, excellentia novi,' ff. 47v–50r.

55. Ibid., f. 48r, '... ex quibus apparet quod Clemens Alexandrinus e, Atticus Platonicus et Eusebius et Aristobolus probant, gentiles videlicett si qua habuerunt egregia dogmata et mysteria, a Iudeis usurpavisse; sed quae apud illos historia simplici continentur, ab his in poeticas fabulas fuisse translata. ... Plato usque adeo Iudeos imitatus est, ut Numenius Pythagoricus dixerit, Platonem nihil aliud fuisse quam Moysen Attica longua loquentem.'
56. Ibid., ff. 48r–9v.
57. Ibid., ff. 41v–2r, 'Prisca gentilium Theologia in qua Zoroaster, Mercurius, Orpheus, Aglaophemus [*sic* Laur. 21, 9; 1559 Aglaus, Phemus], Pythagoras consenserunt, tota in Platonis nostri voluminibus continentur. Mysteria huiusmodi Plato in epistolis vaticinatur tandem post multa secula hominibus manifesta fieri posse. Quod quidem ita contigit, nam Philonis Numeniique temporibus primum coepit mens priscorum theologorum in Platonicis chartis intelligi, videlicet statim post Apostolorum apostolicorumque Discipulorum conciones et scripta. Divino enim Christianorum lumine usi sunt Platonici ad divinum Platonem interpretandum. Hinc est quod magnus Basilius et Augustinus probant, Platonicos Ioannis evangelistae misteria sibi usurpavasse. Ergo certe reperi precipua Numenii, Philonis, Plotini, Iamblichi, Proculi misteria ab Ioanne, Paulo, Hierotheo, Dionysio Areopagita accepta fuisse. Quicquid enim de mente divina angelisque et caeteris ad theologiam spectantibus magnificum dixere manifeste ab illis usurpaverunt.'
58. Ibid., Cap. XXVII, 'Testimonium prophetarum de Christo,' ff. 50r–76v; Cap. XXVIII, 'Solutiones dubitationum circa prophetas,' ff. 76v–83v. Ficino's exegesis is the traditional 'figural' rather than the new philological mode. As such it suited his context and purpose of finding concealed universal meanings.
59. Ibid., Cap. XXIX, 'Contra Iudeos qui miseri sunt in Christi vindictam,' ff. 84r–90r.
60. Ibid., Cap. XXX, 'Confirmatio rerum nostrarum ex Iudaicis, contra Iudeos de sacris libris,' ff. 90r–3v; Cap. XXXI, 'Confirmatio trinitatis Dei et divinitatis Christi ex Iudaicis,' ff. 93v–7r; Cap. XXXII, 'Confirmatio passionis Messiae contra Iudeos ex Iudaicis,' ff. 97r–100v; Cap. XXXIII, 'Confirmatio peccati originali, et ob hoc passionis Messiae ex Iudaicis contra Iudeos,' ff. 100v–5v; Cap. XXXIV, 'Probatio quod testamenti veteris ceremoniae merito consumptae consummataeque sunt adveniente novo: ex Iudaicis contra Iudeos,' ff. 105v–13r.
61. Ibid., Capp. XXX–XXXIV. The statements in this paragraph are based on the information and judgements of U. Cassuto, *Gli Ebrei*, op. cit., pp. 278–81.
62. Op. cit., all of Cap. XXXIV, and espec. ff. 109r–11r.
63. Cf. ibid., Cap. XXXV, 'De auctoritate doctrinae Christianae,' ff. 113r–18v and Capp. XXIV, XXV, XXVI as cited above.

64. Ibid., Cap. XXXVI, 'Quod sacrae Christianorum litterae vitiatae non sint,' ff. 118v–22r; Cap. XXXVII, 'Causa erroris Iudeorum, Mahumetensium, atque Gentilium,' ff. 122r–3v.
65. *In Epistolas Pauli, Opera omnia*, Basel, 1576, pp. 425–72.
66. Ibid., p. 426, Prohemium.
67. Ibid., pp. 427–9, Cap. I.
68. Ibid., pp. 429–30, Cap. II, 'De rationibus Trinitatis'.
69. Ibid., p. 430, Cap. III, 'Rationes quibus divinam verbum assumpsit humanitatem. . . .'
70. Ibid., p. 431, Cap. IV, 'De summa epistolae. . . .'
71. Ibid., pp. 433–4, Cap. V, 'De virtute Evangelii, fide gemina, charitate. Quo modo differant dubium, opinio, scientia, fides, de cultu Gentilium, de lege Mosaica.'
72. Ibid., p. 434, 'Hanc iustitiam neque Gentiles neque Mosaica lex penitus consummavit. Nam et Gentiles pro hominum opinionibus, et Mosaica pro natura et consuetudine populi promulgata videtur. Evangelica vero lex ad iustitiam, id est, universam virtutem perducit, non civilem duntaxat, sed purgatorium atque potius animi iam purgati.'
73. Ibid.
74. Ibid., pp. 434–5, Cap. VI, 'Contra Gentiles, Quomodo Deo ingrati, et de impietate, et quomodo divino lumine Deum cognoverint,' 'Evangelium quoque sive in meditatione, sive in voce, sive in scriptis, Dei verbum est, prolatum quidem afflante spiritu, sed humana meditatione, vel voce, vel scriptura vestitum; videtur autem eiusmodi copula divini verbi cum eiusmodi corpore non solum in Apostolis, sed etiam in Prophetis ab initio extitisse, ut tota divina scriptura per sanctum Spiritum de Christo loquens, quasi ipse sit Christus, ubique vivens et spirans in omnes, qui vehementer quodam affectu legunt, audiunt, meditantur. Quapropter Paulus clam hic admonere videtur, ut ad Evangelium cum summa reverentia, ferme sicut ad Eucharistiam, accedamus.'
75. Ibid., pp. 435–6, 'Deus manifestavit, quoniam communem notitiam divinarum, Deus ipse sicut Iudeis revelaverat per Prophetas, ita Gentibus manifestam effecerat per Philosophos.'
76. Ibid., pp. 436–8, Cap. VII, 'Quomodo invisibilia Dei per visibilia cognoscantur,' cit., p. 438, 'Philosophi, vero, praesertim Platonici, formas in materia mundi considerantes, agnoscunt eas esse similitudines idearum, ut viri per imagines in speculo, si modo sint in speculo, animadvertunt totidem a tergo res esse. Ad quae quidem ideas in alia vita convertentes vultum, perspicaciter, ut inquit Paulus, facie ad faciem contemplantur.'
77. Ibid., pp. 438–9, Chap. VIII, 'Apud hos enim non Leges solum, sed etiam Philosophi Deum unum, omnium conditorem, singulis providentem, principium rerum atque finem aptissime celebrant, ut hoc ignorare nemo debuerit. . . . Animus autem qui primum in seipso quiescere

tentat, ob hanc iniustitiam ne assequitur Deum, neque seipso fruitur, quia caret idea quae verus animus est, in qua et animus formatur.'

78. Ibid., p. 440, 'Platonici enim et Homerus atque Maro corpus nostrum imaginem animae vocaverunt. Apostolus ad hoc alludens Gentiles vituperat, quod nec animam ipsam hominis adoraverunt, nec saltem corpus hominis animatum, quod imago animae nuncupatur, sed corporis similitudinem, id est, statuam picturamque honoraverint.'
79. Ibid., Cap. IX, X, pp. 441–4.
80. Ibid., Cap. XI, pp. 445–6.
81. Ibid., Cap. XII, pp. 446–7.
82. Ibid., p. 447, 'Denique si attributa consideremus horribile forsitan videatur iudicium potentiae paternae concedere, ne forte sententia rigidior expectetur, tribuere vero clementiae spiritus nimium praestaret indulgentiae confidentiam. Ad sapientiam vero iuste iudicaret, simul cum aequitate, spectare videtur.' On Pico's view's of damnation, cf. Garin, *La cultura filosofica*, op. cit., pp. 280–6, 'La "Quaestio de Peccato" di Filippo Callimaco Esperiente.'
83. Ibid., p. 448 to *Rom.* i:7–9, Ficino's Cap. XIII. Missing passage in *Opera* condemning Jews is in P. O. Kristeller, *Supplementum Ficinianum*, op. cit., I, 17–19.
84. Op. cit., p. 449, Cap. XIV, to *Rom.* ii:10–13, 'Deus pensat opera, non personas, Iudeas atque Gentiles aeque damnat, quamvis illi sine lege, hi cum lege delinquant. . . . Culpa quidem Iudei gravior, quia lex Mosaica data divinitus, neque permittit Iudaeum semper ignorantiam excusare, et arctiori vinculo reddit obnoxiam. Itaque peccantes apud Gentiles, qui lege Mosaica nec instructi fuerant, nec abstricti, levius punientur.'
85. Ibid., p. 450, Cap. XV, to *Rom.* ii:14–16, 'Denique nullam legem vel naturalem, vel scriptam habere efficaciam ad iustitiam et salutem, nisi divina gratia, praeter intellectum, moveat et affectum, atque ita moveat, ut ipsius Dei gratia legis praecepta servetur. . . . Profecto lux illa vera, illuminans omnem hominem venientem in hanc mundum, infudii lumen menti veridicum. . . . tanquam iudex sederet in animo, vicemque Dei teneret in homine.'
86. Ibid., p. 451, 'Iam vero conscientiae virtus causam pro anima vel contra animam agitans coram intimo lumine, tanquam Iudice leges habente, testes producit in medium, cogitationes recordationesque frequentes, quae nonnunquam nos accusant, ratione quadam obiicientes aliquid male factum. . . . Atque ita saepe mutua quadam alteratione vicissim, donec his ista sub iudice recognoscente interim conscientia dirimatur. Accusatio vero defensioque et iudicium absque notitia quadam legis agi non possunt. Per haec igitur confirmatur, moralium legem esse mentibus nostris impressam. Per quam prudentior, temperantior aliquis sine scriptis legibus viram quodammodo iustam agat. Scripturae vero leges impru-

dentibus improbisque videntur armatae insuper ad compellandos, qui leges intimas neglexerint.'

87. Cf. Part IV, Chapter XIV, pp. 673–80, above.
88. Ficino, op. cit., p. 451, 'Iniqui sua quadam inclinatione loca suis meritis convenientia petunt, sicut ignis quidem levitate sursum fertur, terra vero deorsum.'
89. Ibid., p. 452, Cap. XVI, to *Rom.* ii:17–24, '... et passim Gentilibus quodammodo deteriores esse significat. Atque ut mihi videtur, eos indignatione quadam interrogat, et quasi quodam invectiva refellit.'
90. Ibid., pp. 457–8, Cap. XX, to *Rom.* iii:9–20, 'Utrique igitur sed Iudei maxime cohibendi Apostolo videbantur.'
91. Ibid., p. 460, Cap. XXI, to *Rom.* iii: 20–26.
92. Ibid., pp. 460–1, Cap. XXII, to *Rom.* iii:27–31, 'Non per meritum legalium operum, sed per Christianam fidem iustus salvusque efficitur, Gentilis pariter ut Iudaeus. ... Fides profecto viva, et per charitatem operans, exhibita Christo, iustitiam praestat perfectam cuilibet ita credenti, etiam si in legis operibus non fuerit conversatus. Necessarium tamen est, ita credentem deinde legitimi operari, nec fide sine operibus mortua iudicetur.'
93. Ibid., p. 462, Cap. XXIII, to *Rom.* iv:1–10, 'Praeterea ex operibus externis acquisitur civilis et humana iustitia, gloriam inter homines, quidem habens, sed non similem apud Deum, quoniam non efficit hominem externa gloria dignum, nisi accesserit et praecesserit ingens fidei et charitatis affectus gratia divina munitus.'
94. Cf. ibid., p. 465, in Cap. XXIV, to *Rom.* iv:11–15, where he says: 'Levius ergo peccant qui sola lege naturali vivunt, quam qui praeterea legi scriptae subiiciuntur. Cum igitur lex eiusmodi culpam quidem praevaricantibus augeat, adminiculum vero adiuvantis gratiae non secum afferat, munus videlicet Christi proprium; consequenter accidit, ut impediat vel differat promissae hereditas effectum. Praesertim quia per notiam lege datam excusatio minuitur in peccatis, et propter libertatis licentiaeque aviditatem nitimur. Atque hoc quidem incommodi per legem in moralibus accidat.' This analysis might be compared with Luther's distrust of externally imposed morality. Ficino, in other words, shares Luther's stress on inwardness and grace, but he does not go so far as to believe that works can be dispensed with, though even these are to attest to the aliveness of faith.
95. Cf. Anders Nygren, *Eros and Agape*, London, 1932, Vol. II, Part II, pp. 445–62.
96. Ficino, op. cit., p. 469, in Cap. XXVI, to *Rom.* v:1–12, 'Quod si charitas in Deum nostra ab ipsa Dei erga nos charitate principium habet, merito et quae charitati necessaria sunt, fidei scilicet atque spes, ab eadem divinitate procedunt. ... Quod autem instinctus ad divina in nobis ab ipsa divinitate procedat, hinc etiam confirmatur, quod omnia circa animum

in terris mortalia, contrarium generant in nobis instinctum, ut non valeat animus mortalibus abrutus, nisi per divinitatem.'

97. Ibid., p. 470, 'Charitatem interea tangit utranque, et qua nos Deus amat et qua nos amamus Deum, utranque vero charitatem per sanctum Spiritum voluntibus nostris inustam esse censet. Nos autem, ut cum Thoma nostro loquamur, sic exponemus. Spiritum sanctum, qui est amor Patris et Filii, dari nobis est nos ad participationem amoris illius adduci, qui sane ipsius Spiritus sanctus existit, qua quidem participatione ipsi Dei amatores efficimur. Iam vero ex hoc quod in ipsum amamus argumentum habemus, quod ipse nos amet. Non quasi primo dileximus Deum, sed quoniam ipse prior nos amat.'
98. Walter Dress, *Die Mystik des Marsilio Ficinos*, Leipzig-Berlin, 1929.
99. Ibid., p. 193, 'Ja darüber hinaus wird die Liebe, die den Menschen in das Reich der Seraphen zieht, nicht einmal als Werk des heiligen Geistes gedacht; umgekehrt vielmehr folgt der Geist der Liebeserregung. Er wird – und man sieht, wie wenig Ficino christliche Gedankengänge verstanden hat – mit der aus der Liebe sich ergebenden Gotteserkenntnis identifiziert.'
100. On Pico and the *Oration*, cf. above, Part III, Chapter X, p. 505, n. 5. I will cite this work in the translation of E. Forbes, *The Renaissance Philosophy of Man*, op. cit., pp. 223–54.
101. Forbes trans. p. 231.
102. Ibid., pp. 231–4.
103. Ibid., p. 248; cf. Wind, *Pagan Mysteries*, op. cit., Chapter 1, pp. 17–25, for Pico's practice of this art, even if he never wrote the promised work. Cf. also his reference to his *Poetica theologia* in his *Commento* [ed. Garin in *De hominis dignitate* etc., op. cit.], p. 546 and p. 581. This work is itself a kind of *theologia poetica* in its exegesis of Benivieni's *Canzone d'amore*.
104. *Oratio*, op. cit., Forbes trans., pp. 242–4.
105. Ibid., pp. 244–45.
106. Ibid., pp. 245–6.
107. Ibid., pp. 246–9.
108. Ibid., pp. 249–50.
109. Ibid., pp. 250.
110. Ibid., pp. 250–1.
111. Cf. Cassuto, *Gli Ebrei a Firenze*, op. cit., pp. 281–323; Nardi, 'La mistica averroistica e Pico della Mirandola', op. cit.
112. *Oratio*, op. cit., in Forbes trans., p. 251.
113. Ibid., pp. 251–2.
114. Ibid., pp. 252–3.
115. Ibid., p. 253.
116. Cf. the article cited in note 111.
117. Wind, *Pagan Mysteries*, rev. ed., op. cit., Appendix 2, 'Pagan Vestiges of the Trinity', p. 255.

Bibliography

I. Ancient, Medieval and Renaissance Authors and Works

PETER ABELARD, *Expositio in Hexaemeron*, 'De sexta die', Migne, *P. L.*, 178, 759 ff.

DONATO ACCIAIUOLI, *Oratione del corpo di Christo*, Bibl. Ricc., Cod. 2204, ff. 181–4v.

AEGIDIUS ROMANUS [GILES OF ROME], *Errores Philosophorum*, ed. Josef Koch, Eng. trans. John Riedl, Marquette, 1944.

—— *De humani corporis formatione tractatus*, Paris, 1515; Venice, 1523; Rimini, 1626; Bibl. Vatic., Cod. Vat. lat. 845, ff. 1–36, owned by Coluccio Salutati.

—— *In librum I sententiarum*, Bibl. Vatic., Cod. Vat. lat. 836, ff. 1–259v, owned by Coluccio Salutati.

—— *In secundum sententiarum*, Venice, 1521.

——*Tractatus de Predestinatione, Prescientia, Paradiso, Purgatorio et Inferno*, in *Opuscula*, Naples, 1525, ff. 23v–40r.

ALBERTUS MAGNUS, *Summa de creaturis*, in *Opera*, ed. Borgnet, Paris, 1890 ff., Tomes 34 and 35 [includes *De homine*].

ALCHERUS OF CLAIRVAUX, *Liber de spiritu et anima*, Migne, *P. L.*, 40, 779–832; Cap. 35, 'Dignitas humanae conditionis', 805–6.

GIROLAMO ALIOTTI [JERONIMO ARETINO], *Epistolae et opuscula*, Arezzo, 1769.

ST. AMBROSE OF MILAN, *De bono mortis*, Migne, *P.L.*, 14, 567–96.

—— *De fuga saeculi*, Migne, *P.L.*, 14, 597–624.

—— *Hexaemeron*, Bibl. Vatic., Cod. Pal. lat. 317 owned by Giannozzo Manetti.

PSEUDO-AMBROSIUS [ALCUIN?], *De dignitate humanae conditionis*, Migne, *P.L.*, 17, 1105–08.

ANONYMOUS, *Tractatus de fine hominis in hoc seculo*, Bergamo, Bibl. Civica, Cod. Lambda V 24.

——*Tractatus de miseria hominis*, Bergamo, Bibl. Civica, Cod. Delta V 42.

PSEUDO-APULEIUS, *Asclepius*, in A.D. Nock and A. J. Festugière, *Corpus Hermeticum*, II, Paris, 1945, 296–355.

THOMAS AQUINAS, *Commentum in quattuor libros sententiarum*, I, Parma, 1856.

ARISTEAS, *De septuaginta interpretibus*, Latin trans. by Mattia Palmieri of Pisa, Bibl. Vatic., Cod. Urb. lat. 566; Italian trans. by Bartolommeo della Fonte, Florence, Bibl. Naz., Cod. Magl. Strozzi 40, 43, ff. 1–34v; Bibl.

Vatic., Codd. Ottob. lat. 1558, Ross. 407; Rome, Bibl. Angel., Cod. 1003.

ARISTOTLE, *De animalibus* [*varia opera*], Bibl. Vatic., Cod. Pal. lat. 1068, owned by Giannozzo Manetti.

ST. AUGUSTINE [AURELIUS AUGUSTINUS], *Opera* in Migne, *P.L.* 32–46. Of special importance:

—— *Confessionum libri XIII*, Migne, *P.L.*, 32, 659–868

—— *De civitate Dei libri XXII*, Migne, *P.L.*, 41;

—— *De doctrina Christiana libri IV*, Migne, *P.L.*, 34, 15–122;

—— *De Genesi ad litteram*, Migne, *P.L.*, 34, 245–486;

—— *De quantitate animae*, Migne, *P.L.*, 32, 1035–80;

—— *De Trinitate libri XV*, Migne, *P.L.*, 42, 819–1098.

—— English translations: *A Select Library of Nicene and Post-Nicene Fathers*, New York, 1887–1902; *Basic Writings of St. Augustine*, ed. Whitney J. Oates, New York, 1948; *St. Augustine on Christian Doctrine*, trans. with introd. by D. W. Robertson, Indianapolis, 1958.

PSEUDO-AUGUSTINUS, *Liber de spiritu et anima*, see Alcherus of Clairvaux.

ANTONIO DA BARGA, *Antonii Bargensis Cronicon Montis Oliveti*, ed. by Placido M. Lugano, Florence, 1901.

—— *Historia Tusciae*, Ms cit. of *Opera*, ff. 50–60.

—— *Libellus de dignitate et excellentia humane vite*, Ms cit. of *Opera*, ff. 61–78v.

—— *De magistratibus et prelatis*, Ms cit. of *Opera*, ff. 17–36.

—— *Opera*, in un-numbered Ms of Archivio of Monte Oliveto Maggiore, near Siena.

ST. BASIL, *Homiliae in Hexaemeron*, Latin trans. by Rufinus, Bibl. Vatic., Cod. Urb. lat. 485, ff. 2–61 for Federigo da Montefeltre.

ST. BERNARD OF CLAIRVAUX, *De diligendo Deo* and *De gradibus humilitatis et superbiae*, ed. W. W. Williams and B. R. V. Mills, *Select Treatises of St. Bernard of Clairvaux*, Cambridge, 1926; also Migne, *P.L.*, 182, and *The Steps of Humility*, ed. with Eng. trans. by G. B. Burch, Cambridge, Mass., 1940, repr. Notre Dame, 1963.

BERNARD SILVESTRIS, *De universitate mundi*, ed. C. S. Barach and J. Wrobel, Innsbruck, 1876.

SAN BERNARDINO OF SIENA, *Quadragesimale de Christiana religione*, *Opera omnia*, I, Florence-Quaracchi, 1950.

GABRIEL BIEL, *Commentarium in sententias*, Brescia, 1574.

VESPASIANO DA BISTICCI, *Vita di Giannozzo Manetti* and *Commentario della vita di Giannozzo Manetti* in his *Vite di uomini illustri del secolo XV*, ed. L. Frati, Bologna, 1893 (*Collezione di opere inedite o rare dei primi tre secoli della lingua*, 69), II, 33–201.

GIOVANNI BOCCACCIO, *Genealogia deorum gentilium libri XV*, ed. V. Romano, 2 vols., Bari, 1951.

—— *On Poetry, Being the Preface and the Fourteenth and Fifteenth Books of Boccaccio's Genealogia Deorum Gentilium*, Eng. trans., with introductory essay and commentary, by Charles G. Osgood, Princeton, 1930, repr. Indianapolis, 1956.

St. Bonaventura, *In sententias Petri Lombardi, Opera omnia,* II, Florence, 1885, and sep. Quaracchi, 1916.

Aurelio Brandolini [Lippo], *Carmina,* Bologna, Bibl. Univ., Cod. 2948, pp. 115–18; Rome, Bibl. Naz. V.E., Cod. S. Giovanni e Paolo 7 (1823), 108 folios owned by Raffaello Brandolini; Bibl. Vatic., Cod. Vat. lat. 5008, Cod. Urb. lat. 739.

—— *Dialogus de humanae vitae conditione et toleranda corporis aegritudine,* Basel, s.a., 1498, 1541, 1543; Vienna, 1541; Paris, 1562.

—— *Epithomas in sacram judeorum historiam ex volumine quam Bibliam appellant et Josepho historico fidelissimo,* Bibl. Vatic., Cod. Ottobon. lat. 121 [autograph working copy], Cod. Ottobon. lat. 438 [the dedication copy].

—— *Oratio in cena domini,* Siena, Bibl. Comm., Cod. H VI 30.

—— *Oratio pro Sancto Thoma Aquinate Romae in templo Sanctae Mariae Minerviae ad Cardinales et populum habita,* s.l.a. [Ges. Kat. 5016].

—— *Oratio de virtutibus domini nostri Jesu Christi,* Rome, 1596 and 1735; Volgare edition, Venice, 1596.

—— *Paradoxa Christiana,* Budapest, Library of National Museum, Cod. Oct. 232; Bibl. Ricc., Cod. 1235 and Cod. 1277; Bibl. Vatic., Cod. Vat. lat. 739, Cod. Pal. lat. 382; Basel, 1543; Cologne, 1573; Rome 1498, 1531, 1581.

—— *De ratione scribendi,* Siena, Bibl. Comm., Cod. H VII 13; Basel, 1549, 1573, 1585; Rome 1735.

Raffaello Brandolini [Lippo], *De laudibus musice et Petriboni,* Lucca, Bibl. Capitolare, Cod. 525, ff. 177–81.

—— *De musica et poetica opusculum,* Rome, Bibl. Casanatense, Cod. 805, ff. 84v–7v [containing the life of Aurelio Brandolini].

—— List of his writings in Bibl. Vatic., Cod. Vat. lat. 3590.

Stefano Breventano, *Dell'eccelenza e felicità dell'uomo* and *Della di lui miseria ed infelicità,* both in Bibl. Ambros., Cod. P 17 sup.

Leonardo Bruni, *Epistolarum libri VIII,* ed. L. Mehus, Florence, 1741.

—— *Humanistisch-philosophische Schriften,* ed. Hans Baron, Leipzig-Berlin, 1928.

—— *Isagogicon moralis disciplinae,* in *Humanistisch-philosophische Schriften,* pp. 20–41.

—— *Oratio adversus hypocrisim,* Florence, Bibl. Laur., Cod. 52, 3, ff. 25–30; Lyons, 1679; ed. with Italian trans. by Giulio Vallese, Naples, 1946.

—— *De recta interpretatione,* in *Humanistisch-philosophische Schriften,* pp. 81–96.

Giovanni Caldiera, *Catonis expositio pro filia erudienda,* Modena, Naples, Bibl. Govern. dei Gerolamini, Cart. 29; Bibl. Est., Cod. 299 (Gamma N 8 4 8); Padua, Bibl. del Seminario Vescovile, Cod. 39

—— *De concordantia poetarum, philosophorum et theologorum libri II,* Fossombrone, Bibl. Civica Passionei, Cod. IV F; Bibl. Vatic., Cod. Urb. lat. 1178, Cod. Pal. lat. 985; Venice, 1557.

—— *Expositio in Psalmos,* Modena, Bibl. Est., Cod. 1000 (Alpha K 3 6).

—— *Liber canonum astrologaie ac totius orbis descriptione*, Bibl. Marciana, Cod. VIII, 72 (3273).

—— *De praestantia Venetae Politiae, et artibus in eadem excultis, tam mechanicis quam liberalibus, et de virtutibus quae maxime Respublicae Venetae debentur*, Florence, Bibl. Ricc., Cod. 669; Oxford, Bodl. Cod. 846.

—— *De Veneta oeconomio*, Oxford, Bodl., Cod. 846.

—— *De virtutibus moralibus et theologicis*, Oxford, Bodl. Cod. 846.

JEAN CALVIN, *Institutio Christianae Religionis*, [1559 version], ed. W. Baum, E. Cunitz, E. Reuss, Brunswick, 1869.

PIETRO CAVRETTO [PETRUS HAEDUS], *De miseria humana libri V*, Venice, 1558 *et aliae.*

M. T. CICERO, *De natura deorum libri III*, ed. A. S. Pease, 2 vols., Cambridge, Mass. 1955–8; and in Bibl. Vatic., Cod. Pal. lat. 1518 (with *De fato* and *De divinatione*) owned by Giannozzo Manetti; Eng. trans. H. M. Poteat, Chicago, 1950.

—— *Libri philosophici* (*De amicitia, De senectute, Paradoxa, De finibus, De officiis, Disputationes Tusculanae, De natura deorum, De divinatione, De fato, De legibus*), in Bibl. Vatic., Cod. Pal. lat. 1524 owned by Giannozzo Manetti.

LOTHARIUS CONTI [INNOCENT III], *De miseria humanae conditionis*, ed. Michele Maccarrone, Lugano, 1955, also Migne, *P.L.*, 217, 702 ff.

NICHOLAS OF CUSA [CUSANUS], *Opera omnia*, pub. by Heidelberger Akademie der Wissenschaften, Leipzig-Hamburg, 1932 et seq. in progress.

—— *Nicholaus von Cues, Texte seiner philosophischen Schriften*, ed. Alfred Petzelt, Vol. I, Stuttgart, 1949.

JOHANNES DAMASCENUS, *De orthodoxa fide*, Latin trans. by Burgundio of Pisa and by Cerbanus, ed. E. M. Buytaert, (*Franciscan Institute Publications*, Text Series, 8 [1955]). Interp. Burgundio in Bibl. Vatic., Cod. Pal. lat. 309 owned by Coluccio Salutati and then by Giannozzo Manetti.

PETER DAMIANI, *De bono religiosi status et variorum animantium tropologia*, Migne, *P.L.*, 145.

PIER CANDIDO DECEMBRIO, *De anima et eius immortalitate*, Bibl. Ambros., Cod. R 88 sup., ff. 158v–63v; Berlin. Cod. lat. oct. 159, ff. 2–27 [now in Marburg]; Modena, Bibl. Est., Cod. Campori App. 110 (Gamma E 5 7), ff. 55v–68: Munich, Cod. CLM 508, ff. 167v–78. See Alcherus and Kristeller.

DIONYSIUS EXIGUUS, Latin trans. of Gregorii Nyssensis, *De hominis opificio* entitled *De imagine, id est de hominis conditione*, Migne, *P.L.*, 67, 347–408.

LORENZO DOMENICHI, *Libri delle antiche religione*, Florence, Bibl. Naz., Cod. Magl., 37, 319 [Book I only].

EADMER, MONK OF CANTERBURY, *Liber de sancti Anselmi similitudinibus*, Migne, *P.L.*, 159.

EGIDIO DA VITERBO [GILES OF VITERBO], *Commentarii in Petri Lombardi sententias ad mentem Platonis*, Bibl. Vatic., Cod. Vat. lat. 6325, 216 fols.; Naples, Bibl. Naz., Cod. VIII F 8, 277 fols.; Rome, Bibl. Ang., Cod. 636, 233 fols. Excerpts edited by Eugenio Massa in *Testi umanistici sul 'De anima'* and in his *I fondamenti metafisici della 'Dignitas hominis' e testi inediti di Egidio da Viterbo*, Turin, 1954, and in *Testi umanistici sul 'De Anima'*, ed. Garin, Padua, 1951.

—— *Historia viginti saeculorum*, Rome, Bibl. Ang., Cod. 502.

—— *Scechina e Libellus de litteris hebraicis*, ed. François Secret, Rome, 1959.

ERASMUS OF ROTTERDAM, *Enchiridion militis Christiani*, *Opera omnia*, V, Louvain 1704; Eng. trans. Raymond Himelick, Bloomington, Ind., 1963.

EUSEBIUS OF CAESAREA, *De preparatione evangelica libri XV*, Migne, *P.G.*, 21.

BARTOLOMEO FACIO, *Dialogus de vitae felicitate*, Bibl. Vatic., Cod. Urb. lat. 227, ff. 112r–48v; also Leyden, 1628 and in *Dialogi decem variorum auctorum*, s.l. 1473.

—— *De hominis excellentia ad Nicolaum Quintum*, Bibl. Vatic., Cod. Urb. lat. 227, ff. 150–69; and in Felino Sandeo, *De Regibus Siciliae et Apuliae epitome*, Hanover, 1611, pp. 149–68.

ANTONIO DE FERRARIIS [IL GALATEO], *De distinctione et nobilitate humani generis*, *Epistola* 13, pp. 559–69, Angelo Mai, *Spicilegium Romanum*, VIII, Rome, 1842 [based on Vat. lat. 7584, ff. 1–129v]. See now the edition of his *Epistole* ed. by A. Altamura, Lecce, 1959, pp. 104–20.

MARSILIO FICINO, *In Convivium Platonis, sive de amore*, ed. with French trans. by Raymond Marcel, *Marsile Ficin, Commentaire sur le Banquet de Platon*, Paris, 1956.

—— *In Epistolas Pauli*, in *Opera omnia*, Basel, 1576, I, pp. 425–72.

—— *De religione Christiana*, in Bibl. Laur., Cod. 21, 9; *Opera omnia*, Basel, 1576, I, 1–77; Paris 1559.

—— *Supplementum Ficinianum*, ed. P. O. Kristeller, 2 vols., Florence, 1937.

—— *Theologia Platonica de immortalitate animorum*, in *Marsile Ficin, Théologie Platonicienne de l'immortalité des âmes*, texte critique établi et traduit par Raymond Marcel, vols. I and II, Paris, 1964.

BARTOLOMEO DELLA FONTE, *Donatus sive de poenitentia ad Julianum Medicem*, in Wolfenbüttel, Herzog August Bibliothek, Cod. Guelferbytanus 43 Aug. Fol., ff. 118v–40v; Florence 1488 [3 eds. Hain]; variant *Dialogus de poenitentia ad Johannem Archiepiscopum Histrigomensis*, in Oxford, Bodl. 7227, 8, 9, Ms. D'Orville 59 (Western 16937), ff. 226v–35r; Perugia, Bibl. Com., Cod. 706 (I 100), ff. 289v–301v; Bibl. Vatic., Cod. Vat. lat. 13679, ff. 270v–8v; Bibl. Laur., Cod. Ashb. 918 (849), ff. 95–115; *Sermone di Penitentia*, Bibl. Naz. Cod. Magl. 35, 20, ff. lxv bis rcv.

—— *Epistolarum libri III* ed. Ladislas Juhàsz, Budapest, 1931.

—— *De poetice libri III*, C f. under Trin Kaus below.

GIOVANNI GARZONI, *De Christiana felicitate libellus*, Bologna, Bibl. Univ., Cod. 739 (Frati 431), ff. 3–23v, Cod. 1622 (842), ff. 181–91, Cod. 2648 (1391), ff. 75–85. [Also titled *De Christianorum felicitate*.]

—— *De contemptu mundi et felicitatis religione* (sic), Bologna, Bibl. Univ., Cod. 1622 (842), ff. 153–7.

—— *Epistola de contemptu mundi*, Bologna, Bibl. Univ., Cod. 742 (434), ff. 124–5v, Cod. 1622 (842), ff. 394–6.

—— *De miseria humana*, Strassbourg, 1505; also a variant version, Bologna, Bibl. Univ., Cod. 752, III, ff. 121–43.

—— *De miseria mundi libellus*, Bologna, Bibl. Univ., Cod. 742, (434), ff. 162–70v.

—— *De summo bono*, Bologna, Bibl. Univ., Cod. 752 III, ff. 143v–56v, Cod. 1622 (842), ff. 118–124.

—— *De varietate fortunae*, Bologna, Bibl. Univ., Cod. 740 (432), ff. 1–30v, Cod. 2648 (1391), ff. 9 seq.

—— *De vera felicitate* [unlocated or unidentified].

—— *Vitae sanctorum*, in Bologna, Bibl. Univ., Codd. 738, 739, 741, 744, 746.

Bartolommeo Goggio, *De nobilitate humani animi*, Modena, Bibl. Est., Fondo Campori Cod. 134 (Gamma S 6 7).

Gorgias of Leontini, *Laus Helenae*, Greek work in Giannozzo Manetti's library, Bibl. Vatic., Cod. Pal. graec. 179.

Gregory of Nyssa, *De hominis opificio*, Migne, *P.G.*, 44, 137–256; Interp. Lat. by Dionysius Exiguus, Migne, *P.L.*, 67, 347–408, and in Bibl. Ambros., Cod. s 51 sup; Bibl. Vatic., Cod. Urb. lat 485, ff. 62–105 for Federigo da Montefeltre. Fr. trans. by Jean Laplace with notes and introd. by Jean Daniélou, *La création de l'homme*, Paris, 1943.

—— *Oratio in verba 'Faciamus hominem etc'* [suppositious work of Greg. of Nyssa], Migne *P.G.*, 44, 257–78 and 278–98.

Gregory of Rimini, *Super primum et secundum sententiarum*, St. Bonaventure, New York, 1955, [facsimile of Venice, 1522 edition].

Robert Grosseteste, *Hexameron*, Oxford, MS lat. th. c. 17; also published in part, 'The Hexameron of Robert Grosseteste: the First Twelve Chapters of Part Seven [Eight]', ed. with introd. by J. T. Muckle, *Mediaeval Studies*, VI (1944), pp. 151–75.

Hesiod, Greek works in Giannozzo Manetti's library, Bibl. Vatic., Cod. Pal. graec. 190.

Hippocrates, *Opuscula* [including *De natura hominis* etc.], Greek works in Giannozzo Manetti's library, Bibl. Vatic., Cod. Pal. graec. 192.

Homer, *Iliad*, *Odyssey*, *Homerica*, *Batrachomyomachia*, *Homeric Hymns*, '*Musaeus*', Greek works in Giannozzo Manetti's library, Bibl. Vatic., Codd. Pal. graec. 179, 180, 181.

Innocent III, *see* Conti.

St. Jerome, *Epistola LVII ad Pammachium: De optimo genere interpretandi*, Migne, *P.L.*, 22, 568–79.

—— *Praefatium in Pentateuchum*, Migne, *P.L.*, 28, 181–2.

—— *Praefatium ad Sophronicum*, Migne, *P.L.*, 28, 1184–5; *Psalterium secundum Hieronymum de Hebraica veritate*, Migne, *P.L.*, 28, 1189–1306.

Firmianus, Lactantius, *Institutiones divinae*, in Migne, *P.L.*, 6, *C.E.S.L.*, 19.

—— *De opificio Dei*, in Migne, *P.L.* 6, *C.S.E.L.*, 27. Both works also in Bibl. Vatic., Cod. Pal. lat. 162 owned by Giannozzo Manetti.

Cristoforo Landino, *De anima*, Bibl. Ricc., Cod. 417, 134 folios [with autographic corrections but fragmentary]; Bibl. Vatic., Cod. Urb. lat. 1370, 193 folios; Books I and II ed. by A. Paoli, *Annali delle Università Toscane*, XXXIV (1915); N.S. I, fasc. 2 (1916); and Book III by G. Gentile, ibid. N.S. II, fasc. 3 (1917).

—— *Disputationes Camaldulenses libri IV*, Bibl. Laur., Cod. 53, 28; Bibl. Vatic., Cod. Urb. lat. 508 [dedication copy].

—— *Interpretationes in P. Vergilii opera*, Bibl. Laur., Cod. 53, 37 [dedication copy].

—— *Sermone in commemoratione del corpo di Christo*, Bibl. Ricc., Cod. 2204, ff. 173v–81.

—— *De vera nobilitate*, Rome, Bibl. Corsiniana, Cod. 433.

Lodovico Lazzarelli, *De gentilium deorum imaginibus*, Bibl. Vatic., Codd. Urb. lat. 716, 717; Florence, Bibl. Naz., Cod. Nuovi Acquisti 272.

Peter Lombard, *Sententiarum libri quattuor*, Migne, *P.L.*, 192 [Passages on Trinity, Image and Similitude: Lib. I, Dist. II, 'De mysterio Trinitatis et Unitatis', 525–9; Dist. III, 'Incipit ostendere quomodo per creaturam poterit cognosci Creator', 529–33; Lib. II, Dist. XVI, 'De hominis creatione', 683–5; Dist. XVII, 'De creatione animae', 685 ff.]

Lucian of Samosata, Greek Works in Giannozzo Manetti's library, Bibl. Vatic., Cod. Pal. graec. 174.

Giannozzo Manetti, *Adversus suae novae Psalterii traductionis obtrectatores apologetici libri V*, Bibl. Vatic., Codd. Pal. lat. 40, 41, Cod. Urb. lat. 5.

—— *Contra Iudeos et Gentes libri X*, Bibl. Vatic., Cod. Urb. lat. 154 [unique].

—— *De dignitate et excellentia hominis libri IV*, Bibl. Laur., Cod. San Marco 456, ff. 1–51v; Bibl. Vatic., Cod. Urb. lat. 5, ff. 109–59v; Basel, 1532.

—— Catalogue of Greek works in his library, Bibl. Vatic., Cod. Pal. lat. 1916, ff. 530–51v.

—— Latin translation of Greek New Testament, Bibl. Vatic., Cod. Urb. lat. 6; Cod. Pal. lat. 45.

—— *Nova totius Psalterii de Hebraica veritate in Latinum traductio ad Alphonsum clarissimum Aragonum Regem*, Bibl. Vatic., Codd. Pal. lat. 40, 41 [dedication copy], 42, 43, Cod. Urb. lat. 5; Florence, Bibl. Marucelliana, Cod. C 336 [fragmentary]; Brussels, Bibl. Royale, Ms 10745.

Luigi Marsili, Letters in *Lettere del B. Giovanni delle Celle*, ed. P. Sorio, Rome, 1845.

Galeotto Marzio di Narni, *De homine*, Bologna, 1475, Basel, 1517 etc.

—— *Refutatio obiectorum in librum de homine a Giorgio Merula inchoata*, Bibl. Vatic., Cod. Urb. lat. 1385.

Giorgio Merula, *In librum de homine Galeoti Narniensis opus*, Basel, 1517.

Benedetto Morandi, *De felicitate humana* and *In calumniatorem naturae humanae secunda reluctatio*, both in Bibl. Vatic., Cod. Urb. lat. 1245, ff. 1–29, and ff. 32v–81, Cod. Ottob. lat. 1828, ff. 154–77, 178–216. Also in Vat. lat. 4569 [poor 16c. copy] and Bologna, Bibl. Univ., Cod. 2948, vol. 15 [18c. copy].

NALDO NALDI, *Vita Iannotii Maneti*, Bibl. Ricc., Codd. 891, 910; Ital. trans., Bibl. Naz., Cod. Magl. 8, 45.

NEMESIUS OF EMESA, *De natura hominis*, Migne, *P.G.*, 40, 504–817; Greek Ms in Giannozzo Manetti's Library, Bibl. Vatic., Cod. Pal. graec. 385; Latin trans. by Burgundio of Pisa, Bergamo, Bibl. Civica, Cod. Delta IV 10 (s. XV); Bologna, Bibl. Coll. di Spagna, Cod. 19 (s XIV); Bibl. Vatic., Cod. Urb. lat. 485, ff. 105–56 for Federigo da Montefeltre, Eng. trans., *Of the Nature of Man*, ed. William Telfer (*Library of Christian Classics*, IV), Philadelphia, 1955.

NEW TESTAMENT, *Novum Testamentum* and *Evangelistae quattuor*, Greek Mss in Giannozzo Manetti's library, Bibl. Vatic., Codd. Pal. graec., 171, 189, 229; Latin translation by Giannozzo Manetti, Bibl. Vatic., Cod. Urb. lat. 6, Cod. Pal. lat. 45.

ORIGEN, *Hexaplorum quae supersunt*, Migne, *P.G.*, 5 and 6.

ORPHIC HYMNS, Greek texts in Giannozzo Manetti's library, Bibl. Vatic., Cod. Pal. graec. 179.

FRANCESCO PETRARCA, *Opera omnia*, Basel, 1481.

—— *Epistolae familiares – Le Familiari*, ed. V. Rossi and U. Bosco, 4 vols., Florence, 1933–42; ed. G. Fracassetti, 3 vols., Florence, 1859–63.

—— *Epistolae seniles*, Bibl. Vatic., Cod. Urb. lat. 331; Ital. trans. by G. Fracassetti, *Lettere senili*, 2 vols., Florence, 1869–70.

—— *Invective contra medicum*, ed. P. G. Ricci, Rome, 1950.

—— *De otio religioso*, ed. Giuseppe Rotondi [completed posthumously by Guido Martellotti], (*Studi e Testi*, 195), Città del Vaticano, 1958.

—— *Prose*, ed. G. Martellotti and P. G. Ricci, E. Carrara, E. Bianchi, Milan and Naples, 1955.

—— *De remediis utriusque fortunae libri II*, Bibl. Vatic., Cod. Urb. lat. 334.

—— *De secreto conflictu curarum mearum libri III*, ed. E. Carrara, in F. P. *Prose*, pp. 22–215.

—— *De sui ipsius et multorum ignorantia*, ed. L. M. Capelli, *Le traité De sui ipsius et multorum ignorantia*, Paris, 1906; Eng. trans. by Hans Nachod, in E. Cassirer et al., eds. *The Renaissance Philosophy of Man*, Chicago, 1948, pp. 47–133.

—— *De vita solitaria libri II*, ed. Guido Martellotti in F. P. *Prose*, pp. 286–590; Eng. trans. with introd. by Jacob Zeitlin, *The Life of Solitude*, Urbana, 1924.

PHILO JUDAEUS, *De opificio mundi*, in *Philo*, ed. and trans. by F. H. Colson and G. H. Whitaker (*Loeb Classical Library*), Vol. I, London and New York, 1929.

—— Greek works in Giannozzo Manetti's library, Bibl. Vatic., Cod. Pal. graec. 183. [Includes *De opificio hominis.*]

—— *Opera*, Latin trans. by Lilius Tifernate, Bibl. Vatic., Codd. Vat. lat. 180, 181, 182, 183, 184, 185; Cod. Barb. lat. 662 (XVIs.), partial.

GIOVANNI PICO DELLA MIRANDOLA, *Commento alla Canzone d'Amore di Girolamo Benivieni*, in Garin, ed., *De dignitate hominis* etc., pp. 443–581.
—— *Disputationes adversus astrologiam divinatricem*, ed. with Italian trans. by Eugenio Garin, 2 vols. Florence, 1946, 1952.
—— *De hominis dignitate, Heptaplus, De ente et uno, e scritti vari*, ed. with Italian trans. by Eugenio Garin, Florence, 1942.
—— *Oratio de dignitate hominis*, Eng. trans. by Elizabeth L. Forbes in Cassirer et al., eds. *The Renaissance Philosophy of Man*, pp. 223–54.
PLATO, Greek dialogues in Gianozzo Manetti's library, Bibl. Vatic., Codd. Pal. graec. 173, 174, 175, 177.
PLUTARCH, *Sermones et opuscula*, Greek works in Giannozzo Manetti's library, Bibl. Vatic., Codd. Pal. graec. 170–8.
POGGIO BRACCIOLINI, *Dialogus contra hypocritas*, ed. with Italian trans. by Giulio Vallese, from Lyons, 1679 edition, Naples, 1946.
—— *De miseria humanae conditionis libri II*, Bibl. Vatic., Cod. Urb. lat. 224, ff. 130–61; *Opera omnia*, Strassbourg, 1513, ff. 33v–49v.
SICCO POLENTON, *De confessione Christiana libri IV*, Modena, Bibl. Est., Cod. lat. VII F 17, Cod 914 (Alpha S 9 14); Padua, Bibl. Antoniana, Cod. scaff. XXII, 565; Venice, Bibl. Marc., Cod. lat. III, 81 (2772), Cod. lat. III, 82 (2773), Cod. lat. III, 137 (2239); Bibl. Vatic., Cod. Vat.lat. 7781, ff. 1–76v.
—— *Scriptorum illustrium latinae linguae libri XVIII*, ed. B. L. Ullman, Rome, 1928.
PIETRO POMPONAZZI, *Libri quinque de fato, de libero arbitrio et de praedestinatione*. ed. Richard LeMay, Lugano, 1957.
—— *De immortalitate animae*, ed. G. Gentile (*Opuscoli filosofici: testi e documenti inediti o rari*, I), Messina and Rome, 1925; ed. G. Morra, Bologna, 1954; Eng. trans. by W. H. Hay, Jr. with fascimile of *editio princeps*, Haverford, 1938, and in Cassirer et al., eds. *The Renaissance Philosophy of Man*, pp. 280–381.
—— Also cf. under Nardi below for his commentaries.
GIOVANNI GIOVIANO PONTANO, *Aegidius*, in *I dialoghi*, ed. C. Previtera, Florence, 1943, pp. 245–84.
PROCLUS, *Hymnes*, in Greek Ms in Giannozzo Manetti's library, Bibl. Vatic., Cod. Pal. graec. 179.
E. REUSCH, ed., *Die Indices Librorum Prohibitorum des sechszehnten Jahrhunderts*, Tübingen, 1886, photo-repr. Nieukoop, 1961.
BARTOLOMMEO DE' SACCHI [IL PLATINA], *De vero et falso bono*, Cologne, 1568.
COLUCCIO SALUTATI, *Epistolario*, ed. F. Novati, 4 vols., Rome, 1891–1911.
—— *De fato, fortuna et casu*, Bibl. Vat., Cod. Urb. lat. 201, ff. 2–74v; Cod. Vat. lat. 2928, ff. 1–83 [with autographic corrections].
—— *De laboribus Herculis*, ed. B. L. Ullman, Zurich, 1951.
—— *De nobilitate legum et medicinae*, ed. E. Garin, Florence, 1947.
—— *De seculo et religione*, ed. B. L. Ullman, Florence, 1957.
JOHANNES SCOTUS ERIUGENA, *De divisione naturae*, Migne, *P.L.*, 122, 441–1022.

Sermons, Collections of humanist sermons: Florence, Bibl. Naz., Cod. Magl. Strozzi 35, 211, ff. 90–183; Bibl. Ricc., Cod. 2204, ff. 131–219.

Lorenzo Valla, *Adnotationes in Novum Testamentum, editio princeps* by Desid. Erasmus, *Laurentii Vallensis . . . in Latinam Novi Testamenti interpretationem ex collatione Graecorum exemplarum Adnotationes apprime utiles*, Paris, 1505; Basel, 1541.

—— *Apologia*, i.e. *De falsa in eundem haeresis objectione ad summum pontificem libellus*, Bibl. Vatic., Cod. Ottobon. lat. 2075, ff. 238–47.

—— *Dialecticarum disputationum libri III, Opera omnia*, Basel, 1540, also separately by Badius Ascensius, Paris, 1509; Simon Colynaeus, Paris, 1530; Joannes Gymnicus, Cologne, 1530 and 1541. Original Ms version: *Repastinatio dialecticae et philosophiae libri III*, Bibl. Vatic., Cod. Urb. lat. 1207, ff. 39v–174; revised Ms version: *Reconcinnatio dialecticae et philosophiae libri III*, Bibl. Vatic., Cod. Ottobon. lat. 2075, ff. 1–124v. [First sheet of proem is missing. Lib. III, f. 93v, uses same title as Urb. lat. 1207, i.e. *Repastinatio* etc.].

—— *Dialogus de libero arbitrio*, ed. Maria Anfossi, Florence, 1934 (*Opuscoli filosofici: testi e documenti inediti o rari pubblicati da Giovanni Gentile*, VI); Eng. trans. by C. Trinkaus with Introd. and notes in Cassirer et al. eds. *The Renaissance Philosophy of Man*, pp. 147–82.

—— *Encomium Sancti Thomae Aquinatis*, ed. J. Vahlen, *Vierteljahrschrift für Kultur- und Litteraturgeschichte der Renaissance*, I, (1886), pp. 387–96.

—— *De falso credita et ementita Constantini donatione declamatio*, ed. Walter Schwahn, Leipzig, 1928; ed. with Eng. trans. Christopher B. Coleman, New Haven, 1922.

—— *Opuscula tria*, ed. J. Vahlen, *Sitzungsberichte der K. Akademie der Wissenschaften*, Phil.-Hist. Klasse. Bd. 61, Vienna, 1868, pp. 9–15 and 50–66; repr. in L. Valla, *Opera omnia*, Tomus alter, Turin, 1962, pp. 135–41 and 176–92.

—— *De professione religiosorum*, Bibl. Vatic., Cod. Urb. lat. 595 [unique], ed. by J. Vahlen, *Sitzungsberichte der K. Akademie der Wissenschaften*, Phil.-Hist Klasse. vol. 62, Vienna, 1869, pp. 99–134: repr., L. Valla, *Opera omnia*, Tomus alter, Turin, 1962, pp. 287–322.

—— *Scritti filosofici e religiosi*, Italian translations with introduction and notes by Giorgio Radetti, Florence, 1953.

—— *Sermo de mysterio Eucharistiae*, Florence, 1479; and in *Lanctantii opera* Venice, 1521, ff. 158v–9.

—— *De vero falsoque bono*, Bibl. Vatic., Cod. Ottobon. lat. 2075, ff. 141–237v.

Mafeo Vegio, *De perseverantia religionis libri VI*, in *Maxima Bibliotheca Veterum Patrum*, Vol. XXVI, Lyons, 1677, pp. 688–744.

—— *De quattuor hominis novissimis: morte, iudicio, inferno, et paradiso meditationes*, Paris, 1511; and in *Maxima Bibliotheca Veterum Patrum*, Vol. XXVI, Lyons, 1677, pp. 745–54.

—— Saints' Lives and Offices [St. Augustine, Beata Monica, Beato Niccolo Tolentino, Celestine V, San Bernardino], Bibl. Vatic., Cod. Ottobon. lat. 1253 [*Opera* of Mafeo Vegio], ff. 52–181v.

WILLIAM OF ST. THIERRY, *De natura corporis et animae libri duo*, Migne, *P.L.*, 180, 695–726.

II. Scholarly Studies and Interpretive Works

GIOVANNI DEGLI AGOSTINI, *Notizie istorico-critiche intorno le vite e le opere degli scrittori veneziani*, Tom. II, Venice, 1754.

DON CAMERON ALLEN, *Doubt's Boundless Sea: Skepticism and Faith in the Renaissance*, Baltimore, 1964.

E. AMANN, A. MICHEL, Article: 'Penitence', *Dict. de Théologie Catholique*, XII, i, Paris, 1933, 722–1050.

CARLO ANGELIERI, *Il problema religiosa del Rinascimento*, Florence, 1952.

S. E. ASSEMANI, *Codices Ebraici et Samaritani, Bibliothecae Apostolicae Vaticanae Codicum Manuscriptorum Catalogus*, Partes Primae, Tom. I, Rome, 1756.

HERSCHEL BAKER, *The Image of Man: A Study of the Idea of Human Dignity in Classical Antiquity, the Middle Ages and the Renaissance*, Cambridge, Mass., 1947; repr. New York, 1961.

C. S. BALDWIN, *Medieval Rhetoric and Poetic*, New York, 1928.

—— *Renaissance Literary Theory and Practice*, ed. D. L. Clark, New York, 1939.

FLORIO BANFI, 'Un umanista bolognese e i domenicani. A proposto dell'opera inedita su Giovanni Garzoni del P. Vincenzo Domenico Fassini', *Memorie Domenicane*, Florence, 1936.

LUISA BANTI, 'Agnolo Manetti e alcuni scribi a Napoli nel secolo XV', *Annali della R. Scuola Normale Superiore di Pisa*, Serie II, VIII (1939), Fasc. IV.

—— 'Annotatori del manoscritto vaticano Pal. lat. 889 della "Historia Augusta" ', *Studi in onore di Ugo Enrico Paoli*, Florence, 1955, pp. 59–70.

HANS BARON, *The Crisis of the Early Italian Renaissance*, 2 vols., Princeton, 1955; revised one volume edition, Princeton, 1966.

—— 'The Evolution of Petrarch's Thought', *Bibliothèque d'Humanisme et Renaissance*, XXIV (1962), pp. 7–41.

—— 'Franciscan Poverty and Civic Wealth as Factors in the Rise of Humanistic Thought', *Speculum*, XIII (1938), pp. 1–37.

—— Petrarch's *Secretum:* Was It Revised – and Why?, *Bibliothèque d'Humanisme et Renaissance*, XXV (1963), pp. 489–530.

—— 'Leonardo Bruni: "Professional Rhetorician" or "Civic Humanist"?' *Past and Present*, No. 36 (April 1967), pp. 21–37.

—— *From Petrarch to Leonardo Bruni, Studies in Humanistic and Political Literature*, Chicago, 1968.

LUCIANO BAROZZI AND REMEGIO SABBADINI, *Studi sul Panormita e sul Valla*, Florence, 1891.

LÉON BAUDRY, *Guillaume d'Ockham: Sa vie, ses oeuvres, ses idées sociales et politiques* (*Études de philosophie médiévale*, XXXIX), Paris, 1949.

—— *Lexique philosophique de Guillaume d'Ockham: Étude des notions fondamentales*, Paris, 1958.

MARVIN B. BECKER, 'Florentine Politics and the Diffusion of Heresy in the Trecento: A Socioeconomic Inquiry', *Speculum*, XXXIV (1959), pp. 60–75.

E. BENZ, *Marius Victorinus und die Entwicklung des abendlandischen Willenmetaphysik*, Stuttgart, 1932.

GIUSEPPE BILLANOVICH, *Petrarca letterato*, I, *Lo scrittoio del Petrarca*, Rome, 1947.

J. L. BLAU, *The Christian Interpretation of the Cabala in the Renaissance*, New York, 1944.

M. W. BLOOMFIELD, *The Seven Deadly Sins*, E. Lansing, 1952.

PHILOTHEUS BOEHNER, *Collected Articles on Ockham*, ed. E. M. Buytaert, St. Bonaventure, N. Y., 1958.

—— *Ockham: Philosophical Writings*, Edinburgh and London, 1967; repr. Indianapolis, 1964.

—— 'The Realistic Conceptualism of William of Ockham,' *Traditio*, IV (1946), pp. 307–35.

L. BORGHI, 'La dottrina morale di Coluccio Salutati', *Annali della R. Scuola Normale Superiore di Pisa*, Serie II, III (1934), pp. 75–102.

UMBERTO BOSCO, *Petrarca*, Turin, 1946.

WILLIAM J. BOUWSMA, *Concordia Mundi: The Career and Thought of Guillaume Postel*, Cambridge, Mass., 1957.

SAMUEL BRANDT, 'Uber die Quellen von Lactanz' Schrift *de opificio Dei*', *Wiener Studien*, XIII (1891), pp. 255–92.

WILLIAM J. BRANDT, *The Shape of Medieval History: Studies in Modes of Perception*, New Haven and London, 1966.

QUIRINUS BREEN, *Christianity and Humanism: Studies in the History of Ideas*, Grand Rapids, 1968.

C. O. BRINK, *Horace on Poetry, Prolegomena to the Literary Epistles*, Cambridge, 1963.

GERARDO BRUNI, *Egidio Romano e la sua polemica antitomista*, Milan, 1934. *Le opere di Egidio Romano*, Florence, 1936.

AUGUST BUCK, *Italienische Dichtungslehre vom Mittelalter bis zum Ausgang der Renaissance*, Tübingen, 1952.

—— 'Das Problem des christlichen Humanismus in der italienischen Renaissance', *Sodalitas Erasmiana*, I, Naples, 1949, pp. 181–92.

JACOB BURCKHARDT, *The Civilization of the Renaissance in Italy*, Eng. trans. by S. G. C. Middlemore, New York, 1929; repr. in 2 vols., New York, 1958.

KONRAD BURDACH, *Vom Mittelalter zur Reformation*, Vol. III, part 1, 'Der Ackermann aus Böhmen', Berlin, 1917.

GIUSEPPE CAGNI, 'I codici Vaticani Palatino-latini appartenuti alla biblioteca di Giannozzo Manetti', *La Bibliofilia*, Anno LXII (1960), pp. 1–43.

CARLO CALCATERRA, 'Il Petrarca e il Petrarchismo', *Problemi ed orientamenti critici di lingua e di letteratura italiana*, Vol. III, Milan, 1949, pp. 167–271.

DELIO CANTIMORI, *Eretici italiani del Cinquecento*, Florence, 1936.

ERNST CASSIRER, *Individuum und Kosmos in der Philosophie der Renaissance*, Leipzig and Berlin, 1927; Eng. trans. by Mario Domandi, New York, 1964.

ERNST CASSIRER, PAUL OSKAR KRISTELLER, JOHN HERMAN RANDALL, Jr., eds. *The Renaissance Philosophy of Man*, Chicago, 1948.

UMBERTO CASSUTO, *Codices Vaticani Hebraica. Codices 1–115*, Città del Vaticano, 1956.

—— *Gli Ebrei a Firenze nell'età del Rinascimento*, Florence, 1918; repr. 1965.

—— *I manoscritti palatini ebraici della Biblioteca Apostolica*, Città del Vaticano, 1935.

ENRICO CASTELLI, ed., *Testi umanistici inediti sul 'De anima'*, Rome, 1951.

—— *Testi umanistici sul'Ermetismo*, Rome, 1955.

—— *Umanesimo e ermeneutica*, Padua, 1963.

—— *Umanesimo e esoterismo*, Padua, 1960.

—— *Umanesimo e Machiavellismo*, Padua, 1949.

—— *Umanesimo e simbolismo*, Padua, 1958.

ANDRÉ CHASTEL, *Art et humanisme à Florence au temps de Laurent le Magnifique*, Paris, 1959.

HENRI COCHIN, *Le frère de Petrarque et le livre Du repos des religieux*, Paris, 1903.

NORMAN COHN, *The Pursuit of the Millenium*, New York, 1957; repr. 1961.

ANDREW THOMAS COLE, *Democritus and the Sources of Greek Anthropology*, American Philological Association, *Philological Monographs*, 25 (1967).

ANTONIO CORSANO, 'Note sul "De voluptate" del Valla', *Giornale critico della filosofia italiana*, II serie, VIII (1940), pp. 166–84.

—— *Il pensiero religioso italiano dall'umanesimo al giurisdizionalismo*, Bari, 1937.

SOCRATE CORVI, ed., *Studi su Mafeo Vegio*, Lodi, 1959.

P. COURCELLE, 'Petrarque entre Saint Augustin et les Augustins du XIVe siècle', *Studi petrarcheschi*, VII (1961).

F. EDWARD CRANZ, 'St. Augustine and Nicholas of Cusa in the Tradition of Western Christian Thought', *Speculum*, XXVIII (1953), pp. 297–315.

ERNST ROBERT CURTIUS, *European Literature and the Latin Middle Ages*, Eng. trans. by W. R. Trask, New York, 1953; repr. 1963.

RICHARD C. DALES and SERVUS GIEBEN, 'The Prooemium to Robert Grosseteste's *Hexaemeron*', *Speculum*, XLIII (1968), pp. 451–61.

TH. DEMAN, Article: 'Péché', *Dict. de Théologie Catholique*, XII, i. Paris, 1933, 140–275.

HERMANN DIELS, *Der antike Pessimismus*, (Schule und Leben herausgegeben vom Zentralinstitut für Erziehung und Unterricht), Berlin, 1921.

SAMUEL DILL, *Roman Society from Nero to Marcus Aurelius*, London, 1920.

J. F. DOBSON, 'The Posidonius Myth', *Classical Quarterly*, 12 (1918), pp. 179–95.

C. H. DODD, *The Bible and the Greeks*, London, 1934; repr. 1964.

B. DOMANSKI, *Die Psychologie des Nemesius* (*Baeumker Beiträge*, III), 1900.

RICHARD B. DONOVAN, 'Salutati's Opinion of Non-Italian Latin Writers', *Studies in the Renaissance*, XIV, (1967), pp. 185–201.

ANDREW H. DOUGLAS, *The Philosophy and Psychology of Pietro Pomponazzi*, Cambridge, 1910.

WALTER DRESS, *Die Mystik des Marsilio Ficinos*, Leipzig-Berlin, 1929.

LUDWIG EDELSTEIN, *The Idea of Progress in Classical Antiquity*, Baltimore, 1967 [with important bibliography].

—— 'The Philosophical System of Posidonius', *American Journal of Philology*, 57 (1936), pp. 286–325.

H. W. EPPELSHEIMER, *Petrarca*, Bonn, 1926.

A. FERRO, 'La dottrina dell'anima di Nemesio di Emesa', *Ricerche Religioso*, I, Rome, 1925, pp. 227–38.

FRANCESCO FIORENTINO, 'Egidio da Viterbo ed i Pontaniani di Napoli', *Atti dell'Accademia Pontaniana*, XVI, I, (1881), pp. 249–71.

—— *Pietro Pomponazzi*, Florence, 1868.

MARCEL FRANÇON, 'Petrarch, Disciple of Heraclitus,' *Speculum*, XI (1936), pp. 265–71.

L. FRATI, 'Le polemiche umanistiche di Benedetto Morandi', *Giornale Storico*, 75 (1920), pp. 32 ff.

—— *Studi italiani di filologia classica*, XVI (1905), pp. 103–432; XVII (1909), pp. 1–171 [Catalogues of Latin Mss of Bologna, Biblioteca Universitaria].

FRANCO GAETA, *Lorenzo Valla: Filologia e storia nell'Umanesimo italiano*, Naples, 1955.

EUGENIO GARIN, *La cultura filosofica del Rinascimento italiano, Ricerche e Documenti*, Florence, 1961.

—— 'Desideri di riforma nell'oratoria del Quattrocento', *La cultura filosofica*, pp. 166–82.

—— 'La "Dignitas Hominis" e la letteratura patristica', *La Rinascita*, I (1938), pp. 102–46.

—— 'Donato Acciaiuoli, cittadino fiorentino', *Medioevo e Rinascimento*, pp. 211–87.

—— 'Le "Elezioni" e il problema dell' astrologia', *Umanesimo e esoterismo*, pp. 7 ff.

—— 'Le favole antiche', *Medioevo e Rinascimento*, pp. 66–89.

—— *Giovanni Pico della Mirandola*, Florence, 1937.

—— *Medioevo e Rinascimento, Studi e Ricerche*, 2nd ed., Bari, 1961.

—— ed., *Il pensiero pedagogico dell'Umanesimo*, Florence, 1958.

—— 'Il problema dell'anima e dell'immortalità nella cultura del Quattrocento in Toscana', *La cultura filosofica*, pp. 93–126 [originally in *Archivio di Filosofia*, 1951, *Testi umanistici sul "De anima"*].

—— 'Problemi di religione e filosofia nella cultura fiorentina del Quattrocento', *La cultura filosofica*, pp. 127–42.

—— 'A proposto di Coluccio Salutati', *Rivista critica di storia della filosofia*, XV (1960), pp. 73–82.

—— 'La "Quaestio de Peccato" di Filippo Callimaco Esperiente', *La cultura filosofica*, pp. 280–6.

—— 'Ricerche su Giovanni Pico della Mirandola', *La cultura filosofica*, pp. 231–89.

—— *Studi sul Platonismo medievale*, Florence, 1958.

—— 'I trattati morali di Coluccio Salutati', *Atti dell'Accademia Fiorentina di Scienze Morali, 'La Columbaria'*, 1943, pp. 53–88.

—— *L'Umanesimo italiano*, 2nd ed., Bari, 1958.

Salvatore Garofalo, 'Gli umanisti italiani del secolo XV e la Bibbia', *La Bibbia e il concilio di Trento (Scripti Pontifici Instituti Biblici*, 96), Rome, 1947, pp. 338–75.

L. Gasparetti, 'Il "De fato, fortuna et casu" di Coluccio Salutati', *La Rinascita*, IV (1941), pp. 555–82.

Giovanni Gentile, 'Il concetto dell'uomo nel Rinascimento' (1916), repr. in his *Il pensiero italiano del Rinascimento*, Florence, 1940, pp. 47–113.

P. P. Gerosa, *La cultura patristica del Petrarca*, Turin, 1929.

—— *L'Umanesimo agostiniano del Petrarca*, Turin, 1927.

Servus Gieben, see under Dales.

Felix Gilbert, 'Cristianesimo, Umanesimo e la bolla "Apostolici Regeminis" del 1513' *Rivista Storica Italiana*, 79 (1967), pp. 976–990.

—— *Machiavelli and Guicciardini*, Princeton, 1965.

Neal W. Gilbert, *Renaissance Concepts of Method*, New York, 1960.

Étienne Gilson, 'Notes sur une frontière contestée', *Archives d'Histoire Doctrinale et Litteraire du Môyen Age*, 33 (T. 25) (1958), pp. 59–88.

E. H. Gombrich, 'The Debate on Primitivism in Ancient Rhetoric', *Journal of the Warburg and Courtauld Institutes*, XXIX (1966), pp. 24–37.

—— '*Icones symbolicae*. The Visual Image in Neo-Platonic Thought', *Journal of the Warburg and Courtauld Institutes*, XI (1948), pp. 163–92.

M. Grabmann, *Die Geschichte der scholastischen Methode*, 2 vols., Freiburg, 1909–11.

Karl Gronau, *Poseidonios und die jüdisch-christliche Genesis-exegese*, Leipzig, 1914.

Johannes Gründel, *Die Lehre von den Umständen der Menschlichen Handlung im Mittelalter (Baeumker Beiträge*, XXXIX) (1963), No. 5.

Godfrey Habery, *De Sancti Hieronimi ratione interpretandi*, Freiburg-im-Breisgau, 1886.

E. H. Harbison, *The Christian Scholar in the Age of the Reformation*, New York, 1956.

saak Heinemann, *Poseidonios' metaphysiche Schriften*, 2 vols. Breslau, 1921–8.

Klaus Heitmann, *Fortuna und Virtus, Eine Studie zu Petrarcas Lebensweisheit, Studi italiani*, I, Köln-Graz, 1958.

—— 'Insegnamenti agostiniani nel "Secretum" ', *Studi petrarcheschi*, VII (1961).

Peter Herde, 'Politik und Rhetorik in Florenz am Vorabend der Renaissance, Die ideologische Rechtfertigung der Florentiner Aussenpolitik durch Coluccio Salutati', *Archiv für Kulturgeschichte*, XLVII (1965), Heft 2, pp. 141–220.

F. Hilt, *Des heilige Gregor von Nyssa Lehre vom Menschen*, Cologne, 1890.
Albert Hyma, *The Christian Renaissance: A History of the Devotio Moderna*, Grand Rapids, 1924.
Matteo Iannizzotto, *Saggio sulla filosofia di Coluccio Salutati*, Padua, 1959.
E. F. Jacob, *Essays in the Conciliar Epoch*, rev. ed. Notre Dame, 1963.
—— ed., *Italian Renaissance Studies*, London, 1960.
Werner Jaeger, *Humanism and Theology*, Milwaukee, 1943.
—— *Nemesius von Emesa, Quellenforschung – zum Neuplatonismus und seinen Anfängen bei Poesidonios*, Berlin, 1914.
——*Paideia; The Ideals of Greek Culture*, trans. Gilbert Highet, second edition, 3 vols., New York, 1945.
R. Javelet, *Image et ressemblance au douzième siècle de saint Anselme à Alain de Lille*, 2 vols., Strassbourg, 1967 [with important bibliography of studies of patristic and medieval 'image-theology' and the exegesis of *Gen.* i:26].
Sears Jayne, *John Colet and Marsilio Ficino*, London, 1963.
Pearl Kibre, 'Giovanni Garzoni of Bologna (1419–1505), Professor of Medicine and Defender of Astrology', *Isis*, LVIII (1967), pp. 504–14.
K. E. Kirk, *The Vision of God*, London, 1931; repr. New York, 1966.
Adolf Kleingunther, Πρῶτος Εὑρετής, *Philologus, Supplementband* XXVI, Heft 1 (1930).
Raymond Klibansky, *The Continuity of the Platonic Tradition during the Middle Ages*, London, 1939.
Richard and Trude Krautheimer, *Lorenzo Ghiberti*, Princeton, 1956.
P. O. Kristeller, 'Augustine and the Early Renaissance', *Studies in Renaissance Thought and Letters*, pp. 355–72.
—— *Eight Philosophers of the Italian Renaissance*, Stanford, 1964.
—— 'Ficino and Pomponazzi on the Place of Man in the Universe', *Journal of the History of Ideas*, V (1944), pp. 220–6; reprinted in *Studies in Renaissance Thought and Letters*, pp. 279–86.
—— 'Giovanni Pico della Mirandola and His Sources', in *L'opera e il pensiero di Giovanni Pico della Mirandola nella storia dell'Umanesimo*, Florence, 1965.
—— 'Humanism and Scholasticism in the Italian Renaissance', *Byzantion*, XVII (1944–5), pp. 346–74, reprinted, *Studies in Renaissance Thought and Letters*, 553–83, and in *Renaissance Thought, Its Classical, Scholastic and Humanist Strains*, pp. 92–119.
—— 'The Humanist Bartolomeo Facio and His Unknown Correspondence', in *From the Renaissance to the Counter-Reformation: Essays in Honor of Garrett Mattingly*, New York, 1965.
—— *Iter Italicum*, 2 vols., London and Leiden, 1963, 1967.
—— 'Lay Religious Traditions and Florentine Platonism', *Studies in Renaissance Thought and Letters*, pp. 99–122.
—— 'Marsilio Ficino e Lodovico Lazzarelli: Contributo alla diffusione delle idee ermetiche nel Rinascimento', *Studies in Renaissance Thought and Letters*, pp. 221–48.

—— 'The Modern System of the Arts', *Renaissance Thought II*, New York, 1965, pp. 163–227.

—— 'Paduan Averroism and Alexandrism in the Light of Recent Studies', *Atti del XII Congresso Internazionale di Filosofia*, Vol. IX, Florence, 1960, pp. 147–55.

—— 'Paganism and Christianity', lecture 4 of *The Classics and Renaissance Thought*, Cambridge, Mass., 1955, pp. 70–91, repr. in his *Renaissance Thought, Its Classical, Scholastic and Humanist Strains*, pp. 70–91.

—— 'Il Petrarca, l'umanesimo e la scolastica a Venezia'. *La civltà veneziana del Trecento*, Venice, n.d. [1956], pp. 149–78.

—— 'The Philosophy of Man in the Italian Renaissance', *Italica*, XXIV (1947), pp. 93–112, repr. in *Studies in Renaissance Thought and Letters*, pp. 261–78.

—— *The Philosophy of Marsilio Ficino*, New York, 1943; Italian trans.: *Il pensiero filosofico di Marsilio Ficino*, Florence, 1953.

—— 'Pier Candido Decembrio and His Unpublished Treatise on the Immortality of the Soul', *The Classical Tradition: Literary and Historical Studies in Honor of Harry Caplan*, Ithaca, 1966, pp. 536–58.

—— *Renaissance Philosophy and the Medieval Tradition*, Latrobe, 1966.

—— *Renaissance Thought, Its Classical, Scholastic and Humanist Strains*, New York, 1961.

—— *Renaissance Thought II*, New York, 1965.

—— 'The Scholastic Background of Marsilio Ficino', *Studies in Renaissance Thought and Letters*, 35–55.

—— *Studies in Renaissance Thought and Letters*, Rome, 1956.

—— ed., *Supplementum Ficinianum*, 2 vols., Florence, 1937.

—— *Le Thomisme et la pensée italienne de la Renaissance*, Montreal and Paris, 1967.

—— 'A Thomist Critique of Marsilio Ficino's Theory of Will and Intellect', *Harry A. Wolfson Jubilee Volume*, Jerusalem, 1965.

—— 'An Unknown Humanist Sermon on St. Stephen by Guillaume Fichet', *Mélanges Eugène Tisserant* [*Biblioteca Vaticana Studi e Testi* No. 236], Vol. VI (1964), pp. 459–97.

Gerhart B. Ladner, *Ad imaginem Dei, The Image of Man in Medieval Art*, Latrobe, 1965.

—— '*Homo Viator:* Medieval Ideas on Alienation and Order', *Speculum*, XLII (1967), pp. 233–59.

—— *The Idea of Reform*, Cambridge, Mass., 1959.

Marie Laffranque, *Poseidonios d'Apamée, Essai de mise au point*, Paris, 1964.

Georges de Lagarde, *La naissance de l'esprit laïque au déclin du Moyen Age*, 6 vols., Paris, 1942–8.

F. Lammert, 'Zur lehre von den Grundeigenschaften bei Nemesius', *Hermes*, LXXXI (1953), pp. 488–91.

Gordon Leff, *Bradwardine and the Pelagians*, Cambridge, 1957.

—— *Gregory of Rimini: Tradition and Innovation in Fourteenth Century Thought*, Manchester and New York, 1961.

—— *Medieval Thought*, London, 1958.

Philip Levene, 'Two Early Versions of St. Gregory of Nyassa's Περι Κατασκευης Ανθρωρον', *Harvard Studies in Classical Philology*, LXIII (1958), pp. 473–92.

A. O. Lovejoy, G. Chinard, G. Boas, R. S. Crane, eds., *A Documentary History of Primitivism and Related Ideas*, Baltimore, 1935.

Henri de Lubac, *Exégèse médiévale*, 4 vols., Paris, 1959, 1961, 1964.

Georg Luck, *Der Akademiker Antiochos* (*Noctes Romanae*, 7), Bern, 1953.

Placido M. Lugano, ed., *Antonii Bargensis Cronicon Montis Oliveti*, and with biographical introduction, Florence, 1901.

—— 'De vita scriptisque Antonii Bargensis', in *Antonii Bargensis Cronicon Monti Oliveti*, xxv–li.

Girolamo Mancini, *Vita di Lorenzo Valla*, Florence, 1891.

Guglielmo Manfré, 'La Biblioteca dell'umanista Bolognese Giovanni Garzoni', *Accademie e Biblioteche d'Italia*, Anno XXVII (1959), No. 4, Anno XXVIII (1960), Nos. 1, 2, 3.

E. Mangenot, E. Vacandard, P. Bernard, Article: 'Confession', *Dict. de Théologie Catholique*, III, Paris, 1923, 828–926.

Raymond Marcel, *Marsile Ficin*, Paris, 1958.

—— 'Les Perspectives de l' "Apologétique" de Lorenzo Valla à Savonarole', in *Courants religieux et Humanisme*, Paris, 1959.

Concetto Marchesi, *Bartolommeo della Fonte* (*Bartholomaeus Fontius*), *Contributo alla storia degli studi classici in Firenze nella seconda metà del Quattrocento*, Catania, 1900.

Ugo Mariani, *Il Petrarca e gli Agostiniani*, Rome, 1946.

Henri Marrou, *Saint Augustin et la fin de la culture antique*, Paris, 1938.

Guido Martellotti, 'Introduzione', 'Nota bibliografica', 'Nota critica ai testi', in Francesco Petrarca, *Prose*, ed. by G. Martellotti, P. G. Ricci, E. Carrara, E. Bianchi, Milan and Naples, 1955, pp. vii–xxv and 1161–79.

Alfred von Martin, *Coluccio Salutati und das Humanistische Lebensideal*, Leipzig and Berlin, 1916.

—— *Mittelalterliche Welt—und Lebensanschauungen im Spiegel der Schriften Coluccio Salutatis*, Leipzig and Berlin, 1913.

Francis X. Martin, 'The Problem of Giles of Viterbo: A Historiographical Survey', *Augustiniana*, IX (1959), pp. 357–79: X (1960), pp. 43–60.

Lauro Martines, *The Social World of the Florentine Humanists, 1390–1460*, Princeton, 1963.

Louis L. Martz, *The Poetry of Meditation*, New Haven, 1954.

F. Masai, *Pléthon et le platonisme de Mistra*, Paris, 1956.

Eugenio Massa, 'L'anima e l'uomo in Egidio da Viterbo e nelle fonti classiche e medievali', in *Testi umanistici sul 'De Anima'*, ed. Garin, Padua, 1951.

—— 'Egidio da Viterbo e la metodologia del sapere nel Cinquecento', *Pensée humaniste et tradition chrétienne*, Paris, 1950, pp. 189–94.
—— see also Egidio da Viterbo.
NICOLA MATTIOLI, *Studio critico sopra Egidio Romano*, Rome, 1896.
ELISABETTA MAYER, *Un umanista italiano della corte di Mattia Corvino, Aurelio Brandolini Lippo*, Rome (Accademia d'Ungheria), 1938.
UBALDO MAZZINI, 'Appunti e notizie per servire alla bio-bibliografia di Bartolomeo Facio', *Giornale Storico e Letterario della Liguria*, IV (1903), pp. 400–54.
MILLARD MEISS, *Painting in Florence and Siena After the Black Death*, Princeton, 1951.
K. MICHALSKI, 'Le problème de la volonté à Oxford et à Paris au XIVe siècle', *Commentariorum societatis philosophicae Polonorum*, II, Lemberg, 1937, pp. 233–365.
GEORG MISCH, *Geschichte der Autobiographie*, 3 vols. (3rd ed.), Bern, 1949–62.
THEODOR E. MOMMSEN, *Medieval and Renaissance Studies*, ed. E. F. Rice, Jr., Ithaca, 1959.
—— 'Petrarch's Conception of the "Dark Ages"', in *Medieval and Renaissance Studies*, pp. 106–29; *Speculum*, XVII (1942), pp. 239 ff.
—— 'Petrarch and the Story of the Choice of Hercules', *Medieval and Renaissance Studies*, pp. 175–96.
RODOLFO MONDOLFO, *La comprensione del soggetto umano nell'antichità classica*, Florence, 1958.
ENGELBERT MONNERJAHN, *Giovanni Pico della Mirandola, Ein Beitrag zur philosophischen Theologie des italienischen Humanismus*, Wiesbaden, 1960.
G. M. MONTI, *Le confraternite medievali dell'alta e media Italia*, 2 vols., Venice, 1927.
ERNEST A. MOODY, *The Logic of William of Ockham*, London, 1935.
J. T. MUCKLE, 'The Doctrine of Gregory of Nyssa on Man as the Image of God', *Mediaeval Studies*, VII (1945), pp. 55–84.
—— 'The Hexameron of Robert Grosseteste: The First Twelve Chapters of Part Seven', *Mediaeval Studies*, VI (1944), pp. 151–75.
SALVATORE MUZZI, *Annali della Città di Bologna dalla sua origine al 1796*, Vol. V, Bologna, 1845.
GIOVANNI DI NAPOLI, '"Contemptus Mundi" e "Dignitas Hominis" nel Rinascimento', *Rivista di filosofia neoscolastica*, XLVIII (1956), pp. 9–41.
—— *Giovanni Pico della Mirandola e la problematica dottrinale del suo tempo*, Rome, 1965. [Comprehensive and fundamental.]
—— *L'immortalità dell'anima nel Rinascimento*, Turin, 1963.
BRUNO NARDI, *L'Aristotelismo Padovano*, Florence, 1955.
—— 'La mistica averroistica e Pico della Mirandola', in *Umanesimo e Machiavellismo*, ed. E. Castelli, Padua, 1949, pp. 55–74, and in B. Nardi, *L'Aristotelismo Padovano*, pp. 127–46.
—— *Saggi sull'Aristotelismo padovano dal secolo XIV al XVI*, Florence, 1958.

—— *Studi su Pietro Pomponazzi*, Florence, 1965.

Benjamin Nelson, *The Idea of Usury: From Tribal Brotherhood to Universal Otherhood*, Princeton, 1949.

Wilhelm Nestle, 'Der Pessimismus und seine Überwinding bei den Griechen', *Neue Jahrbücher für das klassische Altertums*, 47 (1921), pp. 81–97.

Arthur Darby Nock, 'Posidonius', *Journal of Roman Studies*, 49 (1959), pp. 1–15.

Bartolomeo Nogara, *I codici di Mafeo Vegio nella Biblioteca Vaticana*, Milan, 1903.

Pierre de Nolhac, *Pétrarque et l'humanisme*, 2nd ed., 2 vols, Paris, 1907.

Anders Nygren, *Agape and Eros*, Eng. trans., London, 1932.

Heiko A. Oberman, *Archbishop Thomas Bradwardine: A Fourteenth-century Augustinian: A Study of his Theology in its Historical Context*, Utrecht, 1958.

—— *Forerunners of the Reformation: The Shape of Late Medieval Thought*, New York, 1966.

—— *The Harvest of Medieval Theology: Gabriel Biel and Late Medieval Theology*, Cambridge, Mass., 1963.

—— 'Some Notes on the Theology of Nominalism with Attention to its Relation to the Renaissance', *Harvard Theological Review*, LIII (1960), pp. 47–76.

John W. O'Malley, 'Giles of Viterbo: A Reformer's Thought on Renaissance Rome', *Renaissance Quarterly*, XX (1967), pp. 1–11.

—— 'Giles of Viterbo: A Sixteenth Century Text on Doctrinal Development', *Traditio*, XXII (1966), pp. 445–50.

—— *Giles of Viterbo on Church and Reform, A Study In Renaissance Thought*, Leyden, 1968.

Walter J. Ong, *Ramus: Method and the Decay of Dialogue*, Cambridge, Mass., 1958.

Maristella di Panizza [Lorch], 'Le tre redazioni del *De voluptate* del Valla', *Giornale storico della letteratura italiana*, CXXI (1943), pp. 1–22.

—— 'Le tre versioni del *De vero bono* del Valla', *Rinascimento*, VI (1956), pp. 349–64.

Erwin Panofsky, *Gothic Architecture and Scholasticism*, Latrobe, 1951.

—— *Hercules am Scheidewege und andere antike Bildstoffe in der neueren Kunst*, (*Studien der Bibliothek Warburg*, X), Leipzig and Berlin, 1930.

—— *Renaissance and Renascences in Western Art*, Stockholm, 1960.

—— *Studies in Iconology*, New York, 1939; repr., 1962 with corrections.

Gioacchino Paparelli, *Feritas, Humanitas, Divinitas: Le componenti dell'Umanesimo*, Messina and Florence, 1960.

Alberto Pinerchle, 'La religione nel Rinascimento', *Atti del III Convegno Internazionale sul Rinascimento*, Florence, 1953, pp. 173–206; pp. 206–9.

P. Piur, *Petrarcas 'Buch ohne Namen' und die päpstliche Kurie*, Halle, 1925.

Max Pohlenz, *Die Stoa*, 2 vols., Göttingen, 1948–9.

M. Quartana, 'Un umanista minore della corte di Leone X, Raphael Brandolinus', *Atti della Società italiana per il progresso delle scienze*, XX riunione, II, Rome, 1932, pp. 466 ff.

GIORGIO RADETTI, 'L'epicureismo di Callimaco Esperiente nella biografia di Gregorio di Sanok', *Atti del Convegno italo-ungherese di studi rinascimentali* (September, 1964) in *Ungheria d'Oggi*, V, 1965, pp. 46–53.

—— *L'Epicureismo nel pensiero umanistico del Quattrocento*, in *Grande Antologia Filosofica*, VI, Milan, 1964, pp. 839–961.

—— 'La religione di Lorenzo Valla', in *Medioevo e Rinascimento, Studi in onore di Bruno Nardi*, Florence, 1955, Vol. II, pp. 595–630.

—— See L. Valla, *Scritti filosofici e religiosi*.

LUIGI RAFFAELE, *Mafeo Vegio, Elenco delle opere*, Bologna, 1909.

JOHN HERMAN RANDALL, JR., *The Career of Philosophy from the Middle Ages to the Enlightenment*, New York, 1962.

—— 'The Place of Pomponazzi in the Padua Tradition', *The School of Padua and the Emergence of Modern Science*, Padua, 1961, pp. 69–114.

ELENA RAZZOLI, *Agostinismo e religiosità nel Petrarca*, Milan, 1937.

KARL REINHARDT, *Kosmos und Sympathie*, Munich, 1926.

—— *Poseidonios*, Munich, 1921.

—— 'Poseidonios von Apamea', Paully-Wissowa, *Real-encyclopädie für klassischen Altertums-Kunde*, XXII, (1953), 558–826.

AUGUSTIN RENAUDET, *Préréforme et humanisme à Paris pendant les premières guerres d'Italie (1494–1517)*, 2nd ed., Paris, 1953.

EUGENE F. RICE, JR., 'The Humanist Idea of Christian Antiquity: Lefèvre d'Étaples and his Circle', *Studies in the Renaissance*, IX (1962), pp. 126–60.

—— *The Renaissance Idea of Wisdom*, Cambridge, Mass., 1958.

VITTORIO ROSSI, *Il Quattrocento* (6th revised edition), Milan, 1956.

WALTER RÜEGG, 'Entstehung, Quellen und Ziele von Salutatis "*De fato et fortuna*"', *Rinascimento*, V (1954), pp. 143–88.

REMIGIO SABBADINI, *Cronologia documentata della vita di Lorenzo delle Valle, detto il Valla*, Florence, 1891.

—— See Barozzi.

GIUSEPPE SAITTA, *Marsilio Ficino e la filosofia dell'Umanesimo*, 3rd expanded edition, Bologna, 1954.

—— *Nicolo Cusano e l'Umanesimo italiano*, Bologna, 1957.

—— *Il pensiero italiano nell'Umanesimo e nel Rinascimento*, Bologna, 1949.

M. SCHIAVONE, *Problemi filosofici in Marsilio Ficino*, Milan, 1957.

J. B. SCHOEMANN, 'Gregors von Nyssa theologische Anthropologie als Bildtheologie', *Scholastik*, 1943, pp. 31–53, 175–200.

G. SCHOLEM, 'Zur Geschichte der Anfänge der christlichen Kabbala', *Essays presented to L. Baeck*, London, 1954.

G. M. SCIACCA, *La visione della vita nell'Umanesimo e Coluccio Salutati*, Palermo, 1954.

FRANÇOIS SECRET, 'L'"Emithologie" de Guillaume Postel', *Umanesimo e esoterismo*, pp. 381–437.

—— 'L'hermeneutique de Guillaume Postel', *Umanesimo e ermeneutica*, pp. 91–145.

—— *Les Kabbalistes chrétiens de la Renaissance*, Paris, 1964.

—— 'Pico della Mirandola e gli inizi della cabala cristiana', *Convivium*, N.S. I (1957), pp. 31–47.

—— *Le Zôhar chez les Kabbalistes chrétiens de la Renaissance*, Paris, 1957.

ARNALDO SEGARIZZI, *La Catinia, le Orazioni e le Epistole di Sicco Polenton' umanista Trentino del secolo XV*, Bergamo, 1899.

MICHAEL SEIDLMAYER, 'Religiös-ethische Probleme des italienischen Humanismus', *Germanisch-Romanische Monatsschrift*, N.F. VIII (1958), pp. 105–26.

—— ' "Una religio in rituum varietate" Zur Religionsauffassung des Nikolaus von Cues', *Archiv für Kulturgeschichte*, XXXVI (1954).

JERROLD E. SEIGEL, ' "Civic Humanism" or Ciceronian Rhetoric?', *Past and Present*, No. 34, (July 1966), pp. 3–48.

—— 'Ideals of Eloquence and Silence in Petrarch', *Journal of the History of Ideas*, XXVI (1965), pp. 147–74.

—— *Rhetoric and Philosophy in Renaissance Humanism: The Union of Eloquence and Wisdom, Petrarch to Valla*, Princeton, 1968.

JEAN SEZNEC, *The Survival of the Pagan Gods*, Eng. trans., New York, 1953; repr. 1961.

ALBERT SIEGMUND, *Die Überlieferung der griechischen christlichen Literatur in der lateinischen Kirche bis zum zwölften Jahrhundert*, Munich, 1949.

PAUL E. SIGMUND, *Nicholas of Cusa and Medieval Political Thought*, Cambridge, Mass., 1963.

GIUSEPPE SIGNORELLI, *Il Cardinale Egidio da Viterbo, Agostiniano, umanista e riformatore*, Florence, 1929.

BERYL SMALLEY, *The Study of the Bible in the Middle Ages*, 2nd ed., Oxford, 1952.

SUSAN SNYDER, 'The Left Hand of God: Despair in Medieval and Renaissance Tradition', *Studies in the Renaissance*, XII (1965), pp. 18–59.

C. SPICQ, *Esquisse d'une histoire de l'exégèse latine au moyen âge*, Paris, 1944.

LEWIS W. SPITZ, *The Religious Renaissance of the German Humanists*, Cambridge, Mass., 1963.

HENRY STEVENSON, SR., *Codices manuscripti Palatini Graeci Bibliothecae Vaticanae*, Rome, 1885.

HENRY STEVENSON, JR., ed. *Codices Palatini Latini Bibliothecae Vaticanae*, Città del Vaticano, 1886.

COSIMO STORNAJOLO, ed. *Codices Ubinates Latini Bibliothecae Vaticanae*, vols. 1–3, Città del Vaticano, 1902–21.

HENRY BARCLAY SWETE, *An Introduction to the Old Testament in Greek*, Cambridge, 1900.

FRANCESCO TATEO, *Dialogo interiore e polemica ideologica nel 'Secretum' del Petrarca*, Florence, 1965.

—— *'Retorica' e 'poetica' fra Medioevo e Rinascimento*, Bari, 1960.

—— *Tradizione e realtà nell' Umanesimo italiano*, Bari, 1967.

E. H. R. Tatham, *Francesco Petrarca, the First Modern Man of Letters*, 2 vols., London, 1926.

Margaret Taylor, 'Progress and Primitivism in Lucretius', *American Journal of Philology*, vol. LXVIII (1947), pp. 180–194.

Alberto Tenenti, *Il senso della morte e l'amore della vita nel Rinascimento*, Turin, 1957.

Lynn Thorndike, *A History of Magic and Experimental Science*, 6 vols., New York, 1923–41.

—— '*Lippus Brandolinus de Comparatione Reipublicae et Regni*, a Treatise in Comparative Political Science', *Science and Thought in the Fifteenth Century*, Chapter XIII.

—— *Science and Thought in the Fifteenth Century*, New York, 1929; repr., 1963.

Giuseppe Toffanin, *Perchè l'Umanesimo comincia con Dante*, Bologna, 1967.

—— *Storia dell'Umanesimo*, 3 vols., Bologna, 1950.

—— *Ultimi saggi*, Bologna, 1960.

Damasus Trapp, 'Augustinian Theology of the Fourteenth Century', *Augustiniana*, VI (1956), pp. 146–274.

Charles Trinkaus, *Adversity's Noblemen: The Italian Humanists on Happiness*, New York, 1940, reissued with new Preface, 1965.

—— Article: 'Humanism, Humanism and Renaissance Art', *Encyclopedia oj World Art*, Vol. VII, cols. 702–34, with extensive bibliography of Renaissance humanism, cols. 734–43.

—— 'A Humanist's Image of Humanism: The Inaugural Orations of Bartolommeo della Fonte', *Studies in the Renaissance*, VII (1960), pp. 90–147.

—— 'Humanist Treatises on the Status of the Religious: Petrarch, Salutati, Valla', *Studies in the Renaissance*, XI (1964), pp. 7–45 [now incorporated in this book, Part IV, Chapter XIV.].

—— 'Petrarch's Views on the Individual and His Society', *Osiris*, XI (1954), pp. 168–98.

—— 'The Religious Foundations of Luther's Social Views', *Essays in Medieval Life and Thought*, New York, 1955, pp. 71–87.

—— 'Renaissance Problems in Calvin's Theology', *Studies in the Renaissance*, I (1954), pp. 59–80.

—— 'The Unknown Quattrocento Poetics of Bartolommeo della Fonte' *Studies in the Renaissance*, XIII (1966), pp. 40–122.

Berthold L. Ullman, *The Humanism of Coluccio Salutati*, Padua, 1963.

—— *Studies in the Italian Renaissance*, Rome, 1955.

—— See also under Sicco Polenton and Coluccio Salutati.

Mario Untersteiner, *The Sophists*, Eng. trans. by Kathleen Freeman, Oxford, 1954.

G. Urbano, *Lorenzo Valla e Fra Antonio da Bitonto*, Palermo, 1911.

Graf Woldemar von Uxkull-Gyllenband, *Griechische Kultur-Entstehungslehren* (*Bibliothek für Philosophie*, XXVI), Berlin, 1924.

ALDO VALLONE, *Cortesia e nobilità nel Rinascimento*, Asti, 1955.

SOPHIA VANNI-ROVIGHI, 'Alberto Magno e l'unita della forma', *Medioevo e Rinascimento*, Florence, 1955, pp. 755–78.

CESARE VASOLI, 'Le "Dialecticae Disputationes" del Valla a la critica umanistica della logica Aristotelica', *Rivista critica di storia della filosofia*, Anno XII (1957), pp. 412–34, Anno XIII (1958), pp. 27–46.

—— *La dialettica e la retorica dell'Umanesimo, 'Invenzione' e 'Metodo' nella cultura del XV e XVI secolo*, Milan, 1968.

—— 'Polemiche Occamiste', *Rinascimento*, III (1952), pp. 119–36.

—— [Discussion of Averroism and Paduan culture], 'Tavola rotonda', *Atti del Convegno italo-ungherese di studi rinascimentali, Ungheria d'Oggi*, V, 1965, pp. 111–13.

—— 'Temi e fonte della tradizione ermetica in uno scritto di Symphorien Champier', *Umanesimo e esoterismo*, pp. 235–89.

F. VERNET, J. DE GHELLINCK, E. MANGENOT, L. GODEFROY, Article: 'Eucharistie', *Dict. de Théologie Catholique*, V, Paris, 1924, 1209–56.

LASZLO VERSÉNYI, *Socratic Humanism*, New Haven, 1963.

BRUNO VIGNATI, *Mafeo Vegio, umanista cristiano (1407–1458)*, Bergamo, 1959.

PAUL VIGNAUX, *Justification et prédestination au XIVe siècle*, Paris (*Bibliothèque de l'École des Hautes Études*, 48), 1934.

—— *Nominalisme au XIVe siècle*, Paris, 1948.

D. P. WALKER, 'Orpheus the Theologian and Renaissance Platonists', *Journal o the Warburg and Courtauld Institutes*, 16 (1953), pp. 100–20.

—— 'The *Prisca Theologia* in France,' *Journal of the Warburg and Courtauld Institutes*, 17 (1954), pp. 204–59.

—— *Spiritual and Demonic Magic from Ficino to Campanella*, London, 1958.

ERNST WALSER, *Coluccio Salutati, der Typus eines Humanisten der italienischen Frührenaissance*, Leipzig, 1912: repr. *Gesammelte Studien*, Basel, 1932.

—— *Poggius Florentinus*, Leipzig and Berlin, 1914.

SIEGFRIED WENZEL, 'Petrarch's *Accidia*', *Studies in Renaissance*, VIII (1961), pp. 36–48.

—— *The Sin of Sloth: 'Acedia' in Medieval Thought and Literature*, Chapel Hill, 1967.

KARL WERNER, *Der Augustinismus in der Scholastik des späteren Mittelalters*, Vienna, 1883.

ERNEST HATCH WILKINS, *Life of Petrarch*, Chicago, 1961.

—— *The Making of the 'Canzoniere' and Other Petrarchen Studies*, Rome, 1951.

—— *Petrarch's Eight Years in Milan*, Cambridge, Mass., 1958.

—— *Petrarch's Later Years*, Cambridge, Mass., 1959.

—— *Petrarch at Vaucluse*, Chicago, 1958.

—— *Studies in the Life and Works of Petrarch*, Cambridge, Mass., 1955.

EDGAR WIND, 'Maccabean Histories in the Sistine Ceiling', *Italian Renaissance Studies*, pp. 312–17.

—— 'Michelangelo's Prophets and Sibyls', *Proceedings of the British Academy*, LI (1967), pp. 47–84.
—— *Pagan Mysteries in the Renaissance*, revised [and expanded] edition, London, 1967.
—— 'The Revival of Origen', *Studies in Art and Literature for Belle da Costa Greene*, Princeton, 1954, pp. 412–24.
FRANCES A. YATES, *Giordano Bruno and the Hermetic Tradition*, London and Chicago, 1964.
VLADIMIRO ZABUGHIN, *Il cristianesimo durante il Rinascimento*, Milan, 1924.
GIANNI ZIPPEL, 'La "Defensio questionum in philosophia" di Lorenzo Valla e un noto processo dell'Inquisizione napoletana', *Bulletino dell'Istituto italiano per il Medioevo e Archivio Muratoriano*, No. 69 (1957), pp. 319–47.
—— 'Lorenzo Valla e le origini della storiografia umanistica a Venezia', *Rinascimento*, VII (1956), pp. 93–133.
—— 'Note sulle redazione della "Dialectica" di Lorenzo Valla', *Convegno di studi per il V Centenario della morte di Lorenzo Valla, Archivio storico per le Province Parmensi*, Quarta serie, IX (1957), pp. 301–14.

Index of Manuscripts

*(With few exceptions Mss are also listed in the Bibliography under authors. Those listed only in the Bibliography are indicated by *)*

Index of Names and Works

(Bold type indicates quotation)

(Asterisk indicates work appears in Bibliography only)

Index of Subjects

(Bold type indicates quotation.)